BRITISH JOURNAL OF PHOTOGRAPHY ANNUAL 1987

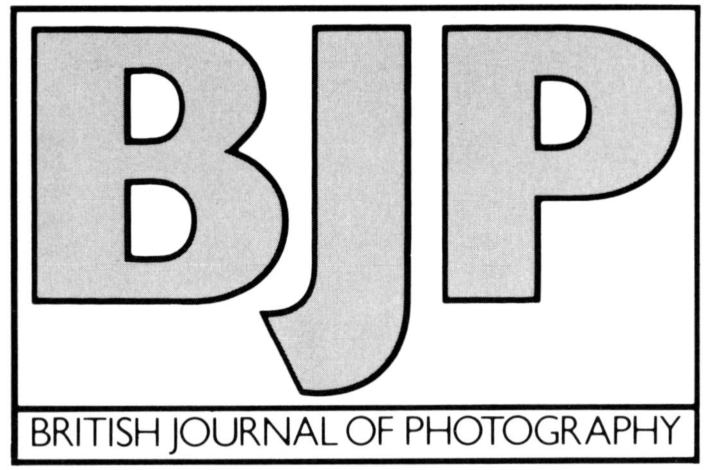

ANNUAL 1987

HENRY GREENWOOD & CO LTD

To
Mr Dalladay
best wishes from
Geoffrey Crawley

EDITOR
Geoffrey Crawley

PICTURE EDITOR
Colin Osman

ASSOCIATE EDITOR
Tim Hughes

PRODUCTION
Sue Dimmock

ISBN 0 900414 34 0
Published by Henry Greenwood & Co Ltd
28 Great James Street, London WC1N 3HL
Distributed in the USA by Writer's Digest Books
9933 Alliance Road, Cincinnati, Ohio 45242

Printed and bound in Great Britain by
Manor Park Press Ltd, Eastbourne

SUCCESSIVE EDITORS OF THE ANNUAL:

1861-62	Samuel Highley
1863	James Martin
1864	Emerson J. Reynolds
1865-79	J. Traill Taylor
1880-86	W. B. Bolton
1887-96	J. Traill Taylor
1897-1905	Thomas Bedding
1906-1934	George E. Brown
1935	H. W. Bennett
	P. C. Smethurst
1936	H. W. Bennett
	Arthur J. Dalladay
1937-67	Arthur J. Dalladay
1968-	Geoffrey Crawley

PICTURE EDITORS:

1964	Bryn Campbell
1965-67	Normal Hall
1968	Ainslie Ellis
1969	Anna Körner
	Geoffrey Crawley
1970-71	Anna Körner
1972-73	Mark Butler
1974-76	Anne Owen
1977-78	Judy Goldhill
1979	Geoffrey Crawley
1980	Jan Turvey
1981-82	Christine Cornick
1983-86	Anna Tait
1987-	Colin Osman

THE ANNUAL'S HISTORY
The *British Journal of Photography Annual* is the oldest photographic yearbook in the world. It appeared first in the form of a wall calendar for the year 1860 and was published as a supplement to *The British Journal of Photography* issue of 15 December 1859. In the following year the *British Journal Photographic Almanac,* 1861, as it was then titled, with the sub-title *Photographer's Daily Companion,* appeared as a pocket book, 4 × 2½in in size, issued free of charge to subscribers of the *Journal.* The 1886 issue was produced in the Crown 8vo format, 4½ × 7in, and sold as a separate publication with 118 pages of text and 44 of advertising, priced 6d. This format remained unchanged for 97 years until the 1964 issue, when the book was enlarged to 8 × 11in, enabling photographs to be properly displayed, selected by a picture editor also responsible for the layout of the book. With the 1980 edition, the book adopted a new, 255 × 240mm, format. Last year for the first time it was published as a paperback.

CONTENTS

AS EDITOR of the weekly *British Journal of Photography* and this, its associated *Annual,* I would like to disclose two ambitions. The first is to publish a test report on a British-made precision camera system of world class and market appeal, and the second is to be able to note in the foreword to this Annual one year soon that with a steady sustained growth in the country's economy and reduction in unemployment, interest in photography and sales in the photographic industry are also steadily growing. As things are turning out the second hope is rather more realistic than the first although there is likely to be a very long haul indeed before the description 'flourishing' is likely to be applied to the UK. Looking back over the year we can say that the beginning of 1986 probably marked the bump on the bottom, as it is called, for the UK photographic industry and trade. Our sector had held up longer than many in the inflationary period with its accompanying developing depression, and as a result it reached bedrock later than some other sectors. Since then reports coming in indicate that there are signs of a new stability and from that the hope of gradual growth.

Nevertheless it would not be right to give the reader of these pages in future years the impression that the bad times left the industry more or less unscathed. Major firms, household names, have had to contract rapidly and ruthlessly. Fat which accumulated during the years when photography was expanding like a balloon has had to go. In fact the rapidity of that growth in the 70s meant that expansion was not always carried out in the most logical and cost effective manner, so it is hardly surprising that when the nation's economic conditions finally affected the photographic industry, it should find itself with the need to slim down and become much more efficient.

Having set that overall scene it would be wrong to give the impression that photography is in the doldrums, either in its practice at amateur or professional level, or in the launching of new products and materials by the manufacturers. In fact 1986 saw important new developments. This time last year the photographic world was still marvelling at Minolta's brave auto-focus venture the 7000 AF camera, known in the States as the Maxum. On the other hand some sage heads wondered whether automatic focusing, proven as a useful aid to the less experienced photographer, would really appeal to the enthusiast and the professional. Now, just a year later, such doubts seem very strange. Minolta have added two other models to their AF series, a professional camera — a scaling up of the 7000 — and a simpler version of it, the 5000. Nikon have confirmed the new 35mm SLR era with their 501 model, which has the appeal that earlier Nikon lenses can be used via an adaptor, whereas the Minolta cameras require a new lens range to be used. It is well known that Canon are working on an automatic focusing 35mm SLR and the photographic world waits with great interest to see just how it turns out.

From the Canon stable has come during the year a real milestone in the history of photography — the first fully integrated electronic still video camera. A few years back when Sony showed their Mavica prototype, the industry more or less agreed worldwide on a standard for the magnetic recording of still photographic images. The Canon system conforms to this and no doubt others which come along will also do so. But, before anyone runs along to the corner shop to buy one, it has to be said that the system costs around £25 000, and the image quality it gives is nowhere near that of a medium price standard 35mm camera. However, for that outlay the commercial, press and industrial users for whom it is really designed, can obtain quite an outfit. It allows 50 images to be recorded on a floppy disc, each image with 20 seconds of sound. Those images can be transmitted more or less anywhere in the world over telephone lines or via satellite and be printed out at the receiving end. A colour printer is part of the system and this can produce a 3 × 5in colour print in about 4½ minutes. Pictures can also be displayed on the TV screen with the accompanying sound recording. The amount of detail that can be recorded is only about 3% that of the standard 35mm film frame but the introduction of the SSE, Solid State Electronic, camera system must still be classed with the major milestone steps taken by Daguerre and Fox Talbot in laying foundations for the future in the 19th century. Very major technical advances will have to be made before you can go down to your photographic dealer and see a system at an affordable price demonstrated, but there is no doubt that in the long run — perhaps the next 20 years — SSE photography will broaden the scope and interest of the photographic craft. Whilst that research and development is going on, traditional silver film will continue to improve and there are many fascinating developments in the pipeline. The world's leading scientists believe that cameras using film will remain indefinitely the most convenient way of obtaining a really high quality picture.

Turning to photography itself, taking pictures that is, what is the message for this year? Many people in the photographic world feel that in some way we are resting on our laurels. In the immense popularisation of photography over the last 15 years — remember that this year over 1000 million colour prints are likely to be handed in wallets over the counter to hopefully satisfied customers — too much emphasis has been placed on what we call point-and-shoot photography. Naturally it was necessary to make it clear that with modern cameras, anyone can go out and take a large percentage of sharply focused, nicely exposed pictures on each roll of film, but it means that photography has been put across, more or less to a whole generation, as a rather superficial pursuit. Readers of this Annual will hardly need to be told that it can be very very far from that. With photography now firmly established as something which *can* be carried out successfully by anyone who can hold a camera, point it in the right direction and press the shutter release. That is only the beginning. It is a craft and a skill which, with increasing knowledge, experience and understanding can be creatively fulfilling. 'Creatively fulfilling' sounds rather high flown but is quite true. It can never be too often repeated that photography is literally an eye-opening way of life and a craft which can influence the world. But to make pictures which really interest people outside your own family circle requires more than a point-and-shoot knowledge of photography. That is not to say that the snapshot cannot be of lasting value, many of them taken in years gone by are proving to be exactly that. But there is a great difference between accidentally producing a significant image and setting out to do so with the acquired knowledge and skill required.

What we need to do now, and by 'we' is meant not only the industry and trade but, more importantly, photographers themselves, is to spread that message. We can do this by sitting down with relatives and friends who own cameras and trying to explain to them how they can use them more fully. Most cameras today, including the widely successful compact 35mm viewfinder cameras, have a potential of control by the user of which only a fraction is ever exploited. Show them the photographs in this Annual and try and get them thinking. If you have a darkroom then take relatives and friends who own cameras and show them how the process works and the fun and satisfaction which can be had. Make yourself known to local groups. Conservation and historical societies are on the whole quite badly served by photography, since they usually do not know much about it. It is not an area in which the professional normally becomes very much involved except voluntarily, so there is no reason why knowledgeable photographers should not put their services at the disposal of these societies. In some areas there may be socially involved groups whose work could be greatly assisted by having a photographer to call on. Then there are the schools, the real seeding grounds for future interest in photography. The industry is taking time to encourage pupils to take an interest in photography and many schools would welcome offer of assistance from local individuals or camera societies. These are just a few suggestions. The message from this Annual is 'Spread the word!'. There are so many competing leisure interests nowadays, most of them uncreative and sterile, that we in photography are fully justified in promoting our craft which is one that develops the individual and gives him or her a creative outlet, and a whole family interest.

Well, these remarks commenced with two personal ambitions of the Editor. It is unlikely that this time next year much progress will have been made with the first, but let us very much hope that a significant step forward has been made with the second, and the sapping of society's health and future strength seen in the unemployment figures of the young, will at least have ceased to spread and, hopefully, be on the mend.

Geoffrey Crawley

Editor, September 1986

THE COMPUTERISED CAMERA

Now that they are well entrenched in cameras, microprocessors are expanding their empire, L. A. Mannheim relates.

'COMPUTER-control' — like 'electronic control' — crept into the list of copywriters' superlatives back in the days of simple photocell circuits and electrical switches. More recently that control has become not only more complex but also shifted its emphasis.

The camera continues to do clever automatic tricks; however now it feels obliged to tell its owner at increasing length what is going on. Often it does so in computer jargonese, as function designers have probably fed passingly on programmer wisdom. Lay users — that is, snapshooters — are getting understandably confused! Reminded generation after generation of George Eastman's exhortation just to press the button, they now have to cope with miniature video displays bearing unpronounceable messages (Tv, Av, PSAM) or ambiguous pictograms. So the camera owner is being pressurised into a dialogue with his technical toy, in a language that he is finding difficult to understand.

The irony is that today's sophisticated cameras really are computerised, with the virtues and vices that this implies. The virtues are the increased versatility and — in theory at least — greater precision of control functions, from DX code film cartridge input (film speed etc) to exposure programming and autofocus. The vice is the need for the dialogue and for decisions by the photographer that sophisticated automation was supposed to eliminate.

Even the computer dialogue is becoming literally that: the Command Back of Canon's T90 camera stores automatically all the picture taking information that a few conscientious photographers used to write down in their notebooks. Through an interface unit it can then download the data into a personal computer for display on the PC's screen.

Children now learn computer literacy in school; so, technologists argue, the new generation should have no difficulty in handling the new information interchange. That is valid where preserving the information matters: the T90's memory and computer interface are more elegant (and possibly more convenient) than a notebook. But most of photography is concerned with preserving visual impressions. The dialogue therefore tends to get in the way.

In current photo hardware, computerisation more mundanely means micro-processor control with integrated circuit chips looking after more and more functions. In latest cameras that trend is making life both more difficult for the user and easier — with exposure programming on the one hand and autofocus on the other.

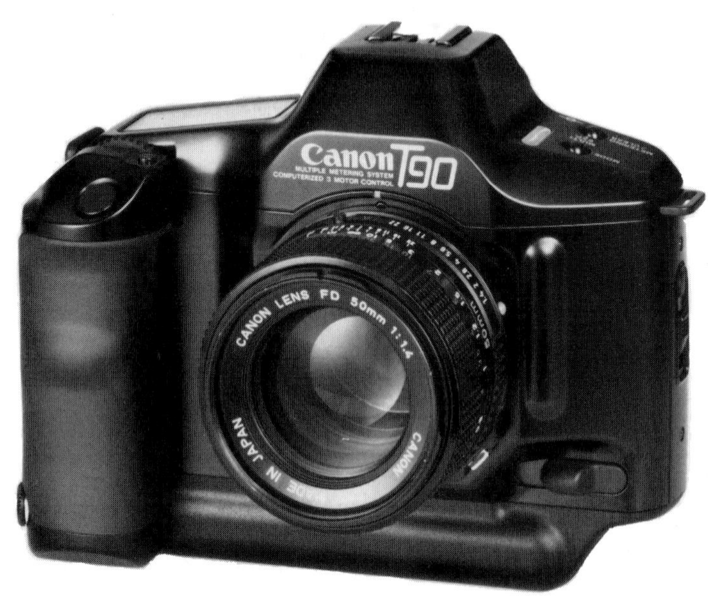

Canon T-90.

The program inflation

Originally an exposure program was a way for the camera to select a correct exposure without reference to the user. When users demanded faster shutter speeds for shake-free exposures with long-focus lenses, they got a choice of alternative automatic programs — selected by the lens input. When photographers still objected to being overridden, they got multiprograms with program shift.

The Canon T90 and Minolta 9000/7000 are the two camera systems again in the forefront of this program manipulation. It is fractionally simpler on the Canon for this has one basic program of a normal 45° gradient — i.e. apertures and shutter speeds increment equally. In normal program (P) mode the program runs from 1/15sec at f/1.4 (EV 5) to 1/2000sec at f/16 (EV19) or 1/4000sec at f/22 for lenses that stop down that far. Above and below this range the aperture stays at its highest or lowest f/number respectively and only the shutter time shifts.

The program shift displaces the whole program along the time axis. There are six shift positions labelled — for convenience only — in terms of focal length definition (W-3 to T-3 for wide-angle to tele). The W-3 program starts at EV-1 (4sec at f/1.4) and ends at EV 13 (1/30sec at f/16), the T-3 program runs from EV 11 (1/1000sec at f/1.4) to EV 15 (1/4000sec at f/2.8), because after the top speed the camera can only close down the aperture.

Minolta superimposes a similar shift on to whichever program the lens input has selected. On both cameras the electronic input control wheel or lever, which in

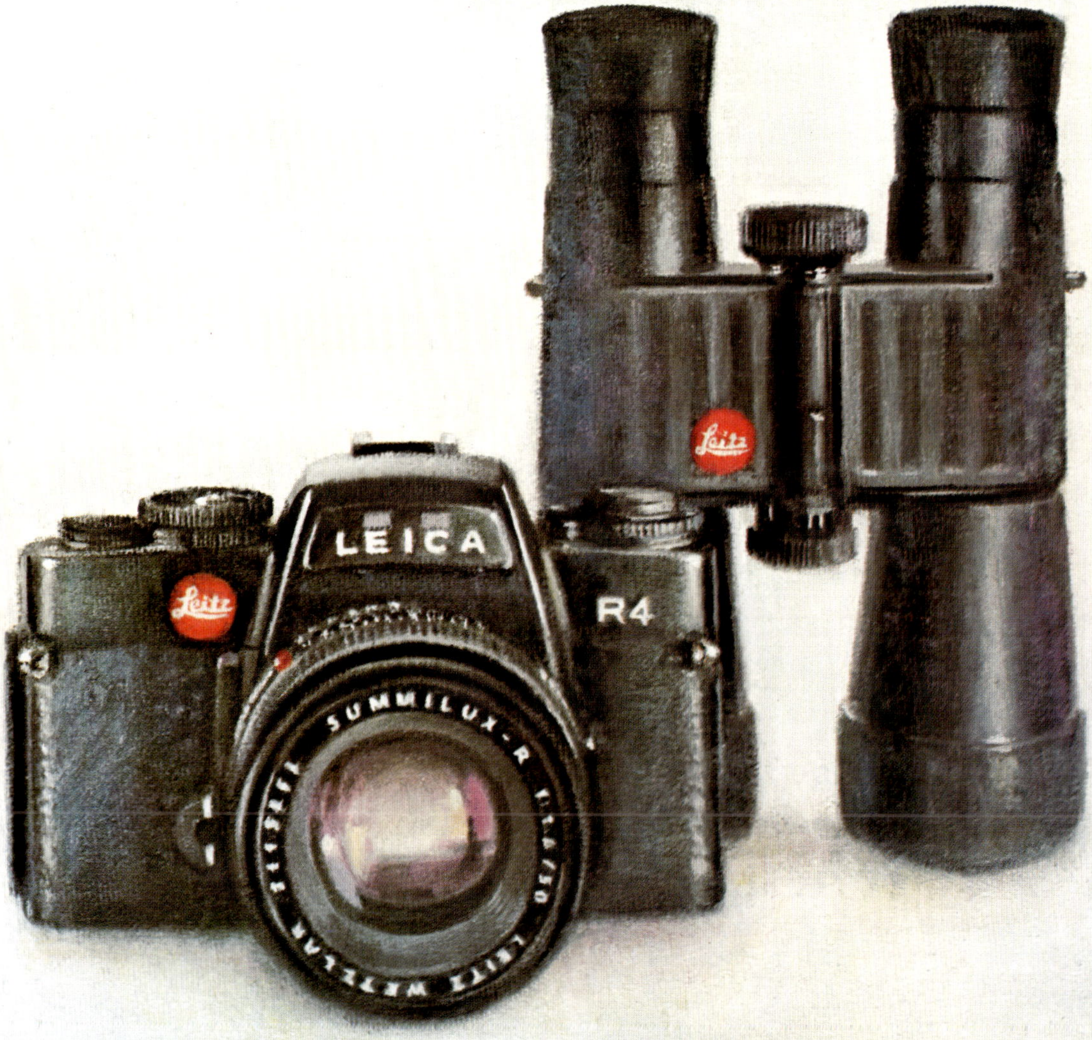

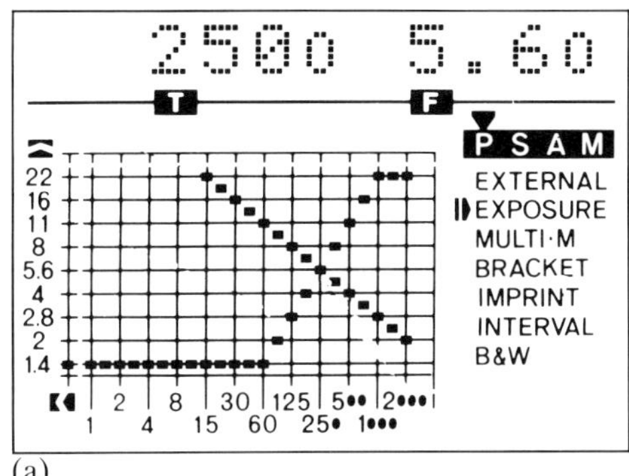

(a)

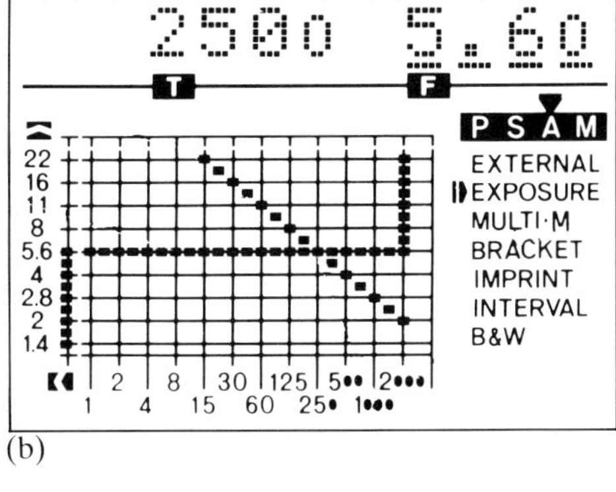

(b)

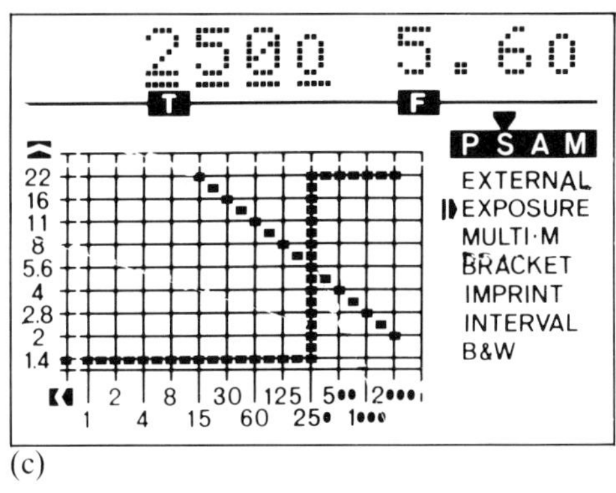

(c)

Program mapping on Minolta's Program Back Super 90. In Programmed AE mode (a) the LCD displays the program curve (running from 1sec at f/1.4 bottom left to 1/2000sec at f/22 top right), and the EV line going from top left to bottom right. You can shift the program along this EV line for alternative aperture/speed combinations; the curve will move accordingly in the display. The display in aperture priority AE mode (b) has a different curve shape (aperture remains constant over the whole shutter speed range). The intersection with the oblique EV line again indicates the actual exposure set by the camera. The principle is the same for shutter speed priority AE, with curve shape and priority reversed (c). In manual mode (d) aperture and speed lines cross; when the oblique EV line intersects the crossing point, you have the correct exposure setting. Multiple memory function (e) display changes to show separate spot readings above and below horizontal bar line indicating exposure latitude.

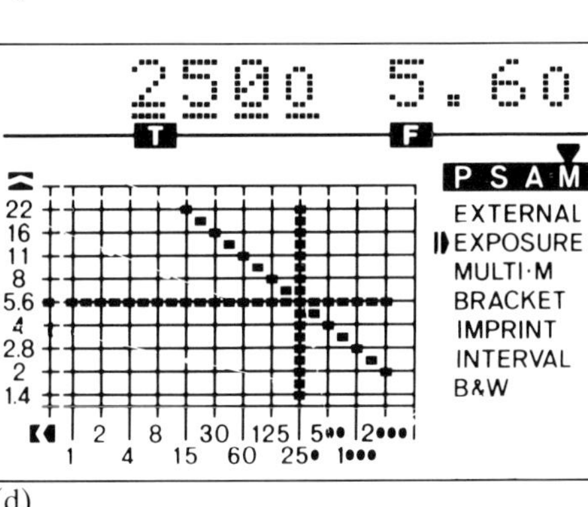

(d)

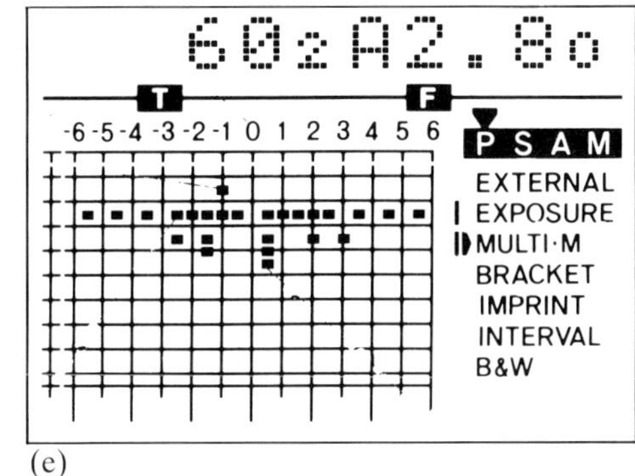

(e)

manual mode would be expected to change apertures and/or speeds, selects alternative programs.

With either camera the shift adds a dimension to the setting range. But the user does not really know were exactly he is at any time in this extended territory. The finder singles the actual aperture/speed combination set. But one would have to carry in one's head a program map similar to that illustrated here to know which part of which program is actually in use.

Taking computerisation a step further, the Program Back Super 90 accessory back for the Minolta 9000 displays just such a program map. It indicates available exposure combinations in each mode (program, aperture-preferred AE etc), allows preselection of maximum and minimum apertures that the program should not go beyond and displays the actual combination set, all on a bit-mapped LCD. In a multiple memory mode it even displays on that map multiple readings that are averaged or otherwise adjusted for the correct exposure.

All this certainly gets more mileage out of exposure programs. It also becomes at least as involved as choosing settings in aperture or shutter priority AE mode. This technical overkill negates the decision-free purpose of programming.

Lens-compatible autofocus

After years of heartsearching by designers and engineers, the market impact of Minolta's 7000 (and further models of the '1000' series) proved the value of getting priorities right. Sharpness metering on its own was not good enough: autofocusing cameras had to offer focusing speed and convenience that translated into easier picture taking.

The Data Memory Back of the Canon T90 is the first system to be able to memorise exposure data as input into, or set by, the camera and to download them into a Personal Computer.

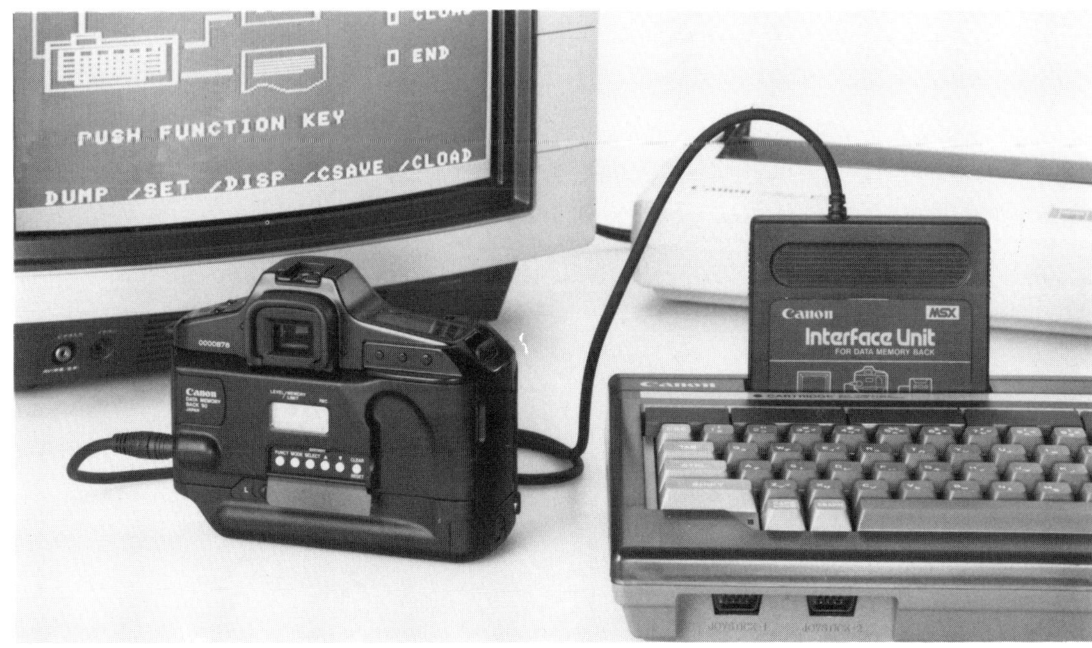

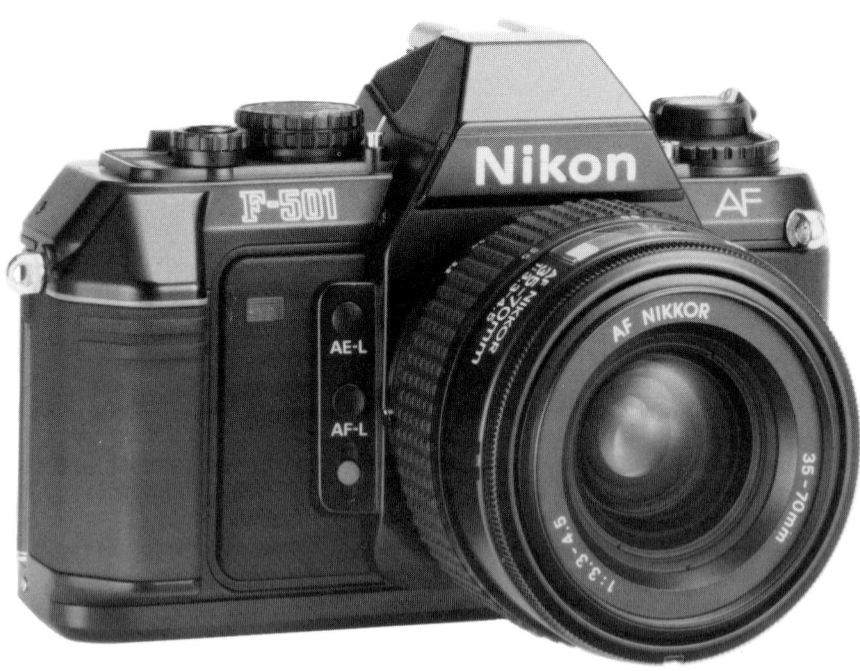

Lens-compatible AF: Nikon's 501 AF (N 2020 in the USA) autofocuses with new range of Nikon lenses but can also operate (in part with AF) with most existing Nikon AT-mounted optics.

The argument has now shifted from relative merits of different measuring systems (contrast v. phase shift) to lens compatibility and camera model policy. This does not mean that the technology has become unimportant; but sharpness metering as used in SLR cameras has not changed fundamentally in the last five years. At best it has improved a little here and there: the autofocus sensitivity in the most recent Minolta 5000 is significantly better than in the original 7000 a year and a half ago. (Present 7000s have probably been upgraded, too.) But this is not that relevant to the comparatively lay user who wouldn't know how to measure autofocus limits, anyway.

Relevant, however, is what lenses the photographer can use with his AF camera. The Pentax (MF) and Canon (T80) experience on the one hand — and of course Minolta on the other — proved clearly that the focusing motor power has to be not in the lenses but in the camera. As the first to appear on the market Minolta could get away with a new lens system incompatible with what there was before. Nikon and Canon — with a much larger established and professional lens selection to look after — could not.

In its autofocusing 501 AF camera, Nikon — like Minolta in the 7000/9000/5000 range — uses a sharpness metering system based on phase shift detection. This is the electronic way of noticing that two halves of a split image are displaced relative to each other. The ways of evaluating the output signals of the measuring module differ of course. Nikon also uses two rows of CCD detectors — one to deal with the image at lens apertures larger than f/2.8 and the other for lenses for maximum apertures between f/2.8 and f/4.5. The electrical input from the lens on the camera determines which CCD set is used. The larger-aperture system is more sensitive — i.e. usable at lower lighting levels, quite apart from the lens aperture itself, but not

Program shifting means that you can move the standard program curve (top) to a number of additional positions for — in this case — altogether seven alternative programs. The exposure locus can move in two dimensions instead of one — but becomes almost as complex to understand in practice as it looks on paper. (This is Canon T90 — the Minolta 9000 program shift differs slightly in detail but is similar in principle.

Standard Program AE Characteristics Graph

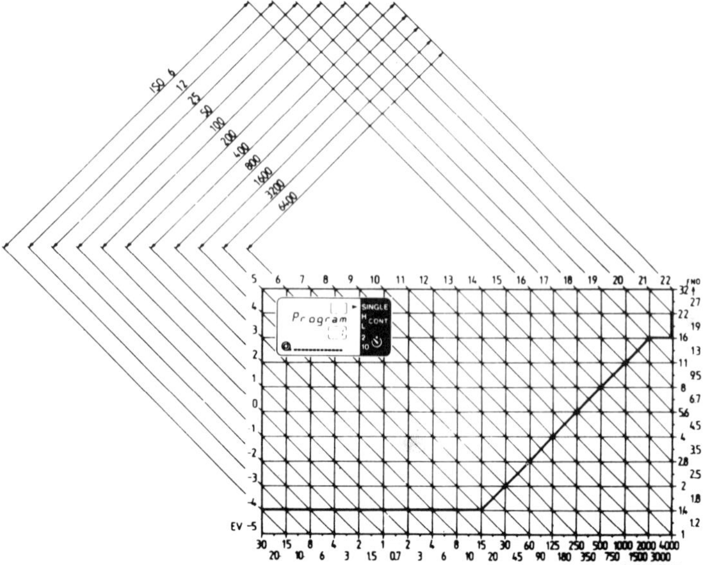

Variable-shift Program AE Characteristics Graph

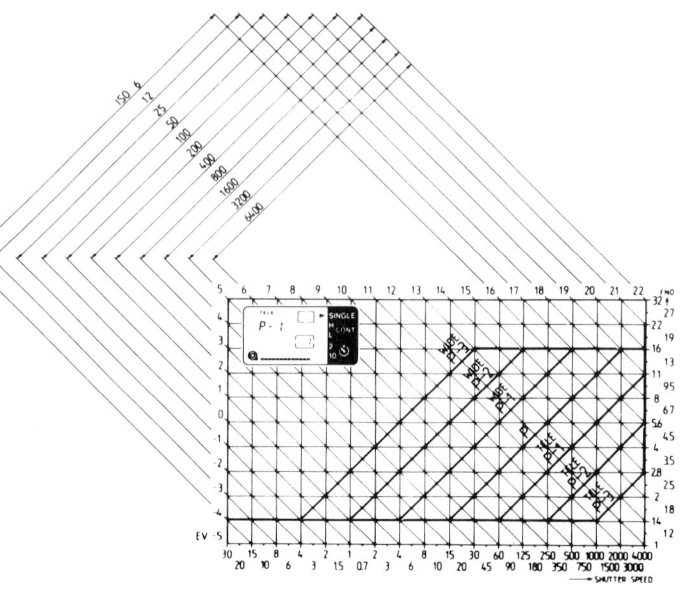

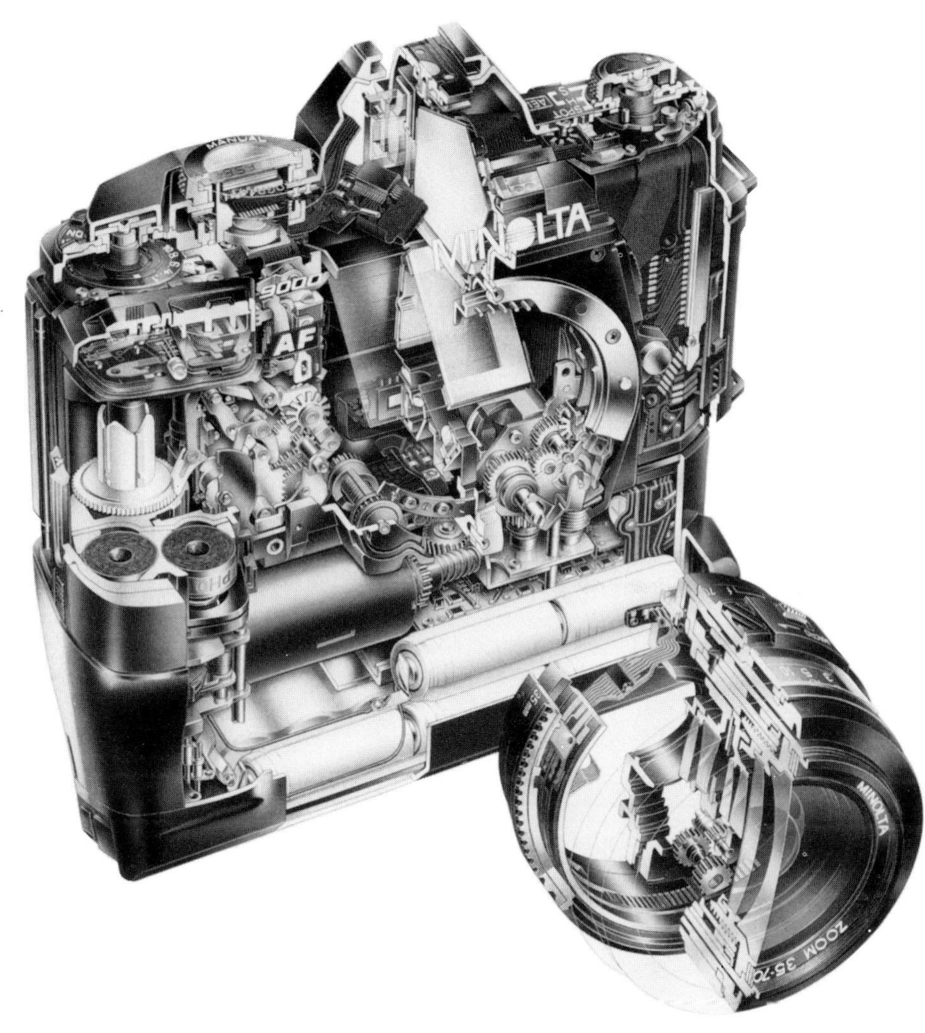

The computerised camera: microchips drive motors, exposure settings and digital displays.

sufficiently accurate with a slower lens — hence the alternative set. This is analogous to the relative advantage of high-angle and low-angle rangefinder wedges and microprisms for faster and slower lenses respectively.

For the 501 AF Nikon cleverly solved the compatibility problem three ways:

1. The autofocusing motor built into the camera drives a new set of dedicated autofocus lenses for full AF functioning;
2. The TC-16A autofocus converter provides autofocusing with over 30 existing (non-AF) Nikon lenses;
3. All non-AF Nikon lenses remain usable on the camera, most in focus assist mode, i.e. with the sharpness metering system providing a sharp/unsharp signal in the camera's viewfinder.

The TC-16A converter follows the same optical principle as the TC-16 introduced a couple of years ago for the Nikon F3AF. Internal movement of the teleconverter elements (by the camera's focusing motor in the case of the TC-16A) focuses whichever lens is attached to the converter. It is also subject to the same optical limitations. Firstly, autofocusing only works with lenses of f/2.8 or faster — which the converter turns to f/4.5, the limiting aperture for autofocusing in the Nikon system. (Sharpness metering with regular Nikon lenses does not work with systems slower than f/4.5, either). Secondly, longer focal lengths have inconveniently distant near focusing limits.

For marketing, Minolta's timing of its Autofocus cameras was even more important. The 7000 could hardly have gained the phenomenal market shares it did during 1985 if Nikon had had its 501 AF ready a year earlier. On the other hand Nikon's approach looks like being the model for future autofocus SLRs. That is, now that Nikon has proved the practicability of camera-driven AF compatible with the camera's previous lens range, Minolta's lens solution is unlikely to become a new industry standard. There was intense speculation on this possibility about a year ago. Certainly Canon cannot afford to bring out an autofocus camera that would not be compatible with the existing Canon lens range, which is as widely used among professionals as is Nikon's.

The other camera makers showing — and possibly even marketing — new autofocus SLRs by photokina 1986 would also appear to have better reason to follow Nikon's rather than Minolta's lens policy example.

Can there be life without AF?

At the time of writing the Minolta 5000/7000/9000 models and the Nikon 501 AF are the only popular SLR cameras on the market with autofocusing. They are of course unlikely to keep this unique position. In a couple of years at the latest, middle- and

The computerised through the lens automatic flash output control in the Minolta 9000 shown in this diagram with its dedicated flash unit.

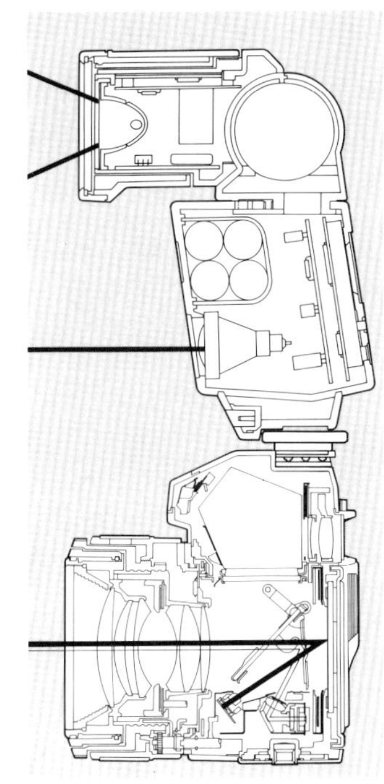

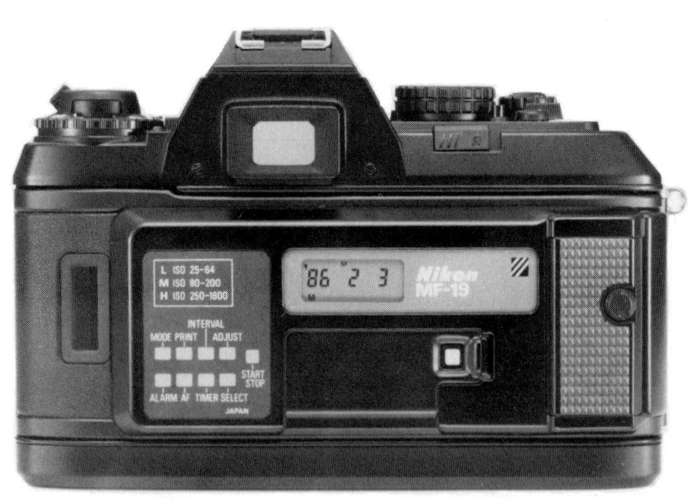

Several cameras now take command backs that control both data imprinting and interval timing for automatic time lapse photography and similar applications.

upper-price SLRs will have little chance on the mass market if they do not offer AF. Current sophisticated models especially are now obsolescent, though some of them will take a little time to disappear altogether. But the introduction of new non-AF reflexes should — except in the lowest price range — dwindle to negligible levels. Even this price cut-off point is uncertain. Evidently Minolta planned AF models for all price levels and introduced them as soon as production capacity allowed. There are even rumours of a Minolta 3000. Autofocusing will be viewed as something as indispensable as exposure automation.

Lens compatibility makes matters easier for independent lens makers than incompatible lens ranges — licensing of the Minolta mount is still very restricted — but only slightly easier. On the one hand the focusing drive shaft and its coupling in the lens should not pose major patent problems. On the other, Nikon — like Minolta — took the opportunity of the new AF facilities to install a ROM chip in its autofocus lenses to assist exposure programming. So an independent-make AF lens without ROM chip is a poor second-best on the market.

'Compatible' independent ROM chips are in the same position as IBM-compatible personal computers: In some applications they do not quite offer the facilities of the original equipment. The deviation is not clearly definable but will show up sooner or later. Minolta have hinted that the ROM in its lenses contains provision for functions not yet utilised in current Minolta cameras.

Further autofocusing SLRs, even if compatible with lenses from earlier cameras, will have different ROM (or other information storage) configurations. Nikon can afford to tell buyers of the 501 AF that they can with specific restrictions use older lenses; independent lens suppliers must offer full current compatibility. On the other hand budget-conscious photographers tend to select cameras for which they can buy lower-priced independent lenses. Paradoxically it is in the economy camera maker's interest to encourage the independent lens producer.

A curious sidelight on the program control surfeit is the effect of what could be called electronic pollution. The multitude of static, magnetic and radiation fields that abound in locations where electronic and electric control processes take place. The flood of stray signals is beginning to cause interference with information flow in portable computers and may do so in more sophisticated cameras. Aircraft operators have long been nervous of passengers using radios in flight. Passengers may get cause to worry about what the plane's electrical system is doing to their portable computing equipment. Electronic and X-ray security systems at airports could eventually pose greater risks to the ICs and chips in the hardware than to the film.

The electronic-image generation

In past progress reviews we repeatedly remarked on the potential of electronic image recording to analyse and control its recording modes. We did, and still, expect automation and computerisation there to execute more elegantly the exposure and sharpness programming functions of present hybrid systems.

Meanwhile Canon has announced the RC 701 — the first still video camera likely to reach the market. The point it most strongly illustrates is that, unlike visionary flights of fancy, technological evolution rarely advances at more than a very pedestrian step at a time.

In fact, the RC 701 is a traditional SLR concept with very little of the expected high-flying computerisation. It simply has a CCD instead of film — photography's new motorised horse carriage. Perhaps it is just as well; electronic recording is scaring the photographic industry, as motors scared the horses. For the present it should be enough of a miracle that it works. Imaginative engineering will come later.■

The Canon RC 701, the first still video camera on the market, part of a £25-30 000 system for the magnetic recording, modem transmission, and inkjet printout of colour pictures.

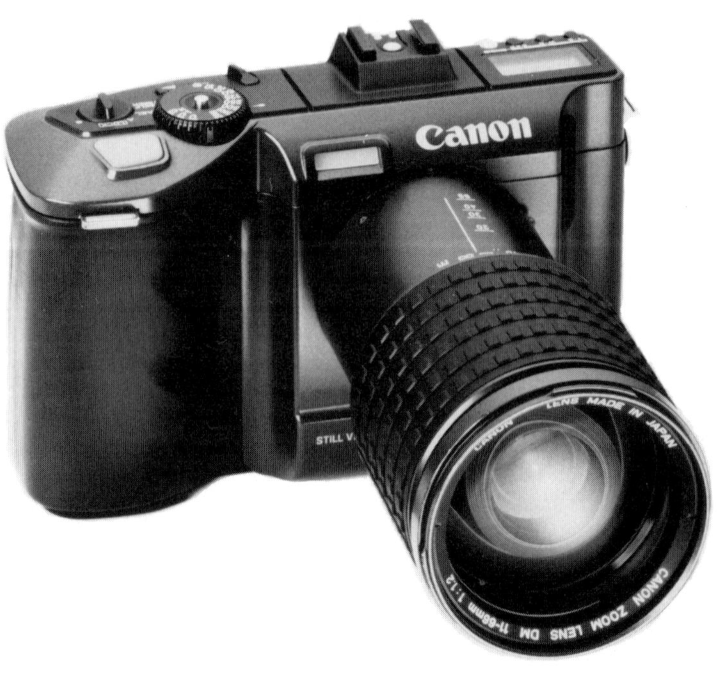

CAR PHOTOGRAPHY

Tim Imrie looks at a specialised field full, he says, of contradictions and anomalies.

HALFWAY THROUGH researching for this article, I almost began to wish that I had never started. Car photography seemed to be quite a straightforward subject, but in practice it is such a mass of contradictions and anomalies that it is impossible to come up with a nice clean-cut set of generalisations that summarise the business.

Cars get to be photographed in a studio or on almost any kind of location you care to mention, and on almost any format you care to mention. The shoot can be constrained by a vice-tight brief, with art directors and clients hovering like expectant fathers around every emerging Polaroid, or it can be as loose as a thumbnail sketch advising the photographer where the copy will fall. The transparencies can be used complete and unretouched, or as only one element in a complex and heavily retouched montage.

And that is just on the advertising side. Editorial car photography is different again, and the differences between the two are greater than you might expect. True, editorial photographers do also work on advertising commissions, and some agencies do use editorial photographs to sell cars (although one major publication refuses on principle to release any of its material for advertising purposes) but the requirements are different and that shows up in the style of some of the images.

Advertising shots are almost never taken with a wide angle lens, which would distort the proportions of the car, whereas in editorial work, it sometimes seems as if they never use anything else. Again, in advertising the car is only rarely shot in motion, while the better magazines are full of superb panning shots with just the right balance of blur and sharp detail.

Good editorial outlets for car photography are in fact very limited. The majority of prestige books on cars concentrate on historic vehicles and use archive photographs or illustrations, while the number of motoring magazines that take their photography seriously can be counted on the fingers of one hand. *Car* and its sister magazines *Supercar* and *Truck* are the best and the best known. In little more than a decade, the publishers have acquired a reputation for a quality of work that gives them the unstinting co-operation of vehicle manufacturers when they want to do a feature on their models, and enables them to bring in the volume of advertising they need to produce a well-finished mazazine.

The present art-director for all three publications is Adam Stinson who took over from Wendy Harrop when she moved to *World of Interiors.* Between the two of them, they have built up a small network of eight photographers who are very strong on the atmospheric, slightly oblique style of photography that sets the magazine apart from the more prosaically descriptive work of their rivals.

The strength of the current team makes it difficult for other photographers to break into working for *Car,* though Stinson does try to find time for everyone who asks to show their folio. However, he is generally disappointed by what he sees, by the lack of fresh ideas and by the tendency for photographers to allow the subject itself to do all the work and to assume that an exciting piece of machinery will automatically make an exciting photograph.

This is precisely what *Car* is not about. It is true that the magazine features a lot of what one might call fantasy cars, which can take a degree of photographic

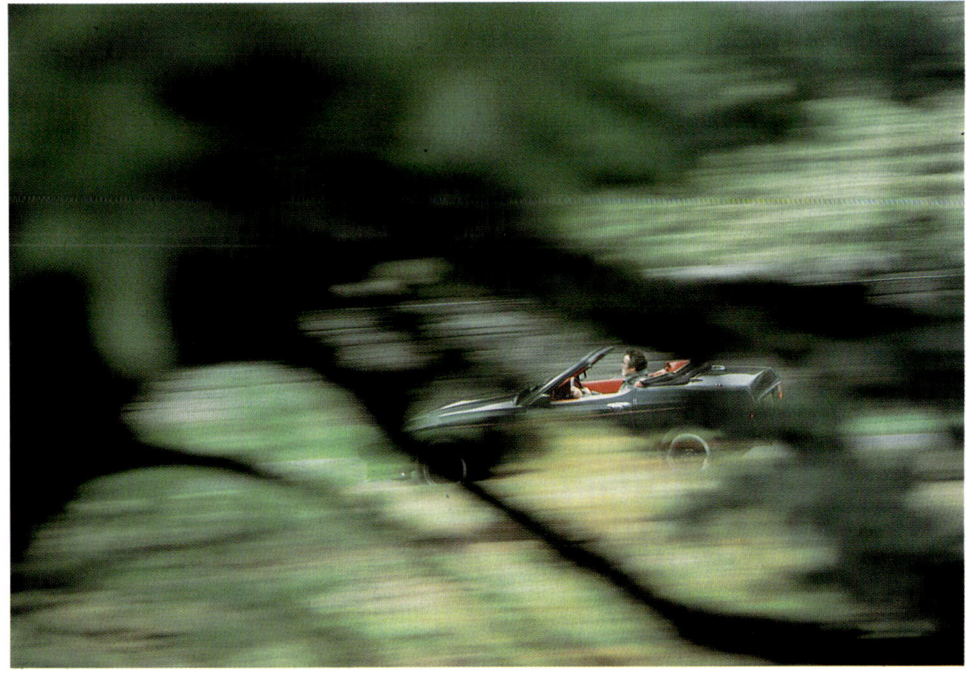

TVR Coupe — John Mason.

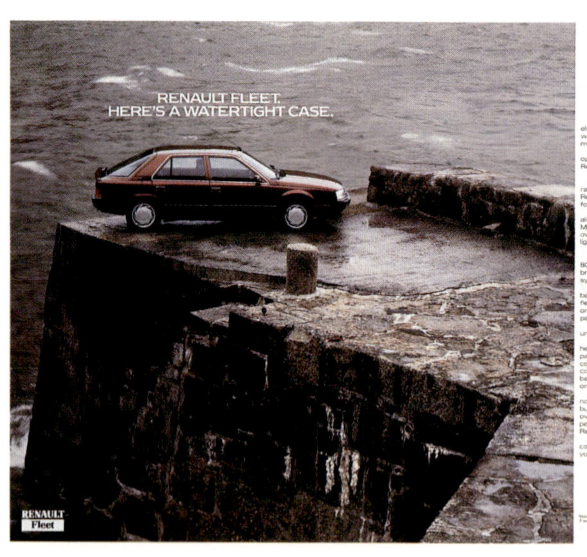

experimentation and flamboyancy that would just look silly if applied to a Ford Fiesta, but *Car*'s photographers are expected to produce the unexpected, no matter what the car or the circumstances. It generates the sort of pressure the magazine's favourite photographers, such as John Mason, thrive on — late afternoon, beginning to rain, the car has to be back with the supplier tomorrow morning, and you still haven't found the right location. Yet for him, it is this sort of semi-anarchy and the necessity for turning disadvantage into advantage that often produces the most dynamic images.

The photograph of the TVR Coupé he took at Blackpool was made in perfect British holiday weather: driving rain, a biting wind and a sky full of clouds. As Mason parked the car on the promenade in the hope that the mud-coloured sea and leaden sky might provide some sort of backdrop, he noticed a man with a folded deck-chair some distance off, struggling against the wind as he moved slowly in his direction. And he knew that, human nature being what it is, that man would have to turn and stare as he passed by at the incongruous piece of exotica parked on the

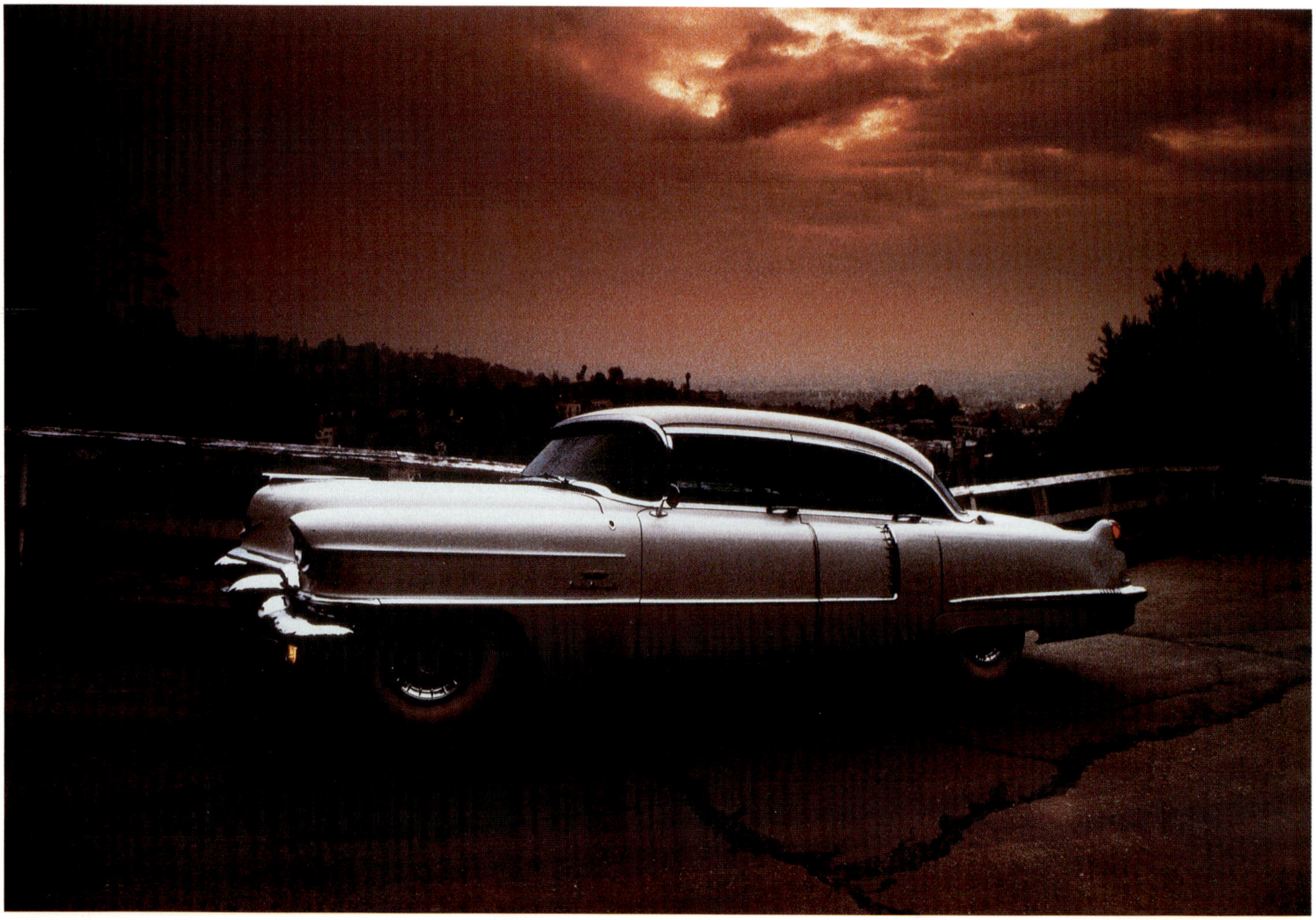

Top: Renault fleet advertisement. Above: Old American car — Jake Wallis.

PHOTOGRAPHY AND THE LAW

Robin Fry on legal matters of concern to photographers.

IT IS probably a very familiar feeling: a wonderful editorial shot appearing before you, but the rather nervous feeling that the ticket you have in your hands, at the concert, says 'no photography'. What does one do?

Is one allowed to take the photographs? Even if one does take the photographs, covertly, can they be reproduced; if so, is there a possible injunction against you or maybe a liability for royalties to the owner of the land or the person shown in the photograph?

The position highlights, really quite clearly, what copyright is all about. The most important and central matter, of course, is who is entitled to reproduce the photographs and, as a corollary, in what circumstances could someone prevent you from reproducing them. The rules for this are in the Copyright Act 1956. This says that the first copyright owner of a photograph is the 'author' but the Act goes on to define that person not as the photographer but as the person who owned the film on which the photograph was taken. This is a somewhat unusual definition for an author and, certainly, in literary, dramatic and other artistic areas, the first copyright owner is, naturally, the author of those works.

In fact, the latest government White Paper published in May 1986 has decided, simply, to define the author of a photograph as 'the photographer' but, until those proposals come into law, one should be extremely careful about using a borrowed camera or, being lent film stock by friends or film companies; you could find yourself in these circumstances without the copyright in 'your' photographs.

Who owns the copyright is important: copyright is the right to prevent other people copying your work and if a person does not have copyright in photographs even if, say, that person is the subject shown, he or she cannot prevent publication of these photographs unless the photographer has, somehow, breached other rules, e.g. in libel or contract.

This definition of the first owner of copyright does not relate, in any way, to the circumstances in which the photograph was taken. Therefore, if you are on someone else's land, the fact that no specific permission has been obtained to take photographs does not mean that the basic rules as to ownership of copyright has changed. If you are the original photographer, then you will be the copyright owner and you will be able to reproduce the photographs as you wish without payment of royalties to other persons.

It is interesting to note that, unlike in the USA, people do not have any rights to their own appearance; accordingly, rock stars, political figures and TV stars can all be photographed and printed up on T-shirts, posters, mugs and other merchandised items without the need for obtaining permission from that person and without payment of any form of royalty. Adverts for Trivial Pursuit, for instance, have shown photographs of Margaret Thatcher and David Owen pondering some trivia and neither of them would be in a position to ask for a model fee or any form of royalty for being shown in the adverts.

Because of the very large amounts of money available in so-called merchandising, use has to be made of other copyright material and so often one will note that some form of logo, original drawing or trademark has been incorporated so that celebrities, doing their own merchandising, can, at least, establish some form of merchandising which can be protected by law against copying.

The Pope, for instance, in his visit to England had established a substantial merchandising business through Mark MaCormack's IMG organisation, the income from which was used to subsidise the tour. Many items were put out as 'official' Papal souvenirs showing the Pope's tour logo (protected in copyright). The organisation would not have been in a position, however, to prevent books, pamphlets and other items, simply, showing photographs of Pope John Paul (as opposed to the logo) since there is no copyright in his appearance. The copyright is owned by the photographer and not by the subject (however divine).

If one looks, for example, at the position of a photographer taking shots at a race meeting, rock concert or, in the gardens of a National Trust house, the copyright in all such photographs will normally belong to the photographer.

That said, it may well be that the owners of the land take exception to somebody taking photographs 'without permission' and may ask the photographer to leave. That permission may be required, explicitly, as a condition of entry, e.g. as in 'no photographs' or 'camera fee: £5' but if one fails to obtain the necessary permission, this does not invalidate the laws in relation to ownership of the copyright in the photographs.

Editorial photographers, therefore, should not easily be intimidated by threats that film be confiscated, or payments made in situations where the police or other authorities assert that the photographer is trespassing or that his permission to be there has been revoked.

One major exception to this is in connection with the Official Secret Act 1916 which may make it a criminal offence to take photographs of certain military installations although, as is well known, the statute is so widely drafted that it could, possibly, be used against the photographer in a very wide variety of situations where national security may not be in issue.

I did mention above the basic provision in the Copyright Act 1956 as regards ownership of copyright but this is subject to the following main exceptions:

i Where a photographer has been commissioned 'for money or money's worth' and a photograph is taken in pursuance of that commission then the commissioner has the copyright.

ii Photographs taken in the

course of employment, as a staff photographer, will be owned by the employer.

iii If there is a contract or agreement, in advance, as regards ownership of copyright then this will override the usual copyright provisions.

iv Copyright can, in any case, be assigned in writing.

Recently, there has been considerable pressure from the NUJ/AFAEP and other photographic bodies for a new Copyright Act to abandon the automatic right of commissioners to receive copyright in commissioned photographs. The provision operates, at the moment, at the time the photograph is taken, and therefore the injustice is that the commissioner has copyright whether or not the photographer ever gets paid.

The position is considerably confused for advertising photographers because if, say, a shot is commissioned for brochure use in the UK only, then the commissioner will still have the entire copyright in that photograph and it will be up to the photographer to try to establish that the commissioner had specifically contracted not to use the photographs in other areas; this may be difficult to prove where there was an oral commission and very little in writing.

Shots taken on location will always remain the property of the photographer (subject to the specific exceptions above) but a photographer should be aware that he or she has no more nor no less a right than any other member of the public to enter on someone's land, cause an obstruction or take photographs. 'Freedom of the press' does not exist, as a positive right, but one should be aware that once the photographs have been taken, there should not, in general, be any bar on their publication.■

Robin Fry is a partner in the firm of Stephens Innocent, Solicitors, St Mary's Clergy House, 2 Whitechurch Lane, London E1.

COPYRIGHT PROPOSALS

First reactions from the respected and highly professional Association of Fashion, Advertising and Editorial Photographers to the Governments 1986 White Paper on the reform of the copyright law.

THE Committee of the Association of Fashion, Advertising and Editorial Photographers on Photographic Copyright welcomed the proposal in the Government's White Paper on Copyright — *Intellectual Property and Innovation* — that the photographer should be deemed the author of a photograph. The photographer was the only creator hitherto not granted this essential recognition. However, to make the law uniform in all respects for all authors, the term of copyright for photographers should now be as for other authors: fifty years from the end of the year in which the photographer dies, not fifty years from the date when the photograph is taken.

The major disappointment with the White Paper was that, despite many representations from the bodies concerned, the Government has chosen to leave the exceptions to the original ownership of copyright unchanged. Thus in cases of employment, contract of service or apprenticeship and commissioned work, the owner of the copyright is still the commissioner of the photograph. Professional photographers earn their living from these areas.

AFAEP feel strongly that in all cases the author should be the first owner of copyright and that the assignment of copyright should be covered by contractual agreement. This part of the present law serves to protect the rights of large, powerful corporations against those of the individual photographer, which is contrary to the original intent of copyright legislation. AFAEP intends to continue to press for these exceptions to be removed from the Copyright Law.

AFAEP's view is that the failure of the White Paper *Intellectual Property and Innovation* (April 1986) to redress the injustices of the 1956 and 1911 Copyright Acts as far as freelance photographers are concerned, is appalling. They go on to criticise current laws as well as the proposals of the White Paper.■

Members and Observers of the Committee on Photographic Copyright

Association of Fashion, Advertising and Editorial Photographers, British Association of Picture Libraries and Agencies, British Institute of Professional Photography, Institute of Journalists, Institute of Medical and Biological Illustration, Master Photographers Association, National Union of Journalists, Royal Photographic Society, Society of Industrial Artists and Designers, Society of Picture Researchers and Editors, British Sports Photographers Association.

VIDEO TODAY

Reginald Miles relates the year's main developments and looks at what may be coming.

1986 WAS a year of several important anniversaries in television and video, of events from fifty years to five years ago. The first was the advent of television broadcasting itself, first in Germany and then in England in 1936. The former service ran until 1944, whereas the BBC pulled the plug at the outbreak of war — apparently in the middle of a Mickey Mouse cartoon without even a 'goodbye'. In 1951 Bing Crosby Enterprises were credited with the first demonstration of black-and-white video recording, using a longitudinal VTR. Five years later the Ampex Quadruplex became the first VTR with a performance that made it suitable for marketing. For this 3M produced the first proper video tape — 2in wide. 1976 saw the birth of JVC's Video Home System format which now dominates the domestic market and has moved into the lower end of the industrial one. All told, about 100 million VHS machines have been sold worldwide. Finally, five years ago saw the launch of Sony's Betacam and Matsushita's M-format camcorders for electronic news gathering. And the appearance of Sony's electronic still camera prototype, Mavica.

At the time of writing the Mavica still hasn't been launched (although the Mavigraph printer has) but Canon have gone ahead with a professional ESC for press and TV news-gathering use in Japan. It was going to be launched here in 1986, but it's now been put back, quite possibly because part of the system is a telephone transmitter, and British Telecom tend to be rather slow in licensing such things for use over their network.

In the mean time, the newspapers have taken a step into video by employing image-grabbing systems and doing deals with the BBC and commercial stations to allow them to grab video frames and turn them into newspaper pictures. Once they've got used to the method, it will be interesting to see what, if any, difference there will be between those and run-of-the-mill newspaper pictures. And whether this easy-come approach will cause a change in photographic coverage of events (and eventually redundancies).

There is further scope for the development of image grabbing as satellite programming increases. 1986 saw a sudden upsurge in interest in this medium with both large and small companies offering dish receivers. One company, Connexions Satellite Systems, broke the £1000 price barrier, and then further reduced the system to £895 (including VAT), while Thorn EMI Ferguson began renting them through their chain of rental outlets. The Government also did their bit and made it unnecessary to have planning permission to erect dishes of 90cm and less — although such small sizes will only become practicable when the high power satellites are launched: the present ones need at least a 1.2 metre dish for reasonable reception.

Satellite transmission will be necessary for the future high definition TV system proposed for the nineties. Unfortunately, there are two conflicting systems: one developed by the IBA known as C-MAC; the other developed by NHK (Japanese Broadcasting Corporation) called Hi-Vision. Naturally Japan and also the States have adopted the latter, while the USSR is said to be interested in it. In Western Europe, however, there is a general preference for the C-MAC system. So the dream of one international TV standard may have to wait until well into the 21st century to be realised.

On the bright side, stereo sound may be transmitted in the London area in time for Christmas 1986, if the Department of Trade gives the

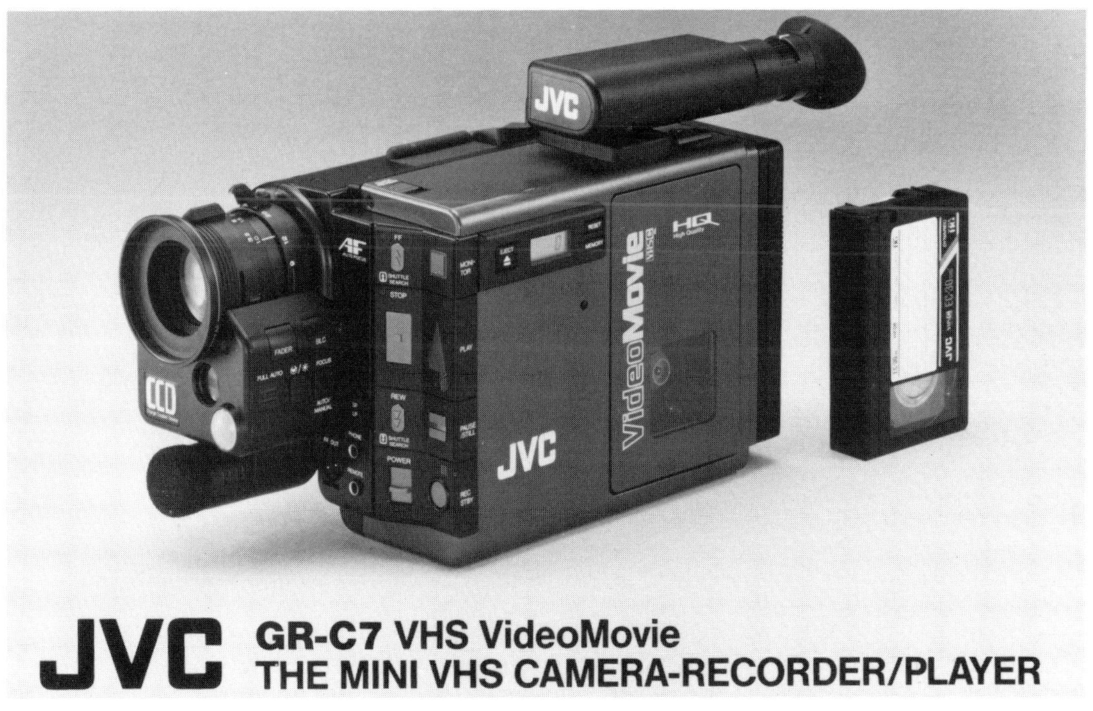

go-ahead to the BBC. The digital system, called 728-Nicam, has also been agreed to by the IBA. But which will come first, the transmissions or TVs with suitable tuners?

Another bit of good news for video users is that there will be no levy charged on blank tapes, because they're mainly used for timeshifting. Only audio cassettes incur a penalty.

Of more academic interest was the news from Philips that the Video 2000 format was officially dead. It was probably doomed from the outset, even if there hadn't been the delay between its announcement and introduction which allowed the Japanese companies to offer competitive features and if the early machines had provided decent picture quality. The continuing decline of the Beta format implies that the majority of people think that one format is quite sufficient.

Which doesn't auger well for 8mm video — particularly after the major VHS companies, like Hitachi and Matsushita, changed their minds about launching it in '86 and are continuing to concentrate on VHS Movie camcorders instead. The Hitachi VHS Movie is the one that both Minolta and Pentax chose to use for their UK video debut. But it was JVC's VideoMovie, using a VHS-C cassette, that grabbed the news: the GR-C7 squeezes a camera and a recorder with full playback facilities into a package that's remarkably small and light (1.4kg). And, by the time that you read this, they should have launched an even smaller and lighter one (under 800g) in Japan with very simple features similar to Sony's 8mm Handycam — which weighs 1kg. However, 8mm certainly isn't finished, for the list of companies marketing 8mm camcorders and mains machines continues to grow, and a few more — like Sanyo — joined Canon and Sony in actually manufacturing them.

Despite the fact that 8mm is still very much at the beginning of its development curve, there has already been a rumour that companies are starting to develop 4mm video, using the Digital Audio Tape format cassette. This is apparently intended for camcorder use to bring the size and weight down still further, although this quest for miniaturisation could result in equipment so light that it can't be held steady, and a lot of disappointed users.

In the more practical broadcast market, Hitachi have designed a camcorder for electronic news gathering around the 8mm cassette — although that is the only similarity with the domestic 8mm format. Meanwhile Bosch have finally launched their Quartercam format, using the Compact Video Cassette with quarter-inch tape developed by Funai and Fuji and briefly flirted with in the amateur market by Canon, Grundig and Technicolor.

Whether these new ENG camcorder formats can make any impression on a market that is largely dominated by Sony's Betacam with Matsushita's M-format trailing along remains to be seen. In the past broadcasters have always put pressure on manufacturers to standardise their products. Now there seems to be no stopping the process of incompatibility; already M-format has begot M-II, jointly developed by Matsushita and NHK and now also adopted by JVC, which is incompatible with its predecessor (it still uses the VHS cassette, but this is now loaded with expensive metal tape).

In the domestic market VHS recorders with High Quality image enhancement are compatible with non-HQ tapes and vice-versa. Which is a good thing, because a high proportion of the latest VCRs and some camcorders now make use of it. Sony's Super Beta recorder is also compatible.

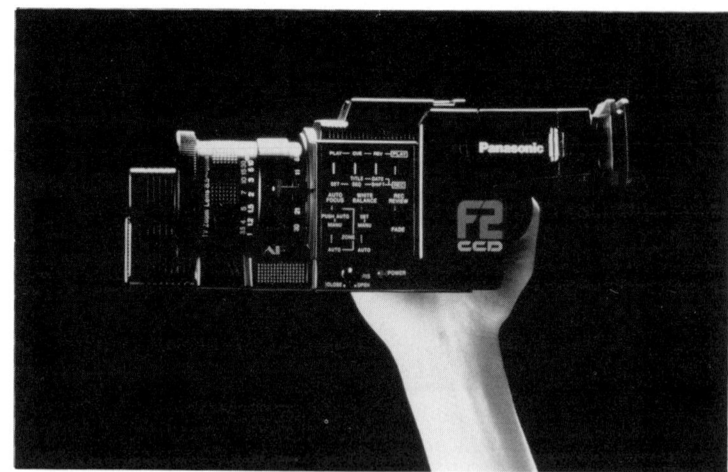

Panasonic WVP-F2.

But incompatibility seems to be a growth area: there is a new video disc format called Laser Film Disc jointly developed by McDonnell Douglas Electronics, Sansui and Nissho-Iwai. It's intended to be a DIY system, using photographic printing technology, and operating in a manner akin to the optical soundtrack of a motion picture film — although in this case it's a laser shining through the density variations. Its one limitation is that it can only carry up to seventeen minutes of programming on its single side. There is also a 3-D variant on JVC's Video High Density capacitive disc. This has alternate left and right eye images recorded on it, which are viewed on a normal TV through liquid crystal shutter glasses developed by Sharp that blank off each eye in turn by remote control from the player. Or, in the case of the projection version, blank off each tube in turn so that the screen can be viewed through normal polarising glasses. Finally, Thomson Brandt of France and Nakamichi are developing recordable versions of the Philips laser disc and the Compact audio disc.

The use of video disc — and tape — in interactive video systems is on the increase as companies and institutions realise the potential for education, training, marketing and selling.

The camera side has also seen some interesting developments. The first 13mm CCD has appeared (previous solid-state pick-up devices were 17mm) in the Panasonic WVP-F2 and their JVC GR-C7 camcorder, while Sony's DXC3000 ENG camera has three 17mm CCDs. Panasonic's WV-V3 is their second industrial camera to have three small 13mm Newvicon tubes, and the first of any industrial camera to borrow self-adjusting white balance from the amateur cameras. Going back to their WVP-F2, this is the first camera on the UK market to make use of the CCD pick-up for autofocusing; and giving a choice of three focusing areas — small, medium and virtually full area — for different subjects.

Finally, 1986 saw a considerable increase in the number of computer graphics systems being offered, with more features for less cost, a number of them with resolution of 4000 lines or more to enable high quality transparencies to be produced.

1986 turned out to be a rather fruitful year for video developments. It was a shame about the loss of the V2000 format; but Philips have already gained a very nice market share with their VHS recorders to make up for it, and Grundig aren't doing too badly either. So in general things continue to look up. And to become more relevant to photographers — for better or worse.■

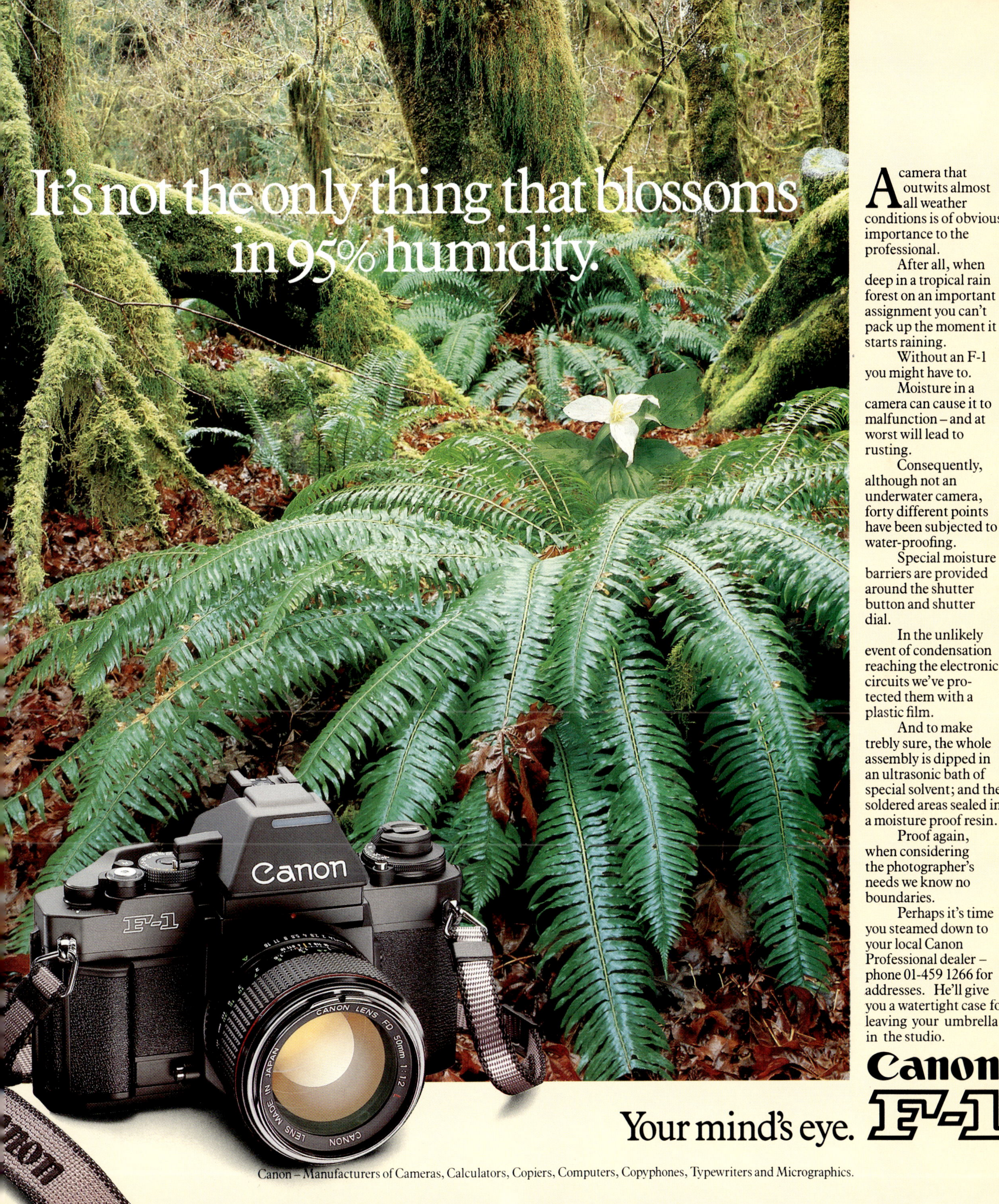
It's not the only thing that blossoms in 95% humidity.
A camera that outwits almost all weather conditions is of obvious importance to the professional.
After all, when deep in a tropical rain forest on an important assignment you can't pack up the moment it starts raining.
Without an F-1 you might have to.
Moisture in a camera can cause it to malfunction – and at worst will lead to rusting.
Consequently, although not an underwater camera, forty different points have been subjected to water-proofing.
Special moisture barriers are provided around the shutter button and shutter dial.
In the unlikely event of condensation reaching the electronic circuits we've protected them with a plastic film.
And to make trebly sure, the whole assembly is dipped in an ultrasonic bath of special solvent; and the soldered areas sealed in a moisture proof resin.
Proof again, when considering the photographer's needs we know no boundaries.
Perhaps it's time you steamed down to your local Canon Professional dealer – phone 01-459 1266 for addresses. He'll give you a watertight case for leaving your umbrella in the studio.
Canon
F-1
Your mind's eye.
Canon
F-1
CANON LENS FD 50mm 1:1.2
LENS MADE IN JAPAN
Canon – Manufacturers of Cameras, Calculators, Copiers, Computers, Copyphones, Typewriters and Micrographics.

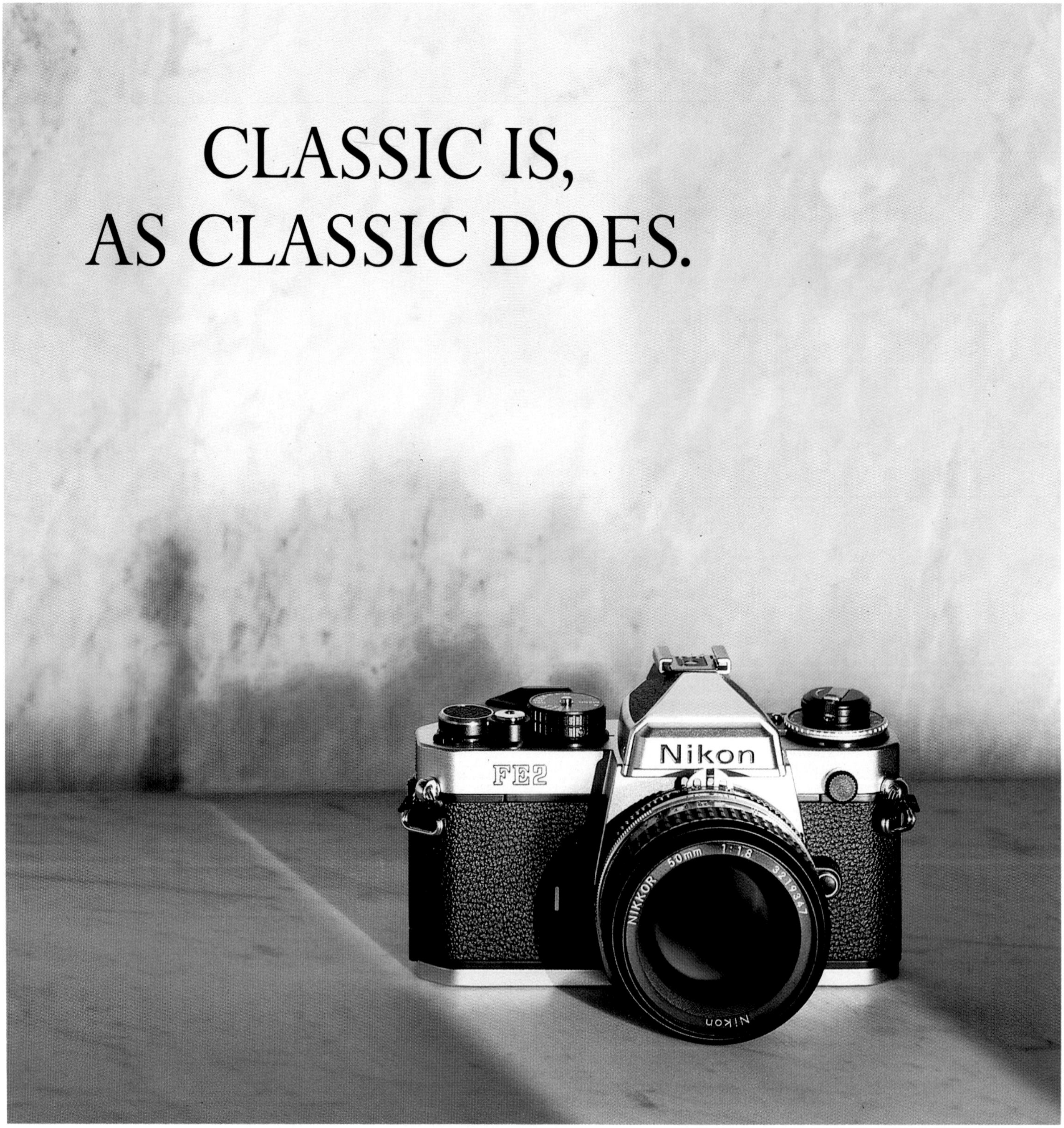

A THOUSAND AND ONE NIGHTS

Tom Ang looks at the book and exhibition which attracted great acclaim in the year

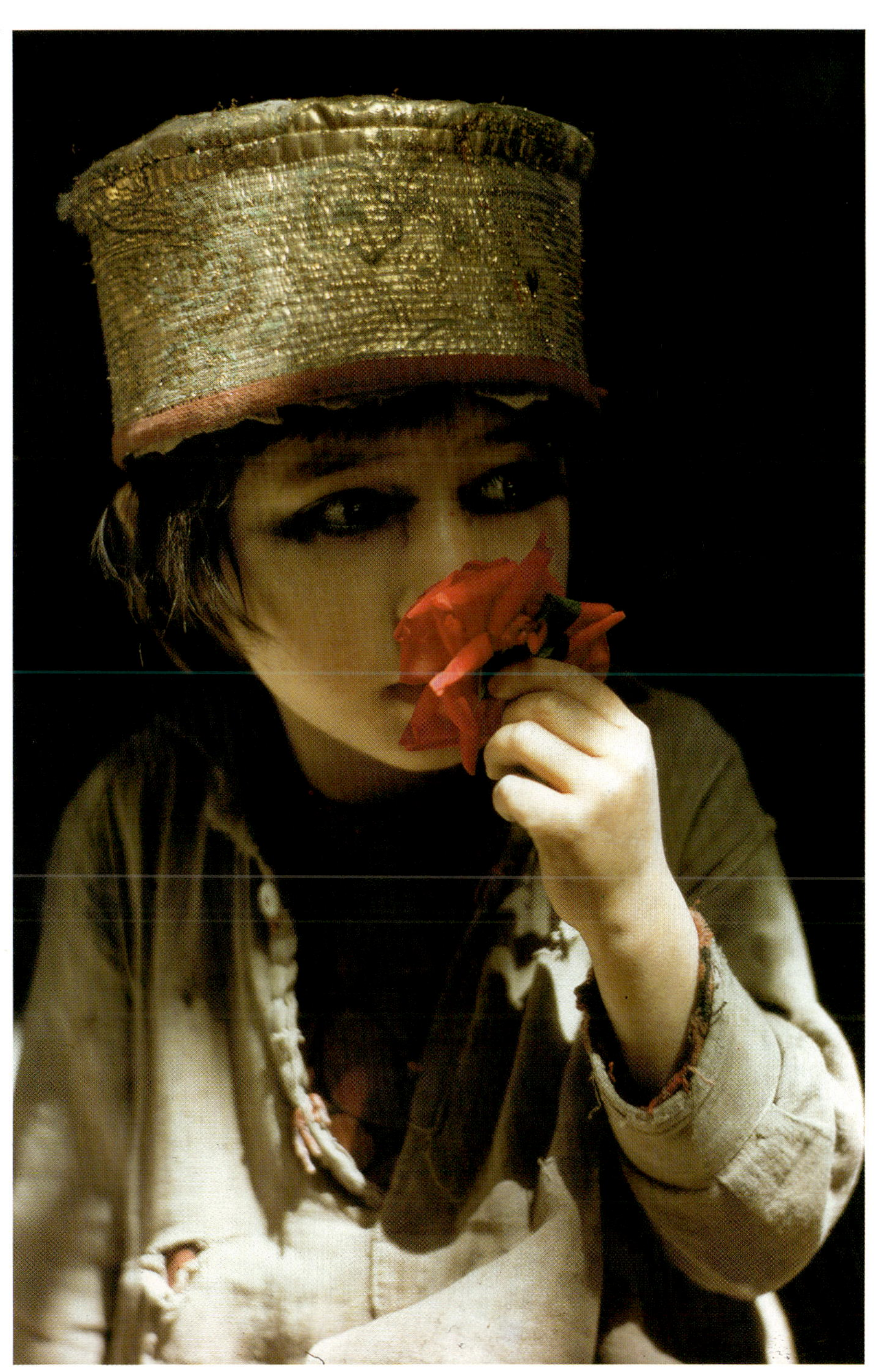

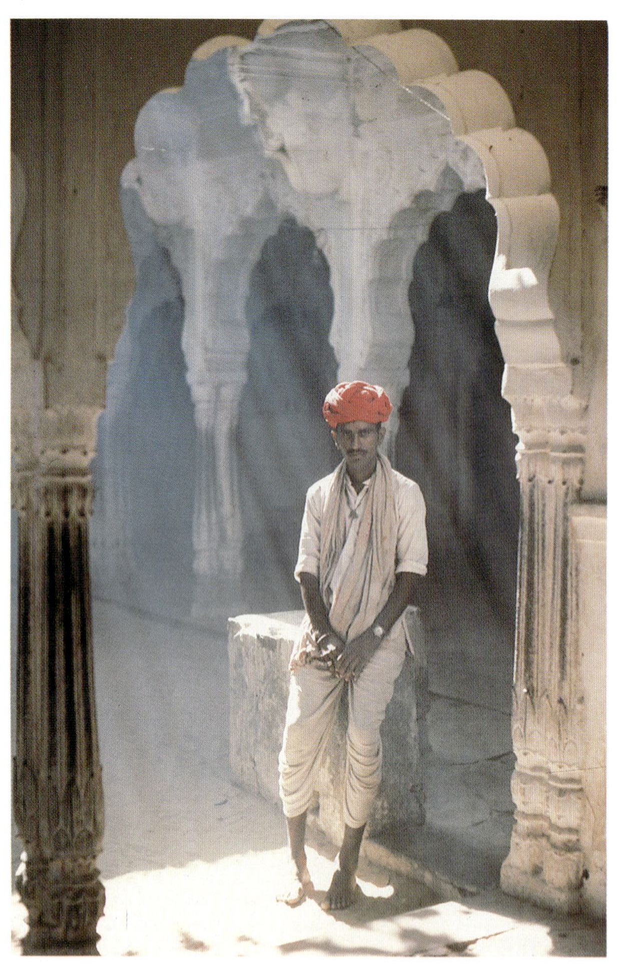

TRAVELLERS in thought and imagination, voyagers in creativity, all photographers traverse expanses of their mind and senses as they search out those features of life before them with which they may clothe their conceptions and aspirations. Photography may thus be just so much theatre: a medley of one-act vignettes making you cry or laugh or ponder, playing momentarily to inattentive houses in the theatre-lands of gallery and journal. We agree to the rules, pay the admission fee, keep silent and adjust to the dark of the theatre. With photographs we accept the medium's limited form, we accede to interpretation from the photographer, and we adjust to the mannerisms imposed by the picture's production.

Within this scheme of more-or-less cosy reciprocations, travel photography drifts by like a much-loved but unattached vagabond. In an open and loose sense almost all photography is travel photography, as space and time and frontiers of all sorts must be crossed. Travel photography in the usual sense implies foreignness: that photographers are strangers to their subjects and that a certain innocence and ignorance on the

Previous page, Nur Jahan.
Above, Pushkar, Rajasthan Noontime in the courtyard of a stately residence.
Below, Rohri, Sind Portrait of a Fisherman.
Photographs ©Roland and Sabrina Michaud. Courtesy of Zamana Gallery.

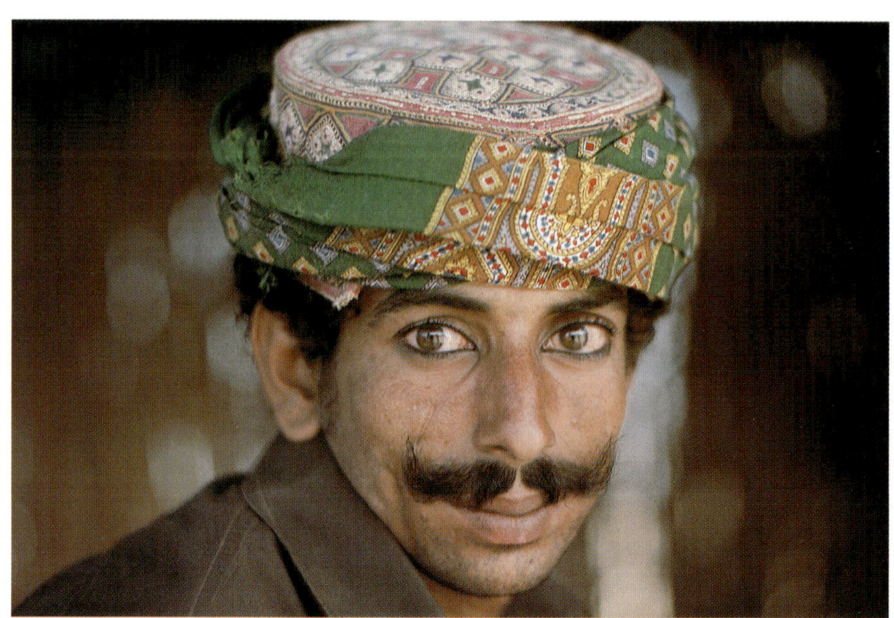

India of One Thousand and One Nights ***by Roland Michaud and Sabrina Michaud is published by Thames and Hudson, London and New York. Price £30 in UK.***

part of the photographer are almost quintessential.

So what are the rules for this theatre of operations? It's seldom clear whether a photographer may enter into reciprocal relations with his 'foreign' subjects as the gulf between them is doubtless wide: at least cultural and linguistical if not also personal. Whether a travel photographer may subsume any right to personal interpretation of such subjects (let alone whether it's possible, given the cultural hurdles) is not clear either. For better or worse, theoretical unease has never seriously ruffled the progress of film through camera. It is very likely that, for example, just being present to take pictures endangers the very substance of a culture which we find so attractive and interesting that we will take great expense and pains to visit and photograph. But that problem in itself will never stop travel photographers from travelling and taking pictures.

One of the achievements of Roland and Sabrina Michaud is that they faced some of these issues. With a penetration that is wholly Gallic and with a thoroughness that has to be characterised by breathtaking stubbornness, they have tried to weld together the several irreconcilables of travel photography.

Their work as known and widely celebrated in several previous books culminates now in the *India of One Thousand and One Nights*. The Michauds are unrepentant dreamers. 'In the dimness of our furnished rooms in Paris' they explain, 'the Thousand and One Nights is our bedside book . . . Like beads of a giant rosary, the tales spread out night after night . . . We dream of the Orient until the day we decide to measure our dream against reality.' It was no short-lived dream, this: it took the couple the better part of their working lives (twenty years) and many journeys to India to photograph the book.

Driven by their eye for light and colour and pictorial tempo, as well as their desire to really understand the people and the country, to capture the spirit — they return again and again to the same places in search of the pictures that can be measured up to clothe their dreams. Thanks to an enormous investment in time, they can take their leisure with people — the strangers who are their subjects — to talk with them and make friends even. The final result is a sumptuously photographed book, artfully designed by Sabrina Michaud and beautifully produced.

Open it and picture after picture makes you ponder: when *will* the dream end? The India of the Michauds' dream is dazzlingly beautiful spectacle where brilliance of colour parade and cavort, where doorways are filled with dizzyingly seductived faces a-glow with warmth and humour. It is an ecstatic book, powered by idealism and is, in short, a remarkable achievement of unmannered photography. Comparison with a typical tourist's pictures of India is very instructive: hard and indifferent lighting, dusty dull colours and a purposeless untidiness characterise almost all 'snaps'. It's not easy to accept that the Michaud pictures must have sprung from the same well of reality. Their lyrical compositions bear as much resemblance to tourist's snaps as a distinguished malt whiskey does to the burn from which it's born.

The Michaud tale begins twenty-five years ago with the spluttering of a *Deux Chevaux* (Citroën 2CV) as it galumphed over the last cobbled streets of France carrying a young teacher and his wife to Ethiopia and a holiday planned to last six months. Seventeen months later, they return *Deux Chevaux* much the worse for wear with Roland's interest in photography heated to a passion by what he'd seen and felt in the Orient. Sabrina took the back-seat until Roland realised that without her, many pictures would be impossible to take. In Somalia, a shy face smiles and pops into a hut. Roland cries 'We *must* have a picture of her. Sabrina, you take it'. With instructions on exposure and framing shouted through the doorway, Sabrina takes her first pictures. One of the secrets of this couple's success as a team is the way their photographic styles are more than complementary, they're nearly identically direct in style and meticulously framed. And latterly their son, Romain, appears to be growing into the team: first as a sort of innocent conduit to family sympathies — a young child travelling with photographers helps win acceptance — and now as critic of his parents' work.

It is easy to characterise their work. It is unique: uniquely ambitious, uniquely *'sympa'* — sympathetic and understanding. They tell proudly that a portrait of an Afghanistani patriach was received by the King as a portrait of the country. On the strength of their pictures we can given them the benefit of the doubt when they claim to strive to 'really understand the people and the country'.

Their understanding is shaped by their dreams, of course. Their dreams are beautiful dreams and their pictures are beautiful pictures, brimming over with the entire thesaurus for loveliness. This uncovers a paradox. There is so much beauty it is not at all easy to accept it can be true. A handsome fisherman haloed with red and proudly wearing beads of many shapes and colour; an almost sniffable haze over the bustle and noise of a camel market; dusty shafts of sunlight shower a courtyard with a beautifying sheen. Too much. Of course, it's based on a reality but equally clearly it's one that's by now so highly distilled, the merest whiff is enough to drunken you and bathe the senses. The worse aspect about intoxication is the loss of trust: senses fail the sensibilities and intellect; you are left entranced and yet uneasy.

Like all good paradoxes, the answer lies within the conundrum. All this beautiful reality is somehow unsettling because, in truth, it isn't real or not true-to-life at least. Like an anthology of prose which strings together all the purple, pink and poetic passages of novels having snipped away painful passages into a bin, like 'Bambi' without the mother's death, like love stories without sulks and rows, like symphonies without dissonance . . . 'India of One Thousand and One Nights' is just too lovely, just too good. Well, in a way it's not meant to be true: it is, after all, the Michauds' *dream*. 'And what a gap there is between imagination and experience' they sigh: 'so many contradictions and disappointments, so much frustration.' This touching moan is not merely the typical travel photographer's tired lament of lost opportunities and fraility of body, but an apologia for all photographers who forsake their comfy home for strange lands.

Travel photography is neither easy nor as unproblematical as we thoughtlessly imagine: if the Michaud's work stimulates some unease as it delights the eye, it has done great service for the understanding of photography. Not in this book, nor anywhere else for that matter, can beauty and loveliness ever be taken for granted.■

MICHAEL JOSEPH

The top commercial photographer talks to John Morrison.

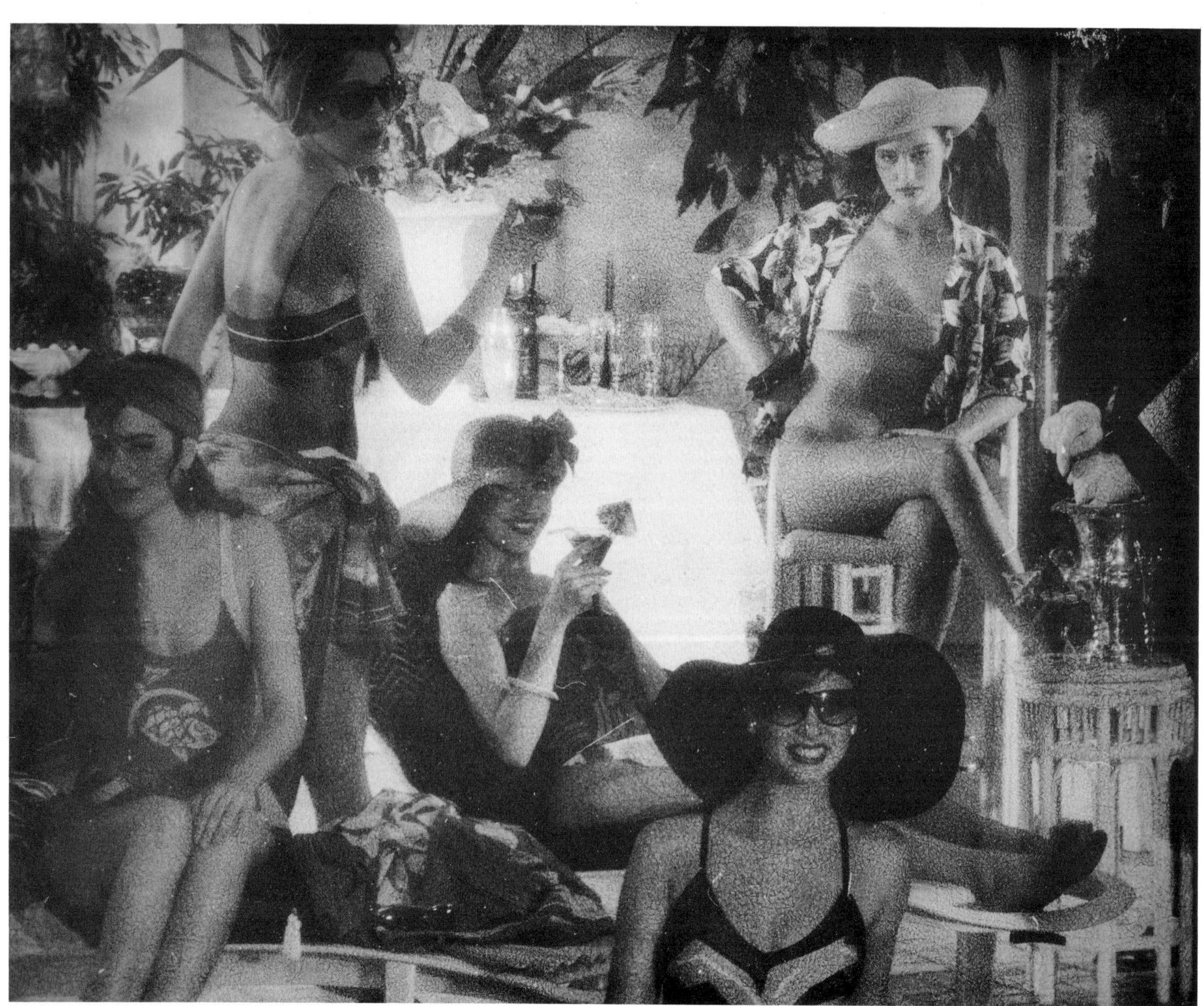

Pool Ladies, for Franca von Munster. Art Director Peter von Schalkwyck. Agency, McCanns agency of Milan.

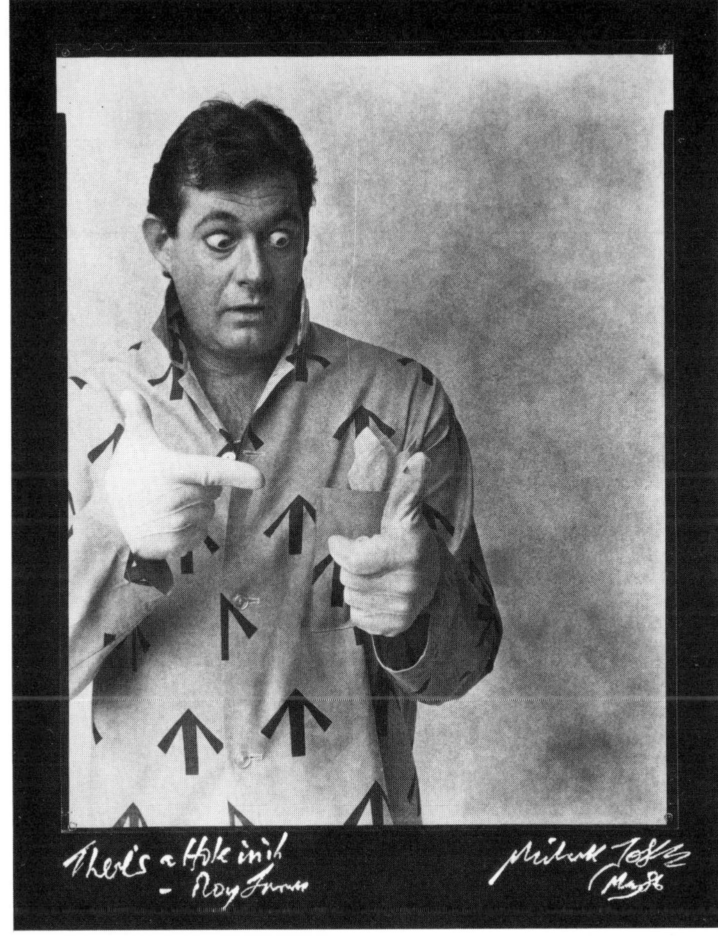

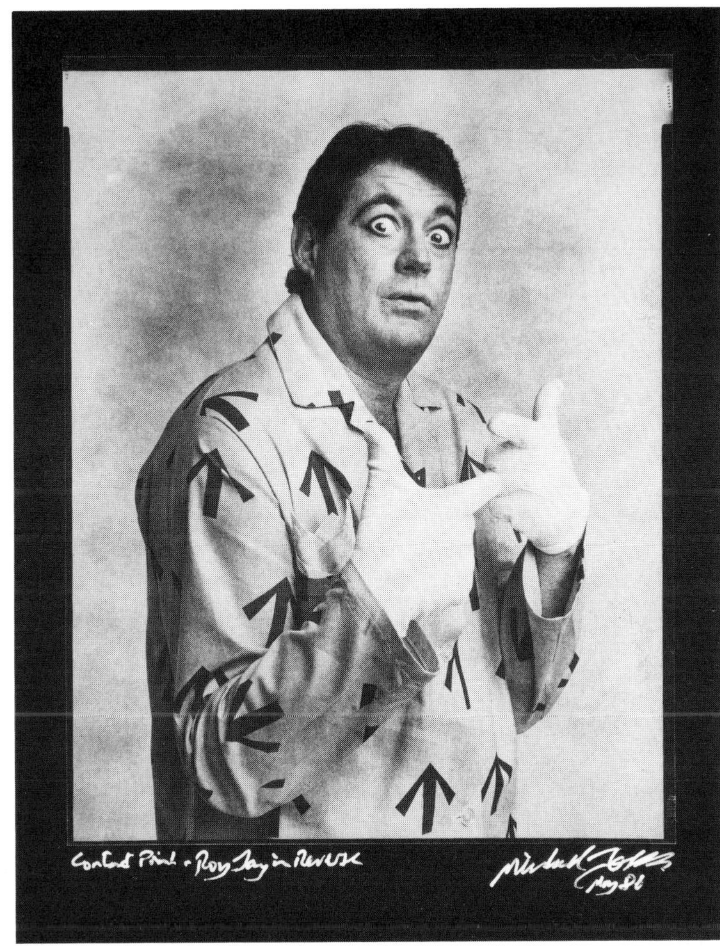

Roy Jay, comedian. For Saatchi & Saatchi.

FROM THE roof garden atop his London home Michael Joseph enjoys a panoramic vantage over the capital: the green acres of Clapham Common on one side, and a bird's-eye view of bustling city streets on the other. The house itself is enormous, but then it has to serve as both workplace and family home.

It's something of an understatement to say that Michael Joseph has his studio there, since almost every room (Michael has never got round to counting them . . .) has been pressed into service, at one time or another, as settings for his photographs. Not as empty studio spaces, but as fully-furnished locations to be peopled.

The kitchen has provided a setting for domestic and food shots; upstairs rooms have been used for more spacious interiors. There are even false walls which can be detached at will if the decor needs to be changed. It's a matter of living in — rather than over — the shop, so Michael has ensured that the house serves efficiently in its dual role. With a number of staff on the payroll he accepts the responsibilities that commercial success inevitably brings.

People are his forté: the more the merrier. Over the years he's earned the soubriquet of 'The Orgy Man', and with good reason . . . He has a reputation for orchestrating complex human tableaux to advertise a wide

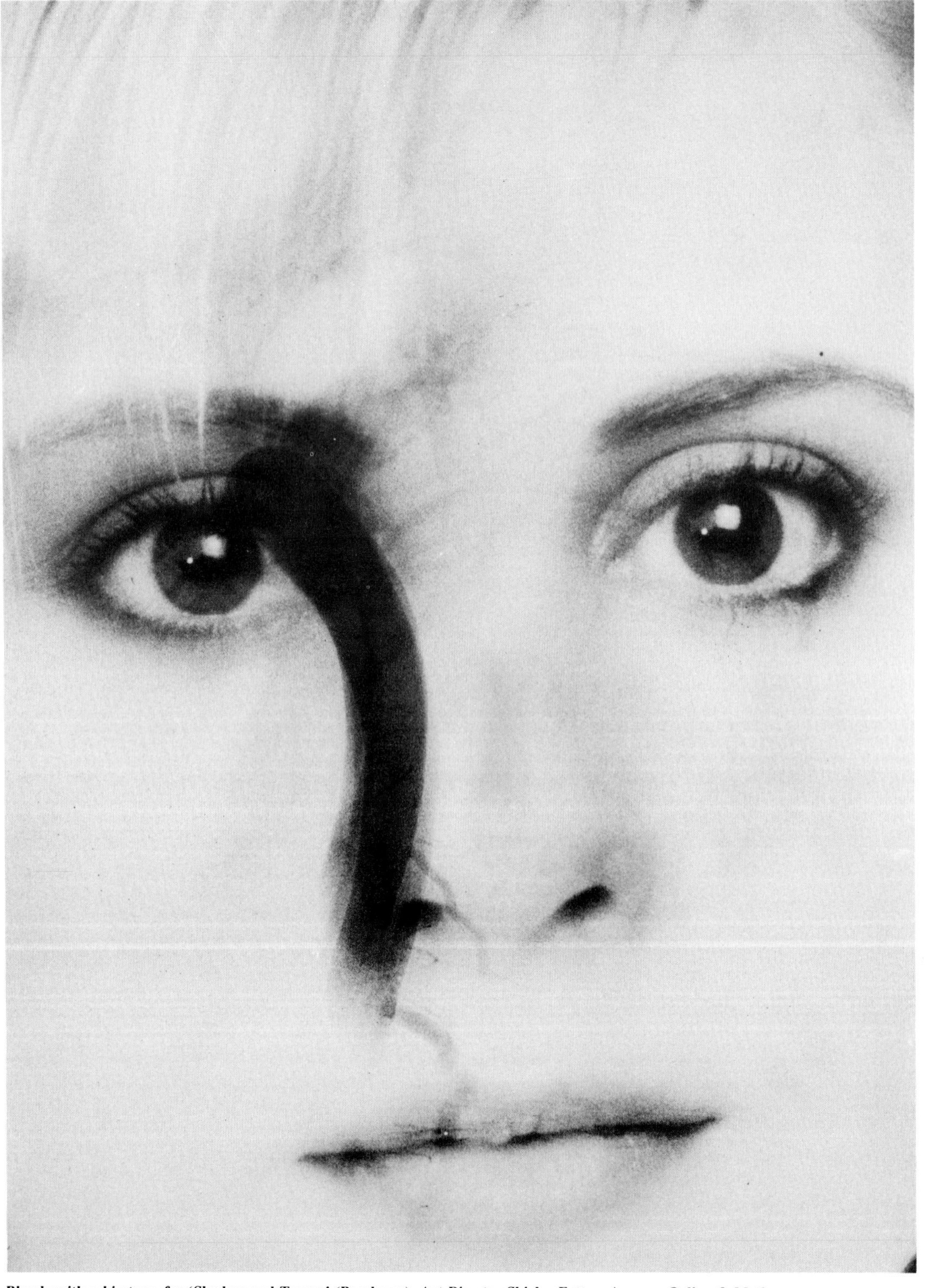

Blonde with a big tear, for 'Shaders and Toners' (Beechams). Art Director Shirley Futter. Agency, Oglivy & Mather.

variety of products, with as many as forty people to accommodate within a single shot.

The logistics of organising — and entertaining — large groups of people would reduce most photographers to a state of nervous collapse. But Michael's home has, by now, witnessed more orgies than Sodom and Gomorrah, and practice — in the specialised world of group photography — makes perfect.

The brief is to present a highly organised chaos: adding and subtracting people and props to provide a convincing illusion of movement and excitement. An illusion it has to be, however, since every element in every picture must be inch-perfect in its positioning for the final shoot. One misplaced gesture could hide a model's face, or reveal scars, watches and tattoos that might destroy all semblance of authenticity — especially in a supposedly historical setting.

The art is to make the result look artless, so that the viewer is drawn into the scene without being aware of the blood, sweat and tears that went into its making. And the craft often involves keeping large numbers of models in that transient state between sobriety and drunkenness; it's vital that their patience doesn't run out before the shot's in the can.

Capturing the appropriate expressions of body and face is difficult enough with just a single model, but add a few dozen more characters and you would appear to have produced a scenario that would defeat all but the most experienced photographers. It's to Michael Joseph's credit that he thrives in conditions where other photographers might be tempted to give up.

His group photographs often resemble stills from an unmade movie: suggesting a story-line through the interaction of characters. So it was a natural progression for him to direct TV commercials. That's behind him

35

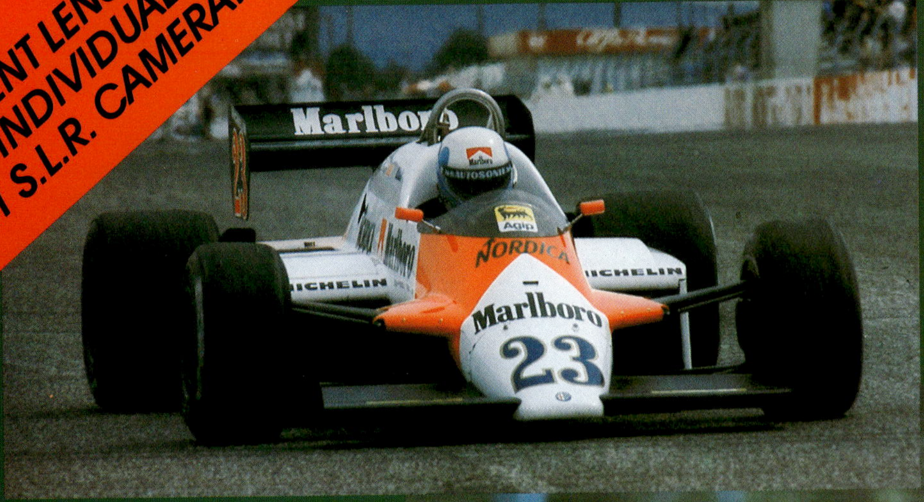

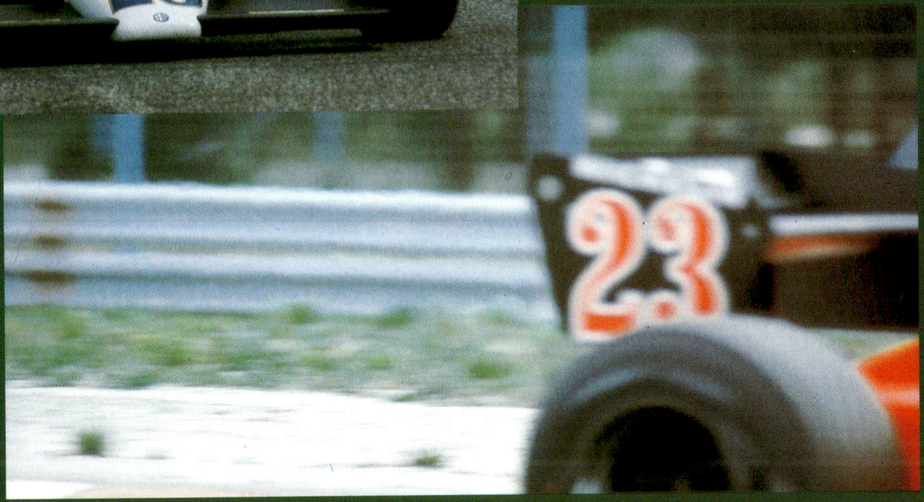

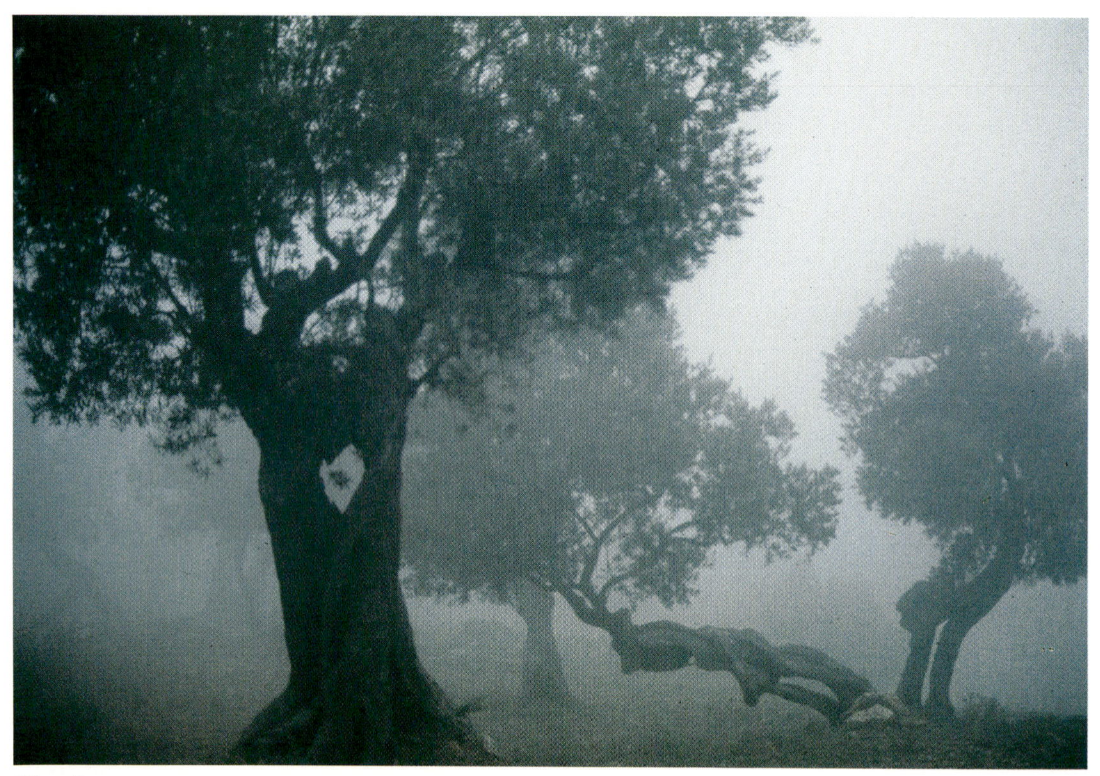

Misty olives.

Old Bushmills drinkers, for Old Bushmills Whiskey. Art Director Cliff Goodenough. Agency Ted Bates, New York.

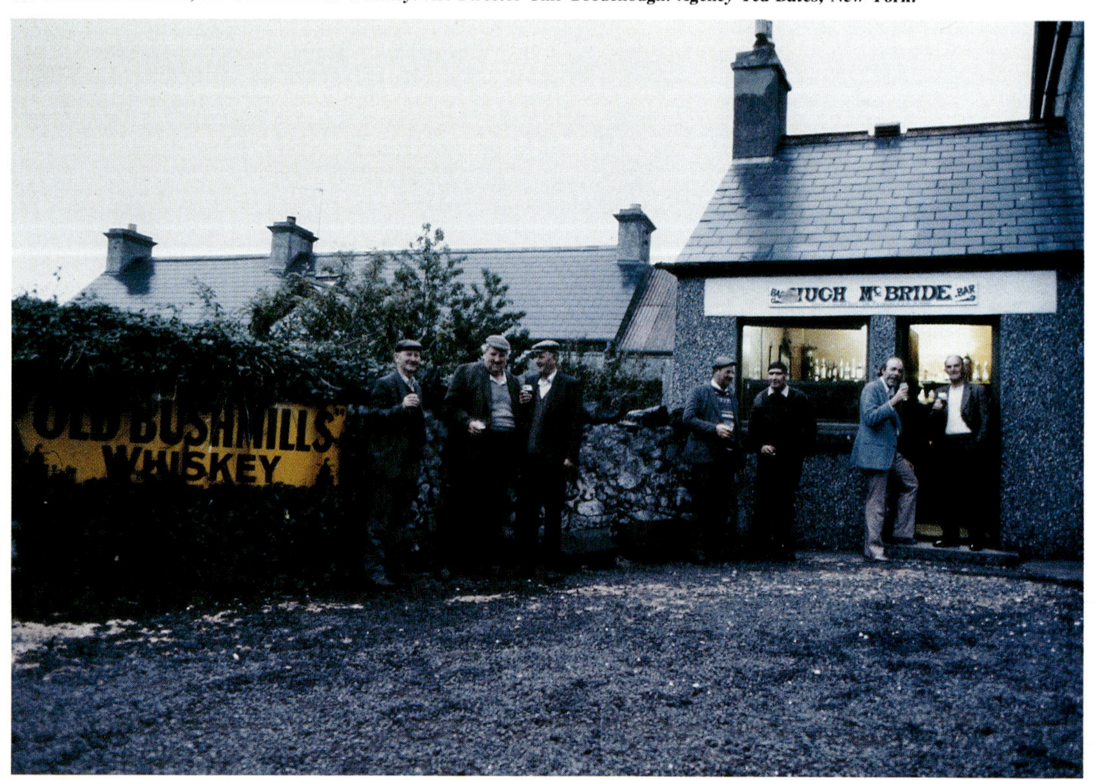

now, though, since he gradually became frustrated by the lack of control he was able to have over the results. Despite the problems of still photography it still allows Michael the chance to run the show more or less on is own terms. Advertising has supplied with him a good living for twenty-one years now, and it's a branch of photography in which he still has a great faith . . .

'Advertising photography has legitimately been called an art form. Just because it exists to sell products doesn't mean that it can't be exciting and authentic. I'm sensitive to peoples' opinions about my work and I still enjoy taking pictures: the knowledge that I've done my very best, whatever the client decides to do with my photographs.

'But advertising is hard graft, a cut-throat business. It's always been like an assault course: working with different clients every day and having to meet restrictive deadlines. I feel that my advertising work has helped to make me something of a stage-manager, a diplomat. I've had twenty-one years of being "Mr Nice", trying to please too many people.'

I wondered whether Michael's reputation was a help or a hindrance when he took on a new assignment.

'If anything it can be a hindrance, because people naturally expect you to be able to do the impossible on every occasion. You've got to be very resourceful and hope for the luck that every photographer needs. Advertising has given me a certain position in photography, but it is all too easy to find yourself being pigeon-holed into one particular style. All photographers get type-cast to some extent, so I'm very grateful that there are a few art directors around who realise that I can shoot more that just orgies . . . '

Success, in Michael's terms, is being asked to take on assignments that are both

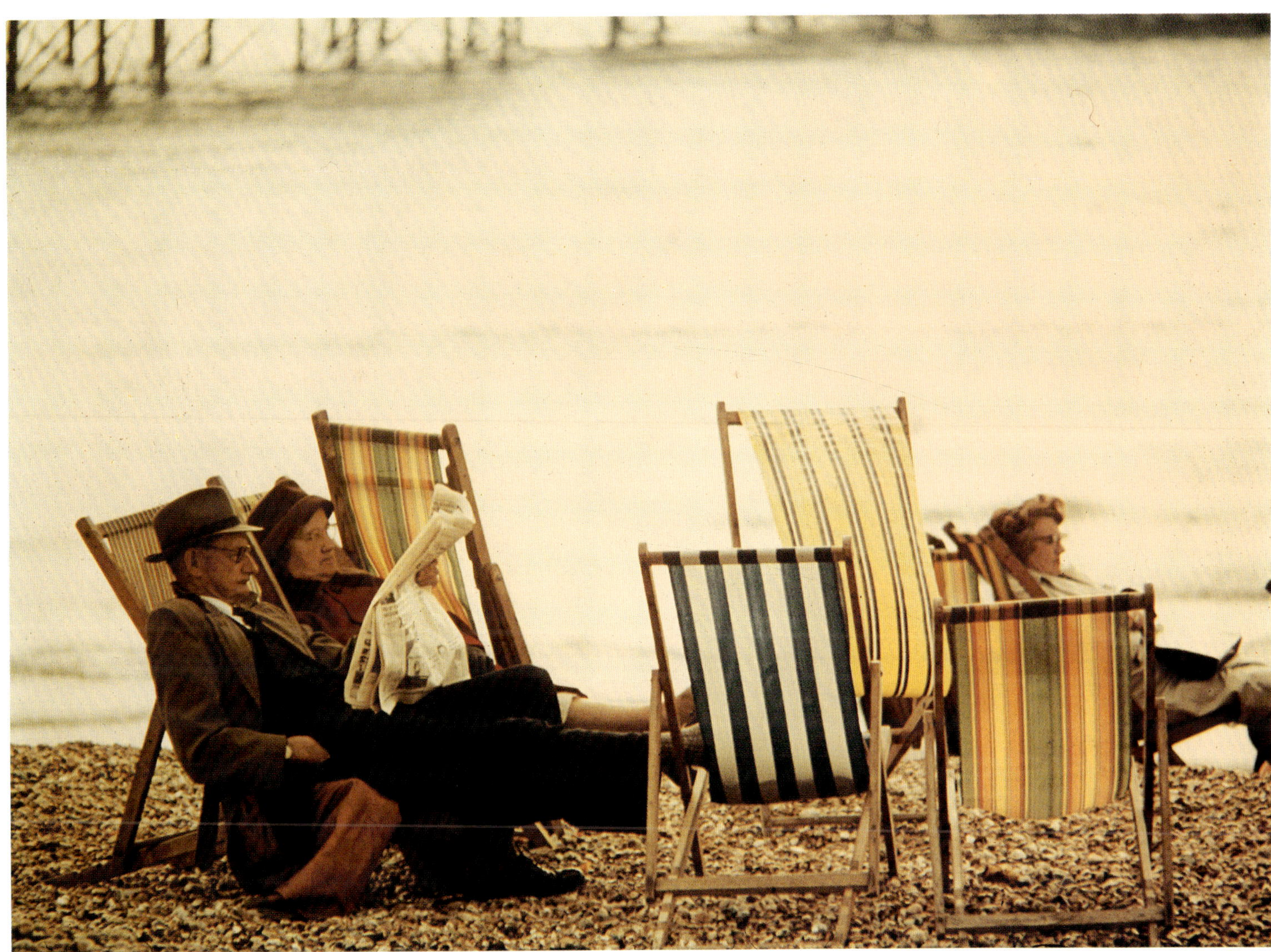

Brighton beach.

prestigious and entertaining. He's been involved in countless campaigns that meet both criteria, but campaigns are, by their very nature, ephemeral. Some are remembered — particularly within the advertising profession — but most meet immediate needs and are quickly consigned to the archives or, worse, to the dustbin.

'Art directors get so involved in campaigns that your pictures, once used, may simply be thrown away. A lot of good photography can disappear in this way, since the photographer concerned is unlikely to hold copyright. Your clients don't always realise that your pictures may have a future once they have finished with them. Rather upsetting . . .'

Michael's more notable images deserve better than this, and he has tentative plans to gather together as many as possible — even if it means buying back the copyright — for publication as a book. He also plans to pursue some personal projects which have been held in abeyance by the exigencies of earning a living.

'I feel I'm really beginning to enjoy photography, and I want to shoot pictures that I haven't had time to take before now. For example, I want to set up dramatic and emotional scenes for publication as posters: the kind of pictures that people want to hang on their walls. And I recently returned from an assignment in Malaysia with the desire to do a book about the country: it would be an interesting challenge. It's time I started shooting pictures that *I* consider important. On the other hand, if for some reason I had to give up photography then at least I'd know that I'd taken maybe a hundred pictures that are OK.' ■

The Winning Hand..

64

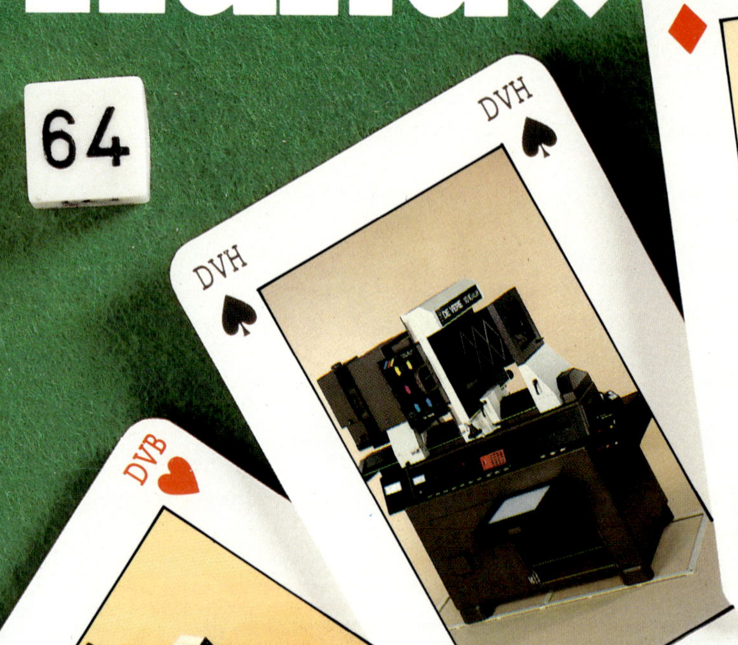

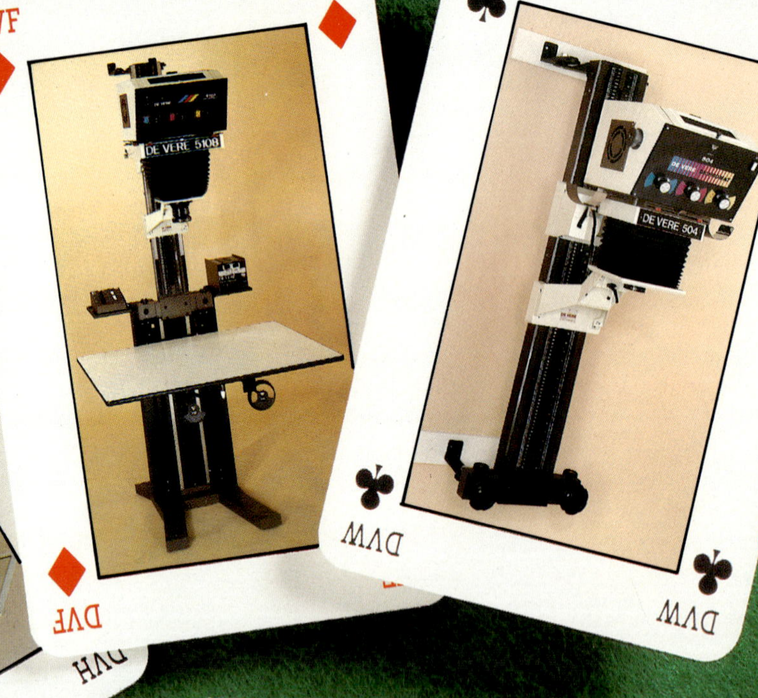

DVB

..with a range of Enlargers to suit you!

- **DVB BENCH ENLARGERS** Disc to 15″x12″ (40x30cm) Prints to 20″x24″ (50x60cm)
- **DVW WALL ENLARGERS** Disc to 15″x12″ (40x30cm) Prints to 40″x80″ (100x200cm)
- **DVF FLOORSTANDING ENLARGERS** Disc to 15″x12″ (40x30cm) Prints to 40″x60″ (100x150cm)
- **DVH HORIZONTAL ENLARGERS** 35mm to 15″x12″ (40x30cm) Prints to giant mural any size

You'll see a great Deal with DE VERE

Manufacturers and Suppliers of Precision Photographic Equipment

Head Office: DE VERE (Kensington) Ltd, De Vere House, 100-108 Beckenham Road, Beckenham, Kent BR3 4RH.
Telephone: 01-658 7511. Telex: 946252.

WILLIAM SKEOCH CUMMING

Yeoman Photographer and Painter of the Boer War by Jane Carmichael, Keeper of Photographs, Imperial War Museum

THE Boer War was the first major British conflict to be recorded photographically by both professionals and amateurs. The professional, working for the illustrated press, used the large plate format suitable for reproduction through the half tone process perfected in the 1880s. The range of cheap small-format Kodak cameras introduced in the same decade brought photography within reach of the amateur. During the war the professional attempted to cover it at the general level while the amateur, naturally enough, took photographs within the limits of his own experience. William Skeoch Cumming, serving with the Imperial Yeomanry, recorded his service with a particular gifted eye.

War had broken out in October 1899 over the rights of the 'Uitlanders' the largely British immigrant mining community of the Transvaal and the Orange Free State, the two Boer republics of South Africa. In fact the contest was a struggle between two irreconcilables; British imperialism and conviction of the justness of her rule and the independent, introverted republicanism of the Boers. After the disasters of 'Black Week', the reverses suffered by the British at Stormberg, Magersfontein and Colenso between 10 and 17 December 1899, it was apparent that the Army needed urgent reinforcements, particularly of mounted troops, in a campaign which was becoming unexpectedly prolonged. Civilian volunteers were called for and the response was overwhelming. In a new departure it was decided to send the Yeomanry, who were expected to be able to ride and to provide much of their own equipment, overseas. These civilian volunteers of means and education introduced a new element between the exclusive officer caste and the ignorant other ranks of the regular army.

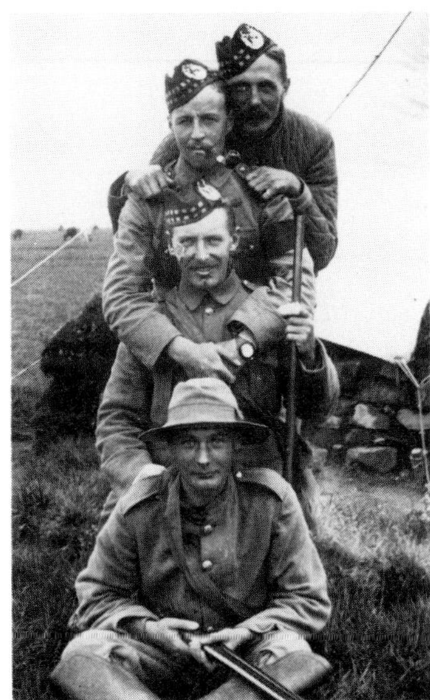

William Skeoch Cumming (top) with three friends wearing Gordon Highlander caps, probably swapped during an unexpected meeting in South Africa. Note the black armband worn for the death of Queen Victoria *(IWM Neg No Q 72532)*

William Skeoch Cumming was an Edinburgh based artist who, in 1900 at the age of 35, had established his reputation as a competent though not outstanding specialist in military and figure painting. He had joined the Lothian and Berwickshire Yeomanry before the war and in January 1900 he volunteered to go with his unit, now the 19th Company of the 6th Scottish Battalion of the Imperial Yeomanry, to South Africa. He was overseas from March 1900 until May 1901, serving first as a Lance Corporal and later as a Sergeant. From a series of letters which he wrote to his friend and mentor the sculptor James Pittendrigh MacGillvray it is possible to gauge something of Skeoch Cumming's reactions to the war and his own part in it. The 6th Scottish Battalion arrived in Cape Town on 19 March when the tide of war was apparently beginning to turn in Britain's favour. After passing through the camps at Maitland and Worcester his company was attached to General Sir Archibald Hunter's column to take part in the determined advance of the Commander-in-Chief, Field Marshal Lord Roberts, from Cape Colony into the Transvaal to Johannesburg and on to the capital Pretoria. Initially he saw more marching than fighting, 'After we left Worcester in Cape Colony we took a train to Warrenton-Fourteen Streams then marched to Christiana right up to Lichtenburg, Vryburg, Ventersdorp, Potchefstroom, Klerksdorp, and back to Potchefstroom and thence to Krugersdorp. We have been moving between Klerksdrop and Krugersdorp ever since'. (8 August 1900).

The Boers' tactics were irritating, 'We have not fired a shot at the Boers although they skipped off again and again just as we got in touch with them . . . ' (1 July 1900). Roberts occupied Pretoria on 5 June but the expected Boer surrender did not come. That winter one of the brilliant Commando leaders Christiaan de Wet eluded all British efforts to capture or persuade him to surrender while successfully harassing British forces in the vicinity including Skeoch Cumming's company.

From October onward Skeoch Cumming was increasingly involved in what he referred to as 'scraps' and eventually his unit became part of Major General John French's (later Field Marshal Sir John) attempt to clear the Transvaal of the Boer commandos using several mobile columns. It is possible to detect the emergence of the seasoned campaigner who noted, 'This life has certainly knocked some of the nonsense out of me and steeled my soul against those things that one is better without' (18 January).

The new Commander-in-Chief, General Lord Kitchener, had ordered the rounding up of civilians and the destruction of their property in order to deprive the commandos of their support. Skeoch Cumming took part in the burning and looting of farms and forage and wrote to MacGillvray, revealing how the war was breaking down normal codes of behaviour:

> *'I think you would enjoy the looting, at first you would have executor's scruples but you would soon get over that and when you entered a house*

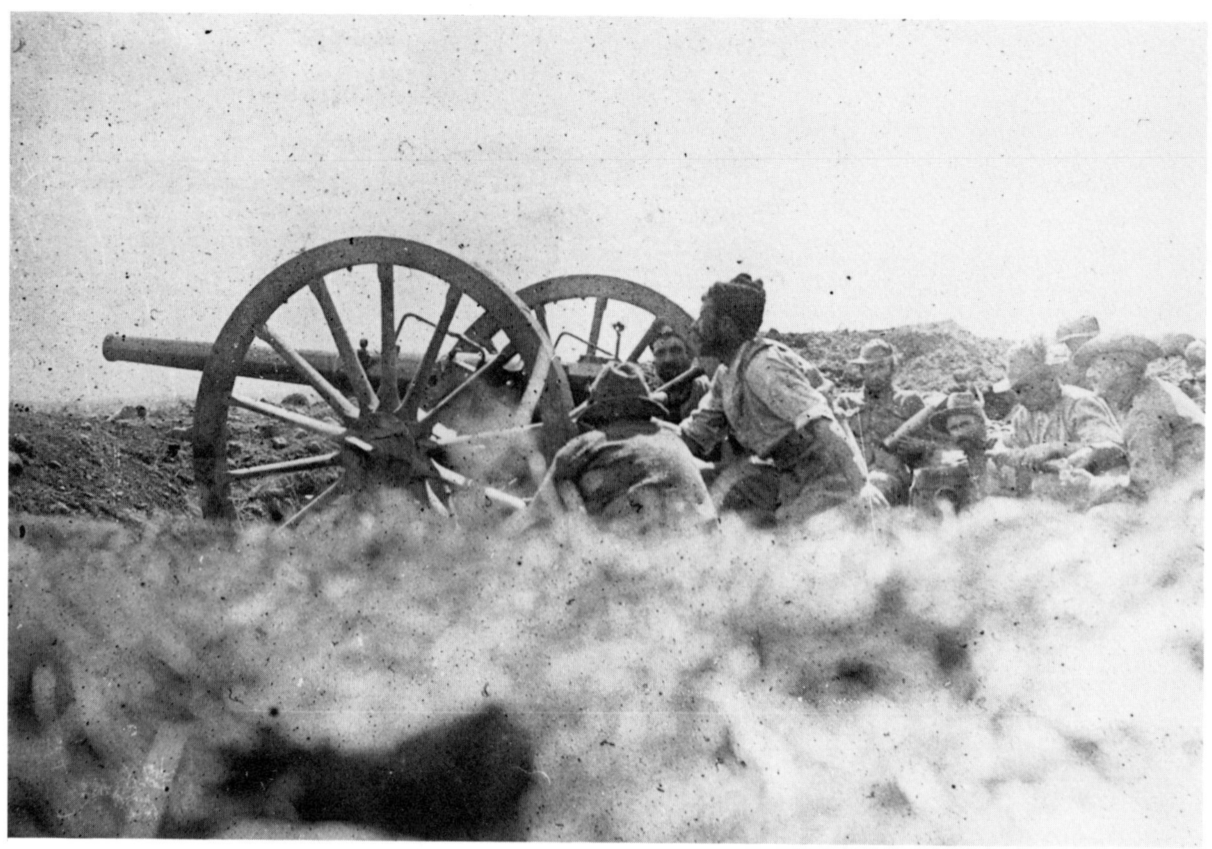

The Gunpit-Colonials Working The Guns: Defence of Wepener. Photograph/Painting *(IWM Neg No Q 72331)*

would be as handy as the next man at helping yourself'. (18 January 1901).

At the beginning of 1901 the end of the war seemed only a matter of months but the determined guerrilla tactics of the 'bitter enders' carried on the struggle for another year. British sovereignty in South Africa was finally asserted at the Peace of Vereeniging in May 1902.

In nearly every one of his letters Skeoch Cumming reiterated that he had no time for sketching and went so far as to say, 'maybe it's good for me that I left off work' (29 January 1901) but he did lament the lack of a camera. His father, besides being a designer, had run a successful

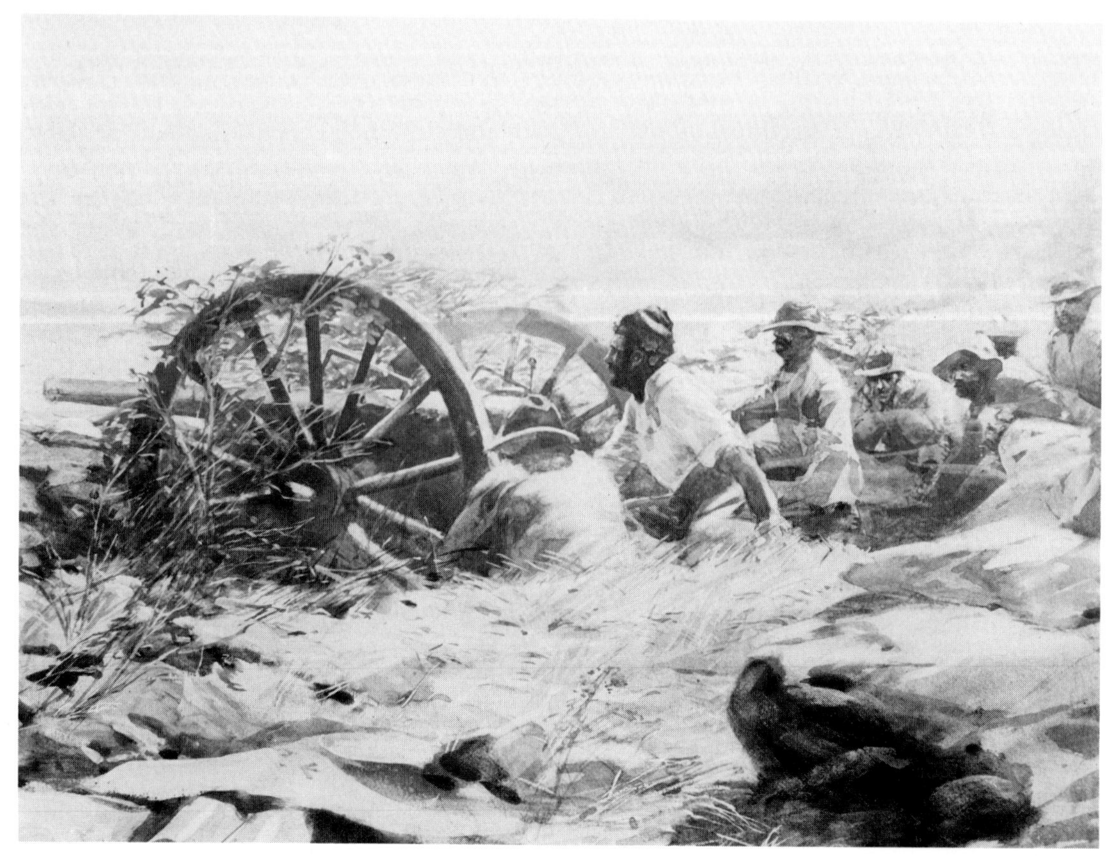

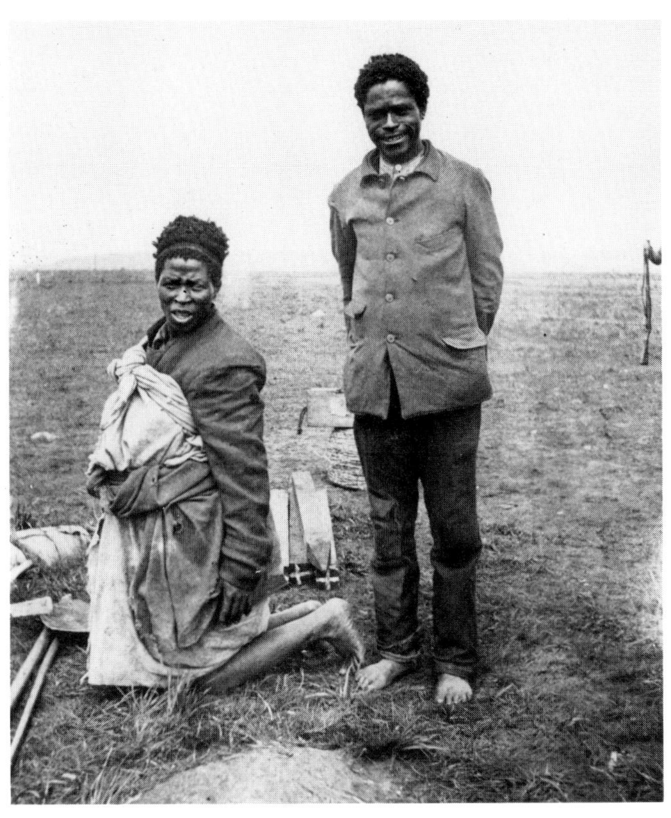

photography business at No 1 Hannover Street in Edinburgh, and Skeoch Cumming was accustomed to having cameras available. He was therefore delighted when his sister sent him a Kodak, probably one of the popular 'pocket' series which took $4\frac{1}{4} \times 2\frac{1}{2}$in roll film negatives in January 1901. His collection of photographs now at the Imperial War Museum also includes some 5×4in glass negatives and it is likely that these were taken with one of his father's cameras while the Lothian and Berwickshire Yeomanry were undergoing the last stages of their pre-South African training on the beaches at Dunbar in East Lothian. During the war Skeoch Cumming's attitude was clearly that he was taking pictures for his private pleasure and not with any particular aim in mind, he wrote 'I have been snap shooting. I do hope they will come out. It would be nice to show Ina and Erna (MacGillvray's daughters) scenes in the Veldt'. (29 January 1901) although it must have occurred to him that the photographs might provide material for later printings. In the five months before his departure he took some 300 photographs which are notable for their range of subjects and the unselfconscious spontaneity of their composition.

His coverage of the yeomanry suggests both the scale and the detail of the life of the mounted troops. He was daring in his use of the camera and successfully captured the excitement of a mass of horsemen in a practice gallop. His eye for composition selected the right moment to 'snap' half a dozen men in the act of mounting and he caught the effort of transport across the Veldt in the

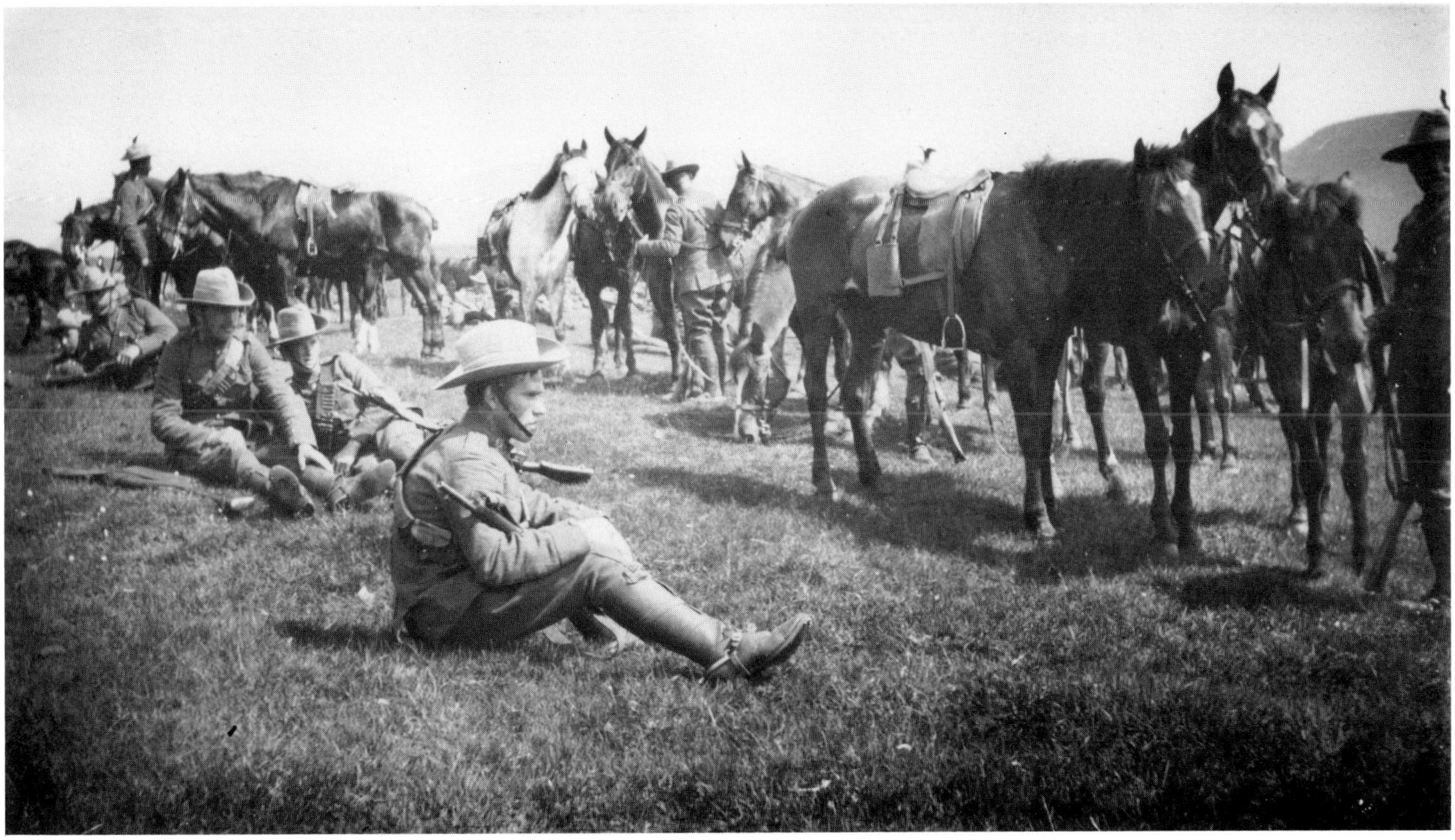

A group of Mounted Infantry pausing for a rest. *(IWM Neg No Q 72037)*

Camp theatricals: Yeoman Impersonate Boer prisoners of war. *(IWM Neg No Q 72455)*

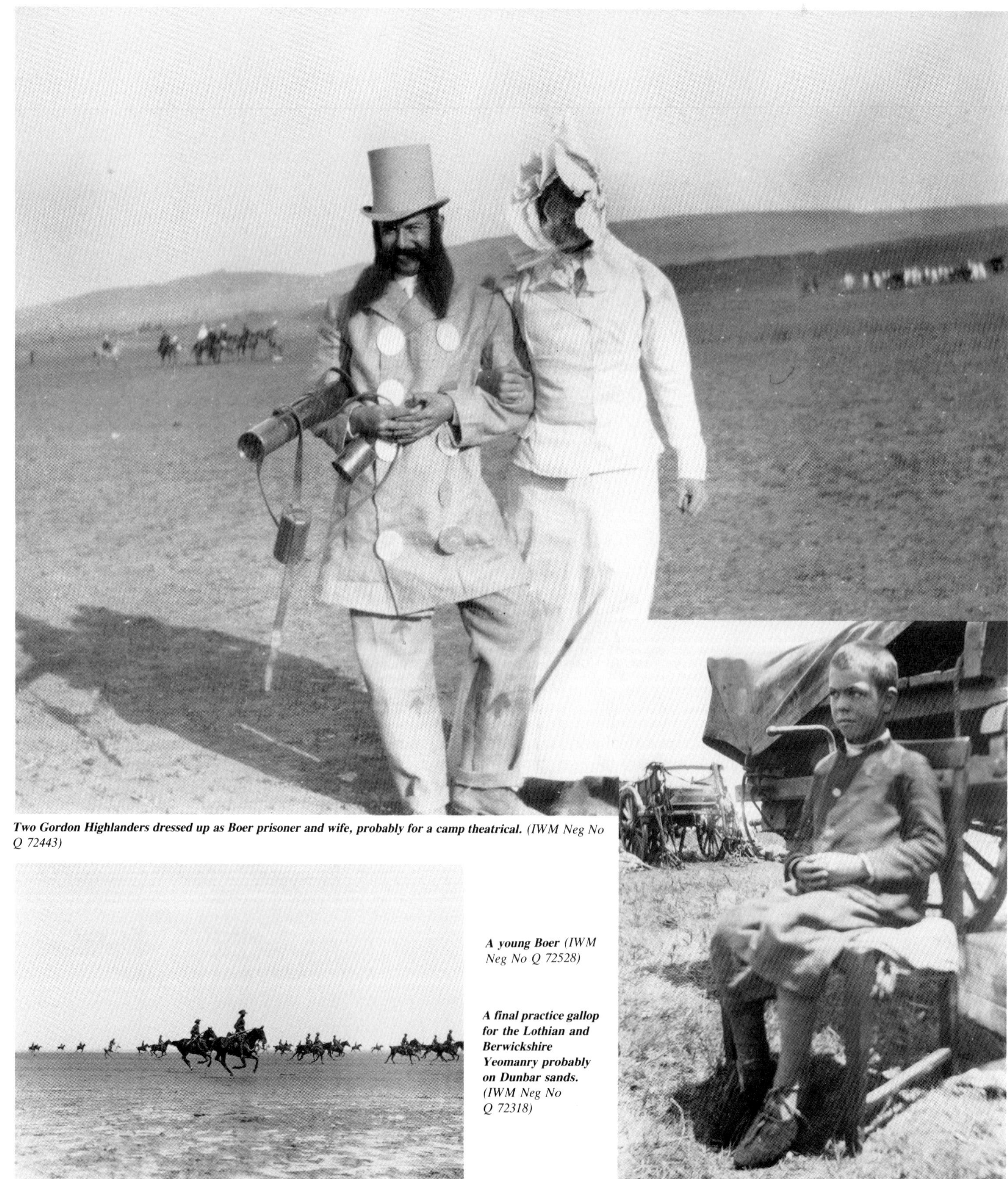

Two Gordon Highlanders dressed up as Boer prisoner and wife, probably for a camp theatrical. *(IWM Neg No Q 72443)*

A young Boer *(IWM Neg No Q 72528)*

A final practice gallop for the Lothian and Berwickshire Yeomanry probably on Dunbar sands. *(IWM Neg No Q 72318)*

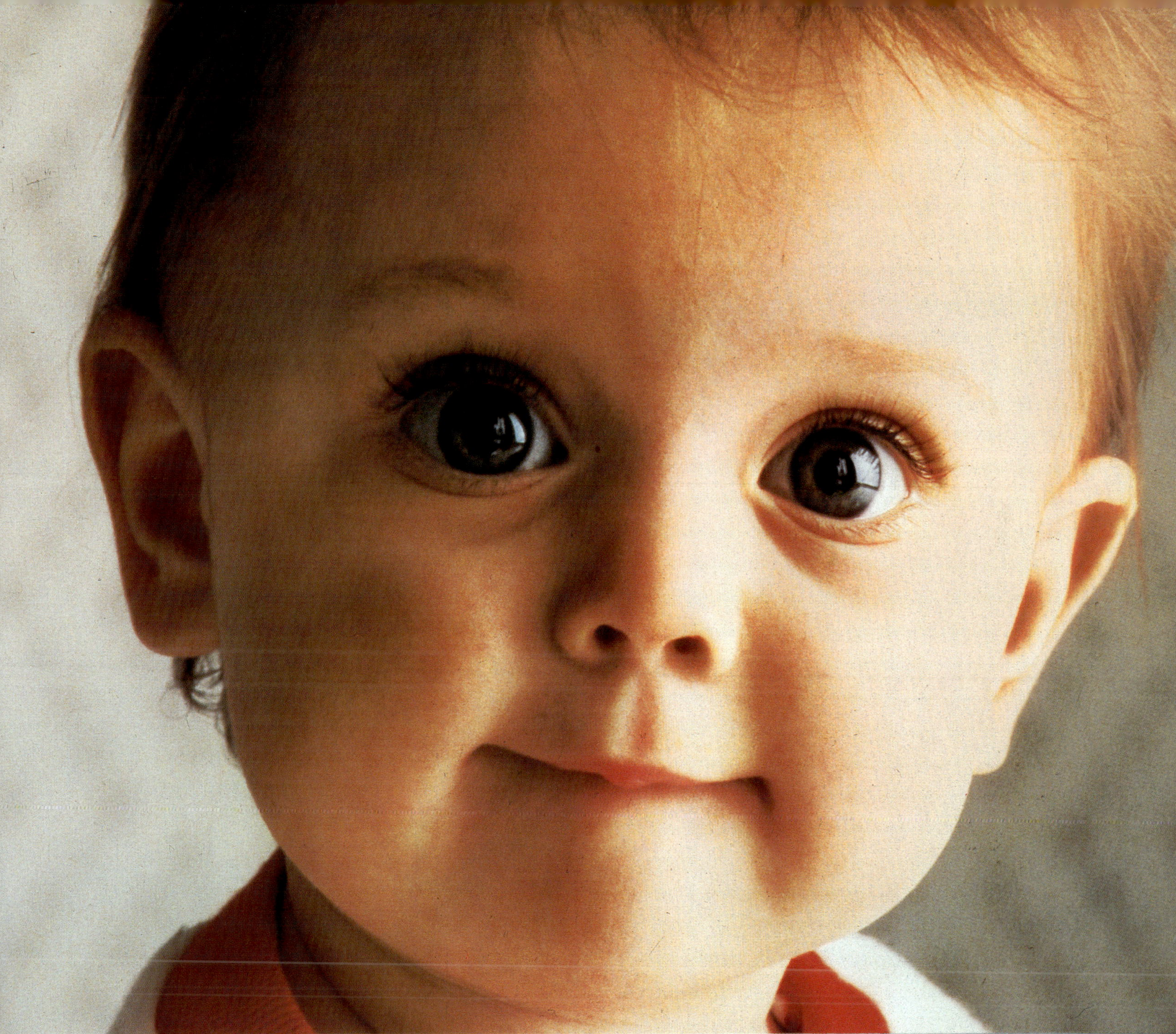

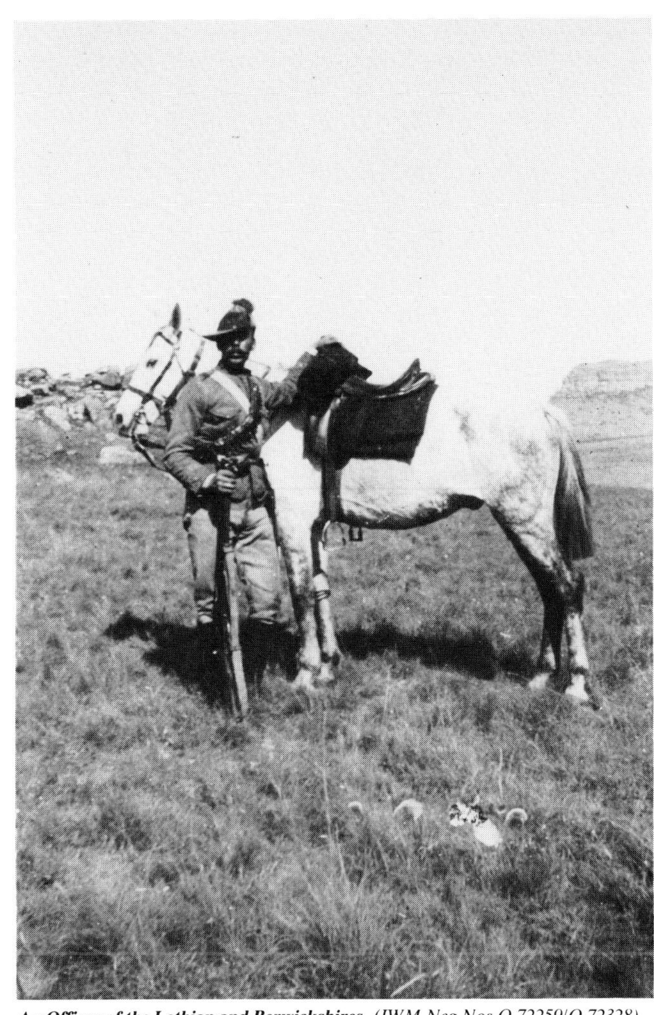

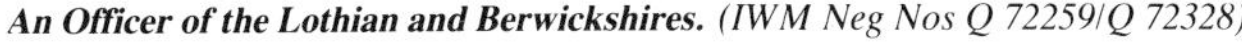

An Officer of the Lothian and Berwickshires. *(IWM Neg Nos Q 72259/Q 72328)*

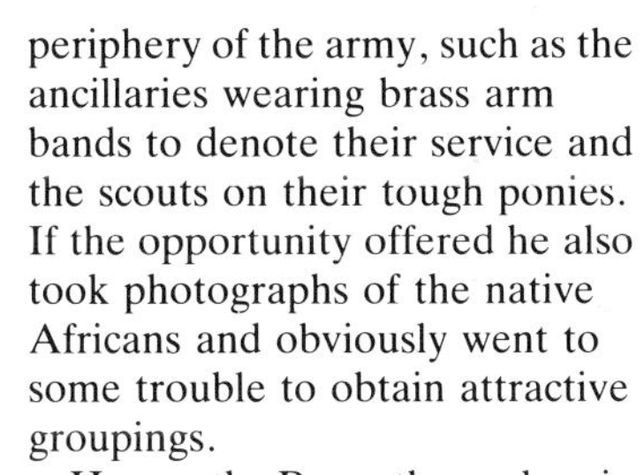

dust stirred up by a mule train.

His own pride in his service showed in his portraits of his smart comrades but he also took them 'off guard' at the moment of a welcome breather on patrol and conveyed their sense of relief. Several photographs show the weapons of war such as the guns and signalling equipment, usually with their operators in easy poses in the style of informal portraiture. Photographs of his own friends in camp or on patrol demonstrate his knack of making people relax in front of the camera and show the hard but in many ways enjoyable life in the clear South African air. He also portrayed successfully the Africans serving with or on the periphery of the army, such as the ancillaries wearing brass arm bands to denote their service and the scouts on their tough ponies. If the opportunity offered he also took photographs of the native Africans and obviously went to some trouble to obtain attractive groupings.

He saw the Boers themselves in two ways; as the military enemy and as refugees in their own country. He took pictures of prisoners of war squatting in the traditional Boer manner on the quayside at Cape Town about to be shipped off to Bermuda and caught the truculence of their expressions. In contrast his photographs of refugees, whether portraits of children beside their wagon or of a family surrounded by their possessions at a railway station suggest both a response to their picturesque qualities and a sympathy for their plight which balances the impression given by the battle-hardened letter writer.

After his return Skeoch Cumming painted some twenty works depicting scenes from the war, many of which were exhibited at the Royal Scottish Academy between 1903 and 1906. Of these at least nine were almost exact 'matches' with a particular photograph and the remainder were clearly influenced by reference to his 'snaps' or, occasionally, to other photographs widely available in the popular stereo sets produced on the war by the publishing firm of Underwood and Underwood. For example, the painting *'The Gunpit-Colonials working the guns — defence of Wepener'* has a corresponding photograph as does his portrait of a yeoman standing beside his horse. If ts suited him he would take elements from a photograph and incorporate them into a painting to give himself some artistic licence with events at which he may not have been present; for instance a snap showing a company of horsemen in an interesting V-shape becomes the basis for a dramatic composition on the evacuation of a hillside position with landscape detail both removed and added.

Interestingly, he does not seem to have chosen the best of his photographs for 'conversion', several are somewhat blurred and lacking the quality which distinguishes his best work. It is possible that he felt he could add nothing to these through the medium of painting as there was no scope for the use of his creative imagination in the straight copying of a good photograph. His Boer War paintings attracted favourable critical notice as the best work of his career so far, but for the rest of his life Cumming remained a second- rather than a first-rate painter. He became involved with the revival of tapestry weaving in Scotland and remained a prolific worker until his death in April 1929.

Skeoch Cumming's photographs of his service with the Imperial Yeomanry reflect a personal experience of war and having been trained to think in terms of composition he was particularly successful with his small Kodak. He also seems to have had a photographer's natural sense of timing probably developed as the result of training from his father which allowed him to 'see' the best moment to press the shutter. His own intelligence and interest in the events in which he was taking part led him to take pictures across as broad a range as possible and they deserve to be assessed as some of the best among the work of amateur photographers of the Boer War. The far flung nature of the war and its protracted elusive character made it particularly difficult for the professionals seeking news pictures and they seem to have rather lost interest in the closing stages. In retrospect, the work of amateurs recording their own personal view of events comes into its own as a particularly telling part of the historical record. William Skeoch Cumming's photographs are both informative and attractive, offering an insight into the Imperial Yeomanry's role in the history of the war, his evolution as an artist, and a demonstration of what a talented amateur photographer could achieve at the turn of the century.■

Notes

For permission to quote from his great uncle's letters now in the custody of the National Library of Scotland I would like to thank Mr Ronald Cumming. I would also like to acknowledge help received from the National Library of Scotland, the Scottish United Services Institute, the Scottish Photography Archive and the National Army Museum.

Examples of Skeoch Cumming's Boer War paintings may be found in the following collections: the Scottish United Services Institute, the City of Edinburgh Art Collection, the National Army Museum, London, and the Africana Museum, South Africa. Other works are in private hands. His most ambitious tapestry design for the Dovecote Tapestry Company 'The Lord of the Hunt' is held at Mount Stuart, Rothesay.

Sources

Ryno Greenwall — William Skeoch Cumming (*Africana Notes and News* September 1984 Vol 23 No 3)

Robert Paton — *Memoir of William Skeoch Cumming* (Constable 1933)

Thomas Pakenham — *The Boer War.*

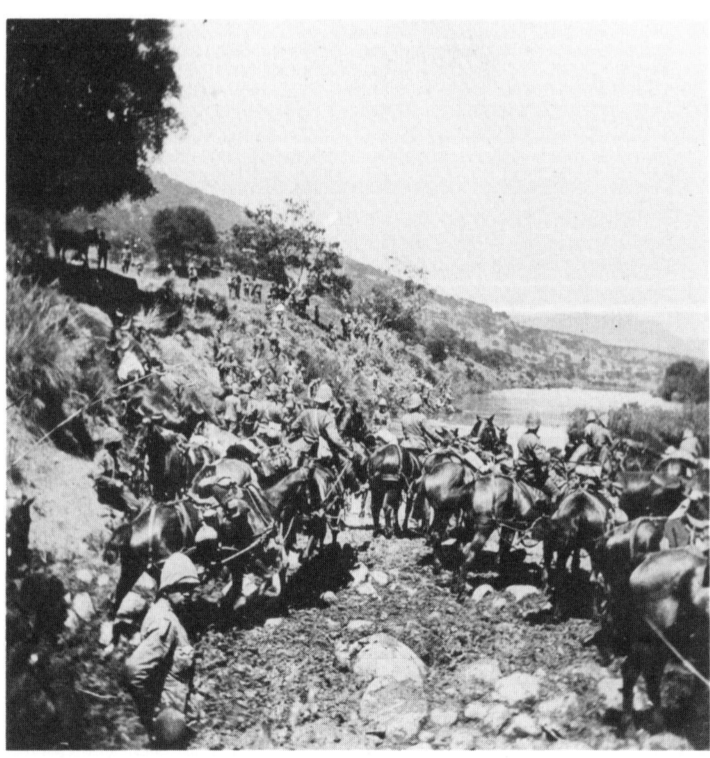

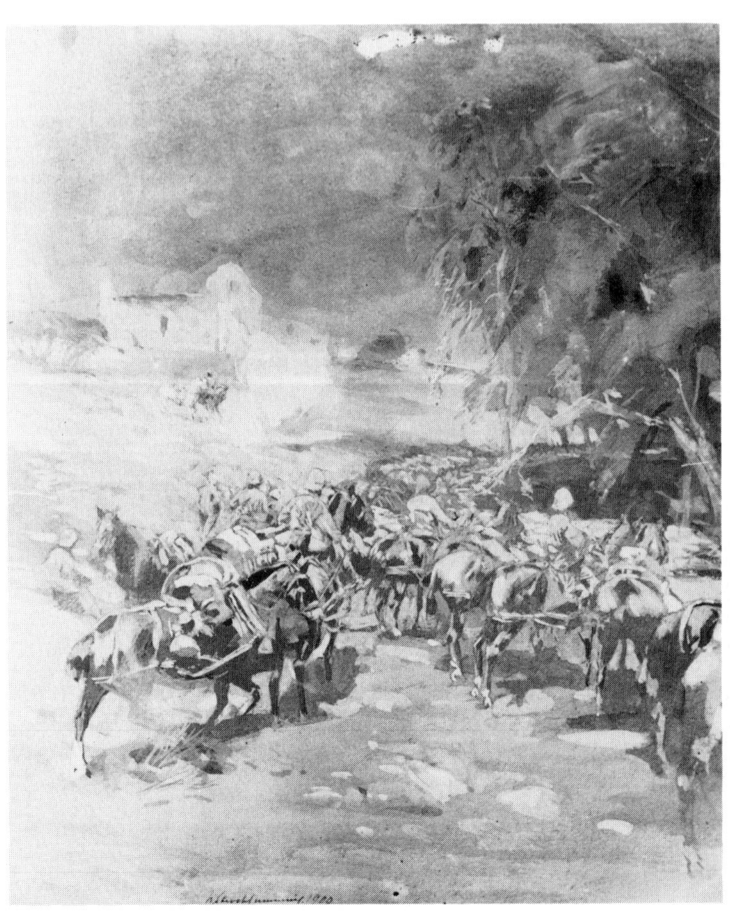

The Photograph shows the fording of a river. The Painting shows the evacuation of a hillside position. Note the 'match' of the horses' formation.
(IWM Neg Nos Q 72269/Q 72326)

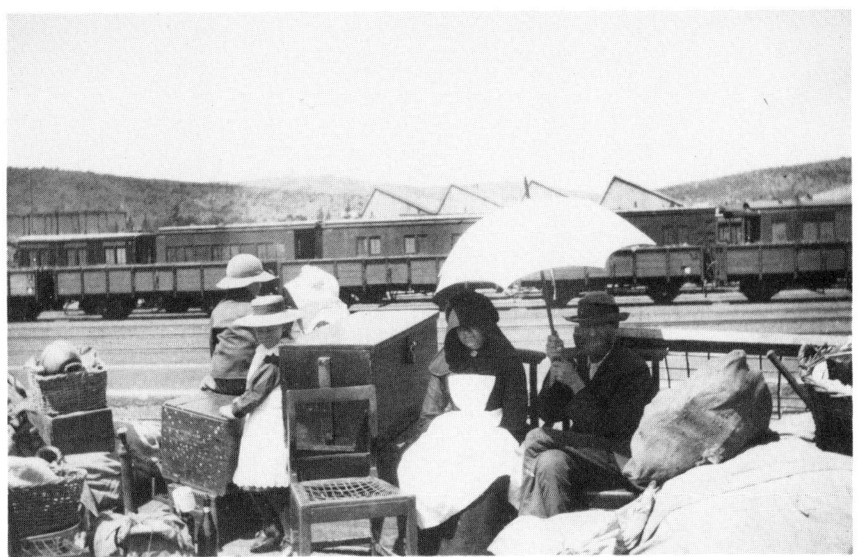

A refugee Boer family, the wife in traditional costume, surrounded by their possessions at a railway station. *(IWM Neg No Q 72378)*

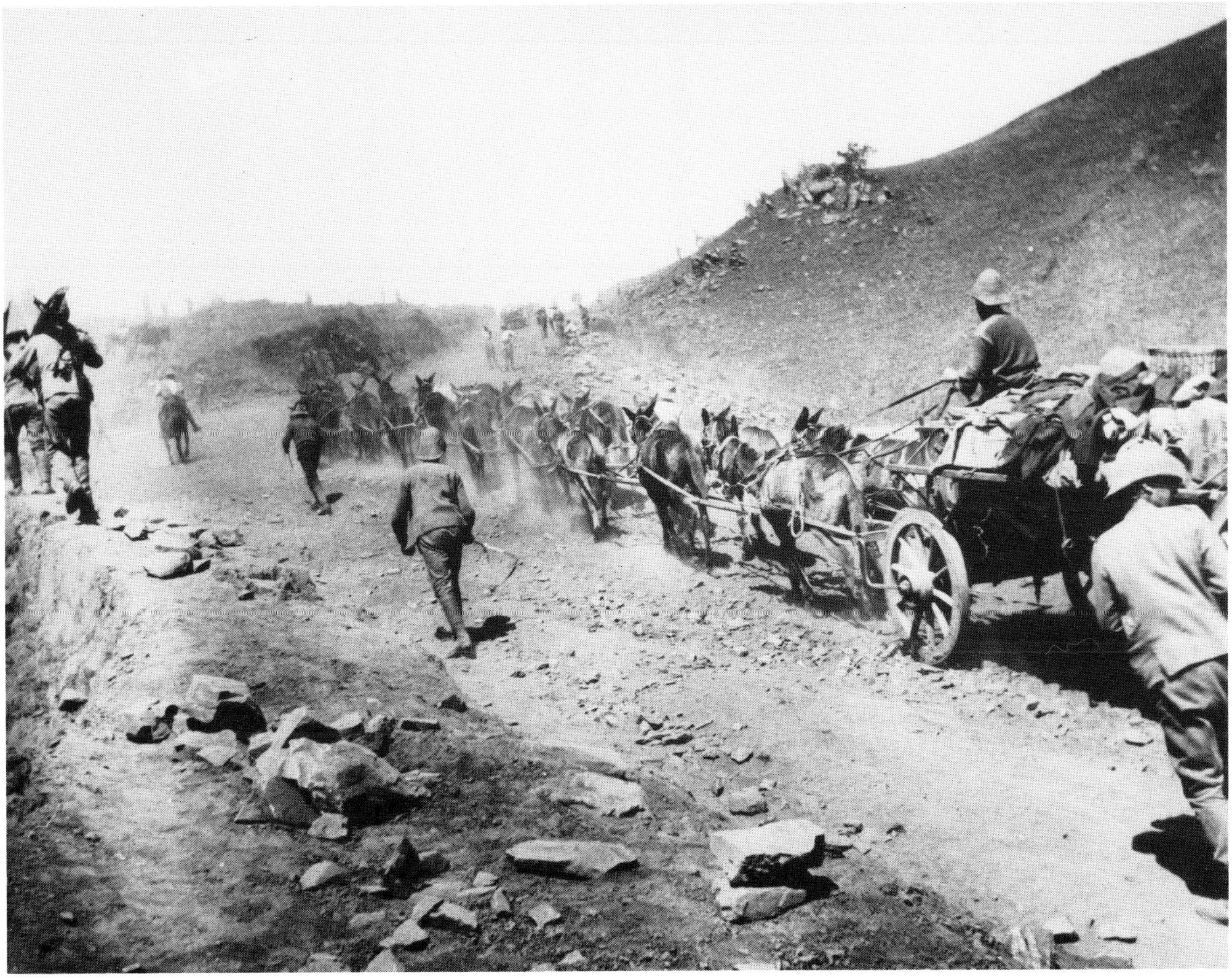

A mule train stirring up the dust as it toils up an incline. *(IWM Neg No Q 72044)*

THE YEAR OF THE COMET

H. J. P. Arnold reviews the modern image techniques — and finds a link with W. H. F. Talbot.

DR HALLEY's Comet has come and gone — now being beyond the reach of all but the most powerful telescopes as it heads towards the depths of the solar system once again. Throughout the second half of 1985 and well into 1986 it was studied by the almost one thousand professional astronomers and institutions, together with numerous amateurs, gathered together in the International Halley Watch — which made it the most comprehensively studied apparition of a comet in history.

It was the first one of the space era, too, and in March 1986 a flotilla of five dedicated spacecraft (to say nothing of the contributions from vehicles in Earth orbit and elsewhere which were put to good use) flew past the comet in a fine demonstration of international co-operation and obtained a wealth of information which will take many years to analyse. The most spectacular success among the fly-by vehicles was ESA's *Giotto* which is now metaphorically limping somewhat as a result of dust impact at the time of closest approach but is nonetheless unbowed. It has already been put in an orbit which will bring it back to the vicinity of Earth in 1990 whence it could be directed to another (though less famous) cometary target in 1992.

The astronomical fraternity warned the public that 1985-86 would not be a dramatic apparition. Nonetheless the intense media attention in the early period of the comet's visit led to a sub-conscious expectation of a spectacular object ('it must be, mustn't it, if the media are giving it so much attention' was the feeling) which could not possibly be fulfilled in the northern hemisphere. Those keen amateurs and others in the UK in November/December 1985 who pointed their telescopes at the diffuse ball in Taurus and then Pisces when weather permitted and who invited dear ones, friends and neighbours to view it received gratitude but no amount of diplomacy or good manners could hide the sense of disappointment felt by many of the guests. Those who had been unwise enough to buy telescopes for the occasion and then discovered the problems for the inexperienced in locating celestial (and particularly dim) objects through such an instrument must have been despondent indeed.

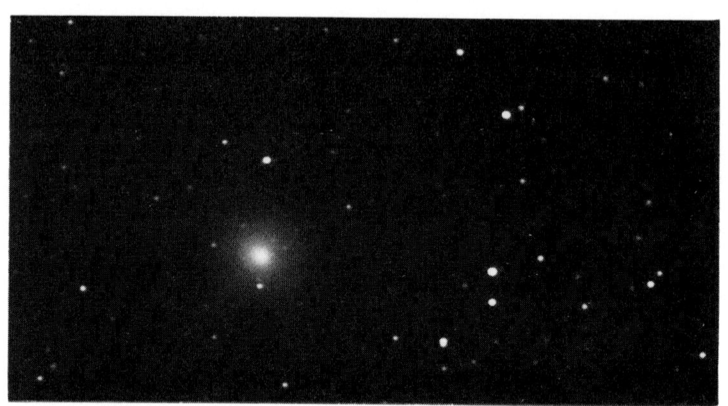

Compared with the other more exotic images reproduced on the following pages this is a salutary reminder of the appearance of Halley's Comet as it will be remembered by many of those who observed the visitor from the UK using binoculars or a telescope during November/December 1985. This is a section of a 35mm original exposed for ten minutes on hypersensitised 2415 Technical Pan film on 7 December 1985 commencing at 18.58GMT. The camera was a Nikon F3 with a Nikkor f/3.5 400mm ED lens fitted. The unit was mounted on a guided Celestron Super C8 telescope. At this time the comet was tracking along the border between southern Pegasus and northern Pisces.

To be fair, even the astronomically more sophisticated could be heard expressing some dissatisfaction on occasion — as witness the distinguished Californian space artist who, having caught a chill in April 1986 after waiting many hours for a sight of the comet through breaks in cloud, was heard to exclaim: 'Thank God it only comes once every 76 years!' Those who scrimped and saved to go to the southern hemisphere in the spring of 1986 — which was the place to be, we were assured — did not escape entirely, either. The comet 'peaked' a little early in terms of maximum brightness and tail length so that those who arrived in Australia in the first half of April were greeted with the news that 'it was a lot better three weeks ago' — a sure recipe for contentment.

The writer was a member of a party which, having selected Alice Springs in Australia's Northern Territory as an assured haven of crystal clear skies, arrived to be greeted by cloud and rain and comments (depending upon whom you asked) that it was the first rain in nine months, two years or five years. Neither the warmth of the welcome extended by Australian fellow enthusiasts, nor the fact that an 80km drive in the direction of the South Australian border brought one to somewhat clearer skies eased the sneaking suspicion that there might be after all something in the supposed nonsense associating comets with bad luck, if not death and destruction. 'Doesn't the damn thing *want* to be seen?' As to the serious business of astro-photography, was it the comet that caused equipment, which had always performed flawlessly and had been carefully checked beforehand, to misbehave?

So we bid farewell to Dr Halley's Comet. Even if it wasn't a breathtaking object this time, hopefully it won new adherents to the delights of astronomy — and it certainly caused many to see the magnificent skies of the southern hemisphere for the first time. In 2061 there should be numerous space missions that will rendezvous with the comet and bring back surface samples for examination on earth. For those who saw it — or tried to see it — in 1986, there might be some selfish satisfaction in knowing that the 2061 apparition will quite possibly be even worse!

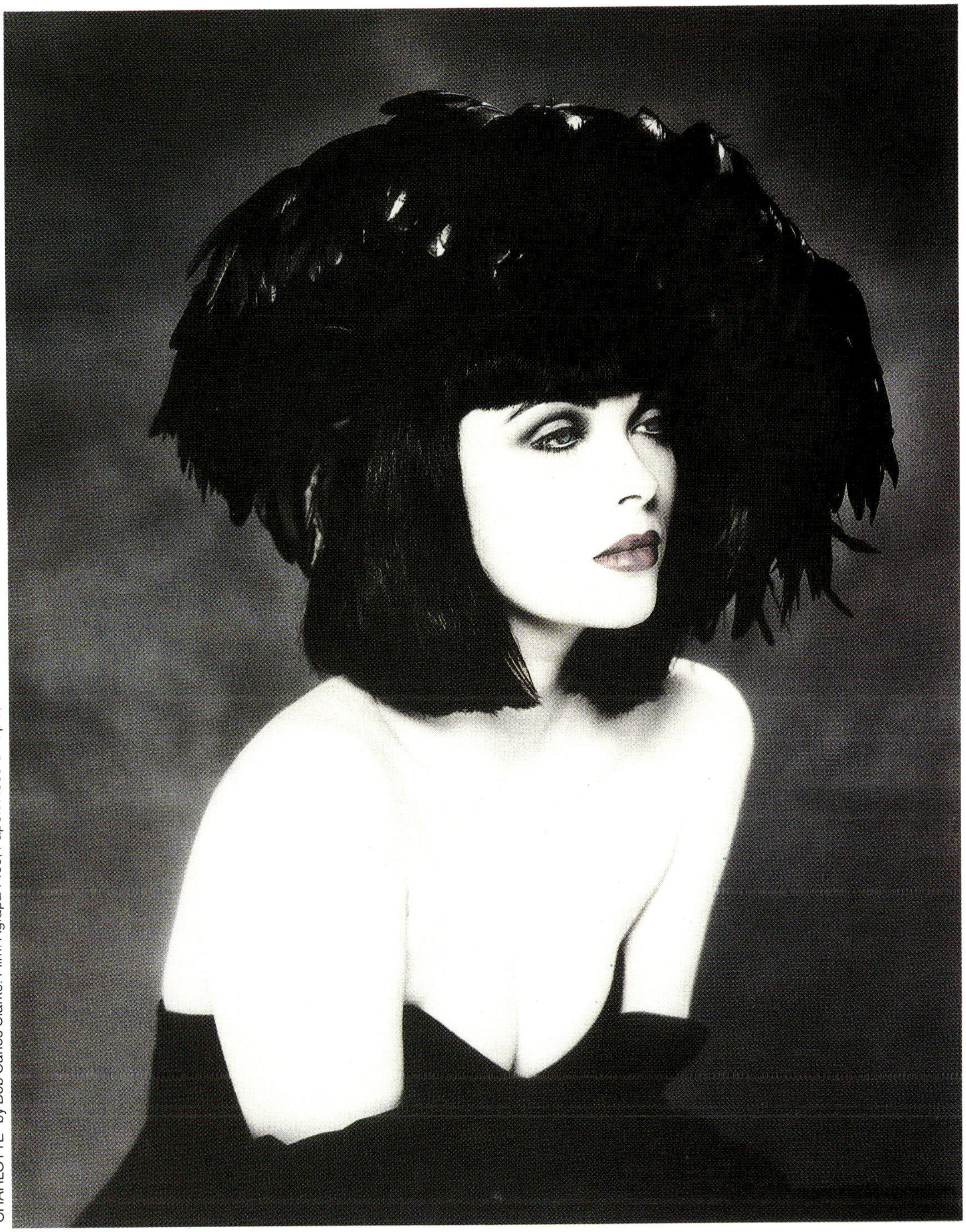

"CHARLOTTE" by Bob Carlos Clarke. Film: Agfapan 100, Paper: Record Rapid, Chemicals: Rodinal & Neutol.

Preferred by those who know

The high standard of reproduction that today's professional quite rightly expects, demands products of exceptional quality – and that's exactly what you get from Agfa Professional Division. Whether you want film, chemicals, black & white or colour paper you'll not find anything to beat the professional performance of Agfa.

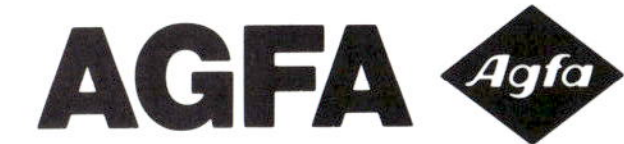

Agfa Gevaert Limited, 27 Great West Road, Brentford, Middlesex TW8 9AX. Tel: 01-560 2131

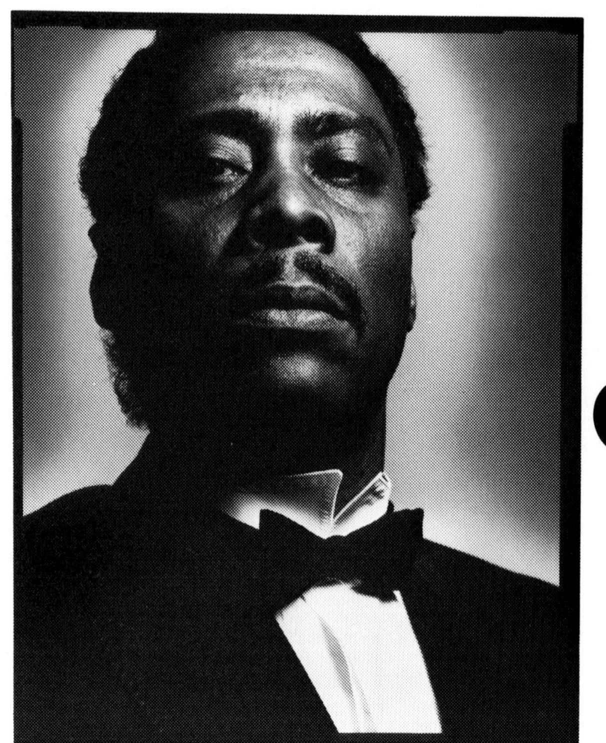

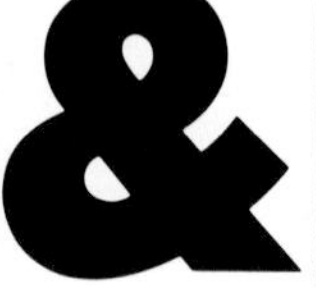

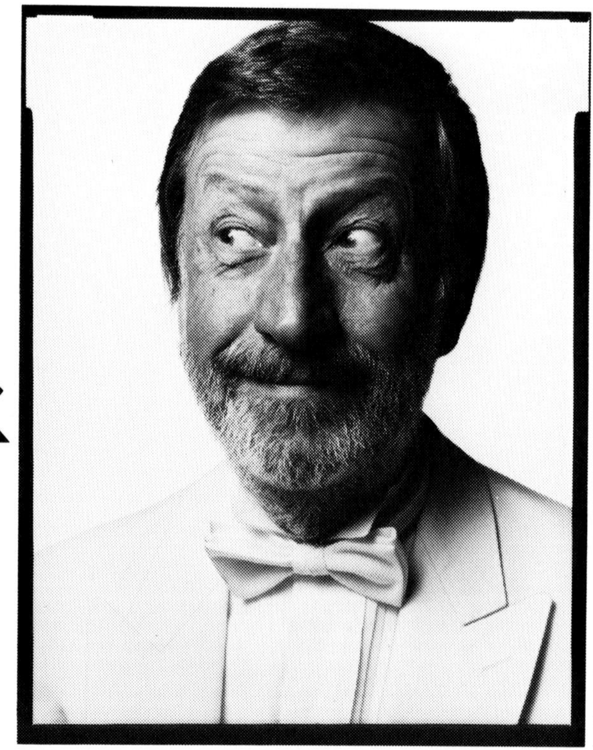

by John Claridge.

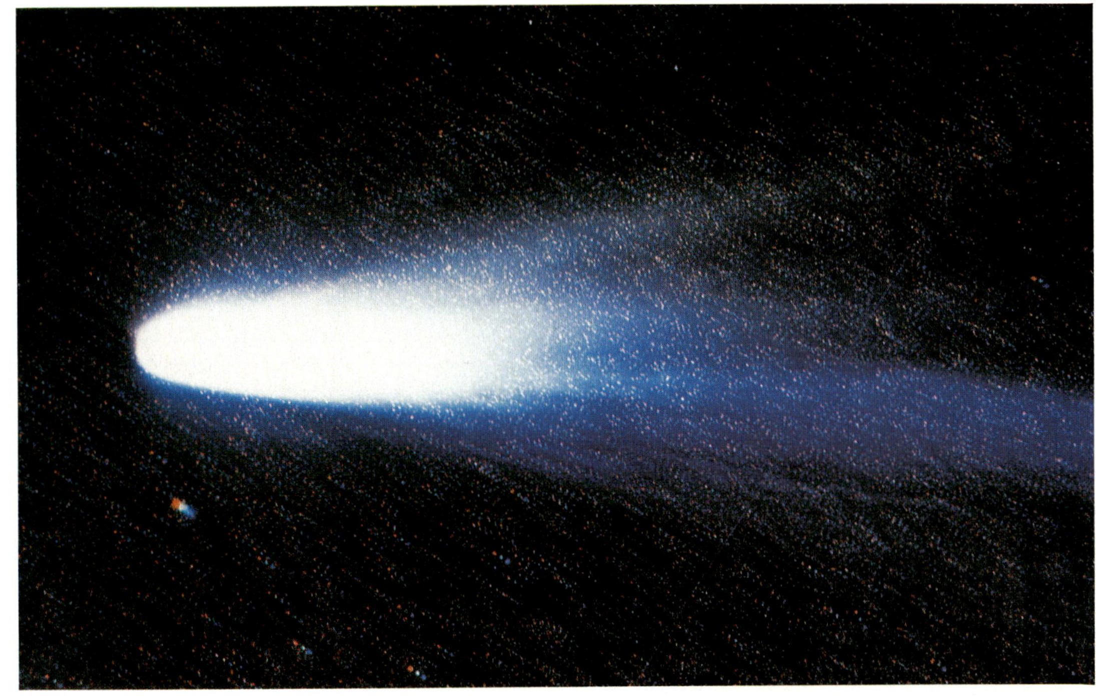

While conventional colour film is convenient, greater spectral accuracy results from combining black-and-white images recording blue, green and red light. This image is such a composite combining blue, green and red plates exposed on the night of 12 March 1986 for 15min, 20min and 20min respectively at the UK 1.2m Schmidt telescope in NSW, Australia. The telescope was tracking the comet hence the trailing of the stars separated into red/green/blue elements. The lower (bluish) tails are ion tails while the tails to the north (top) are formed by dust being swept from the nucleus and shine by reflected sunlight. *(Royal Observatory, Edinburgh)*

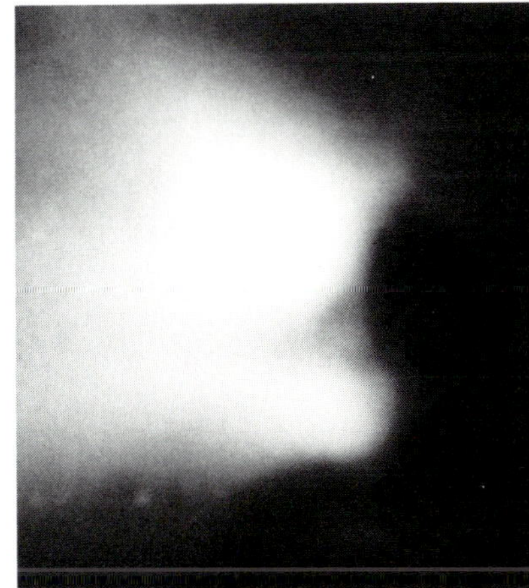

Giotto ***established that Halley's Comet has an albedo of only 2-4% which is comparable to the darkest bodies in the solar system. Released in May 1986, the black-and-white image (top) suggests what a human eye aboard the spacecraft would have discerned during the fly-by in March. (The frame size is 30km sq.) Two bright jets near the northern tip of the nucleus extend toward the Sun and are in stark contrast to the darkness of the night side (lower right). An earlier image in false colours (bottom) hinted at the irregular surface including 'spherical structures, not unlike impact craters, and valleys and hills' which Giotto team scientists claimed to have discerned in the data. The nucleus was larger than had been expected — about 15km along the major axis and up to 10km along the minor — but the appearance of a waist (giving rise to descriptions of the nucleus as being like a peanut in shape) is thought to be an artefact of the dust and lighting conditions existing at the time of the fly-by. Thus 'potato shaped' is considered to be more accurate.*** *(ESA/Max Planck Institut)*

A wide field view of Halley's Comet obtained at the European Southern Observatory on 21 March 1986 by R. Hafner using a Minolta XD7 camera fitted with a 50mm Rokkor lens attached to a mounting provided by the Ruhr University of Bochum. The exposure was for 70min on Perutz ISO100 film and the original frame was subsequently copied and corrected for colour balance by the ESO photo laboratory. At this time, the comet was 118m km from Earth and seen close to the constellation Sagittarius and the band of the Milky Way. The long, straight ion tail is clearly visible but much of the faint light emanating from the outermost parts of the comet are lost in the Milky Way. *(European Southern Observatory)*

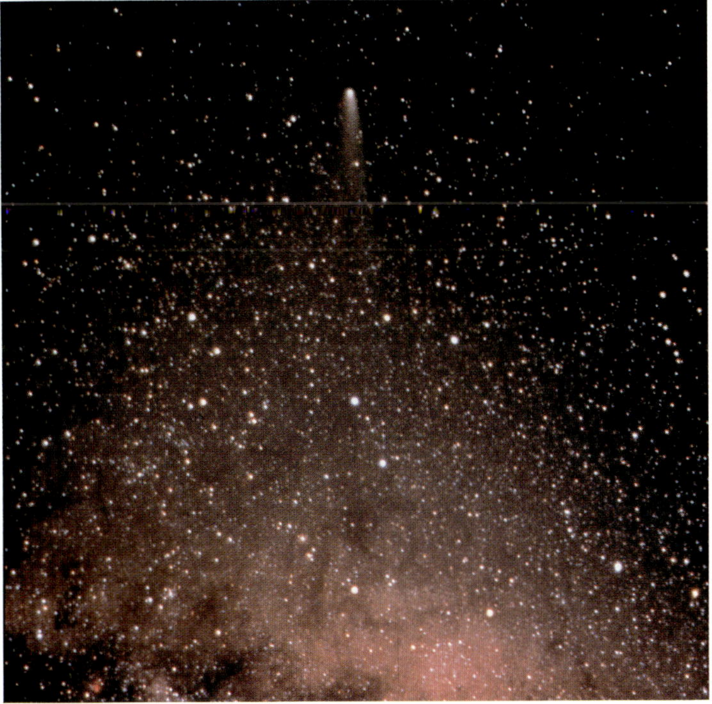

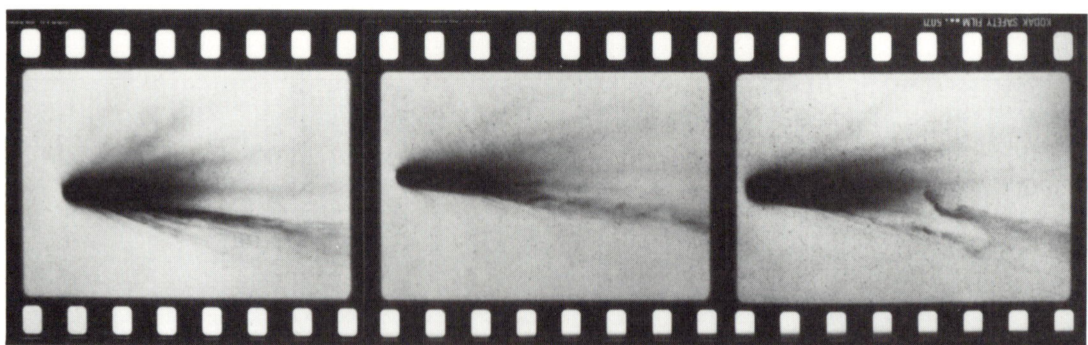

This series of three 30-minute exposures on blue sensitive photographic plates using the European Southern Observatory's 1m Schmidt telescope in Chile shows a spectacular 'disconnection event' over three nights from 8 to 10 March 1986 inclusive. On the first date, the main ion tail has a wiggly structure and there are many narrow streamers further south (below). On the following night, the ion tail has become more disordered and the amplitude of the wiggles has increased, with fewer streamers also. By 10 March part of the ion tail has become detached caused by changes in the solar wind. (ESO)

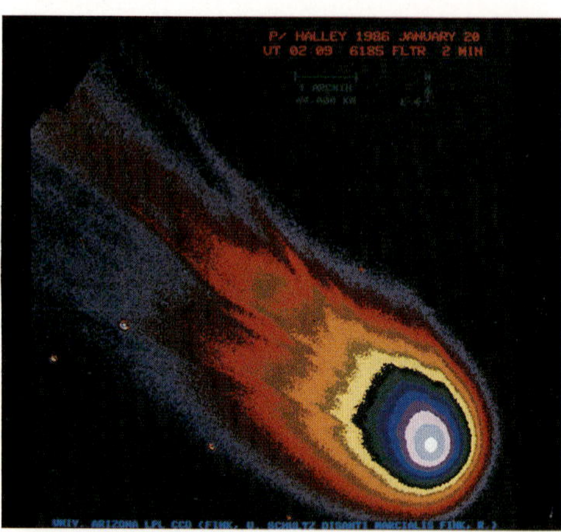

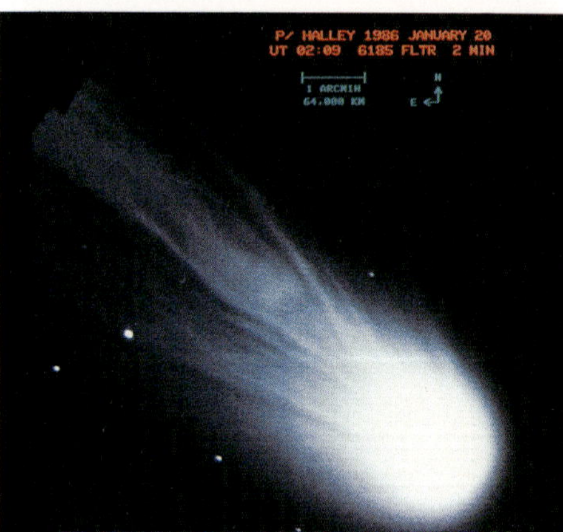

These two images are excellent examples of contemporary quality obtained from the use of a charge coupled device (CCD) imaging system — and the false colour representation of different intensity levels contained in the original black-and-white image. The latter was obtained on 20 January 1986 (i.e. as the comet approached perihelion on 9 February) in a 2min exposure using the University of Arizona's 61in Catalina telescope located on Mount Lemmon, 30 miles from Tucson. At the heart of the system is a Texas Instruments sensor consisting of an array of 800 × 800 individual silicon detectors — each detector being 15μm square.

In the original exposure a filter centred at 618.5nm with a width of 4nm was used. This narrow band pass filter mostly transmits the light from H_2O^+ ions — water molecules with an electron removed — which interact with the solar wind. The interaction produces the sharp tail and fan visible in this image though the exact process involved is not yet completely understood. (Dr Uwe Fink, Lunar and Planetary Laboratory, University of Arizona)

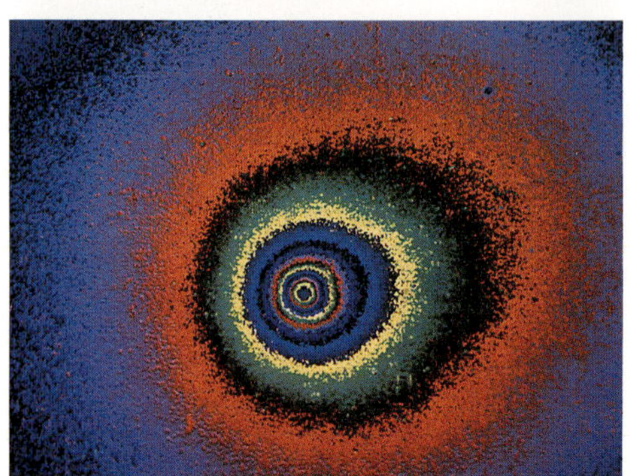

The false colour contours of a far-ultraviolet image of Halley's Comet obtained from a sounding rocket 300km above Earth on 13 March 1986 — thirteen hours before Giotto *flew past the comet. This image at the atomic hydrogen wavelength of 121.6nm shows an immense hydrogen cloud surrounding the comet and extending tens of millions of kilometres.* (US Naval Research Laboratory)

Optimum electronics and photographic lens technology was used to produce this image. The sensor system described (left) was coupled to a 58mm f/1.2 Noct-Nikkor lens for a 5min exposure again using the narrow band pass filter centred at 618,5nm. The unit was 'piggy-backed' on the 61in telescope which tracked the comet during the exposure. Dr Uwe Fink comments on the image: 'We estimate that stars down to about 11th magnitude are readily visible . . . this is probably the characteristic that best distinguishes the present image(s) from other typical Halley pictures . . . We attribute this to the fine quality of the lens and the small pixel size (15μm) of our CCD. We estimate the point spread function (i.e. the full width at half maximum) of the lens to be about 20μm. This is equivalent to an MTF of about 0.50 at 50 line pairs/mm.' (Lunar and Planetary Laboratory, University of Arizona)

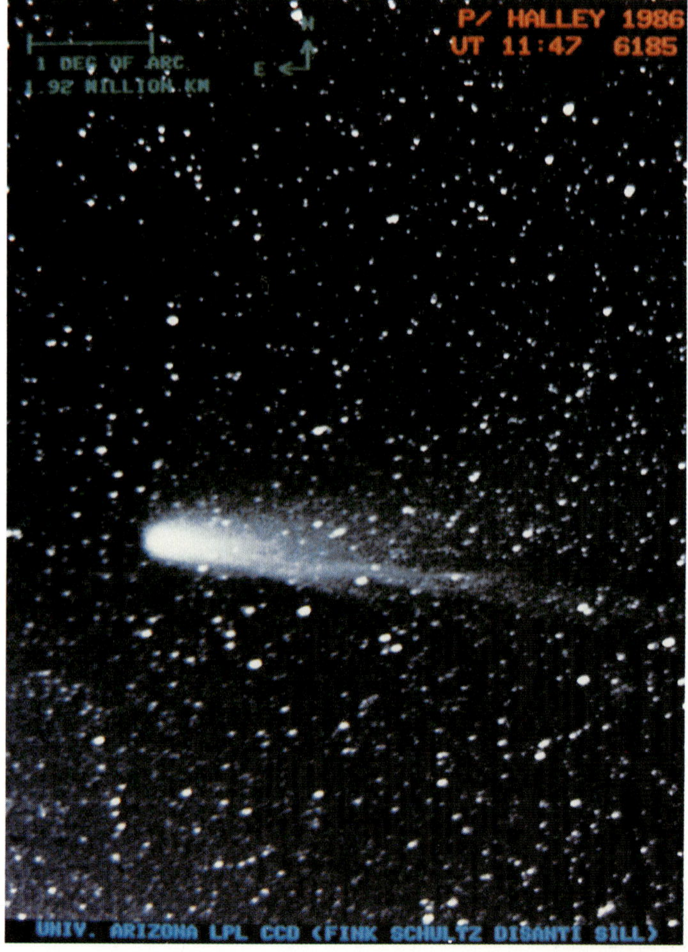

The Talbot connexion

The part played by photography in analysing the latest return of Halley's Comet is obvious from the examples in these pages. The 1910 appearance, too, was well within the photographic era. But even the previous return was already just into the lifetime of photography: William Henry Fox Talbot's achievement in obtaining and preserving a photographic negative — of one of the windows at Lacock Abbey — in August 1835 was accompanied in the very same month in the astronomical world by the 'recovery' of Halley's Comet.

Astronomical matters figured prominently in Talbot's notebooks from the early 1820s onwards — and comets were a favourite topic. He spent time calculating their paths and speculating on their nature. His observations and speculations were competent though not particularly original nor dramatic and — like many others — he suspected a similarity between the tails of comets and the then little understood phenomenon of the nebula. On 9 January 1831, for example, he wrote to his half-sister Horatia of 'seeing such a beautiful Aurora Borealis on the night of the 7th. It was very curious, there were white luminous clouds that shot across the sky from the West to the East; beginning at the West, where the Sun had gone down and in half a minute or less reaching to the east and forming a bright arch over the whole heavens. Whatever is the nature of this luminous substance, I think it likely that the tails of the Comets consist of the same, and perhaps those nebulae in the sky which astronomers describe as consisting of uniformed light'.[1]

The year of 1835 was a period of intense activity for Henry Talbot. Besides his photographic and other experiments he was hard at work on research into the integral calculus which would be published with great success in the following year. It is not surprising therefore that the two pages of Talbot's observations of Halley's Comet in notebook 'N' — which bears the date of 13 October 1835 on the flyleaf — are followed by a body of mathematical research which fills the remainder of the entire book.

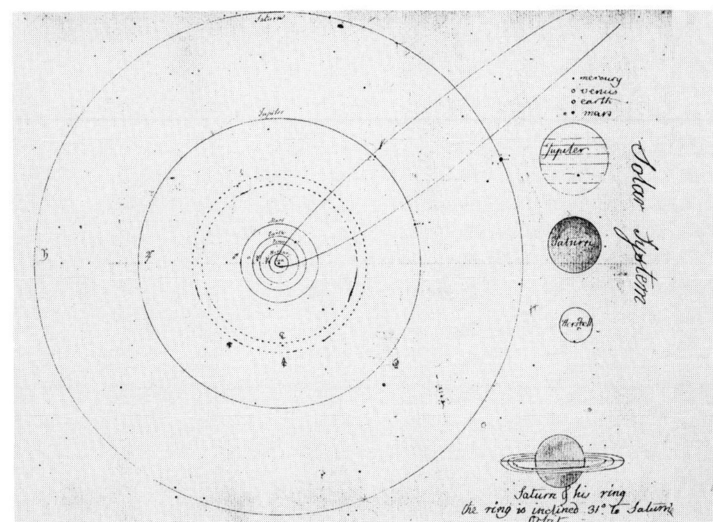

Solar system with comet ellipse. Drawn by the young William Henry Fox Talbot, at the age of nine. (Courtesy Talbot Museum, Lacock and Mr Anthony Burnett-Brown).

Henry Talbot wrote as follows about the Comet:

'Saturday 10th October the comet was beautifully seen. It passed rapidly about one degree north of α Ursa Majoris [the star Dubhe in the Plough]. Its brightness to the naked eye is about equal to one of the stars of Ursa Major but this is owing to its extensive luminous coma, for the nucleus is but a small star, and apparently a shapeless mass, since it will not bear a high magnifying power. The coma is white, the tail very inconspicuous. The three predictions in the Nautical Almanac of Pontecoulant, Damoiseau and Lubbock [the French astronomers Baron Damoiseau and the Count de Pontecoulant, and Talbot's fellow mathematician and scientist J. W. Lubbock] all made the comet pass below Ursa Major whereas it has past above.'

'Sunday 11th. Comet above the middle of Ursa Major.'

M[onday] 12th. Cloudy and so continued till . . .'

M[onday] 19th. Comet in [the constellation] Ophiuchus, having moved an immense distance since the 11th. It passed about 10′ from a fine star. The nucleus of the comet is conspicuous but ill defined, the tail straight not diverging much or fanshaped, shining with white light, directed away from the sun, very regular in form, about two degrees long.'

'Tu 20th Oct. Comet moved about 4 degrees from yesterday's position and not far from a good star which it may have reached after its setting. To the naked eye the comet is about as visible as a star of the second magnitude.'

'Sat 24th October. Comet very bright, with a long tail, seen for a moment between the clouds.'

'Tu 27th. Comet much fainter scarcely visible to the naked eye.' (Two intermediate observations.)

'Tu 10th November. Comet seen in the twilight near ν Ophiuchi, in the field of view with it. The tail faintly visible. Nucleus bright.'[2]

Talbot had seen the comet earlier than these observations because his wife Constance wrote to him on 4 September 1835 from Cowes where she was on holiday whilst he was working in London and at Lacock Abbey: 'What a triumph for you to have espied the Comet one day sooner than the Greenwich Observatory. Tell me in what part of the heavens you discovered it and how soon there will be any use in our looking for it.'[3] *It is now impossible to confirm whether Talbot's claim was valid: William Richardson made the first recorded observation at the Royal Greenwich Observatory on 28 August.*[4]

By the end of November observations of the comet became difficult for northern hemisphere astronomers and with the new year responsibility for studying it passed to southern hemisphere observers — and in particular to Thomas Maclear, Director of the Cape Observatory and to Talbot's scientific colleague and friend John Herschel who had set up a 20ft reflector telescope at Feldhausen near Cape Town.

It was appropriate and perhaps inevitable that two of the leading figures in the history of photography should have provided the link between the old way of recording the appearance of Halley's Comet in 1835 — and the new from 1910 onwards. Photographing a diffuse and often dim object like a comet was (and often still is) a demanding task and it was not until almost fifty years after Talbot's trail-blazing work in 1834-35 that the first high quality comet images began to be made. By 1910, astrophotographers were awaiting the most famous comet of them all with relish.

Sources

1 Lacock Collection.
2 Lacock Collection.
3 Lacock Collection: LA35-25.
4 Information from Miss Janet Dudley, Librarian & Archivist, Royal Greenwich Observatory.

TEACHING & LEARNING

A year of considerations for the future, Michael Hallett discusses the Education scene.

'ESSENTIALLY, the Green Paper is rolling the wicket for rationalisation' was the way that Peter Brooke, then Under Secretary for Higher Education, saw the publication in May 1985 of the Government's Green Paper *The Development of Higher Education in the 1990s*. Rationalisation was also the theme behind the cuts proposed by the National Advisory Body in April 1986. Rationalisation means contraction and links well with the revision of the Robbins principle on access to further and higher education. This suggests that 'ability to benefit' should be the guiding criterion, rather than formal qualifications. There was, however, an important rider — the benefit had to be sufficient to justify the cost.

The Green Paper, sets out the Government's intention to produce a higher education system more attuned to the needs of the economy and warns of the consequences for non-vocational subjects. It denies placing a low value on the general cultural benefits of education and research or, specifically, on the study of the humanities. It warns: 'Unless the country's economic performance improves, we shall be even less able than now to afford many of the things that we value most including education for pleasure and general culture and research as an end in itself.' A thriving economy needs more qualified scientists, engineers, technologists and technicians and intiatives throughout education are geared to producing them. The possibility of financial incentives to encourage students into relevant areas is cited as one item for debate in the forthcoming review of student support.

Great importance is attached to raising standards. The universities are considered the 'principal guardians of pure academic excellence and the main source of creative research' but should not be regarded as the model for higher education as a whole. It is accepted that some public sector institutions have a graduate output superior in quality and fitness to that of the universities.

Three other essentials are identified for all higher education institutions:

- to be concerned with attitudes to the wider world particularly industry and commerce and to beware of 'anti-business snobbery'. Students need a positive attitude to work and to be able to work co-operatively in groups as well as individually, show leadership and respond to it;
- to develop links with industry and commerce along the lines of the best existing practice;
- strong links with their local communities. Sharing of artistic, cultural and recreational facilities is encouraged, as well as close contact with local firms.

The Government has no wish to impose a uniform pattern on higher education and would like to see, on the contrary, more vitality and flexibility. It sees greater financial independence as one step in this direction. 'Adjustments in higher education are undoubtedly needed now', it concludes. 'More will be required as a result of the decline in student numbers that is to be expected in the 1990s. The years between now and then allow opportunity to plan for that situation constructively and to resolve other outstanding policy questions. It is not improbable that some institutions of higher education will need to be closed or merged at some point during the next ten years.'

Acceptance of the revised Robbins Principle is heavily qualified in the chapter on access to higher education. Formal qualification will be replaced by 'the ability to benefit' as a main criterion for entry to advanced courses. But the Green Paper adds a rider: 'So long as taxpayers substantially finance higher education, however, the benefit has to be sufficient to justify the cost.' Two further caveats are included: the student's motivation and maturity must be consistent with the course, which must itself be of sufficient standard; and selection procedures must be rigorous, assessing the ability to benefit those with qualifications as stringently as those without. Deferred entry to higher education is given an approving mention and the Government also declares its intention to simplify transfer from courses such as those validated by BTEC to degrees.

Student numbers are expected to remain roughly constant for the rest of this decade and then to fall from 612 000 (full-time) to 525 000 in 1996/97. Government spending plans are judged adequate to meet such demand in the next few years and there is a commitment to continuing updating of the demand projections. It is accepted that the levels of fees and student support will have a significant impact on future demand, although both are left for discussion in the forthcoming review of student support. The possibility of student loans replacing at least part of the grant is specifically noted. A 'great financial engagement' on the part of students might encourage them to take more care over their choice of study.

The National Advisory Body's Art and Design Working Group was reconstituted in February 1985 to consider, in relation to career opportunities, public expenditure plans and the needs of individuals and society: the philosophy, practice and objectives of higher education in art and design in the public sector; and the range of location of courses. The review that the Working Group was asked to undertake in the context of a major planning exercise for 1987-88 included the following considerations: 'the balance between fine art and design, between the design specialisms, and the relationships not only within art and design but between them and other relevant disciplines' and 'the need to stimulate new courses . . . particularly for design technicians.'

The Working Group's discussion document, *Provision*

for Art Education in Public Sector Higher Education was published in September 1985 and made the following recommendation relating to specialist degree courses. 'The number and size of the specialist Fine Art degree courses at honours level that would remain in their present form are matters for debate . . . Some of the existing Fine Art courses which offer significant opportunities for study in, for example, photography, film and video could be developed further on these interdisciplinary lines, and might with advantage be re-titled to reflect their content more precisely.'

The main impact of the cuts proposed in April 1986 by the National Advisory Body will fall on degree courses but is spread reasonably evenly between polytechnics and colleges. While details are currently unavailable, photography should not fare too badly as most of its courses are under the Design umbrella which is a 'protected' programme area with cuts of 6%. By contrast both Art and the Humanities are in 'unprotected' programme areas both taking some 16%.

The NAB cuts are in fact provisional decisions by the secretariat to cut student intakes, close courses, and in a few cases merge institutions in order to implement the NAB committee's instruction to protect the unit of resource in polytechnics and colleges by reducing the number of first-year students admitted in 1987/88 by 9500 or 7%. Later in the summer the NAB board and then committee will decide whether to endorse, modify or cancel these NAB cuts in the light of the appeals by institutions and the response of the DES. Only then will they be passed on to the Secretary of State for Education and Science, for a final decision.

The most likely outcome of these proposals is that the DES will find at least some of the extra money which the NAB is demanding as the price for cancelling the planned cuts. Maybe not the full £23 million, but something between £12 and £15 million would probably be enough. The NAB could then re-work its calculation and discover that a cut of 9500 students would not be necessary to protect the unit of resource. With the DES providing more money and the NAB adopting a less rigid position most of the cut would be avoided.

Where to Study: Photography, Film, Video, TV is the current edition of the *BJP*'s guide to photographic education published in July 1985. This provides the only source-listing of those courses in the United Kingdom which contain a photographic element. These are covered in nine tabulations giving full information on the colleges, the nature of the courses, the qualifications which may be obtained as well as a description of the courses as a general guide. The following statistical breakdown of these tables gives an indication of the current photographic provision in the United Kingdom: GCE — O-level courses in film study and photography 99; part-time courses in photography, film and television leading to certificate/diploma 36, leading to higher certificate or equivalent 8, leading to a first degree 2; BTEC National Diploma courses and similar full-time courses in photography, film and television 41; BTEC Higher National Diploma courses and similar full-time courses in photography, film and television 14; first degree full-time courses in photography, film and television 13; postgraduate courses in photography, film and television 11; foundation courses in art and design, SCOTEC Ordinary National Diploma in art and design, and BTEC National Diploma courses in general art and design 111; related full-time courses 48; full- and part-time related degree and higher degree courses 63; independent courses and workshops 11; and correspondence courses 2.

Peter Rolls' survey on 'Part-Time Photographic Courses' appeared in the 12 July 1985 issue of the *BJP*. The survey can be summarised as follows:

- Part-time courses are now operating at seven colleges in the London area and in 18 other centres. The erosion of provincial courses continues, although there are plans for a new course at Bournemouth.
- There has been no change in the higher level courses running in London, Edinburgh, Leeds, Sheffield and Belfast. There may be an extension of the C&G Advanced schemes in the London area over the next year or so.
- Ten of the 25 colleges reported increased enrolments, but a count of students suggests a decrease of around 7% across the country.
- The proportion of female students on photographic courses is estimated to be no more than 25-30%. Many part-time classes follow this pattern, but there is an even more marked reduction at the Higher level.
- A sample of 650 students showed that 20% were unemployed and a further 14% were in 'non-photographic' work.
- Student drop-out and the assessment hurdles take a heavy toll. It is suggested that less than half those enrolling on three-year basic courses are likely to obtain awards.
- The national product of the part-time schemes is estimated to be in the order of 250 qualified students a year.

Rolls' survey raises some important issues and concludes: 'part-time courses have a key role in the continuum of education. Employers, colleges and local authorities must ensure that this bridge to the future is kept open. Particular concern is expressed about the limited regional access to higher level education: this could be a serious structural weakness for the industry in years to come.'

Interest in photography in recent years has increased to a level where there is a need for a general provision for the non-professional of any age, from the school child, through youth groups to the camera club member and students taking the subject as a general study which will give the opportunity to study a wide variety of photographic topics on a flexible, short-course, modular basis. The new City and Guilds 923 Certificate in Photography scheme fulfils this need. This scheme is designed mainly for amateurs and is planned in such a way as to enable photographers to achieve practical competence together with appropriate background knowledge which will enable them to develop an interest or pastime to the level of a serious study. The scheme is *not* intended to provide a comprehensive training for those people already employed as photographers or trainees in the profession for whom provision already exists in the C&G 750 Photography Assistants scheme and the C&G 744 General Photography scheme.

Each module has been constructed to provide a single course leading to examination and certification or to be combined with other modules to provide a more integrated course leading to a Grouped Course Certificate. Students may take the modules in any order although the content of some modules will presuppose familiarity with the content of others. The modules currently available are: Starting Photography, Introduction to Black-and-White Printing, Introduction to Colour Photography,. Portraiture, Social/Documentary

Photography, and Landscape Photography. Other modules are planned and consideration may also be given to the submission of centre devised modules.

The Royal Photographic Society and City and Guilds have also announced that an agreement has been reached which links the C&G 923 Certificate in Photography scheme to the distinctions of the Society. Under the new agreement the Grouped Course certificate will be regarded by the Society as a recognised examination. This means that anyone who gains this certificate will, providing he or she joins the RPS or is already a member, be entitled to become a Licentiate of the Society and to use the designatory letters, LRPS.

In September 1986 the General Certificate in Secondary Education (GCSE) replaced the GCE O-level and CSE examination schemes. The first examinations for the new scheme will take place in the summer of 1988. Certification for the examinations in Art and Design will take one of two forms:

1 Art and Design (Unendorsed), where the work submitted for assessment will be from a broad area of study;
2 Art and Design (Endorsed), where the work submitted for assessment will indicate a single area of study from *one* of the following: Drawing and Painting, Graphics, Textiles, Three Dimensional Studies and Photography.

A major innovation of the new system is the introduction of national criteria governing all GCSE syllabuses. The criteria are in two parts. First, there are the General Criteria, which set out the general frame-work for all syllabuses and examinations, as well as a number of ground rules for the conduct of examinations — such as eligibility for entry to examinations, a mechanism for appeals and provision for handicapped candidates. Second, there are criteria specific to each of twenty major subjects, including art and design, which lay down certain requirements for every GCSE syllabus in those subjects. These requirements cover five areas: aims of courses leading to the GCSE in each subject, assessment objectives, content, the relationship between assessment objectives and content, and techniques of assessment.

In the context of general education the aims of Art and Design education are to stimulate, encourage and develop:

- the ability to perceive, understand and express concepts and feelings in visual and tactile form;
- the ability to record from direct observation and personal experience;
- the ability to form, compose and communicate in two and three dimensions by the use of materials in a systematic and disciplined way;
- the acquisition and understanding of technical competence and manipulative skills, which will enable individuals to realise their creative intentions;
- experimentation and innovation through the inventive use of materials and techniques;
- intuitive and imaginative abilities, and critical and analytical faculties;
- the ability to identify and solve problems in visual and tactile form: to research, select, make and evaluate in a continuum;
- the ability to organise and relate abstract notions (ideas) to practical outcomes;
- awareness and appreciation of relationships between Art and Design and the individual within the historical, social and environmental context;
- the acquisition of a working vocabulary relevant to the subject;
- the individual's special aptitudes and interests and to foster and encourage confidence, enthusiasm and a sense of achievement;
- the understanding of economic considerations which might become limiting factors in the inventive use of materials and techniques.

The Certificate for Pre-Vocational Education is a new award introduced by BTEC and the City and Guilds. It is awarded on completion of a one-year programme which aims to equip students for adult and working life. Young people have the opportunity to acquire basic skills and experience in a work-related context. They are given help to develop the attitudes, knowledge, personal and social maturity which they need and which employers want. CPVE courses involve activity-based learning. Each course includes a minimum of three weeks' actual work experience integrated with other learning activities. Students learn practical skills, basic numeracy, how to express themselves clearly and how to work as part of a team. The programme also provides time for community activities, leisure, recreation and reflection. CPVE is available to all sixteen-year-olds with a positive wish to achieve their full potential. Students will normally embark on the course immediately after completing compulsory secondary education. Although it is designed to provide a practical approach to education, using young people's interests to encourage learning, it is not solely for those who fail to achieve on traditional academic courses. In addition to the Certificate itself, every student will be able to offer an employer a detailed profile which records his or her achievements and a summary of experience and activities.

A pilot project is under way to incorporate CPVE into Youth Training Schemes (YTS) and Youth Training Programmes (YTP). By taking the CPVE during the first year of the two year YTS/YTP programme, young people will have the chance to gain a nationally recognised qualification giving a record of their achievement before going on to achieve job-specific experience and qualifications in the second year of the programme.

Towards the end of 1985, the Conference for Higher Education in Art and Design (CHEAD) published its draft document *Postgraduate Education in Art and Design: A Plan for the Late 1980s.* While currently the provision for postgraduate education in photography, film and television is limited, CHEAD's proposals could expand this. In its introduction the document comments that: 'CHEAD feels strongly that there should be an expansion of postgraduate education in Art & Design, and by postgraduate education, CHEAD means post-graduate research, postgraduate courses and postgraduate practice all three of which should be inter-related.

'In the past, the pattern of postgraduate development in the sector as a whole tended to occur without any central, national planning; and the result of this has been that very little thought has been given questions such as to resource allocation, modes of access, the development of new subject areas, the education role of postgraduate research and postgraduate courses — especially where undergraduate honours degree courses are concerned.'

In the document CHEAD makes the following proposals:

- that there should be an expansion of postgraduate education — research, course *and* practice — in the Art and Design sector;
- that access to postgraduate courses and postgraduate research in the sector should in

future be more flexible and a broader range of possibilities offered;

- that a more rational approach to national policy-making and national funding of post-graduate studies should be devised — involving the UGC, NAB, and perhaps the DES and SED;
- that the policy and funding of postgraduate research should, more appropriately, be directed by a new Art Craft and Design Research Council;
- with this in mind, that an Art Craft and Design Research Council be set up with the aim of attracting and administering funds for research in the sector, and formulating research policy;
- that certain important research projects should be implemented by the Council as a matter of priority, in association with appropriate branches of industry and commerce and other sources of funding;
- that collaboration and joint initiatives between colleges and the Royal College of Art should be encouraged and developed — especially in the area of providing coures for potential research supervisors, and in-course training;
- that postgraduate courses which involve the *practice* of art, craft and design should be awarded degrees or qualifications which match the content of the courses: the most appropriate new titles would seem to be MFA, MDES, DRFA and DRDES.

The role of the British Institute of Professional Photographers towards education and training has been modified over the past few years with the introduction of degree, and more recently BTEC, courses in photography. The Education and Training Committee of the BIPP now has the responsibility for:

- formulating and providing careers information, counselling and liaison with careers advisers in local authorities, schools, further and higher education.
- maintaining an up-to-date position on employers' expectations of students following college courses.
- advising colleges of Further, Higher and Degree education on the profession's immediate and future needs.
- maintaining an industrial influence on education and training establishments, offering Institute recognition, and course recommendation.
- Recognising the need for, formulating content, training tutors and operating a series of post experience training courses including social, technical, photography, selling and business skills.

The BIPP is now taking the initiative along with the Photographer's Charitable Trust and the Professional Photographic Laboratories Association in investigating the current training needs of technicians with the aim of proposing, initiating and monitoring the appropriate remedial action in co-ordination with other Associations and Educational Institutions through funding by the Manpower Services Commission. They suggest that while 'there may well be a sufficient provision of courses preparing photographers, there is a dire shortage in the area of professional photographic laboratory technicians, and a lack of relevant education and training for assistants to advertising, fashion and editorial photographers.' They suggest a 'photographic technician is someone with a skill in one or more specific areas of photographic production techniques. These skills are used to create or convert images, using either conventional silver based techniques or others such as those in video post production.'

It is proposed that a Working Party be set up to determine current supply/demand ratio of photographers and their employment prospects, current supply/demand ratio of professional laboratory technicians and their employment prospects, geographical supply/demand provision for courses for both groups and likely changes *over* the next five years, attempt to assess the quality and appropriate content of existing courses for 1986 and the foreseeable future, assess existing 'commercial' or manufacturer courses, provisions for new technology, provisions for management and marketing, and the level of quality of careers advice.

Following this investigation it would be necessary to develop a pilot scheme at a suitable establishment. There would be open access to the pilot scheme and it is anticipated that courses would admit unemployed adults as well as existing employees and school leavers. The BIPP or the PCT could act as Managing Agents and prepare packaged material for use under the Youth Training Scheme for short intensive courses to meet the needs of AFAEP assistant photographers and BIPP/PPLA technicians.

The Photographic Education Group was established in May 1986 as a 'Voluntary, non-profit-making professional association for everyone who is working as a teacher, lecturer or other educational or training role in the fields of photography, film, video, audiovisual and aspects of media education.' Membership is open to both full and part-time staff. The group aims to promote the personal and professional development of the membership, thereby contributing to the development of educational provision, standards and the appreciation by the public of this area of work. PEG is organised on a regional basis with regional representation on the management group.

The group proposes to offer courses, conferences, symposia, and workshops. It is planning an industrial release scheme and schemes for the exchange of information and visits to establishments abroad. The provision of careers advice is under consideration. Publications include a termly newsletter and a *Journal of Photographic Education*, and there are plans to produce resource material for classroom use.

The initiative for the formation of PEG has come from Frank Hawkins, OBE, HonFRPS, FBIPP, who until recently was the HMI for Photography. There has been a need for such an organisation since the demise of the Society for Photographic Education several years ago. The aims of the new group are much broader and more in sympathy with the needs of the educational provision of the late-1980s. The general movements in education, including the cuts, are outside the influence of teachers and lecturers of photography but this positive development within photographic education will undoubtedly prove, in retrospect, to be the major thrust of the year. It will give photographic education a much needed identity and focal point which can only improve the quality of its education and training.■

PELLING+CROSS

TRADE NAMES A-Z

Solely imported and distributed through our own branches and appointed dealers

AIR-EVAC Concertina chemical storage bottles

ALTO CUTTER Bevel edge mount cutter

BEATTIE INTENSCREENS Camera focussing screens

BLASTER 4-Bulb magnesium flash unit

BO FLASH Magnesium bulb flash system

BOLITE Economy electronic flash units

BOMETER Inexpensive flash meter

BOWPOLE Background support system

BROOKS Stainless steel tanks, reels, dial thermometers

CAPITAL Digital spot meter

COLORMOUNT Dry mounting tissue (Seal)

COMPUTAR Professional quality enlarging lenses

COPYTRAN Slide copier

DUST-OFF The original aerosol dust remover

EXHIBITEX Seal picture texturising process

FC Photographic paper dryers

FIDELITY Double dark slide film holders

FRONT PRO Front projection system

FUJI Range of professional roll film cameras

FUSION 4000 Special super-bond adhesive sheet (Seal)

HAUPT Laboratory clocks/timers

HI-GLIDE Overhead light tracking system

HORSEMAN Large format camera systems

ILLUMITRAN Transparency duplicator

JEDAM Professional register mounts, punches & metal masks, colour gels

JET STREAM Studio wind machine

LUMEDYNE Modular flash system

MAGNASIGHT Enlarger focus finder

MANFROTTO Still & video tripods & lighting stands

MASTER Masking frames, vacuum easels, borderless easels, light boxes, copy stand, slide copier/rostrum stand

MICROSPLIT Haupt quatz stopwatch

MONOLITES Range of portable electronic flash

OMEGA Enlargers and accessories

PEAK Optical magnifiers plus microscopes

PHOTO GRADATION PAPER Graduated colour background paper

PHOTO JACK Platform for macro & micro photography

PHOTOTROLLY Sturdy carrying trolley

PICTROL Variable diffusion device

PLANET Light pointer

POLEVAULT Background paper support unit

QUADMATIC High power studio electronic flash

SAVAGE Coloured background paper

SEAL Dry mounting equipment and software

SKY HOOK Gaffer-type lighting clamp

SPACE ARM Wall fixed lighting support arm

SSR METER Electronic flash meter

VACUSEAL Vacuum activated mounting & heat sealing press

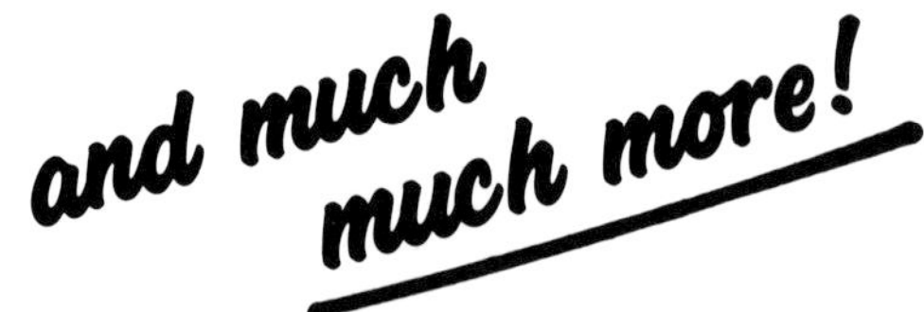

PELLING+CROSS

LONDON
93-103 Drummond St. London NW1 2HJ
Tel 01-380 1144

BIRMINGHAM
Radio House Aston Road North Birmingham B6 4D
Tel 021-359 5751

MANCHESTER
Arundel Street Manchester M15 4JZ
Tel 061-832 4957

BRISTOL
5/9 Welsh Back Bristol BS1 4SP
Tel 0272 24024

HOLOGRAPHY TODAY

This still very modern technique continues to make progress. Graham Saxby reports.

READING again the progress report for last year's BJP Annual, one is reminded of what an exciting year it was, with advances on the technological, commercial and artistic fronts. As copy for the Annual has to be ready well before it is published, venturing a report on an event that has not actually happened can be a risky business, and for this reason nothing was said about the Second International Symposium on Display Holography which took place in July 1985 at Lake Forest College near Chicago, organised by the indefatigable Tung Jeong, Professor of Physics. The College, which is in idyllic surroundings by the shore of Lake Michigan, now miraculously again free from pollution, was at one time known in the UK only for having expelled Bix Beiderbecke in 1921, compelling him to earn his living as a musician and thereby changing the history of jazz. Although the venue was in the USA it was a truly international affair, with participants from more than twenty countries, including a large contingent from the UK. In general, the papers presented at the Symposium broke little new ground, though it was clear that display holography was now consolidating its position. The technical excellence seen in the accompanying exhibition of holograms by the participants showed how far technique has advanced in creative holography. But the great thing about the Symposium was the opportunity to meet in one place almost all the distinguished names in holography, including Emmett Leith, Nils Abramson, Stephen Benton and 'TJ' himself, not to mention all the other enthusiasts from America and elsewhere; for their part, they seemed to be equally pleased to meet us.

Having succumbed to the 'by the time you read this' syndrome last year, it is a pity to have to report that the images in our crystal ball were a little out of focus, and that it has taken a good deal longer that expected for the Royal College of Art's holography facility to get into its stride. Indeed, at the time of writing only one table is in full use, though the second, very large table has been installed and should soon be operational. The pulse laser has produced some first-class master holograms. The optics needed for portraiture have now been installed, and the first open-eye portraits have been made. Using the continuous-wave laser tables some superb multi-image, multicolour work is being turned out by the students under the guidance of Peter Miller, who is the full-time lecturer in charge of day-to-day running of the unit, and Nick Phillips, who has overall technical responsibility and divides his time between the RCA and the Department of Physics at Loughborough University.

Nick recently demonstrated a prototype fringe stabiliser using a transducer mirror based on the piezoelectric diaphragm of a Motorola car radio speaker. This gave an impressive performance. The limitations of fringe-locking devices are that they do not work well where there are several beams illuminating the subject; they have a tendency to 'microphone' or pick up extraneous sound vibrations; and they cannot control fringe movement caused by movement of the plateholder. However, their potential importance in the production of copies of holograms on non-silver material such as dichromated gelatin or photoresist cannot be underestimated. Without such devices the combined problems of fringe drift and fringe jitter have made the obtaining of really high-quality images a hit-and-miss affair, with consequent high cost in both time and material. Basically, a fringe locker is a servo device which detects any movement of the fringes that form the hologram and feeds an amplified signal to a movable optical component (the transducer) which restores the fringes to their original position within a millisecond or so. Its use can lead to dramatic improvements in image quality and to 100% reliability in production work.

The laser industry continues to develop new products, many of which are of interest to holographers. Cambridge Lasers Ltd have introduced a repair service for ion lasers and laser-based systems, from electronic fault finding and repair to plasma tube reprocessing. Glendale Optical Inc have a full range of laser guard goggles which have a density of 6 (ie a transmittance of one-millionth) to the required wavelength but are almost totally transparent to all other wavelengths. Optilas Ltd are marketing tunable helium-neon lasers which can produce coherent light at red, orange, yellow and green wavelengths at the turn of a knob. Spectrolab Ltd have introduced a range of 'Zero-g' isolation tables at very competitive prices, and Ealing Electro-Optics plc has marketed a speckle interferometry camera for research and non-destructive testing applications.

Monomode fibre optics in telecommunications has proliferated to the point where an exhibition can be staged at Olympia dealing with nothing else. Although the communications industry uses wavelengths in the near infrared, the technology for producing a semiconductor laser suitable for holography could be with us within a year or two, according to one specialist at the exhibition — given the industrial incentive, as this is not just a matter of research and development: it is a matter of economics. Telecommunications is very big business indeed; by comparison, holography is a very small market, and the cost of developing a visible-light semiconductor laser suitable for this market has so far not been justifiable to those who pay for the R & D. Such economies even apply to photography: even in this much larger market it is cheaper to buy a microprocessor chip off the shelf than to design and build one especially for a camera; we thus have the logically ludicrous position that the chip that controls exposure on most automatic cameras is capable in theory of taking care of the recording of a month's television programmes, running the central heating system, remembering several hundred telephone numbers and looking after your household accounts as well as masterminding your photography. However, it may well turn out that holography may benefit from other lucrative developments such as the compact disc, which at present uses a small helium-neon laser to read the encoded signal, but could well employ a semiconductor laser in the future. As mentioned in last year's Annual, there are advantages in using monomode optical fibres for light guides in two-beam holography, and it is particularly easy to couple the output of a semiconductor laser ito an optical fibre. For those inclined to experiment, York Technology Ltd of Southampton now produce monomode optical fibres matched to 633nm and will supply small quantities on request, previously one had to buy something like 10km at a time!

Ilford has so far been reluctant to release its new holographic emulsions except in sample batches to bona-fide experimenters. The emulsion originally developed for Applied Holographics plc (who work exclusively with pulse lasers at 694nm) did not give satisfactory results with HeNe lasers owing partly to the mismatch in wavelength, and, more important, to severe low-level reciprocity failure. A new emulsion balanced for 633nm and longer exposures works much better for HeNe; indeed, it works better for pulse lasers too, and has now superseded it. It seems that the emulsion may now appear on a triacetate base which is not optically active, as opposed to polyester base which has to be very thin if birefringence effects are not to mar the quality of transfer holograms. Another important advance not released in time for last year's Annual is that the green-sensitive emulsion has a transmittance of better than 60% to green light, which means that single-beam reflection holograms using argon-ion light are now possible.

After its exhibition of Soviet holograms in the summer of 1985, Light Fantastic reopened its gallery at the Trocadero shortly before Christmas, completely refurbished, with a display of more than 150 holograms in a spacious environment. Some of the holograms were spacious, too; the biggest was a 1 × 1.5m stereogram by the sculptor Alexander, made with the technical co-operation of Dr Hariharan of CSIRO, Sydney. There were several other large holograms, mainly AP-Holographie of Paris, and some excellent portraiture by Richmond Holographic Studios. But perhaps the most exciting exhibit was a real-image hologram of a microscope by Walter Spierings in which it was possible to put one's eye up to the ghostly eyepiece and actually see the greatly magnified image of a microchip just as if the instrument were real. Yes, the theory says it *has* to be so; but the image is still an astonishing technical tour de force. Light Fantastic has recently received an order for two million embossed holograms for inclusion in a new book, 'The Mirrorstone', to be published by Jonathan Cape at about the same time as this Annual. The technical innovations which make it possible to mount holograms flush on credit cards also make it possible to 'print' holograms directly onto the pages of a book, and there are to be seven holograms (one on the cover) incorporated within colour illustrations to the story.

Advanced Holograms continued to produce very high-quality large images, the biggest to date being a 1 × 1.5m image of the Michelin Man. At the opposite end of the market, Light Impressions UK produced a single order for more than 4.8 million small embossed holograms for a promotion by Wilkinsons, the sweet manufacturers. Ian Lancaster parted company with Third Dimension, the company he founded for the mass marketing of silver-halide holograms, to become a free-lance consultant, and the partnership that produced the Ikon holographic viewer (alas, too far ahead of its time) also broke up. Miniature holograms appeared on *every* credit card, and Charles Chatwin of Bradbury, Wilkinson & Co appeared at the RPS Holography Group monthly meeting to tell the members all about the role of holograms in security (BJP, 23 May 1986). The National Geographical Magazine put a hologram of a prehistoric skull on the cover of its November 1985 issue, this time without any eyebrow-raising about the wonders of 3-D images. Two new marketing concerns appeared: Holomart, under the technical direction of Bruce Snyder, and Holoscan, managed by Stephen Crouch, La Société Française d'Holographie is a new production facility with strong British connections (John Webster is a major shareholder), which is moving from DCG hologram production into larger holograms, where it will use a pulse facility for mastering holograms up to 1m square. A new holographic gallery opened in Shepherds Bush, under the direction of Mark Moutafian.

Two books have appeared in the UK this year. The first, *How to Make Holograms* by Don McNair, is published by Tab Books, and was reviewed in the BJP, 12 July 1985; it is notable chiefly for a blow-by-blow account of how to build a sand-table lab. The other, *The Hologram Book*, by Kasper and Feller (Prentice-Hall), reviewed BJP 3 January 1986, is a basic book on the principles of holography, using an approach that relies chiefly on geometrical otics. There are more periodicals concerned with holography this year. In additional to the established *holosphere,* the organ of the Museum of Holography, 11 Mercer Street, New York 10012, there is *Holoblad* from the Museum voor Holografie, Lovelingstraat 56, 2008 Antwerp (with articles in English and Flemish); *Wavefront* from Canada, PO Box 82247, Burnaby, BC; *LASER News* from California, PO Box 42083, San Francisco, CA94101); and *Real Image*, the newsletter of the RPS Holography Group, 4 Macaulay Road, London SW4 0QX. All of them have carried embossed holograms on the covers and are available on subscription.■

EMERSON IN BROADLAND

A controversial figure who lived into the 1930s but remains a 19th century figure — told by Ray Aspin.

FOR A TASTE of 'backwardness' Broadland is the place. Bulging into the North Sea, it is cut off from the rest of the country by a splattering of rivers, lakes and dykes. Four navigable rivers meander through an open landscape of flat grazing marshes and undulating uplands, emptying into the sea at Great Yarmouth. Victorian Broadland was a stronghold of rich landowners employing poor fenmen to farm, fish and fowl for them. Cattle grazed on the marshes while trading wherries carried commerce along the rivers. Then, as town dwellers began drifting into seek rustic tranquility, trading wherries were converted into pleasure boats each summer and let with a skipper and cabin boy. Photographers, too, helped to promote the holiday trade. But for one photographer Broadland was a passion. He dropped his career to be part of it. And Peter Henry Emerson's name will always be associated with his loving arrangements of earth and water beneath East Anglian skies.

Born in Cuba, of an English mother and an American father, Emerson was a young qualified physician of brilliant intellect and with a considerable private income. Yet medicine only filled a corner of his life. He was ever conscious of nature, overwhelmed by its beauty and diversity, and longed to explore the interlacing life patterns of birds, fish, insects and plants. In 1883 he bought a view camera. Head under the focusing cloth, hands fumbling with the knobs, he gasped to see luminuous blurs forming a clear image on the ground glass screen. Breathtakingly beautiful! Here was nature in all its colour, form, light and shade. Here was an art, inferior to painting because it could not record colour, but superior to etching with its ability to resolve almost every subtle tone; an exquisite medium to combine art, science and nature.

While photographing everything everywhere he arrived in Broadland. As the sun broke through the mist he stood transfixed, strangely elated. Nowhere could he remember having seen such a landscape. Yet he felt an uncanny familiarity with the scene. The vast expanse of salt marshes, the turning of a windmill, floating wherries, flying clouds, gliding swans, bleating sheep, were all saying, 'Come home!' Thus Emerson found his vocation. Goodbye medicine.

He cruised the Broads in a hired yacht. Free at last! The medical world behind him, wide horizons before him. Winds swept the wild landscape, tossing the reeds, rippling the waters and chasing fleecy clouds across the blue: everything intoxicated by spring and beating with the tidal pulse of life. He glided along at full sail, savouring the ebb and flow beneath him, the strange clumps of trees, lines of dykes, tints of reeds, fish and flowers which filled the lagoons. He dropped anchor, took an icy swim then took a glass of grog just to celebrate the sheer joy of his new life.

In 1884 Emerson took a cottage in Southwold Common, from where he was to spend the next decade investigating and photographing the landscape. With Broadland he felt something of the intense union which Wordsworth had with the Lake District, Emily Bronte with the Yorkshire Moors: a place of inspiration and fulfilment from which he could never bear to be parted for long. Soon he was a familiar figure there, fishing with the fenmen, forking hay with them, while eagerly learning

A Winter's Morning (By courtesy of The Trustees of the Victoria and Albert Museum.)

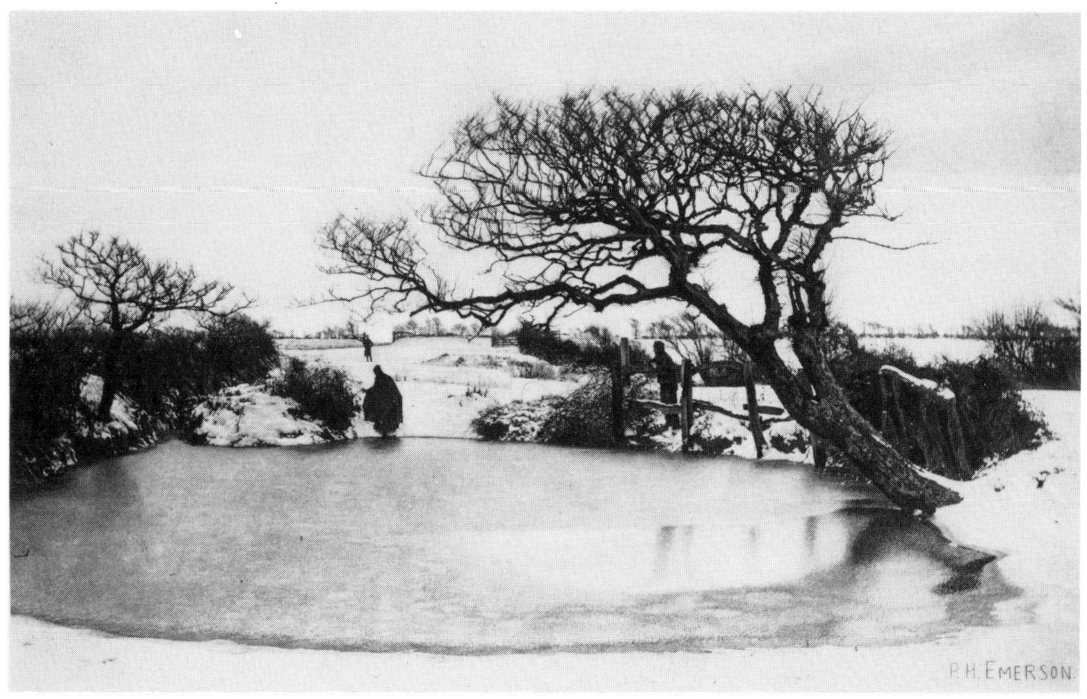

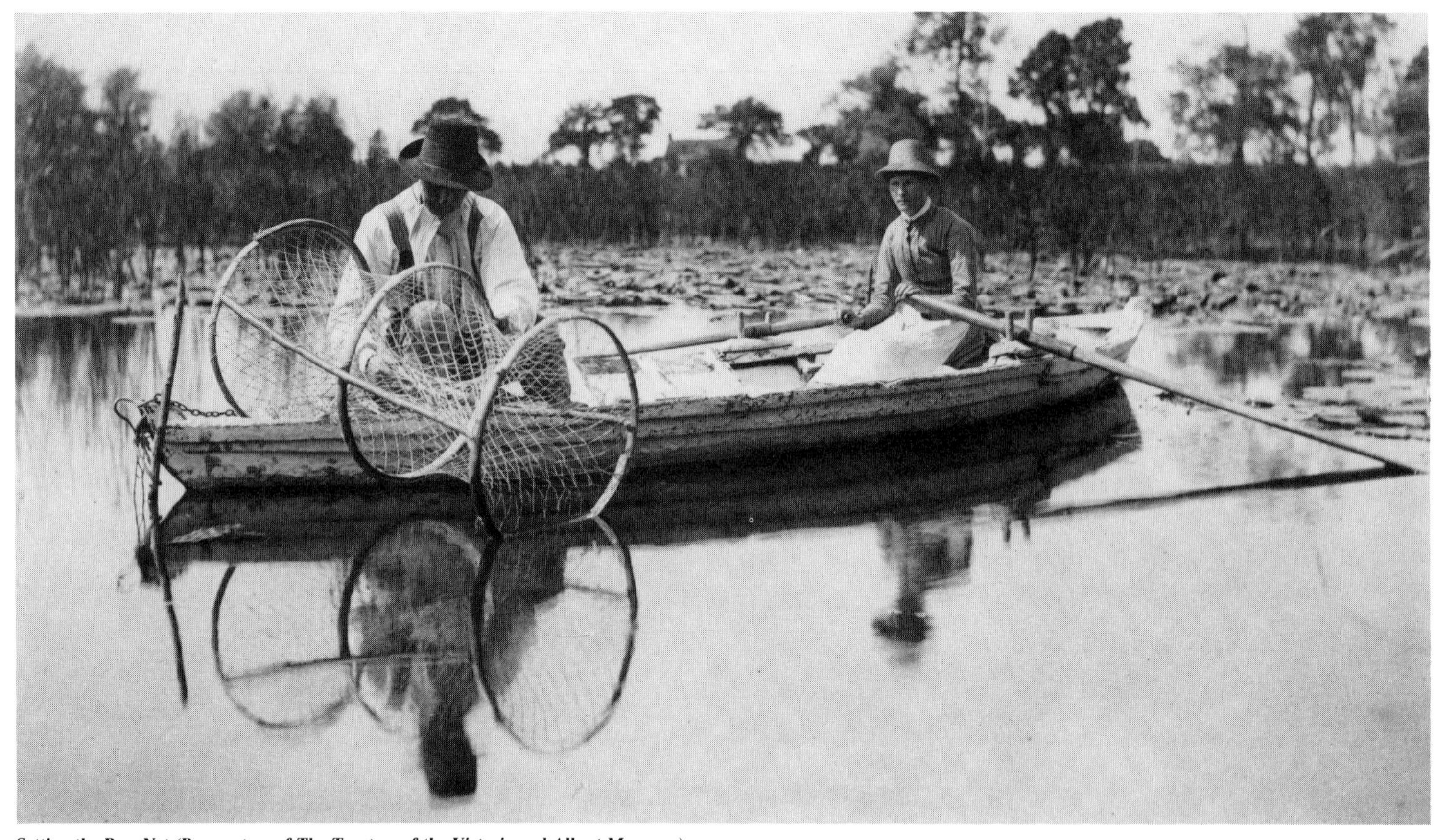

Setting the Bow-Net (By courtesy of The Trustees of the Victoria and Albert Museum.)

about their crafts, lifestyle and folklore.

Frequently he cruised the Broads, photographing and penning his experiences for future publications. The photographs were taken sometimes on a half-plate and sometimes on a 10 × 8in camera, either clamped to the gunwhale or on a tripod with its legs tied to 8ft poles standing in the water. A Dallmeyer long focus lens, sometimes at full aperture, gave an image of soft outline and minimum distortion. He usually developed the plates while on board. When printing he preferred the platinum process for its delicate tonal gradations. His prints were always contacts — enlarging was condemned — and the only permissible doctoring was the printing-in of cloud negatives.

Every flight of birds, every shoal of fish, every cry from the marshes was noted in the log book. He recorded a typical evening, watching from his cabin window, the sun setting, lapwings flying, mists rising. At one in the morning he went on deck, watched the distant lights of Yarmouth dancing in the water as mists enshrouded the horizon and wreathed the stars. . . . I was lost in wonder as I sat on the cabin roof, looking up at the purple sky. Our world is exquisitely beautiful. It is useless sighing for the knowledge that is withheld. Why is man permitted to gaze upon such perfect beauty? Why is he allowed to lift the veil? After such visions the greater part of life must be very prosy indeed.'

Emerson was probably the first photographer-poet. Pioneering the medium of image and words, he yet felt inadequate to convey his depth of feeling for nature: 'The sense of spaciousness was unpaintable, indescribable, wonderful'. Sometimes his reflections rose to the level of mysticism and sometimes he became strangely fused with his subject: 'I could feel before I arose that a south westerly wind was blowing. My skin was no longer dry and smooth like the reed stalks but swollen out and modelled. The light and shade played in and out of the little hollows and hillocks of my arms and all the fluids of my body seemed to flow wildly and healthily just as the sap was rising in the young plants on the marshland.' And while nature seemed to throw pictures at him at every turn, it took all his self control to arrange compositions, calculate exposures and wait for the moment.

Emerson's total immersion into photography was to cause ripples to spread far and wide. He joined the Photographic Society of Great Britain and viewed its exhibition with utter contempt. What ghastly pictures! Bad imitations of bad paintings, dripping with sentiment, affectation and banality. And all taken by members of Britain's top photographic society! A bunch of clumsy incompetent photographers! Well, he, Peter Henry Emerson, was going to wake them up. How? by writing aggressive articles, reviewing exhibitions and thundering from platforms. Above all, he would take photographs beautiful enough to astound the stupid.

British photography was as polite and superficial as a tea party. But Emerson turned it into a brawl. He thrived on stirring up trouble, lashing out at idiots, lambasting opponents with satire and dropping bombshells on convention. From his exhibition

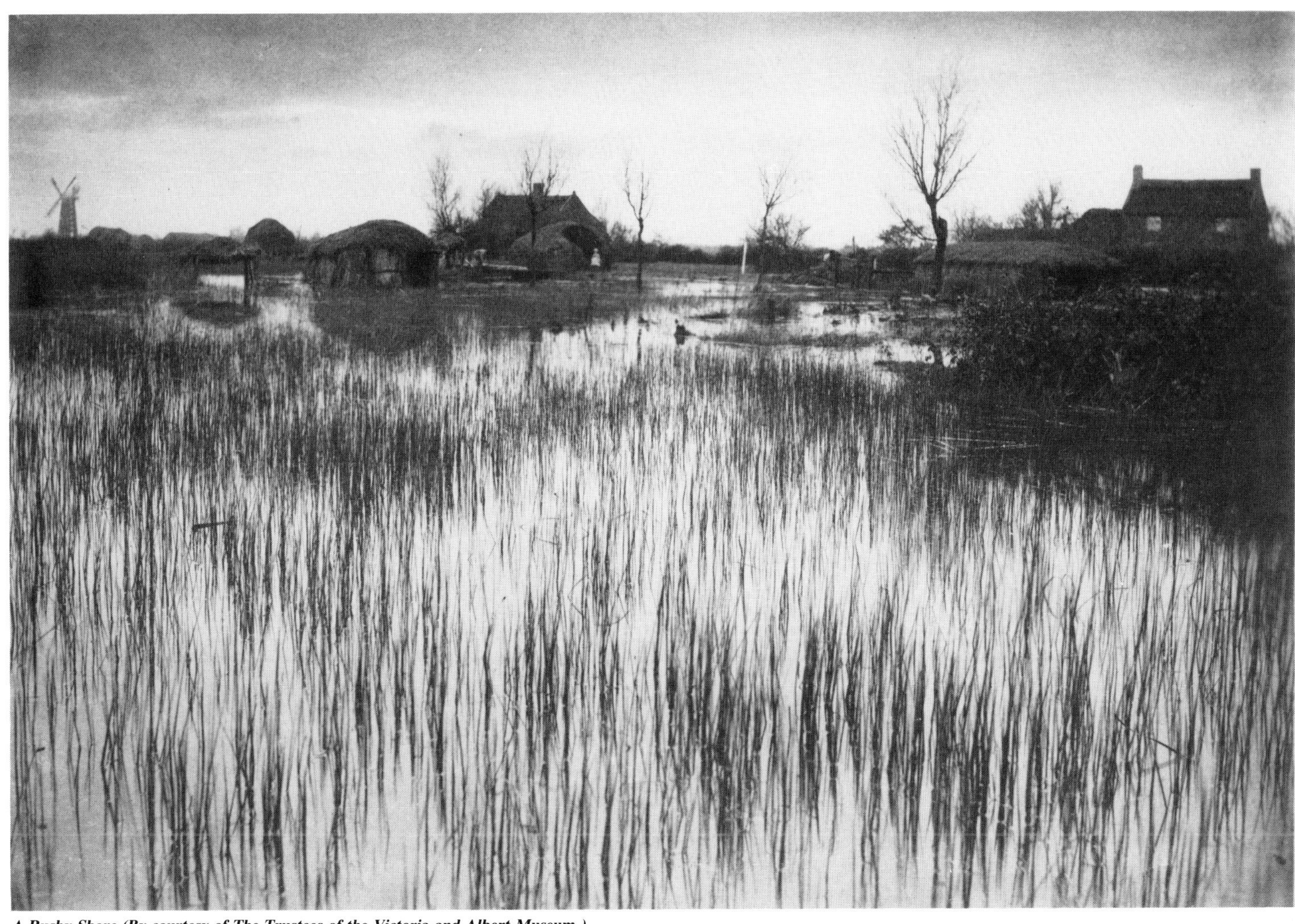

A Rushy Shore (By courtesy of The Trustees of the Victoria and Albert Museum.)

reviews the famous were enraged to find their work described as 'Vapid, bigger, more innane and worthless than ever'. He slammed fancy dress photographers, fashionable fakers, flattering retouchers, preoccupation with technique, commercial manufacture of shoddy goods, photographers cribbing from paintings and painters cribbing from photographs.

Emerson meant business. He would regenerate photography with a new aesthetic and establish it as an art form with its own rules, First, a return to nature, but not just realism — realists kept the notes but lost the sunbeams. The photographer, by applying his appreciation of the picturesque to nature, could imbue ordinary subjects with his personal stamp. For too long personal taste had been dictated by John Ruskin, 'a spasmodic elegant of literature', who promoted merely decorative art, works of imagination. Photography needed a scientific basis. Science was constructive and orderly, so a thing could only be true or false.

'Do not call yourself an "artist-photographer" and make "artist-painters" laugh at you,' he wrote. 'Call yourself a photographer and wait for artists to call you brother. The artist works to record the beauties of nature, the bagman to please the public, or for filthy lucre or for metal medals.'

This was a swipe at Henry Peach Robinson, riding on popularity, rich from royal patronage and decorated with seventy-three medals. He specialised in composite tableaux of remarkable technical achievement, depicting subjects such as a dying girl surrounded by her grieving family on five negatives, a very pregnant Lady of Shalott floating downstream, models in rustic smocks roaming through fields of sentiment, or posed before movable banks of earth tricking with rivulets of print wash water. Reviewing Robinsons's book, *Picture Making by Photography,* Emerson wrote: 'I have looked in vain for a single original idea in his books. The book is not worth criticising in a serious spirit — the writer knows no science, and to take a person whose ability (artistic and otherwise) I honestly consider beneath contempt *au sérieux* here would be ridiculous.'

If Emerson's aggressive writing was fascinating, his thunderous oratory was riveting. His bright blue eyes blazed with a passion to communicate and a conviction that he was right. Arrogant, dogmatic, opinionated, he was, at thirty, an idealist, a reformer, a fanatic, a self-packaged leader with no time for diplomacy. His mind was an impenetrable wall to any idea differing from his own. Lecturing at Yarmouth, he first opened fire on Robinson then stormed through an entire history of art, carefully trimmed to support his theories. Every illustrious artist who failed the Emerson truth-to-nature test was firmly shot down until only Constable, Carot, Rousseau, Miller and Le Page were left standing: pioneers of the naturalistic trend. Then followed a slide show of his Broadland photographs. The audience rose and gave a standing ovation. Never had they seen their landscape so strongly expressed.

In 1887 Emerson produced a sumptuous album, *Life and Landscape of the Norfolk Broads:* a set of forty-nine platinum prints with accompanying text. Bound in green morocco and titled in gold it was the first of many, published in limited editions. And in deference to the Victorian cult of the precious, he destroyed all the negatives and printing plates after each publication.

His real outlet was in these books and portfolios, where, in words and pictures he presented his beloved Broadland in all its moods and seasons. We are shown the simple dignity of farmhands, cattle and sheep, horses pulling ploughs, reed-cutting, basket-making, duck-shooting, fishing, shrimping, thatching, ploughing and poaching. Text and pictures are not always connected, the latter often used as starting points for his decorative prose. Sometimes we are floated on flowery sentences then jolted by bursts of anger at every intrusion of modernity into nature. Closeness to nature gave him a comfortable sense of superiority over major authors, who, he said, 'all smell, more or less, of the lamp or the hospital'.

In photography's history, no book has generated such heat as Emerson's *Naturalistic Photography,* pubished in 1889. It

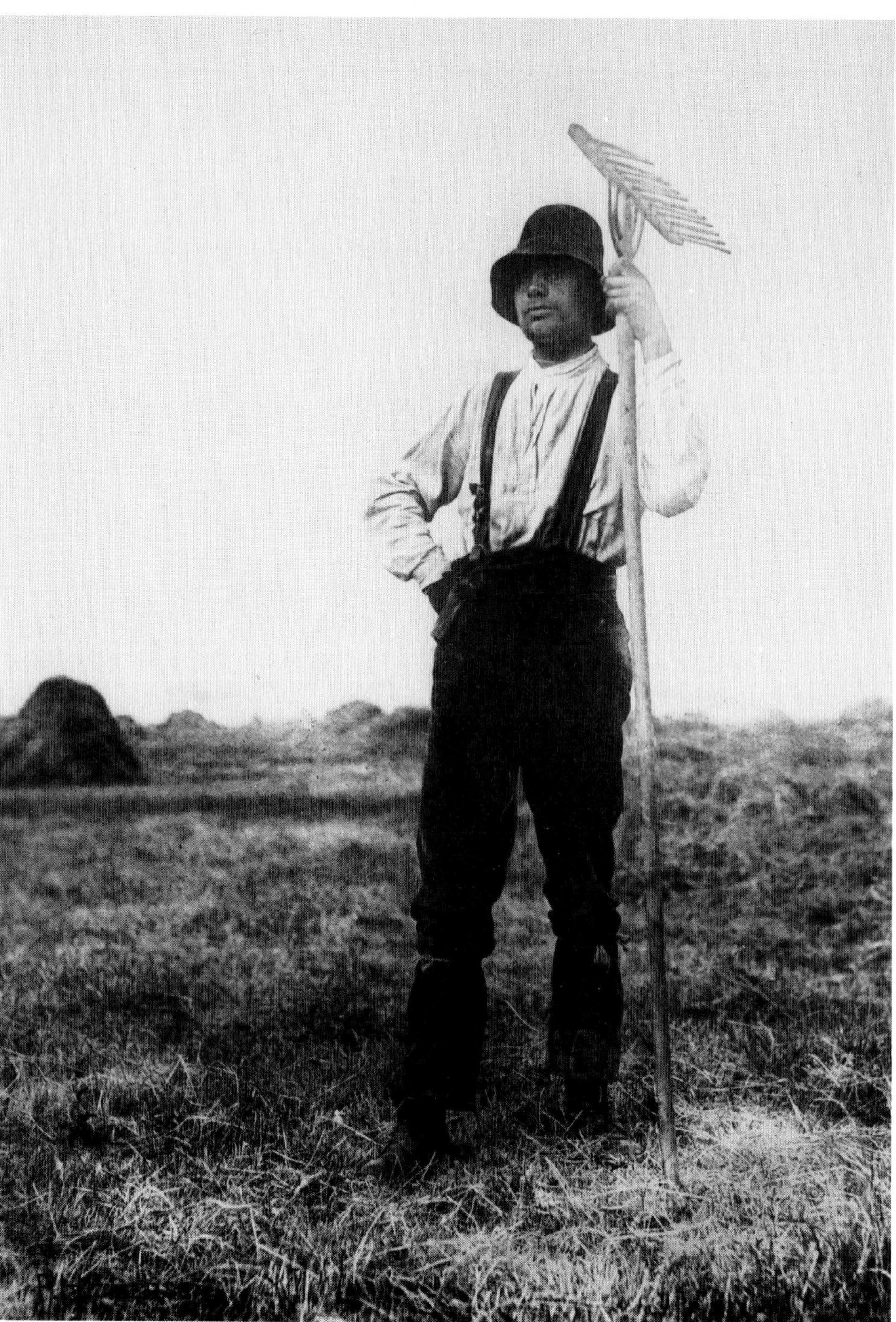

The Haymaker (By courtesy of The Trustees of the Victoria and Albert Museum.)

In the Barley Field
(By courtesy of
The Trustees of the
Victoria and Albert Museum.)

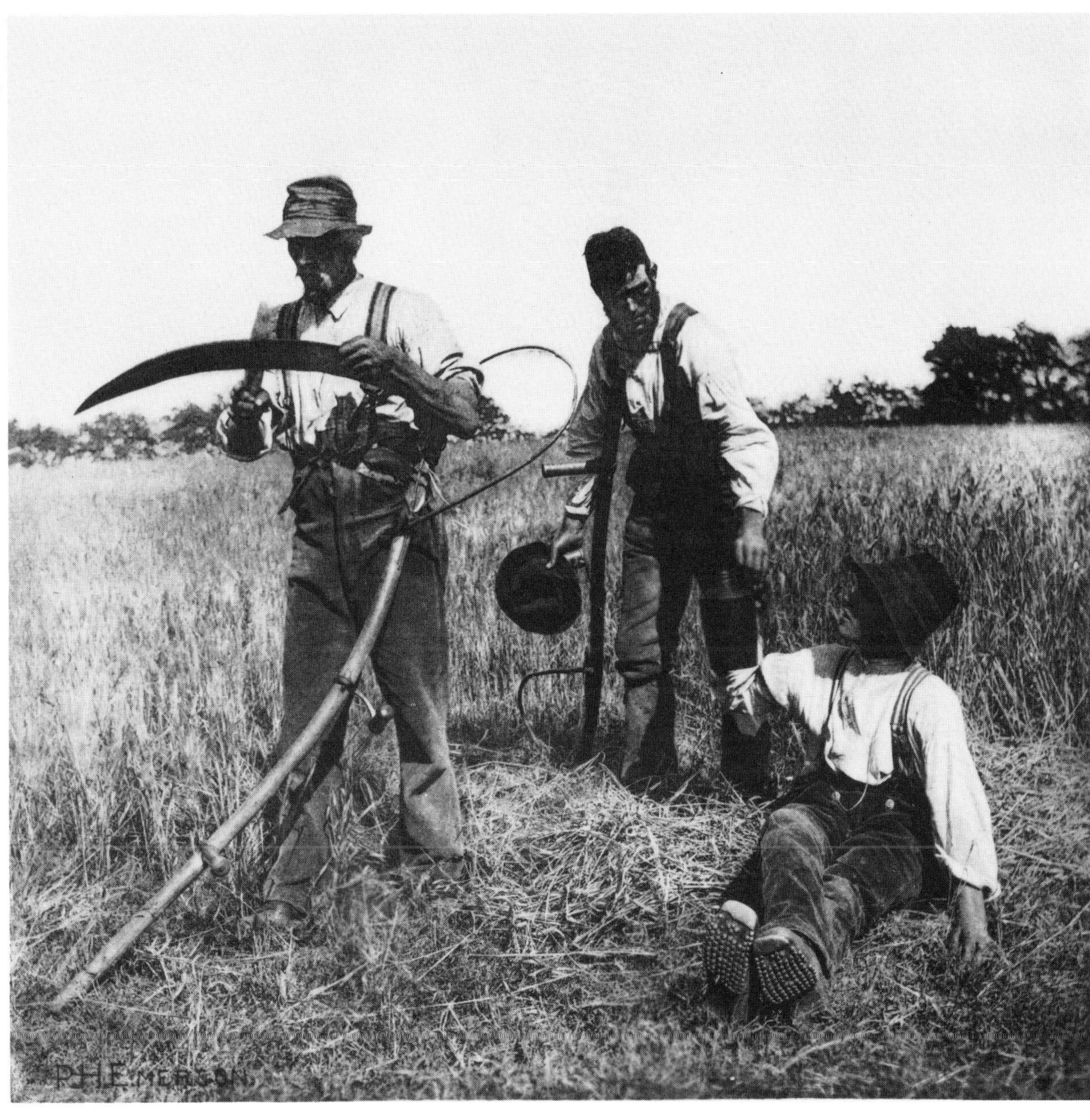

condensed his contempt for pictorialism, romanticism, retouching, cut-and-paste composites, all over sharpness and sitters in painterly compositions. He argued that nothing in nature has a sharp outline. And that because the eye sees only the central area in focus while the edges remain blurred the use of different focusing would give an effect corresponding with natural vision.

So far, the Robinson tea party had stuck to its treacly sentiment, but it was becoming increasingly difficult to pretend that the ill-mannered Emerson was not there. Young photographers, seeking new vision, were gladly responding to him. But this bombshell was the last straw. Robinson, long simmering over Emerson's fire, finally boiled over and fought back. Emerson stepped up his attacks with renewed vindictiveness. Never had the photographic press been so entertaining. It was no longer just Emerson *v.* Robinson. Supporters of both sides were leaving the ringside seats to join the fight. But for Emerson it was getting out of hand. Some of his followers, misunderstanding his theory of focusing, were simply churning out fuzzy pictures. And when George Davidson began to steal Emerson's thunder by advocating his own version of naturalistic photography, Emerson backed out of the fight with a bloodied ego.

The following year, to the incredulity of his supporters, he published his black-bordered *Death of Naturalistic Photography*. With accustomed rhetoric he began: 'I, saner than ever, renounce all theories, teachings and view of art, written and first proculated by me in sundry works, articles etc, and finally collected in a volume entitled *Naturalistic Photography*. I cast them on the dust heap. I am, for the present and future, neither idealist, naturalist, nor impressionist, — *Photographic impressionist indeed!* — a term to consecrate photographic imposters, pickpockets, parasites and vanity-intoxicated amateurs.' (like George Davidson?) And so he went on. Then followed an epitaph 'In Memory of Naturalistic Photography', with waspish statements arranged in line after wicked line:

Which ran a short but active life
Upset many conventions
Produced many prigs and bubble reputations
Exposed the ignorance of the multitudes
Brought out the low morality of certain persons in the photographic world
Encouraged many amateurs to make the words 'art' 'truth' and 'nature' stink in the nostrils of serious artists.'

It all sounded like a cry of anguish. But why was photography no longer an art? He argued that Hurter and Driffield's work on sensitometry meant that one could not exert enough control over plate and print to give a personal interpretation of nature. And that a painter had convinced him that a machine-made picture could never be a work of art. Strange that this scientifically-trained photographer had not considered that H&D could be offering photographers a creative control. And that for 'art' he seemed only to read 'painting'.

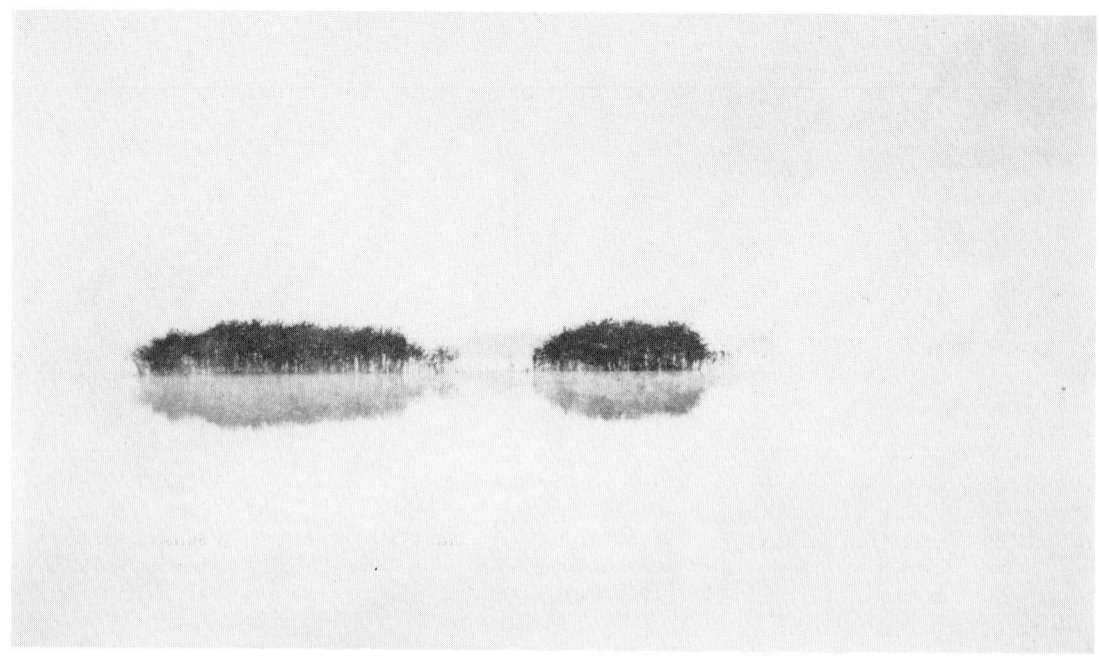

The Lone Lagoon (By courtesy of The Trustees of the Victoria and Albert Museum.)

Despite the painful noises, Emerson arose from self-crucifixion with miraculous alacrity. He was soon back on the Broads, practising the artistry of selection and viewpoint, of waiting for planned lighting effects, of subtle appreciation of line, form, texture, luminosity and atmosphere. He was sensitive, too, to every nuance of colour which he so regretted photography could not then capture: 'A flood of yellow light bathed the marshland, streaming on the bronze-gold crops. The world was transfigured. Blue rims of fairy-like trees were yellowed, the mills were gilded with refined gold, their sails with silvery grey. Even the marsh grasses were veiled in an ethereal golden vapour.' Love and gentleness, seldom expressed to fellow humans, was lavished on every facet of nature as he sought companionship from the winds, the waters, the wildlife: 'The breath of the landscape was delicately scented with a watery perfume, instilling soft desire into the heart of man.'

In 1895 Emerson accepted the Royal Photographic Society's highest honour, the Progress Medal, awarded for artistic achievement. Then he gradually withdrew from photography, seeking new activities to master, new challenges to meet, new axes to grind. In 1925, with customary lack of modesty and flair for the dramatic, he produced a set of silver and bronze medals, each bearing the Emerson profile, to be presented to selected photographers for 'artistic merit'.

Tormented by lumbago, Emerson died on 12 May 1936 on the eve of his eightieth birthday. The photographic world sincerely mourned the man who has so livened up its history. His zeal, sparkle and humour were remembered with affection, and even in his ranting and raving, he seemed, across the years, an endearing figure.

Now, fifty years after this death, his fame is reflected in images of solitary boats in still waters, windmills rising from misty marshlands, waterlillies gathered from sleepy lagoons, rushy shores like brush strokes, all in a world so placid, remote, evanescent. And, with hindsight, these pictures are tinged with melancholy as they tell a story of aggression and loneliness.■

LANDSCAPES OF GIACOMELLI

Jon Chambers interviews the Italian photographer

I FIRST set eyes on works by Mario Giacomelli in a small gallery in the middle of Birmingham, in the mid-seventies, and didn't come across him again until one of his prints turned up in the *View From Above* exhibition at The Photographers' Gallery, London, in 1983. Both times, the result was the same. Here were photos that made an impact.

His style is bold and adventurous, and his opinions are expressed with equal conviction — even if, at times, they falter a little over the language barrier. So, given the surprising shortage of material on Giacomelli, I wanted to find out more about the man and see more of his work.

Giacomelli's recent landscapes are still as graphic as ever, but have become increasingly abstract. Nowadays, he photographs landscapes from aboard an aircraft, which has the effect of disorientating the viewer by alienating him from recognisable elements on the ground. What's more, Giacomelli claims to have been rejuvenated by his discovery of airborne photography, and consequently concentrates most of his efforts on this aspect of his work.

But we shouldn't forget his figurative work, among the most memorable of which, for me, are those that allow movement to distinguish between the animate and inanimate. And also those that employ the same kind of tonal contrasts as are found in his landscapes (Giacomelli thrives on contrast). But it is chiefly in his new landscapes that we are interested here.

J.C. ***Have you been influenced by anyone in particular in your work? That is, are you conscious of any especially strong influence?***

M.G. I don't think I have been influenced by other photographers, by fashions and so on. I look within myself, within the sensations nature gives me. I don't look at big events, but rather at things around me, at relationships, at the emotions I feel looking at whiteness, blackness, light, matter, wrinkles, sweat, work, fortune, happiness, melancholy — everything seems to ask me to be photographed. I also try to realise things that are in my mind, but that I've never seen before in reality. Perhaps it's longing for the possible within the impossible.

New images are arrived at not for pleasure itself, but as a means of reaching an understanding of the mystery within the things which closely surround me. Every landscape of mine is not only space, work, matter and so on, but at the same time a record of the 'existence' of a landscape; it's respecting men who work on the land and (I hope) believe in it.

My early landscapes weren't very original — which is not unusual. But in time, I felt the need to suppress the features one could identify in order to show new sensations, new feelings, new roots, where the roots move from within, inside the folds of imagination, of invention, where a glance doesn't seem to last, when representation seems magical and difficult to get through to and interpret.

Has this always been so, or have your interests and intentions changed over the years?

I still get joy and pleasure out of photography and the sensations I get are stronger than ever. My early landscapes were born out of my interest in the peasant environment — in the hope of the man who works on the land. Each picture is a meditation on existence, life and death.

How important is the region in which you work to you? It would be interesting, I think, to see what kind of results you would have produced had you worked in say, England, where you would have had no emotional roots and a very different character of landscape.

I don't know whether I would have been able to create the same landscapes somewhere else. Perhaps yes. But they would have been about different things. What is important is that the earth should be as interested in me as I am in it.

Some of your earlier photographs appeared, to me at least, to make use of certain darkroom techniques. To what extent are your landscapes artificial?

There is no artifice in my pictures; it's my style, my language. My pictures are only Giacomelli's. Every one of my images is my identity card, the mirror of my sensations.

My photographs are not planned in advance, but they *are* ideas born before the images are. It hasn't always been like this. My past work has taken shape within myself first, then has grown at the moment of taking the picture, to be concluded with the printing on paper.

In 1955, I already tried — using a tractor — to create a design on the land in order to complete, or even totally invent, a landscape all and only mine. And even now, if I can, I look for different designs and new sensations. I started photographing the land from above because I couldn't get any pleasure out of the conventional angles any more. From above, nature lost its known identity, and at the same time, I came to know a new world. I felt like taking pictures again, and I felt like living and penetrating a nature even more sensual, more fantastic. ■

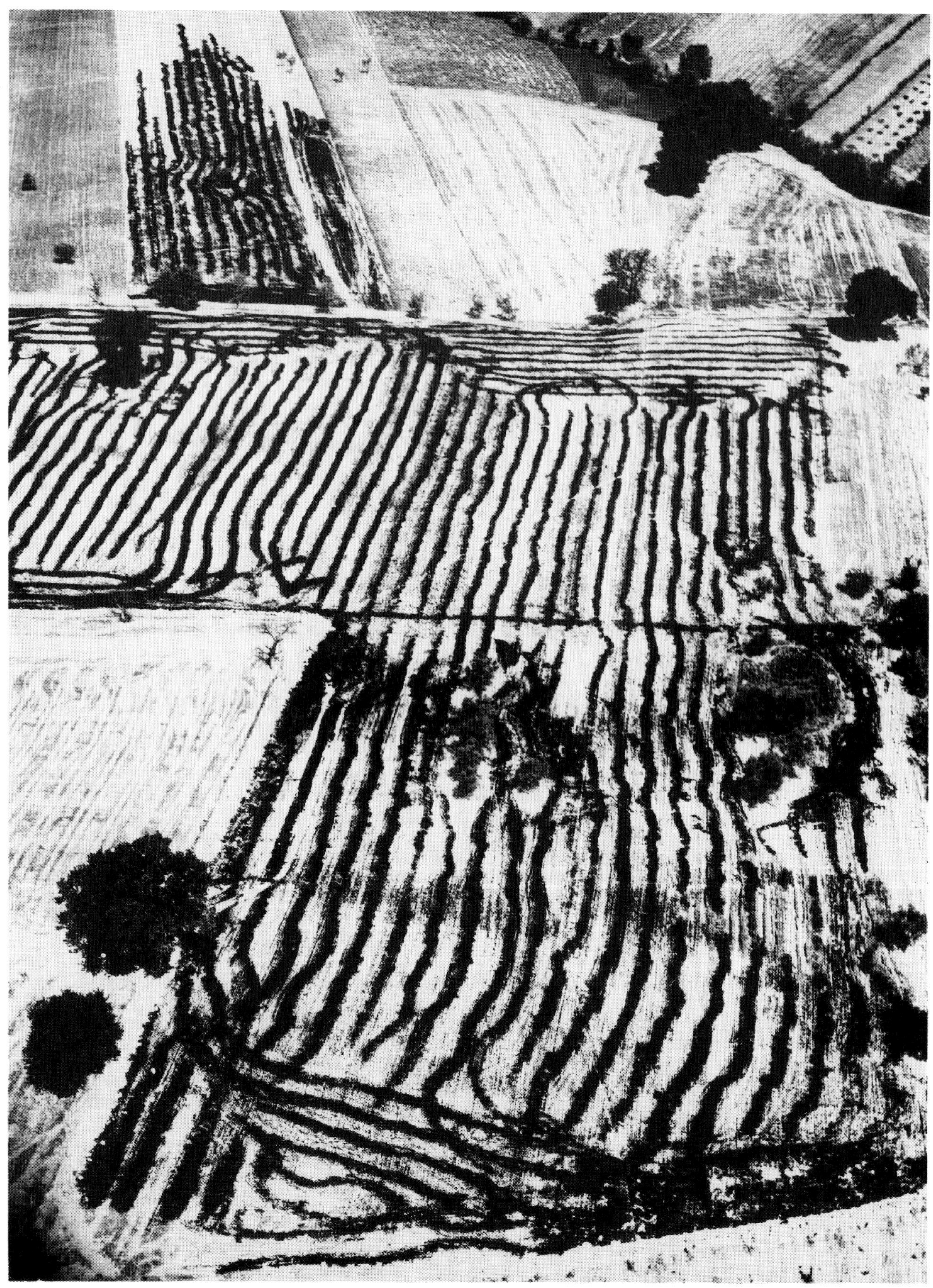

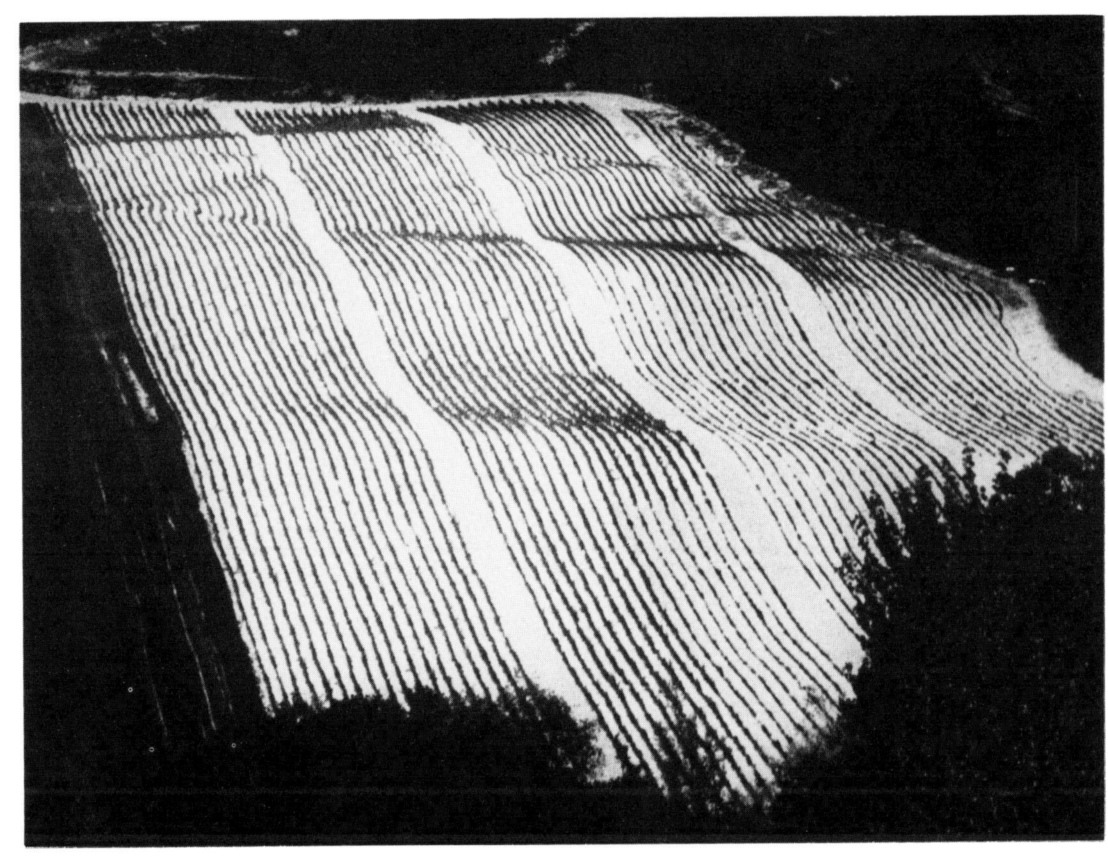

Left: 'Story of the earth'.
Above: 'Pages of a newspaper'.
Right: 'This is one of my first landscapes'.

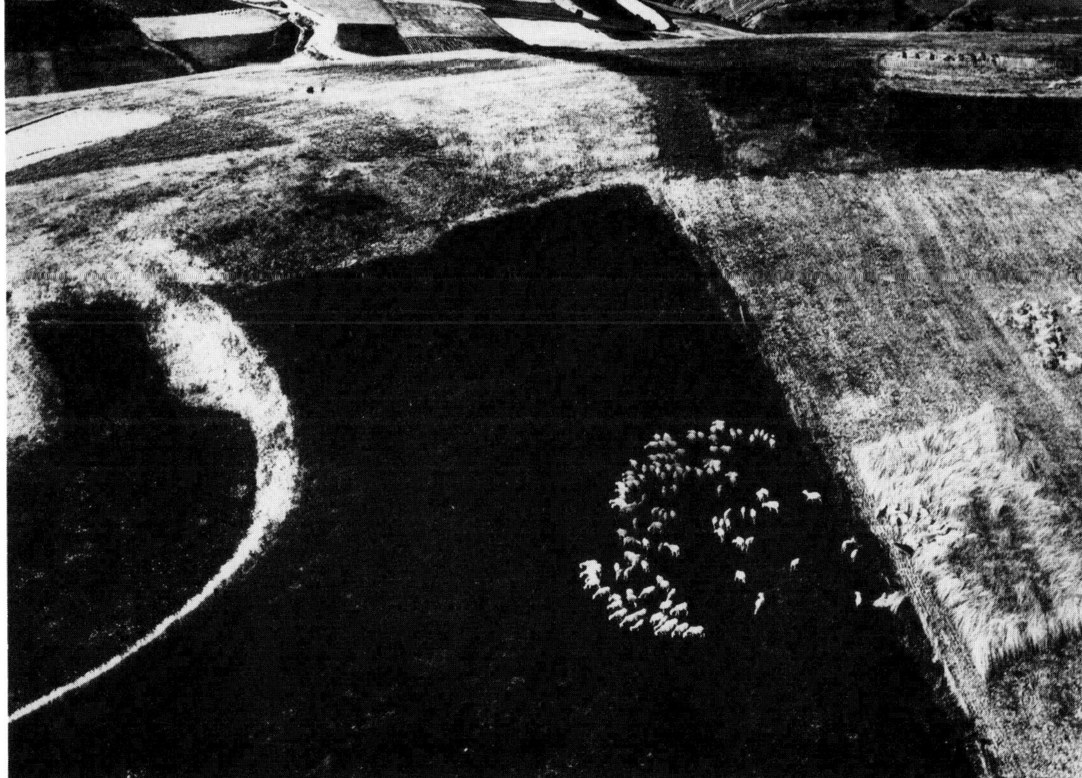

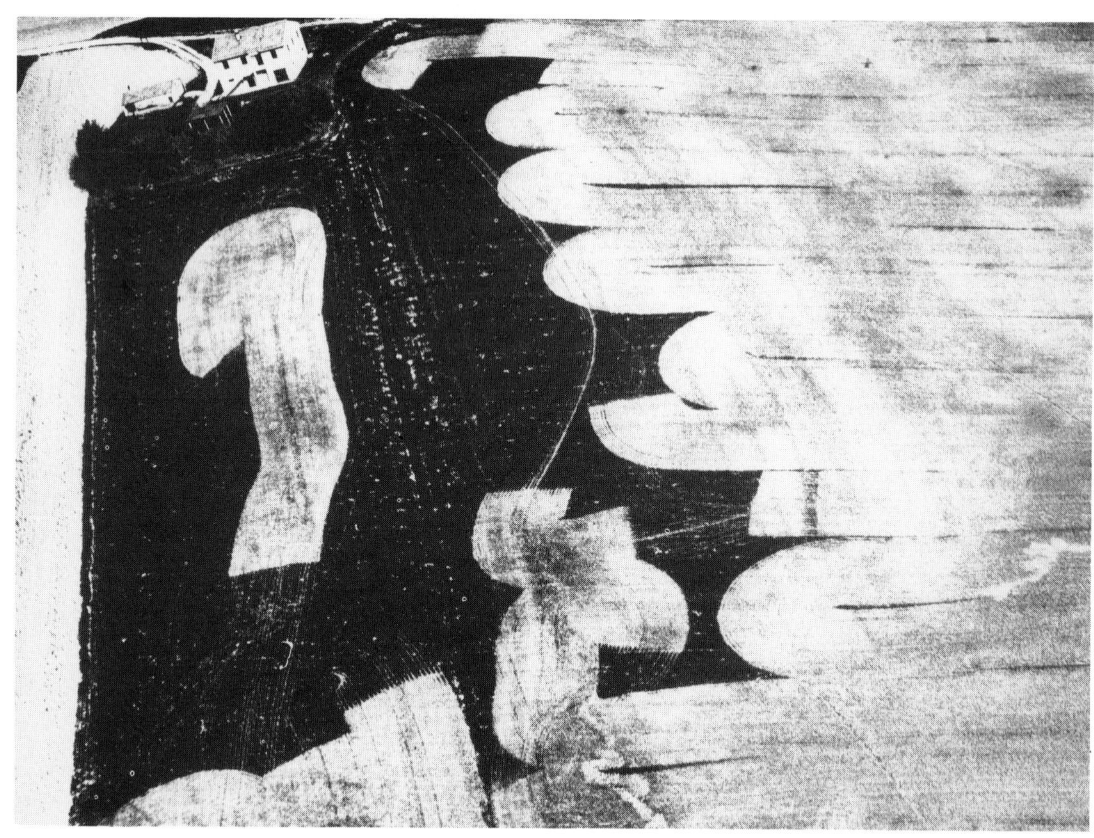

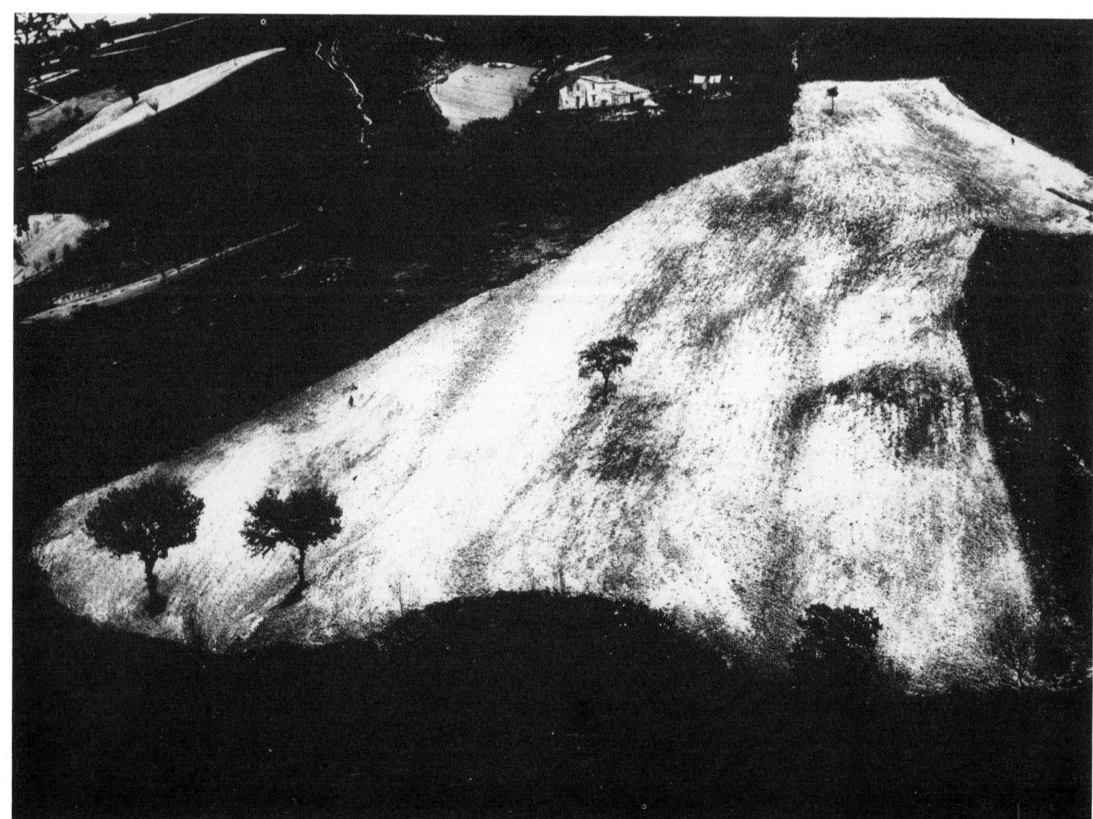

Above: 'Story of the earth'.
Right: 'This is another of my first landscapes'.

Rayco PRESENTS . . .

THE LATEST 'STATE OF THE ART' MICRO-ELECTRONIC DEVICES

Although RAYCO is the oldest established name in the business, with a world-wide reputation for traditional quality, we lead the field into new techniques and present our latest range of micro-electronic products, which take full advantage of the rapid advances in solid-state digital electronics.

Rayco

BRITISH MADE

*ELECTRONIC TIMERS

*AUTOMATIC VOLTAGE STABILISERS

*ELECTRONIC THERMOMETERS

*WE ALSO SUPPLY A VERY WIDE RANGE OF PHOTOGRAPHIC CHEMICALS

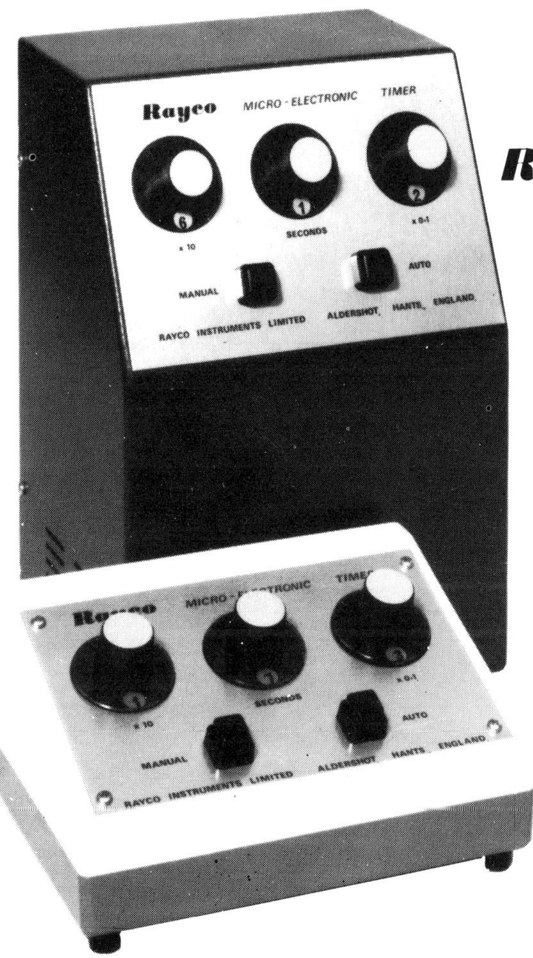

Rayco MICRO-ELECTRONIC TIMER-STABILISER

This is a development of the well established range of RAYCO TIMER-STABILISERS that are used in conjunction with most makes of colour enlargers to give accurate control of lamp voltage and exposure time in colour printing.

These latest units give highly stable voltages, controlled by solid-state electronics, together with times to millisecond accuracy.

All built into a single compact unit which occupies only a few square inches of bench space

These Timer-Stabilisers are supplied to operate with all the leading makes of colour enlarger.

Rayco MICRO-ELECTRONIC 'DIGIDIAL' TIMER

A development of the famous RAYCO 'Precision' Electronic Timer offering millisecond accuracy and solid-state switching.

Using the RAYCO 'Digidial' controls, which show the accurate selected time in digital form.

Any precisely repeatable exposure between 0.1 and 99.9 seconds may be selected.

Rayco ALSO PRODUCE

A wide range of electronic devices and control systems to meet customers' special requirements.

If you have any electronic problems in connection with photographic equipment or processes RAYCO may be able to help you.

JUST RING Rayco

'phone 0252-22725

RAYCO products are available from the leading professional suppliers or direct from the manufacturers. Send now for full details and prices to:

RAYCO INSTRUMENTS LTD.

BLACKWATER WAY, ASH ROAD, ALDERSHOT HAMPSHIRE

BLACK AND WHITE WINNERS

Three outstanding pictures from this year's Ilford Awards

Below: Ilford Student Folio Award 1985, Martin Booker, Young Printer nomination. Right: Malcolm Baker, 1st place in the Industrial and Commercial category. Following page: John Russell, highly commended, Industrial and Commercial category.

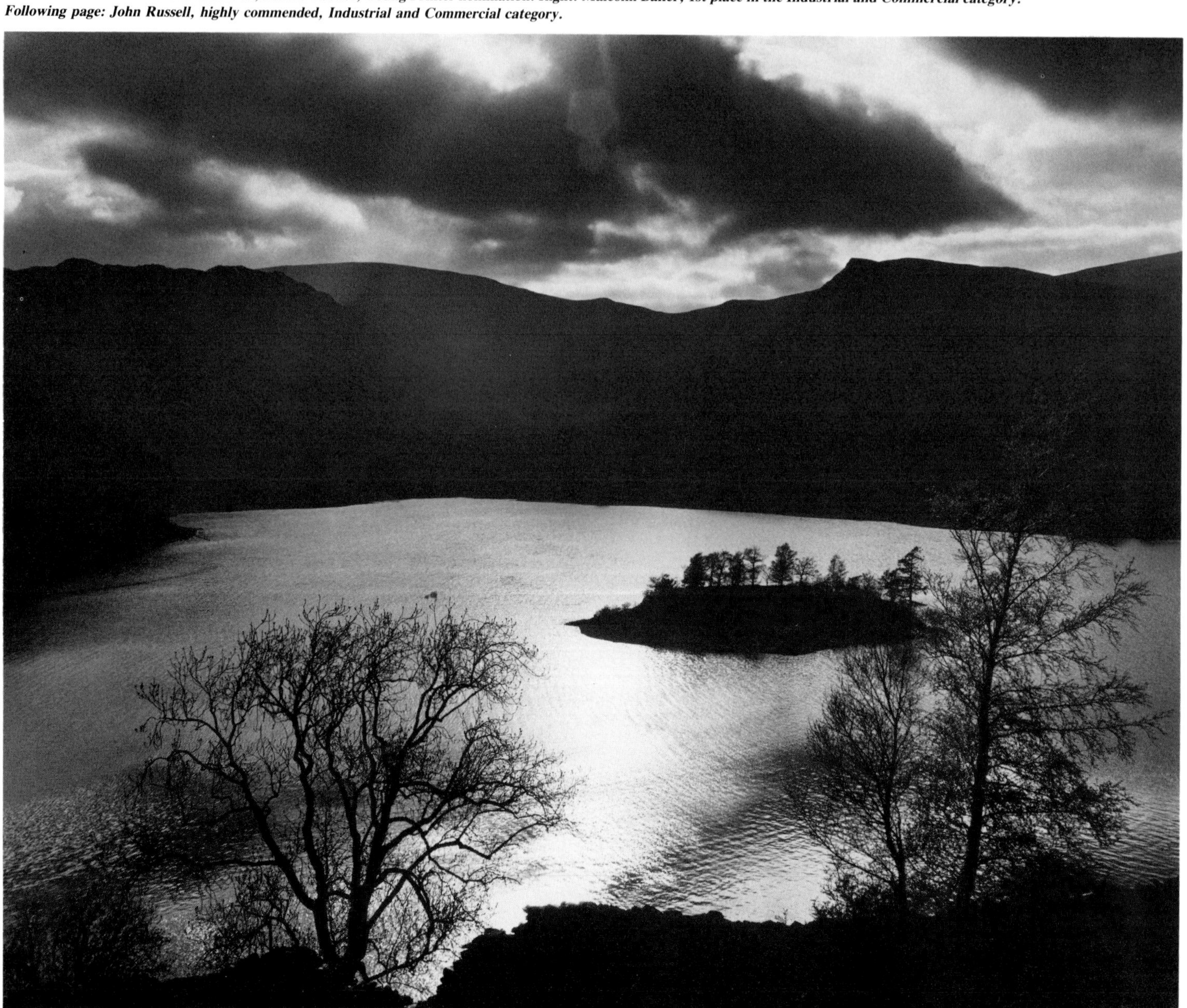

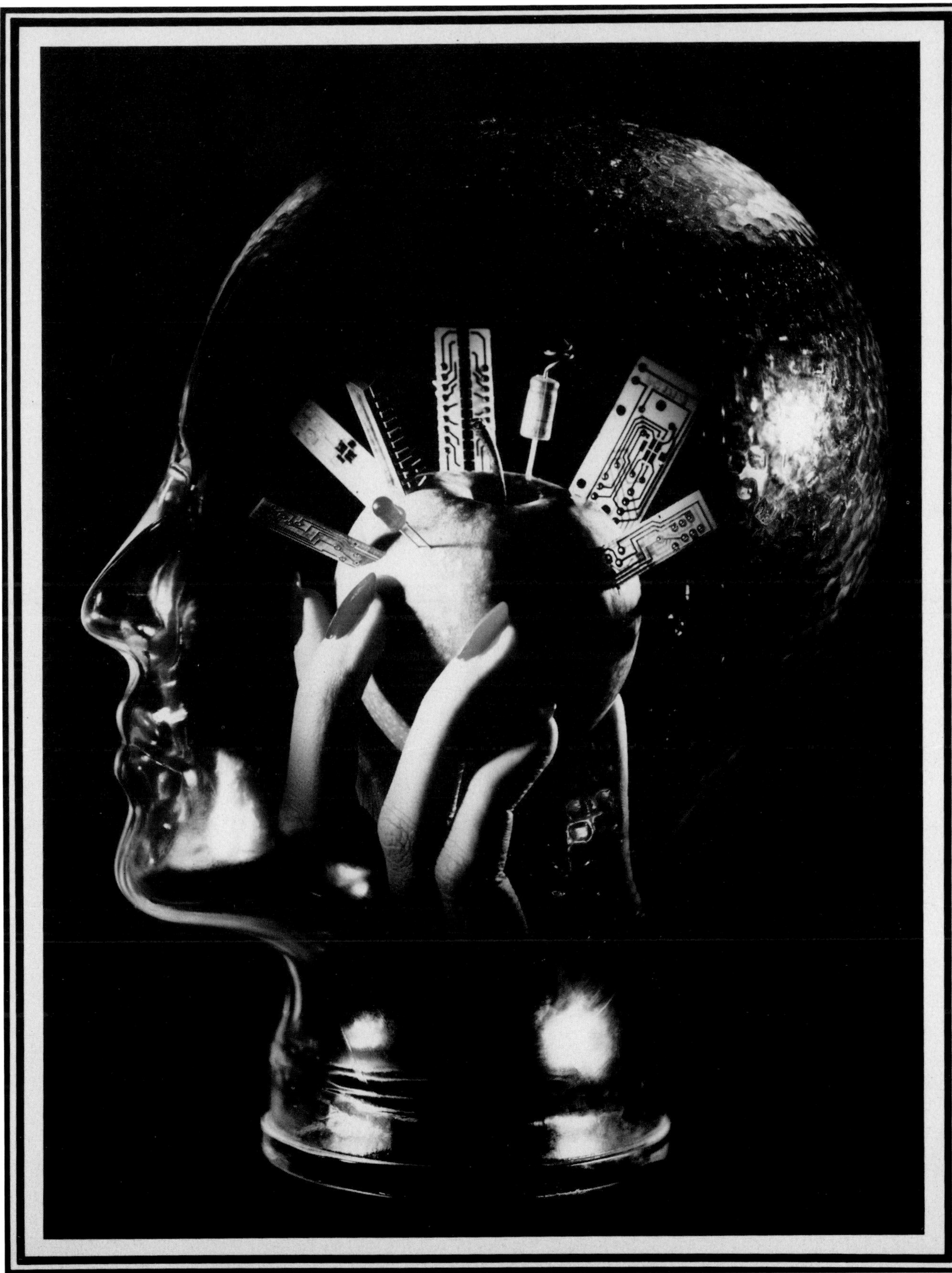

74

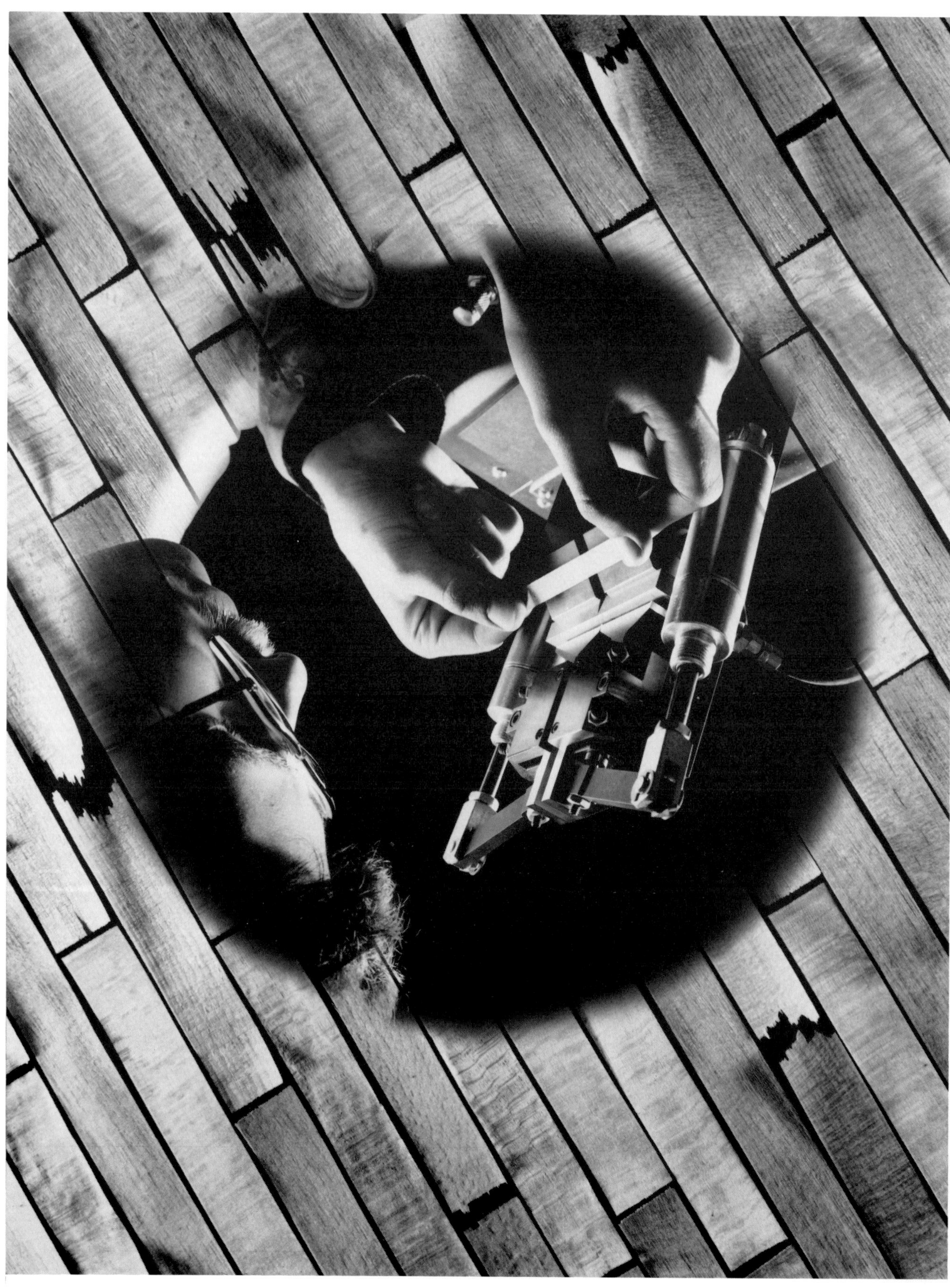

HOME PROCESSING

How to process current colour and black-and-white reversal and negative films and papers

THESE pages on the home processing of current photographic materials continue the tradition of well over a century of the *British Journal Photographic Almanac* — although today the range of materials to be processed covers a far wider field than in those early days. General instructions and precautions to be observed in the handling of chemical solutions are followed by detailed formulae for the processing of colour reversal and negative films and papers. A tabulation of black-and-white films and formulations suitable for processing them follows.

Paradoxically the chemically simpler processing of black-and-white films admits of more control and exploitation of the properties of the different film types than does colour processing. For this reason, although the black-and-white table is retained, the lengthy tabulations of colour film type which were a feature of past *Annuals* have been omitted: in practice virtually all general purpose colour materials are compatible with the same processing solutions which are, for convenience, generally known by their Eastman Kodak designations. Thus all **colour negative materials** manufactured in the non-Comecon countries may be processed in **Kodak C-41** or similar solutions. The former usefulness of the tabulations in listing the process required has therefore gone, and any materials designed for the earlier Kodak C-22 process are by now long out of date.

Similarly, all western and far eastern **colour reversal materials** — bar a few Kodak ones — may be processed by **Kodak's E-6** process, although some may be designed to exploit the process's capability of offering effectively enhanced film speed by increasing first development time. These are the extreme high-speed types exemplified by Kodak's Ektachrome P800/1600 and Fuji's Fujichrome P1600 II, which only reach their designated speeds when treated in this way. The remaining Kodak films not compatible with the E-6 process are the **Kodachrome** types — so-called 'non-substantive' colour films which do not incorporate colour couplers in the emulsion layers and which require to be processed by the complex **K-14** process in Kodak Laboratories — and two which still use the old **E-4** process, Ektachrome Infrared and Photomicrography Color Film 2483, intended for scientific purposes. Substitute formulations for the E-4 process are available and copies of these may be obtained, free of charge, on application to the *British Journal of Photography*'s offices. Tabulations of colour film types also appear from time to time in the *Journal*.

The past year has seen a number of interesting advances in colour materials. In mass market colour materials, the major manufacturers have recognised the popularity with the public of films giving brightly coloured prints, and Kodak, Fuji and Agfa have introduced new ranges of colour negative films to fulfil this demand. These are the Kodacolor Gold range (known as Kodacolor VRG in the USA) at speeds of ISO100, 200 and 400, Fujicolor Super HR at ISO100 and 400, and Agfacolor XR100i. At the same time advances in grain crystal structure technology have been exploited to tailor grains to specific requirements: Fuji, for instance, suggest that they are able to render certain sensitivity sites susceptible to the effect of high-intensity short pulses from electronic flash sources and others to the longer-intensity lighting from natural sources. In this way the differing contrast requirements of the two can be individually met. The trend to brighter colour is achieved by exploiting advances in development inhibition reagents so that, for example, the Kodacolor Gold films exhibit a higher contrast in the individual colours, giving brighter colour rendering, while at the same time inhibiting overall contrast build-up which would lead to prints of harsh appearance.

The year also saw the end, for the time being at least, of the ten-year legal battle between Polaroid and Eastman Kodak, the immediate result of which was Kodak's withdrawal from 'instant' photography, leaving Polaroid alone (except in Japan, where, at the time of publication, Fuji continue their Kodak-compatible Fujirama process). Polaroid have not been idle meanwhile on the technical front as well as the legal, and the year saw the introduction of a new self-developing single-sheet print system known as Polaroid Spectra in America and Australasia and as Polaroid Image in Europe. As with many Polaroid introductions the new material is compatible only with a new camera range and is in a new rectangular format. A brighter, sharper colour rendering is claimed, with specific improvements in pastel shades and in the reproduction of natural foliage colours. The novel technical feature of the new film is that, while the magenta and cyan images are formed in the conventional Polaroid way as in their SX-70 and 600 films by immobilising migrating dyes where they are not required for image formation, the yellow image is formed by the reverse process. A temporarily immobilised yellow dye, linked to a thiazolidine group, is released by an exchange reaction when reversal-image silver ions from the blue-sensitive layer reach the dye. This, claim Polaroid, enables inter-image effects between the yellow layer and the other two to be reduced and permits fine tuning of, particularly, green colour rendering.

In colour reversal films, the year's main news was the announcement, fifty years after the first Kodachrome still camera film, that a new ISO200 Kodachrome Professional 35mm film would be introduced to supplement the existing ISO25 and 64 versions (and the elusive ISO40 artificial light Type A).

Even more surprising was the imminent extension of Kodachrome Professional film to larger sizes, specifically 120 rollfilm and 70mm bulk. It had been widely believed, ever since the withdrawal of Kodachrome sheet film some forty years earlier, that the economic and technical difficulties of extending Kodachrome bulk processing, with its requirement of a substantial semi-continuous throughput of material, to wider formats would effectively inhibit any such move. The move was enthusiastically welcomed in professional circles.

The principal black-and-white introduction of the year was Ilford's baryta-coated fibre-based version of their variable-contrast Multigrade paper under the designation Multigrade FB as a direct competitor for Kodak's recently-introduced Polyfiber. The new Ilford paper is available in three surfaces on a double-weight base and in glossy only on a single-weight paper. A particular feature of Ilford Multigrade FB is the high density of the maximum blacks, ascribed to a more tightly controlled immobilisation of the fluorescent brightener incorporated in virtually all modern printing papers.

General Instructions

Making up solutions

Glass, plastic, new enamel or stainless steel vessels should be used. The chemicals should be taken in order and each completely dissolved before adding the next, using about three-quarters of the final volume of water. Cold or tepid (35-40°C) water should be used, *not* hot water (exceptions are given below). Distilled or deionised water should preferably be used in making up the solutions, particularly the first and colour developers, but this is not essential, and tap water may be used. If the water supply is too hard, it is helpful to add, particularly to water destined for black-and-white and colour developers, *before* dissolving any other chemicals 2g/l of a sequestering agent: Calgon, sodium hexametaphosphate, or sodium tripolyphosphate.

Anhydrous carbonate should be dissolved separately in about three times its own bulk of hot water. Hot water must also be used to make up a hardener-bleach, which may throw down a white precipitate when cold, but this does not affect its working; stop baths are best made up cold. Time can be saved by using 20% solutions of thiocyanate and bromide instead of solid reagent. Phenidone should be dissolved after the hydroquinone and alkalis.

All solutions should be allowed to stand for about 30min and filtered before use.

Practical metric measures (g = grams; ml = millilitres (= cm^3 or cc for practical purposes); °C = Celsius) are used throughout.

Colour developing agents

The following colour developing agents are those which are, or have been, in common use; others are used in some specialised colour processes, such as Kodachrome K-14, but are not supplied or needed for those processes which are generally available.

N,N-Diethyl-*p*-phenylenediamine hydrochloride = Activol H (Johnson),
Colour Developer 1 (chloride) (Merck), CD-1 (Kodak).

N,N-Diethyl-*p*-phenylenediamine sulphate = Colour Developer 1 (sulphate) (Merck). More sulphate than hydrochloride will be needed in the ratio 262:200.

N,N-Diethyl-*p*-phenylenediamine sulphite = Genochrome
(May & Baker), Activol No. 1 (Johnson), S28 (3M/Ferrania).

2-Amino-5-diethylaminotoluene hydrochloride = Tolochrome
(May & Baker), Colour Developer 2 (Merck), CD-2 (Kodak).

4-Amino-N-ethyl-N-(β-methanesulphonamidoethyl-*m*-toluidine sesquisulphate monohydrate = Mydochrome (May & Baker); Activol No 3 (Johnson), Colour Developer 3 (Merck); CD-3 (Kodak).

4-[N-Ethyl-N-2-hydroxyethyl]-2-methylphenylenediamine sulphate = Colour Developer 4 (Merck), CD-4 (Kodak).

N-Ethyl-N-(β-hydroxyethyl)-*p*-phenylenediamine sulphate = Droxychrome (May & Baker), Activol No 8 (Johnson), T32 (Orwo), Colour Developer 32 (Merck).

N-n-Butyl-N(4 sulpho-n-butyl)1,4-phenylediamine = Ac60 (Agfa), Colour Developer 60 (Merck).

This list is retained although some of the chemicals are no longer available under the trade names indicated here, since readers have found it of assistance in tracking them down. The main suppliers are: Rayco Ltd, Ash Road, Aldershot, Hants. Telephone: 0252 22725 and Hogg Laboratory Supplies, Sloane Street, Birmingham B1 3BW.

Chemical names and synonyms

As far as possible the current preferred names have been used for chemicals. These are the names under which they will generally appear in manufacturers' catalogues. However, earlier editions of the *Annual* and *Almanac*, and formulae from other sources, may make use of alternative names. The most important of these are listed here:

Acid EDTA (see EDTA)
Borax (= disodium tetraborate)
Calgon ([trade name] = sodium hexametaphosphate)
Caustic soda (= sodium hydroxide)
Chlorquinol (= chloroquinol *or* chlorhydroquinone)
Chrome alum (= chromic potassium sulphate)
Diethylene glycol (= digol)
2,5-Dimethoxytetrahydrofuran (= tetrahydro-2,5 -dimethoxyfuran)
Disodium phosphate (= disodium hydrogen orthophosphate)
EDTA (= ethylenedinitrilotetra acetic, often called ethylenediaminotetra acetic acid *or* ethylene bisiminodiacetic acid). The acid has been referred to variously at times as Acid EDTA, EDTA, EDTAA, Ethadimil, Acide tetracémique. Havidote and tetramic acid. Trade names include Irgalon and Sequestrene or Sequestrol (Geigy), Versene (Dow), Questex, Tetrine, Kalex, Trilon B, Komplexon, Complexone, Nervanaid (ABM Industrial Products Limited). Salts of this acid used photographically are EDTA NaFe (= EDTA ferric monosodium salt) and EDTA Na_4 (= EDTA tetrasodium salt). The name edetic acid for the acid, the salts being edetates, has made its appearance in the British Pharmacopoeia Codex and the US Pharmacopoeia.
Ethylene diamine (= 1,2 diaminoethane)
Formaldehyde (= formalin)
Glycin (= para-hydroxyphenylglycine *or* para-hydroxyphenyl aminoacetic acid)
IBT ([trade name]) = benzotriazole)
Kodalk ([trade name] = sodium metaborate)
Monopotassium phosphate (= potassium dihydrogen orthophosphate)
Monosodium phosphate (= sodium dihydrogen orthophosphate)
Potash or potassium alum (= aluminium potassium sulphate)
Pyrocatechin (catechol *or* 1,2-dihydroxybenzene)
Sequestrene NaFe ([trade name] — see EDTA)
Sodium bisulphate [sodium hydrogen sulphate]
Sodium bisulphite [= metabisulphite]
Sodium hydrosulphite [sodium dithioniote]

Hydrated salts

Many of the salts used in these formulae may be obtained alternatively in anhydrous or hydrated forms, in some cases in several states of hydration. Some of the principal of these are as follows:
Disodium hydrogen orthophosphate—available with $2H_2O$, $7H_2O$ (relatively rare) or $12H_2O$. The

relative quantities required are 1.00, 1.50, 2.00.
Ethylenediamine—in its hydrated form contains 80% of the pure substance: relative quantities to be employed are therefore 1.00 and 1.25.
Magnesium sulphate—has $1H_2O$ in its hydrated form or $7H_2O$ ('Epsom salts'). The relative quantities required are 1.00, 1.15, 2.05. The so-called dried form is of variable composition.
Sodium acetate—has $3H_2O$ in its hydrated form. The quantity relative to anhydrous required is 1.66:1.00.
Sodium carbonate—available anhydrous. $1H_2O$ (soda ash) or $10H_2O$ (washing soda). The relative quantities required are 1.00, 1.26, 2.69. Although specifications are frequently quoted in terms of the anyhydrous salt, this is more difficult to dissolve than the stable monohydrate, sold as soda ash (note: this is available in a range of purities—many too impure for photographic use). The decahydrate, washing soda, tends to lose water of crystallisation and go powdery: its composition is then indefinite.
Sodium dihydrogen orthophosphate—usually with $2H_2O$. The quantity required relative to the anhydrous material is 1.30:1.

Sodium sulphate is available in the anhydrous form and with $10H_2O$. The relative quantities are 1.00 and 2.27. The anhydrous form may be unreliable unless dried before use.
Sodium sulphite—anhydrous, $7H_2O$ or $10H_2O$. Relative quantities required are 1.00, 2.00, 2.27.
Sodium thiosulphate—has $5H_2O$ in hydrated form. Quantity required relative to anhydrous is 1.57.
Trisodium phosphate—has $12H_2O$ in hydrated form. Anhydrous and hydrate are not interchangeable by equivalent weight as the latter is more alkaline.

Alkali solutions
Sodium hydroxide—although the traditional form of sodium hydroxide is as sticks or pellets, a convenient form of purchase for the small user is as a 40 or 50% weight/volume solution, which keeps indefinitely if stoppered. The weights specified for pellets should be multiplied by 2.5 or 2 respectively. The pellets and sticks absorb both CO_2 and moisture readily.
Ammonium hydroxide—the standard form is '880 Ammonia', a reference to its density. This solution is 35% weight/volume. Dilution to 20 and 25% requires dilution with water in the ratios 100:75 and 100:40 respectively.

Activity
When strict accuracy is essential, the pH-value may be checked with a pH-meter (test papers are not suitable) and adjusted to the standard value by the addition of caustic soda (sodium hydroxide) pellets or flakes or the 40 or 50% solutions mentioned above—it is safest to use the dilute solutions—to raise the pH-value or, if necessary, sodium metabisulphite or acetic acid to lower it. Liquid pH indicators, eg BDH, available from pharmacies, may be useful to the amateur.

Chemical suppliers
Most chemicals quoted in *The British Journal of Photography Annual* are available from Rayco Limited, Rayco Works, Blackwater Way, Ash Road, Aldershot, Hants, telephone 22725. Rayco are willing to add to their chemical lists, which can be obtained by sending a stamped addressed envelope, according to user requirements. Koch-Light Laboratories Limited, Colnbrook, Buckinghamshire SL3 0BZ, telephone: Colnbrook 2262-5, stock a very complete range of chemicals, especially organic ones, and are suppliers to the large scale user, trade, and industry. The Rexolin Division of W. R. Grace Ltd, Northdale House, North Circular Rd, London NW10 7UH supply EDTA, EDTA salts and chelating agents. Ubichem, 281 Hithermoor Road, Stanwell Moor, Staines TW19 6AZ, telephone: 0753 685117, supply most photographic processing chemicals.

Times
All times, including those for washing or rinsing, should be adhered to in order to obviate the possibility of colour casts. The specified treatment items include 10-15sec drainage.

Temperature
Maintenance of constant temperature throughout first (black-and-white) development in reversal processing and (colour) development in negative processing is absolutely essential if consistent results are to be achieved. In the other solutions, the tolerance is wider, although the specified limits should be respected. Even so, it is important that excessive temperature differences between successive solutions and wash water, especially in transferring to the wash following colour development, be avoided, otherwise there is a risk of reticulation. The washing times given in the procedures apply at the recommended temperatures; if water at lower temperatures is used times must be extended by 50% per 5°C.

Agitation
The recommended agitation is indicated immediately after the procedure. It should be adhered to strictly in the developers but in other solutions should be regarded as a minimum; more vigorous agitation can only be advantageous in expediting solution changes in the emulsion.

Lighting
The individual procedures clearly show at what stage normal room lighting may be resumed when use of an open processing tank necessitates initial darkroom working. At the same stage, the lid of a light-tight tank may be removed.

Second exposure
Where second exposure to light is the manufacturer's recommended procedure the recommended lamp wattage and distance are shown at the appropriate point. The film should preferably be removed from the spiral and see-sawed through a dish of cold water below the lamp, front and back being exposed approximately equally. If the exposure is carried out with the film in a transparent-ended spiral, best immersed in cold water in a white bowl, the time should be extended 1½ (35mm) or 2½ (120) times. Care should be taken not to splash the hot lamp with water and not to work near the sink or taps unless the lampholder is properly earthed. Three or four electronic flashes on each side of the film may also be used although this may give odd colour casts with some films.

Wetting agents
If a final wash completes the procedure, the material should be passed for about 1min through water containing around 1ml/l of wetting agent in order to accelerate draining and drying, thereby inhibiting drying marks. The wetting agent may be either of the anionic type — eg American Cyanamid Aerosol OT (sodium di-iso-octysulphosuccinate), Union Carbide Tergitol 7 and Ciba Invitol — or the non-ionic type — eg Rohm and Hass Triton X-100, Francolor Sunaptol OP and Union Carbide Tergitol NPX. The wetting agent is conveniently stored as a 10% solution and made up as a 10% solution of this, thus forming a 1% solution. The working strength solution keeps indefinitely but should be discarded after use.

Drying
Should be performed under protection from air currents and dust.

Storage
The keeping time of used solutions may be diminished by 20-65% depending upon conditions of use and storage (fullness and sealing of bottles, darkness and temperature). Well stoppered dark glass bottles should be used at temperatures not exceeding 20°C. However, first and colour developers should, in any case, be used as fresh as possible. If bleach and fixer are made up as triple-strength stocks, they will be found to have excellent storage properties.

General
The formulae quoted produce results closely corresponding with those from official kits, but deviations occasionally occur owing to variations in reagents from different suppliers. To compensate for these, where necessary, or to provide controls to suit the individual user's taste, the following notes on the less usual ingredients may be helpful:

Citrazinic acid (CZA or 2,6-dihydroxyisonicotinic acid) is employed as a *specialised restraining agent* and serves to prevent what would otherwise be an excessively dense and contrasty dye image. A deficiency produces a dense greenish image, but an excess produces a thin pinkish image; a 10% change in concentration shows markedly in the result.

Ethylenediamine tetra-acetic acid tetrasodium salt (EDTA Na_4) acts as an *accelerator*. A deficiency produces a thin yellowish image, whereas an excess produces a heavy bluish image; a 10% variation has a quite noticeable effect.

Benzyl alcohol acts as a *penetrating agent* making the otherwise waterproof dye-former particles accessible to the colour developer products. It is particularly important to ensure that this liquid is completely dissolved before any othèr reagent of the colour developer is added.

Variations in the amount of *colour developing agent* produce effects rather similar to those of the EDTA salt, the balance travelling from thin and warm to dense and cool as the concentration is increased.

Precaution
Colour developers contain derivatives of paraphenylenediamine, which in certain persons may produce a form of skin irritation. Persons who are

sensitive to chemicals of this kind should take precautions to avoid contact with the developer by using rubber gloves. In all cases, when the skin has been in contact with the solution, it should be rinsed well in clean water, preferably made acid with a few drops of acetic or hydrochloric acid, before using soap. Where processing chemicals are used in premises subject to the provisions of the Health and Safety Act, 1974 (eg in professional use or in commercial processing plants) the Act should be consulted for the safety precautions to be observed. In all cases warnings printed on chemical package labels should be strictly complied with. Fuller details of precautions to be observed in the handling of particular materials may be found in the Royal Society of Chemistry publication, *Hazards in the Chemical Laboratory* (3rd edition) by L. Bretherwick.

COLOUR FILMS

KODAK EKTACHROME FILMS

The generic name for Kodak user-processable reversal materials is Ektachrome and all current materials of this type except two—Ektachrome Infrared and Photomicrography Color Film 2483—are processed by **Process E-6**. These two exceptions continue to use the earlier **Process E-4**, which introduced for the first time the use of a chemical reversal bath to replace reversal by a second exposure. The reversal bath used in Process E-4, however, contains components which are toxic and require care in handling which may not be appropriate to some amateur circumstances.

EKTACHROME E-6

The Ektachrome E-6 process, like its predecessor the E-4 process, is intended for machine use and is usefully shorter, needing around 40min in the solutions. The shorter process time is achieved by raising the solution temperatures to 38°C. From the user's point of view the process has been improved in two directions; the somewhat aggressive preliminary hardener has been eliminated by hardening the film emulsion in manufacture and the highly toxic tertiary-butylaminoborane used as a reversing agent in the colour developer has been replaced by the much less dangerous stannous chloride in a reversing bath which precedes the colour negative stage.

Like the C-41 process for colour negative development the E-6 process uses separate bleach and fix stages but with the bleach action performed by a ferric-EDTA complex as is now common in bleach-fix solutions. Intermediate rinses are practically eliminated, and washing times are shortened, thus permitting substantial economies in water consumption (and probably in energy also, despite the high working temperature). And, thanks to the hardened emulsion, which is more resistant and less retentive of water, drying is much more rapid, the more so as it withstands the necessary higher air temperatures.

Formulae

These formulations give results of comparable quality to those obtained by the use of the manufacturers' formulae. In one or two of the baths deriving from the E-6 process we propose some variants as in the first developer and the bleach. They are both derived from E-4 and only require adaptation for the new products; this should make the work of preparation easier. Quantities are indicated in grammes per litre or ml per litre.

Stock concentrated solutions

Solutions prepared as concentrates and diluted just before use have markedly increased shelf life—by a factor of two or three. The solutions we have used are as follows and they give a worthwhile saving of time and effort.

	Concentration	Dilution
First developer	X2	1+1
Colour developer	X4	1+3*
Reversal	X20	1+19
Conditioner	X10	1+9
Bleach	X2	1+1
Fixer	X5	1+4
Stabiliser	X20	1+19

*The CD-3 or CD-4 may be kept separately by making a 20% solution from which may be measured the required quantity by pipette.

CD-3 or CD-4	20.0g
Potassium metabisulphite (crystalline)	3.0g
Water to	100.0ml

Influence of pH

The E-3 process used solutions whose pH differed considerably from one bath to the next. These variations were considerably reduced from E-4. The high temperature working proposed with E-6 allows only minor pH differences between baths—with the exception of the first and colour developers. Fluctuations, intentional or not, in the colour developer pH, can result in variations in the colour balance of the subject matter of the exposures. Variations in first developer pH chiefly affect its activity, raising or lowering its reducing power, and resulting in an increase or reduction in the speed of development.

Colour Developer
- pH too low: blue cast
- pH too high: yellow cast
- Colour developer too dilute: magenta cast
- If the reversing bath is too dilute or exhausted: green cast.

First developer (pH: 9.6±0.1)

Calgon	2.0g
Sodium sulphite (anhydrous)	15.0g
Potassium hydroquinone monosulphonate (pure)	20.0g
Diethylene glycol	15.0ml
Potassium carbonate (anhydrous)	15.0g
Phenidone	0.4g
Sodium thiocyanate (20% solution)	8.0ml
Potassium bromide	1.8g
Potassium iodide (1% solution)	4.0ml
Water to	1000.0ml

Alternative first developer (pH: 9.6±0.1)

Calgon	2.0g
Sodium sulphite (anhydrous)	15.0g
Potassium carbonate (anhydrous)	15.0g
Hydroquinone	6.0g
Phenidone	0.4g
Sodium thiocyanate (20% solution)	8.0ml
Potassium bromide	2.0g
Potassium iodide (1% solution)	5.0ml
Water to	1000.0ml

Reversal bath (pH: 5.8±0.1)

Propionic acid	12ml
Stannous chloride	1.65g
p-Aminophenol	0.5g
Sodium hydroxide	4.8g
BDH Calcium Complexing Agent No 4	15ml
Water to	1000ml

Notes: 1 The very small quantity of p-Aminophenol can best be measured by making a 0.1% solution (1g/1000ml) in 1% (10ml/1000ml) of propionic acid. This solution does not keep well and should be discarded after a week or so. **2** If the solution, particularly when made up as a 20x concentrate, does not clear on adding the calcium complexing agent in the above quantity a little more should be added slowly until it does. **3** If reversal is carried out by exposure to light the reversal bath must be replaced by a stop bath consisting of 2% acetic acid for 1min at 38°C, followed by a rinse for the same time and temperature in running water. The operation is carried out in the dark.

Colour developer (pH: 11.6±11.7)

EDTA Na_4	3.0g
Potassium carbonate (anhydrous)	40.0g
Sodium sulphite (anhydrous)	4.0g
Potassium bromide	0.5g
Potassium iodide (1% solution)	3.0ml
Citrazinic acid	1.2g
Hydroxylamine hydrochloride	1.5g
Water to	1000.0ml
Add before use: CD-3	10.0g
or CD-4	7.5g

These two chemicals can be kept without difficulty as 20% stock solutions with the addition of 2-3g per litre of potassium or sodium metabisulphite.

Conditioning bath (pH: 6.1±0.1)

Sodium sulphite (anhydrous)	10.0g
EDTA Acid	8.0g
Thioglycerol	0.5ml
Water to	1000.0ml

Notes: 1 If only EDTA Na_4 is available or EDTA Na_2 then 12g of the former or 10g of the latter may be used with the pH adjusted with dilute acetic acid. **2** The inclusion of thioglycerol is optional. **3** For our purposes, perfect results have been obtained with the use of the E-3 clearing bath with a small modification and with the pH adjusted if necessary by adding alkali—sodium or potassium carbonate. The bath is as follows:

Potassium metabisulphite (crystalline)	15.0g
Hydroquinone	1.0g
Water to	1000.0ml

Bleach (pH: 5.5-5.7)

Potassium nitrate (crystalline)	30.0g
Potassium bromide	110.0g
EDTA NaFe or NH_4Fe (Merck)	110.0g
Water to	1000.0ml

Note: The nitrate is optional and acts as a protection for stainless steel tanks.

Alternative bleach (pH: 6.7-6.9)

The formulae established for the E-4 process also gives excellent results. Here is a simple and efficient variant of it:

Potassium ferricyanide (crystalline)	100.0g
Potassium bromide	35.0g
Disodium phosphate (crystalline)	20.0g
Water to	1000.0ml

Fixer (pH: 6.6-6.7)

Ammonium thiosulphite (crystalline)	70.0g
Potassium metabisulphite (crystalline)	12.0g
Sodium sulphite (anhydrous)	7.0g
Water to	1000.0ml

Note: The E-3 or E-4 fixing baths work just as well.

Stabiliser

Wetting agent (Aerosol OT, anionic or any similar product) (10% solution)	5.0ml
Formaldehyde (35-40%)	6.0ml
Water to	1000.0ml

Notes

A The *temperature* of the developer must be maintained with the utmost possible accuracy. We recommend the use of a stainless steel tank immersed in a tank of water at a temperature of 39°C, from which it is removed for agitation and immediately re-immersed.

B The *times* given include the time needed to empty the tank: this should not exceed a maximum of 10sec.

C Each operation should be timed from the moment the tank is filled with the processing solution.

D An initial agitation of 20sec should be given, during which the tank should be tapped on a hard surface (table or sink) to disperse the bubbles of air trapped in the spiral against the emulsion surface.

E For *drying*, the spiral should, after removal from the stabiliser, first be well shaken to remove so far as possible loose drops of solution; the film is removed and then allowed to dry in a well aired but dust free situation (left overnight at a temperature of 20-25°C) or stretched in special drying clips for this purpose, or otherwise suspended. (At 20-25°C drying will then take about ½hr.)

Processing at temperatures other than 38°*C*

The physico-chemical processes which are involved in processing photographic material are intrinsically related to working temperature. In other words, there is a relationship between the speed of a chemical and physical reaction and the temperature at which it occurs, the speed increasing with the temperature.

For black-and-white development stage it is particularly necessary to have as exact a knowledge as possible of this parameter (speed), since it is this which determines the quality of the image: gradation, colour, rendering, density of the silver image deposit in the various zones of the image and hence the dyes in the final image.

The diagram illustrating the relation between temperature and development time is the result of our own experimental work; it can be of use to those who wish (or who are obliged) to work at a temperature other than 38°C. This must not however be below 32-33°C since this will seriously affect the colour rendering of the transparency. (The permeability of the emulsion diminishes too greatly to permit adequate exchange of solutions through the gelatine.)

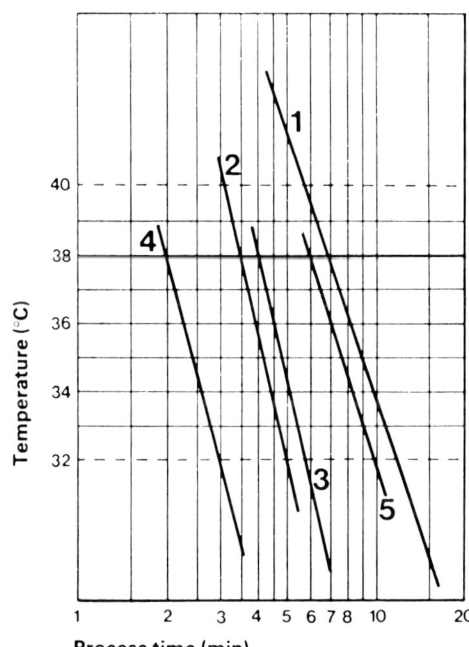

Processing times as a function of temperature in the range 32-40°C. Line 1—black-and-white developer and EDTA Fe bleach; 2—ferricyanide bleach; 3—fix; 4—reversal bath and conditioner; 5—wash.

Modification of processing procedure

A Reversal: It is possible to dispense with *chemical* reversal and instead have recourse to the classic procedure of re-exposure of the emulsion to light: 2 electronic flash exposures to each side of the tank spiral after removal from the tank and preferably kept immersed in water, at a distance of about 30cm; or two 2min exposures to a photoflood at a distance of about 1 metre; or yet again intermediate drying in diffused light (not direct sunlight!)

B Should the re-exposure procedure be adopted in place of chemical reversal, this soaking treatment should be replaced by 1min in a stop bath of 2% acetic acid and followed by 1min wash before opening the tank.

C Recourse may be had to *intermediate drying* in order to defer completion of processing to a later time. After drying, the film should be kept in relative darkness. For completion of processing, it is rewound into the spiral and, preferably, soaked in water for 1min before treatment in the colour developer (this is recommended but not obligatory).

D Bleach: It is possible to bleach the film in 2-3 minutes by treatment in a potassium ferricyanide bleach bath of the E-3 or E-4 type, adjusted to a pH of 6.4± 0.2 followed by 2min rinse before fixing. The temperature of 38°C should also be maintained throughout these stages.

E Where it is desired to *keep* these various solutions, in view of the fact that there is a risk of each solution being contaminated by traces of the previous bath, we recommend an *intermediate rinse* of ½ to 1min after each bath excepting reversal and conditioner solutions where the action must be allowed to continue in the following solutions. The small increase in overall processing time thus occasioned can only be of benefit to working capacity and keeping quality.

Exposure for a speed other than the nominal rating

Films compatible with the E-6 process can be 'uprated' to higher emulsion speeds by up to 2 stops or downrated by 1 stop compared with nominal values. To compensate for this, first development should then be modified in accordance with the table below:

Exposure	Relative speed	Development modification
−2 stops	4x	+5½min
−1 stop	2x	+2min
+1 stop	0.5x	+2min

Colour rendering is slightly affected:

+1 stop	overexposure:	reduction of contrast and deterioration of colour rendering
−1 stop −2 stops	underexposure:	diminution of maximum density diminution of exposure latitude shift of colour rendering increase of contrast

From our personal experience, underexposure by 1 stop (as for example ISO800 for Ektachrome 400) still gives excellent results, of quality not perceptibly inferior to that resulting from correct exposure. Not all E-6 process films from other manufacturers behave identically and these development times may require modification in the light of experience. Special recommendations and process control strips are made for the recently introduced **Ektachrome Professional P800/1600** material which is designed for this type of 'push-processing'.

Keeping properties and working capacities

	dm² per unit of 0.5l	1l	2l	Keeping
First developer	22	46	100	8-10 weeks
Colour developer	22	46	100	12 weeks
Reversal or stop bath	50	130	280	8 weeks
Conditioner	50	130	280	8 weeks
Bleach	50	130	280	6 months
Fixer	50	130	280	4-6 months
Stabiliser	preferably use fresh			

NB: one 36exp 35mm film = 5.8 dm²; one 20exp 35mm film = 3.8 dm²; 1 × 120 film × 5.1 dm²; 1 × 220 film = 10.2 dm².

Partially used solutions and working solutions generally have their keeping life reduced by 50% and their useful capacity reduced by 20%.

Procedure for large tanks (exceeding 2 litres)

Stage	Time min	Temp °C	Agitation
1 First development	6	38±0.3	1 × 20sec, then 2 × 5sec, per min
2 Rinse	2	33-39	1 × 10sec then leave undisturbed
3 Reversal	2	33-39	1 × 10sec then leave undisturbed
4 Colour development	6	38±0.6	1 × 20sec then 2 × 5sec/min
5 Conditioner	2	33-39	1 × 10sec then leave undisturbed
6 Bleach	6	,,	2-4 × 5sec/min
7 Fix	4	,,	2-4 × 5sec/min
8 Wash, running water	4	,,	at least 2 changes per min
9 Stabiliser	½	,,	no agitation
	32.5		

Procedure for small tanks (½ litre)

Stage	Time	Temp
1 First development	7	38±0.3
2 Rinse	2	33-39
3 Reversal	2	,,
4 Colour development	6	38±0.6
5 Conditioner	2	33-39
6 Bleach	7	,,
7 Fixer	4	,,
8 Wash	6	,,
9 Stabiliser	1	,,
	37	

Agitation: as for large-scale processing (above); agitation may be by inversion, if tank is water-tight.
Drying: max 49°C

KODAK COLOUR NEGATIVE FILM PROCESSES

All Kodak colour negative emulsions currently available—and those from most other major manufacturers—are designed for **Process C-41.** These include amateur **Kodacolor VR100, VR400** and **VR1000** and professional **Vericolor II** and **III** films in cartridge, miniature, roll and sheet formats as well as specialised materials for making intermediate negatives from colour transparencies and print transparencies from colour negatives.

C-41 PROCESS

Introduction

During 1983 a new range of Kodacolor VR films was introduced, with speeds of ISO 100/21 DIN, ISO200/24 DIN, ISO400/27 DIN and ISO1000/31 DIN. Improved sharpness and colour rendering, coupled with reduced graininess is claimed for the three slower films. They incorporate experience and methods gained during development of materials for the ultra-miniature 'disc' format. Kodacolor VR1000 incorporates thin plate-like silver halide grains which, aligned parallel to the emulsion surface, show enhanced sensitivity without as large a penalty in graininess as shown by conventional emulsions.

Vericolor II Professional Films Type S (daylight balance, exposures shorter than 1/10sec) and Type L (3200K balance, exposures, from 1/50 to 60sec) were introduced in June 1975. The Type S material

(ISO100) is available in 35mm, 120/220 and 70mm roll formats and in sheet sizes up to 8 × 10in: Type L (ISO25-80, dependent on exposure time) is supplied in 120 roll and in sheet sizes. In 1979 Vericolor Commercial Type S in 120 and sheet formats had a higher contrast than Type S—in this it resembles Type L—but a similar ISO100 speed rating. Improved Veriocolor III materials were announced at photokina in October 1982 and have now superseded Vericolor II films.

Most manufacturers now produce materials compatible with C-41 processing. Reference should be made to the instruction leaflet or the film carton and cartridge.

The brevity of the processing steps of the C-41 process may well *a priori* worry the amateur: it is true that it is difficult simultaneously to maintain a high processing temperature together with regular agitation for a time calculated 'to the second', especially in colour development. This is a process intended primarily for automatic processing installations with a view to increasing throughput and profitability. Oue experiments have confirmed that the C-41 procedure *can* be carried out efficiently in a small tank—so long, that is, as the time, temperature and agitation recommendations are carried out. One advantage, however, is that the solutions contain only chemicals of weak toxicity; environmentally undesirable substances have been banished from the formulation.

C-41 Procedure (after Kodak)

1 Colour development	3min/15sec	37.8±0.15°C
2 Bleach	4min/20sec	24-40°C
3 Wash	1min/05sec	24-40°C
4 Fix	4min/20sec	24-40°C
5 Wash	3min/15sec	24-40°C
6 Stabilisation	1min/05sec	24-40°C
7 Dry	—	<43°C
Total	17min/20sec	

Operational Steps

1 Prepare a water bath at 41°C: this provides a thermal reservoir.
2 Bring the solutions up to 38°C before use.
3 Fill the the developing tank with the necessary quantity of developer, agitate continuously for 20sec, then plunge it in the water bath to within 2-3cm of the top of the lid.
4 Take the tank out again and agitate—preferably by inversion—for 5sec. Put it back in the water bath. Repeat this cycle giving 6 agitations each minute.
5 Empty the tank 10sec before the elapse of the required time. Shake it well so that as little colour developer as possible is left inside.
6 Pour in the bleach and carry out the same agitation rhythm as above.
7 When the bleach stage is finished, the tank may be opened to simplify washing.
8 Once it has come out of the stabilising bath, the film is hung up to dry in the usual manner. In a normally heated and ventilated room it will be dry in about 30-40min.

Variations

When processed mechanically, the film is wiped before passing into the bleach bath. When working with a spiral tank this is unfortunately not possible, so that a rapid contamination of the bleach oxidising solution takes place, together with rise in pH. We have therefore introduced a small variation to overcome this inconvenience: after the end of colour development, we pour into the tank a stop—1% acetic acid or the C-22 stop bath—and agitate continuously for 30sec. The solution is then poured out and a 30sec wash in water at 38°C given before pouring in the bleach bath. The Kodak procedure is then resumed. It is also possible to work with the classic ferricyanide bleach bath, using the following procedure:

1 Colour development	3min/15sec	38±0.2°C
2 Stop bath C-22	0min/30sec	38±0°C
3 Wash in running water	2min/30sec	38±3.0°C
4 C-22 bleach	2min/30sec	38±3.0°C
5 Wash in running water	1min/30sec	38±3.0°C
6 C-22 fix	4min/20sec	38±3.0°C
7 Wash in running water	3min/15sec	38±3.0°C
8 Stabilisation	1min/05sec	38±3.0°C
9 Drying	—	<43°C
Total	18min/55sec	

Results with this procedure are identical to those obtained following the official process.

Formulae

The quantities are given in grams per litre. The chemicals are dissolved in the indicated order.

Colour Developer (pH: 10.0-10.1)

Calgon	2.0g
Sodium sulphite (anhydrous)	4.25g
Potassium bromide	1.5g
Potassium carbonate (anhydrous)	37.5g
Hydroxylamine sulphate	2.0g
Water to make	1000.0ml

Add 6hr before use:

CD-4	4.75g
or CD-4 (20% solution)	24.0ml

CD-4 stock solution

The following keeps well for about 2 months in the cool away from light.

CD-4	20.0g
Potassium metabisulphite (crystalline)	3.0g
Water to make	1000.0ml

Bleach

EDTA NaFe	100.0g
Potassium bromide	50.0g
Ammonia 20%	6.0ml
Water to make	1000.0ml

Fix (pH: 5.8-6.5)

Ammonium thiosulphite	120.0g
Sodium sulphite (anhydrous)	20.0g
Potassium metabisulphite (crystalline)	20.0g
Water to make	1000.0ml

Stabiliser

Wetting agent (10% solution)	10.0ml
Formaldehyde (35-37% solution)	6.0ml
Water to make	1000.0ml

Capacity (1 litre) and shelf life of fresh solutions

		Working capacity				
Solution	**Keeping**	**110/** 20ex	**126/** 20ex	**135** 36ex	**120**	**dm²** approx
Colour developer without CD-4	6 weeks	—	—	—		—
Colour developer with CD-4	1 month	30	12	5	6	30
Bleach	8-12 weeks	120	45	20	24	100-120
Fixer	8-12 weeks	60	22	10	12	60
Stabiliser	1 year	use once only				
Stop bath	1 year	use once only				

Notes

1 Partially used solutions have a 30/50% lower shelf life, depending on the actual storage conditions (darkness, well-stoppered bottle, temperature 14-20°C).
2 Work whenever possible with fresh solutions to ensure optimum consistency of results. However, for 110 format film, Kodak advise the division of 1 litre of development into two 500ml quantities. This enables films to be developed in batches of 3, and 5 or 6 batches can be processed before throwing the developer away. If this is done, processing times should be modified according to the following table.

Development time for 110 format (min/sec)

Film	No of films developed at once	1st batch	2nd	3rd	4th	5th	6th	Total films (in 500ml)
110/20ex	3	3/15	3/22	3/30	3/37	3/45	—	15
110/12ex	3	3/15	3/20	3/26	3/31	3/37	3/43	18

3 It is desirable to keep the bleach solution, unlike others, in a half full container. It should be shaken vigorously after use for about 10sec to reoxidise the ferrous complex Fe^{++} (formed during bleaching) to the ferric complex Fe^{+++}, so that its activity can be maintained. Replenishment is not advisable in amateur usage and the solution should therefore be thrown away after the indicated number of films has been processed.
4 The C-41 colour developer is also suitable for processing Ektacolor 78RC Paper, adding 45ml/l benzyl alcohol.
5 Instead of separate Bleach and Fixing baths, the use of a combined bleach/fix is possible. That given for 78RC paper is suitable (4min): pH 5.8-6.2.■

PROCESSING COLOUR PRINT PAPERS

EKTACOLOR

Introduction
The substitute formulae appearing here may be used with papers designed to use Kodak Ektaprint-2 process or other manufacturers' equivalents (e.g. Fuji process CP21). The current Kodak papers are Ektacolor Plus and Ektacolor Professional: note that Ektacolor 2001 designed for minilab use requires the appropriate Ektacolor RA-4 process. The compatible Fuji papers are Fujicolor HR, 01-P and 02, from Agfa CN Type 7 and from 3M Color Paper High Speed.

Procedure
1 Dish processing
The times given below include 20sec for draining at the conclusion of each processing stage.

Solution	Time (minutes)	Temperature(°C)
Colour developer	3½	31.1±0.3
*Bleach fix	1½	31.1±1.2
Wash	2	31.1±1.2
Stabiliser	1	31.1±1.2
Total	1	—
Drying		not above 107°C

**To obviate an excessive rate of exhaustion of the bleach fix solution due to carry-over contamination, the print may be treated for one minute in a stop bath (for example Stop Bath C-33, or a 3% solution of acetic acid) followed by one minute rinse.*

Clearing
Normal room lighting may be resumed following the bleach fix stage, or even before it, if the stop bath has been used.

Agitation
If only one print is processed at a time, the dish may be lightly rocked, 3 or 4 times per minute. If a number of prints are processed together, immerse the first print, emulsion side down, then at 20sec intervals, the second print, the third, and so on, in each case emulsion side down. When all prints are immersed, bring the bottom print to the top, and the others in succession. Continue this procedure until the processing time of each has elapsed.

Capacity
One litre of colour developer will develop 3 to 4 20 × 25cm prints. It should then be discarded. So far as the other solutions are concerned, they should served to process (in 1 litre) 7-8 prints of the same format. If the additional stop bath is employed, it is even possible to process at least 1 to 1½m^2 of paper in 1 litre of 'blix'.

2 Processing in small drums
The advantage of this procedure is obvious: the quantity of colour developer used is so very small (60ml for the smallest model, sufficing for development of one 20 × 25cm—8 × 10in—print); this corresponds to a capacity of 0.8m^2/litre. For the other solutions the capacity is at least doubled: that is to say, one could use the 60ml twice, or alternatively use four times as much solution (250ml), permitting the consecutive processing of at least 10-12 prints before discarding it. Bearing in mind the cost of chemicals, the economy this represents is obvious, quickly offsetting the initial cost of the drum. This is over and above the immense advantage of being able to work in ordinary light, once the print has been inserted and the drum closed.

Below is a table of procedure for each of three different temperatures from which the most suitable can be chosen to meet location conditions.

Treatment times (min)

Solution	t=31°C	33°C	38°±03C	Remarks
1 Pre-warming/wetting	¾	¾	¾	
2 Colour developer	3½	3	2	
3 Wash*	¾	¾	½	2 changes
or				
3a Stop Bath C-22	½	½	½	
3b Wash*	½	½	½	2 changes
4 Blix	1¾	1½	1	
5 Wash*	2	1½	1	
6 Stabiliser†	1	¾	½	
Total	10	8¼	6-6¼	

Drying temperature 107°C
**Four changes of water may be considered equivalent to one minute of wash.*
†The use of a stabiliser is now optional. The simplified 2-bath process gives equally good results.
In this case the final wash must be prolonged to 4, 3 and 2min respectively.

Agitation
About 20-30 cycles/min (according to size of drum). The times given include 10-20sec for emptying the drum. Note that in the case of large models, treatment times should be prolonged by 15sec for the developer and 30sec for the other solutions to allow for the greater quantities of liquid which have to be emptied.

Temperature
In the case of drums where this information is provided this will be determined by reference to the nomograms provided with the drum; this takes account of the ambient temperature (=temperature of solutions) to indicate that of the water for pre-warming and washing. Other small drums including the Paterson and the Unicolor are also supplied with full temperature instructions.

Alternative formulae
The formulae which we give below yield results which are comparable both qualitatively and quantitatively, with those obtained with the official procedure. Quantities are quoted throughout in grams or millilitres. Where water is the base of a solution, the components should be dissolved in the order indicated in water at 30-35°C.

Colour developer (pH:10.1-10.2)†

1 Working solution

Calgon	2.0g
Hydroxylamine sulphate	3.4g
Sodium sulphite (anhydrous)	2.0g
Potassium carbonate (anhydrous)	32.0g
Potassium bromide	0.4g
Benzyl alcohol (50% solution)*	30.0ml
Water to	1000.0ml

Add before use:

CD-3	4.4g
(or 22% solution)*	20.0ml

**See preparation of concentrated stock Solutions C.*

2 Preparation of concentrated stock solutions

		Quantity to be taken per litre of working solution
Solution A		
Benzyl alcohol	500ml	
Diethyleneglycol	500ml	30ml
Total	1000ml	
Solution B		
Calgon	20g	
Hydroxylamine sulphate	34g	
Potassium bromide	4g	100ml
Sodium sulphite (anhydrous)	20g	
Potassium carbonate (anhydrous)	320g	
Water to	1000ml	

The potassium carbonate should be added slowly in small amounts because of the evolution of CO_2.

Solution C		
Potassium metabisulphite crystalline	2g	
CD-3	22g	20ml
Water to	100ml	

Bleach Fix (pH: 6.2-6.5)

1 Working Solution

EDTA NaFe or NF_4FE (Merck)	40g
EDTA Acid	4g
Potassium iodide	1g
Ammonia (20% solution)	10ml
Ammonium thiosulphate (crystalline)	100g
Sodium sulphite (anhydrous)	2g
Sodium thiocyanate (20% solution)*	50ml
Water to	1000ml

pH: to be adjusted to 6.2-6.5 by the addition of ammonia or acetic acid as necessary.
**Ammonium thiocyanate may be used in place of the sodium salt in the same proportion.*

2 Preparation of concentrated stock solutions

		Quantity to be taken per litre of working solution
Solution A (pH: 7.2-7.5)		
EDTA NH_4Fe	200g	
EDTA Acid	20g	200ml
Ammonia (25% solution)	60ml	
Water to	1000ml	
Solution B (pH: 5.8-6.2)		
Ammonium thiosulphate (crystalline)	500g	
Sodium (or ammonium) thiocyanate	50g	200ml
Potassium metabisulphite (crystalline)	10g	
Potassium iodide	5g	
Water to	1000ml	

Stabiliser (pH: 3.6±0.1)

1 Working Solution

Sodium carbonate (anhydrous)	2.5g
Acetic acid (glacial)	12.5ml
Citric acid (crystalline)*	7g
Water to	1000ml
*or Tartaric acid	8g

2 Concentrated stock solution

		Quantity to be taken per litre of working solution
Acetic acid (glacial)	170ml	
Citric acid (crystalline)	95g	
(or Tartaric)	106g	75ml
Sodium carbonate (anhydrous)	33g	
Water to	1000ml	

Substitute for CD-3 in the Colour Developer

A number of other colour developing agents currently used in colour laboratories have been examined as possible substitutes for CD-3 in the colour developer. The results obtained with many of them have been excellent and the colour quality has been comparable with that obtained with the original formula with CD-3. The activity of each agent is a function of its chemical structure and account has been taken of this in modifying the concentrations in the colour developer. In addition the effective emulsion speed of the paper is also affected and exposure and activity factors are given based on the use of CD-3 and 4.4g/litre of working solution.

Developing agent	g per litre	pH	Relative activity	Relative exposure
CD-3 Kodak	4·4	10·16	100	1·0
CD-4 Kodak	3·0	10·18	130	0·75
Ethylhydroxyethyl-ppd H_2SO_4	5·0	10·10	115	0·85
Diethyl-ppd H_2SO_4	2·4	10·10	145	0·70
Ac60 Agfa	4·0	10·7	50	2·0
CD-2 Kodak	2·4	10·2	145	0·70

The filtration required during printing was very similar with all the agents examined. Using a test negative on Ektacolor Professional Film Type S, the values were near 80Y 40M, except with Agfa developing agent Ac60 which required a filtration adjustment to 100Y 60M and a correction of the pH of the solution to $10·6 \pm 1·0$ by the addition of 0·5 to 1·0g/litre of caustic soda. The findings are summarised in the table.

Notes

All processing was carried out using the three-bath process. At the concentration given the diethyl-paraphenylenediamine produces a light greenish overall fog. It is necessary to reduce the concentration to 2-2·2g/litre to improve the result.■

PROCESSING COLOUR
REVERSAL PAPERS

CIBACHROME PRINT

Since all those Cibachrome materials which used the P-10 and P-18 processing formulations have now been discontinued for several years it is felt that no useful purpose would be served by reprinting the alternative solution formulas worked out by Ernest-Charles Gehret for these materials. The new Cibachrome II amateur and professional print materials are, respectively, processed in P-30 and P-3 solutions, the formulations for which have not been disclosed. However a number of workers have devised alternatives for some of the processing solutions and of these the recommendations of Carl E. Krupp in *Darkroom Techniques* (Vol 4, No 3) have proved to give good results. The divided developer that Krupp recommends was first proosed for Cibachrome by Richard Bisbey II in *Dignan Photographic Report* for September 1977.

With Cibachrome II the black-and-white developer which is the first solution used in processing has to generate what is in effect, a chemical mask. This novel and elegant improvement to the process has the effect of lowering the rather steep gradation of these silver dye-bleach materials and of improving the blue reproduction and giving more saturated yellows and oranges. In order to produce the masking effect the developer includes a silver halide solvent, sodium thiosulphate.

Alternative developers
Krupp recommends that a fast way to make up an alternative Cibachrome II developer is to take one litre of Dektol, diluted 1:1 and add 1.7g of crystalline sodium thiosulphate. The thiosulphate should be added to the developer just before use; do not add it to the stock solution. This is not the same solution as the Cibachrome II developer marketed by the manufacturer which is more complex in order to keep the sodium thiosulphate from precipitating out the silver in the developing dish.

Where Dektol is not available other print developers such as Ilford PQ Universal, Kodak D 163, May and Baker Suprol or Paterson Acuprint can be used at the dilutions recommended for paper processing.

However, an even better Cibachrome II developer is a two-step solution which acts as a compensating developer — holding down highlights and bringing up the shadow areas. The formula recommended by Krupp is:

Black and white developer

Solution A	
Metol	6.9g
Sodium sulphite	37.0g
Hydroquinone	3.0g
Potassium bromide	3.0g
Sodium chloride	6.3g
Water to make	1 litre
Solution B	
Sodium carbonate (anhyd)	111g
Sodium thiosulphate (cryst)	1.8g
Water to make	1 litre

In mixing, start with about three-quarters of the total volume of water at about 35°C and add the chemicals in the order given, dissolving each before adding the next. Table salt should not be used in place of sodium chloride in Solution A since it now commonly contains additives such as sodium hexaferrocyanate and magnesium sulphate to prevent caking.

Bleach
Since the chemistry in the Cibachrome II bleach solution is hard to duplicate, Krupp suggests that it is preferable to use the manufacturer's product which is available as BL 313 Bleach Starter Kit in 3.5 gallon size and Type 30 in amateur size quantities. The newer Cibachrome II bleaches work faster and better than the older ones.

Fixer
With Cibachrome II the fixer is exhausted more quickly than formerly, probably due to the extra layers in the material. Krupp recommends Edwal Quick-Fix diluted 1:3 which gives reliable fixing in five minutes.

Where Edwal Quick-Fix is not available other rapid fixers, without hardener, can be used. Alternatives are Ilford Hypam, Kodak Rapid Fix, May and Baker Amfix or Paterson Acufix. All these alternatives should be used diluted as for film. Ilford technicians stress that the fixing bath should have a pH near 6.8. If the pH is below 6.0 the fixer will destroy the cyan colour layer and affect both colour and density of the print. A higher pH will soften the emulsion.

Processing procedure (dish)

Developer Solution A	1min 24°C±1
Developer Solution B	3min 24°C±1
Stop bath (4% acetic acid)	30sec 24°C±1
Bleach	4min 24°C±1
Fix	5min 24°C±1
Wash	3min 24°C±1

Working with the developer
It is critical that the print remains in Solution A for one minute and in Solution B three minutes. Using the Dektol formula the print must remain in the developer at least three minutes. Developing 11 × 14 prints in dishes it is best to have at least a litre of each of the two working solutions. There will be an 05Y colour shift between the first and fifth print in this quantity of solutions due to hypo depletion in Solution B. One way to correct this is to add 90ml of fresh Solution B after each print is developed. Then completely replace Solution B after processing eight to ten prints.

Working with the bleach
Krupp found that four minutes in dish processing and six minutes in a drum processor is essential to get good clean whites and pastel colours. Excessive bleaching, more than 10 minutes, will lighten delicate colours.

Working with the fixer
To be on the safe side Krupp uses two-bath fixing. Using the same dilution in both fixing baths (i.e. 1:3 with Edwal Quick-Fix) the print is fixed in the first bath for two minutes and then transferred to the second for the remaining three minutes. In practice after processing about ten 11 × 14 prints per litre the first fixing bath is thrown away, the second fixing bath used as the first and a fresh second bath made up.

EKTACHROME 14RC

Although Ektachrome 14RC paper was introduced as long as ten years ago it has been progressively improved during its life. Now, however, this excellent material is in course of being replaced by a further improved product. Ektachrome 22 paper. Since this introduction is taking place slowly and progressively throughout the world there are likely to be stocks of the older product available for some considerable time. There are, in addition colour reversal papers intended for the Ektachrome R-14 process available from Agfa-Gevaert, Fuji and Konishiroku and these too will, in all probability, continue to be available for some time.

It is important to note that the new product, **Ektachrome 22 paper** can be processed only in a new process, coded **Ektachrome R-3** and this process is not suitable for the older R-14 process paper. The alternative solutions which are given below are, therefore, offered to permit the continued processing of the older material for as long as it continues to be available.

Processing method

Ektachrome 14RC is a resin-coated material and so may be processed rapidly at high temperature. As a general rule Ektachrome 14RC may be processed between 28 and 38°C. In amateur usage, unless a proper temperature control system is available with thermostat-controlled water bath, we recommend the 28-32°C range, which it is easiest to maintain. Dish development is possible, but it is better to work using one-shot baths in a processing drum, for example, a Durst, Jobo, Paterson, Unicolor or similar. Besides, it is more pleasant to work in ambient light than in complete darkness and, anyway, the reproducibility of results is improved, since fresh solution is used each time.

The scheme given below applies to both dish and drum development.

Temperature:	30°C		34°C		38°C	
	min	sec	min	sec	min	sec
1 *Pre-soak	1	—	—	50	—	40
2 B & W development	3	—	2	5	1	30
3 Wash Min 4 changes	3	—	2	45	2	30
4 Re-expose	100W at 40cm, minimum 10sec on face of paper only during last minute of wash					
5 Colour development	3	30	3	15	3	—
6 Rinse 1-2 changes	1	—	—	50	—	40
7 Bleach/fix	3	30	3	15	3	—
8 **Final wash	3	30	3	15	3	—

*Follow the tank manufacturers' recommendations.
**Minimum of 6 changes in a drum, but preferable made in running water in a tank, washbowl, or other container.

The time/temperature graph gives indications for immersion in the baths, for the adopted or necessary working temperatures within a 28-38°C range.

Dish processing

Agitation: a slow, steady rocking motion. When finished, drain the print for 5-15sec, according to format, as it is taken out of each bath.

Temperature maintenance: this is critical in the first developer: ±0.3°C. Use either a water bath, or a dish warmer, equipped with thermostat control.

Safelighting: none. Absolute darkness is essential during first development and the first two minutes of the following wash. The subsequent steps may be carried out in normal lighting.

Re-exposure to light: to be made during the last 30sec of the wash following black and white development. Only expose the emulsion side of the print to the light.

Drum processing

Working with a drum, re-exposure is carried out by taking the print briefly out of the drum. This should be kept filled with water at the indicated temperature, so that work may continue afterwards without delay.

A stop bath

Is not absolutely necessary. However, it is possible to use one between first development and the wash before re-exposure, composed of 2% acetic acid for 30sec.

Drying

After having taken the prints from the final wash in the dish or container, they should be wiped or sponged on both sides to remove most of the water, and then hung freely in the air, or in a drying cabinet; this latter appears, however, clumsy and unnecessary. In passing it may well be noted that a hairdryer works perfectly well and is quite cheap. Care must be taken not to char prints by holding them too close to the outlet!

Capacity

In a drum, allow 45-50ml of black and white or colour developer for each 20 × 25cm sheet (500cm^2). A second sheet may be treated in the same quantity of bleach/fix. In our own practice, we prefer to use double quantities of the baths, using the developers twice and the bleach/fix four times. A litre of black-and-white or colour developer can be used to processs 1-1.1m^2 of paper and the bleach/fix has twice that capacity. These figures include at least a 20% safety margin.

Working in a dish, when it will be necessary to use a relatively large amount of solution, one litre of black and white or colour developer should easily process 12-15 20 × 25cm sheets. The bleach/fix capacity is 2-2.5 times more. It is a good idea to work out the volume needed for the number of prints to be processed at a time, since part-used solutions do not keep.

This time-temperature diagram gives the relationship between time of immersion and temperature for the three baths and the final wash. Curve 1 refers to the first, black-and-white, development, 2 to the colour developer, 3 — identical to 2 — to the bleach-fix, and 4 to the final wash. The corrected times may be considered valid over the range 28-38°C.

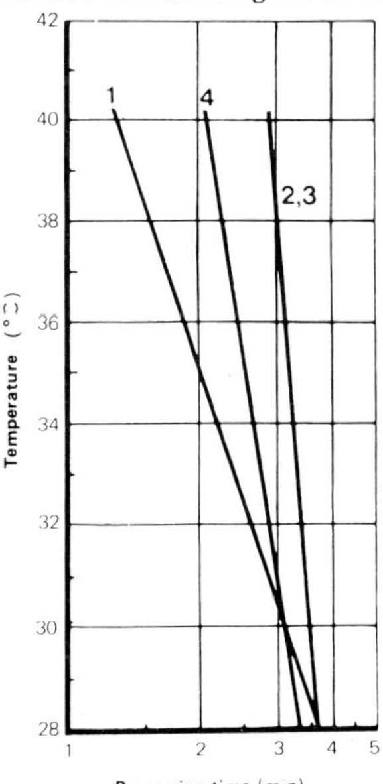

Keeping qualities of unused solutions:

Black-and-white developer: 2-3 months
Colour developer, without CD-4: 3 months
Colour developer made up: 2-4 weeks
Blech/fix made up: 1-2 months
A and B not mixed: 3-4 months

The keeping qualities of part-used bottles are reduced by 30-50%, according to the storage conditions—darkness, well-stoppered bottles and temperature 18-20°C—and exhaustion.

Formulae

Black-and-white developer (pH: 10.1-10.2)

Phenidone	0.5g
(*or* metol: 2.0g)	
Sodium sulphite (anhydrous)	40.0g
Hydroquinone	6.0g
Sodium carbonate (anhydrous)	40.0g
Potassium bromide	1.4g
Sodium thiocyanate 20% solution	7.0ml

Potassium iodide 0.1% solution	6.0ml
Sodium hydroxide 40% solution *as required to adjust pH*	0.5-2ml
Water to make	1000.0ml

Colour developer (pH: 10.1-10.2)

Benzyl alcohol 50%	40.0ml
Hydroxylamine sulphate	3.0g
Sodium sulphite (anhydrous)	2.5g
Sodium carbonate (anhydrous)	30.0g
Potassium bromide	1.0g
6-nitro-benzimidazole nitrate 0.2% soln	10.0ml
Sodium hydroxide 40% *as required to adjust pH*	2.5-3ml
Before use add: CD-4 (Kodak)	4.0g
Water to make	1000.0ml

A 25% CD-4 solution may be conveniently used, taking 16ml per litre:

CD-4	25.0g
Potassium metabisulphite (crystalline)	2.0g
Water to make	100.0ml
	(keeps 2-3 months)

It is best to mix the 50% benzyl alcohol, first by stirring into 700ml of water before adding the solid chemicals. The 50% solution is made up:

Benzyl alcohol	250.0ml
Diethylene glycol	250.0ml
Total	500.0ml

The print base whiteness may be improved by adding 5-10ml/l of a liquid optical brightener, such as Sandoz Leucophore SHR, to this solution.

Bleach/fix (pH: 7.0-7.2)

Solution *A:*	
EDTA acid	6.0g
EDTA NaFe or NH_4Fe (Merck)	60.0g (see note below)
Potassium iodide	2.0g
Ammonia 33% *as required to adjust pH*	12-14ml
Water to make	500.0ml
Solution *B:*	
Ammonium thiosulphite (crystalline)	120.0g
Potassium metabisulphite (crystalline)	5.0g
Water to make	500.0ml

In use take 1 part *A* with 1 part *B*. The pH of this bath when ready to use should be between 6.5 and 6.8. Any adjustment necessary can be made with ammonia or 20% acetic acid.

The ferric-ammonium salt of EDTA is much more easily soluble than Sequestrene NaFe, but the latter may be substituted and costs rather less.

Conclusions and general notes

With the alternative formulae given we have obtained excellent colour prints, comparable with those from the makers own solutions.

Ektachrome 14RC Improved has better thermal stability than its predecessor. It may be kept for 1-2 months in an ambient temperature of 18-25°C without its characteristics being noticeably changed. Nevertheless, it is advisable, as far as possible, to keep it at a lower temperature, around 10°C, or even in a deep freeze −18°C to −22°C, which gives it a life expectancy of up to a year. Do not forget that the main enemy of photographic material is damp. On taking the boxes from the deep freeze or refrigerator, let them temper for 2-4 hr before opening, so as to avoid the formation of condensation.

Exposure latitude has been improved compared with the earlier paper and a 6-12sec bracket gave acceptable prints, when the true exposure was 8sec. However, 4sec gave marked under-exposure. These tests were carried out with a low contrast transparency.

14RC Improved has greatly increased speed, considerably higher than that of Cibachrome—a fact which can sometimes be inconvenient, especially for small and medium-size prints. For instance we found it necessary to work with the following exposure conditions when enlarging an Ektachrome 35mm transparency on to a 20 × 25cm paper: using a Chromega B enlarger with dichroic head and a 48mm Angenieux lens, a 6sec exposure at f/11 with 20Y 20M filtration was required, compared with 14sec at f/5.6 with 50Y 10C filtration for Cibachrome.

The colour balance is very satisfactory, approaching that of Cibachrome. Visual contrast seems to us slightly lower than on the earlier RC14. As regards definition, image sharpness, although entirely acceptable, is not as good as Cibachrome.

In short, our view is that the Ektachrome 14RC Improved paper provides a first-class material for positive/positive printing, easy to handle, simple to process, whose rendition will satisfy many amateur enthusiasts looking for a material with a good quality to price balance.

We must reiterate that Ektachrome 14RC paper is in course of replacement by Ektachrome 22 paper. The new material *cannot* be processed in the Ektaprint R-14 process or the alternative solutions given above but must be processed in the new Ektachrome R-3 process.

REFERENCES

The majority of the formulations given in the colour processing sections derive from independent investigations by the late Ernest Ch. Gehret and were originally published in *The British Journal of Photography*. The author continued to bring these up to date as the materials evolved until his death in April 1981. Subsequent revision has been carried out by George Ashton.

The principal references including those of obsolete processes no longer included in *The British Journal of Photography* are:

Reversal colour processing

Agfachrome 50S/50L, *2 February 1974*
Ektachrome E3, *25 April 1969*
GAF 64, 100, 200, 500, T/190, *11 March 1966*
Orwochrom UT18 and UT21, *28 February 1966*
Peruchrome C18, *9 September 1960*
Etachrome E-6, *28 August and 4 September 1981*

Colour negative films

Kodacolor X, Ektacolor Professional, *13 February 1959 and 15 July 1960*
Kodacolor II, *12 July 1974*

Colour print papers

Ektacolor 37RC, *11 January and 18 June 1974*

Colour reversal papers

Cibachrome Print, *26 December 1975*
Ektachrome 14RC Improved, *15 April 1977.* ■

PROCESSING BLACK & WHITE

IN SPITE of the fact that today the majority of photographs are made on colour film there is still a number of markets where black-and-white film is an essential sensitised material. The majority of pictures made for the 'fine art' photographic market are in black and white, apart from aesthetic considerations, by reason of its greater manipulability and the long life of the images in archive. In the professional markets the newspaper industry is perhaps the best example of continuing B&W practice. The major manufacturers of sensitised products thus produce general purpose black-and-white films for pictorial purposes as well as a range of more specialised products such as x-ray film and the films used for the production of gravure and litho printing plates.

The list which follows is comprehensive in so far as manufacturers is concerned — it includes all those in Europe, Japan and the United States — but covers only those medium contrast films intended for general purpose pictorial photography which are generally available. It does not, therefore, include films for more specialised purposes, such as aerial photography or motion picture photography; nor does it include general purpose films which are available only to special order.

In a number of cases manufacturers actually produce a much wider range of black-and-white films than the listing would seem to suggest; the Eastman Kodak Company and its factories throughout the world, in particular, still list a very large number of monochrome films which are available only with modest or large minimum order requirements for general or specialised use — details of these can best be obtained directly from the companies concerned.

All the films listed are made by the manufacturer named and no 'own-brand' or 'private label' films are included, although a number of manufacturers continue to produce material for sale in this way.

Film	Manufacturer or Distributor	ISO Speed	Sizes									Remarks
			110	126	135	Bulk 35mm	127	120	220	Bulk 70mm	Sheet	
Agfa Isopan	Agfa-Gevaert AG Leverkusen, Germany	125		•	•			•				
Agfaortho 25	Agfa-Gevaert	25			•						•	
Agfapan 25	Agfa-Gevaert	25			•	•		•			•	
Agfapan 100	Agfa-Gevaert	100			•	•		•			•	
Agfapan 200	Agfa-Gevaert										•	
Agfapan 400 Professional	Agfa-Gevaert	400			•	•		•			•	
Agfa Dia Direct	Agfa-Gevaert	32			•							Direct reversal
Efke R and KB 14	Fotokemika, Zagreb, Yugoslavia	20			•	•		•				Adox licence
Efke R and KB 17	Fotokemika	40			•	•		•				Adox licence
Efke R and KB 21	Fotokemika	100			•	•		•				Adox licence
Fortepan 100	Forte, 2601 Vac, Vam u2, POB 100 Hungary	100			•	•		•				
Fortepan 200	Forte	200			•	•			•			
Fortepan 400	Forte	400			•	•		•				
Neopan SS	Fuji Photo Film Co Ltd, Tokyo, Japan	100			•							
Neopan 400	Fuji	400			•							
Pan F	Ilford Ltd, Mobberley, Cheshire	50			•	•		•				
FP4	Ilford	125			•	•		•	•		•	
HP5	Ilford	400			•	•		•	•		•	
XP 1-400	Ilford	50-1600			•	•		•				Chromogenic monochrome
Technical Pan 2415	Kodak Ltd, Hemel Hempstead, Herts HP1 1JU	25-50			•	•		•			•	

Film	Manufacturer or Distributor	ISO Speed	Sizes									Remarks
			110	126	135	Bulk 35mm	127	120	220	Bulk 70mm	Sheet	
Panatomic-X	Kodak Ltd	32			•	•		•				
High Speed Infrared	Kodak Ltd	50-125			•							with filter
Verichrome Pan	Kodak Ltd	125	•	•			•	•				
Plus-X Pan	Kodak Ltd	125			•	•		•	•	•	•	
Tri-X Pan	Kodak Ltd	400			•	•		•	•	•	•	
Recording 2475	Kodak Ltd	1000			•							
Royal-X Pan	Kodak Ltd	1250						•				
Sakurapan SS	Konishiroku Photo Industry Co Ltd, Tokyo	100			•			•				
Sakurapan SSS Professional	Konishiroku	200									•	
Sakurapan 400	Konishiroku	400			•							
Sakura Infrared 750	Konishiroku	—			•			•				
Labaphot SW 100	Labaphot Louis Langebartels GmbH, Berlin	100			•							
Black & White	3M Italia SpA, 20090 Milan, Italy	125			•	•		•			•	
Negrapan 21	Negra Industrial SA, Barcelona	100	•	•	•	•		•				
Tura 22	Tura GmbH, Duren 1, Germany	125	•	•	•							
Tura P150 Professional	Tura GmbH	125			•	•		•				
Tura P400 Professional	Tura GmbH	400			•	•		•				
Valca F-22	Valca SA, Bilbao, Spain	125		•	•	•	•	•				
Valca H-27	Valca, SA	400			•	•		•			•	
Orwo NP 15	VEB Filmfabrik Wolfen, 4440 Wolfen 1, DDR	25			•	•	•	•	•	•		
NP 22	VEB Filmfabrik	125			•	•	•	•	•		•	
Np 27	VEB Filmfabrik	400			•	•	•	•	•		•	
NP 30	VEB Filmfabrik	800						•				
Polapan 35mm	Polaroid Corp, USA	125				•						Continuous tone direct reversal in Autoprocess system

PROCESSING BLACK & WHITE FILMS

Negative Developers

FINE GRAIN FORMULAE

All the formulae included here will give some refinement of grain over the developers in the other sections at a given exploitation of a film's speed. The actual degree of refinement will closely relate to the film speed reached *vis-à-vis* the normal ISO rating. Any increase in speed will give some increase in grain, although this can be kept to a minimum in carefully balanced formulae. On the other hand, very fine grain will only be obtained at some, say ½ stop, loss of film speed. When maximum sharpness and definition are required, refer to the Acutance Developer section; this gain may be at the expense of a slight increase in granularity and some loss of middle-tone gradation.

MEDIUM FINE GRAIN

D-76

Metol	2.0g
Sodium sulphite, anhydrous	100.0g
Hydroquinone	5.0g
Borax	2.0g
Water to	1000ml
D-76 Replenisher	
Metol	3.0g
Sodium sulphite	100.0g
Hydroquinone	7.5g
Borax	20.0g
Water to	1000ml

This developer has come to be taken as a standard against which the granularity, speed, sharpness and definition given by other developers is compared. Thus a formula will be said to give such and such speed increase or loss, increased or less granularity, or higher acutance than D-76. It is also marketed as ID-11. The use of the replenisher quadruples the life of the developer, which is otherwise about ten films per litre. Use of replenisher without dilution to maintain level of solution in tank D-76 gives some rise in activity on use and storage, the addition of 14g/litre of boric acid crystals provides additional buffering, which will even out its action and give greater contrast control, with a 10-20% increase in developing time.

Adox M-Q Borax

Metol	2.0g
Sodium sulphite, anhydrous	80.0g
Hydroquinone	4.0g
Borax	4.0g
Potassium bromide	0.5g
Water to	1000ml

This variant formula of D-76 gives slightly better sharpness with a slower contrast rise. Development times are 10-20% longer. It is closely related to the ISO developer for miniature films, and the Ansco M-Q Borax formula. For a Phenidone variant of this formula, see FX-18 below.

ID-68 Ilford P-Q Fine Grain formula

Sodium sulphite	85.0g
Hydroquinone	5.0g
Borax	7.0g
Boric acid	2.0g
Phenidone	0.13g
Potassium bromide	1.0g
Water to	1000ml

This buffered borax formula gives a marked film speed increase over D-76—about 30-60%, with a minimum increase in granularity, and good sharpness. Times 6-12min at 20° (68°F). The developer, to be used undiluted, has a minimum change of activity with use. Results are comparable to Ilford 'Microphen', development times for which may be used as an 'initial guide'.

D-23

Metol	7.5g
Sodium sulphite, anhydrous	100.0g
Water to	1000ml

Increase development time by 10% after each film, until 8-10 films per litre have been processed. Use of replenisher extends life to 25 rolls per litre. Negligible film speed loss.

D-23 Replenisher

Metol	10.0g
Sodium Sulphite, anhydrous	100.0g
Kodalk	20.0g
Water to	1000ml

Add 20ml for each 36 exposure length or 120 size rollfilm, discarding some developer if necessary. The amount applies to replenishment of 1 litre of developer or more. Replenisher identical to that for D-25.

This developer by R. W. Henn and J. I. Crabtree is the simplest medium fine grain formula. In general it gives good sharpness with slight resolution loss on some films; it is softer working than the D-76 type, and may give a slight increase in granularity; film speed very closely approaches normal. Those workers beginning to weigh and make up their own solutions are recommended to try this formula in use with slow, medium speed films. Diluted 1+3 it resembles the Windisch compensating formula—see page 100—developing time 20-30min approximately for slow and medium speed films. Use once and discard. With the Metol reduced to 5g it becomes Ferrania R23, giving still greater compensation for exposure errors and for high contrast subject.

D-76d, D76b, Agfa 14, Agfa 15

D-76d is a 'buffered borax' version of D-76 (see also notes to D-76) giving greater contrast control, more consistent results on re-use, with a slight speed loss, and 25-50% time increase. Agfa 14 gives results similar to D-23 with similar times. D-76b is a motion picture and variable density sound track developer giving softer results than D-76 with similar times. Agfa 15 is suitable for some modern films notably the slow and medium speed ones, times 25% less than D-76 or ID-11, times which are given in manufacturer's data sheets. The use of these formulae has fallen off in recent years, with the exception perhaps of D-76d. (See also the Ilford published P-Q fine grain formula ID-68 for a Phenidone buffered-borax developer above).

Constituents	Quantities in grams D-76d	Agfa 14	D-76b	Agfa 15
Metol	2	4.5	2.75	8
Sodium sulphite, anhydrous	100	85	100	125
Hydroquinone	5	—	2.75	—
Sodium carbonate, anhydrous	—	—	—	11.5
Borax	8	—	2.5	—
Boric acid	8	—	—	—
Potassium bromide	—	0.5	—	1.5
Water			to 1 litre	

'FX' FINE-GRAIN DEVELOPERS

This series of fine grain formulae was proposed by G. W. Crawley after lengthy research into the development process. (*Brit J Photog,* Vol 107, 2, 9, 16, 23, 30 December (1960) and *ibid*, Vol 108, 6, 13, 27 January (1961)). He found that when the third quality of acutance was added to the requirements of minimum granularity and full film speed, changes might be advantageously made to the type of alkalinity and buffer system employed in a developer. Furthermore, makes and types of film differed in the alkali-buffer restrainer system required to obtain best definition. **FX-4** is a variant of the Adox and ISO evolution of D-76 referred to above, giving higher film speed and more compensation. **FX-5** gives very fine grain with the natural concomitant slight speed loss. **FX-11** is balanced solely to give the fullest possible speed increase with the minimum granularity increase. **FX-19** is a D-23 type formula giving, however, fuller emulsion speed. All modern films may be developed in any of these developers. **FX-15** is the more suitable for the very fastest, as it gives the biggest contrast rise on extended development for low brightness range subjects. **FX-18** is a P-Q version of D-76 claiming slightly higher resolving power, with a slight reduction in grain and minimal speed increase allowing use at stock strength without speed loss. FX-15 is a further development of FX-3, now omitted, giving ⅓rd stop effective speed increase over FX-3, with similar grain and an improved characteristic curve, similar to Paterson Acutol-S, now discontinued.

In the FX-4 and FX-5 formulae dissolve a pinch of the sulphite first, then the metol, next the rest of the sulphite. Always dissolve the hydroquinone with or before the Phenidone, to prevent any temporary oxidation of the latter.

Approximate meter-settings/makers rating

FX-5 −30%; FX-18 +30%; FX-19 +30%; FX-4 +60%;
FX-15 +60%; FX-11 +80%-100%

Constituents	Quantities in grams FX-5	FX-19	FX-15	FX-4	FX-11	FX-18
Metol	5	—	3.5	1.50	—	—
Phenidone	—	0.75	0.1	0.25	0.25	0.10
Hydroquinone	—	7	2.25	6	5	6
Glycin	—	—	—	—	1.50	—
Sodium sulphite anhydrous	125	100	100	100	125	100
Borax	3	—	2.5	2.5	2.5	2.5
Sodium carbonate	—	—	1.0	—	—	—
Sodium metabisulphite	—	—	0.5	—	—	0.35
Boric acid	1.5	—	—	—	—	—
Potassium bromide	0.5	—	1.5	0.5	0.5	1.6
Water			to 1 litre			

Average Capacity

FX-5	4.5 films per 600ml, 20% increase after each film. 8-10 films per 1200ml, 10% increase after each film.
FX-19	5 films per 600ml, 10% increase after each film.
FX-11, FX-15	5-6 films per 600ml, 10% increase after each film.
FX-18, FX-4	6-8 films per 600ml, 10% increase after second or third and the subsequent ones.

Development times

In minutes at 20°C (68°F), using one spiral tank inversion a minute or the recommended normal in larger vessels.

Ilford	FX-19	FX-15	FX-4	FX-11	FX-18
Pan-F (MF)		4	4		6.5
Pan-F (RF)	as for	5	5		7.5
FP4 (MF)	FX-15	5	4.5		9
FP4 (RF)	but	7.5	7		9
HP5 (RF)	slower	8	7	as for	8
HP5 (MF)	contrast rise	7	6	FX-15	7
Mark 5		7	6		7

Kodak	FX-19	FX-11 FX-15	FX-5	FX-4	FX-18
Pan-X (MF)		5	8	5	5.5
Pan-X (RF)	as for	6	9	5.5	6
Plus-X Pan (MF)	FX-15 but	5	9	5	5
Plus-X Pan Prof (RF)	slower contrast	6.5	9	6	7
Veripan	rise	7	10	7	7.5
Tri-X (MF)		7	10	7	8
Tri-X (RF)		9	12	9	10
Royal-X		10-15	Pointless	9-15	15

Changes in development times

Make a note of film batch numbers, and when using a new batch, watch for any unusual contrast change and adjust development time in future accordingly. The brief times above (e.g. on Ilford slow materials) will be found most convenient once temperature and agitation are standardised. Alteration of times by 25% will not affect meter setting in normal work, if required for contrast adjustment FX-18 times are usually very close to those for D-76 and ID-11.

VERY FINE GRAIN

FX-5b

Metol	4.5kg
Sodium sulphite, anhydrous	125.0g
Kodalk (sodium metaborate)	2.25g
Sodium metabisulphite	1.0g
Potassium bromide	0.5g
Water to	1000ml

FX-5b Replenisher

Metol	7.0g
Sodium sulphite, anhydrous	125.0g
Kodalk (sodium metaborate)	25.0g
Sodium metabisulphite	—
Potassium bromide	1.0g
Water to	1000ml

Twenty per cent development time increase after first film until four or five films have been processed per 600ml or 10% increase until eight or ten films have been developed in 1200ml. Use replenisher to maintain level of tank until twenty-five rolls per litre are processed. Visual contrast is lower than the printing contrast. This formula gives true fine grain with good sharpness and the minimum loss of film speed (30-50%) necessary to achieve very fine grain. Results resemble those in the original two-powder pack 'Microdol', found very suitable for Ilford films amongst others, although replaced in Kodak usage by the later formula Microdol-X, giving improved definition on Kodak films.

Development times

In minutes at 20°C (68°F).

Pan F (MF)—10, Pan F (RF)—12, FP4 (MF)—8, FP4 (RF)—12, HP5 (MF)—11, HP5 (RF)—13.

ACUTANCE FORMULAE

For maximum sharpness at some loss of fine grain

Pyrocatechin Surface Developer (Windisch)

Stock A	
Pyrocatechin	80.0g
Sodium sulphite, anhydrous	12.5g
Water to	1000ml
Stock B	
Sodium hydroxide	100g in 1000ml

N.B. The excess Pyrocatechin with minimum sulphite gives the surface development effect.

Working solution

Take 25ml of *A*, 15ml of *B* and make up to 1000ml. Develop 15-20min at 20°C according to film type. The developer keeps reasonably in stock, but deteriorates rapidly when mixed. It is used once and then discarded. Specially recommended by Windisch for Adox/Efke films. Emulsion speed approximately doubled.

N.B. It is not best to make up more of *B* than will be used rapidly since the activity will decrease with solution of atmospheric CO_2. If possible hold only *A* as a stock, and add sodium hydroxide weighed up and dissolved on the occasion of use. Working concentration is 1.5g sodium hydroxide per litre.

The Beutler Developer

Stock A	
Metol	10.0g
Sodium sulphite, anhydrous	50.0g
Water to	1000ml
Stock B	
Sodium carbonate, anhydrous	50.0g
Water to	1000ml

Working solution: 1 part *A*, 1 part *B*, 8 parts water.
Developing times: 8-15min at 20°C (68°F).
See notes on making up FX-1 below for further details of preparing concentrated liquid developers.

'FX' ACUTANCE DEVELOPERS

The following formulae were proposed by G. W. Crawley after research into the design of acutance developers.

FX-1 is fundamentally a variant of the Beutler formula claiming better contrast control, together with a mechanism to enhance 'adjacency' effects; these are also enhanced by the lower concentration of developing agent.

FX-1 High acutance developer, speed increase ½-1 stop

Working solution	
Metol	0.5g
Sodium sulphite, anhydrous	5.0g
Sodium carbonate, anhydrous	2.5g
Potassium iodide 0.001% solution	5.0ml
Water to	1000ml

Use once and discard. Do not use Calgon, etc.

Concentrated stock solutions *(do not use Calgon, etc)*

A Metol	5.0g
Sodium sulphite, anhydrous	50.0g
Potassium iodide 0.001%	50.0ml
Water to	1000ml
B Sodium carbonate, anhydrous	25.0g
Water to	1000ml

Making up

A Use water boiled for just 3min then cooled to about 30°C. Dissolve a pinch of the weighed sulphite before the metol. Filter and bottle. This solution will keep a year unopened or until discoloration begins—a light tint can be ignored. If 50ml of the water is replaced by isopropyl alcohol, keeping qualities are improved and precipitation in extreme cold avoided. (See FX-2, Making up, *A* for general observations on making up concentrated liquid developers.) Amber glass bottles are preferable to plastic ones.

B Dissolve in water prepared as for *A*.

The 0.001% solution of potassium iodide can be obtained by dissolving 1g in 1000ml of water; if 100ml of that solution is diluted to 1000ml, then 100ml of this solution again diluted to 1000ml will give a 0.001% solution. This keeps for two years at least.

Working solution—use once and discard.

One part *A*, one part *B*, eight parts water. Mix for 2min and allow to stand to ensure homogeneity.

Single solution concentrate

Quantities for *A* and *B* may be dissolved together in 1000ml of water to form a single solution developer, reject for use when discoloured. 50ml of the water may be replaced by isopropyl alcohol (see making up *A* above).

Agitation

4 inversions each minute in small tanks up to 300ml capacity, 6-8 in larger ones. (See also notes to FX-2).

General Notes

FX-1 demands first-class lenses, precise exposure and no camera movement; also first-class enlarging lenses. Highest resolution and definition will be obtained on Kodak Technical Pan film which will then resolve a *BJ* classified advertisement page at 10-12ft from a suitable 50mm lens on the 35mm stock.

Development times for FX-1 and FX-2 at 20°C (68°F):

Agfapan 25 (MF)	12min	Ilford FP4 (RF)	14min
Agfapan 25 (RF)	13min	Kodak Technical Pan (MF)	12min
Agfapan 100 (RF)	14min	Kodak Pan-X (MF)	13min
Agfapan 100 (MF)	13min	Kodak Pan-X (RF)	15min
Ilford Pan F (MF)	12min	Kodak Plus-X Pan (MF)	11min
Ilford Pan F (RF)	14min	Plus-X Pan Professional	12min
Ilford FP4 (MF)	13min	Kodak Verichrome-Pan	14min

Equipment contrast variations are more obvious in nonsolvent developers and these times may need individual adjustment, particularly in FX-2. For future 'Changes in development times,' see under that heading in FX series of Fine Grain developers, page 90.

FX-1b* Acutance Developer, ½ stop speed increase

Add to FX-1 working solution (with or without iodide) 40g per litre of anhydrous sodium sulphate. The bare solvent action removes surface flare and image spread. Films faster than ASA160 show a definition and grain disadvantage over normal solvent developers. A 2% acetic acid bath may sometimes be necessary to remove white scum. Times approximately two-thirds FX-1 and 2 (see above).

**Originally numbered FX-13.*

FX-2 Acutance developer, 80% speed increase

Working solution	
Metol	2·5g
Sodium sulphite, anhydrous	3·5g
Glycin	0·75g
Potassium carbonate, crystalline	7·5g
*Pinacryptol Yellow 1:2000 solution	3·5ml
Water to	1000ml

Do not use Calgon, etc.
*See 'Chemical Supplies' in introduction.

Stock solutions (see making up below)

A Metol	25.0g
Sodium sulphite, anhydrous	35.0g

Glycin	7.5g
B Potassium carbonate (crystals, not dried)	75.0g
Water to	500ml
C *Pinacryptol Yellow 1:2000 solution	

Making up
Weigh all constituents of *A* and *B* and place on plain pieces of paper separately.
A In 1400ml of water, boiled for just 3min, then cooled to about 30°C, dissolve a pinch of the sulphite, next the metol, then the rest of the sulphite and add the glycin. If the glycin remains as a yellow suspension after 3min mixing, add a pinch from the weighed carbonate and restir, repeating the operation if it still fails to dissolve. Alternatively replace 50ml of the water by isopropyl alcohol which will dissolve the glycin. (Isopropyl alcohol is available without licence on order from any chemist quite cheaply. Its addition also improves keeping qualities and prevents precipitation in extreme cold, and it is used for these purposes in some commercial developers.) Make up to 500ml. Filter and store in filled bottles. This solution should keep a year unopened, but should be rejected when discoloured to a *deep* yellow (glycin developers are usually a golden tint on making up); partly used concentrate should also be rejected when deeply discoloured. Fresh glycin is a reflectant gold yellow in colour. For best keeping, do not aerate whilst mixing and use spotless vessels. Concentrated liquid developers keep indefinitely until oxidation commences, usually from foreign matter in the solution; deterioration then proceeds rapidly once initiated. The use of distilled water is unnecessary; if used, the mixed solution should still be filtered. Do not use Calgon or other sequestering agents in high dilution developers.
B Dissolve the potassium carbonate crystals (the bulk remaining if any was necessary to dissolve the glycin in *A*) in 400ml water prepared as for *A* and make up to 500ml. This solution maintains activity indefinitely in a full bottle, renew after two months if half used, for consistency.
C Keeps indefinitely away from strong light. After two years, however, reject as an increase in activity may occur thereafter. For working solution, take *A* 50ml, *B* 50ml, *C* 3.5ml to make 1 litre developer. Mix well. Use once and discard.

Development times
As for FX-1.

General notes
If agitation is reduced to every other minute or third minute with an increase in time up to ⅓ to ½, negatives of interesting internal gradation and acutance may be obtained. Agitation can be abandoned altogether with a further increase in time. Dilution may be doubled or trebled to form stand developers over 1-2hr at room temperature. This developer is more 'pictorial' than FX-1, which is designed for maximum resolution and definition primarily; FX-2 is far less sensitive to flare, and less demanding on apparatus.

See also Diluted DK-50, opposite under 'General Purpose Formulae'.

FX-16 (Grain effects on high-speed films)

This developer has been specially designed to produce an obtrusive grain structure on films of ISO400 and over, whilst retaining excellent contour sharpness. This retention of sharpness assists in preventing the loss of image quality often found where grain texture has been utilised to give a special effect. The formula is related to the above FX-2 Acutance Developer for slow and medium speed films.

Working solution

50% speed increase	
Metol	0.5g
Glycin	0.5g
Sodium sulphite, anhydrous	4.0g
Sodium carbonate, anhydrous	50.0g
(vide also General Notes)	
*Pinacryptol Yellow 0.05% solution	250ml
Water to	1000ml
*For Kodak Royal-X Pan 350ml/1000ml.	

*If unavailable, 0.5g/litre potassium bromide must be substituted to balance the formula, at some sharpness loss but giving fluffier grain.

Making up
Dissolve the solids in half the total quantity of water at around 30°C, 90°F. Add the dye and make up to the total volume. Make up when required. Use within 6hr, adding dye just before use. Use once and discard. Pinacryptol Yellow dissolves readily in hot, not quite boiling water. The 0.5% solution—1:2000—keeps indefinitely in a brown bottle away from the light: see note *C* to FX-2.

Development times at 20°C (68°F) in minutes.

Kodak	
Royal-X Pan	20
Tri-X (RF)	12
Tri-X (MF)	12
Ilford	
HP5 (RF)	12
HP5 (MF)	10

Agitation
Should be thorough. 10sec/min either rotation or inversion.

General notes
The grain pattern texture produced by FX-16 disturbs resolution of fine detail but sharpness of contours and medium detail is enhanced markedly, hence print impact is excellent. FX-16 is primarily intended as a developer for operators wishing to experiment with grain structure for special effects, but it can also be used with advantage as an 'acutance' developer for fast films when big enlargements are not required. Texture obtrusiveness can be adjusted by varying the negative area used for enlarging, or using different focal length lenses from the same camera position. With slow and medium speed films there is no gain over FX-2 and 'acutance' developers, and contrast difficulties may occur.
If the carbonate is replaced by 50g/litre of sodium metaborate or 'Kodalk' a fluffier grain texture is produced. Development times remain the same or slightly shorter.

GENERAL PURPOSE FORMULAE

Although Universal formulae can be used for general purpose negative development, 'general purpose' is usually applied to formulae unsuitable for development of enlarging papers, and in which some attempt has been made to obtain contrast control or some particular advantage or negative quality obtainable by the use of a developing agent of special properties. Such developers do not make use of a 'solvent' effect, and therefore are not classed as fine-grain developers (see Fine-Grain Developers), as they do not give the minimum graininess possible at a given film-speed. Best control is obtained when such formulae are buffered against changes of alkalinity, for example, D-61A and DK-50. Both these formulae can be used for Kodak Royal-X Pan.

Ilford General Purpose Negative Developer
free from organic restrainers

Sodium sulphite, anhydrous	75.0g
Hydroquinone	8.0g
Sodium carbonate, anhydrous	37.5g
Phenidone	0.25g
Potassium bromide	0.5g
Water to	1000ml

This concentrated developer is diluted as follows:
For *Dish development of films:* 1+2 water.
Developing time: 4min.

For *Tank development:* 1+5 water.
Developing time: 8min.
Developing temperature: 20°C, 68°F.

Kodak General Purpose Negative Developers

Dissolve chemicals in this order	**D-61A**	**DK-50**
Metol	3.1g	2.5g
Sodium sulphite, anhydrous	90.0g	30.0g
Sodium metabisulphite	2.1g	—
Hydroquinone	5.9g	2.5g
Sodium carbonate, anhydrous	11.5g	—
Kodalk (sodium metaborate)	—	10.0g
Potassium bromide	1.7g	0.5g
Water to	1000ml	1000ml

These buffered developers are recommended for development of medium to highest speed rollfilm, sheet film, and plates. D-61A is used in the dish at 1+1 dilution or in tanks at 1+3. Development times for 1+3, between 5 and 10min at 20°C. DK-50 is normally used as recommended by Kodak at full strength. A diluted form of this developer has been proposed independently as giving a useful balance of natural acutance, gradation and speed qualities with controlled contrast rise, this can be made up as follows:

Diluted DK-50 *Film speed normal, good sharpness*

Working solution	
Metol	0.5g
Sodium sulphite, anhydrous	6.0g
Hydroquinone	0.5g
Kodalk (sodium metaborate)	2.5g
Potassium bromide	0.125g
Water to	1000ml

Stock solutions. Calgon may be used
A Make up DK-50 from the full strength formula on this page or from the packaged powder as directed on the commercial pack.
B Dissolve 80g Kodalk in 1 litre boiled, cooled water.
For working solutions use two parts *A*, one part *B*, seven parts water. Use once and discard.

Development times at 20°C (68°F)

Pan F (MF) 6min	Pan-X (RF) 12min
Pan F (RF) 7min	Veripan 13min
FP4 (MF) 8min	HP5 (MF) 10min
FP4 (RF) 9min	HP5 (RF) 12min
Plus-X (MF) 10min	Tri-X (RF) 13min
Plus-X Prof (RF) 11min	Royal-X Pan 15-20min
Pan-X (MF) 10min	

Print Developers

FX-12

This formula is recommended when a universal formula is more often to be used for developing of printing papers and positive materials of all kinds, since it is balanced to obtain stable image colour over the various grades. The chlorquinol should be obtained as fresh as possible—buff brown not deep brown.
Dilutions are: enlarging paper 1+3; lantern slides 1+4; films in tanks 1+7. Development times for films will closely resemble those in recommended universal developers at the same dilutions. RC, resin coated, and polyester, PE base papers develop in 60-75 seconds, and the benzotriazole may be reduced to 20ml/l for shorter, to 60sec, development. Paper based materials need 9-120 seconds.

Sodium sulphite, anhydrous	60.0g
Hydroquinone	10.0g
Chlorquinol	6.0g
Phenidone	0.5g
Sodium carbonate, anhydrous	60.0g
Potassium bromide	1.5g
Benzotriazole solution*	35.0ml
Water to	1000ml

**A solution of 1% benzotriazole dissolved in hot water containing 10% anhydrous sodium carbonate: e.g. 1g benzotriazole in 100ml water with 10g sodium carbonate. Solution can be speeded by adding the benzotriazole first to a few drops of isopropyl alcohol (cheap and easily available).* ■

Stop Baths

Stop Bath 1

Acetic acid glacial	20ml
or	
Acetic acid 28%	75ml
Water to	1000ml

This bath is recommended for negative development and will remove any surface scum formed. It loses its vinegar smell as activity decreases. It is particularly suitable for use before an ammonium thiosulphate fixer.

Stop Bath 2

Sodium metabisulphite	25g
Water, to make	1000ml

An efficient and inexpensive bath, an acid smell denotes its acidity is maintained.

Stop Bath Hardener

Chromic potassium sulphate (chrome alum)	20g
Water to	1000ml

This stop bath has a hardening action and deteriorates in colour from its original purpose to green blue as its action is lost. It is used for negative emulsions normally, although it can be used as a final hardener for paper based prints processed at high temperatures.

Fixers

1 Ammonium Thiosulphate High-Speed Fixer

Ammonium thiosulphate	175g
Sodium sulphite, anhydrous	25g
Glacial acetic acid (98-100%)	10ml
Boric acid (crystalline)	10g
Water to	1000ml

A high-speed fixer with long working life. If hardening action is required, add 10g per litre of aluminium hydroxychloride after a further 5ml of glacial acetic acid to prevent appearance of a cloudy suspension. Fixing time 30-90sec films, 30-60sec papers. For slower action dilute 1+1.

2 Acid Fixing Bath

Sodium thiosulphate crystals ('Hypo')	250g
Sodium metabisulphite	20g
Water to	1000ml

This acid fixer is of standard composition and will work as a general purpose bath for all fixing purposes. If the acid smell is lost it can be topped up again with a little metabisulphite until it is regained.

3 Acid Fixing Bath (Buffered)

Sodium thiosulphite crystals ('Hypo')	250g
Sodium sulphite, anhydrous	25g
Acetic acid glacial	25ml
or Acetic acid 28%	80ml
Water to	1000ml

This is a 'buffered' fixing bath which has improved efficiency during use as a result—it has great tolerance to carry-over of developer.

4 Buffered Acid Fixer Hardener

Sodium thiosulphate crystals ('Hypo')	300g
Water to	1000ml

Add to the above whilst stirring slowly 250ml of the following stock hardening solution:

Sodium sulphite, anhydrous	75g
Acetic acid glacial	65ml
or Acetic acid 28%	235ml
Boric acid (crystals)	50g
Potassium alum	75g
Water to	1000ml

Dissolve these constituents in the order given in half the total quantity of water at about 50°C to dissolve the boric acid quickly.

Process Developers

These are used for copying and process materials, graticules, photomechanical papers, X-ray development, etc; they are not usually suitable for the development of ordinary general photographic materials.

Ilford formulae

Dissolve chemicals in this order

	High contrast	*Med contrast*
Sodium sulphite, anhydrous	150.0g	72.0g
Potassium carbonate, anhydrous	100.0g	—
Sodium carbonate, anhydrous	—	50.0g
Hydroquinone	50.0g	8.8g
Phenidone	1.1g	0.22g
Caustic soda	10.0g	—
Potassium bromide	16.0g	4.0g
Benzotriazole	1.1g	0.1g
Water to make	1000ml	1000ml
	Dilute 1:1 for use	Use undiluted

Medium high contrast hydroquinone caustic developer

A Stock

Sodium metabisulphite	25.0g
Hydroquinone	25.0g
Potassium bromide	25.0g
Water to	1000ml

B Stock

Caustic soda	45.0g
Water to	1000ml

For use mix equal part of **A** and **B** and develop for 2min at 20°C. Rinse well before acid-fixing to avoid stain or use acid stop bath.

High contrast single solution hydroquinone-caustic developer Kodak D-8

Stock Solution

Sodium sulphite, anhydrous	90.0g
Hydroquinone	45.5g
Caustic soda	37.5g
Potassium bromide	30.0g
Water to	1000ml

For use take 2 parts stock solution to 1 part water. Develop for 2min at 20°C. This developer keeps for several weeks bottled, and retains its energy for several hours in the open dish. Without loss of density, the caustic soda may be reduced to 28g in which case the stock solution will keep longer still. ■

THIS YEAR'S PICTURES

COMING fresh to the selection of pictures for this annual I rapidly came face to face with the problem of deciding what my criteria should be. Differing from previous collections I have edited, it is concerned more with single pictures or small portfolios and all taken within the last year. The first decision was to make it only roughly within the last year because it is quite clearly non-productive if a photographer has been working on an extended project not to include the whole of that project even if only part of it was shot in the current twelve months.

The second decision is to accept that the *BJ* covers the whole spectrum of photography not just creative art photography and that, therefore, good commercial, studio, sports photography and so on should be included. This is easier said than done; there was painfully little commercial photography, while sports photography, like any Fleet Street press photography competition, is better suited to the pages of the weekly *BJ* than to a year book. The portfolio of the 'Sports Photographer of the Year' has its place there because only a single and inevitably unrepresentative picture would be used in the *Annual*. The same applies to a number of portfolios sent in from photographers working on local papers; it does not help to have a bit of everything in front of you. The simple solution is just to pick out one single picture but it is just not possible to present a mixed bag in the limited number of pages available.

What a picture editor looks for, or at least, what I am looking for, is work of imagination and talent; competence should be taken for granted. I am looking for the work of photographers who know what they want to say and how to say it. If I am only able for space reasons to choose one picture from such a submission, this is a usually acceptable compromise because the work being of a piece can be represented even if not entirely adequately by a single picture.

Competence is relatively simple to assess, not so easy is this quality of imagination. As a photographer, I once tried to define it as saying that if I had been standing there it is the picture I might have missed. It is not the predictable, it is not the scene that says 'take me'. Some years ago it used to be possible to buy maps of German towns with little arrows on them telling you where to take pictures, they were the *Fotoführerpunkt* and they guaranteed good pictures. Alas, perhaps good pictures to show the folks back home but not for the *BJP Annual*.

Having something different to say is not the same as being deliberately different; amateur magazines love the word 'impact' but impact is not necessarily what is needed in the *Annual*. You need impact perhaps in the daily press to catch the eye of a lethargic reader. Lethargic readers don't buy the *Annual*. A photo needs enough to capture the interest in those first few seconds of looking to seduce you into looking again and again until the image can be enjoyed in all its complexity. It needs that seduction because no one has a right to demand that the reader look at their images even if there is the right to ask that they be taken seriously.

This is another part of my credo and that is that the job of an editor is to act as a midwife to help in the birth of an image of beauty. His efforts and those of the designer and printer should be to help the image come through. It can only happen if there is an inherent respect for the image and for other photographers. Respect however becomes a little thin after unravelling some of the packaging that pictures come in. No-one expects a photographer to make a new set of prints for the *Annual* but huge mounted exhibition prints do try the patience of the lonely viewer. Even worse are those of any size surrounded by miles of sticky tape that make it almost impossible to enter the parcel. The ideal size is about 12 × 10in for black-and-white, single weight unmounted in case the laser scanner is to be used, and always with the name and address on the back. God bless the little sticky labels! I think it helps if prints have to be made specially that they should have slightly wider borders than usual. It makes the handling of them a little bit easier and gives the printing technicians a better chance.

What of this year's selection, done under some pressure it must be said? One portfolio was misplaced and deserved to be in, many others are only represented by one picture when more could have been used if there had been the space. There are, as explained earlier, gaps in the wide coverage simply because the material was not sent in but for my first experience I was very pleased at the amount of serious work and careful photography that had been sent in. Next year submissions will be invited in the *British Journal of Photography* closing on 1 May 1987; I hope there will be a wide and difficult choice of all possible types of photography. It only needs to be good in its class.

Colin Osman

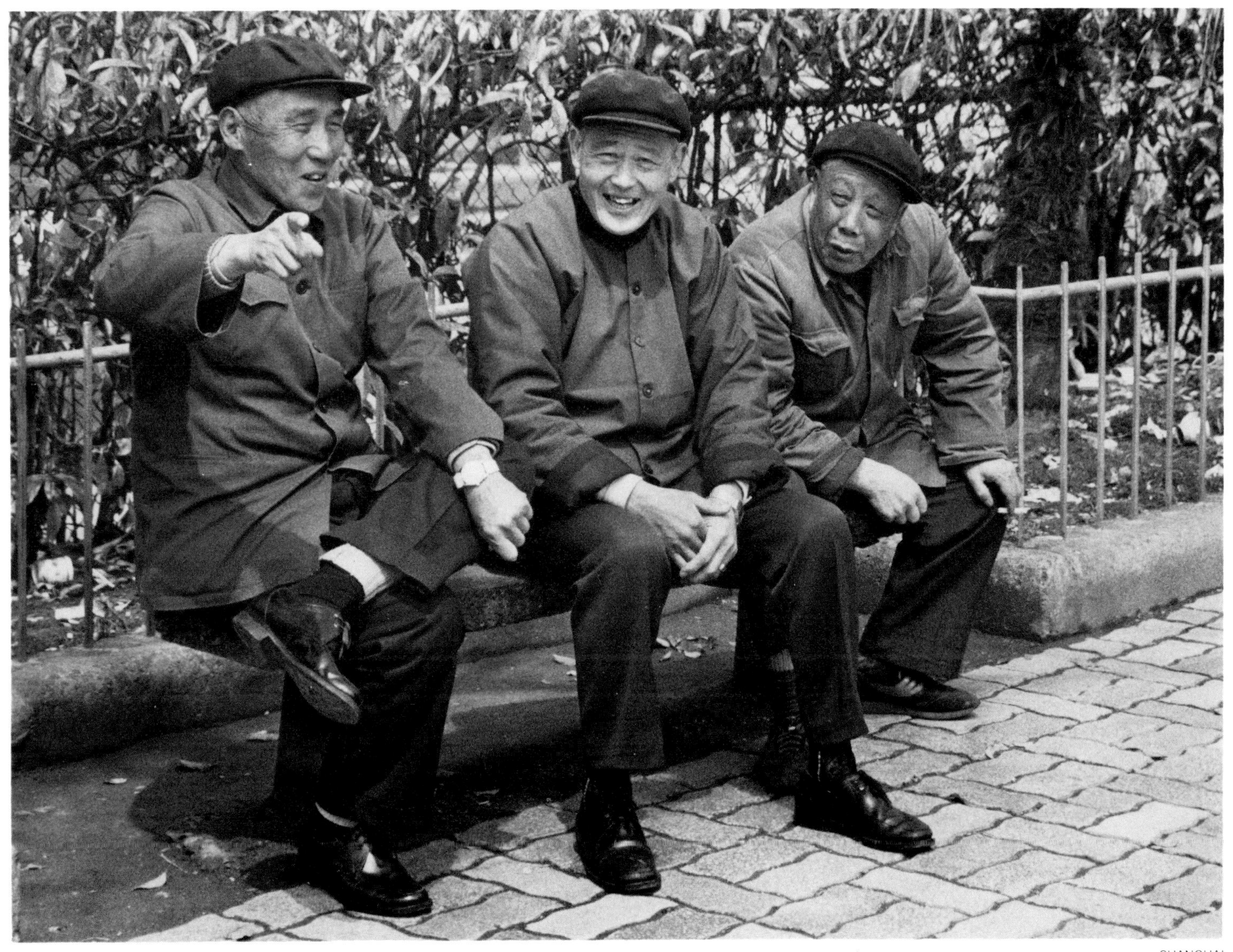

SHANGHAI

MARK RUSSELL WAS TRAINED AT WATFORD COLLEGE AND CITY AND EAST LONDON COLLEGE.
HE IS WORKING AS A FREELANCE PHOTO-JOURNALIST.

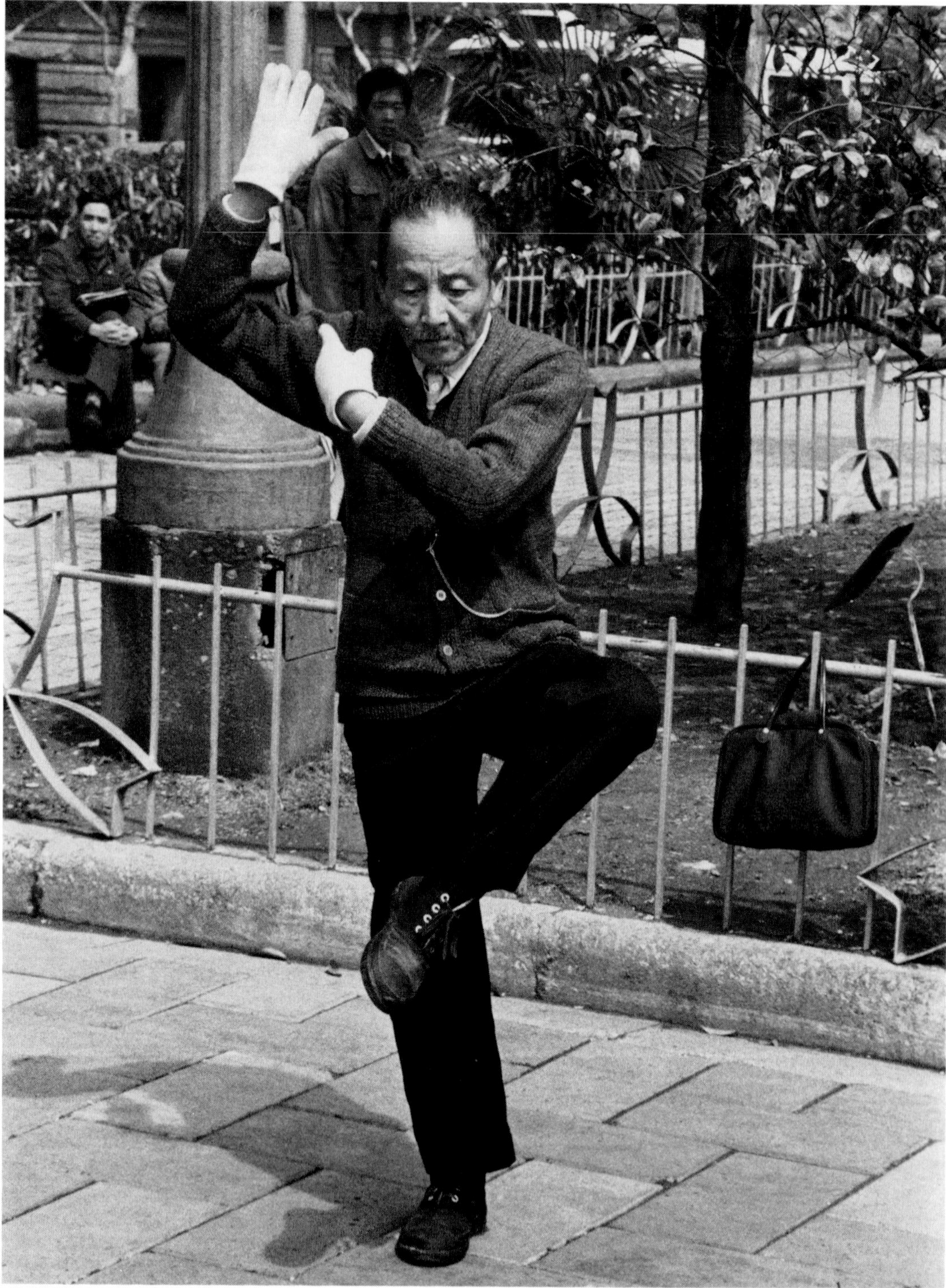

TAI CHI SHANGHAI

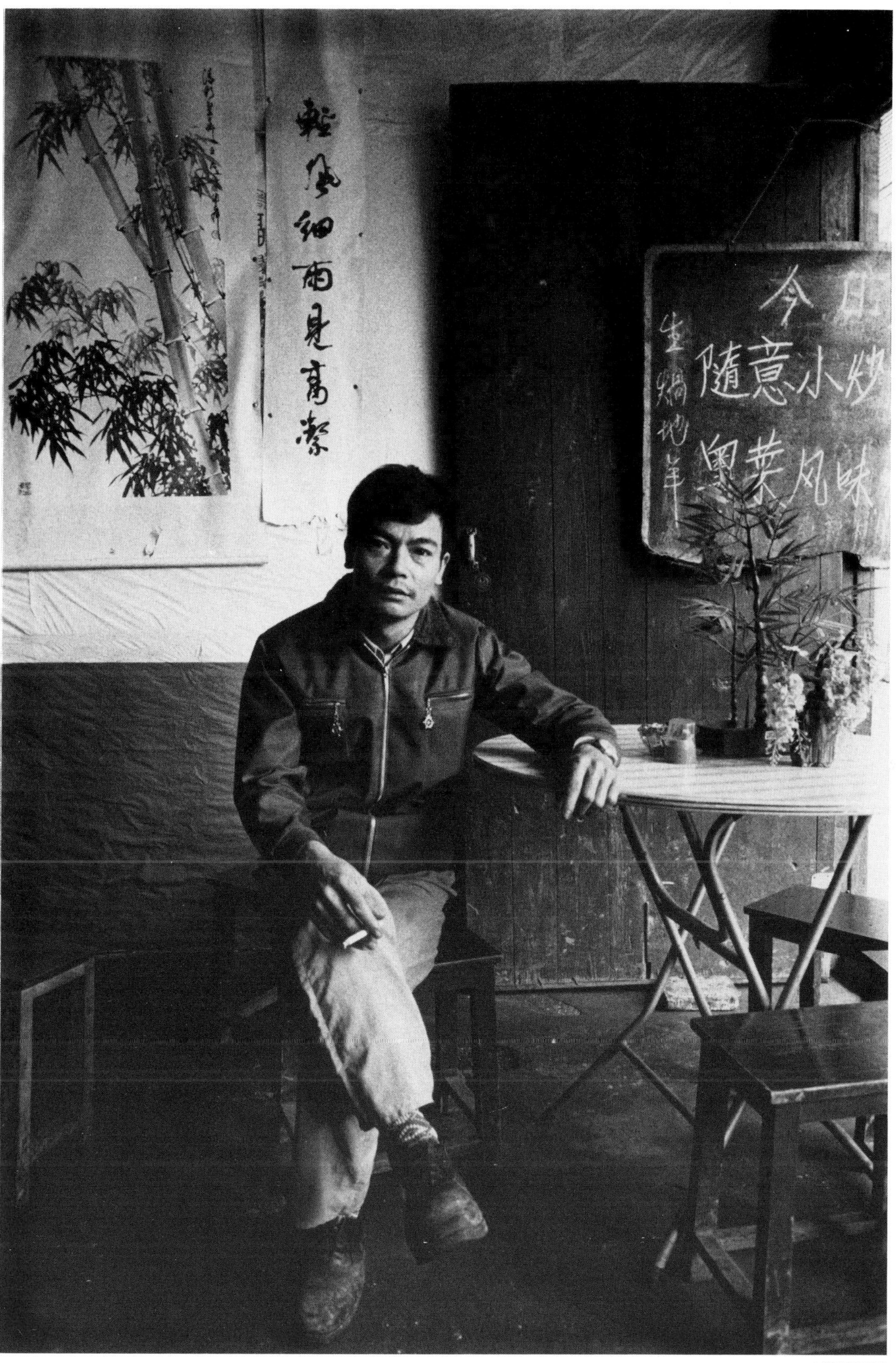

YANGSHOU

MARK RUSSELL

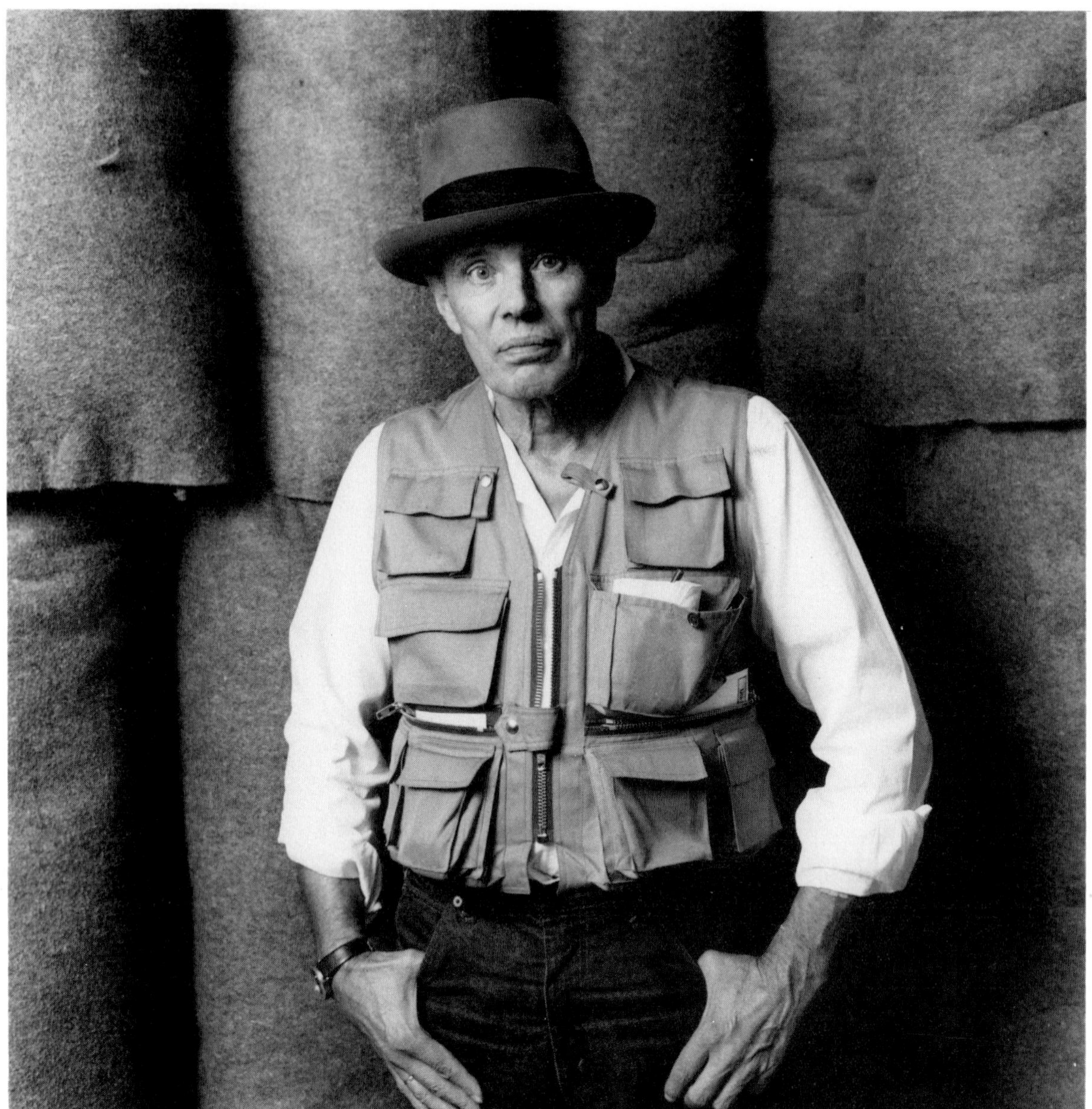

JOSEPH BEUYS

NIGEL MAUDSLEY GRADUATED FROM WOLVERHAMPTON IN 1974. HE IS A PART-TIME LECTURER AT THE CITY OF LONDON POLYTECHNIC AND A FREELANCE PHOTOGRAPHER.

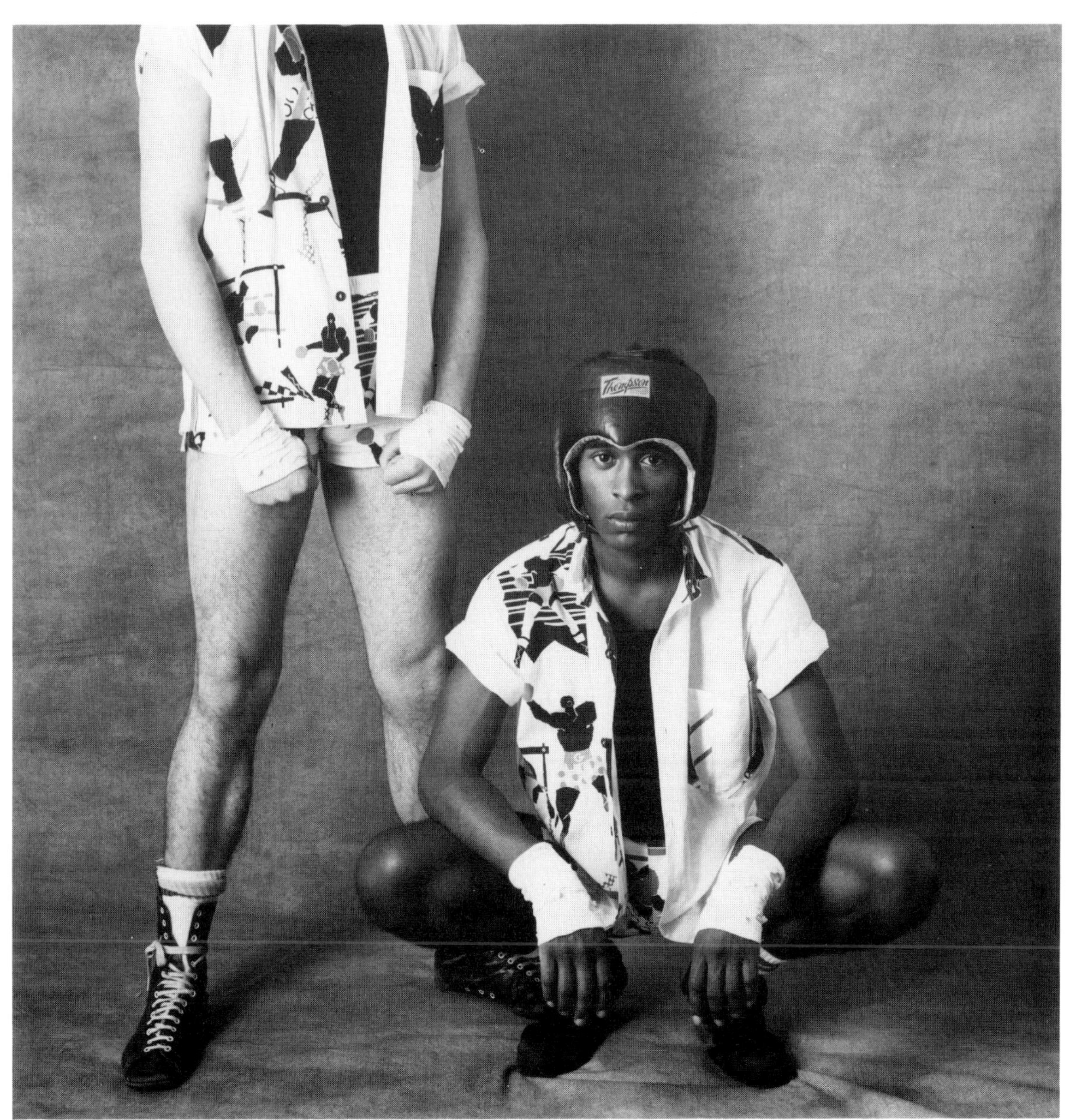

KEITH AND JOHN

102

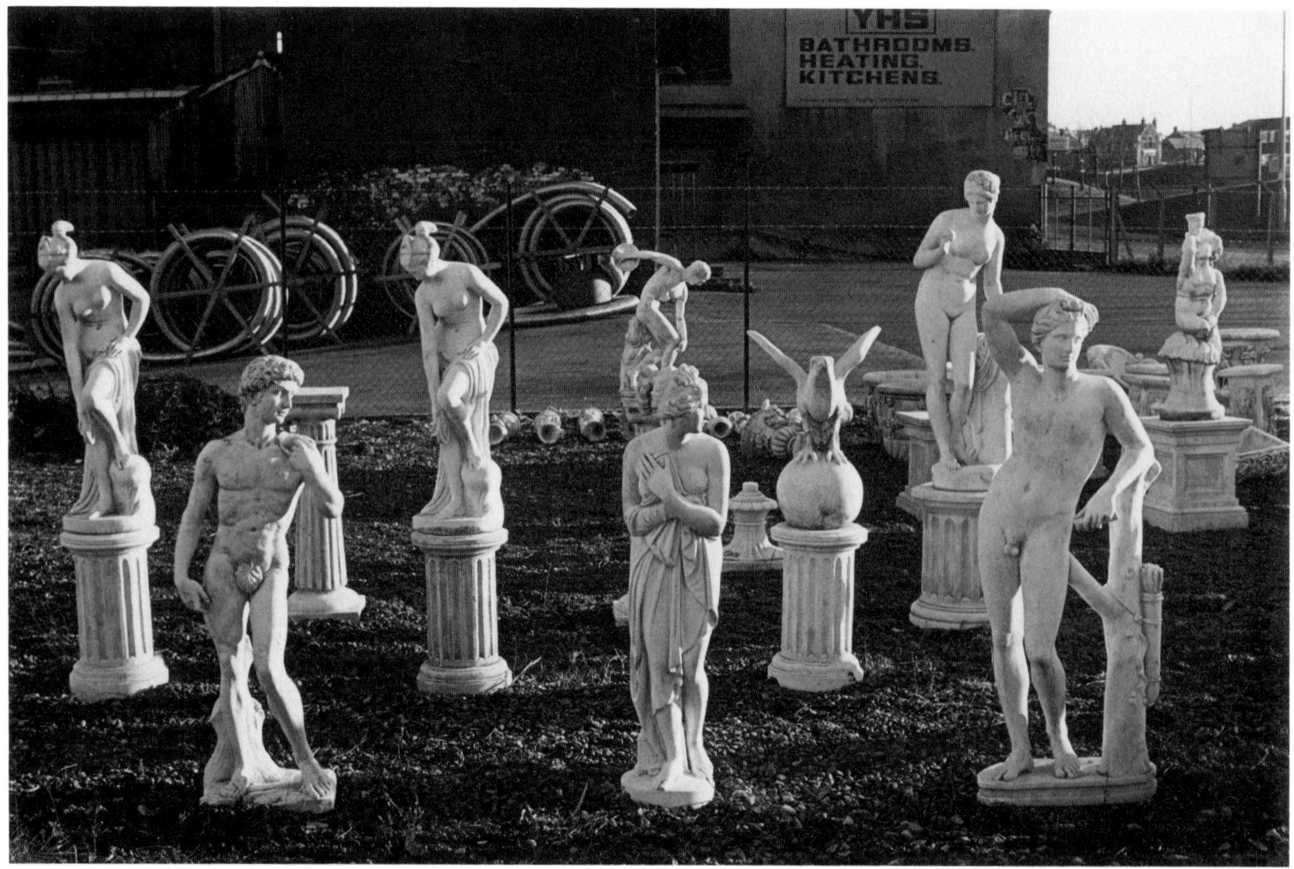

CLASSICAL STATUES, LEEDS

MATT WINTERLICH WAS BORN IN DUBLIN BUT NOW LIVES IN LEEDS WHERE HE STUDIED PHOTOGRAPHY. CURRENTLY WORKING ON SEVERAL PROJECTS INCLUDING MONUMENTS AND ALSO TEACHING YOUNG PEOPLE PHOTOGRAPHY.

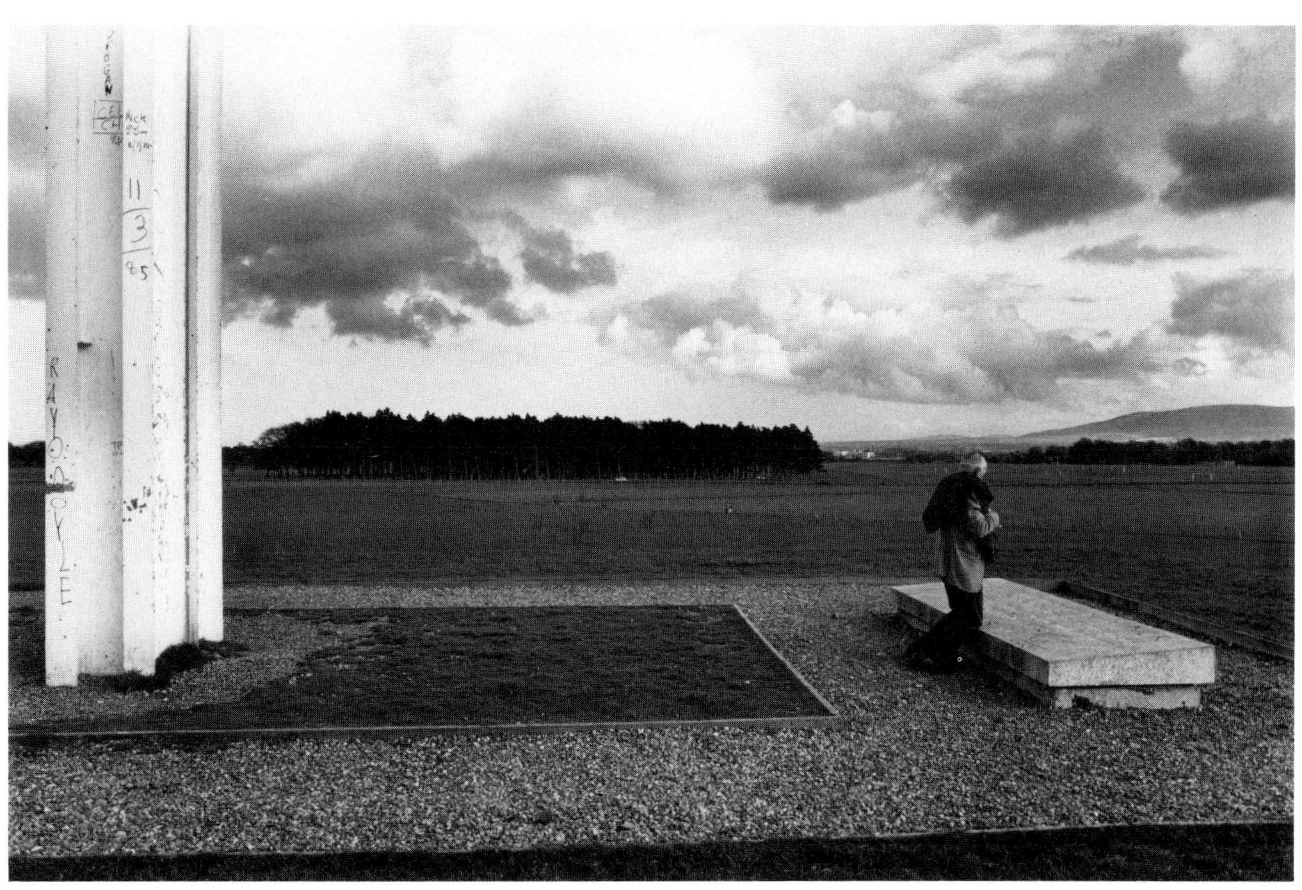

PAPAL CROSS, PHOENIX PARK, DUBLIN

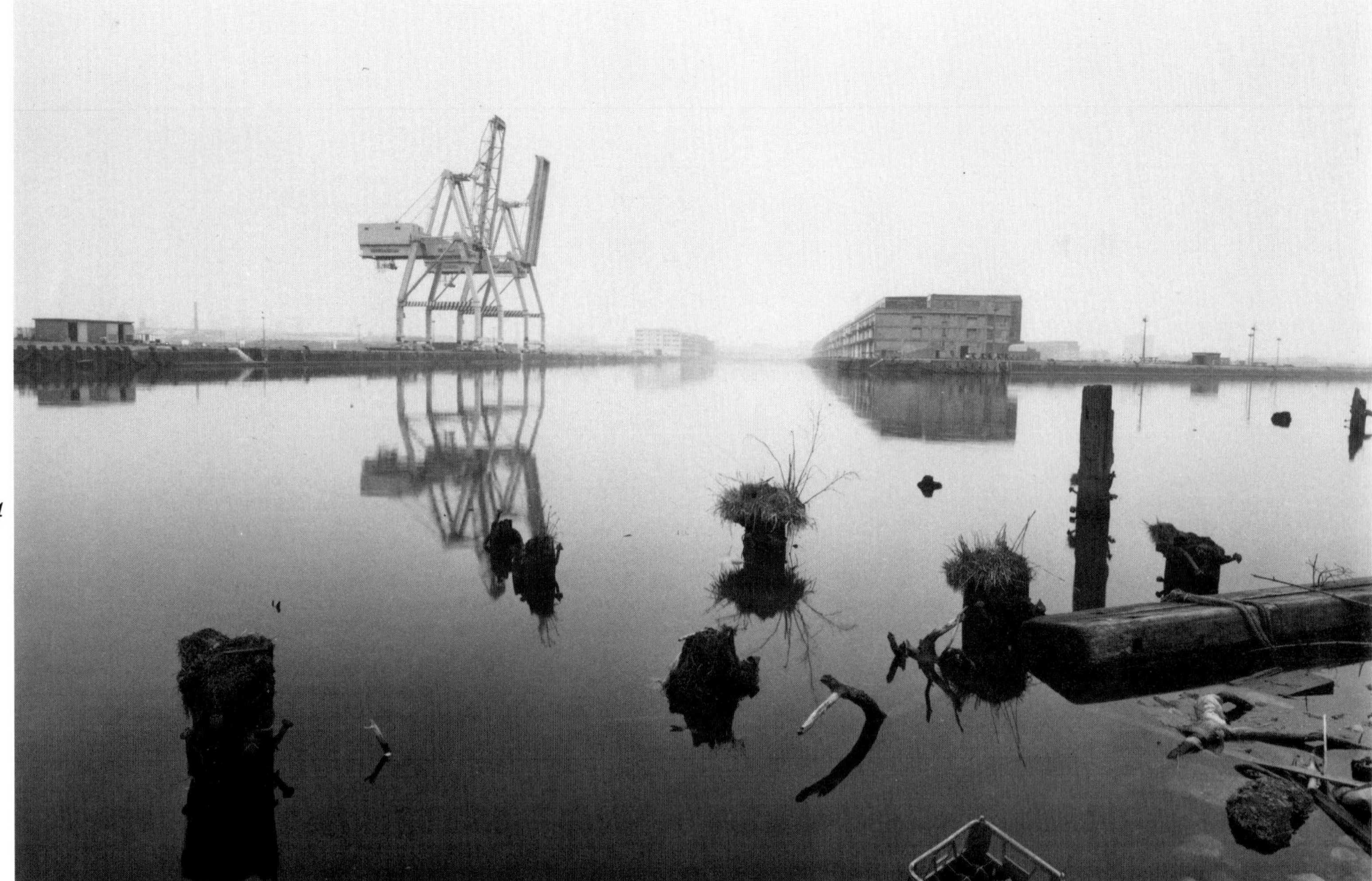

THE DOCKS MANCHESTER SHIP CANAL

JOHN DARWELL LEFT COLLEGE IN 1980 AND IS NOW WORKING ON A TWO-YEAR PROJECT ON THE MANCHESTER SHIP CANAL.

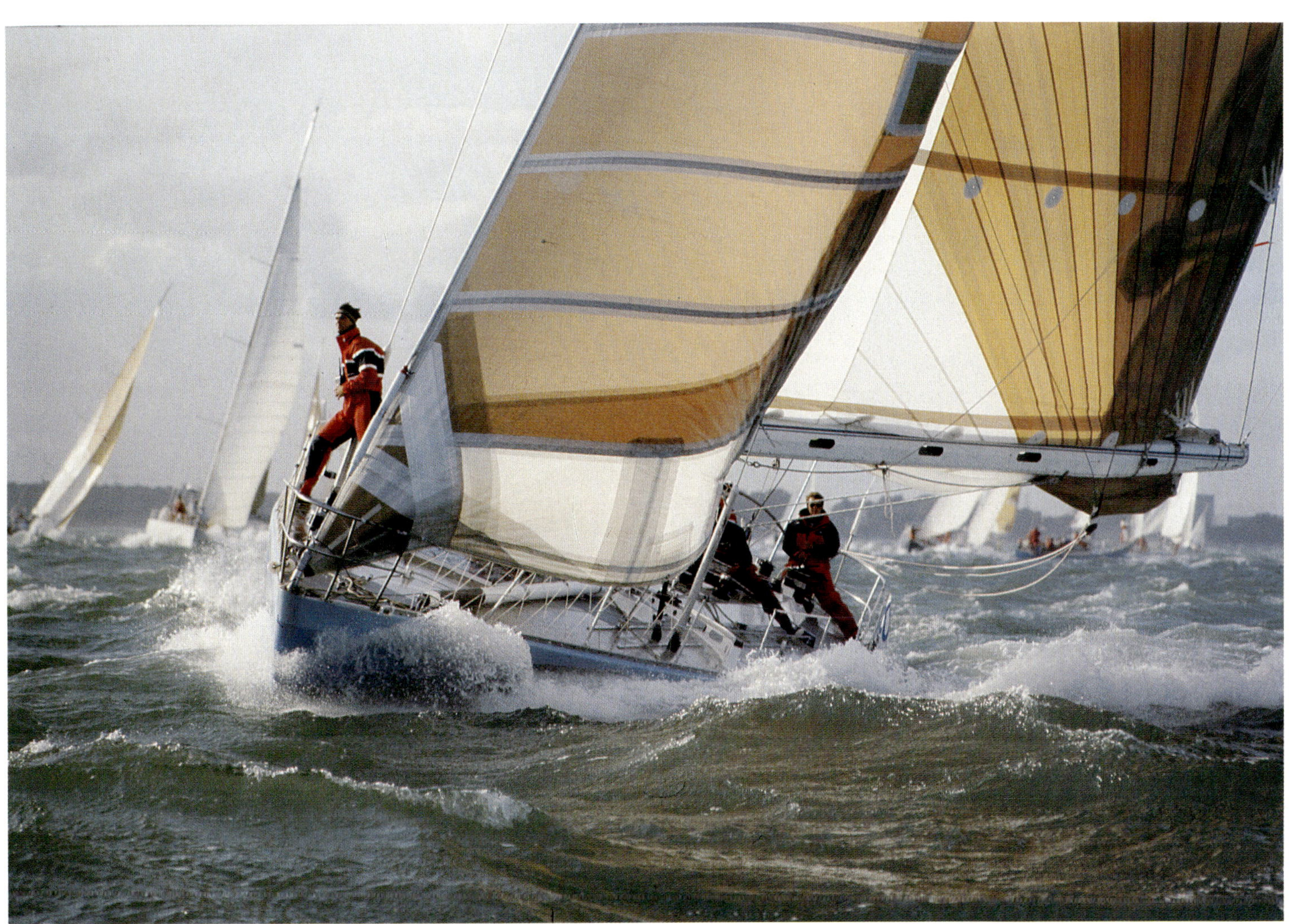

FASTNET START, COWES

105

PATRICK EDEN IS 26 AND HAS BEEN PHOTOGRAPHING FOR MAGAZINES FOR SEVEN YEARS. HE LIVES ON THE ISLE OF WIGHT.

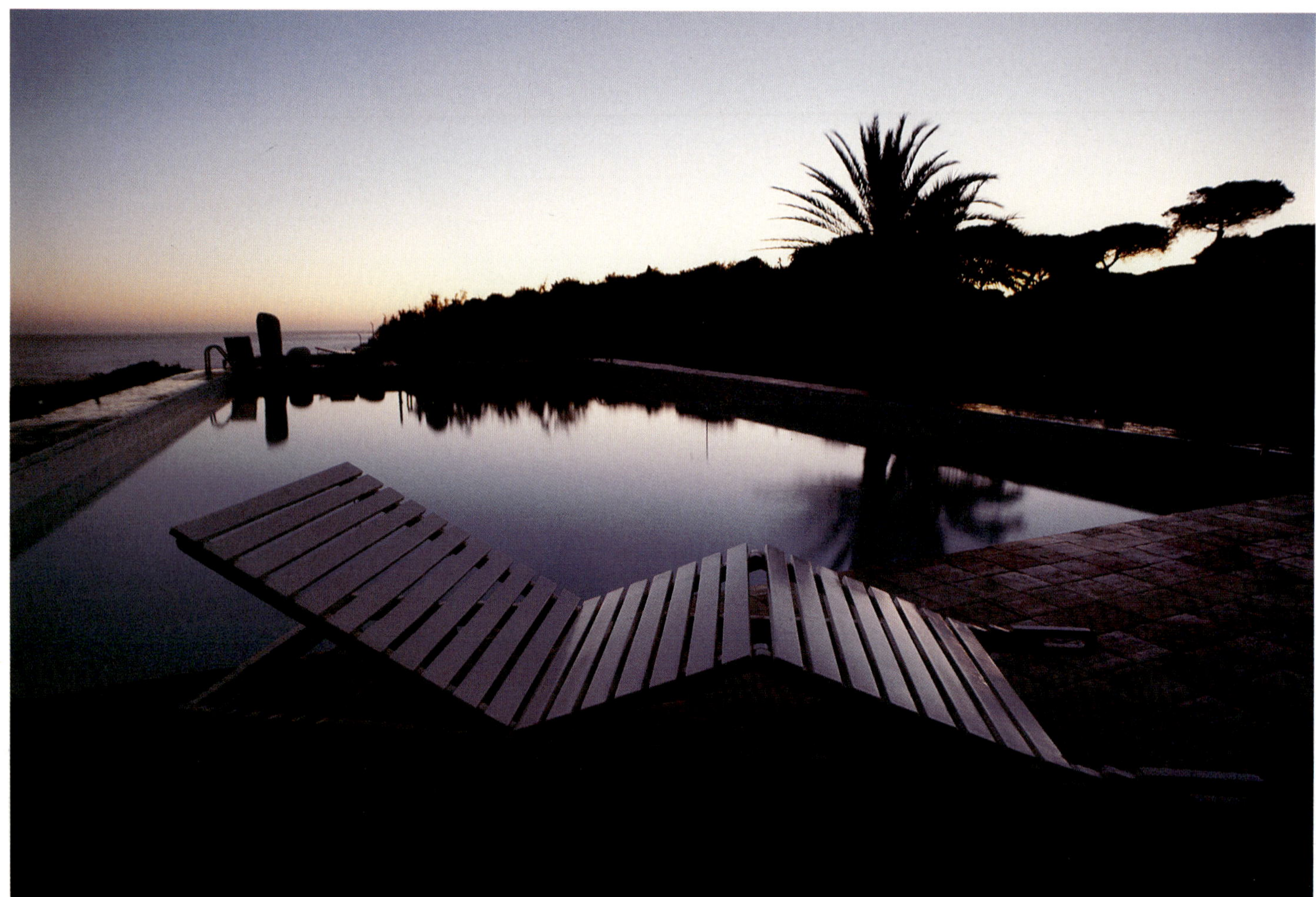

SPAIN

JOHN HESELTINE STARTED PHOTOGRAPHY IN NEW YORK IN THE SIXTIES. NOW HAS A COMMERCIAL STUDIO NEAR KINGS CROSS.

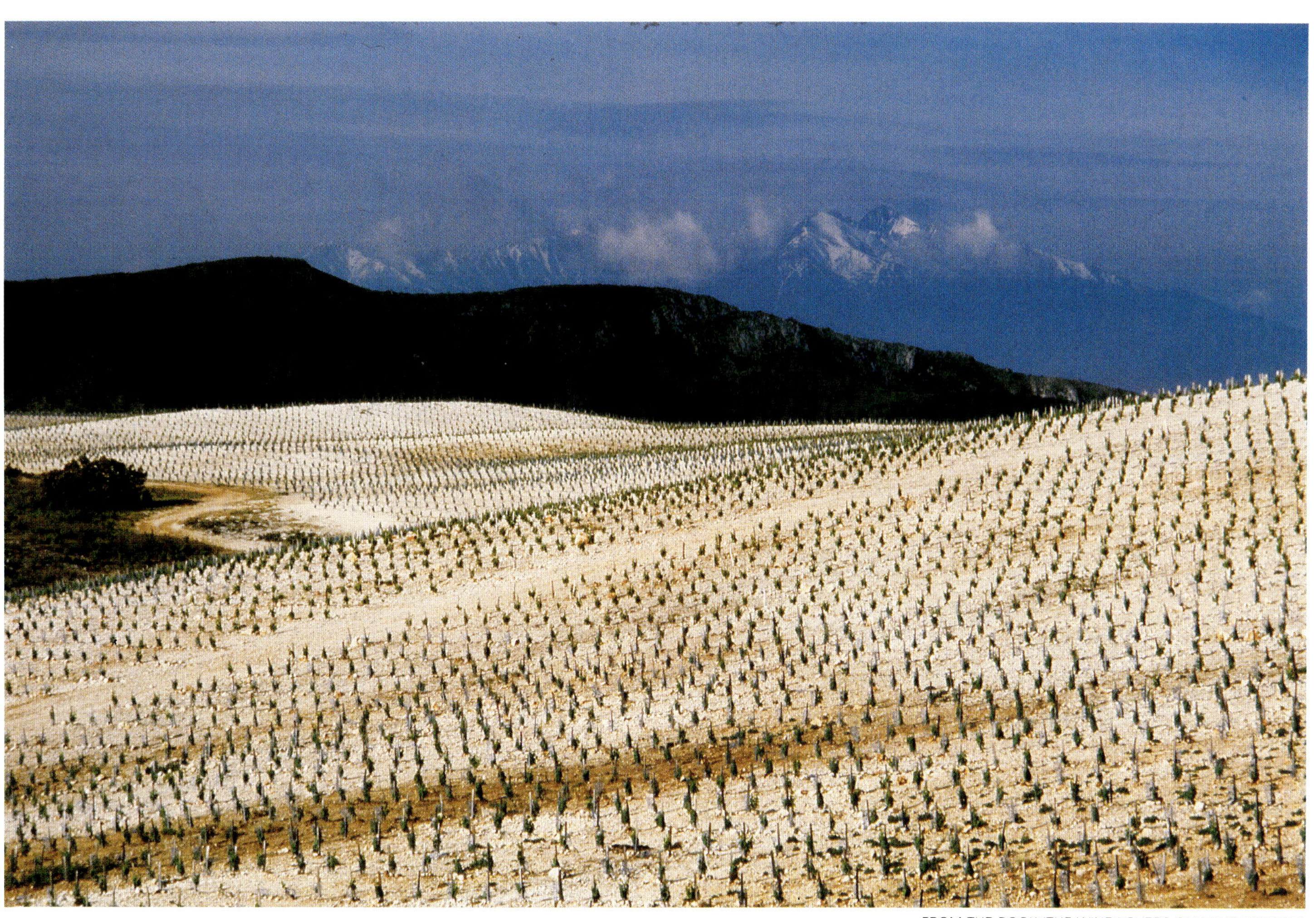

FROM THE BOOK 'THE WINE LOVERS GUIDE TO FRANCE'

MICHAEL BUSSELLE OF SEVENOAKS HAS BEEN PROFESSIONAL FOR 30 YEARS SPECIALISING IN TRAVEL FOR PUBLICATIONS.

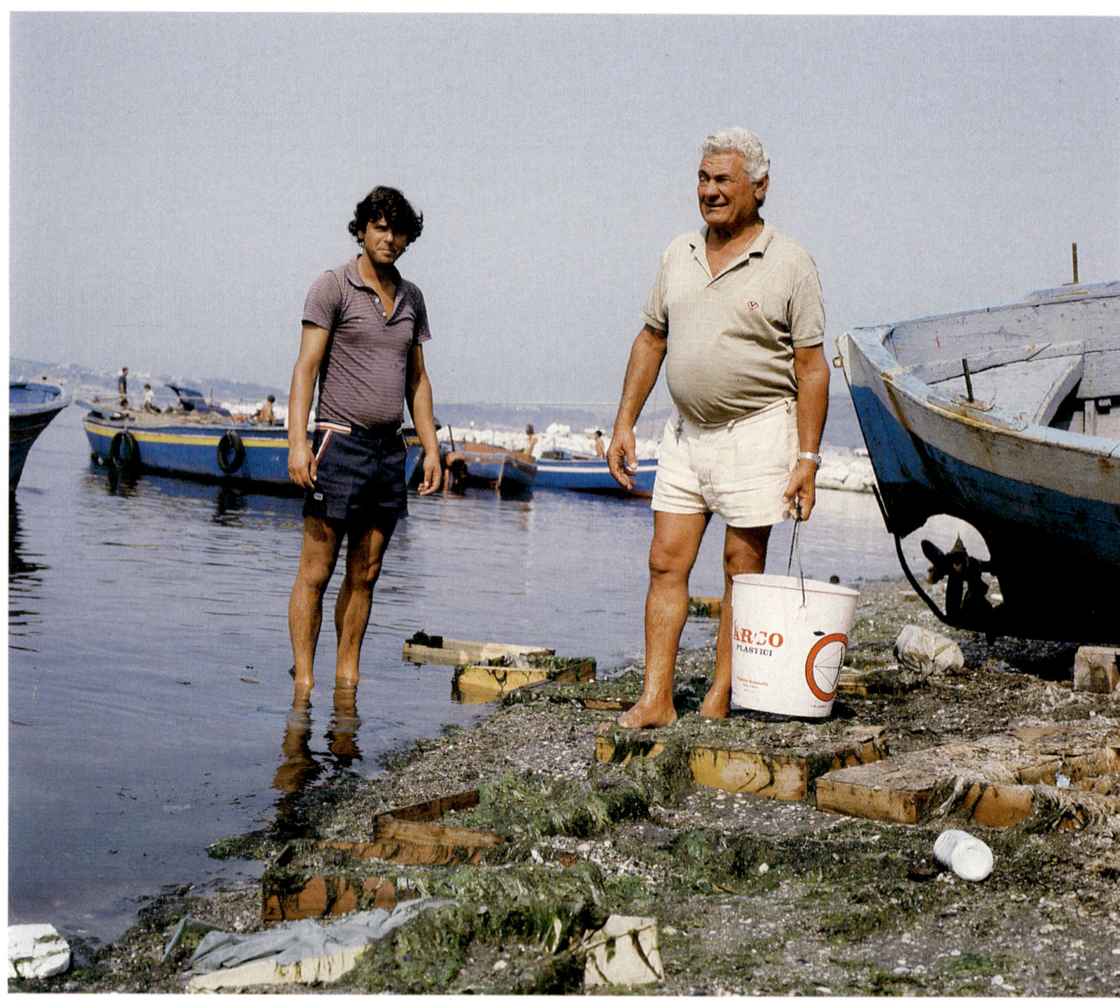

FROM 'THE PROUD PEOPLE OF POZZUOLI'

LONDON-BASED **FABRIZIO PANATTONI** CREATED AN EXTENSIVE DOCUMENTARY ON 'THE PROUD PEOPLE OF POZZUOLI'.
POZZUOLI IS A TOWN ON THE BAY OF NAPLES DEVASTATED BY VOLCANIC AND SEISMIC ACTIVITY FOR HUNDREDS OF YEARS.

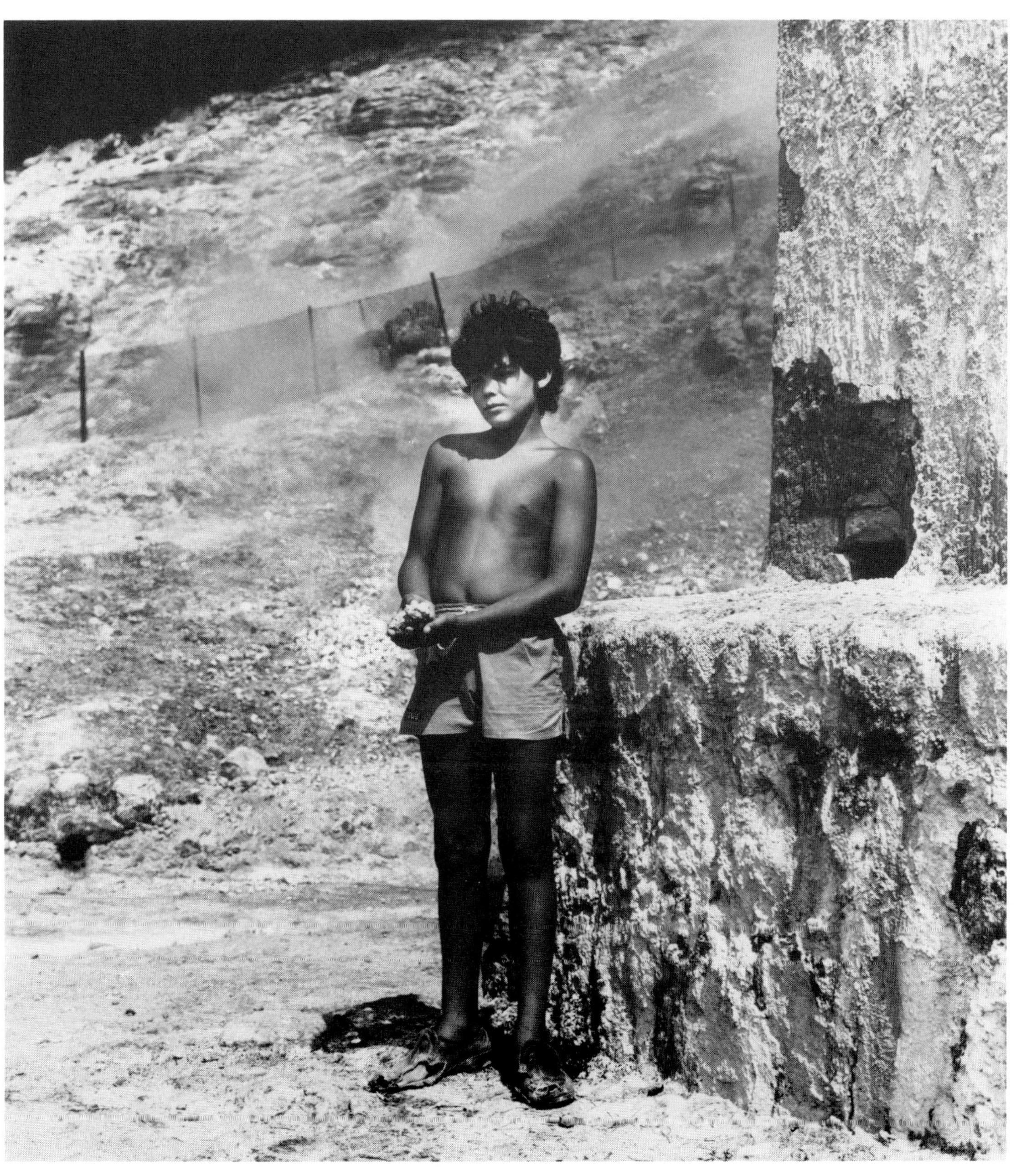

FABRIZIO PANATTONI

110

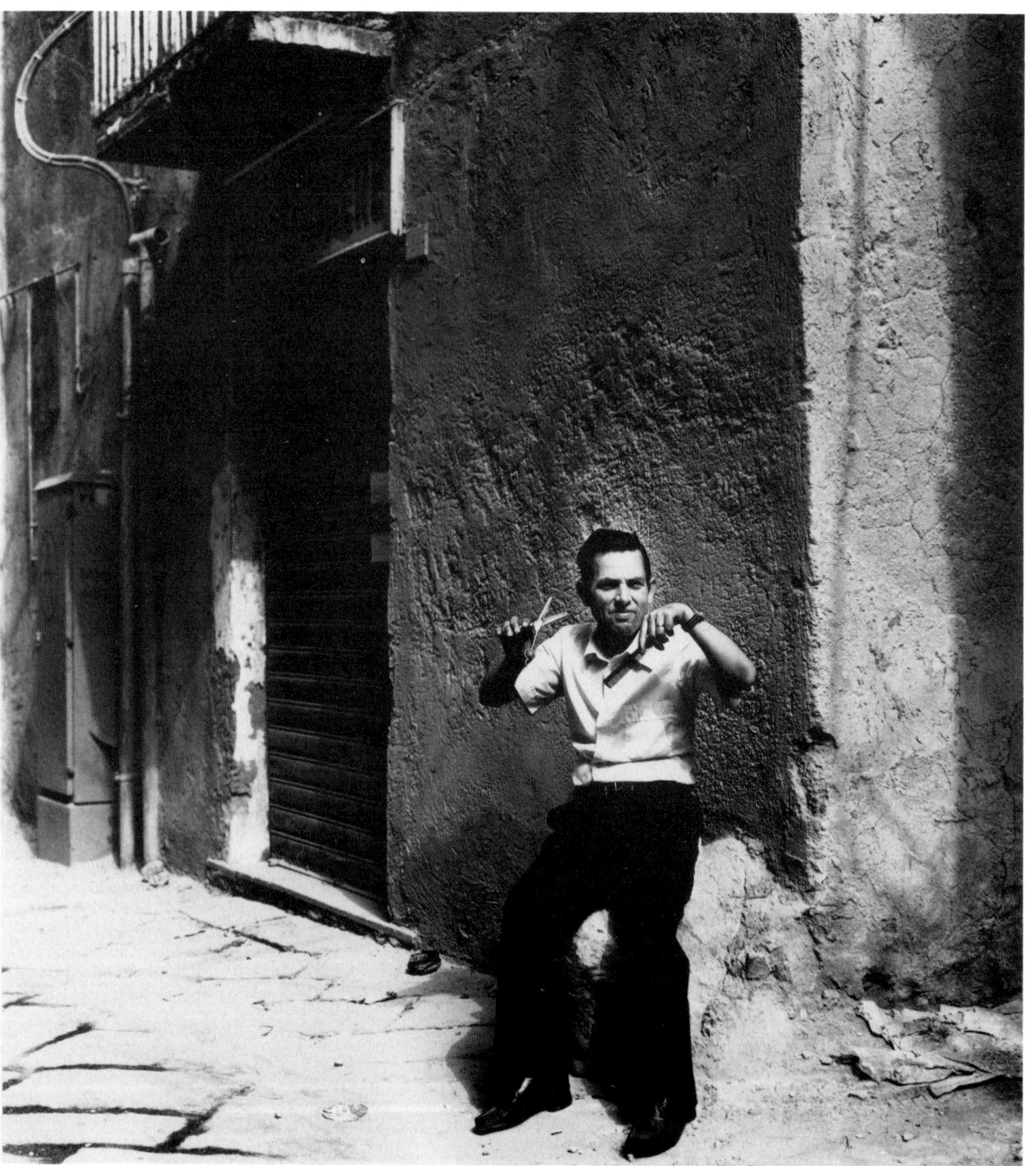

FABRIZIO PANATTONI

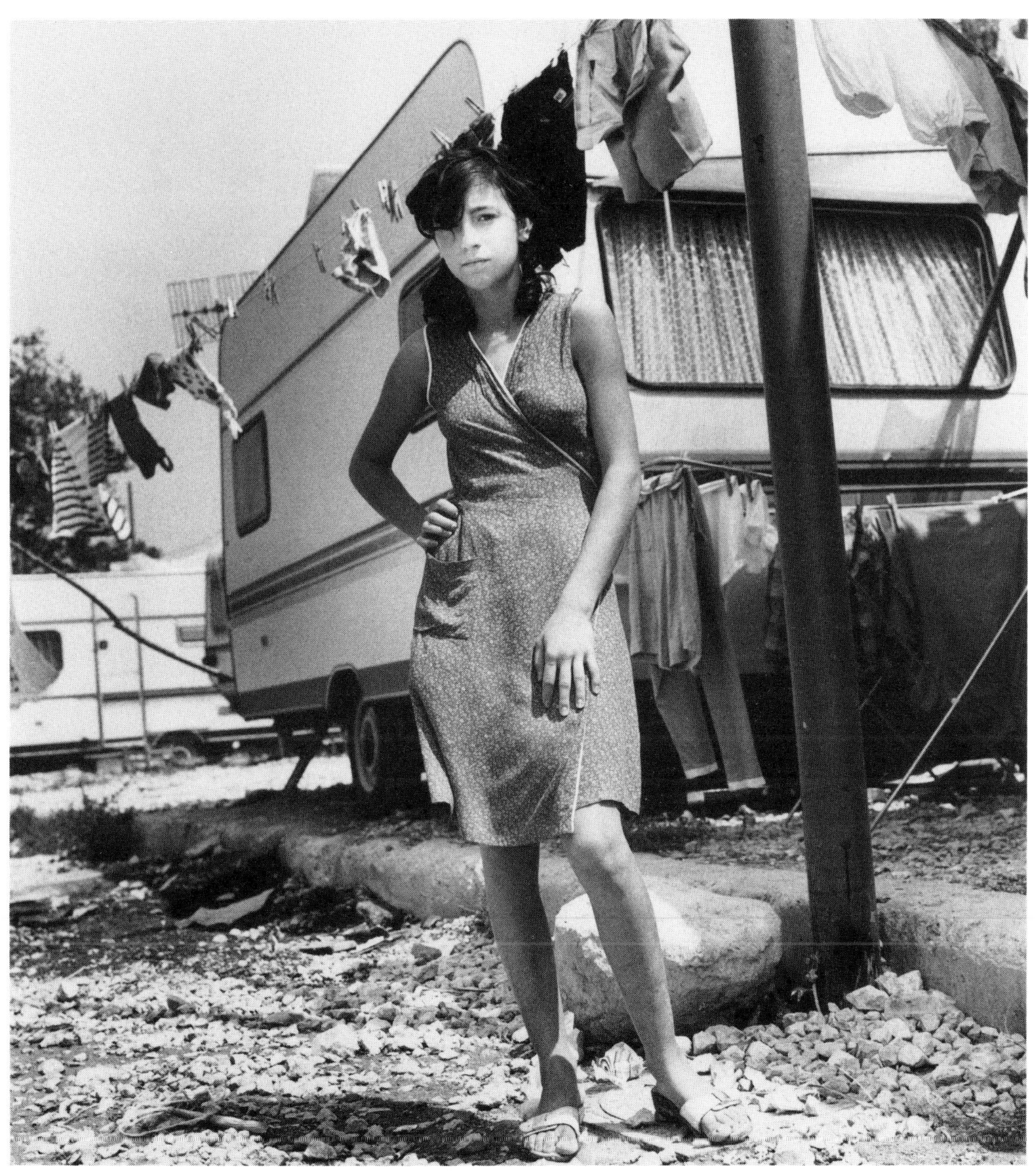

FABRIZIO PANATTONI

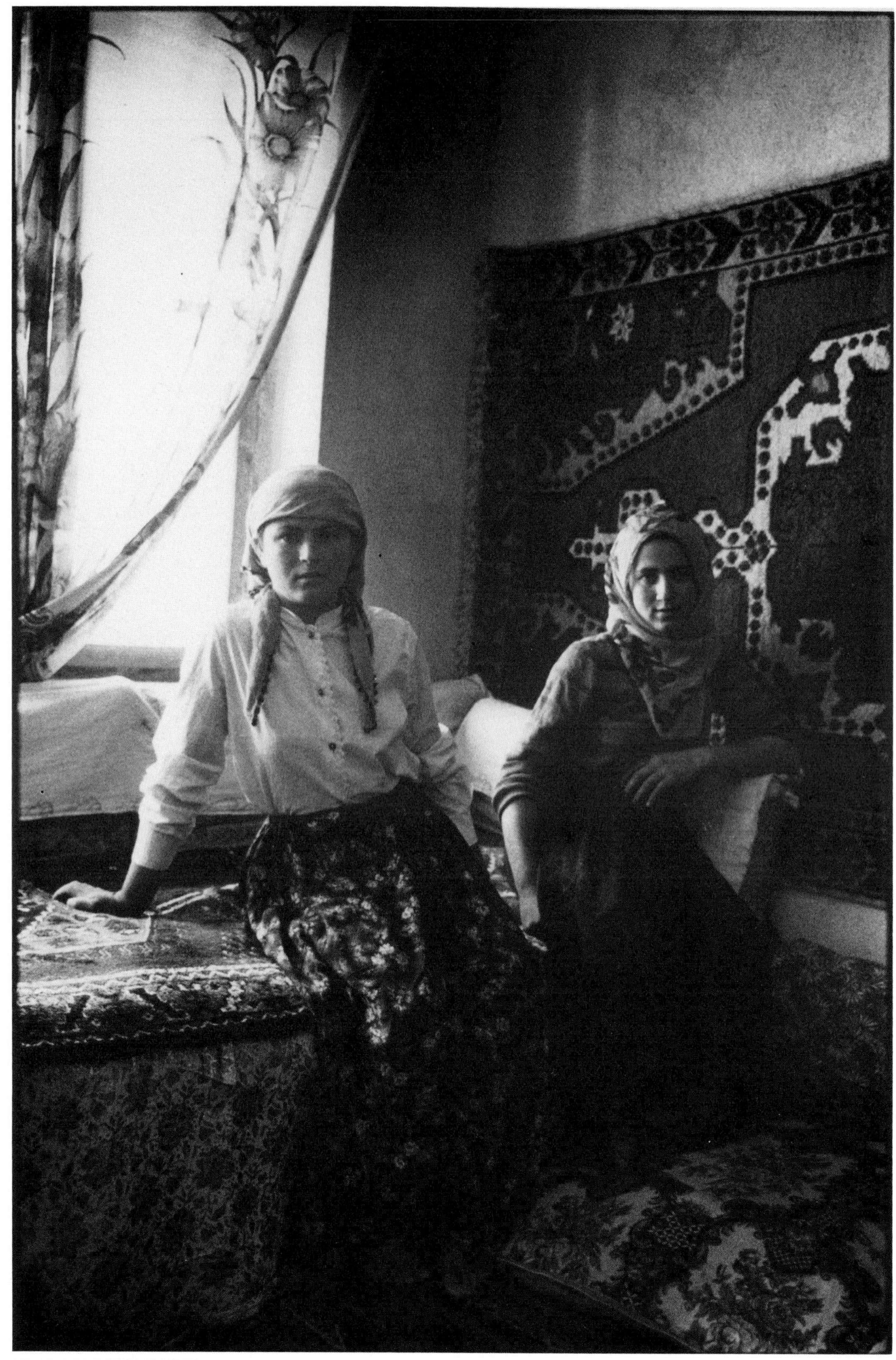

FATIMA AND HANIFE CINGITAS

RICHARD HADLEY LIVES AND WORKS IN SOUTH WEST LONDON. THE PHOTOGRAPHS WERE TAKEN DURING A MONTH LONG TRIP TO TURKEY.

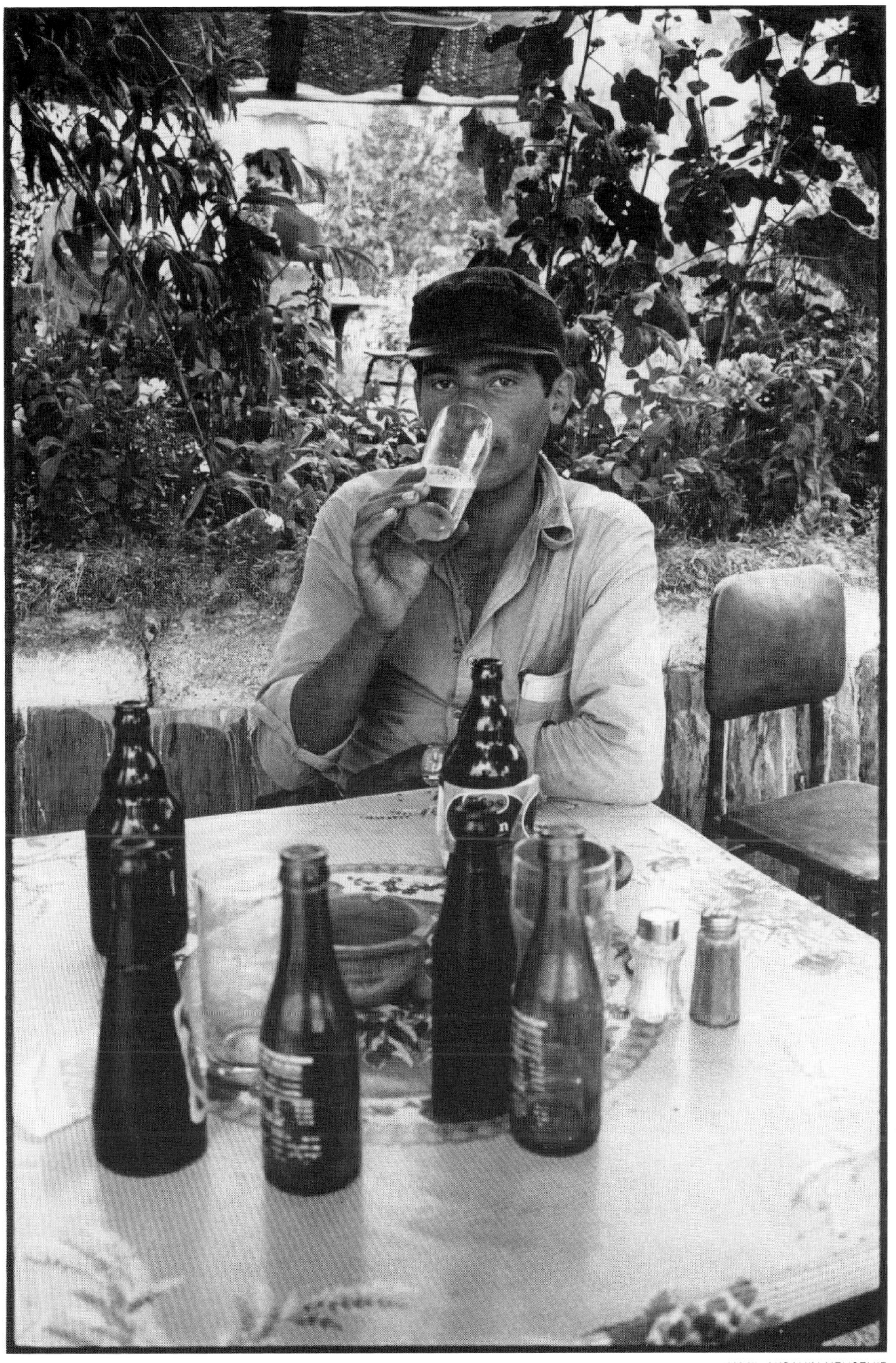

KAMIL AKSAHIN NEUSEHIR

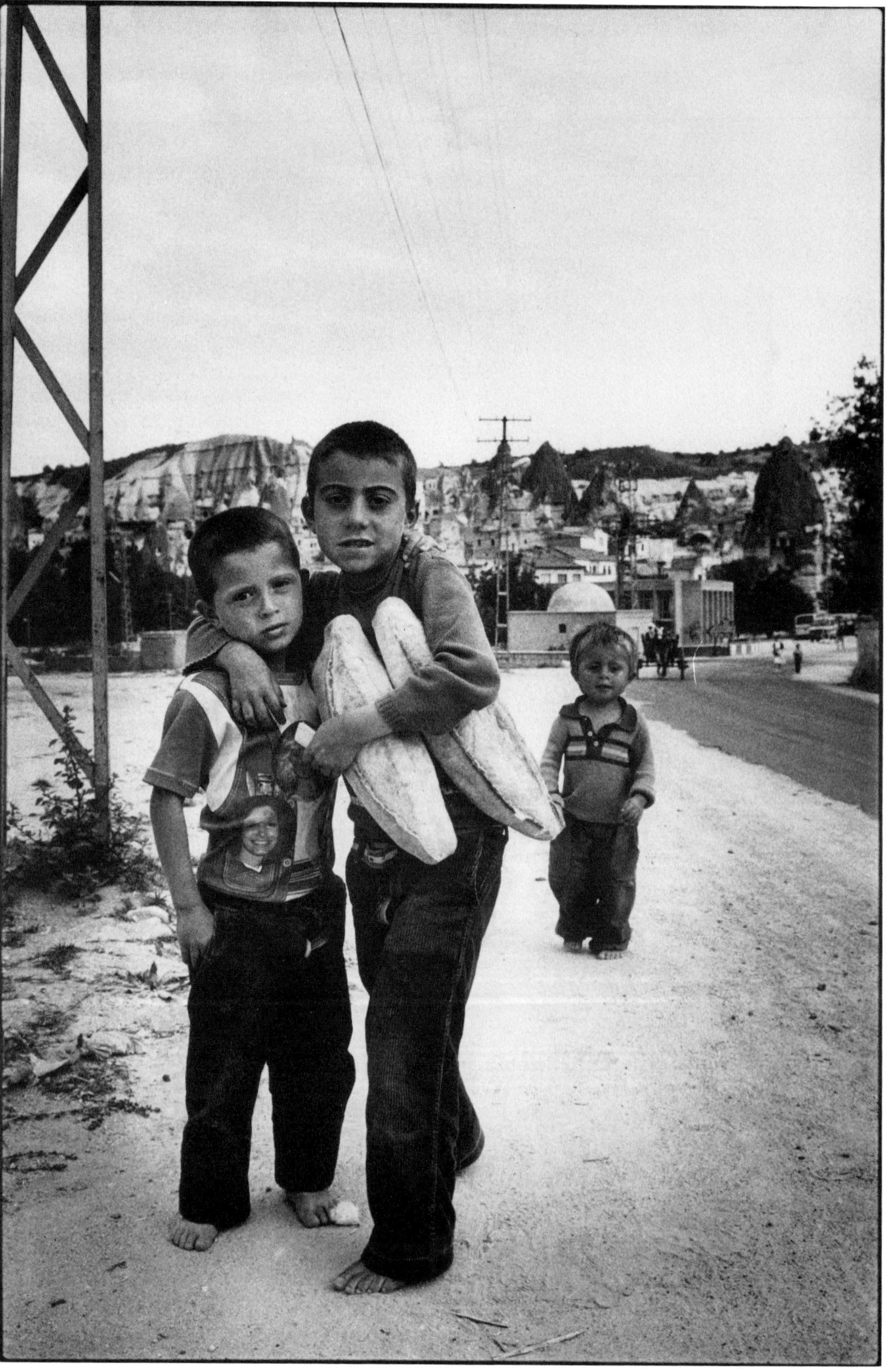

AYNYR AND MEHMET, GÖREME

RICHARD HADLEY

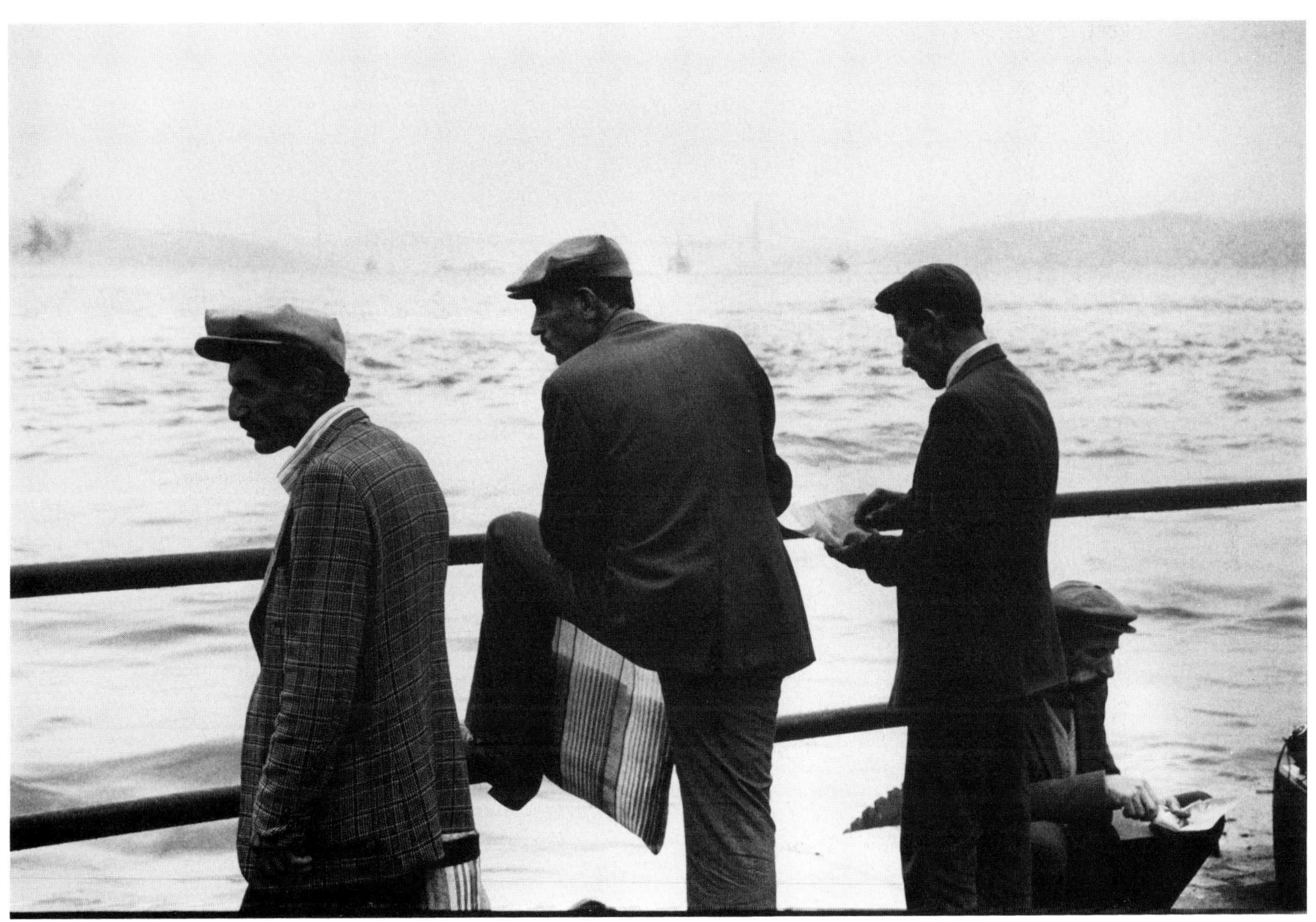

ISTANBUL

RICHARD HADLEY

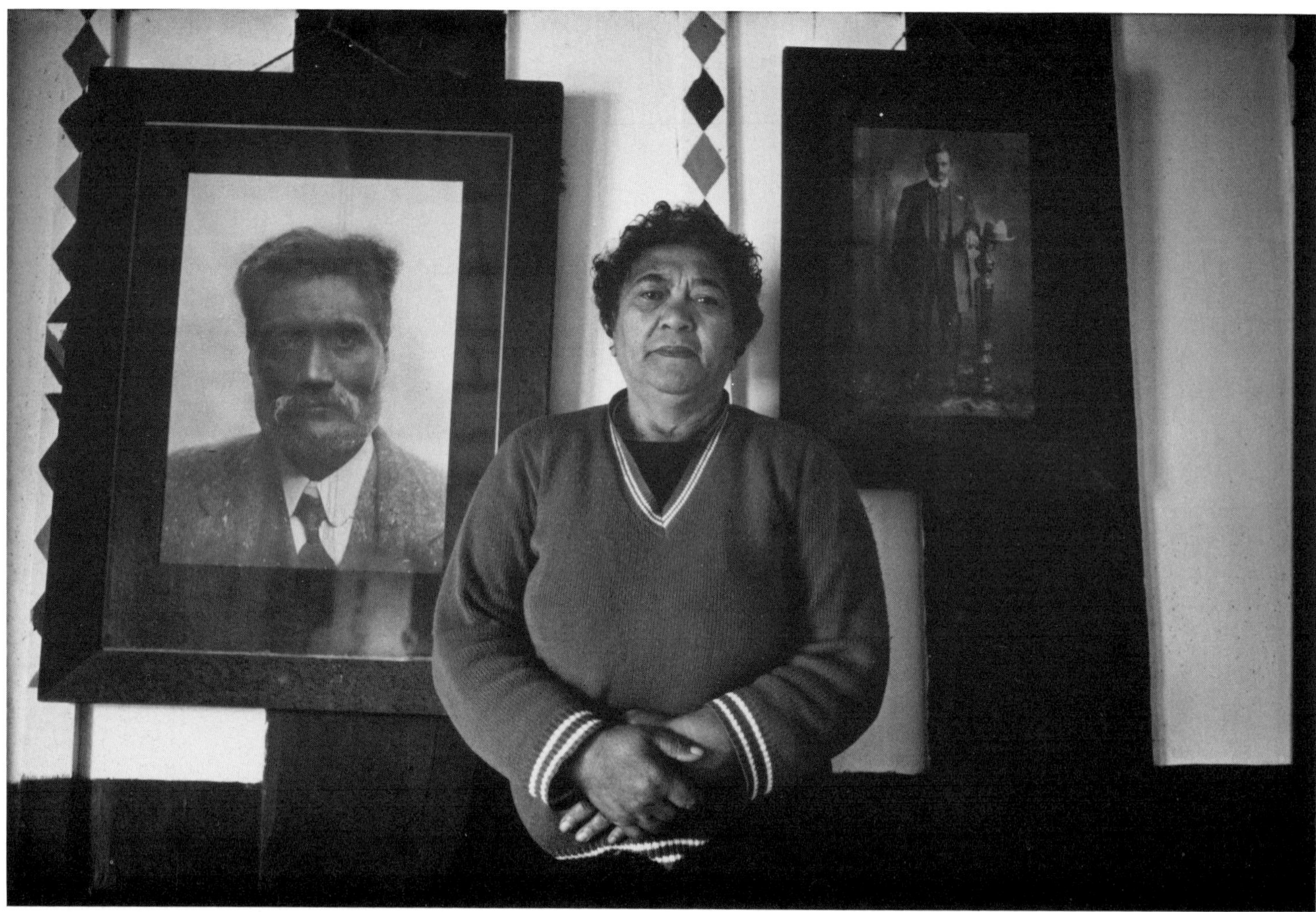

AT MAUNGAPO HATU

TERRY O'CONNOR LIVES IN AUCKLAND, NEW ZEALAND. HIS BOOK DOCUMENTING HEALTH CAMPS FOR NEGLECTED NEW ZEALAND CHILDREN HAS BEEN PUBLISHED.
HE HAS RECEIVED A QUEEN ELIZABETH II (NZ) ARTS COUNCIL GRANT TO MAKE A DOCUMENTARY ON THE TUHOE MAORI TRIBE, HAVING PREVIOUSLY MADE A PILOT ON THE MARAE.

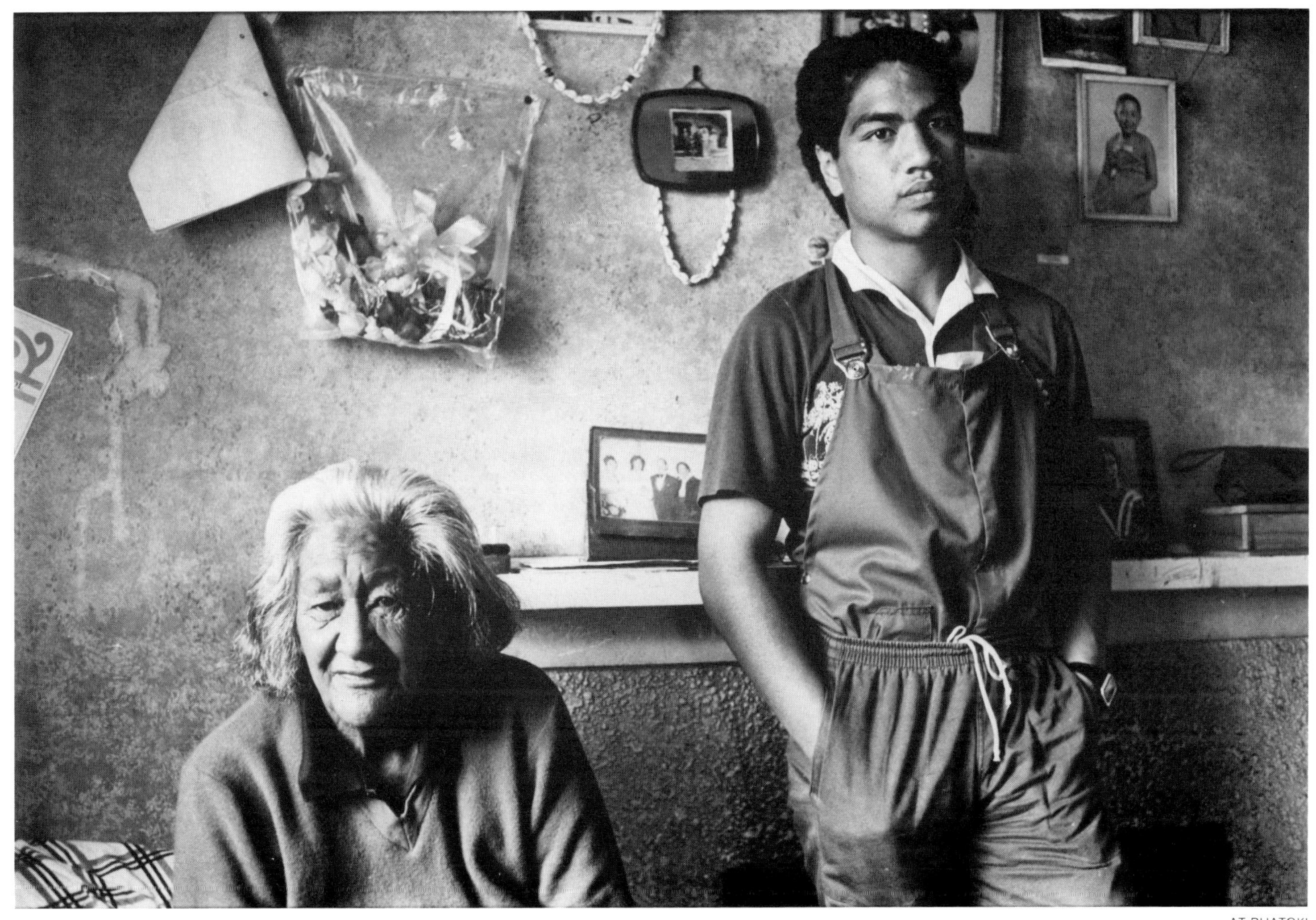

AT RUATOKI

TERRY O'CONNOR

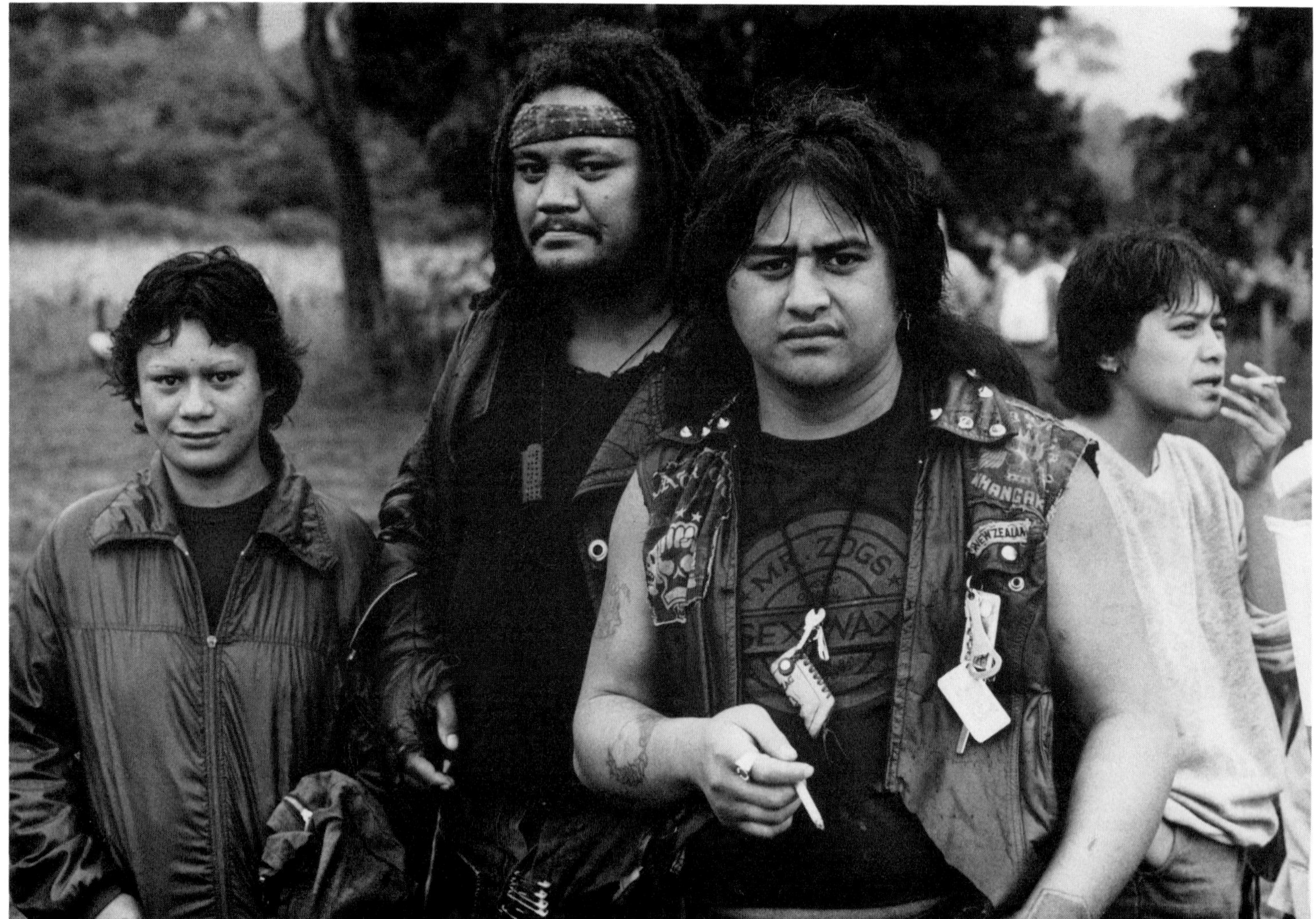

THE BLACK POWER AT RUATOKI

TERRY O'CONNOR

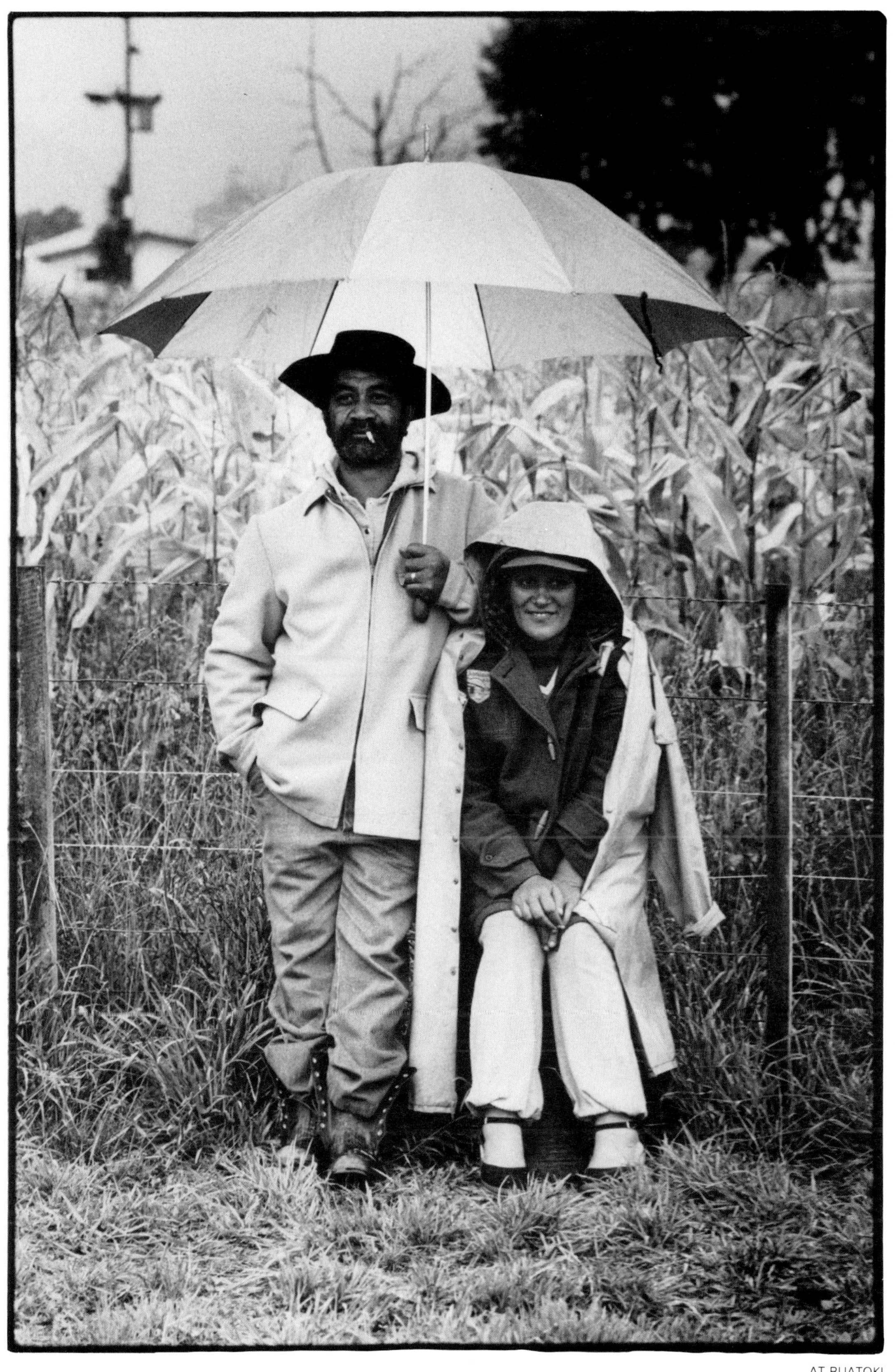

AT RUATOKI

TERRY O'CONNOR

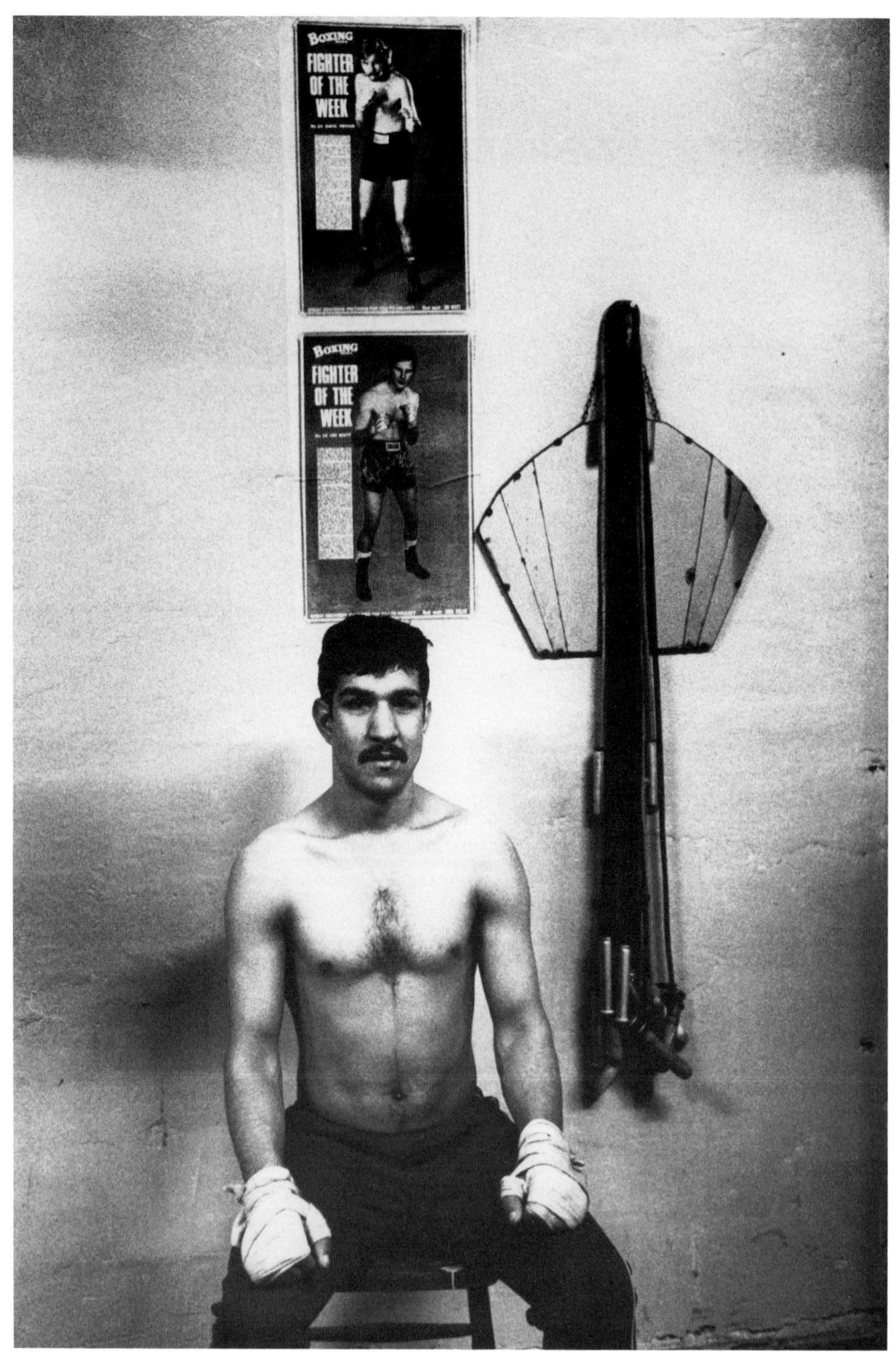

JOHN MIKOL IS 33-YEARS OLD AND STUDIED PHOTOGRAPHY AT READING. HE WORKED IN ADVERTISING AND SCIENTIFIC PHOTOGRAPHY BUT IS NOW A PHOTO-JOURNALIST.

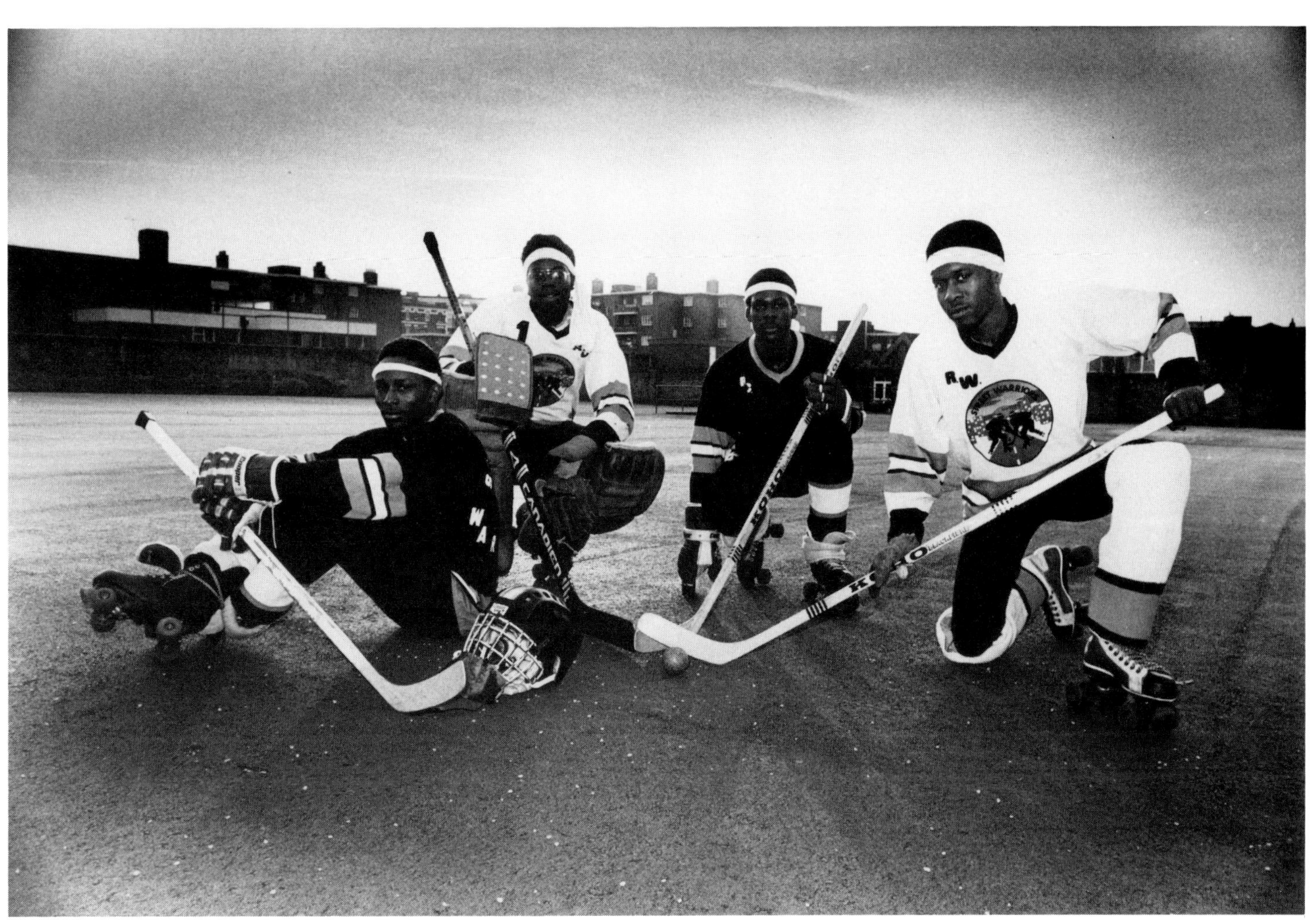

STREET WARRIORS

GEOFF FRANKLIN IS A LONDON-BASED FREELANCE PHOTOJOURNALIST. THE STREET HOCKEY SERIES WAS COMMISSIONED BY *'CITY LIMITS'*.

122

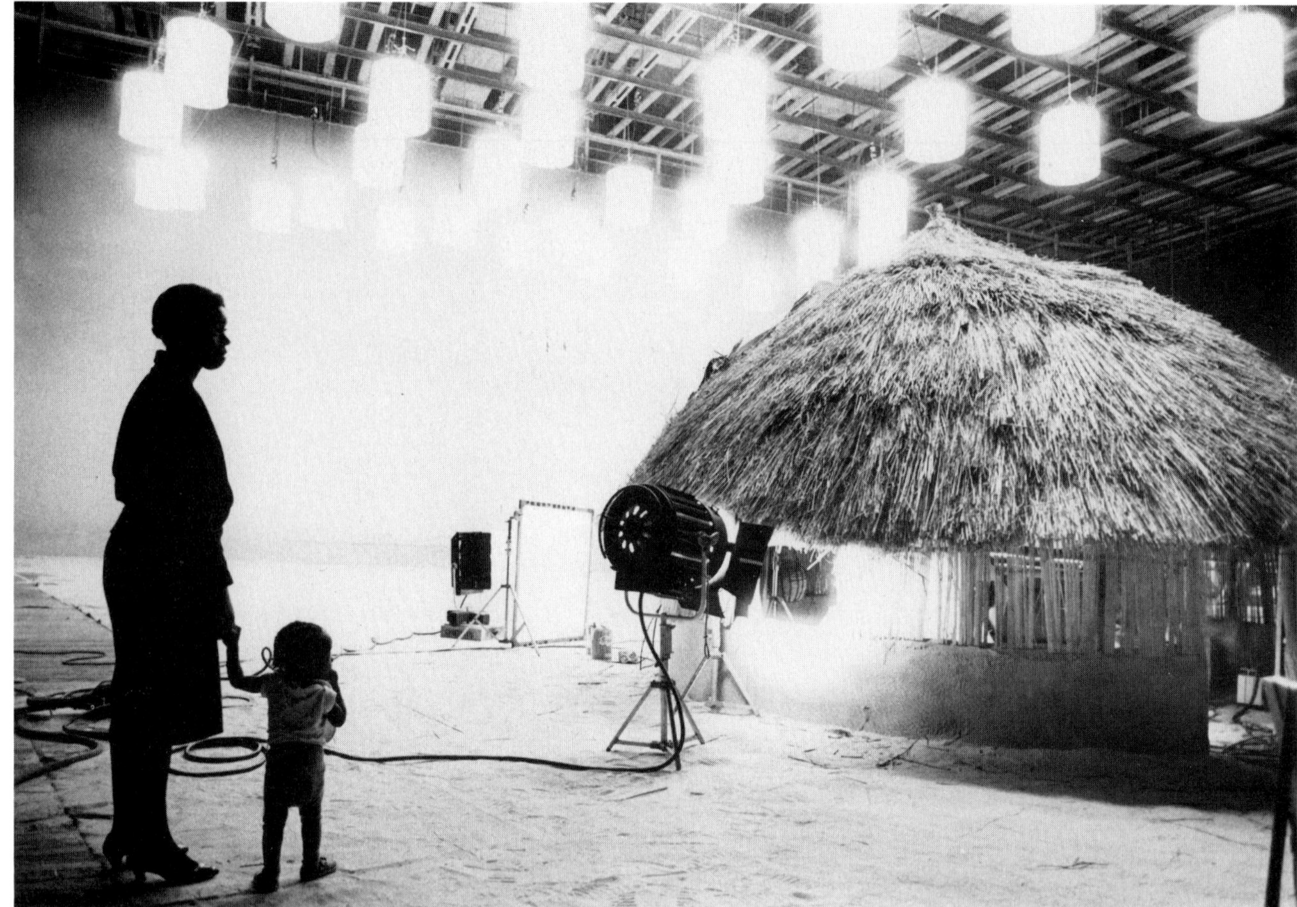

MAKING A COMMERCIAL FOR SPORT AID, SHEPPERTON

CAROLINE PENN IS A FREELANCE PHOTOGRAPHER WORKING FOR NATIONAL NEWSPAPERS AND MAGAZINES.

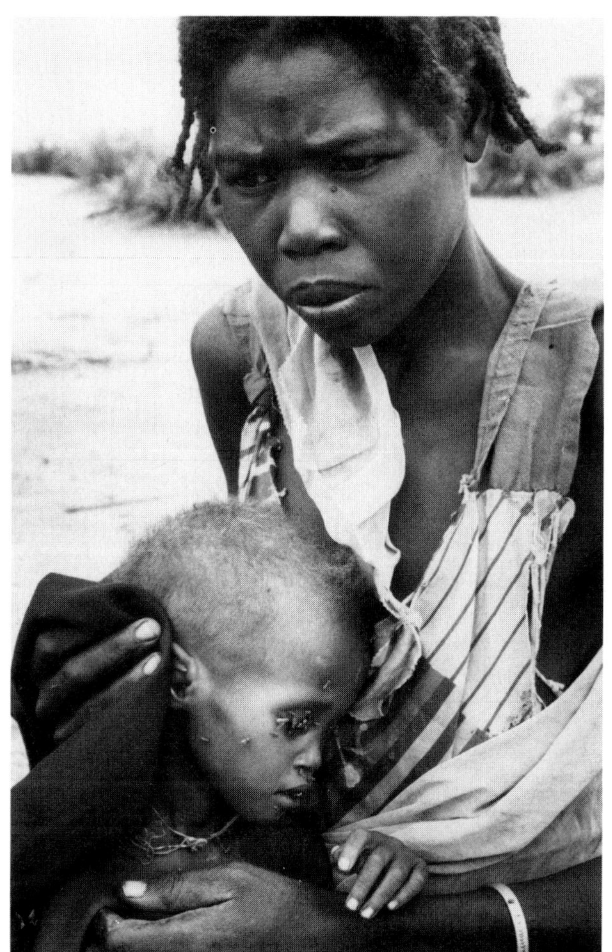

DARFUR, WEST SUDAN

CAROLINE PENN

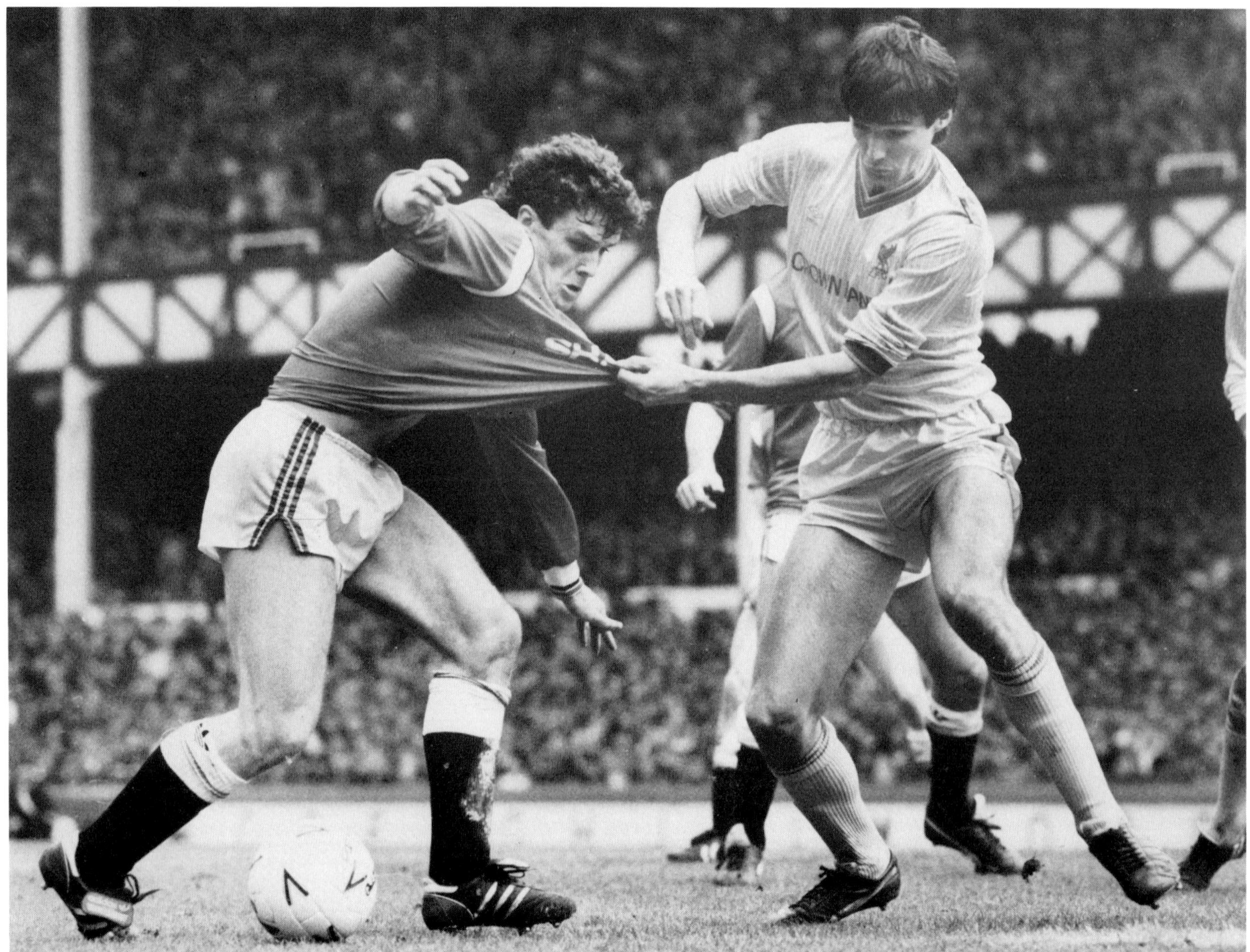

GETTING SHIRTY

CHRIS SMITH WAS JUDGED SPORTS PHOTOGRAPHER OF THE YEAR 1986 IN A COMPETITION PROMOTED BY THE SPORTS COUNCIL AND THE RPS.

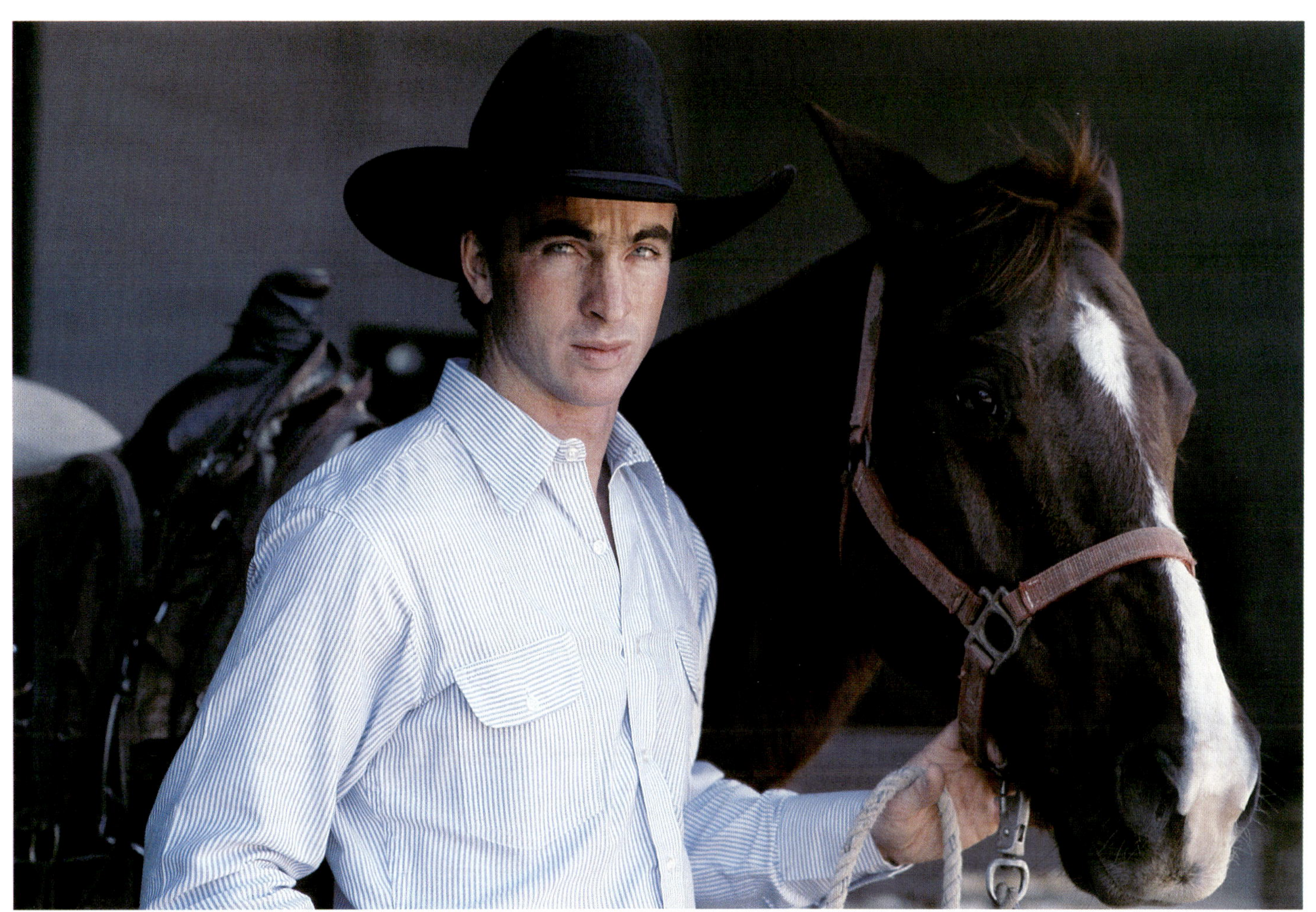

RODEO RIDER

EAMONN McCABE FOUR TIMES 'SPORTS PHOTOGRAPHER OF THE YEAR' IS CURRENTLY PICTURE EDITOR FOR THE NEW MAGAZINE *SPORTSWEEK*.

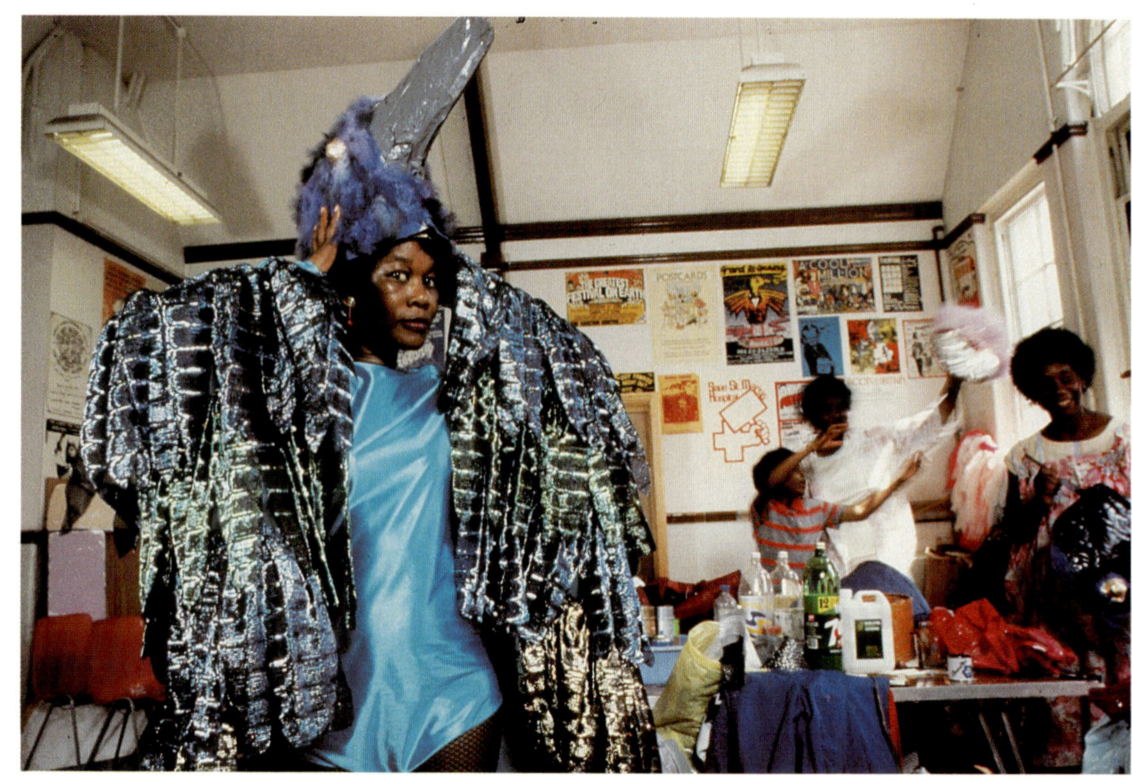

EBONY: LEADER GLORIA WITH HER HUSBAND WIRE BENDING

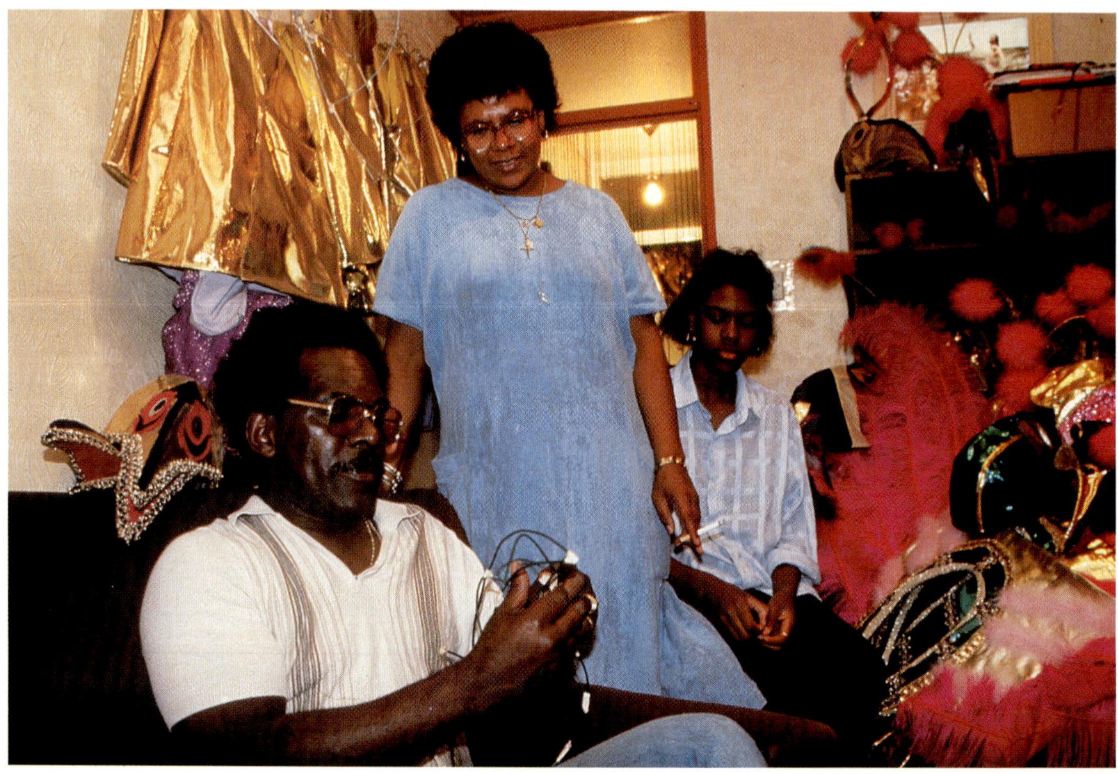

SUNIL GUPTA WAS BORN IN INDIA, IS A CANADIAN CITIZEN BUT HE STUDIED PHOTOGRAPHY AND NOW LIVES IN LONDON.

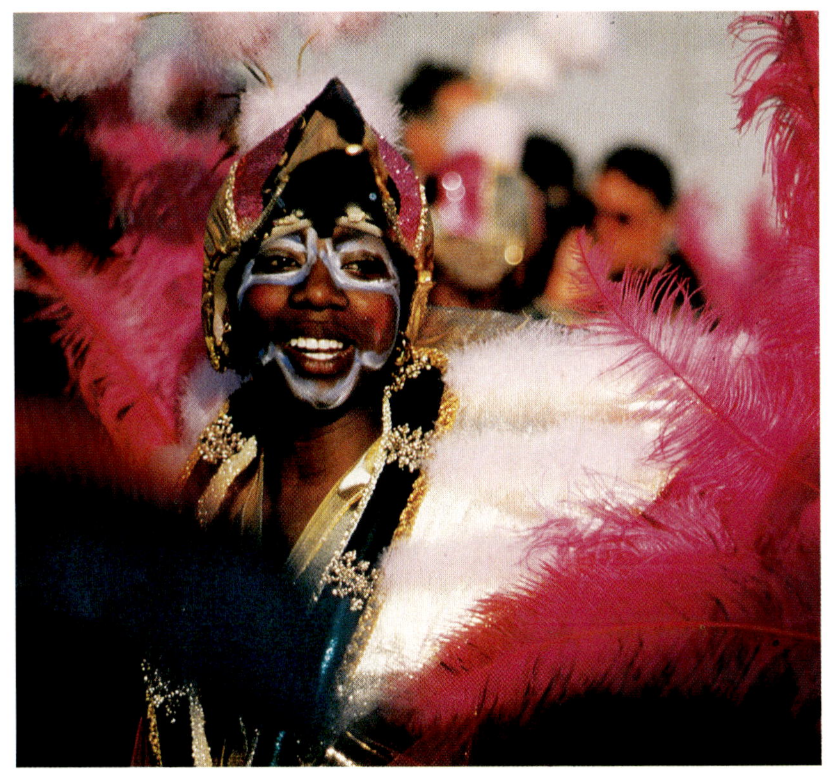

EBONY: GLORIA'S SECTION ON THE STREETS

GRENADA SHORTNEY, SOUTHALL

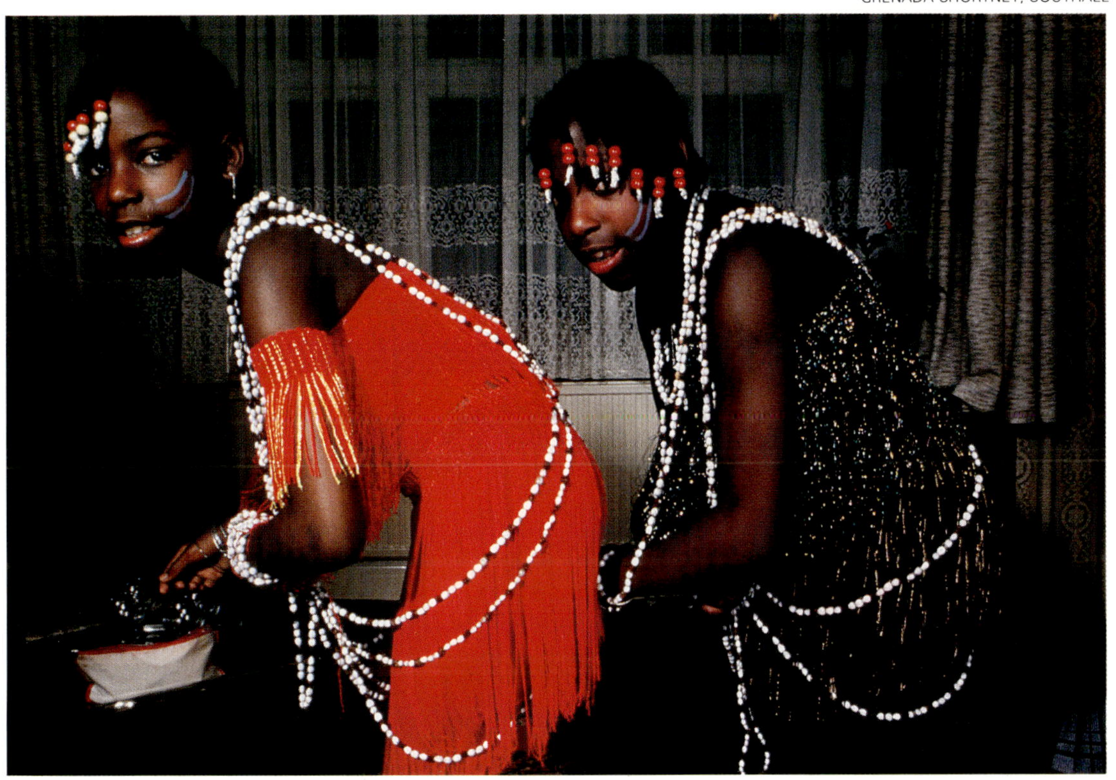

THE CARNIVAL PICTURES ARE PART OF AN ARTS COUNCIL COMMISSION TO RECORD THE PREPARATIONS OF THREE BANDS; EBONY, FLAMINGO AND THE GRENADA SHORTNEY.

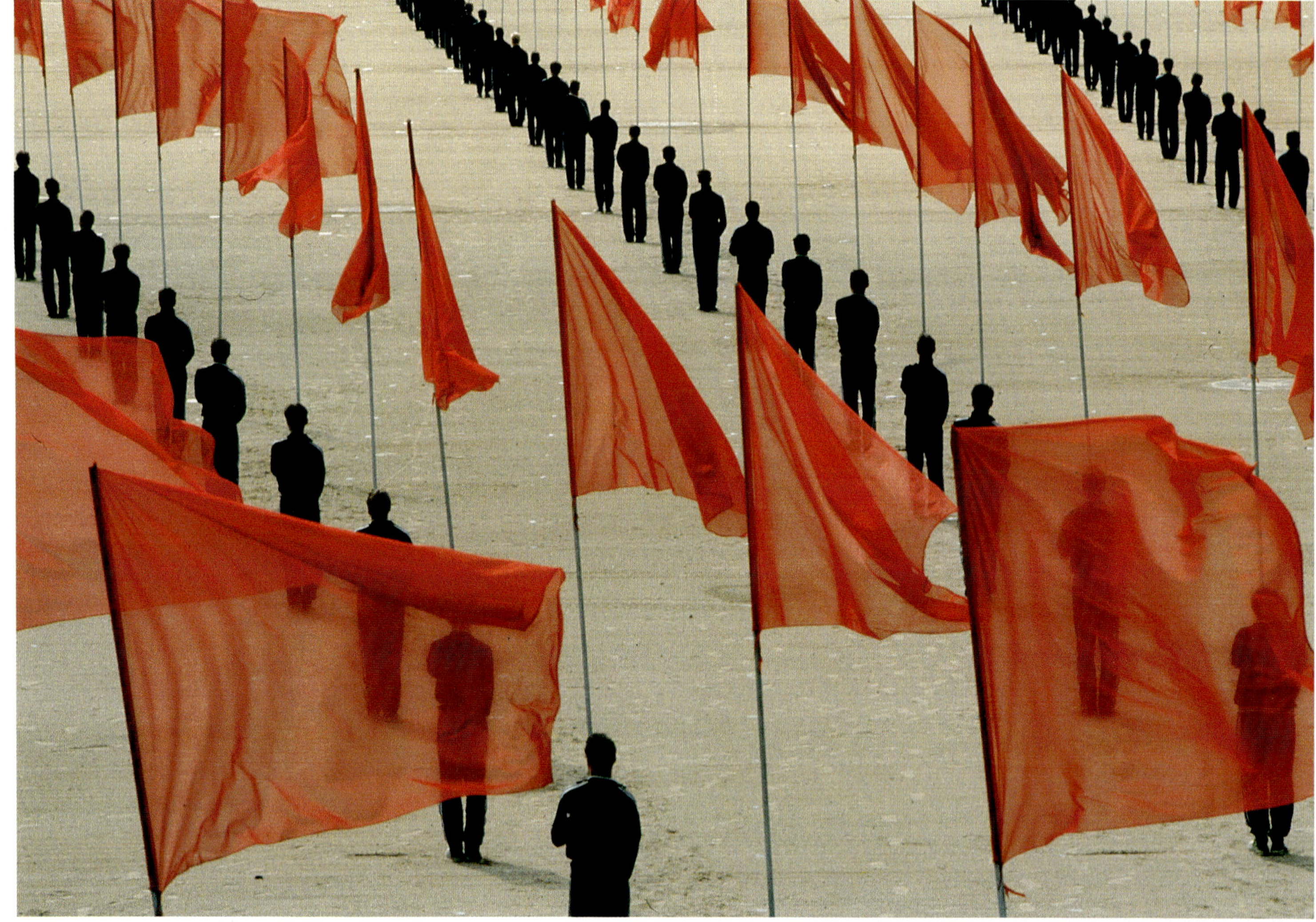

SPARTAKIAD, PRAGUE

LIBA TAYLOR WAS BORN IN CZECHOSLOVAKIA, LIVES IN LONDON AND IS A FREELANCE PHOTOGRAPHER AND WRITER ON PHOTOGRAPHY.

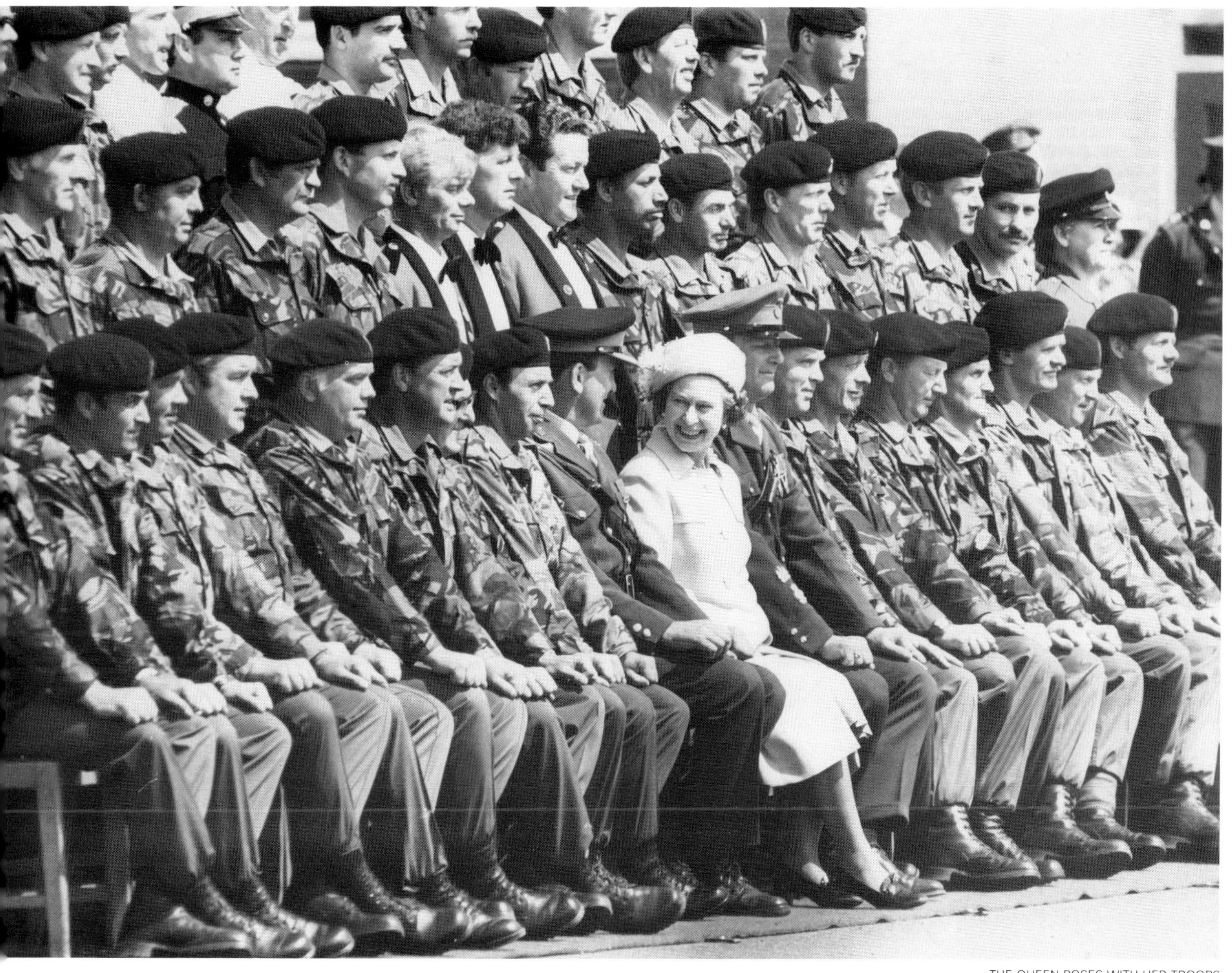

THE QUEEN POSES WITH HER TROOPS

HOWARD WALKER, FRPS, LEFT SCHOOL IN 1969, WAS A PHOTOGRAPHIC APPRENTICE TO THE *BURY TIMES*, WORKED FOR LOCAL NEWSPAPERS AND AGENCIES BEFORE JOINING THE *SUNDAY MIRROR*.

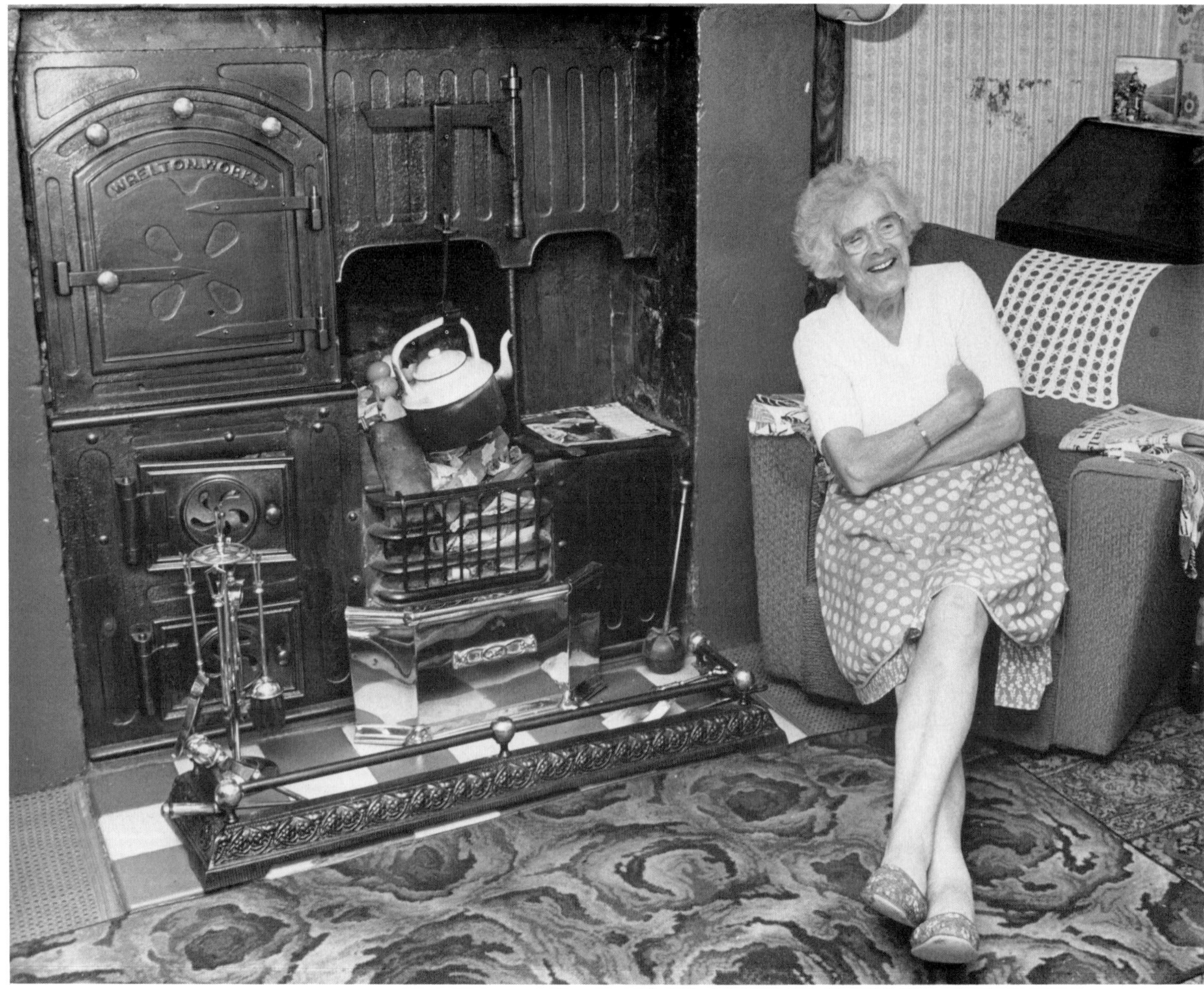

MAGGIE IN HER YORKSHIRE COTTAGE

GLYN BARNEY STUDIED AT WEST SURREY COLLEGE OF ART AND IS NOW A FREELANCE PHOTOGRAPHER LIVING AT GRAY'S ESSEX.

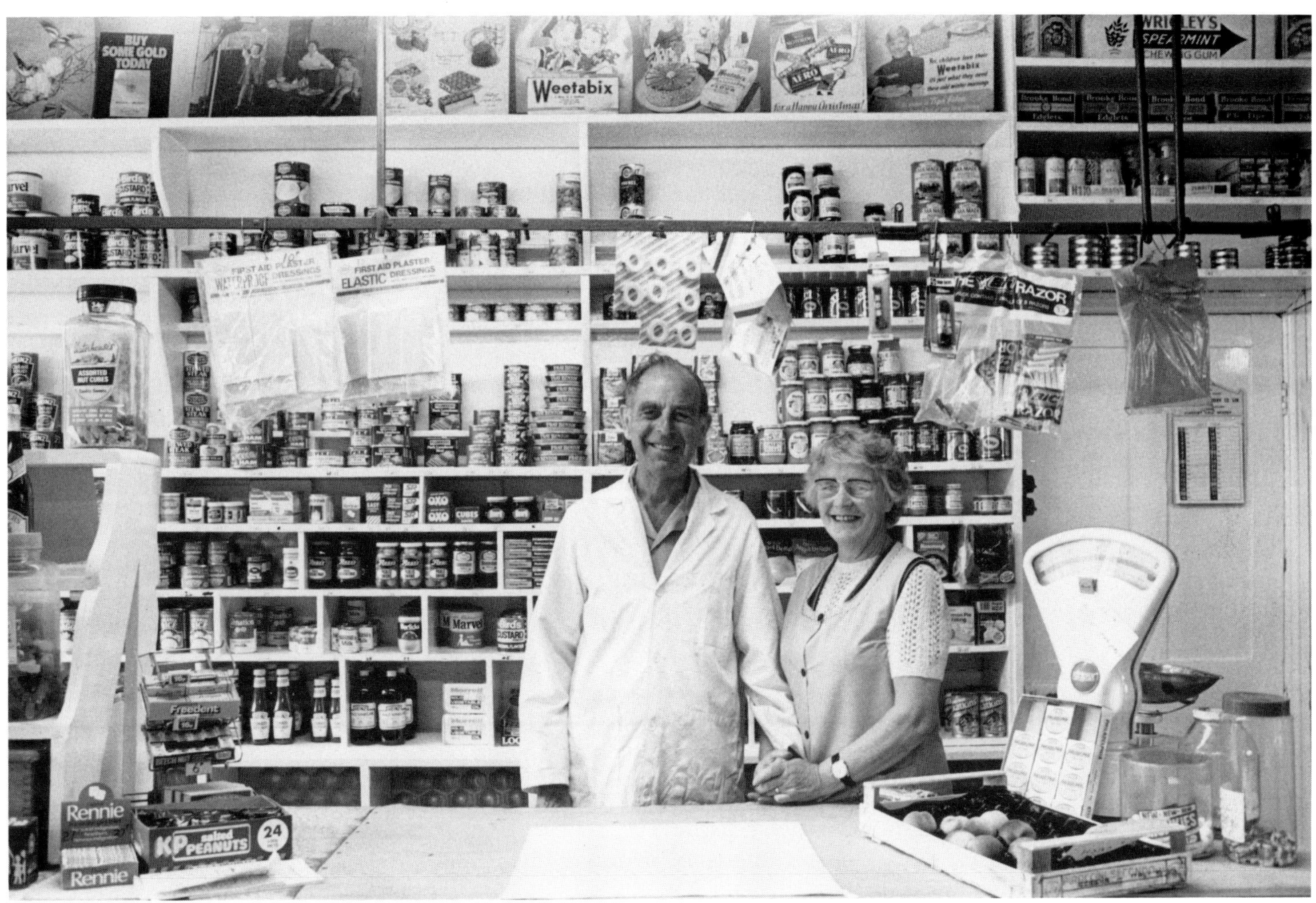

THE LAST DAY AT THE SHOP

GLYN BARNEY

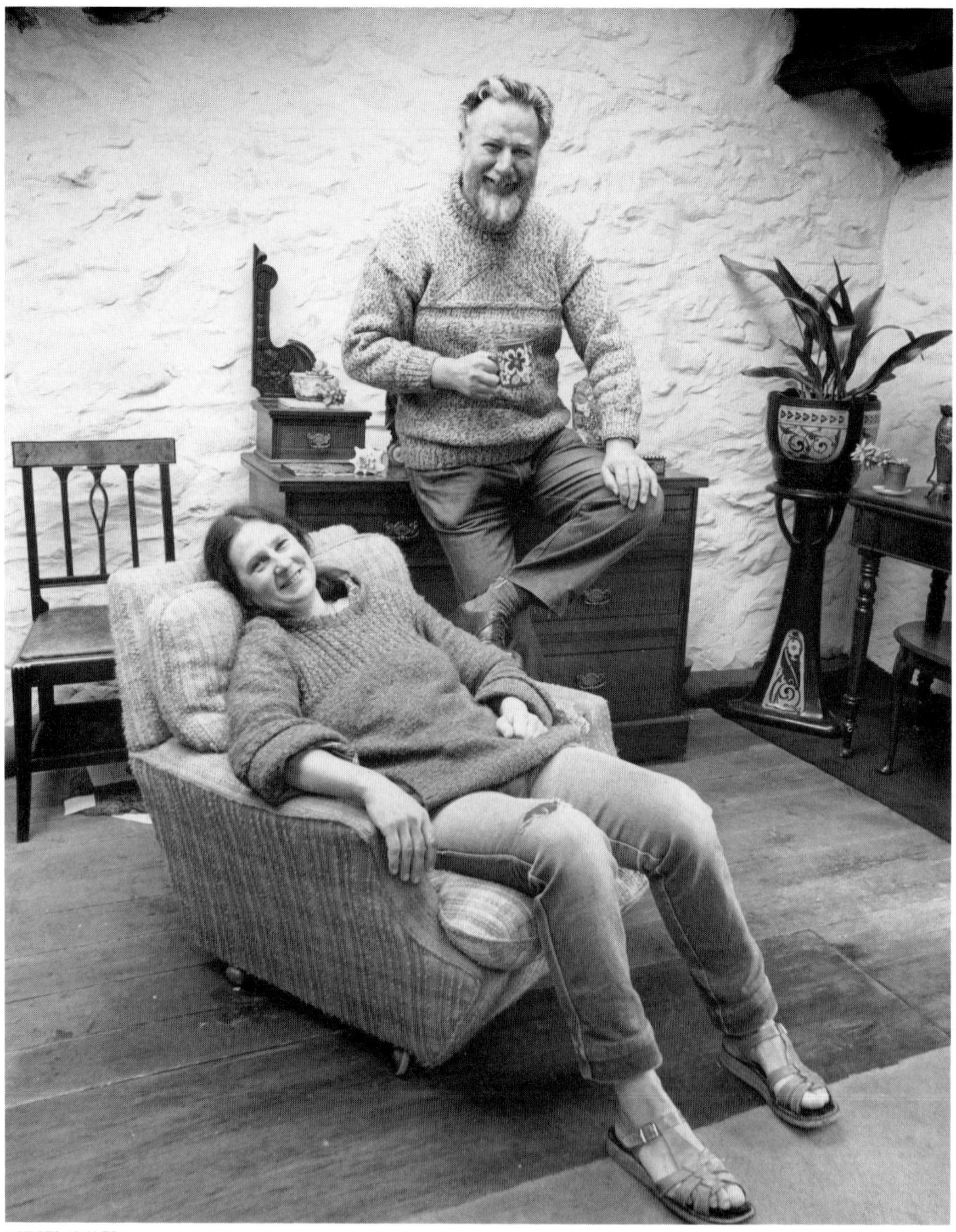

ARTISTS, WALES

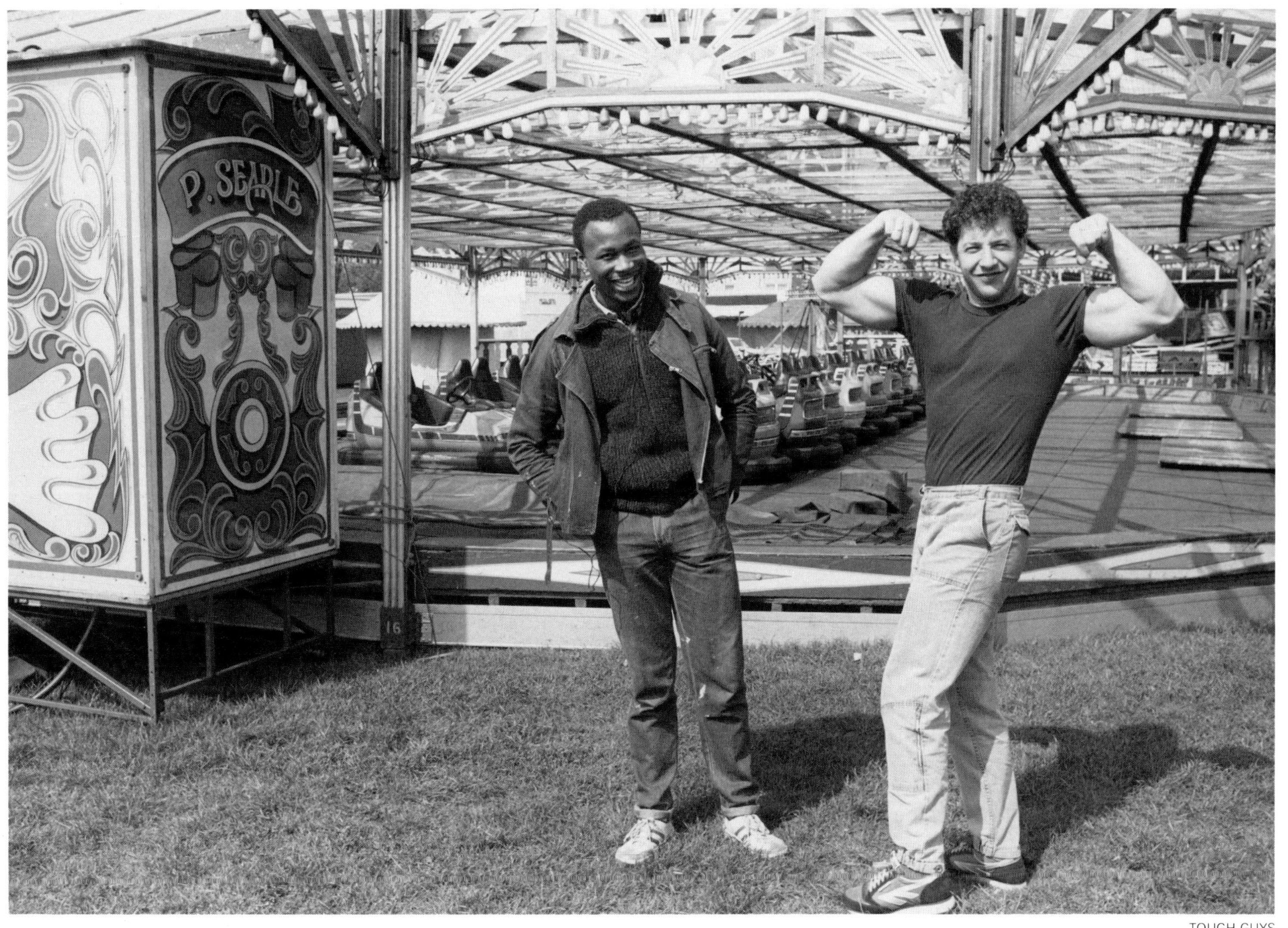

TOUGH GUYS

GLYN BARNEY

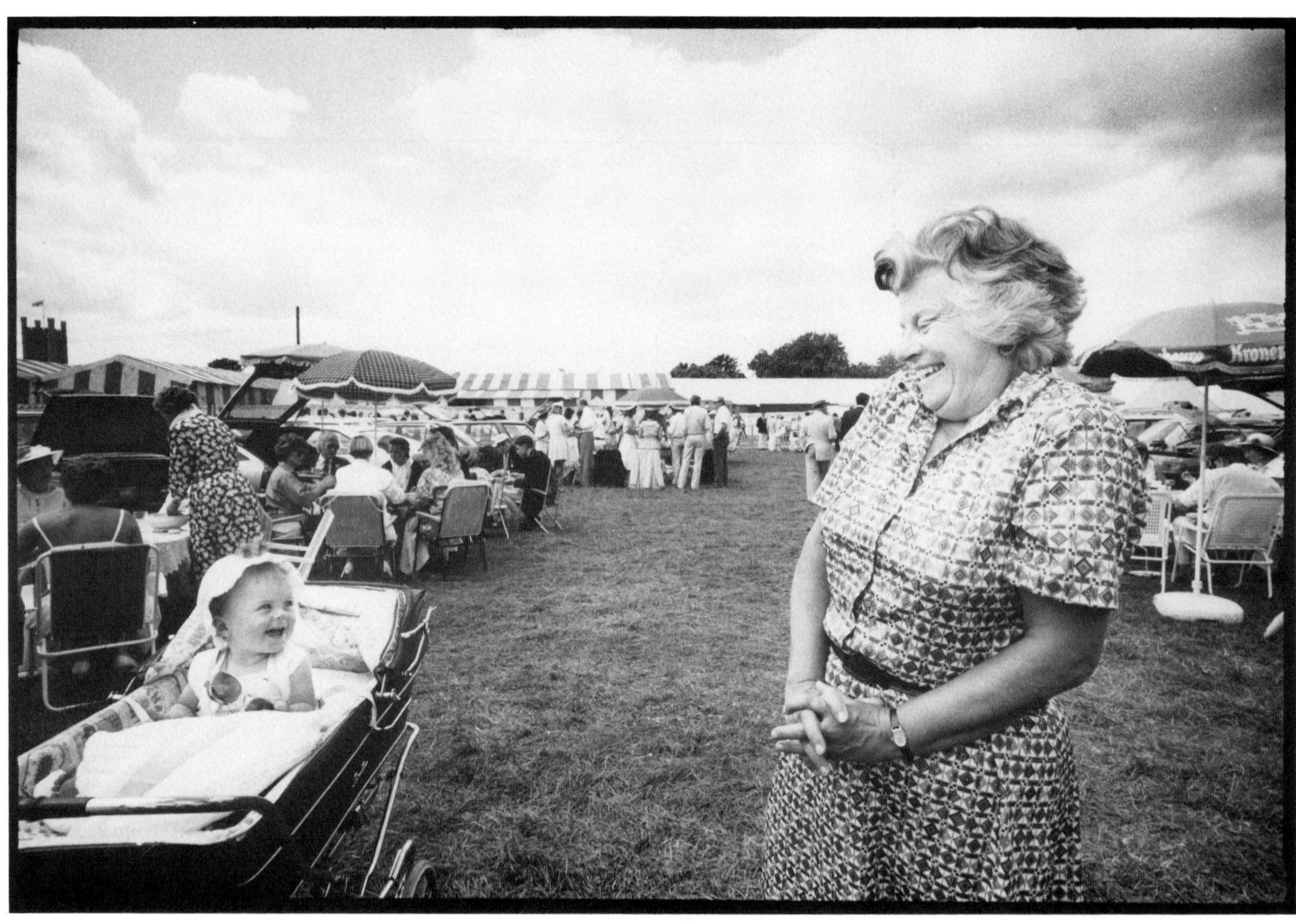

MELCHIOR DIGIACOMO LIVES IN NEW JERSEY AND WORKS FOR ABC-TV, NEWSWEEK, VARIOUS SPORTS JOURNALS AND ADVERTISING AGENCIES.

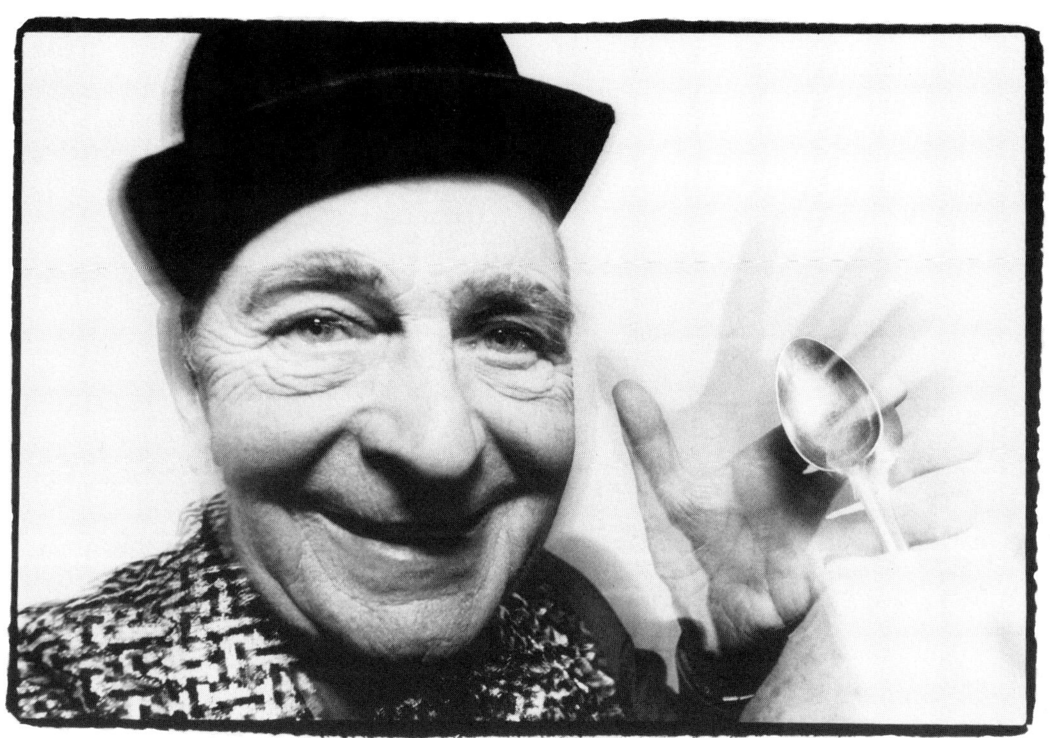

JOHNNY GROVES, MUSIC HALL ARTIST

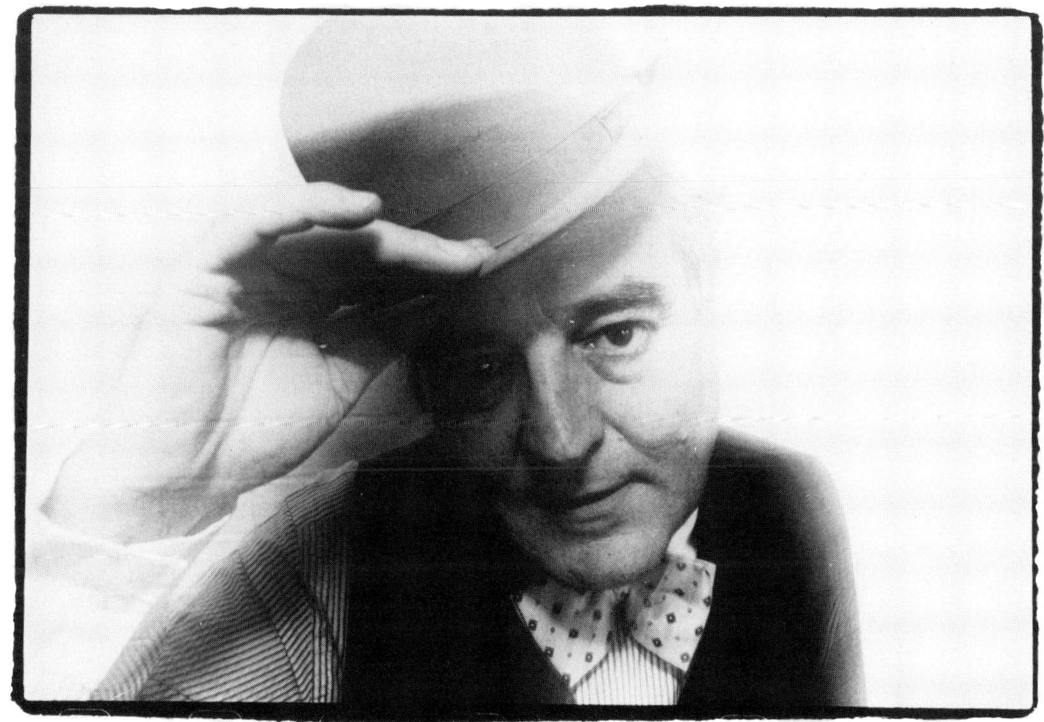

FROM THE MUSIC HALL SERIES

ADRIAN FRANKLIN IS A PHOTOJOURNALIST WORKING FROM LONDON FOR THE LAST THREE YEARS.

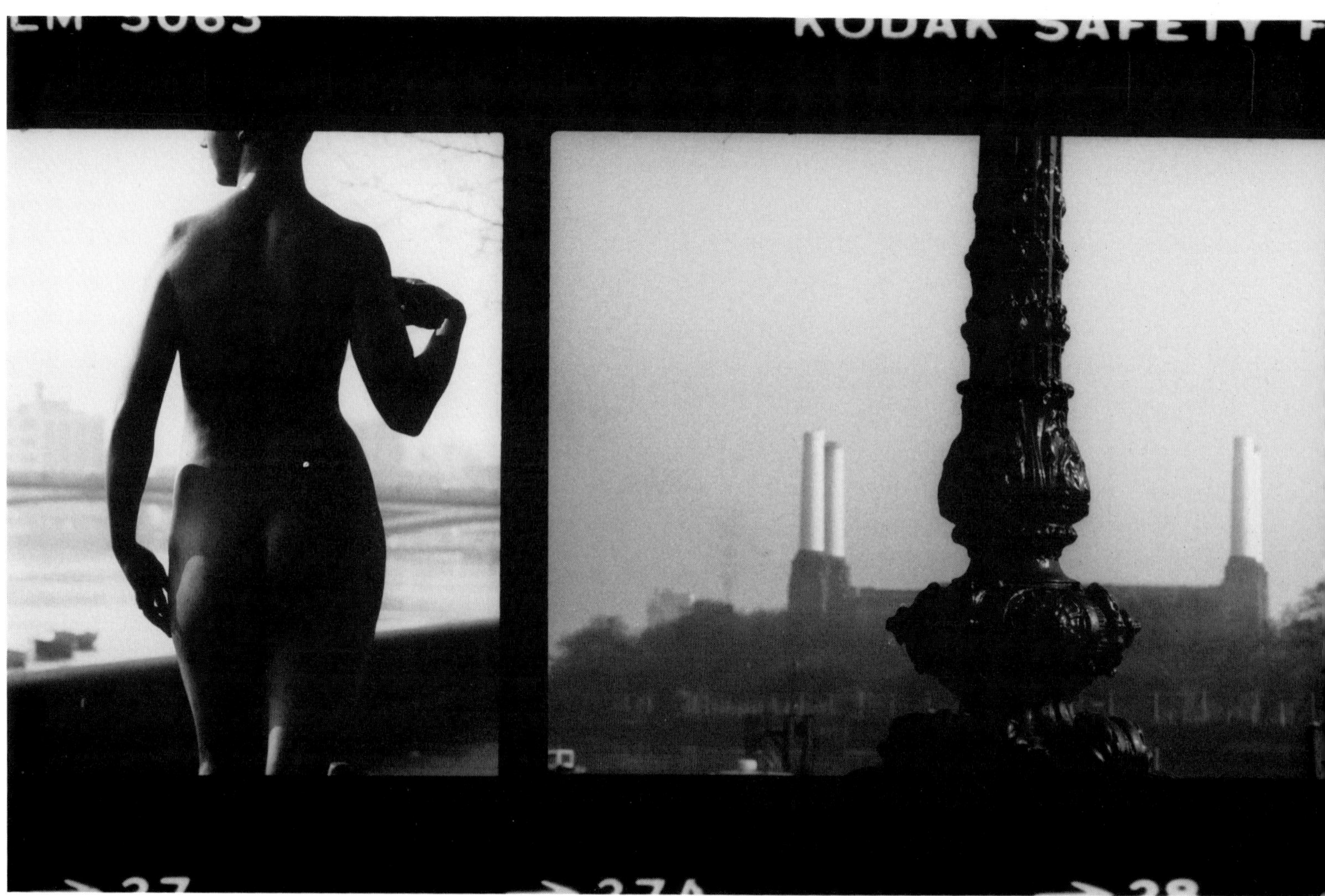

BATTERSEA COMPLICATIONS

JEFF HUTCHINSON IS A SELF-TAUGHT PHOTOGRAPHER LIVING IN SUSSEX. HE HAS HAD LOCAL EXHIBITIONS AND WAS A PHOTO ESSAY CONTEST WINNER AT LAS VEGAS.

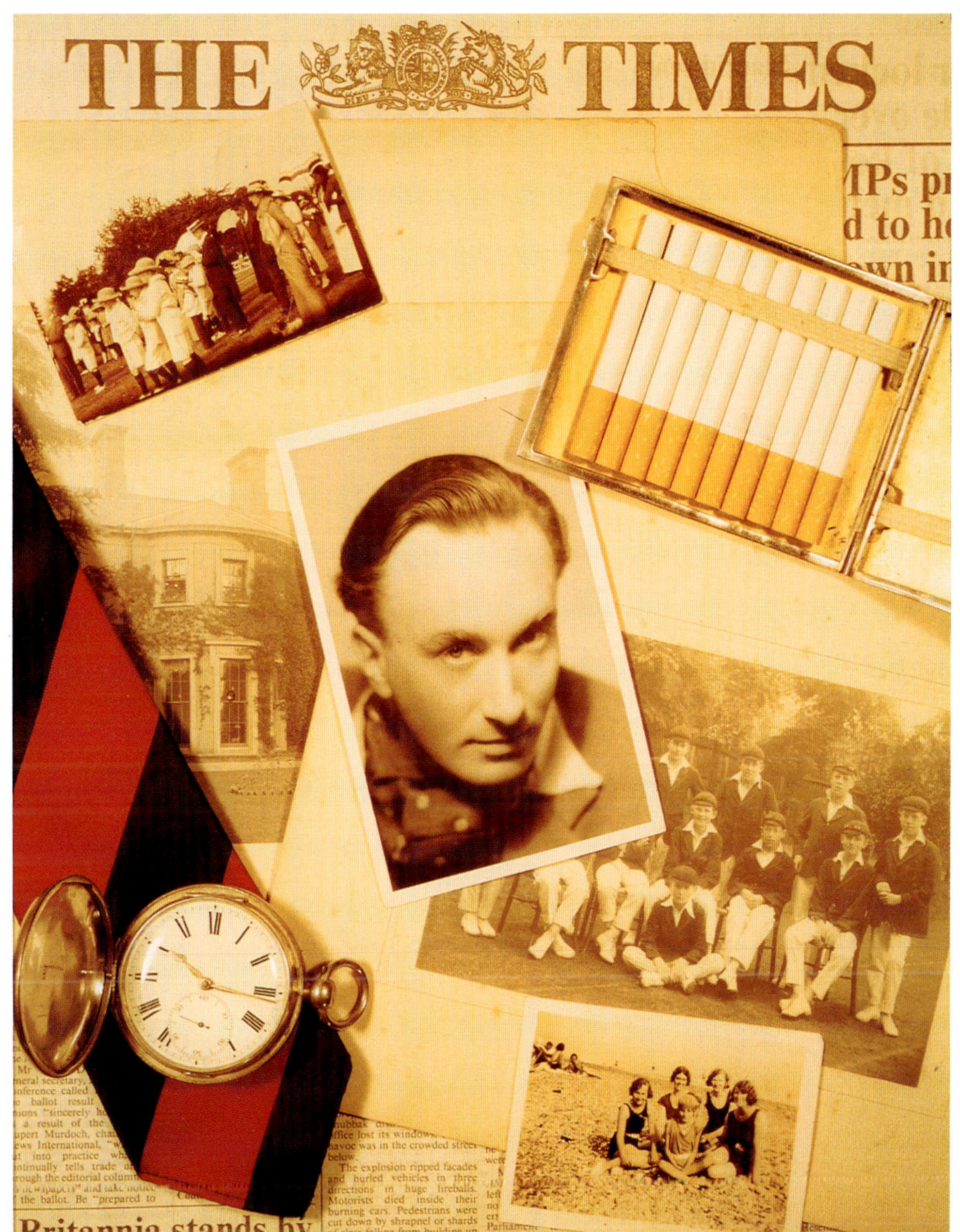

ENGLISH GENTLEMEN

STUART PITKIN WENT BACK TO COLLEGE TO STUDY PHOTOGRAPHY AND HAS RECENTLY STARTED FREELANCING.

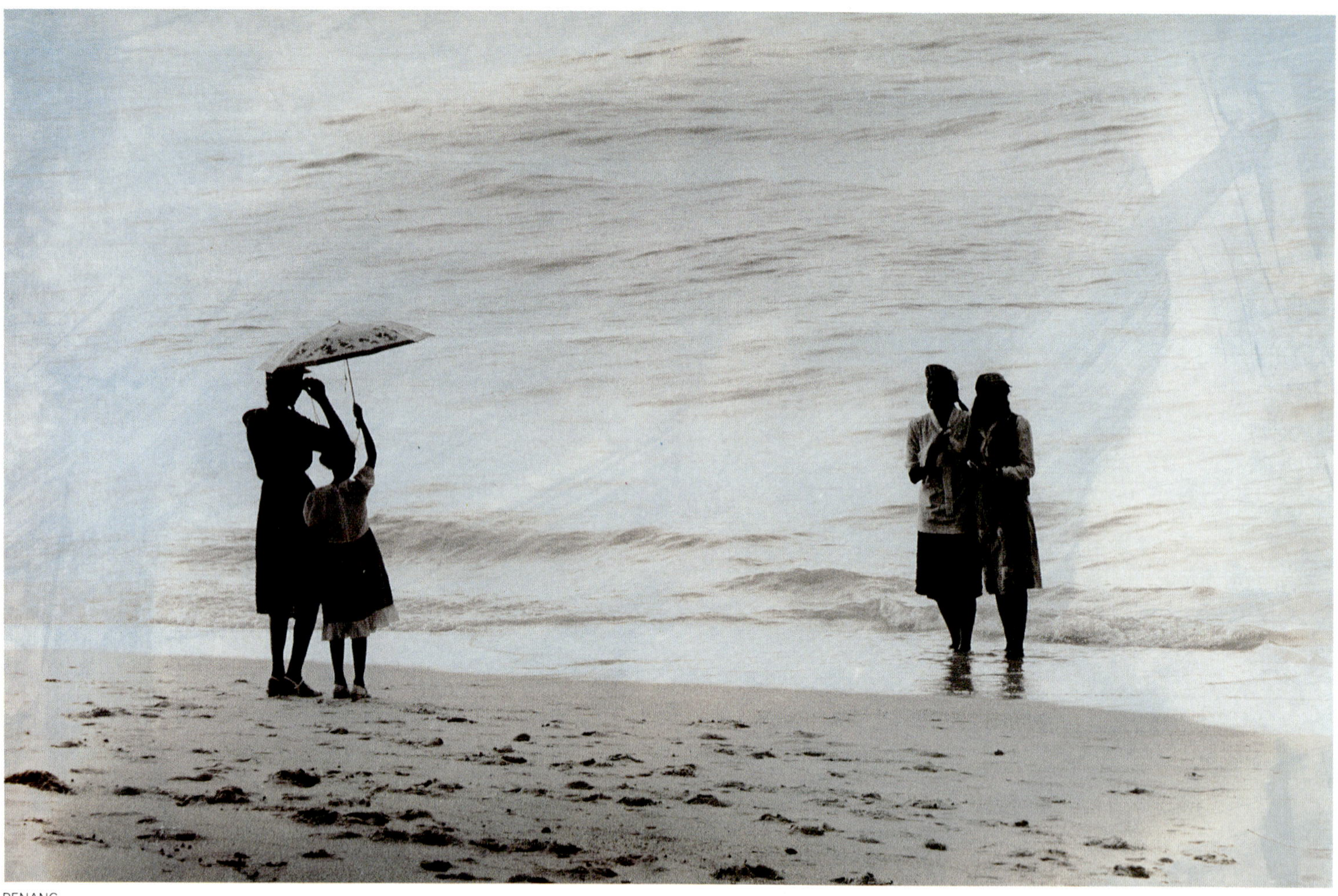

PENANG

BRUCE LITSON IS A FREELANCE PHOTOJOURNALIST WHO MADE THESE PERSONAL PICTURES WHILE ON ASSIGNMENT ABROAD.

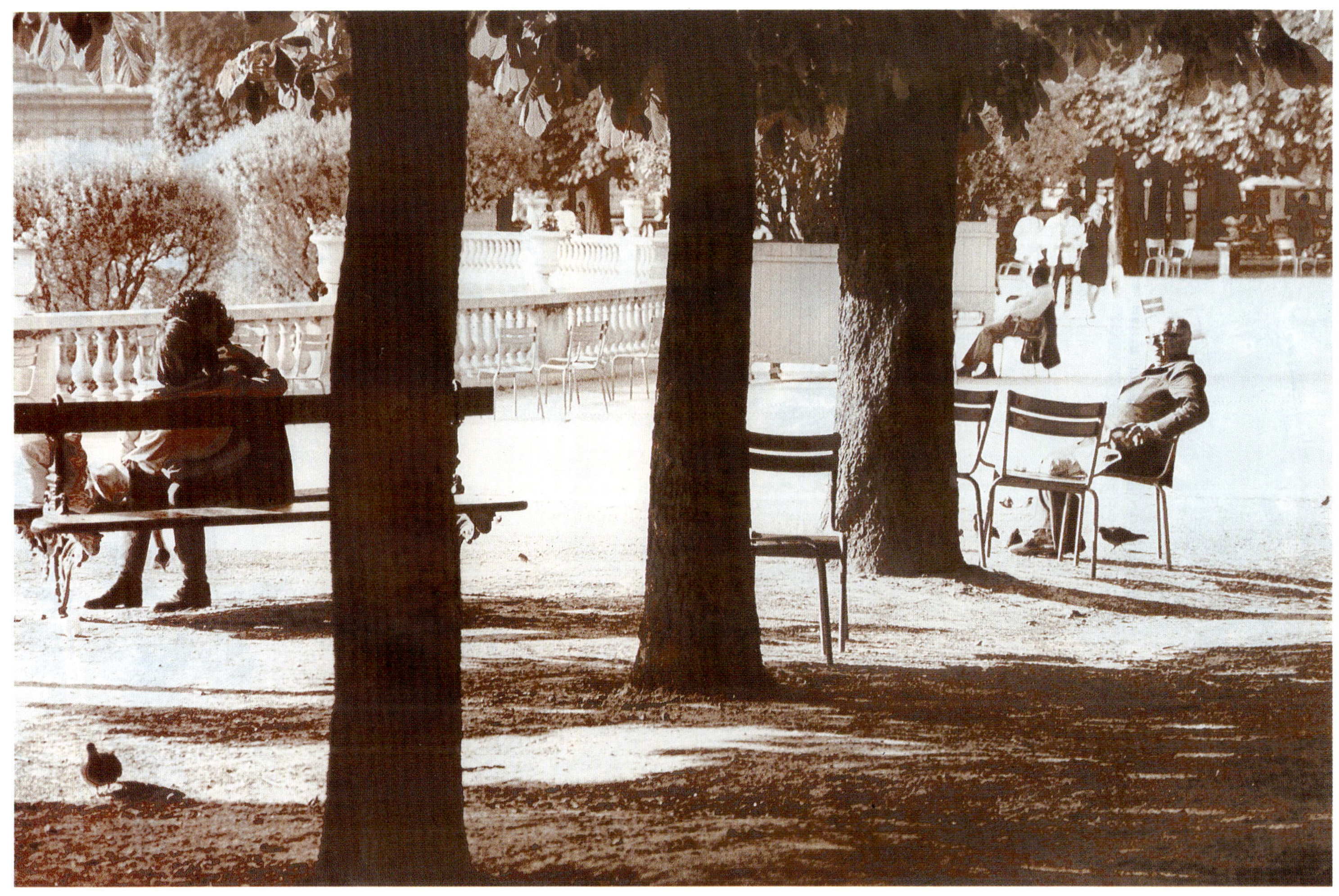

PARIS

BRUCE LITSON

140

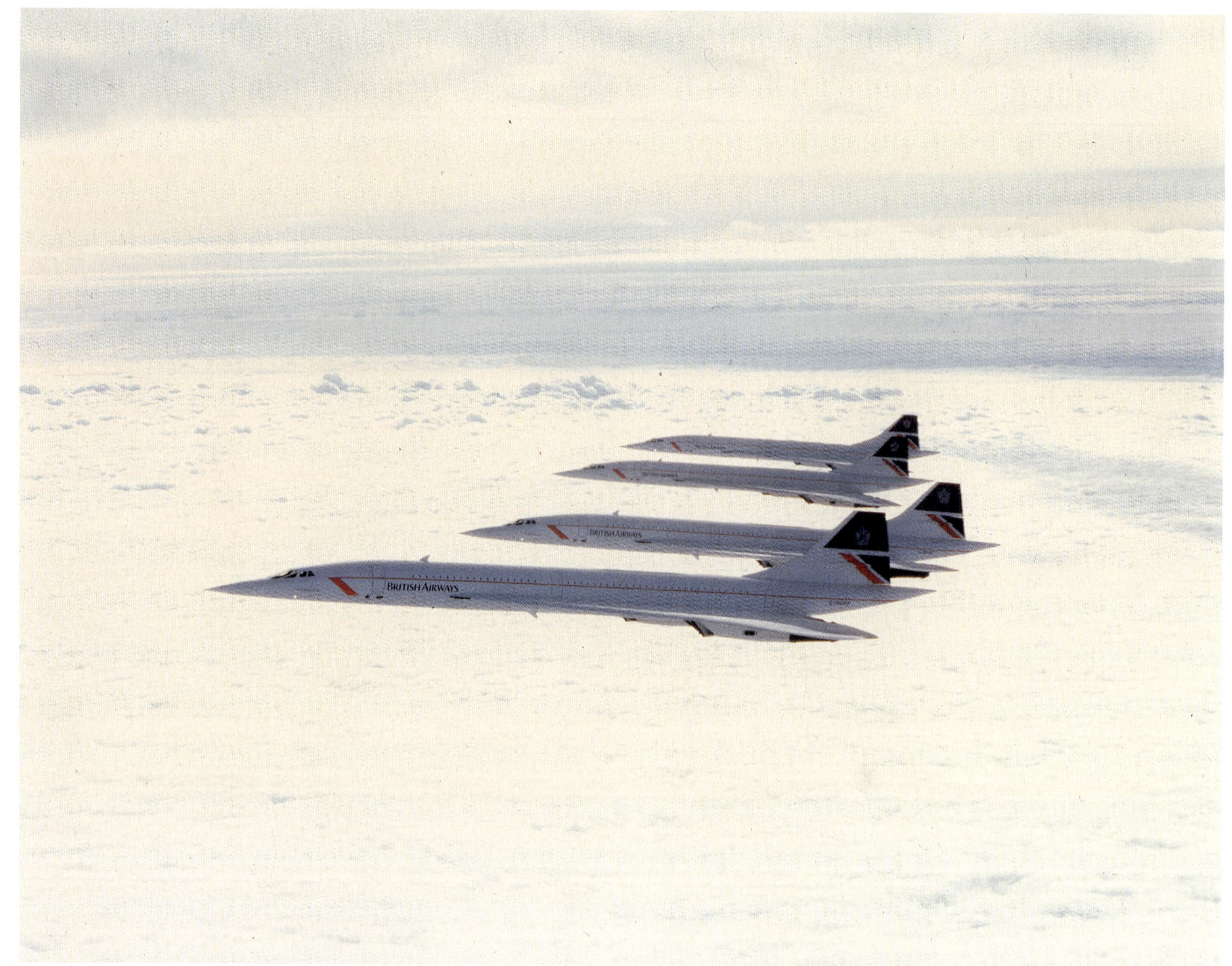

TEN YEARS OF CONCORDE

ADRIAN MEREDITH HAS BEEN WORKING IN PHOTOGRAPHY FOR 20 YEARS. CURRENTLY FREELANCING ESPECIALLY WITH BRITISH AIRWAYS.

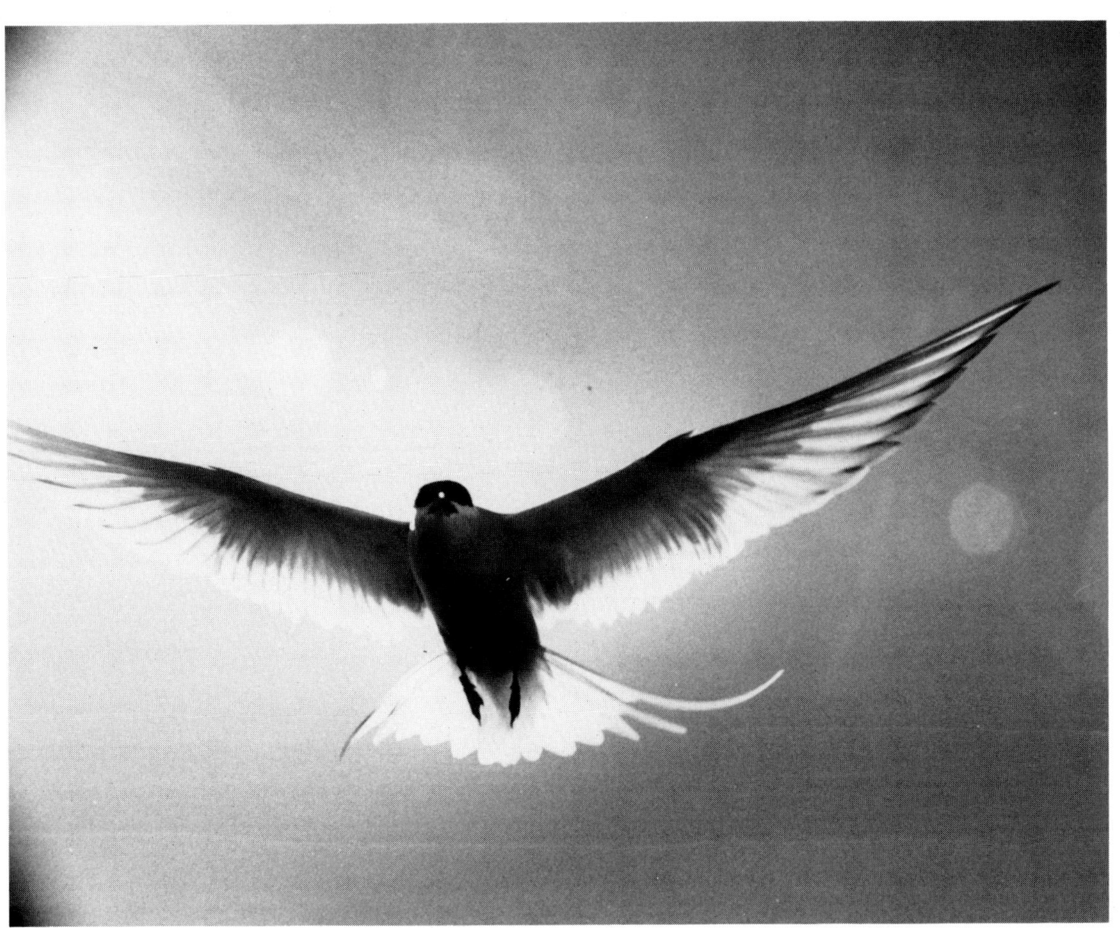

A ROSEAT TERN ATTACKING THE PHOTOGRAPHER

JOHN TOPHAM NO LONGER OWNS THE FAMOUS LIBRARY OF THAT NAME. AT 78 AND DISABLED HE MADE A TRIP TO THE SCOTTISH ISLANDS THAT HAVE GIVEN HIM SIXTY (NOW SIXTY-ONE) PUBLICATIONS TO DATE. HE BEGAN PHOTOGRAPHY AS A POLICEMAN IN THE EAST END BEFORE TURNING FREELANCE IN 1933.

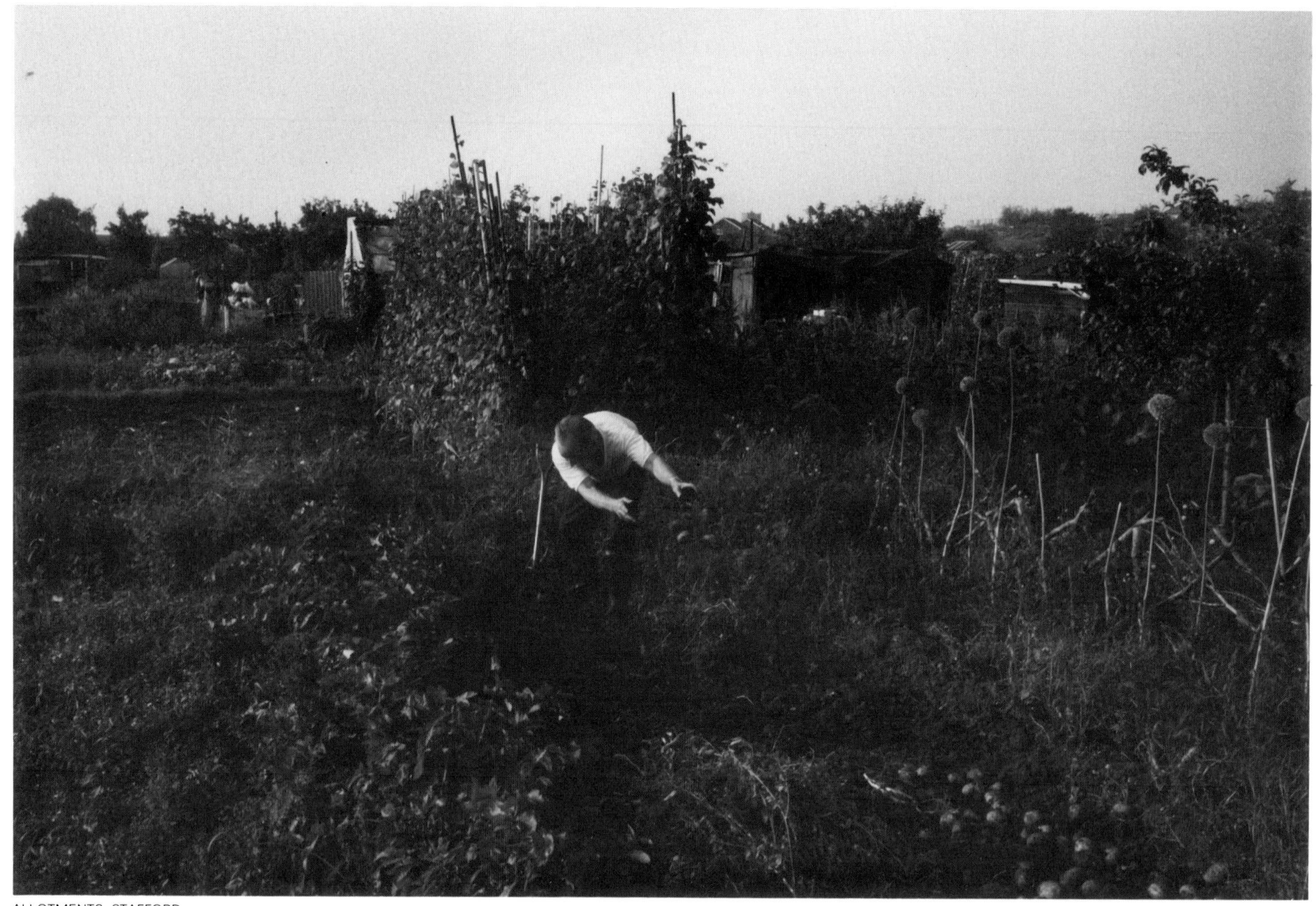

ALLOTMENTS, STAFFORD

MICHAEL PEARSON WAS BORN IN DARLINGTON IN 1956. HE IS A SOCIAL WORKER AND PHOTOGRAPHER LIVING IN STAFFORD. HIS PUBLICATIONS INCLUDE THE FOOTBALL MONOGRAPH 'CITY GO NAP AS QUAKERS HALT SLUMP'.

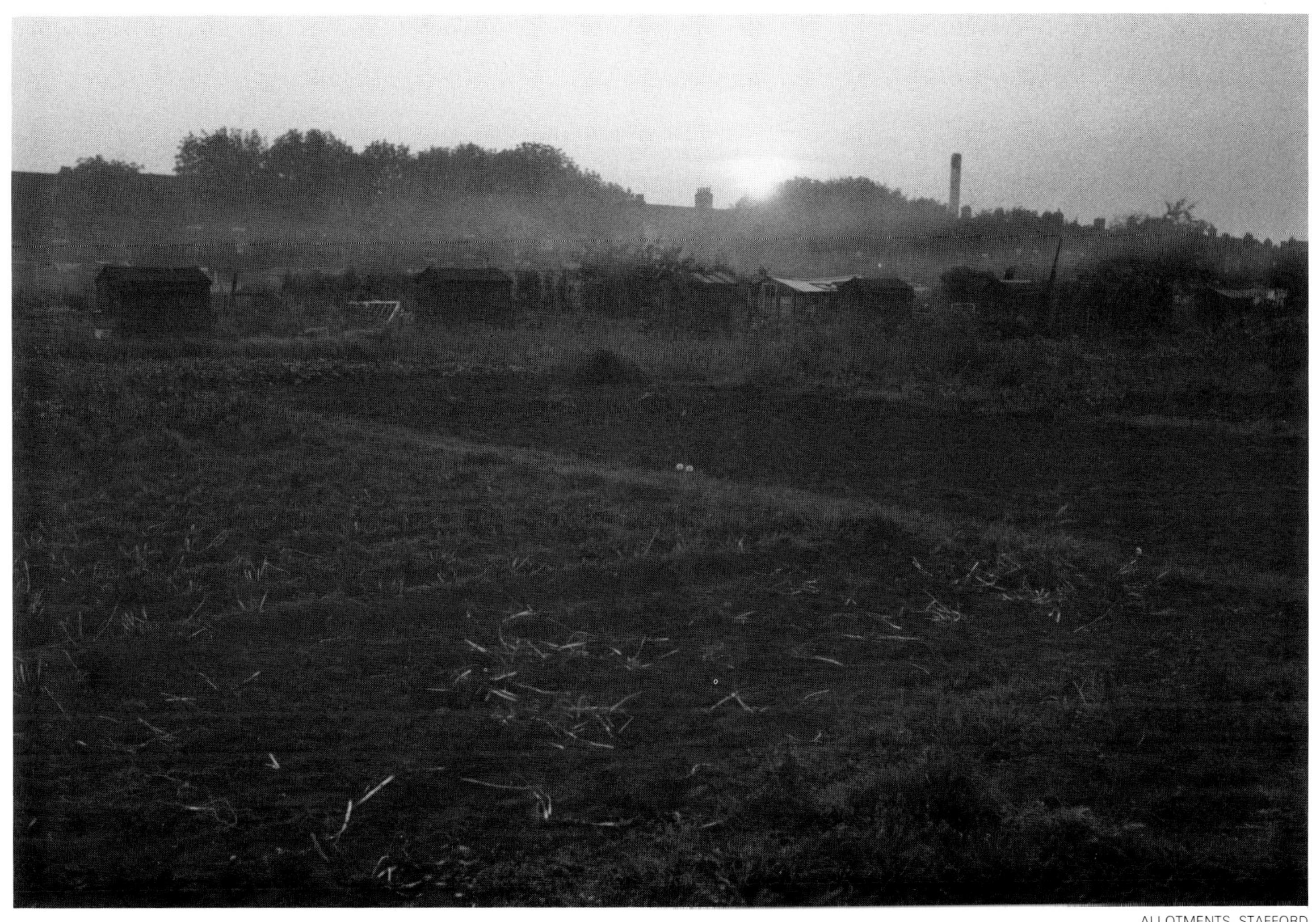

ALLOTMENTS, STAFFORD

MICHAEL PEARSON

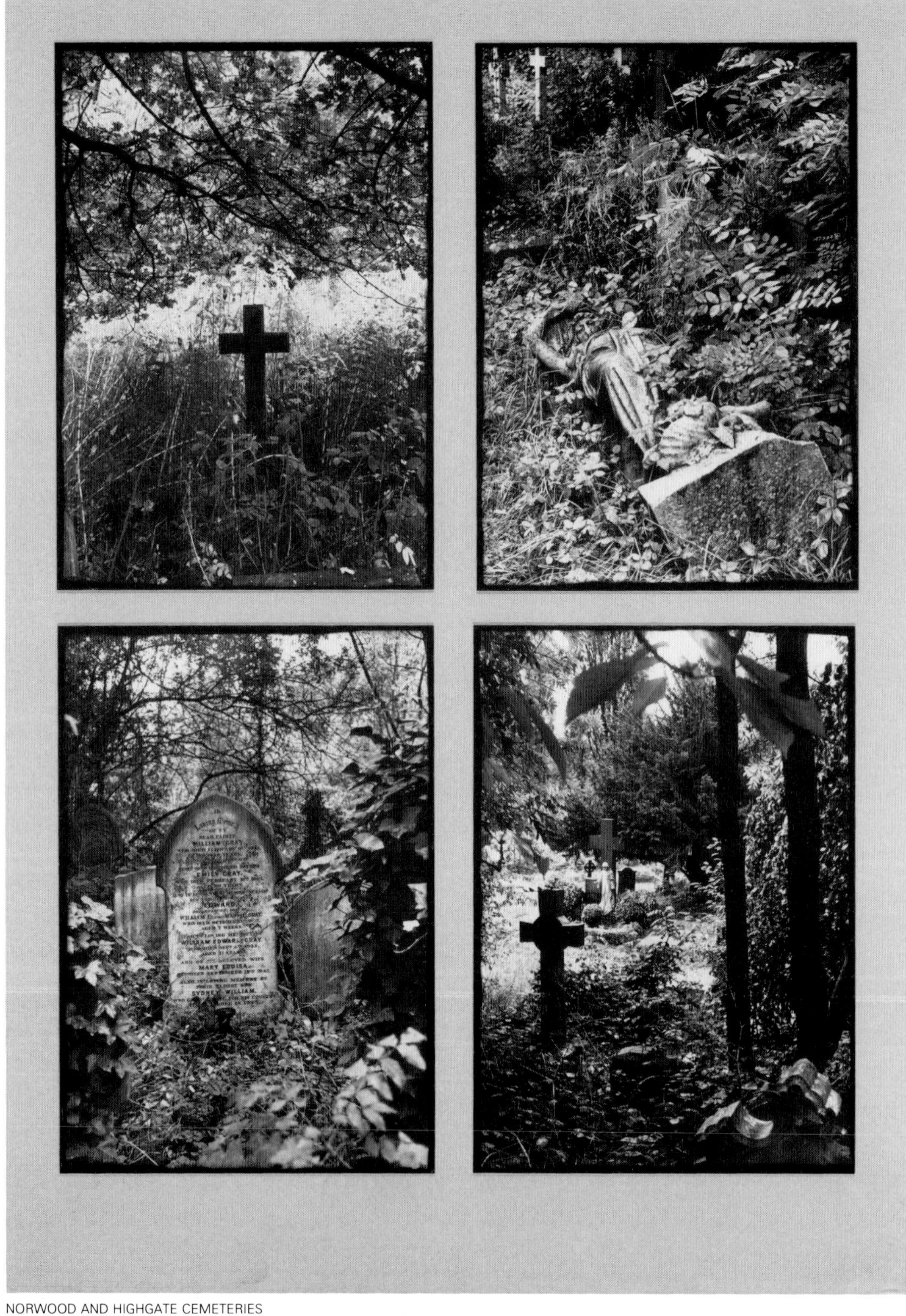

NORWOOD AND HIGHGATE CEMETERIES

A. HOLTZMAN COMES FROM THE HAGUE, HOLLAND AND TOOK AN EXTENDED SERIES IN THE CEMETERIES OF NORWOOD AND HIGHGATE.

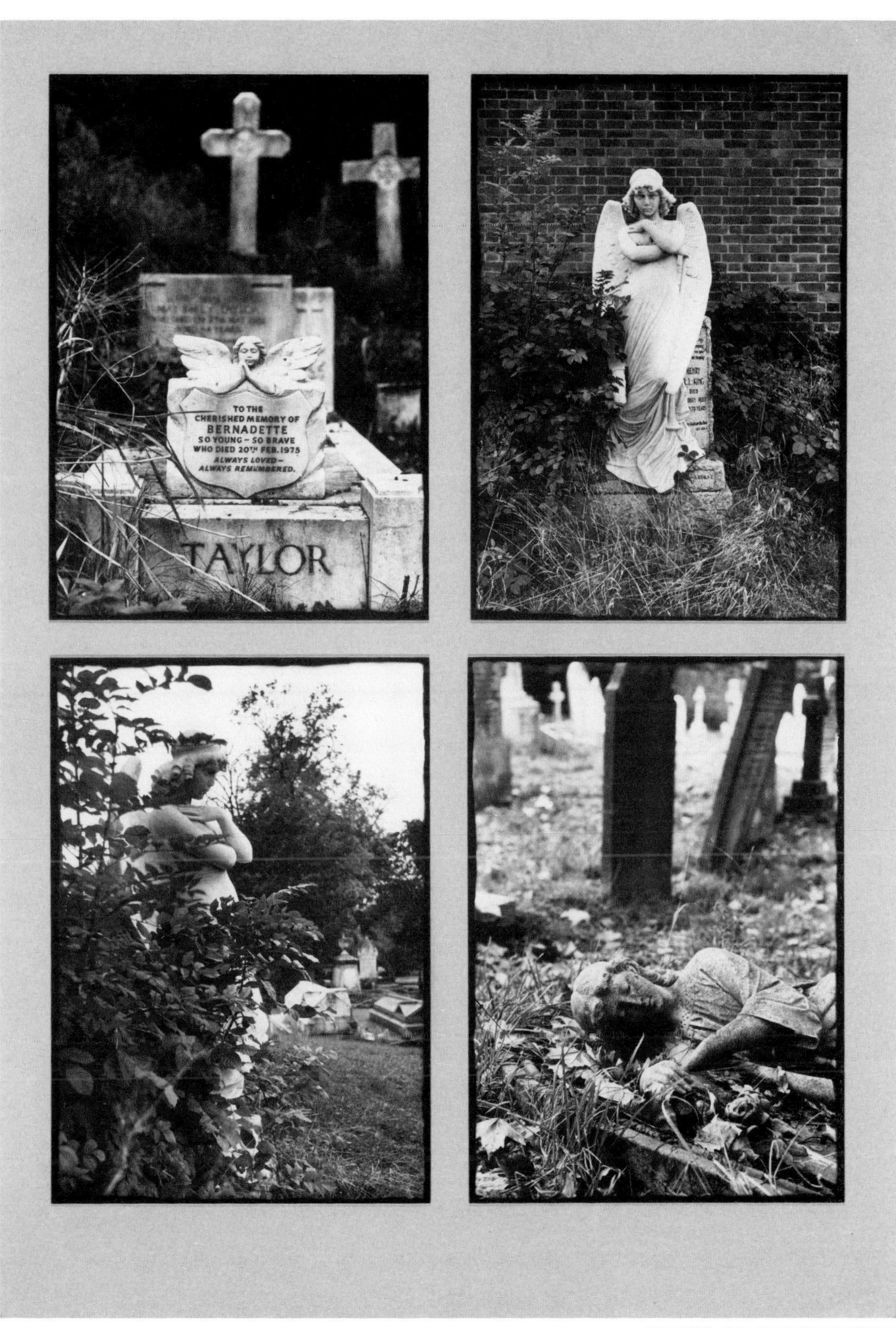

NORWOOD AND HIGHGATE CEMETERIES

A. HOLTZMAN

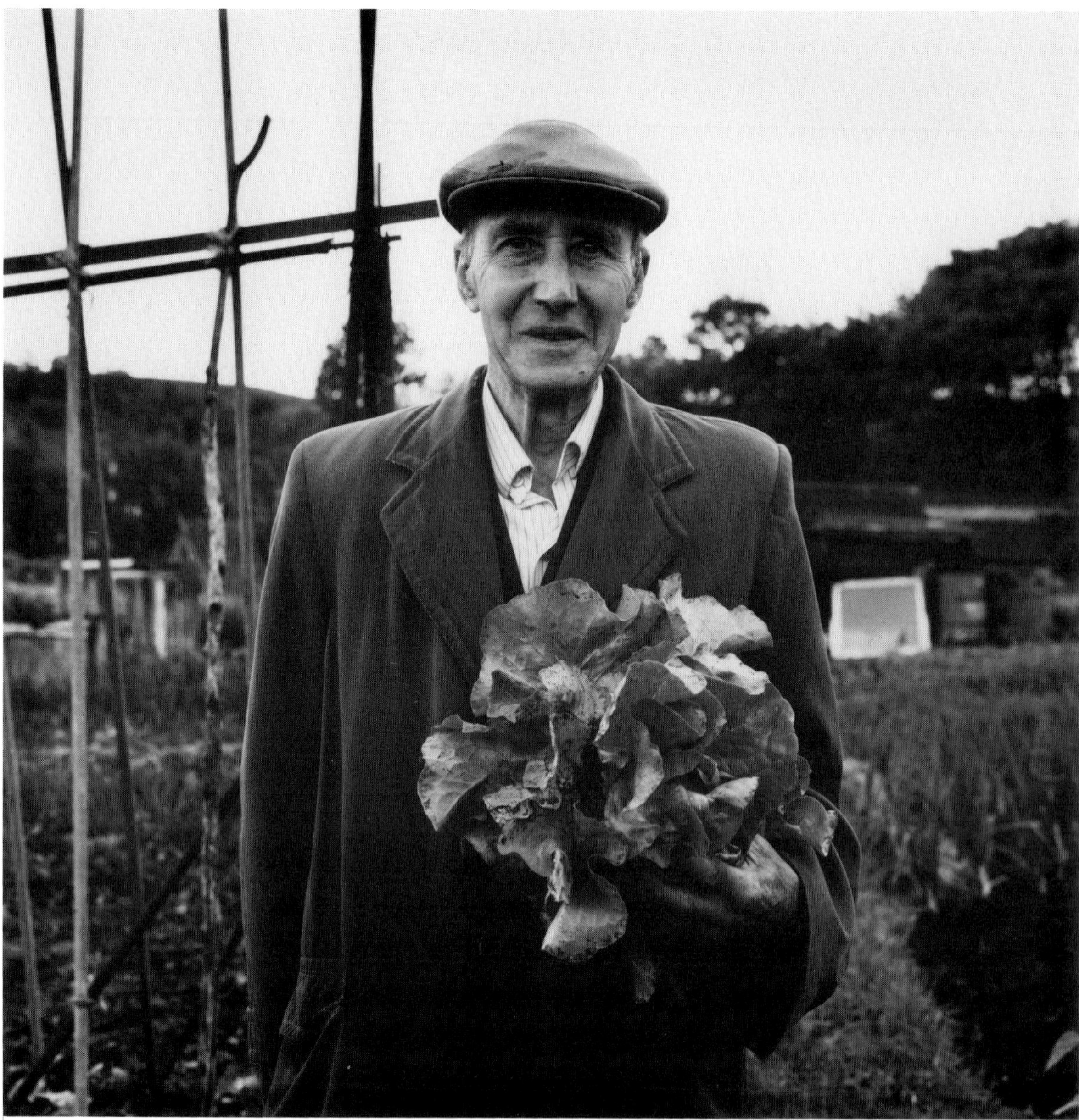

MEMBER OF THE ASHLEY VALE ALLOTMENT ASSOCIATION

ROBERT PULLEN STUDIED AT THE LONDON COLLEGE OF PRINTING 1976-79 AND WORKS AS A HOSPITAL DARKROOM TECHNICIAN. HE LIVES IN SOUTH EAST LONDON AND HAS MADE LOCAL PHOTO DOCUMENTATIONS.

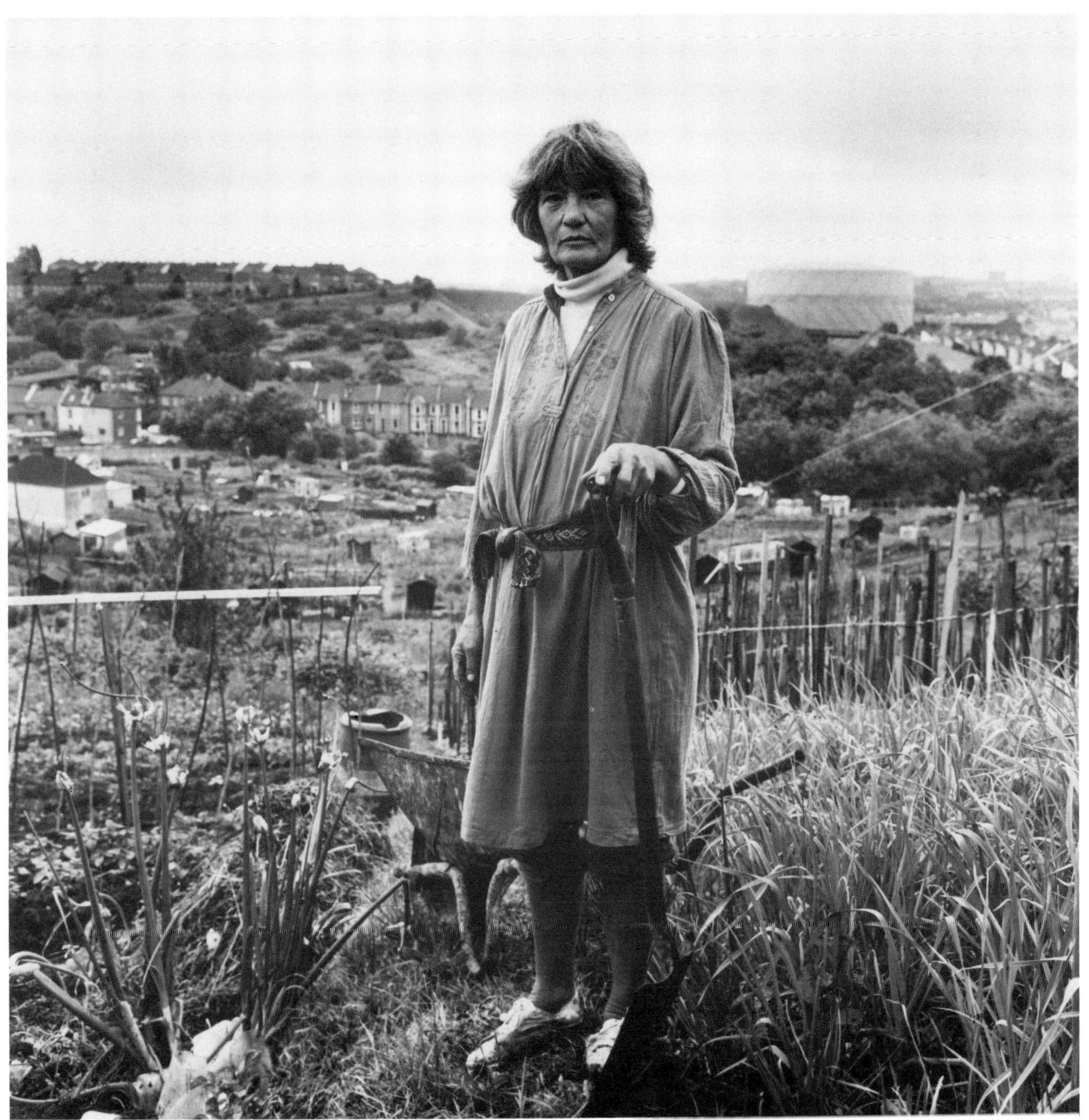

MEMBER OF THE ASHLEY VALE ALLOTMENT ASSOCIATION

ROBERT PULLEN

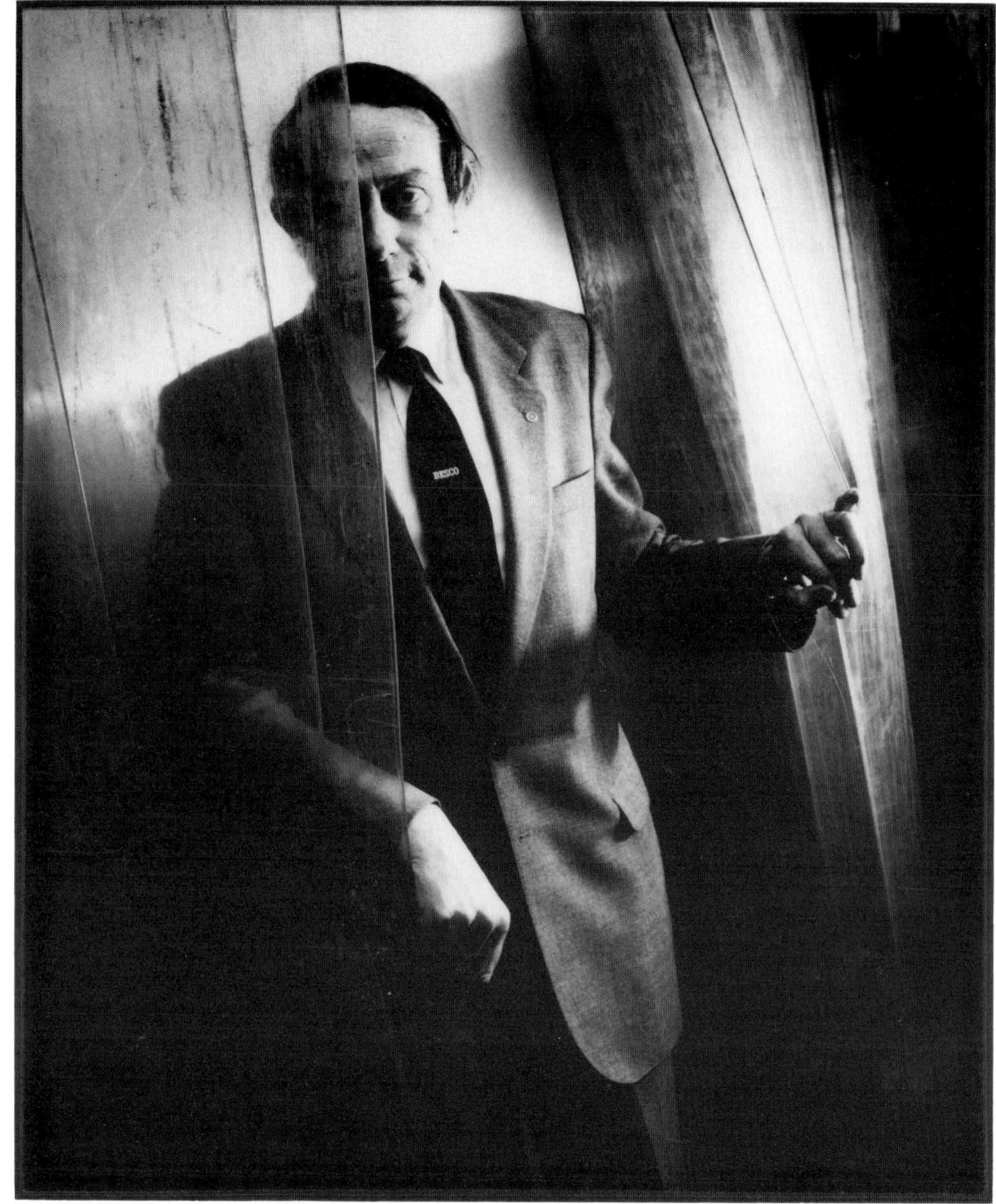

DON WILSON (TAKEN FOR 'TRUCK' MAGAZINE)

STEPHEN MOORS WAS BORN IN LONDON BUT BROUGHT UP IN MERSEYSIDE. HE STUDIED PHOTOGRAPHY AT NEWPORT, AND HAS BEEN A COMMERCIAL PORTRAIT PHOTOGRAPHER FOR TWO YEARS AND BEEN PUBLISHED IN MANY MAGAZINES.

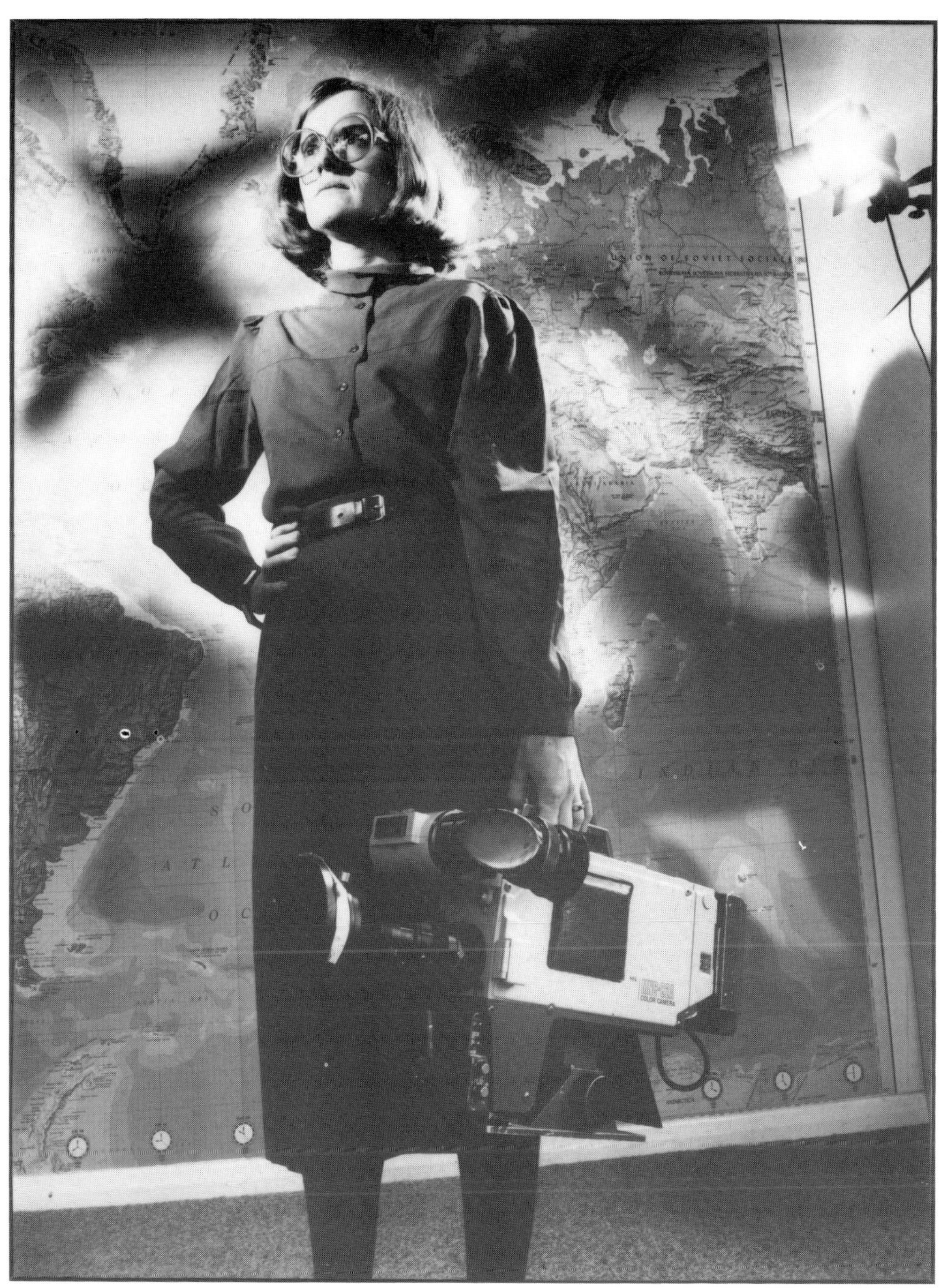

VICKI WEGG-PROSSER

STEPHEN MOORS

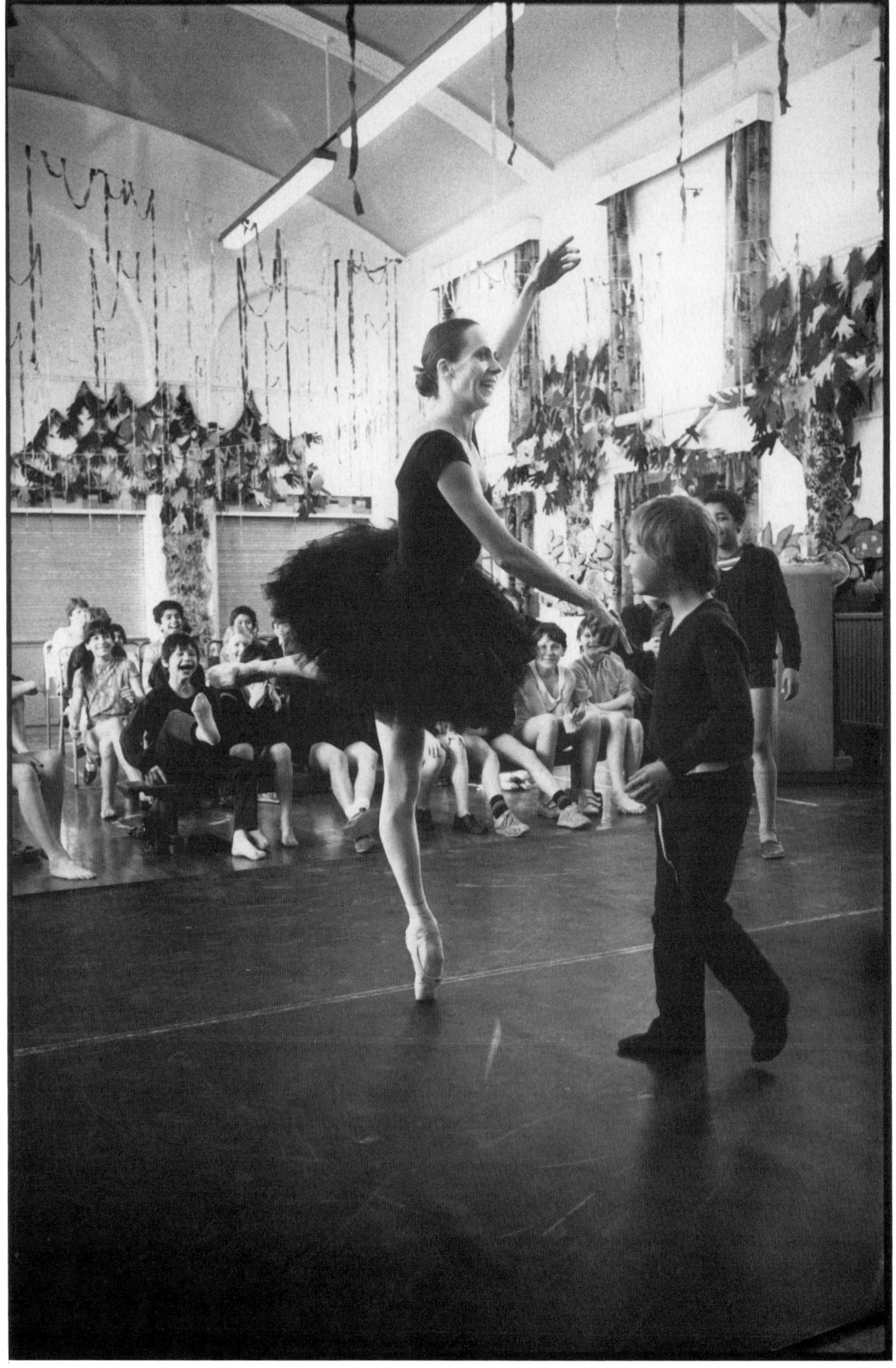

ROYAL BALLET VISIT, LADY BARN PRIMARY SCHOOL

ROB PHILLIPS WAS TRAINED AS A TEACHER FOR THE DEAF AT MANCHESTER UNIVERSITY AND IS CURRENTLY BASED AT A SCHOOL PRODUCING VISUAL TEACHING MATERIALS.
IN FEBRUARY 1986 THE ROYAL BALLET UNDERTOOK A PROJECT WITH MANCHESTER SCHOOLS. HERE MEMBERS OF THE BALLET ARE AT LADY BARN PRIMARY SCHOOL.

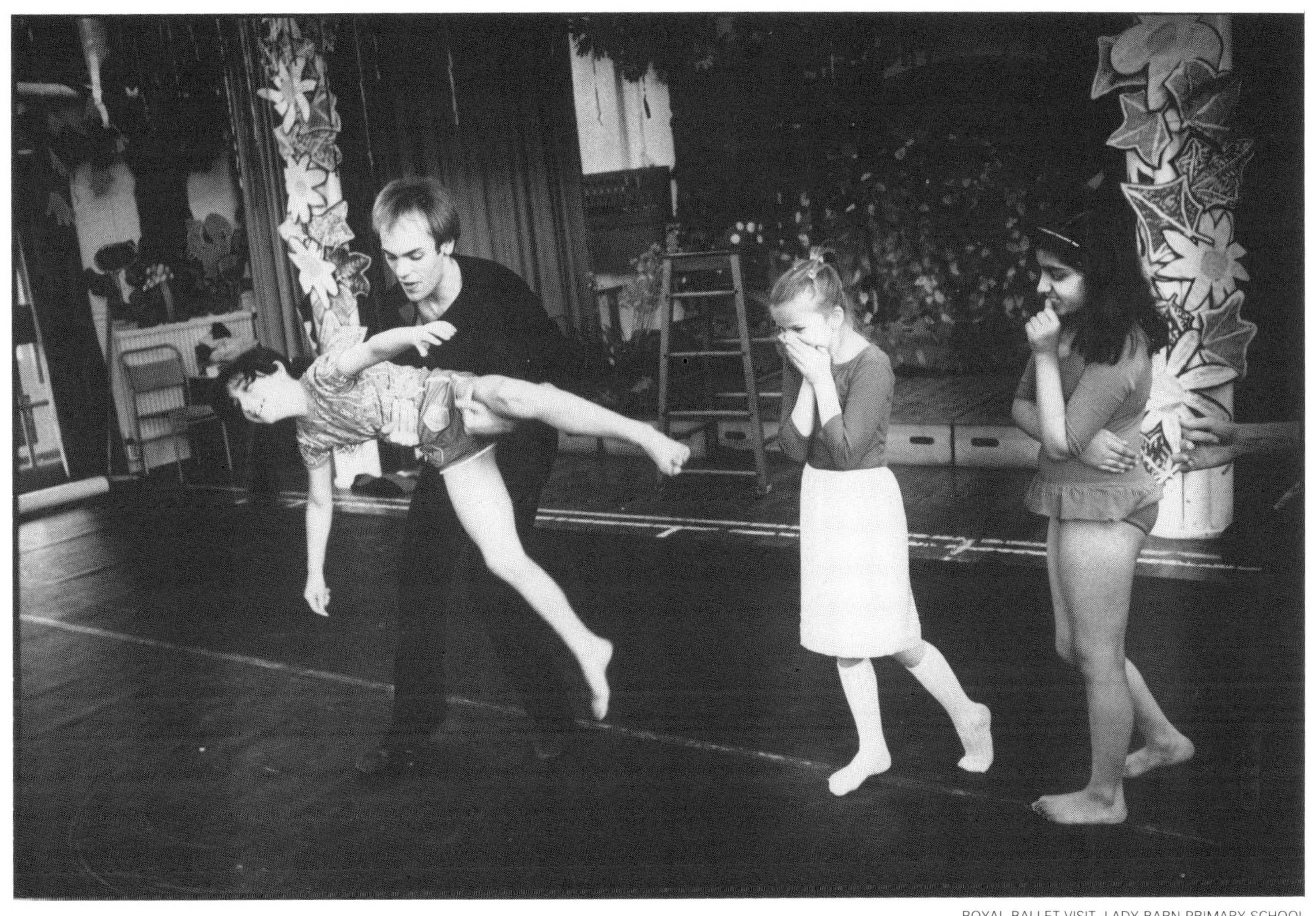

ROYAL BALLET VISIT, LADY BARN PRIMARY SCHOOL

ROB PHILLIPS

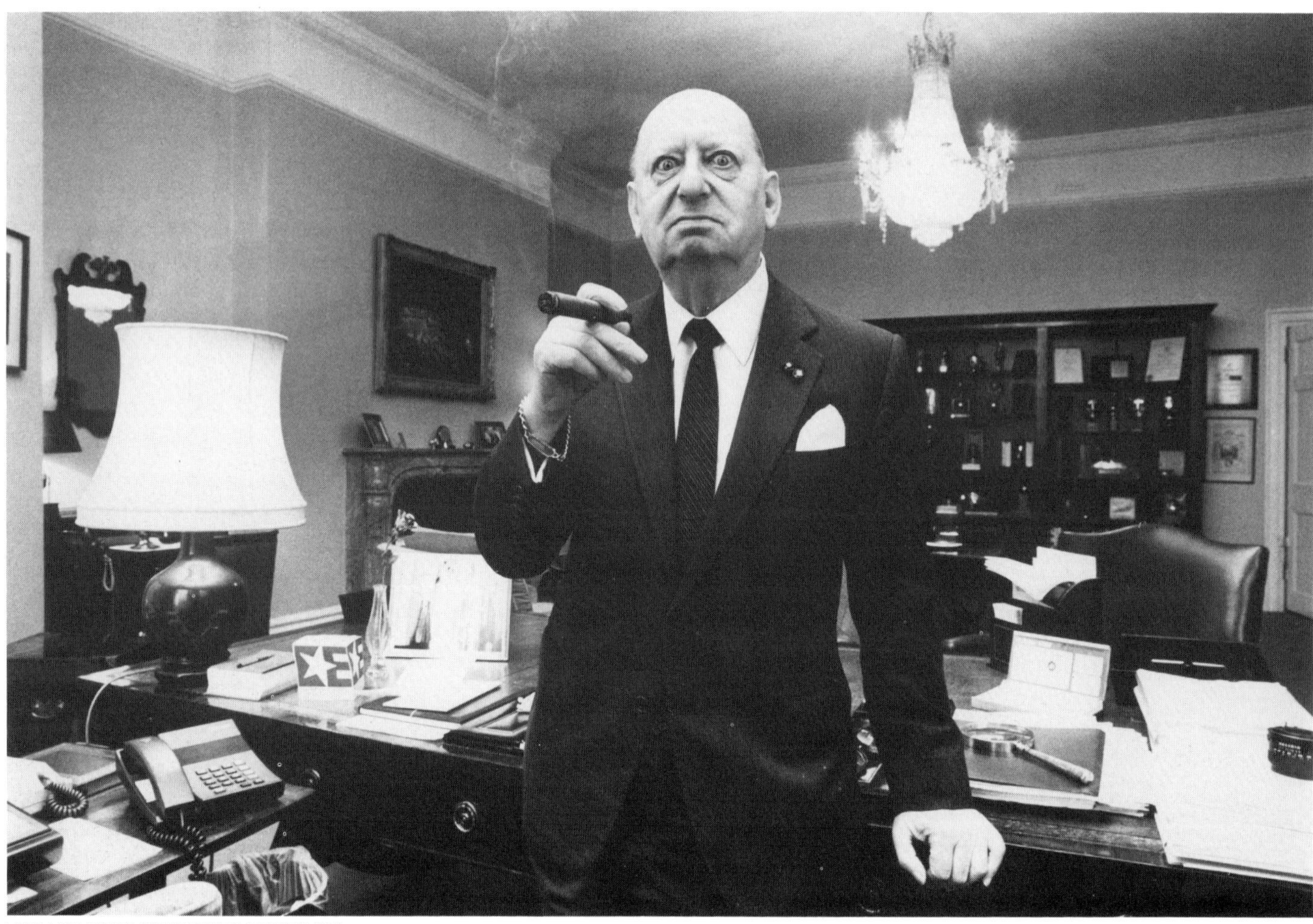

LORD LEW GRADE (COURTESY 'SUNDAY TIMES')

JILLIAN EDELSTEIN WAS BORN IN SOUTH AFRICA AND WORKED FOR THE *RAND DAILY MAIL* THERE AND THE *SUNDAY TIMES* IN LONDON. SHE IS NOW SPECIALISING IN FREELANCE PORTRAITURE.

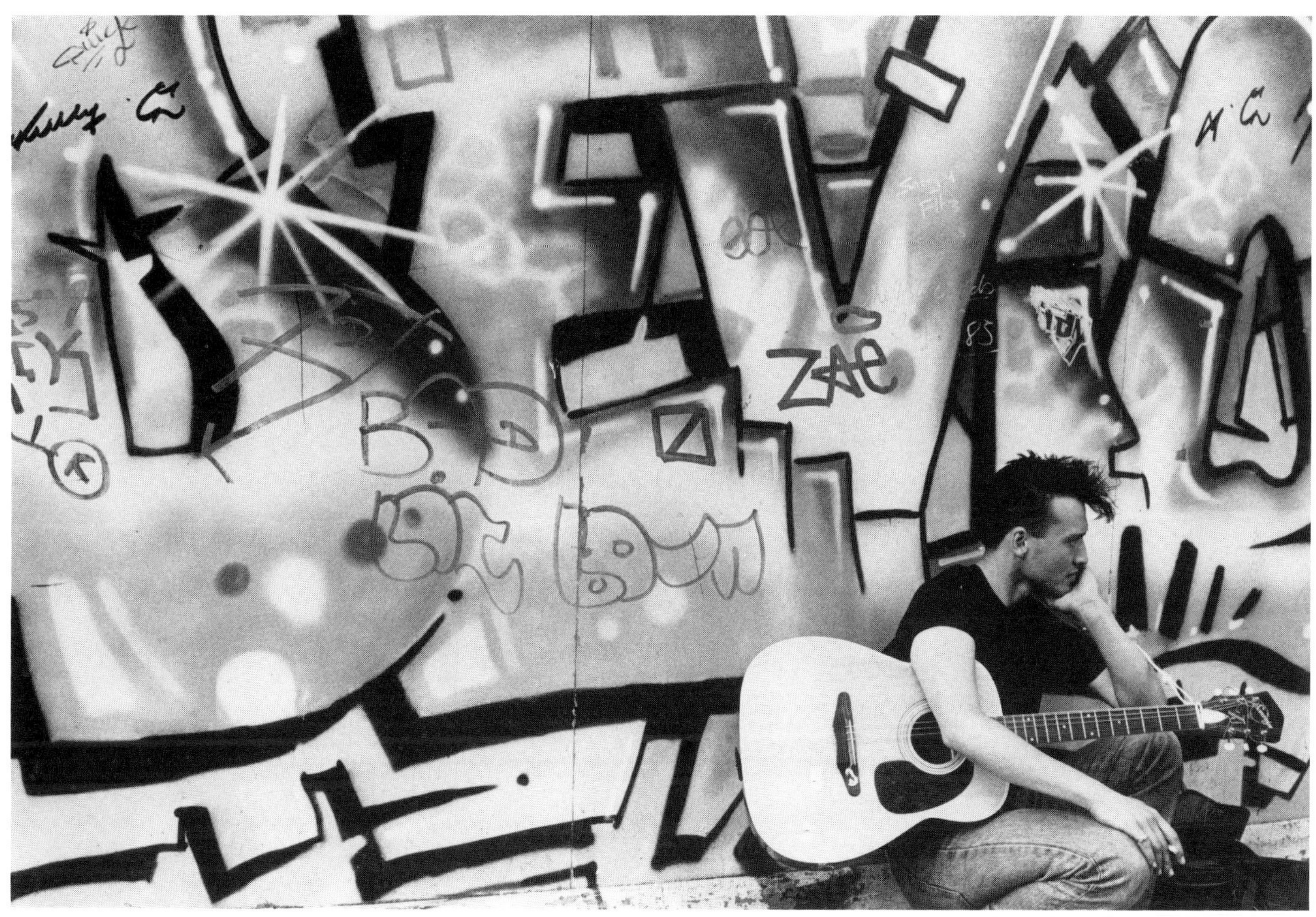

COVENT GARDEN BUSKER

JILLIAN EDELSTEIN

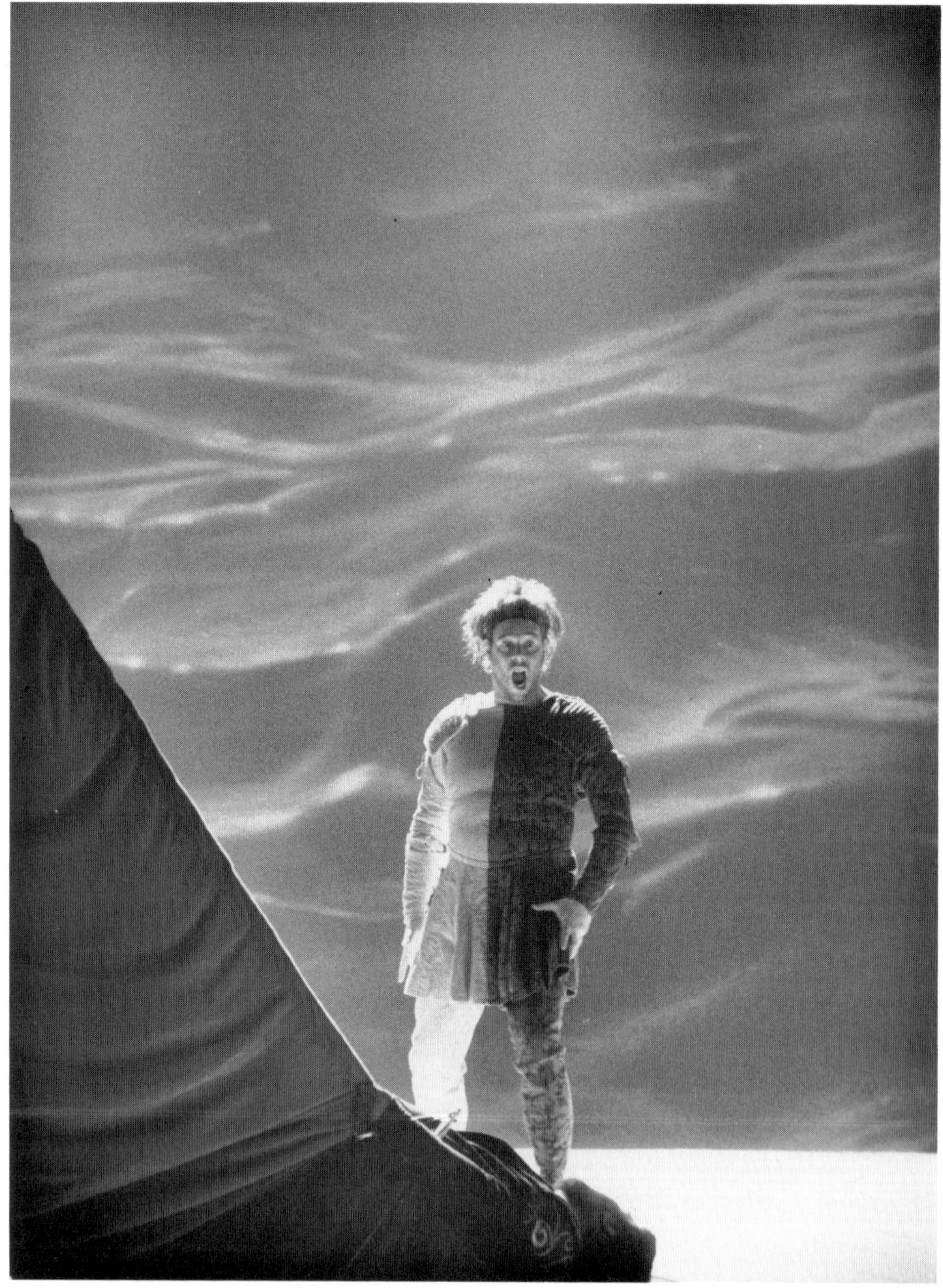

OTELLO, WELSH NATIONAL OPERA

MARTYN HOSKINS HAS RECENTLY COMPLETED HIS HND AT MEDWAY COLLEGE OF DESIGN. HE NOW LIVES AND WORKS IN BRISTOL SPECIALISING IN THE PERFORMING ARTS.

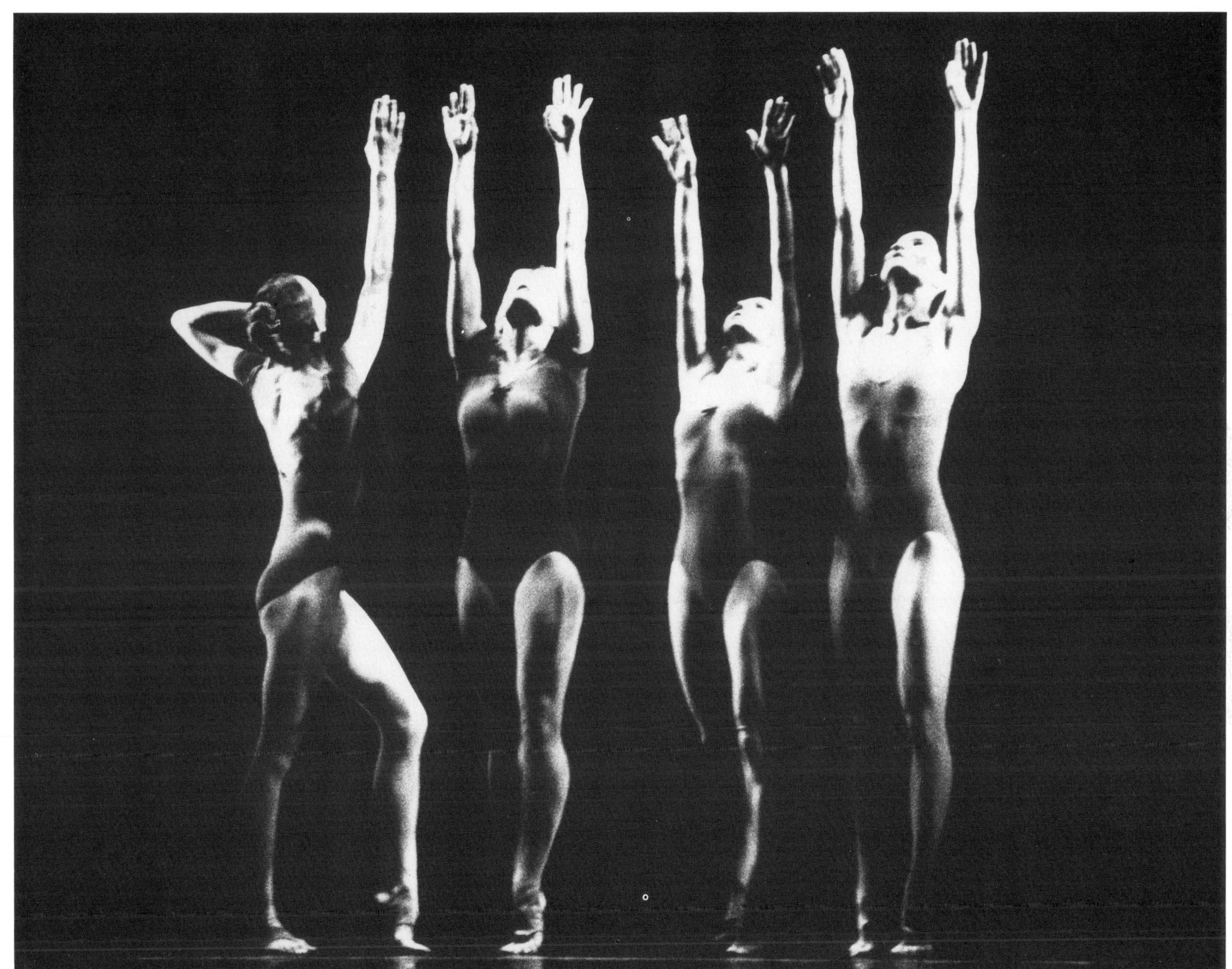

DANCE II

MARTYN HOSKINS

156

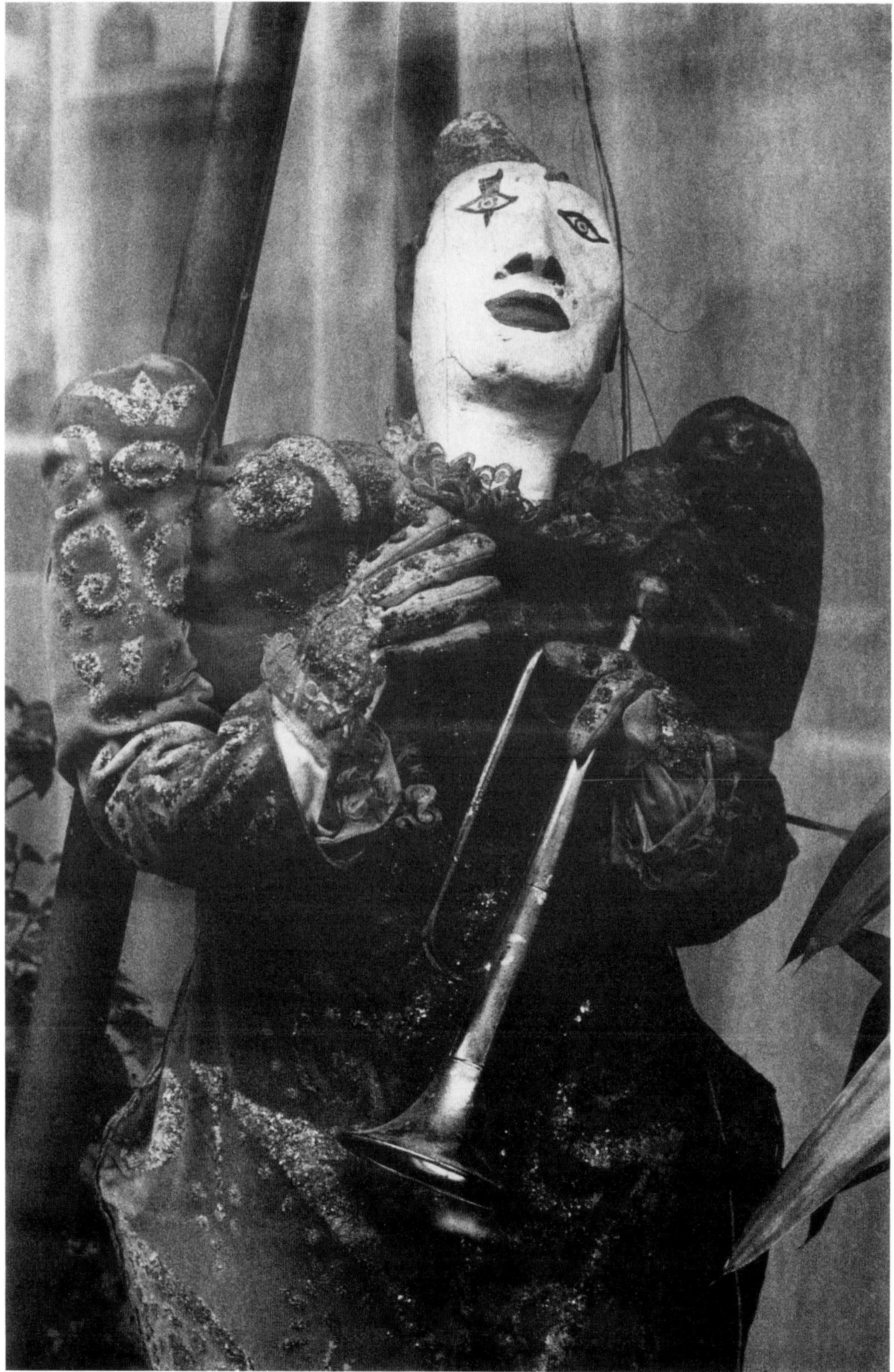

CLOWN PUPPET, PARIS

NICHOLAS SINCLAIR BEGAN HIS SERIES ON THE CIRCUS SOME YEARS AGO AS A DRUMMER IN A CIRCUS BAND. BEFORE THAT HE HAD STUDIED FINE ART AT NEWCASTLE.

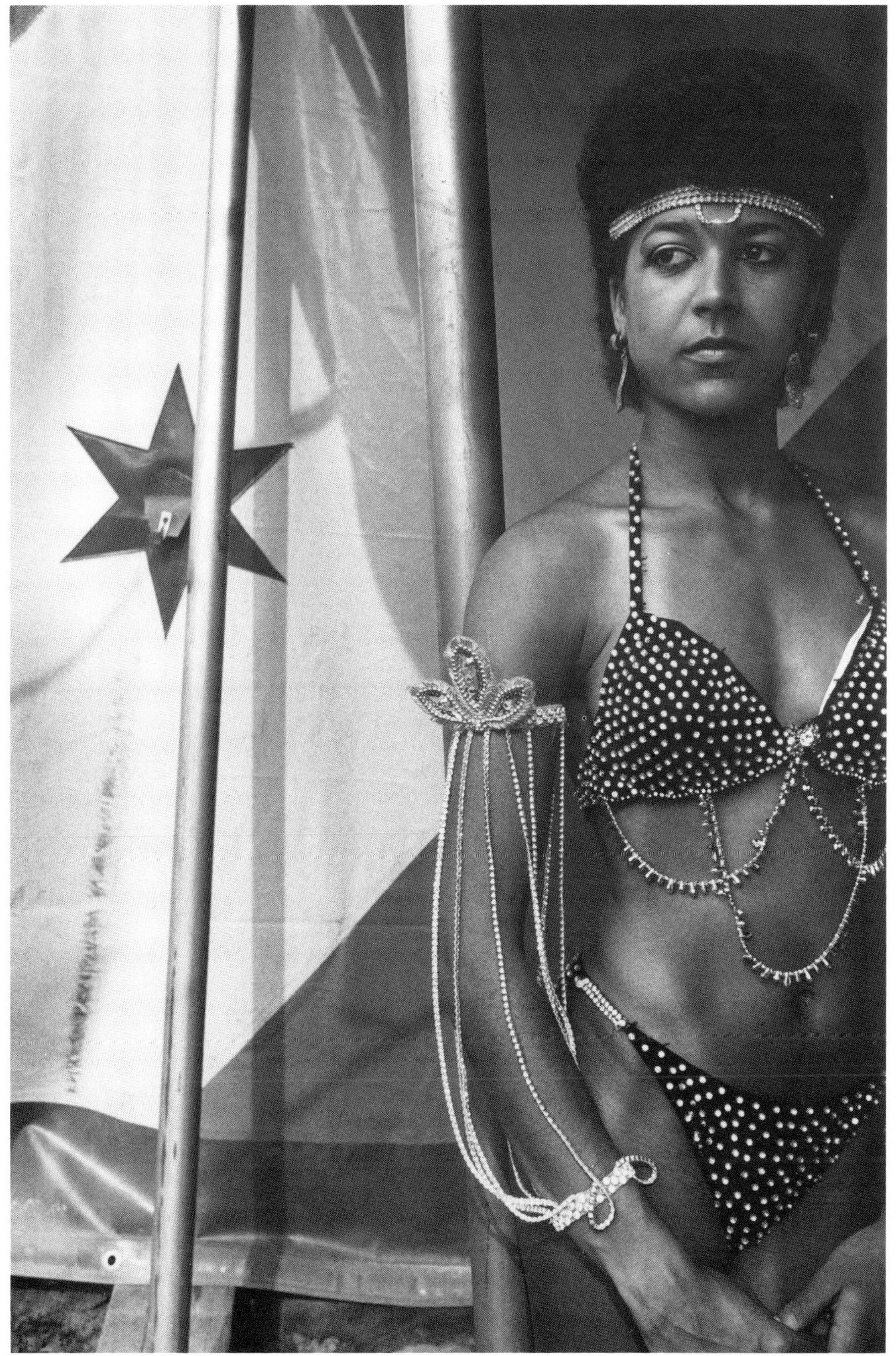

FRENCH TRAPEZE ARTIST, CHESSINGTON

NICHOLAS SINCLAIR

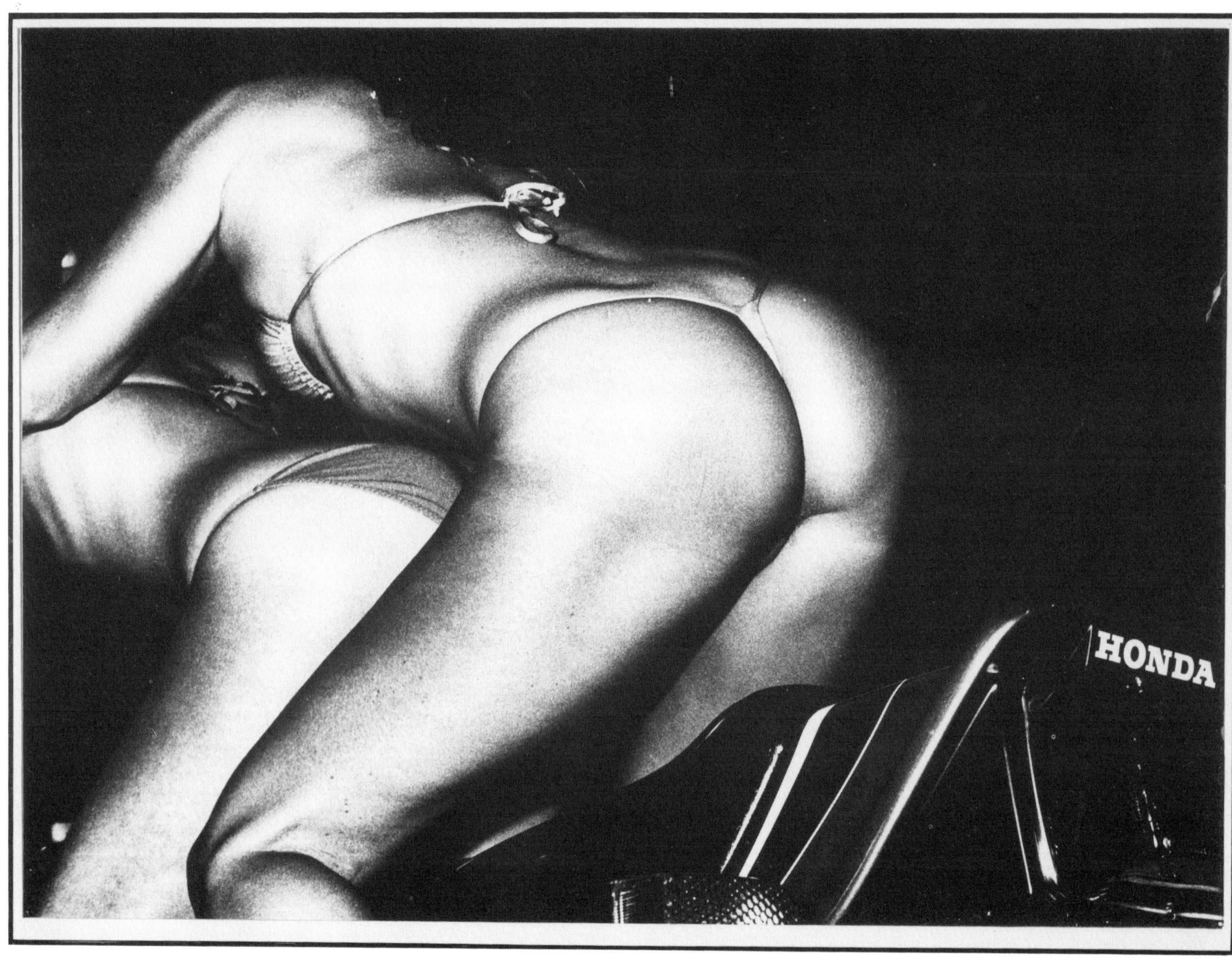

NICHOLAS FISHER STUDIED GRAPHICS 1967-1970. STARTED PHOTOGRAPHY 1979 AND IS NOW WORKING FROM STUDIOS IN DERBY.

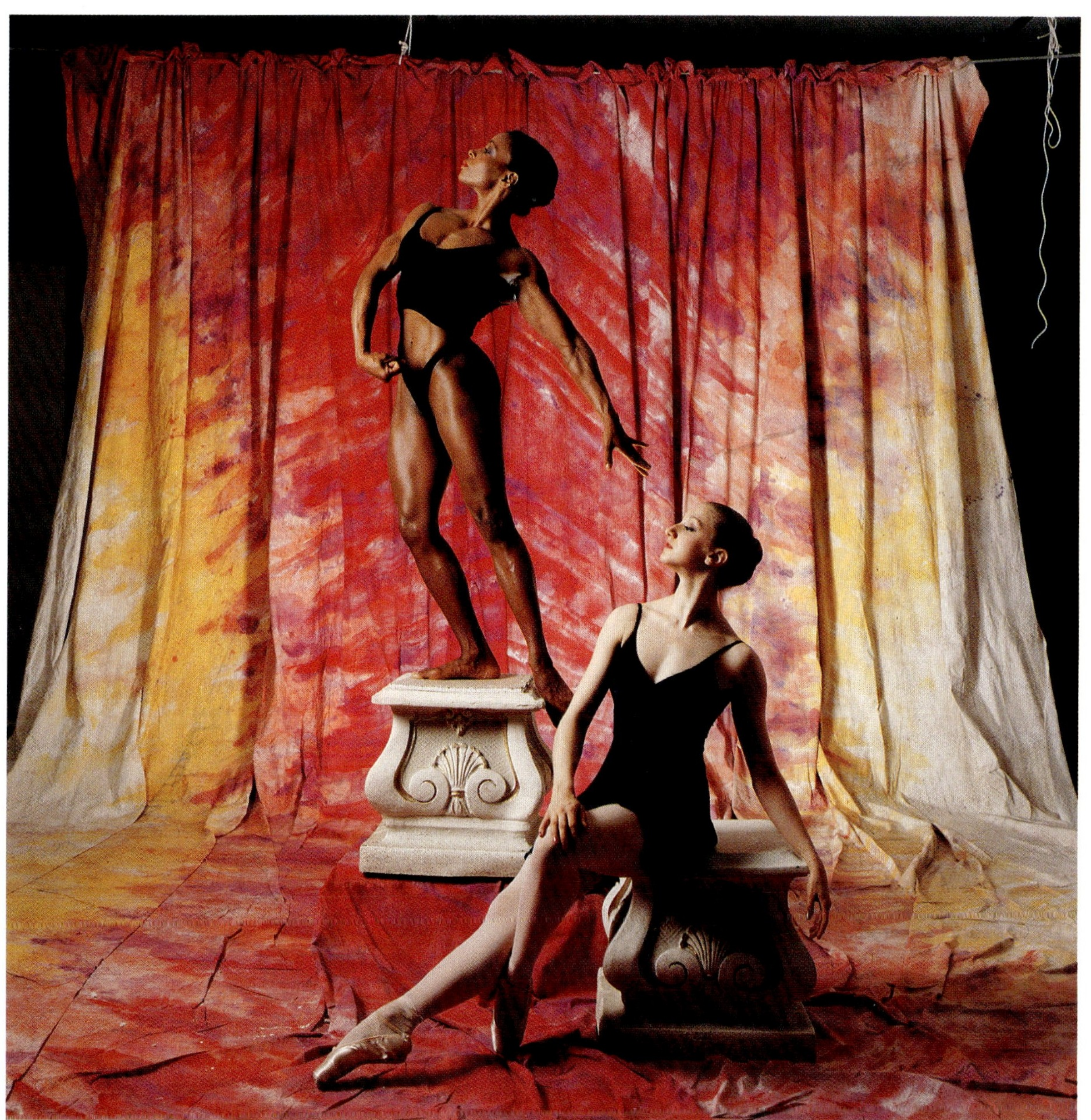

PUMPING IRON

HANS NELEMAN IS 25 AND WAS BORN IN HOLLAND. HE TOOK HIS DEGREE AT PCL AND WON THE KODAK PHOTOGRAPHER OF THE YEAR AWARD BEFORE LEAVING FOR NEW YORK FOR HIS MA. HE NOW HAS A SUCCESSFUL ADVERTISING STUDIO THERE.

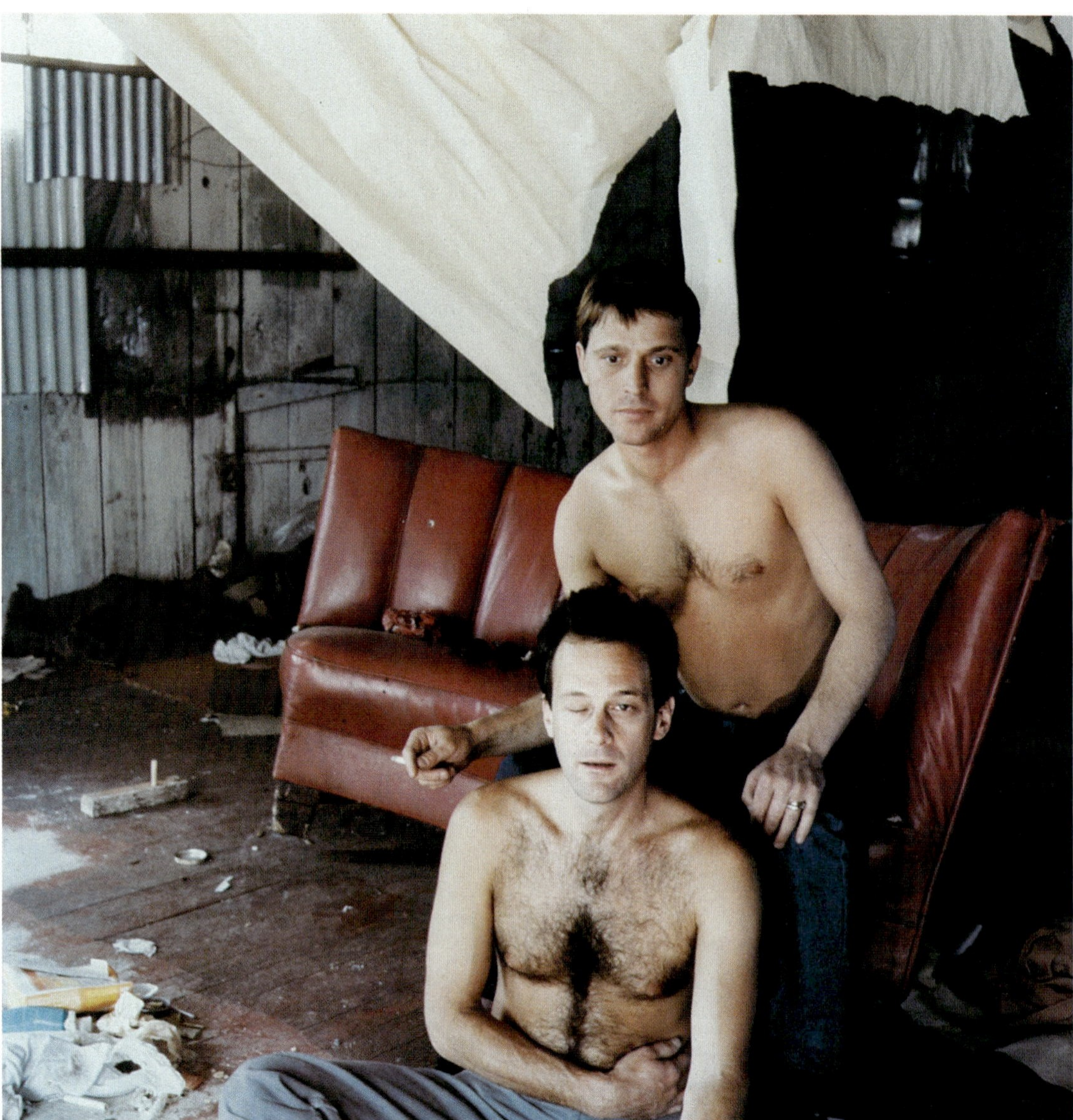

UNTITLED

STEPHEN CHAMPION STUDIED AT BRIGHTON AND BOURNEMOUTH TAKING HIS MFA AT SAN FRANCISCO 1984.

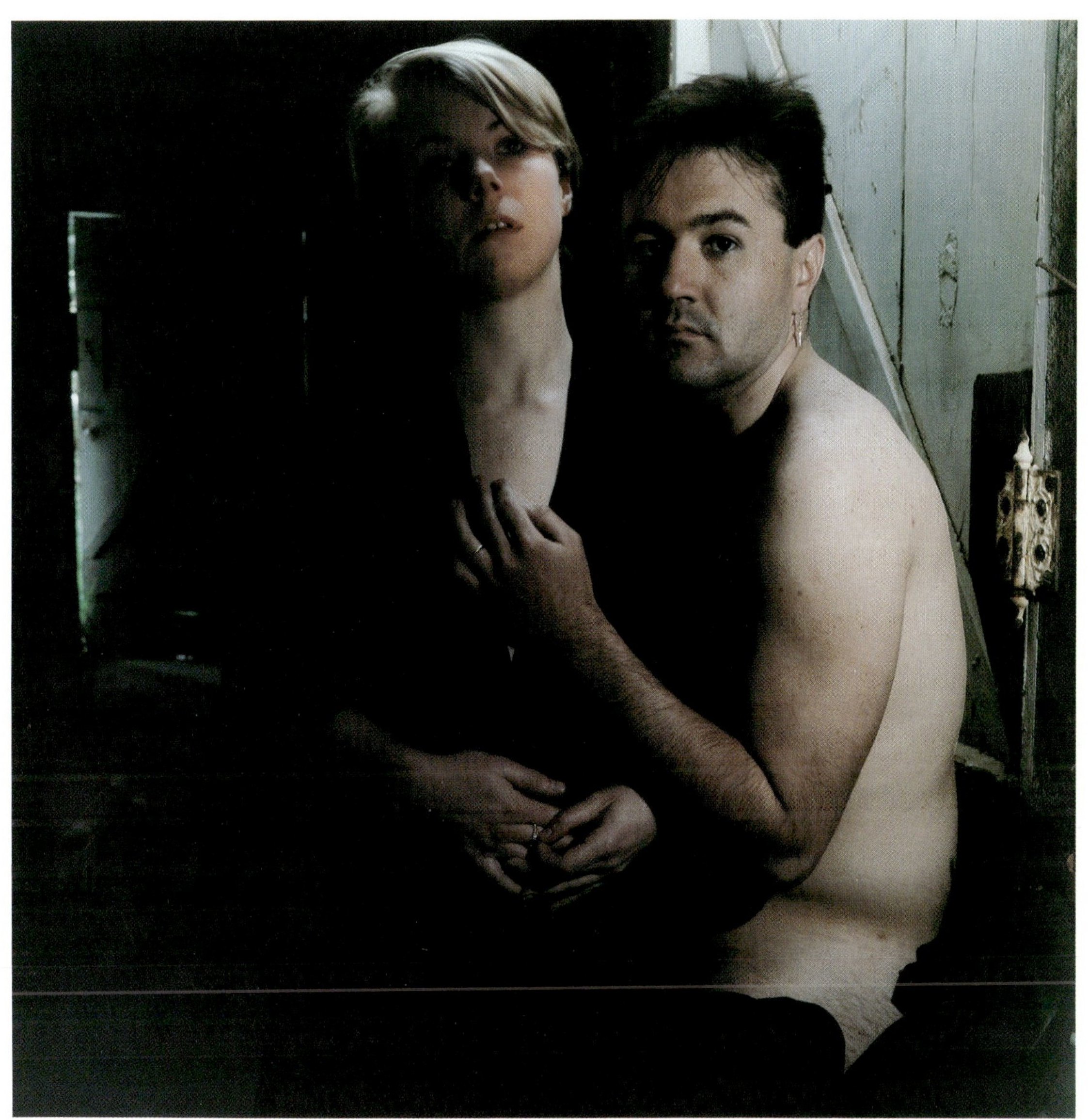

UNTITLED

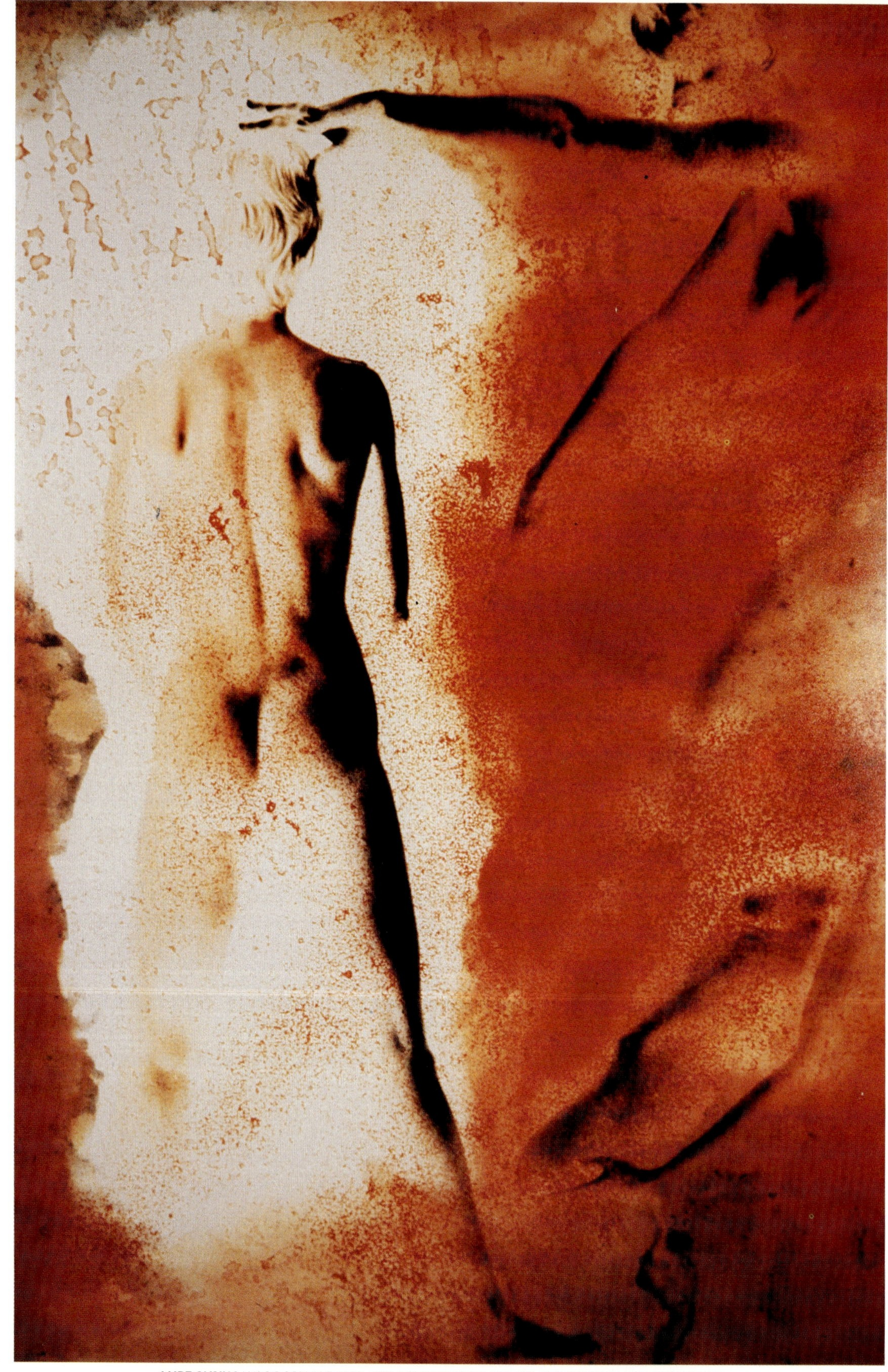

CAVE PAINTING

LUPE CUNHA WAS BORN IN BRAZIL AND NOW LIVES IN LONDON. SHE STUDIED ART AT CHICAGO AND RIO AND BECAME A NEWSPAPER PHOTOGRAPHER. COMING TO ENGLAND SHE CONTINUED MAGAZINE WORK WHILE EXTENDING HER 'PRO ARTE' AT THE CAMERA CLUB.

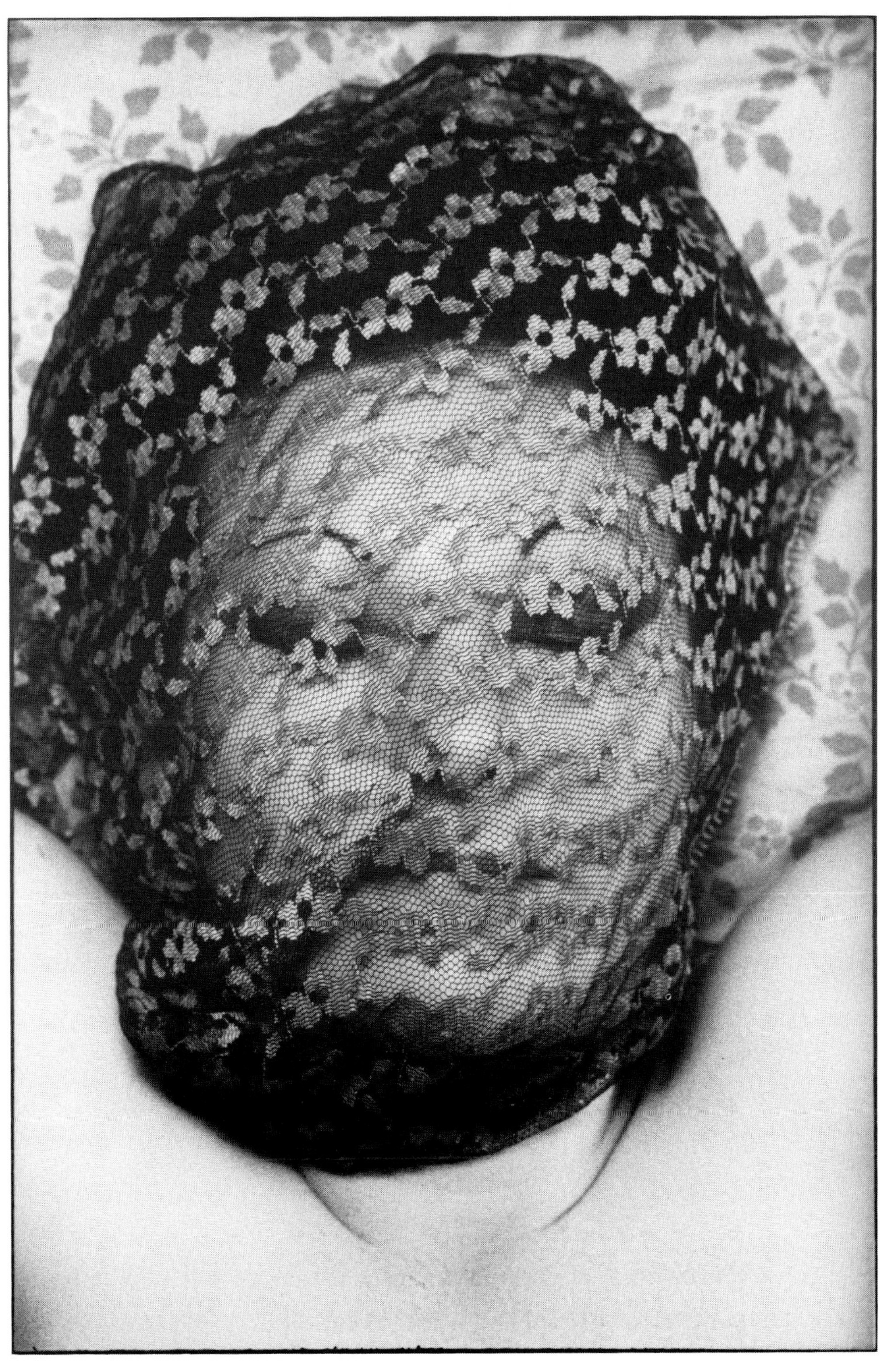

AVA VARGAS WAS BORN IN MEXICO 1952 AND STUDIED PHOTOGRAPHY IN MEXICO AND USA.
HE CAME TO EUROPE 1977 WHERE HE LIVED IN PARIS AND ROME BEFORE MOVING TO LONDON.
HIS WORK HAS BEEN EXHIBITED IN EUROPE, USA, MEXICO AND CHINA.

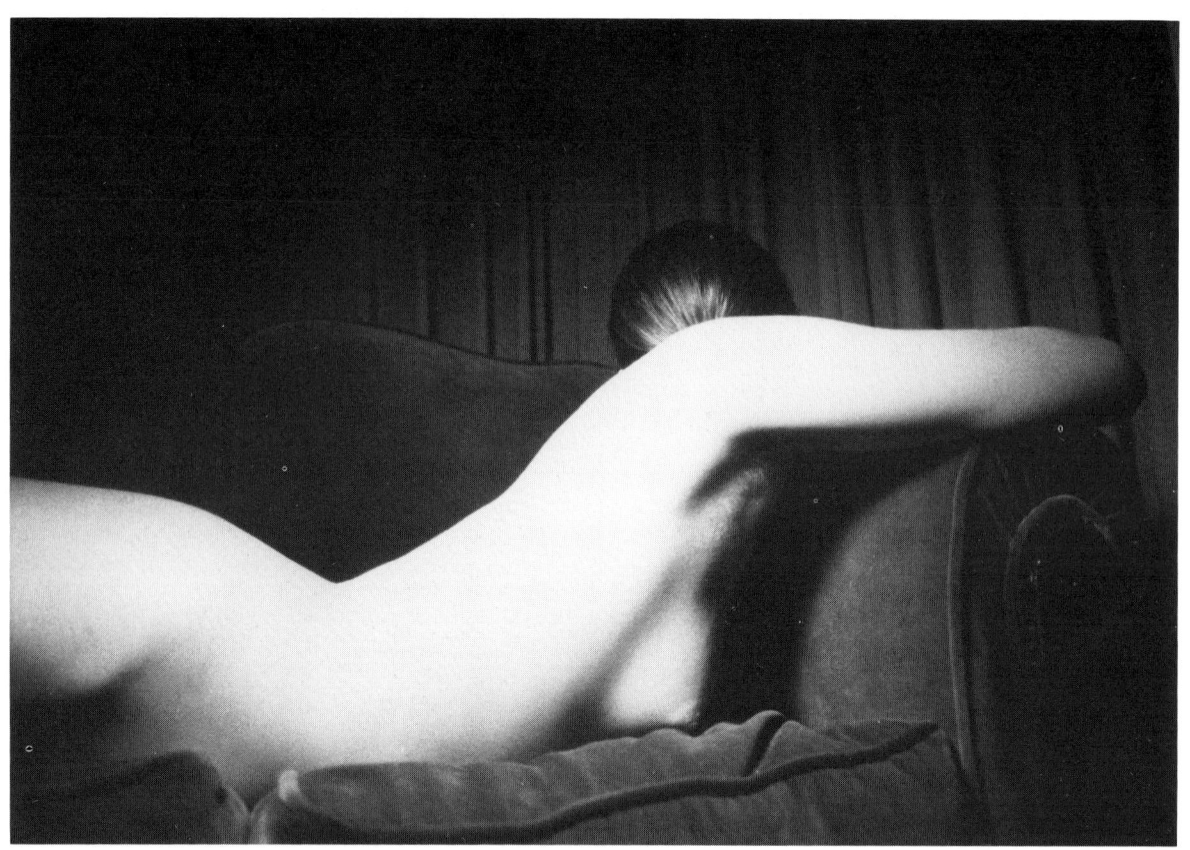

GAVIN BURNS IS A SELF-TAUGHT AMATEUR PHOTOGRAPHER BORN, LIVING AND WORKING IN NORTH LONDON.

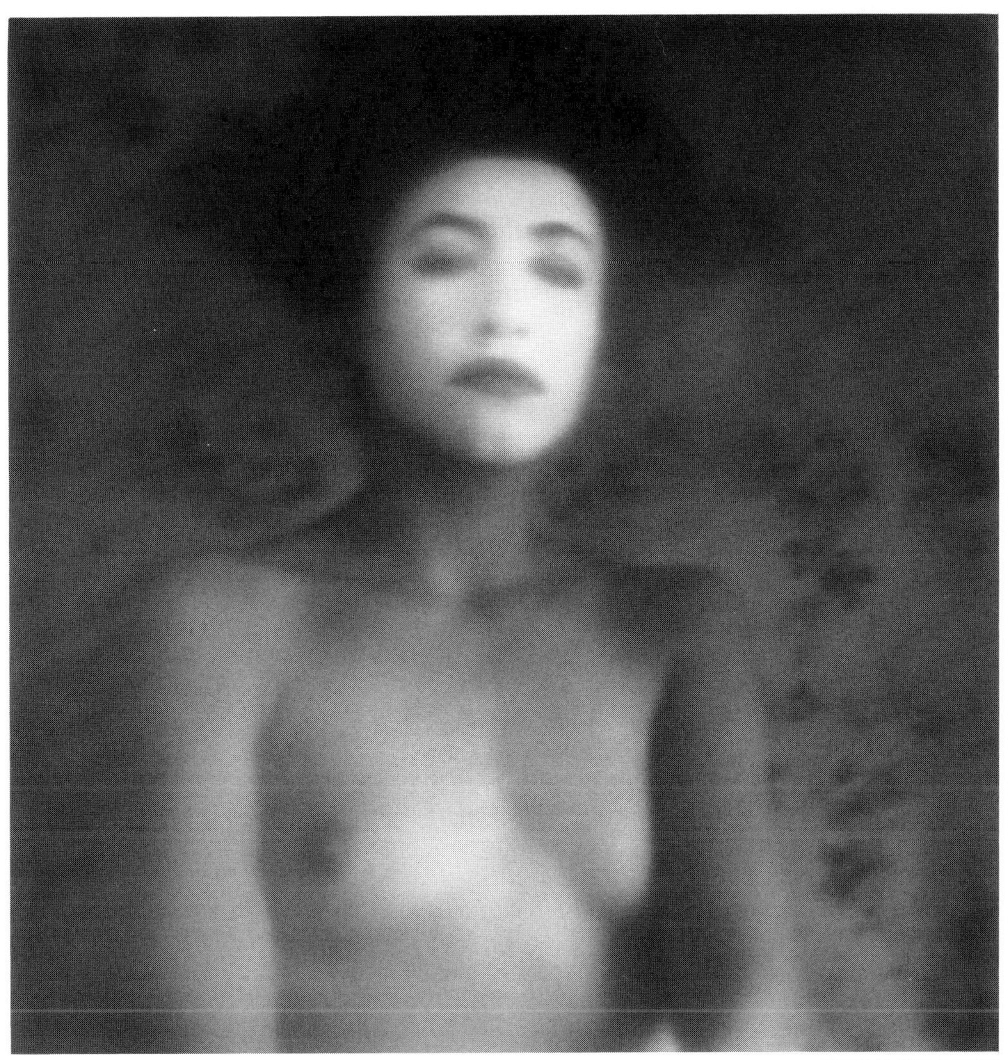

THE HUNDRED ECHOES

GARY HEISS WORKED AS A STAFF PHOTOGRAPHER FOR A CHARITY BUT NOW FREELANCES. THE PICTURE IS FROM A SERIES CALLED 'THE HUNDRED ECHOES'.

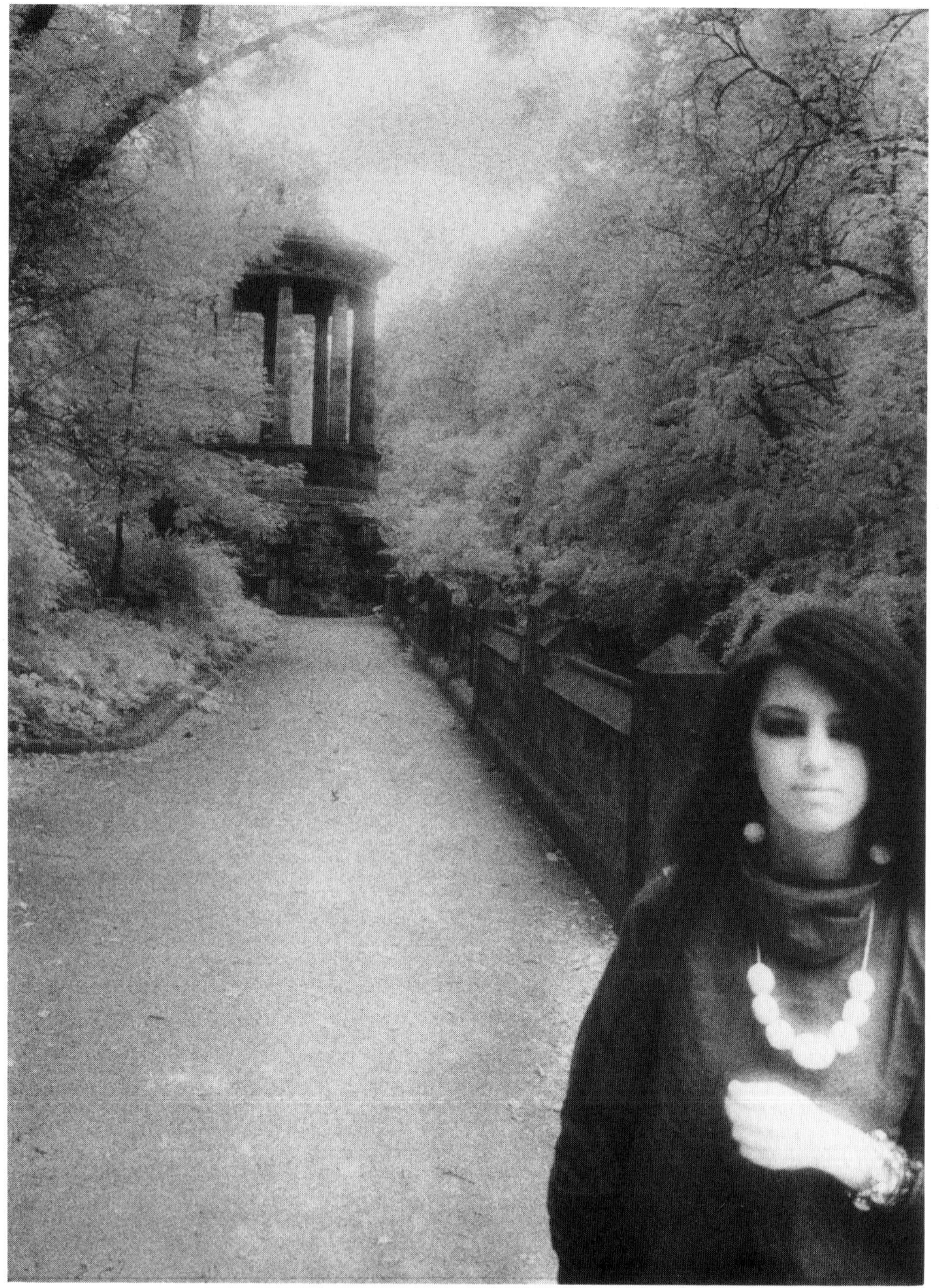

GRAHAM POMPHREY OF EDINBURGH HAS JUST COMPLETED A LEVEL PHOTOGRAPHY AND IS WORKING IN AN ADVERTISING AGENCY.

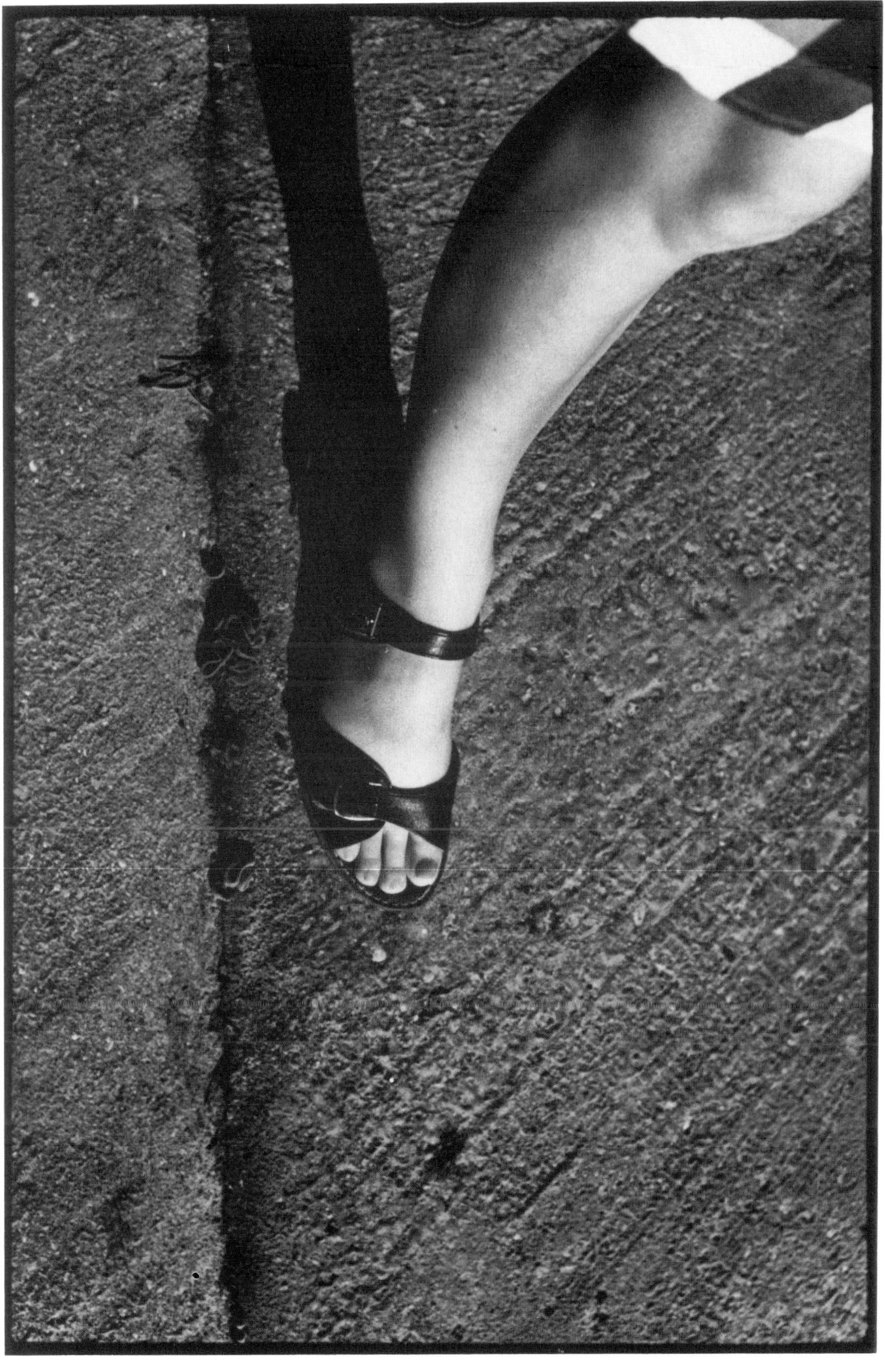

MICHAEL JOVIC IS AN AMATEUR PHOTOGRAPHER AND A PSYCHIATRIC NURSE, 31, MARRIED WITH ONE DAUGHTER.

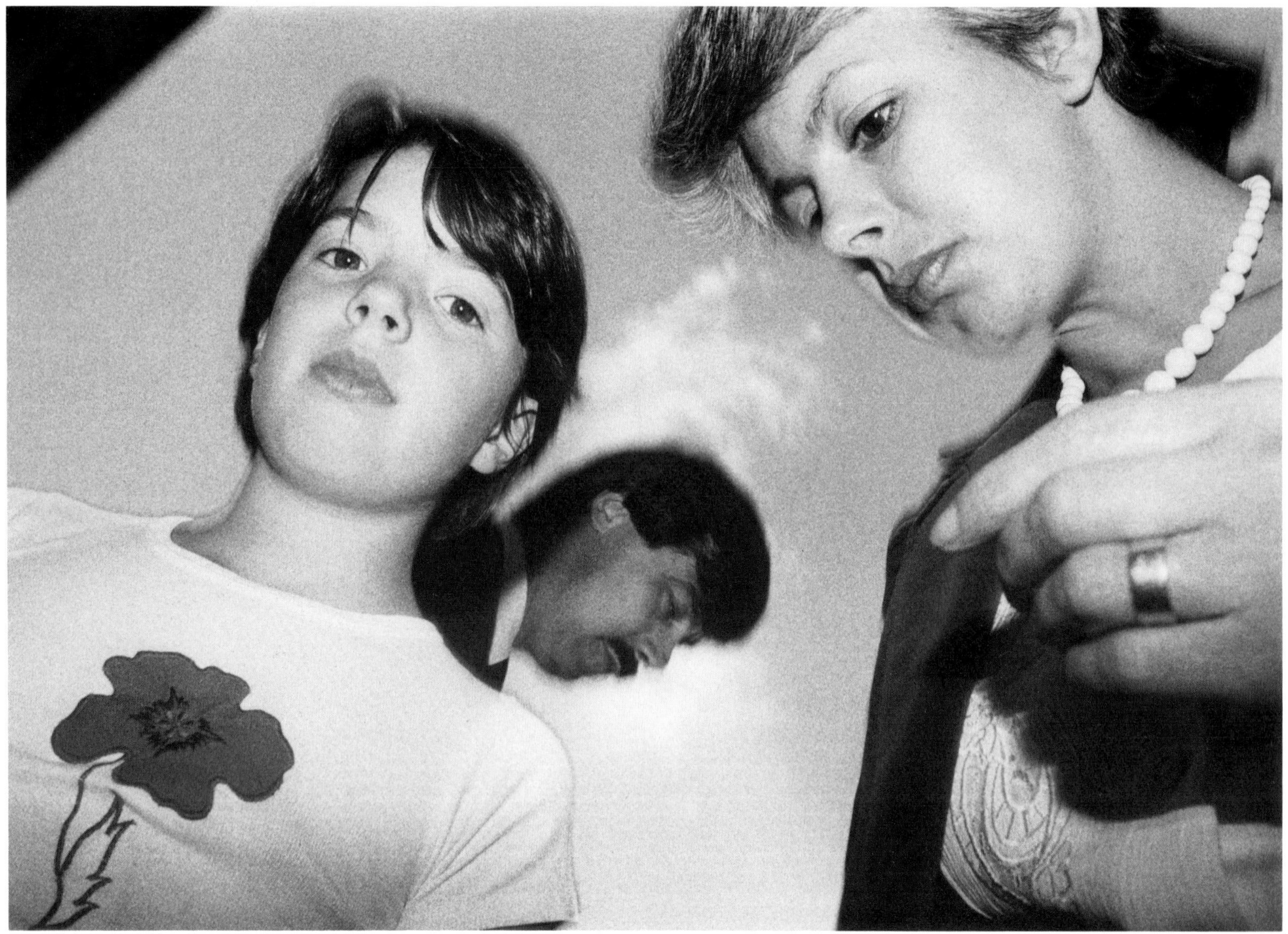

FROM THE SERIES 'UNGUARDED MOMENTS'

MARK WARNER TOOK HIS MA PHOTOGRAPHY AT MANCHESTER POLYTECHNIC 1983 AND IS NOW A PART-TIME LECTURER, PART-TIME GALLERY TECHNICIAN AND PART-TIME FREELANCE.

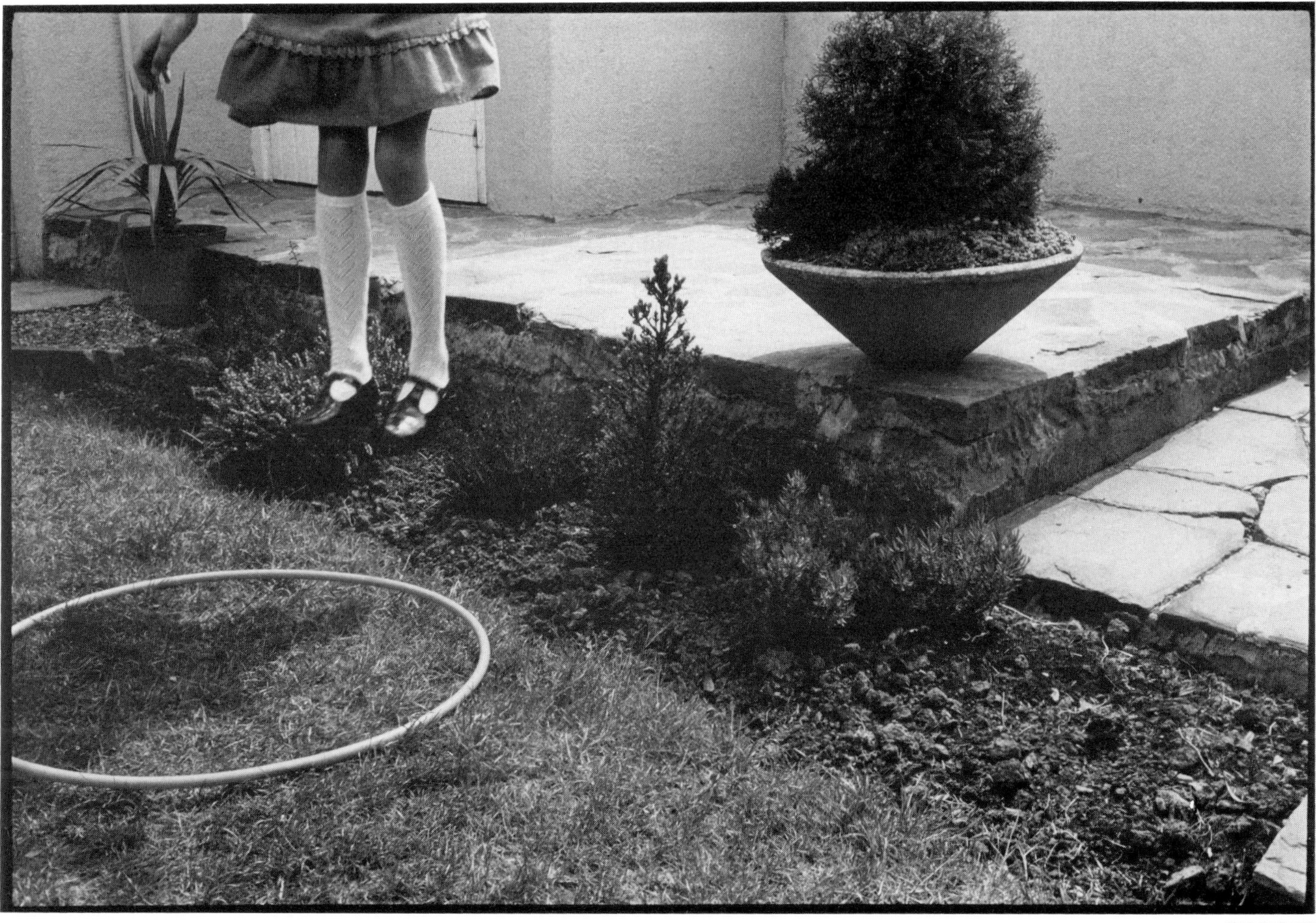

THE SILENCE

ROY SHOESMITH IS AN AEROSPACE PRODUCTION ENGINEER. HE STARTED PHOTOGRAPHY IN THE SIXTIES AT NELSON AND COLNE COLLEGE, WHERE HE IS TEACHING PART-TIME NOW. THE IMAGE IS ONE OF A SERIES INSPIRED BY THE POETRY OF NIKOS KAZANTZAKIS.

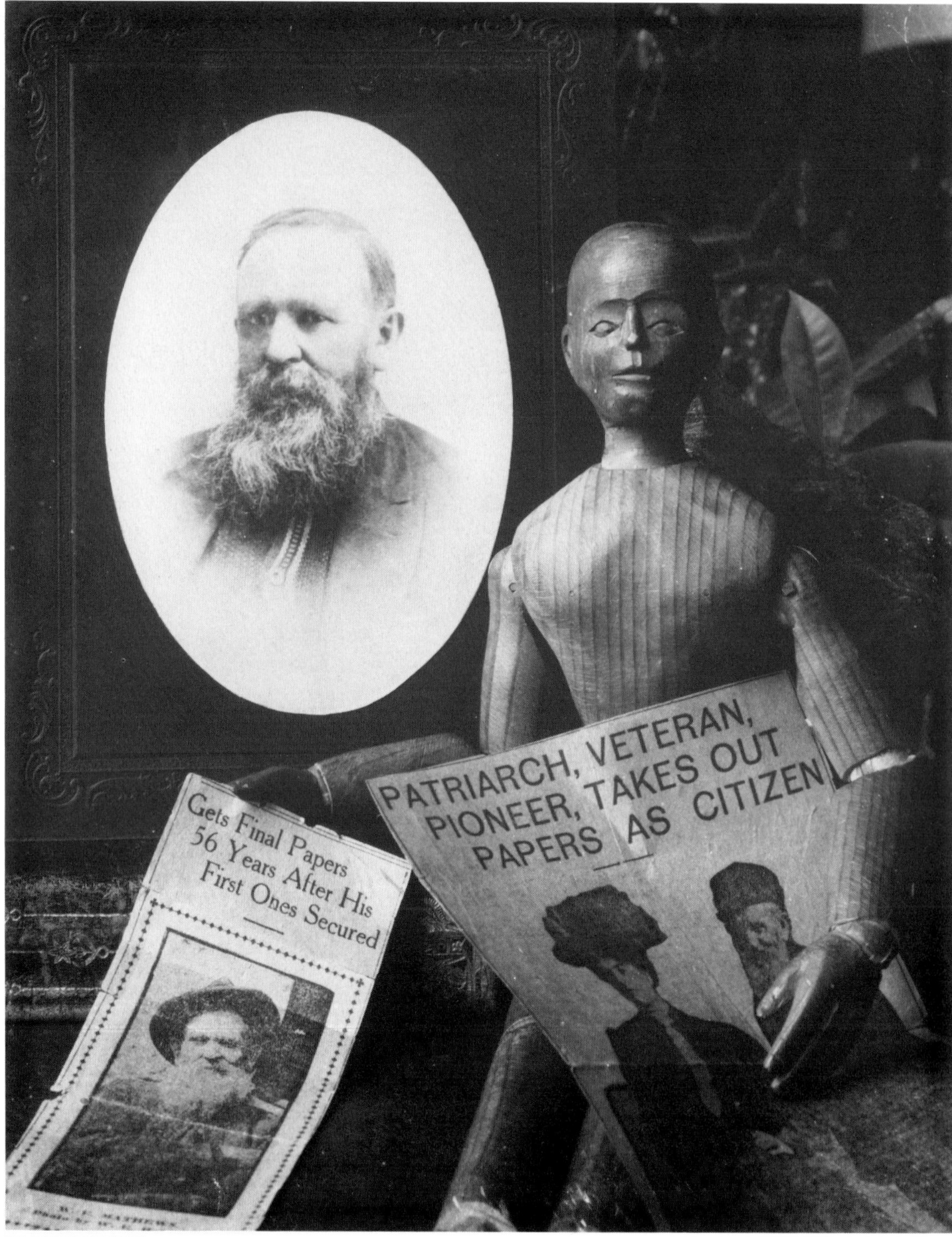

WILLIAM MATTHEWS

VIRGINIA KHURI IS A SELF-TAUGHT PHOTOGRAPHER BUT HAS ATTENDED WORKSHOPS WITH PAUL HILL, RAYMOND MOORE AND THE ANSEL ADAMS LAST IN 1983.
THESE PHOTOS ARE A RECORD OF SIX GENERATIONS OF AMERICAN FAMILY PORTRAITS, PART OF A SERIES OF THIRTY.

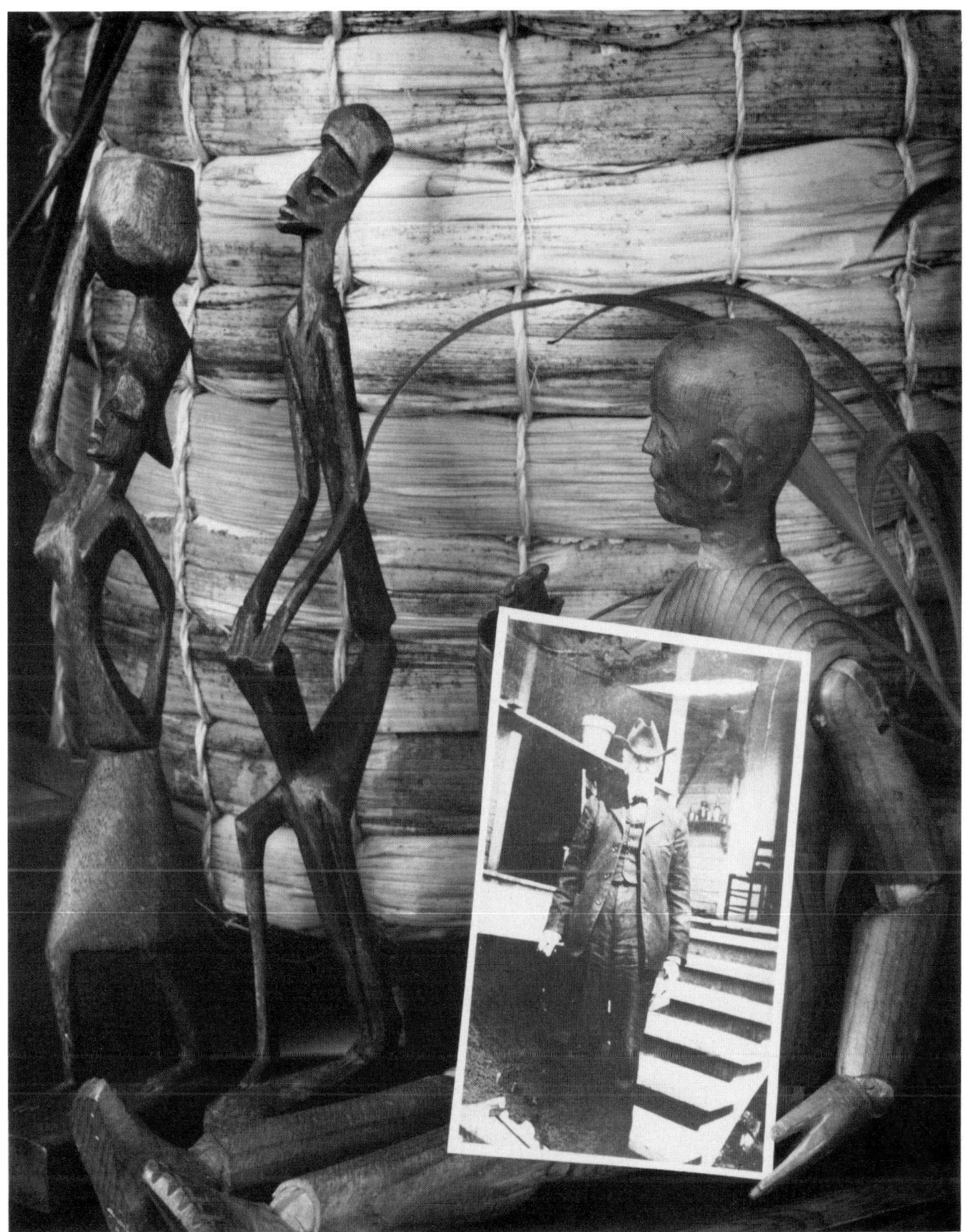

JAMES WASHINGTON ASBURY

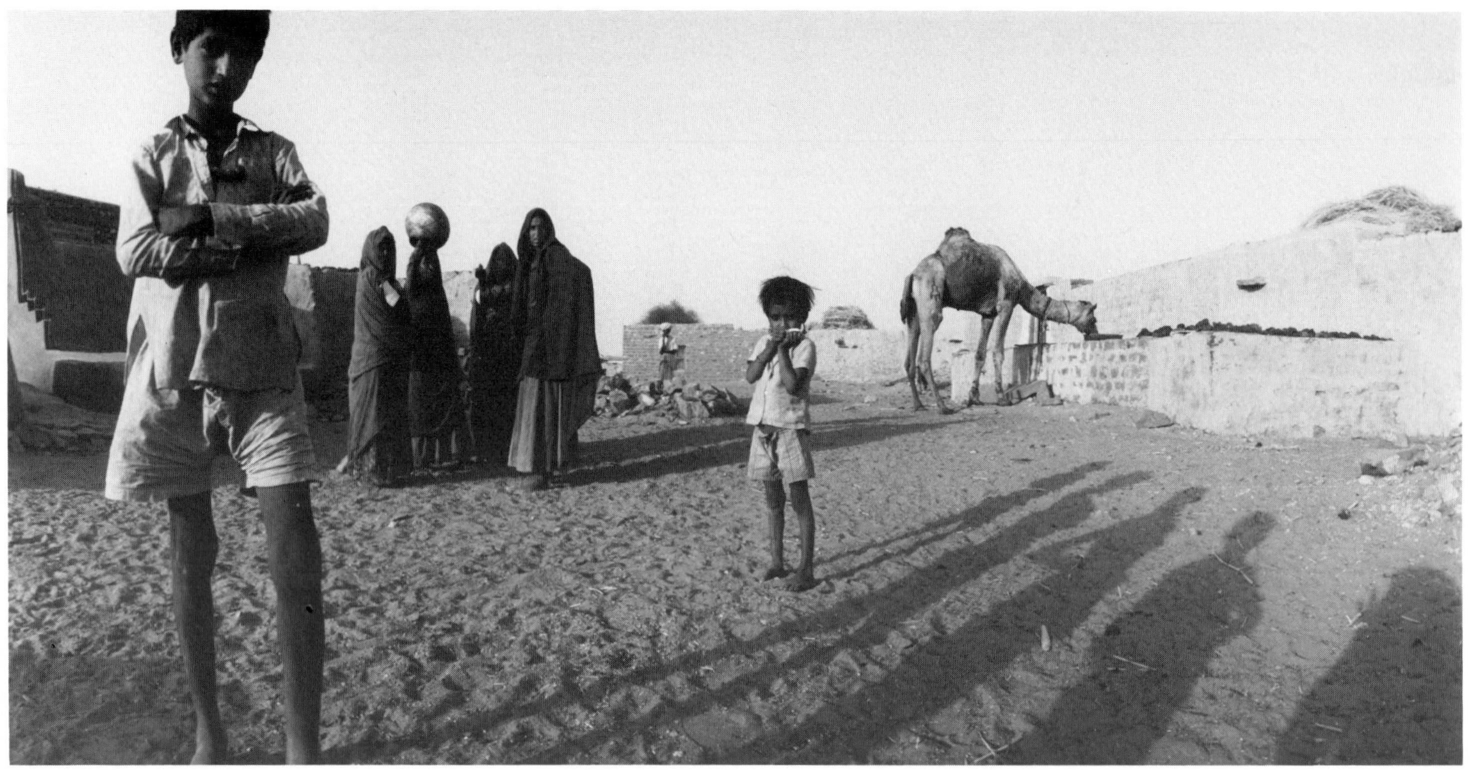

ABOVE: DESERT VILLAGE IN RAJASTHAN

BELOW: PURI, A HOLY CITY NEAR CALCUTTA

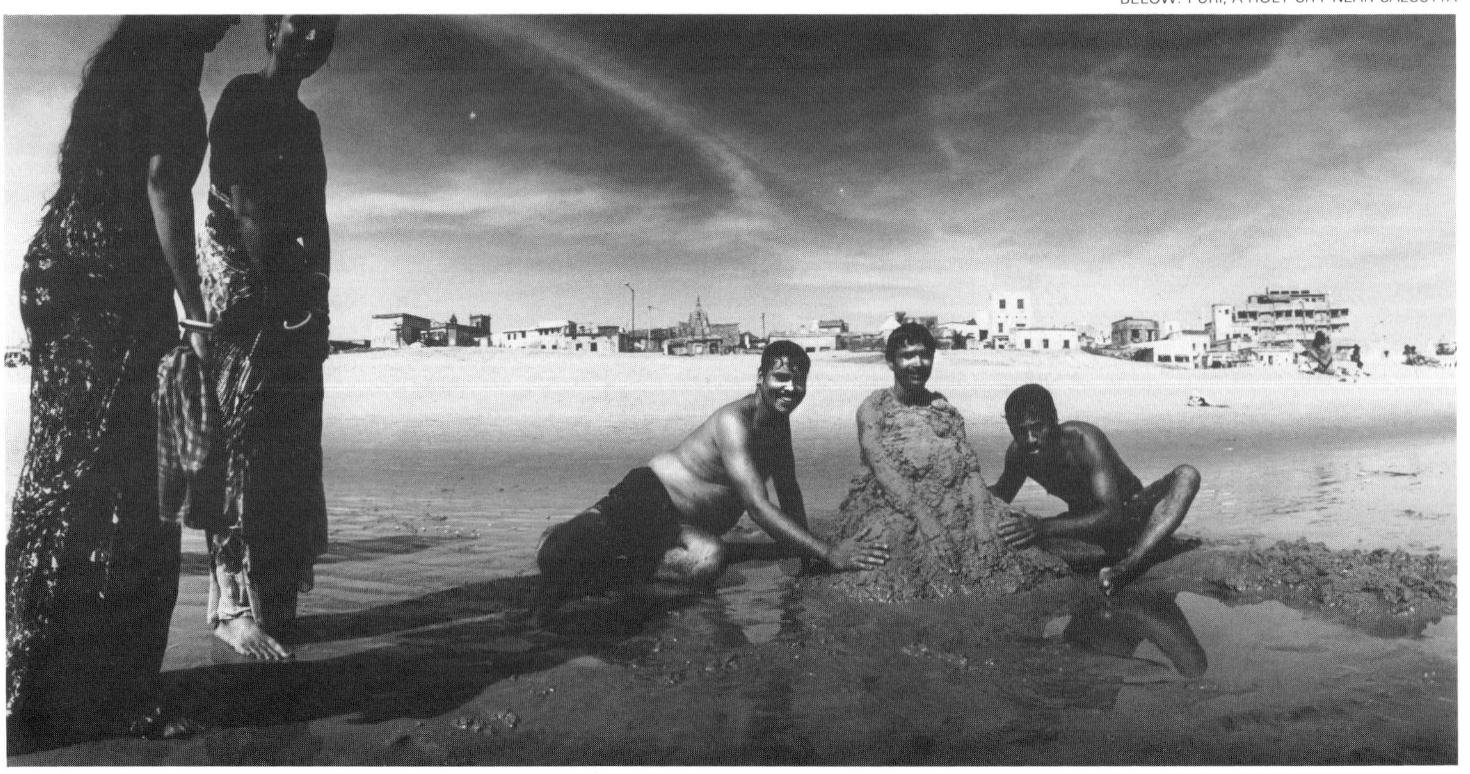

TIM BAUER IS A 25-YEAR-OLD AUSTRALIAN BASED IN LONDON AND WINNER OF A ROTHMAN'S WORLD PRESS AWARD. THESE PICTURES COME FROM A THREE MONTH STAY IN INDIA.

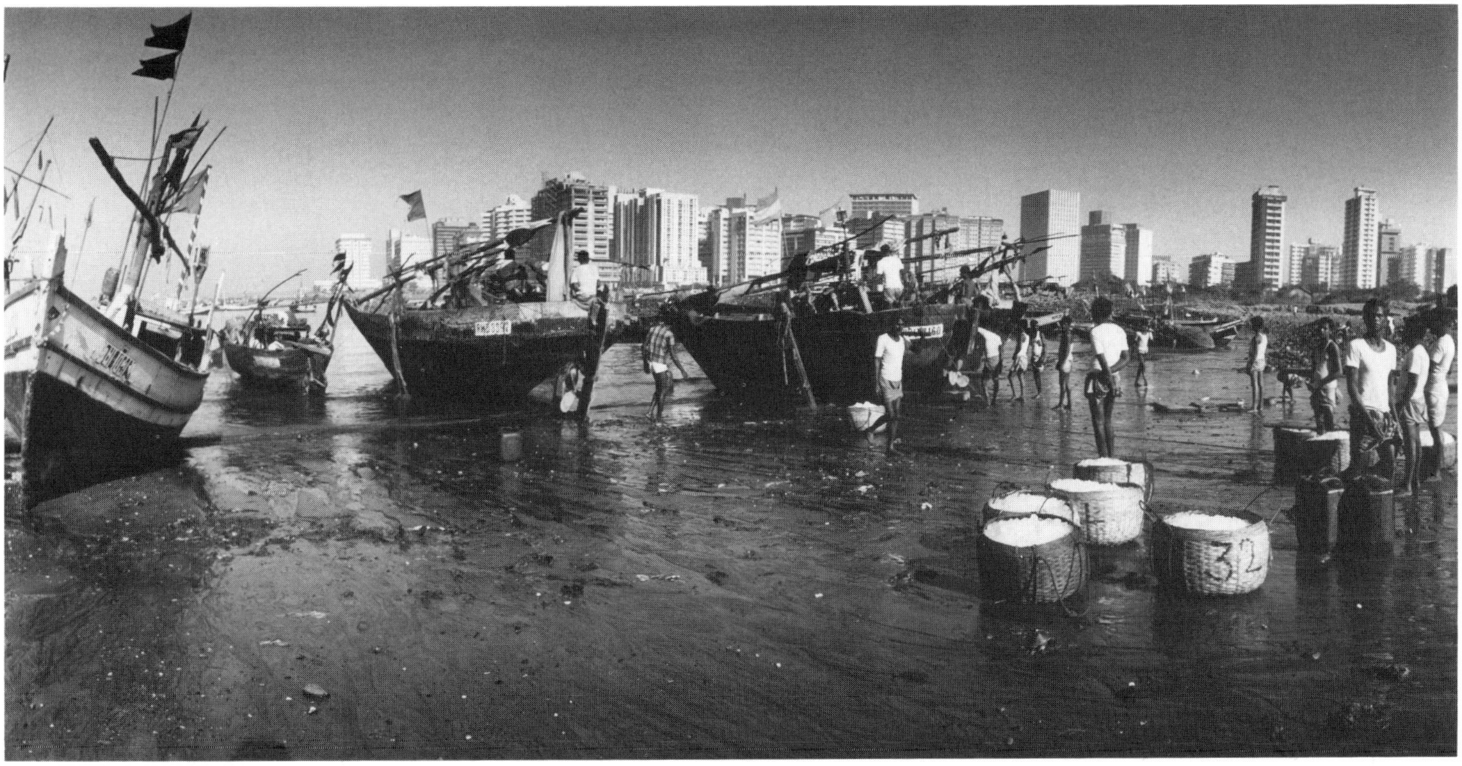

ABOVE: COLABA POINT, BOMBAY

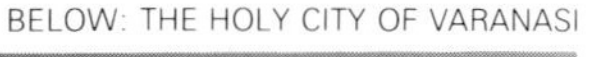

BELOW: THE HOLY CITY OF VARANASI

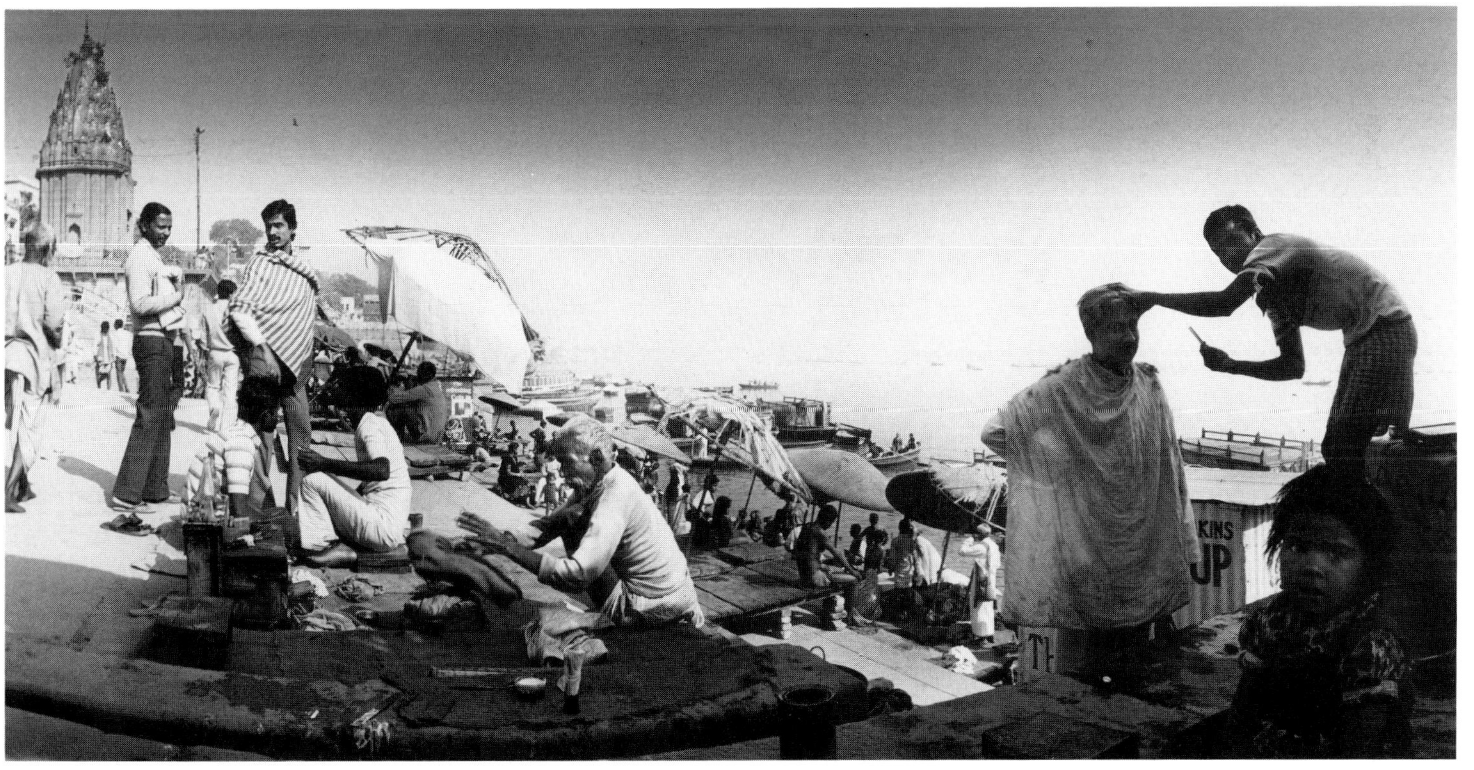

TIM BAUER

174

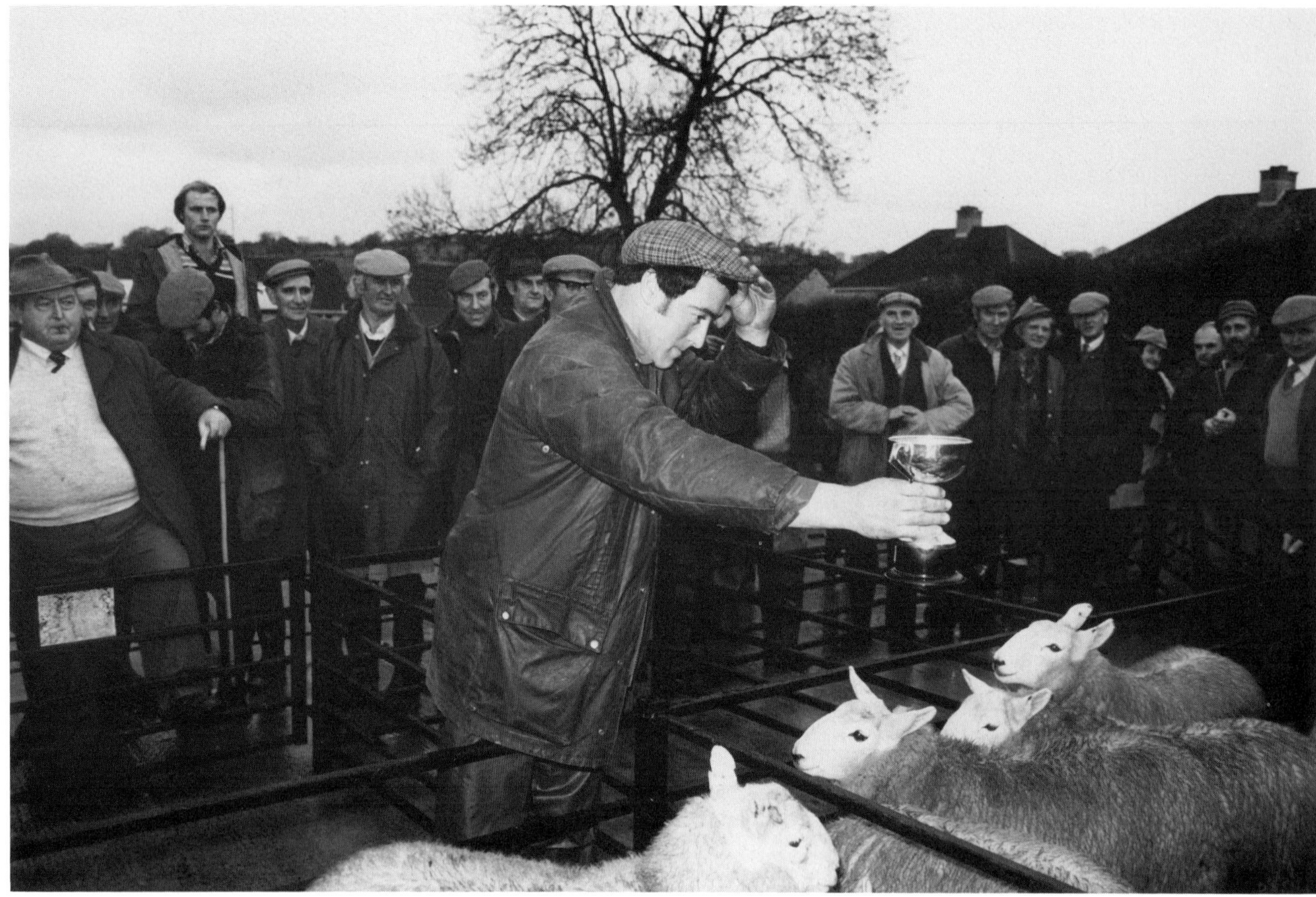

LLANGAOG CHRISTM MART

NIA CLEMENT IS A WELSH-SPEAKING ENGLISH GRADUATE. AFTER WORKING AS AN ADMINISTRATOR AT THE FFOTOGALLERY, CARDIFF SHE BECAME A FREELANCE PHOTOGRAPHER CURRENTLY DOCUMENTING WELSH-SPEAKING WEST WALES.

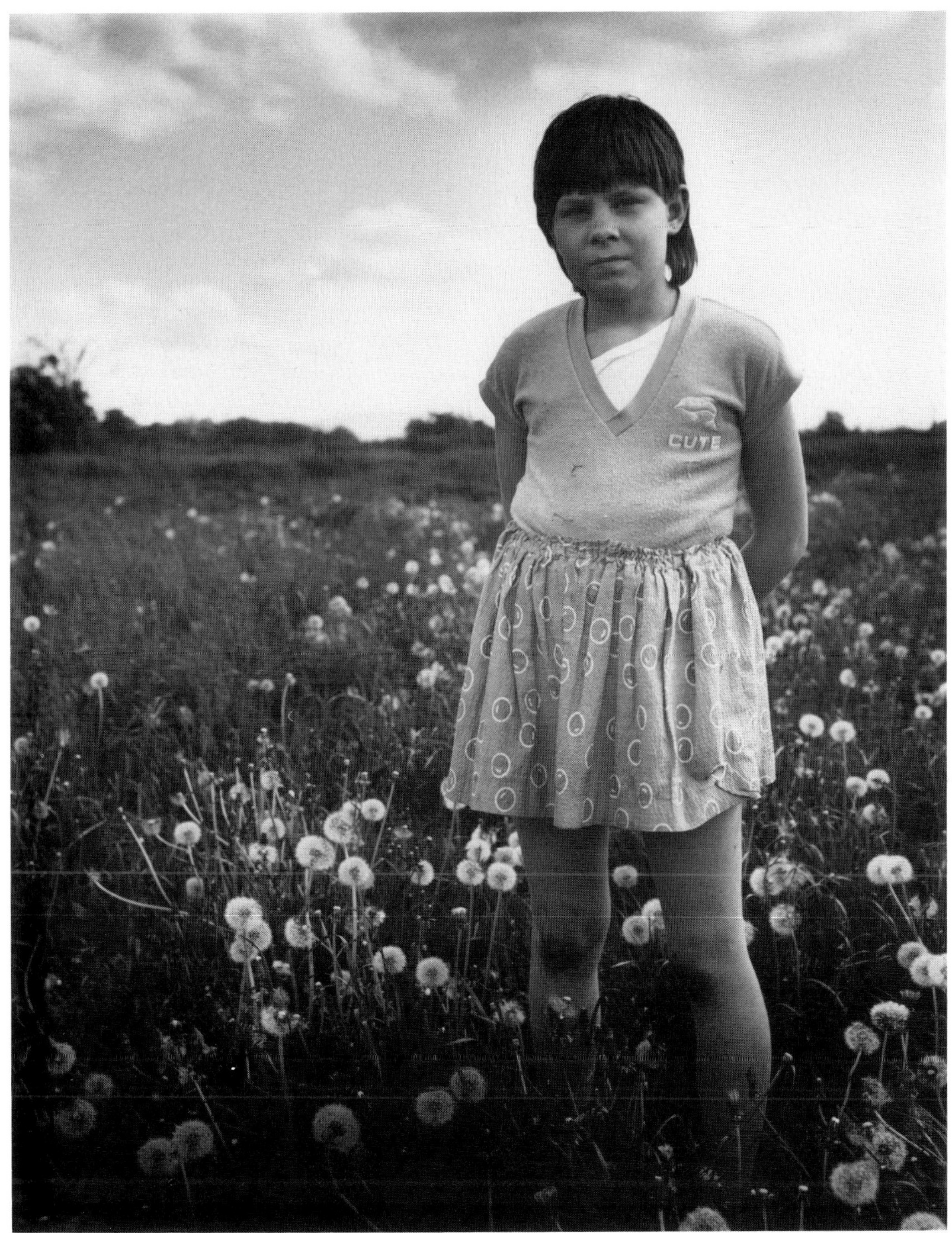

RACHEL EDWARD AGED TEN

MARIANNE MORRIS WAS BORN IN DÜSSELDORF AND STUDIED PHOTOGRAPHY IN ESSEN. FOR 12 YEARS SHE WAS AN ADVERTISING PHOTOGRAPHER IN AMSTERDAM WHILE LIVING IN LONDON, HAS NOW STOPPED ADVERTISING AND IS WORKING ON A VILLAGE PROJECT WITH A GRANT FROM WEST MIDLANDS ARTS.

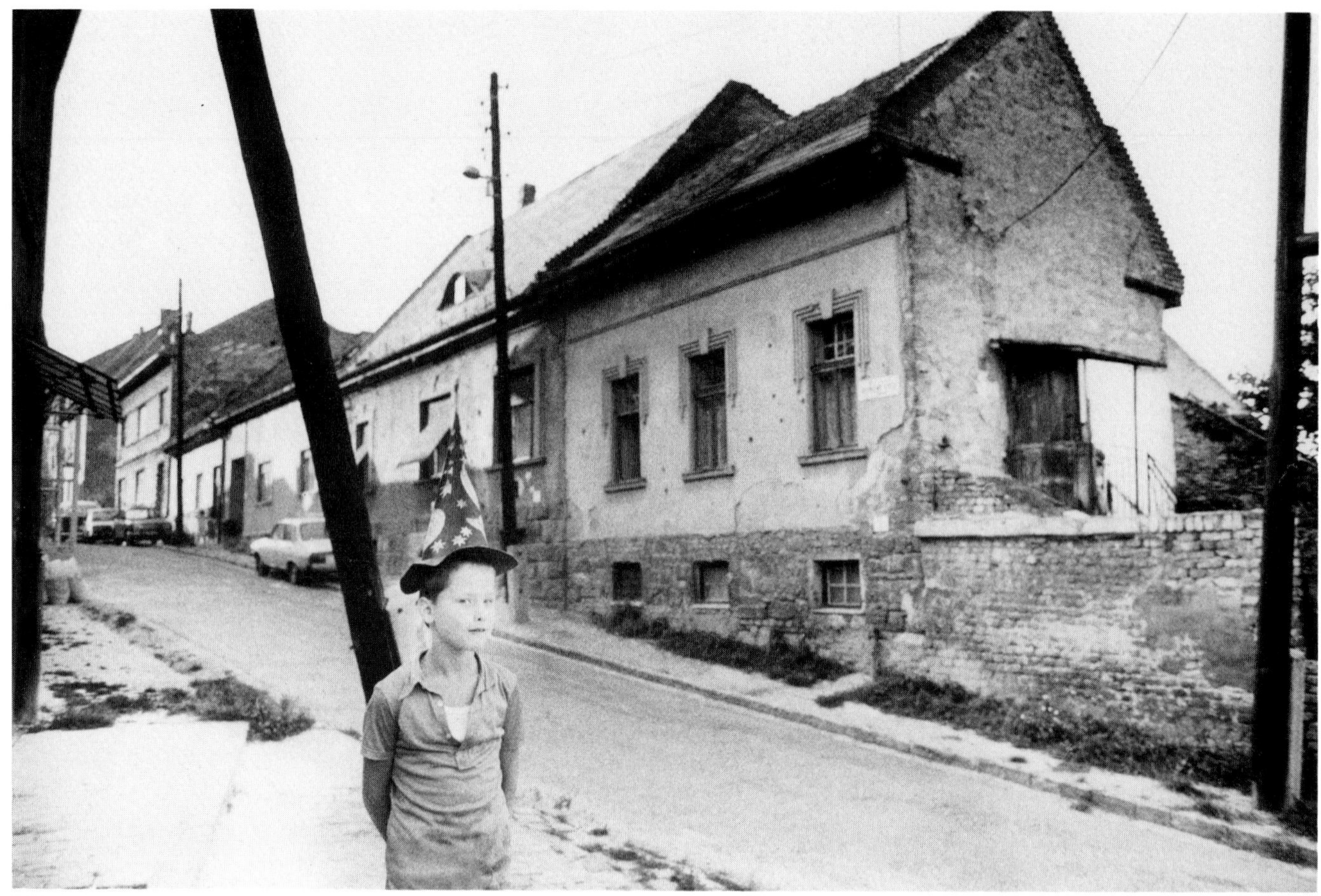

HUNGARY

JOHN CHATER IS 20-YEARS-OLD, UNEMPLOYED LIVING IN THE NORTH OF SCOTLAND. ALL HIS PROJECTS ARE SELF-FINANCED.

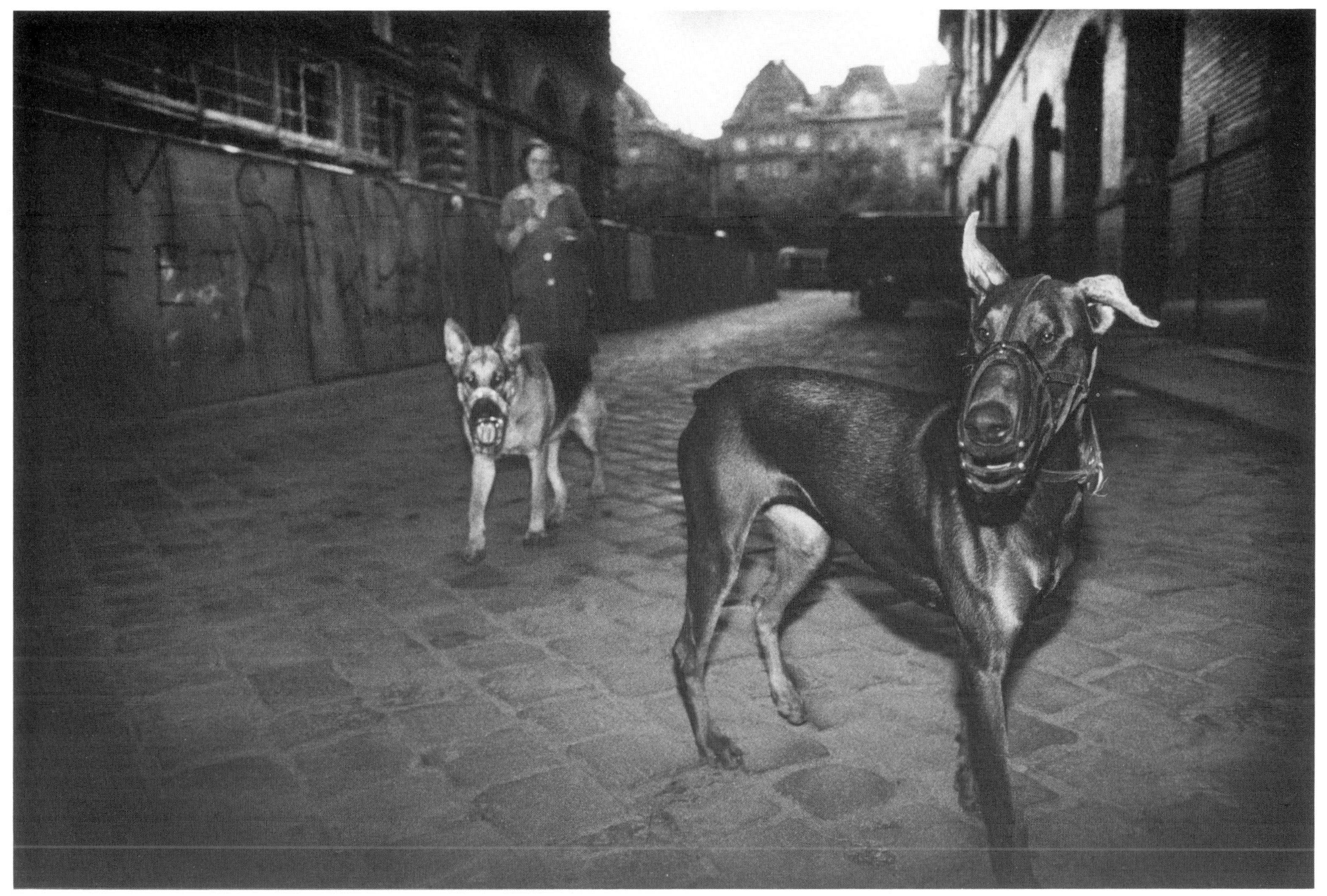

HUNGARY

JOHN CHATER

178

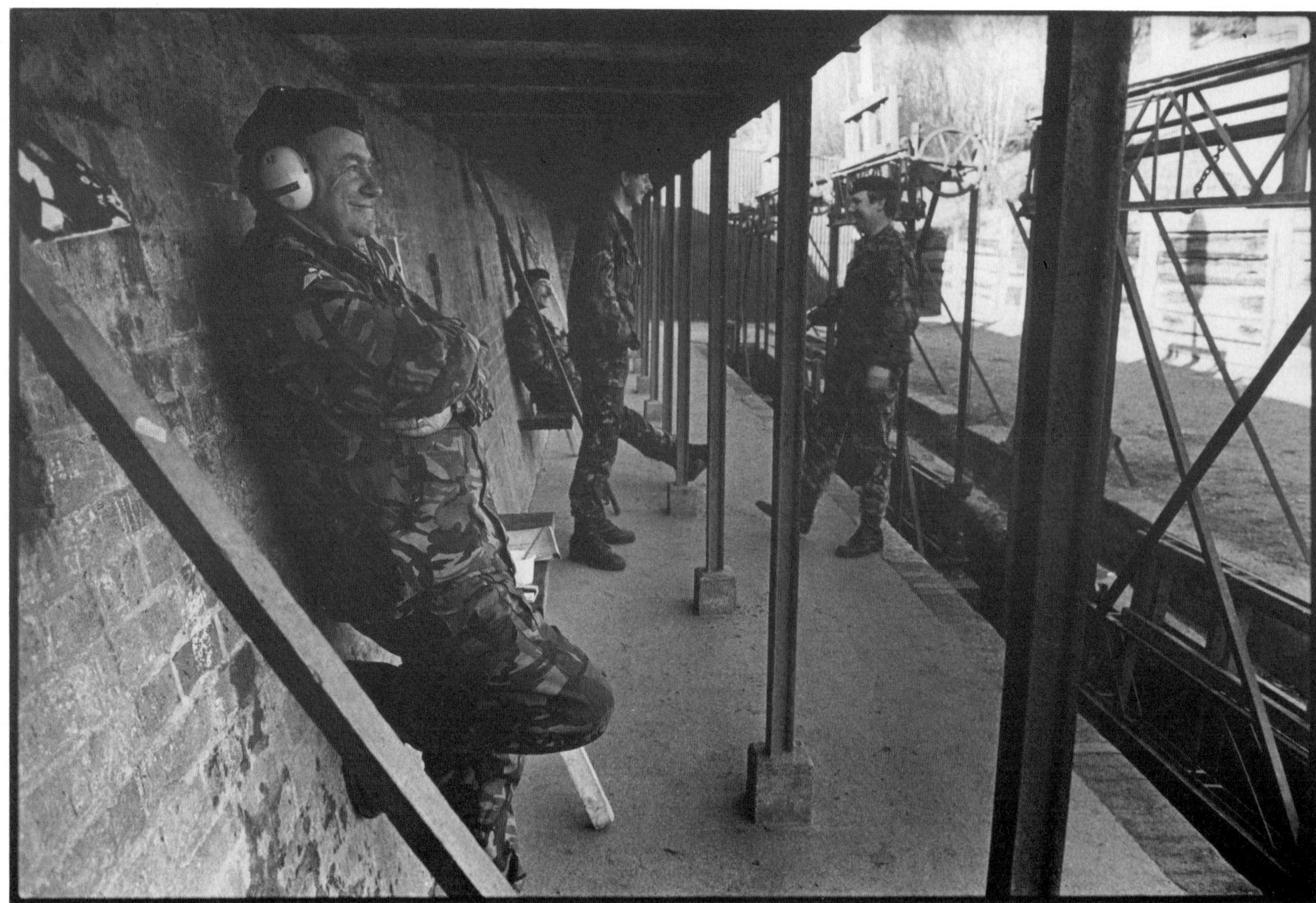

FROM THE SERIES 'THE LIGHTER SIDE OF ARMY LIFE'

NICK DAWE IS CURRENTLY STUDYING AT WEST SURREY COLLEGE OF ART. THE SERIES ON THE LIGHTER SIDE OF ARMY LIFE IS PART OF A LARGER PROJECT ON THE TERRITORIAL ARMY.

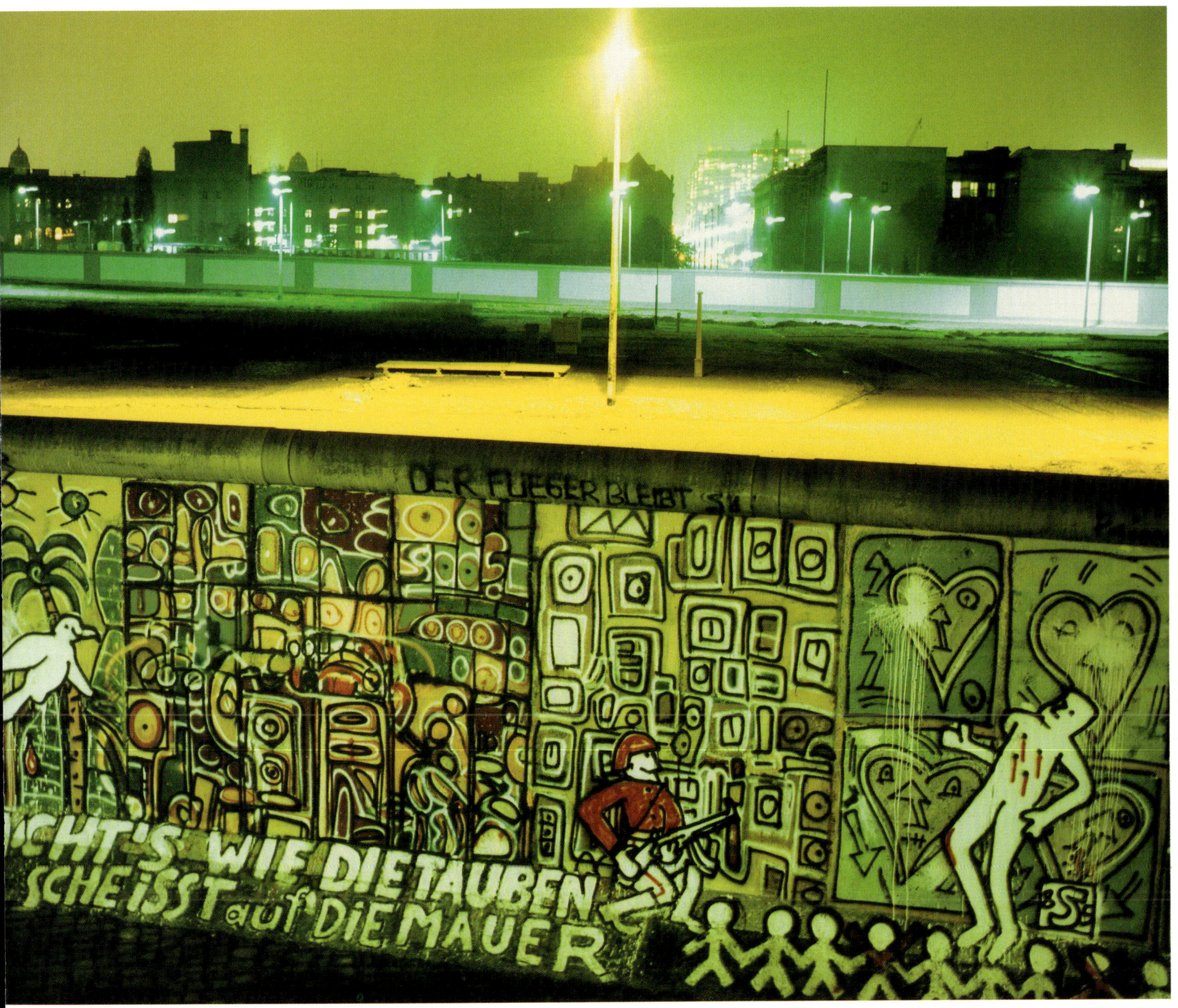

THE WALL AT NIGHT

ROLF RICHARDSON OF HENLEY-ON-THAMES STARTED SHOOTING STOCK TRAVEL PHOTOS 20 YEARS AGO AS AN AIRLINE PILOT. IS NOW A FULL-TIME COMMERCIAL PHOTOGRAPHER.

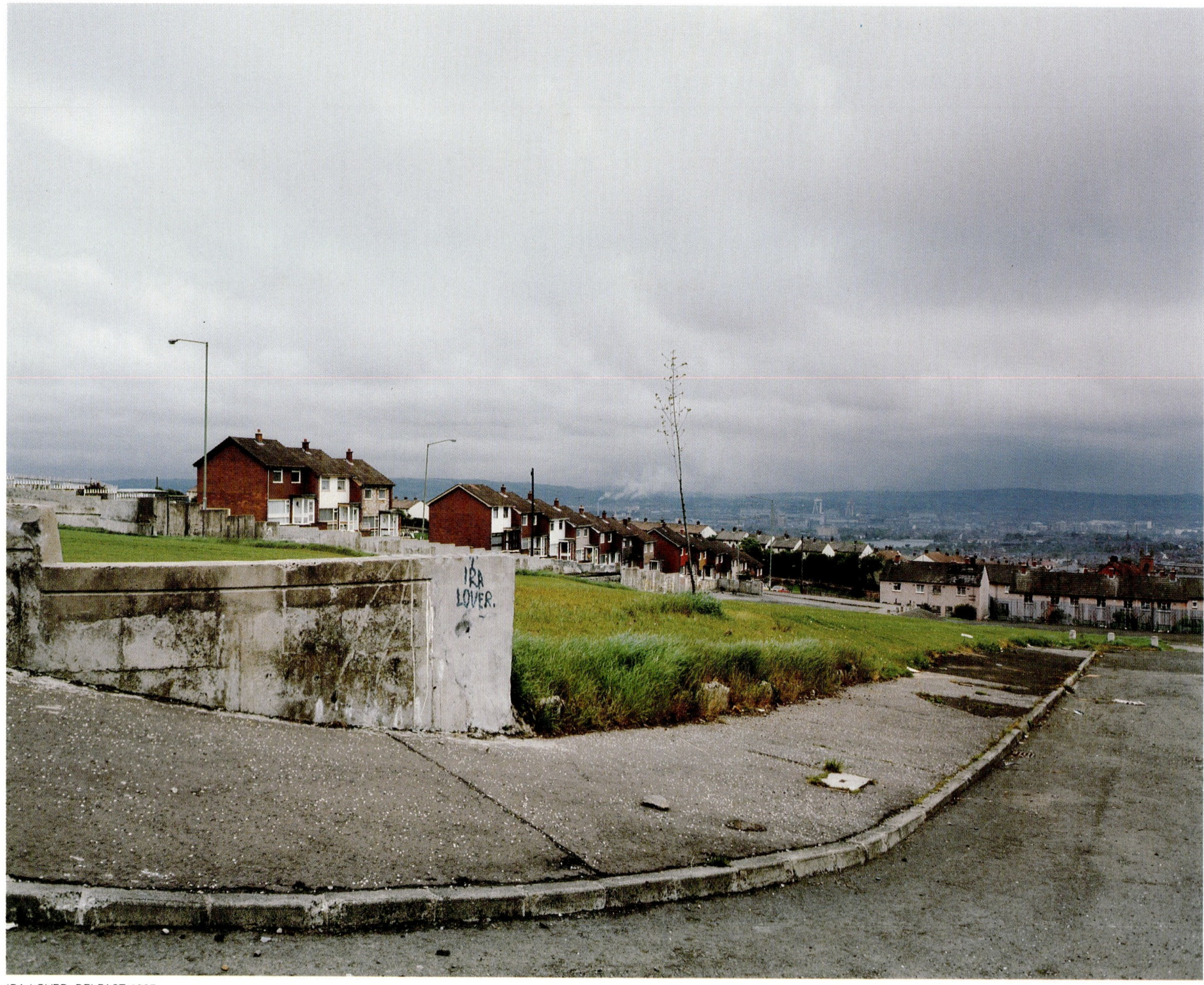

IRA LOVER, BELFAST 1985

PAUL GRAHAM IS ONE OF BRITAIN'S OUTSTANDING DOCUMENTARY PHOTOGRAPHERS. THE SERIES ON NORTHERN IRELAND WAS EXHIBITED AT THE FOTOFEST, HOUSTON.

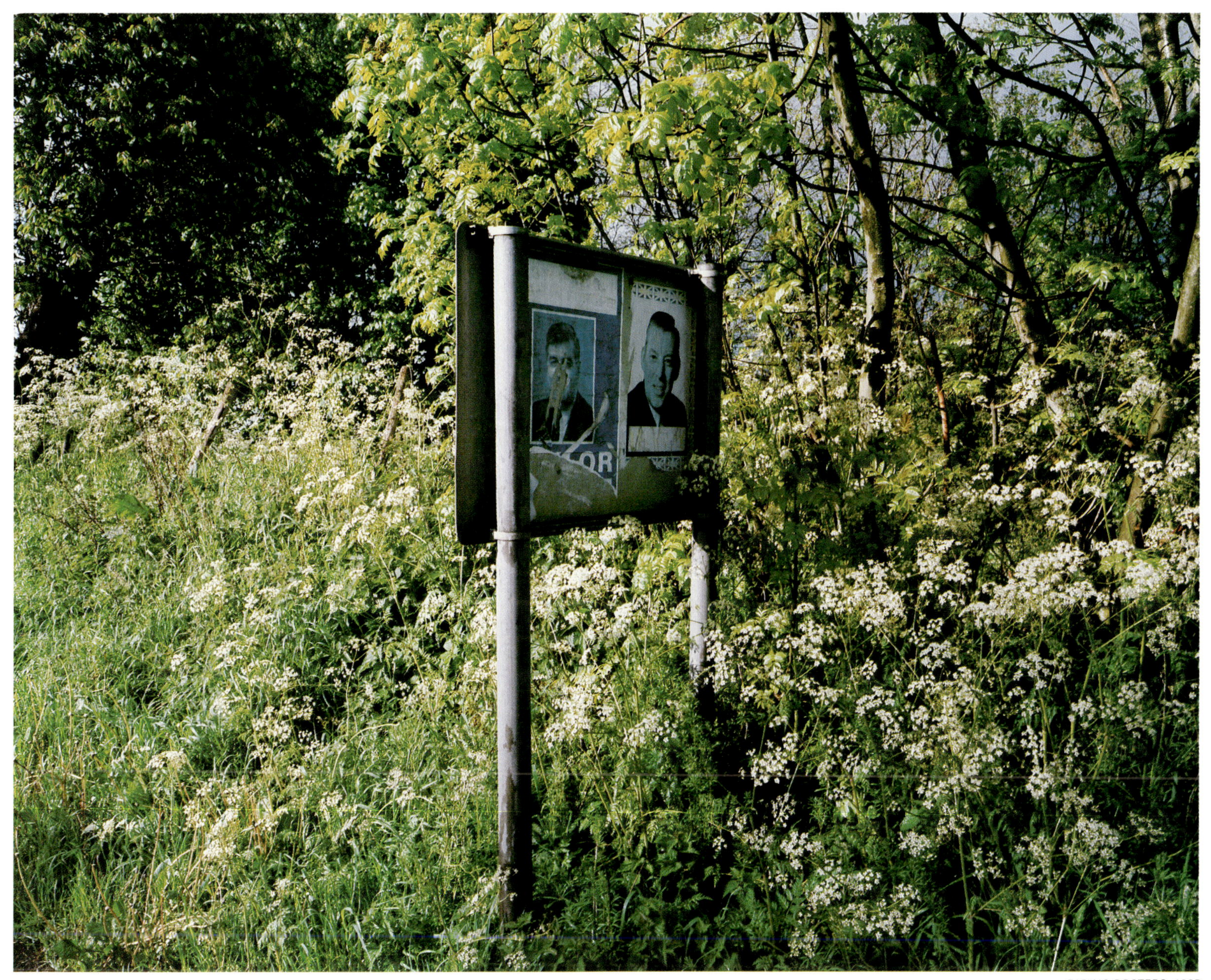

FADING POSTERS, 1985

PAUL GRAHAM

182

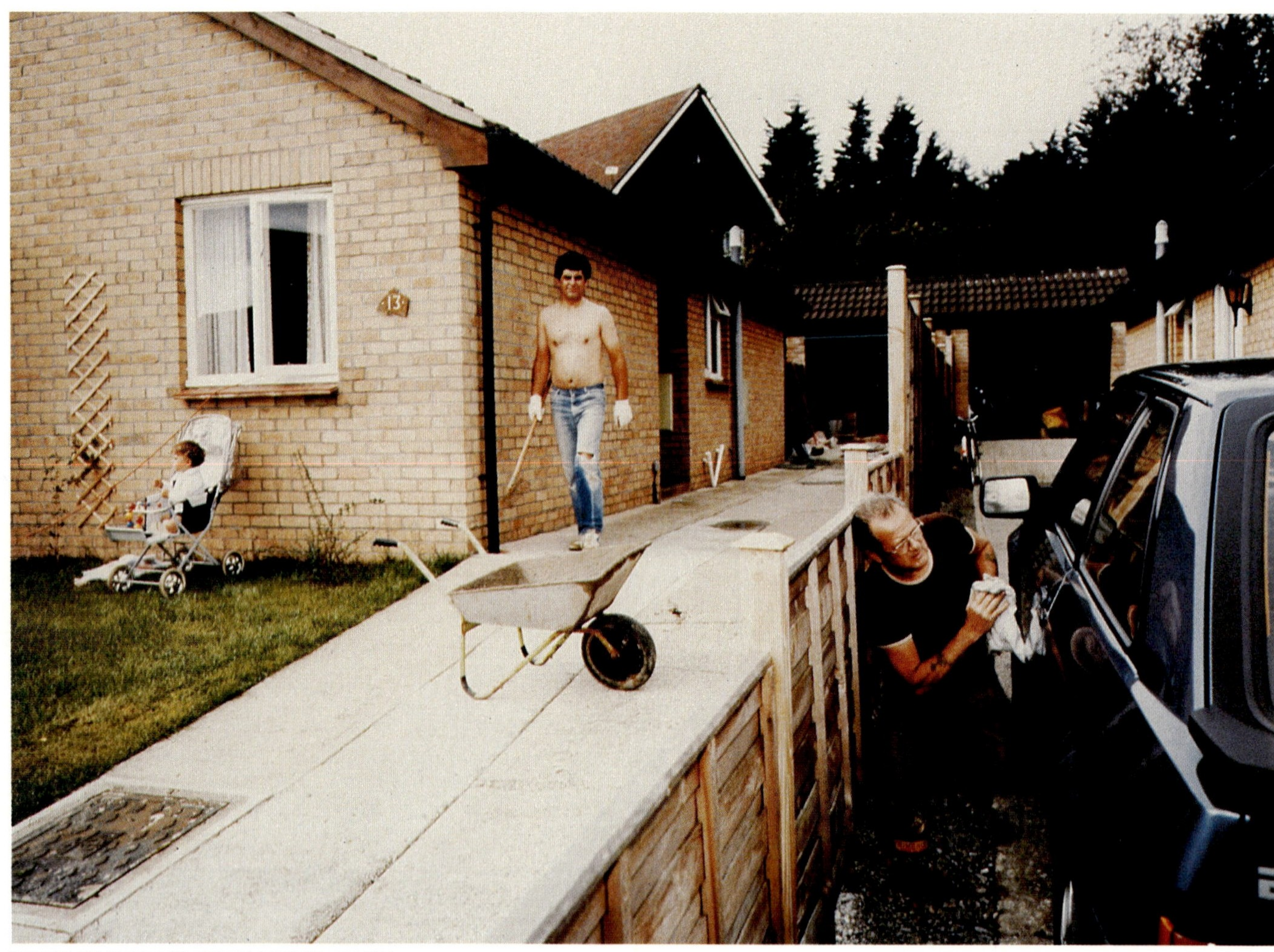
SUNDAY AFTERNOON, ST. MELLONS ESTATE, CARDIFF

PAUL REAS LIVES AND WORKS IN SOUTH WALES. THESE PICTURES ARE FROM A TOURING EXHIBITION 'I CAN HELP' FROM THE CARDIFF FFOTOGALLERY.

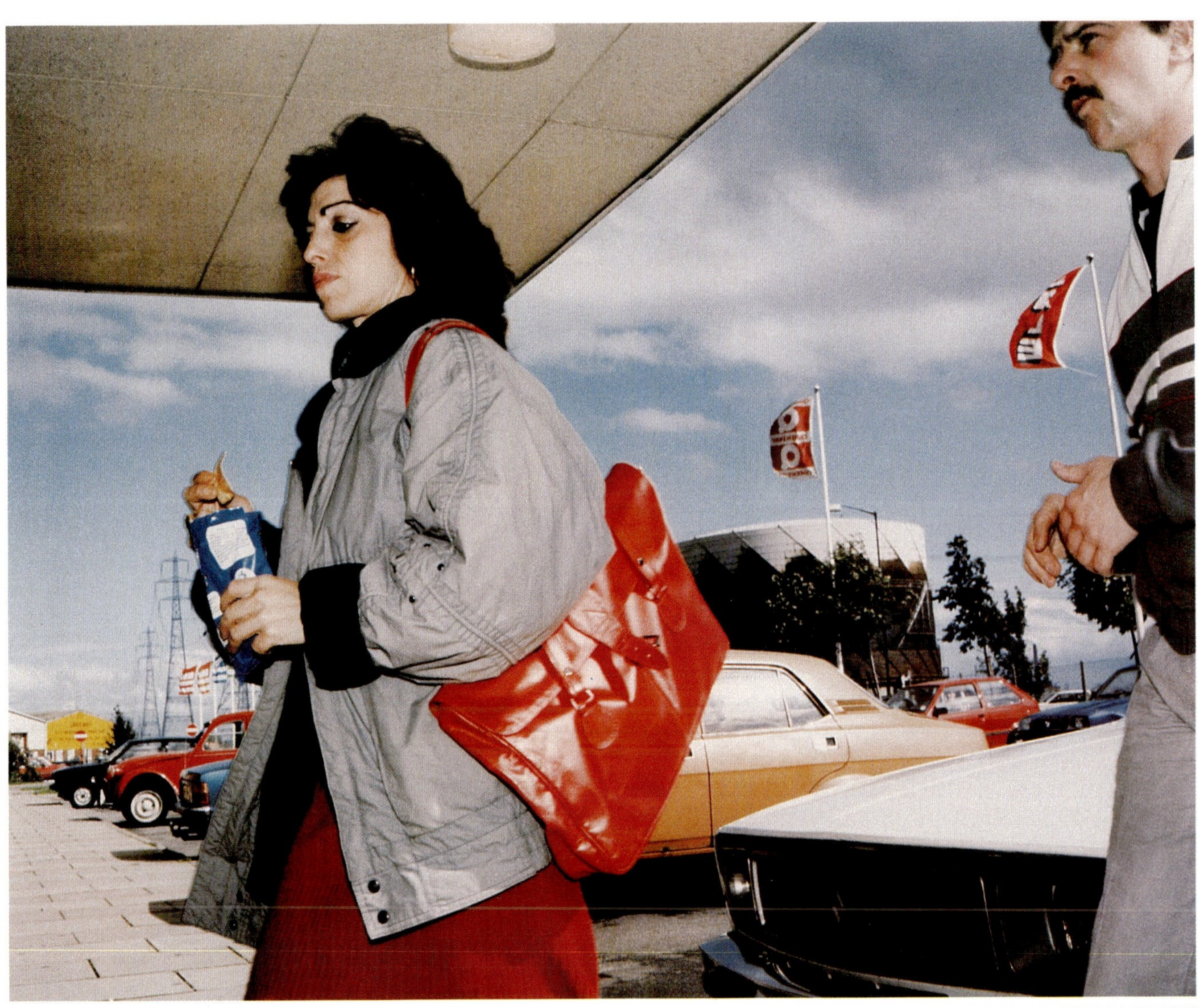

BANK HOLIDAY MONDAY, NEWPORT

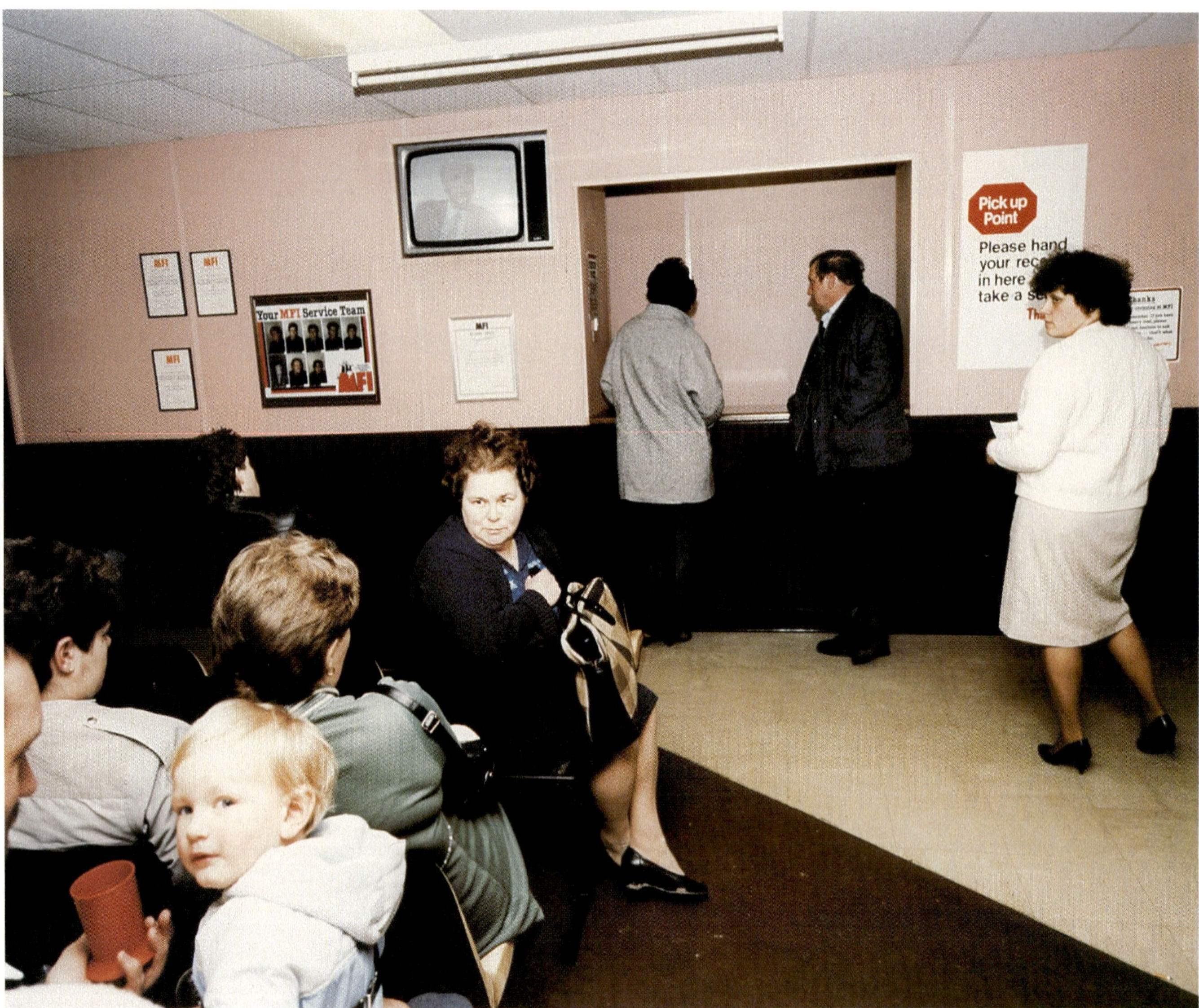

PICK-UP POINT MFI, NEWPORT

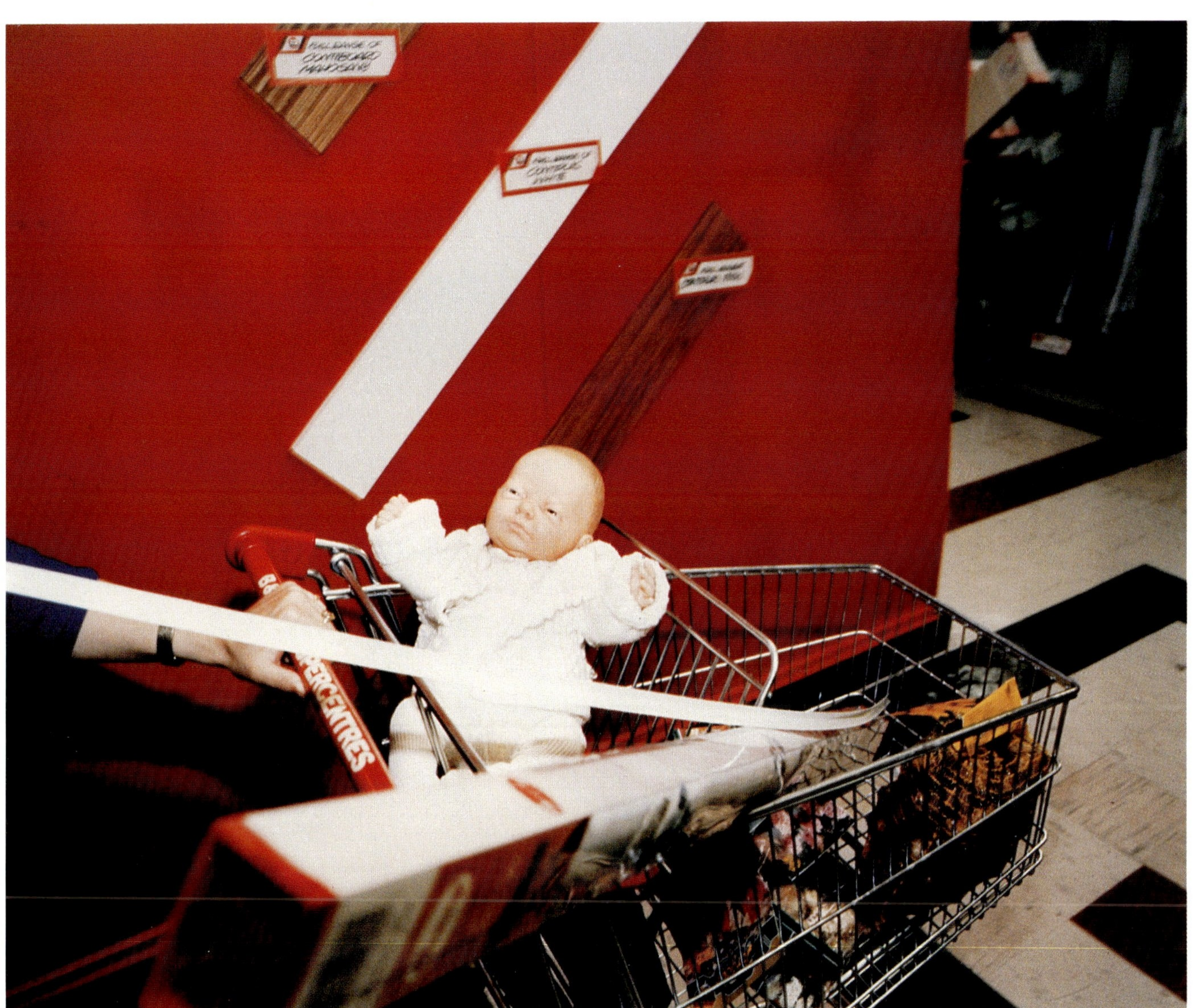

RUFER BABY IN TROLLEY B&Q, CWMBRAN

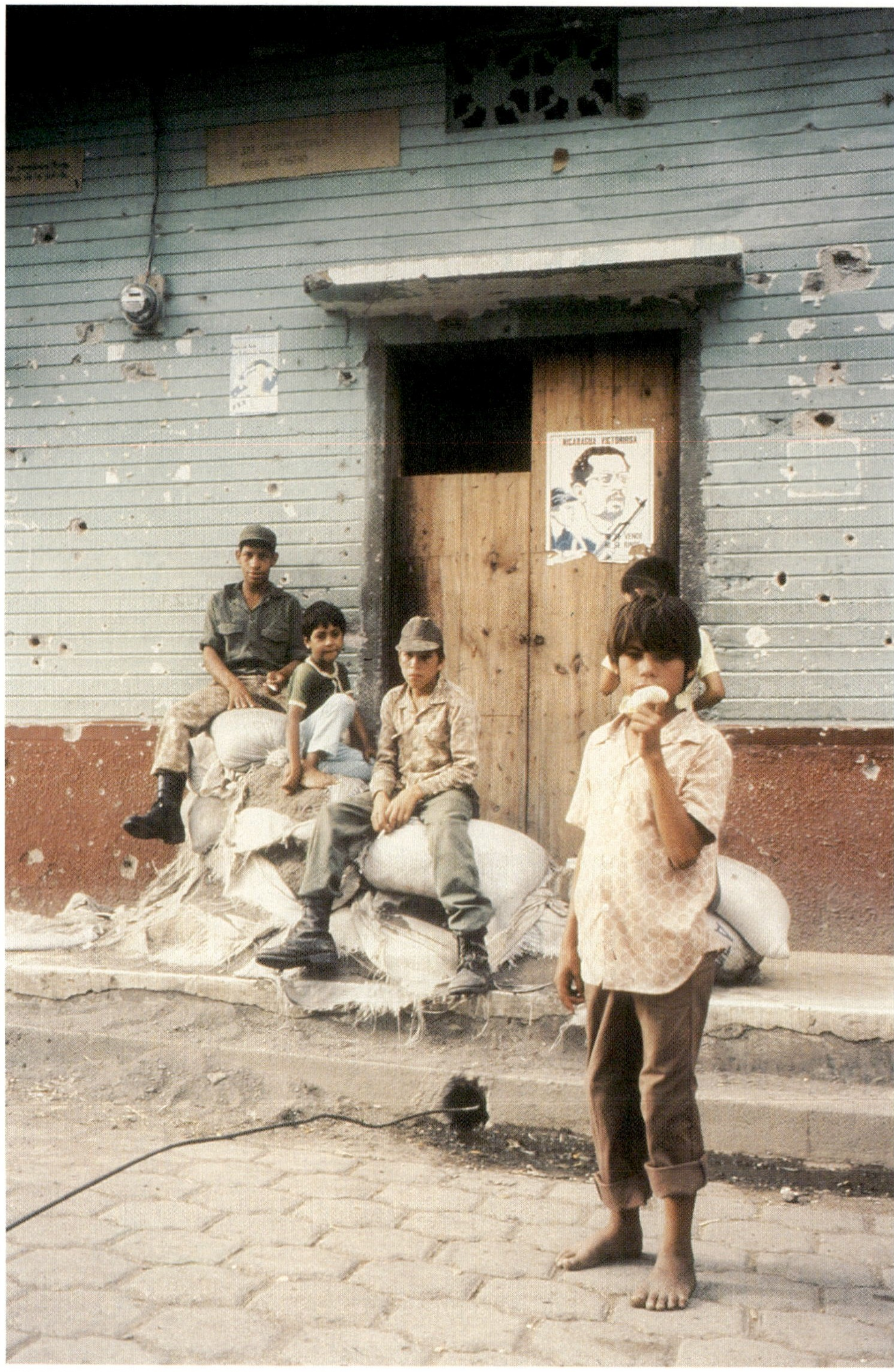

SANDINISTA YOUTH MILITIA OUTSIDE A RECENTLY RAIDED POST, NICARAGUA

TONY PALIOS IS 29 AND WORKS FOR A LONDON-BASED SHIPPING FIRM. HE TRAVELS EXTENSIVELY AND USES THE OPPORTUNITY FOR PHOTOGRAPHY.

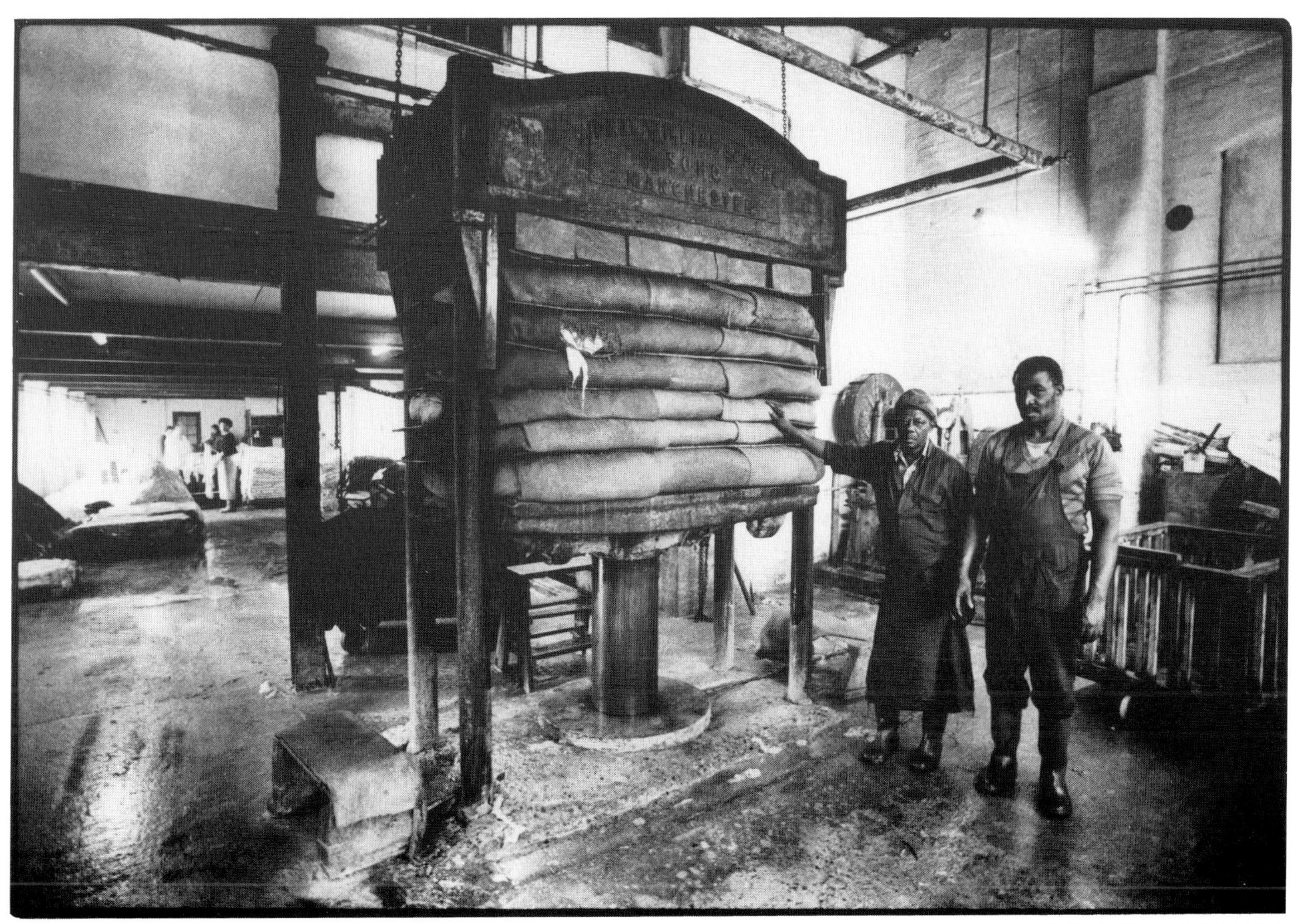

TANNERY WORKERS, HERTFORDSHIRE

BILL SMITH OF STEVENAGE HAS WORKED AS A NEWSPAPER PHOTOGRAPHER FOR 13 YEARS. HE HAS WON AWARDS FOR SPORTS PHOTOGRAPHY AND HAS HAD A TOURING EXHIBITION OF OTHER PHOTOGRAPHS.

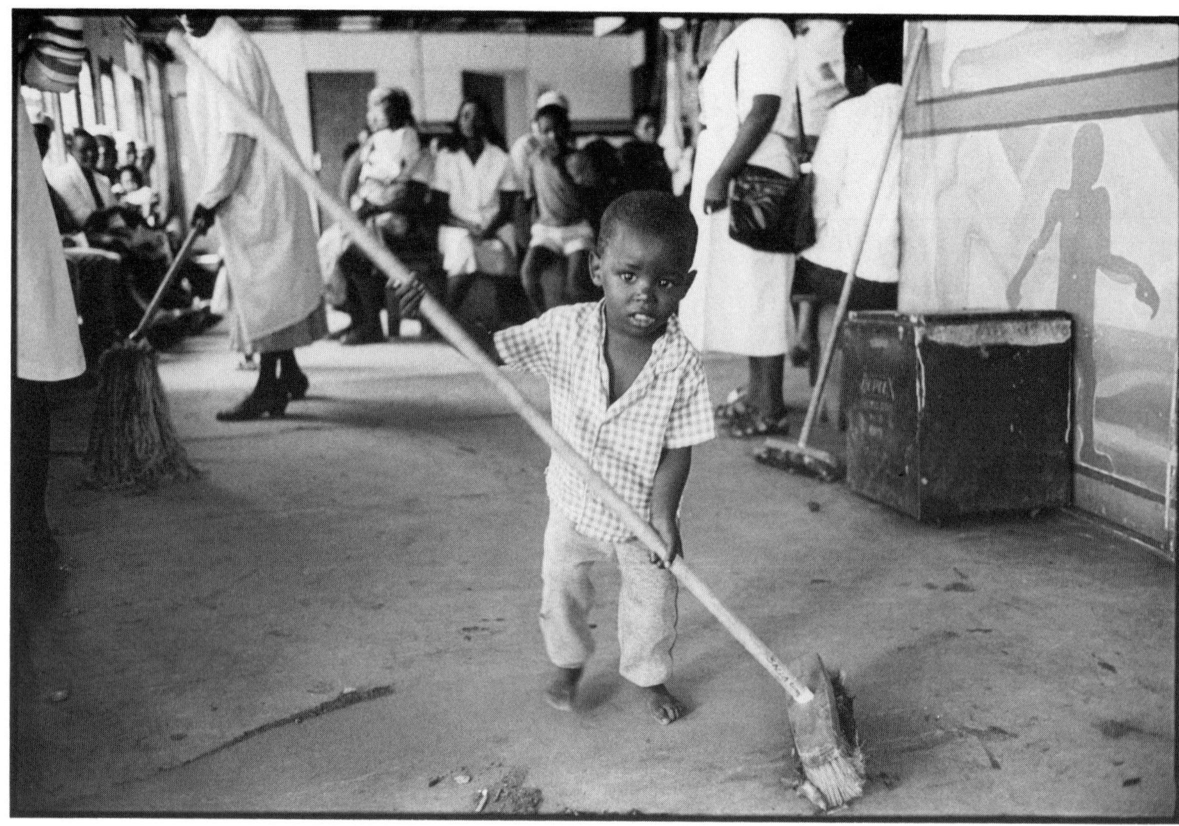

EMPILISWENI CLINIC, CROSSROADS NEAR CAPETOWN

MICROCEPHILIC CHILD HAVING PHYSIOTHERAPY

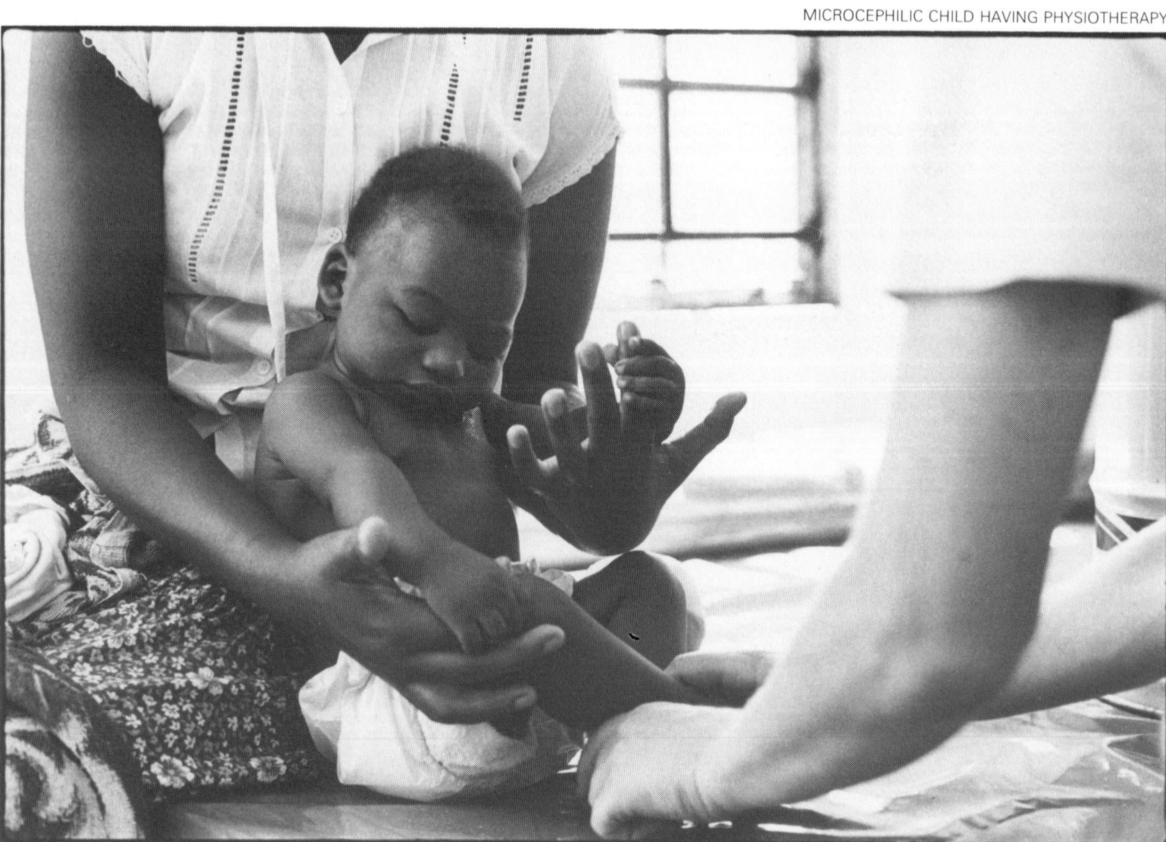

RICHARD OLIVIER WAS BORN IN SOUTH AFRICA AND NOW LIVES IN ENGLAND, WORKING AS A SELF-EMPLOYED FREELANCE PHOTOGRAPHER. HE ALSO TAKES ON ASSIGNMENTS IN COMMERCIAL AND INDUSTRIAL FIELDS.

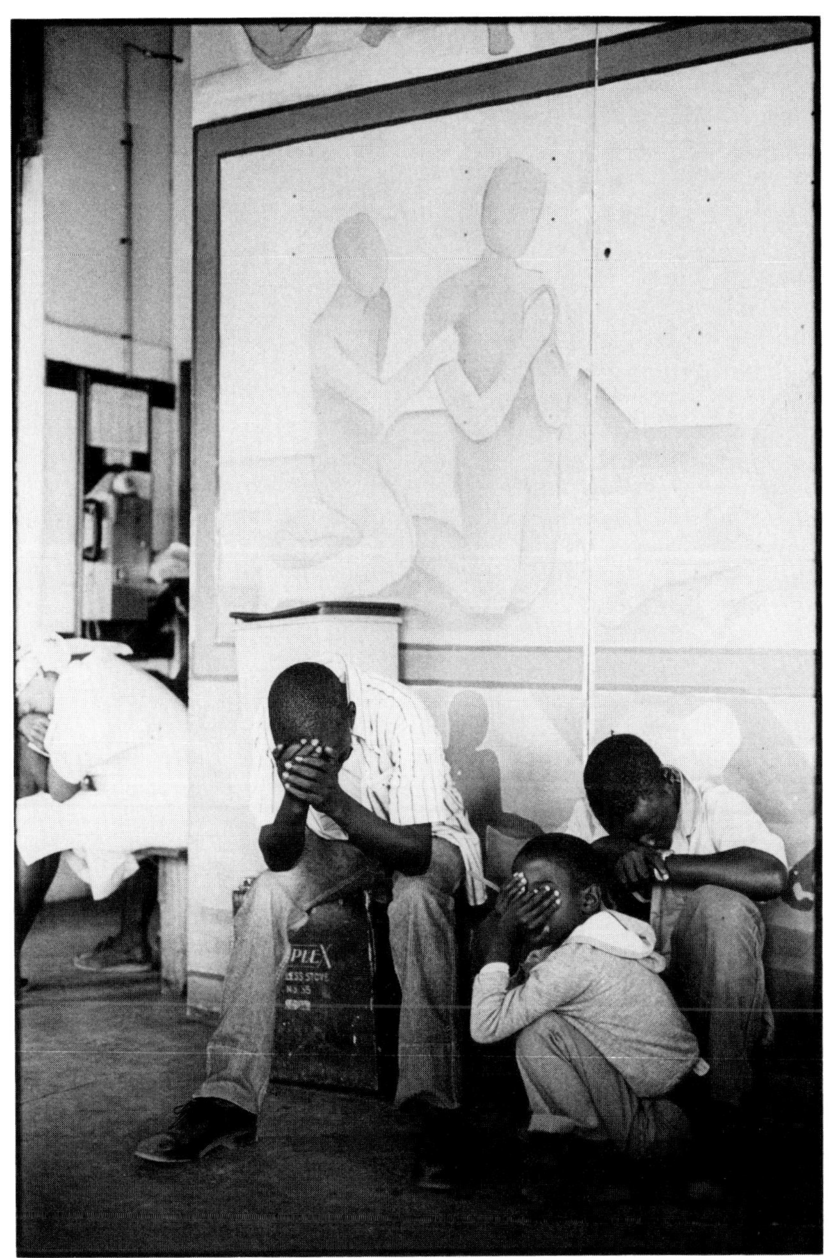

PRAYER MEETING AT THE EMPILISWENI CLINIC

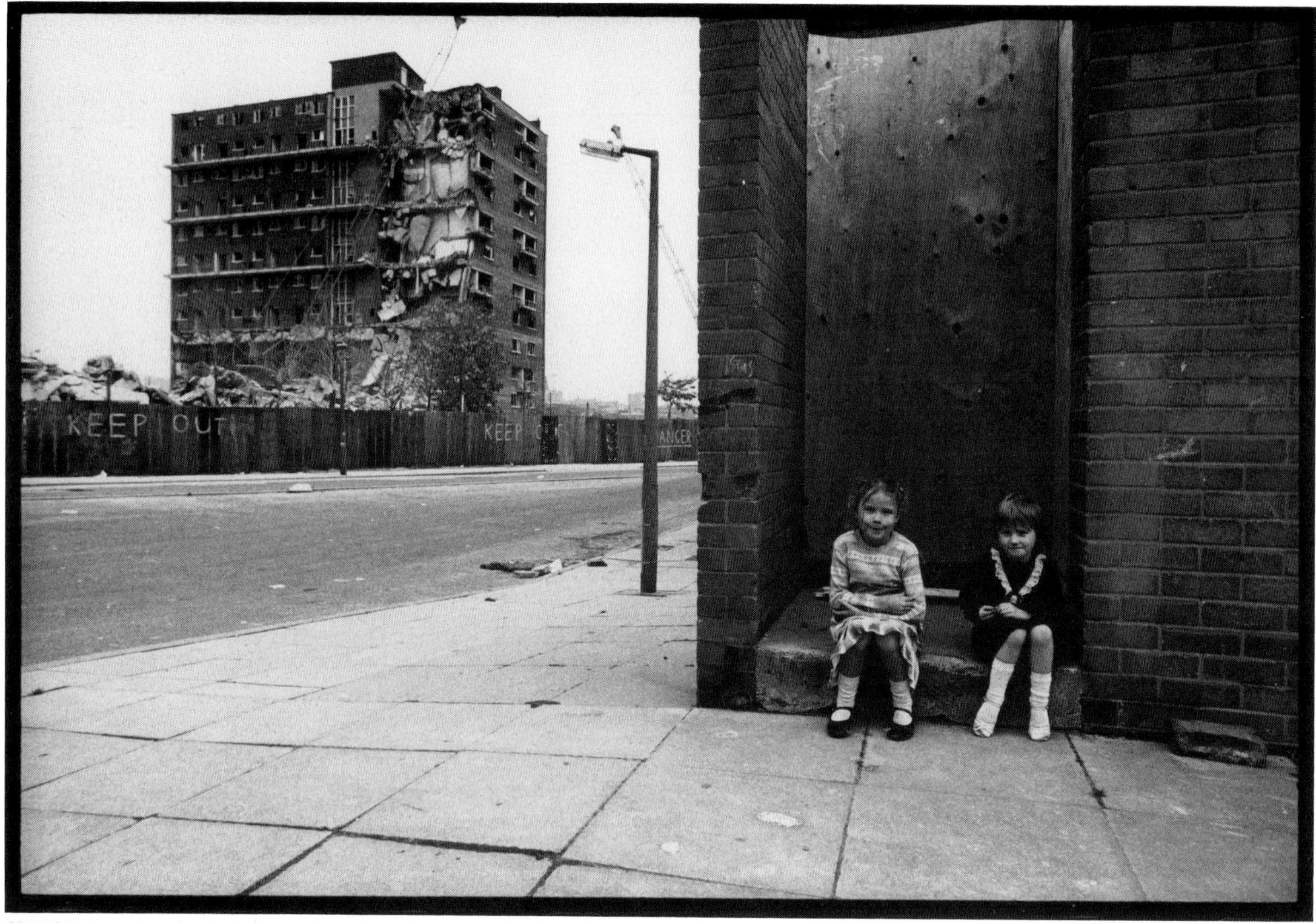

BRAUNSTONE, LEICESTER. SAMANTHA & JASON

MARK POWER TOOK THESE PICTURES AS PART OF A PROJECT, CURRENTLY TOURING, FOR THE CHILDREN'S SOCIETY. HE IS WORKING ON A SERIES ON POVERTY IN BRIGHTON, WHERE HE LIVES.

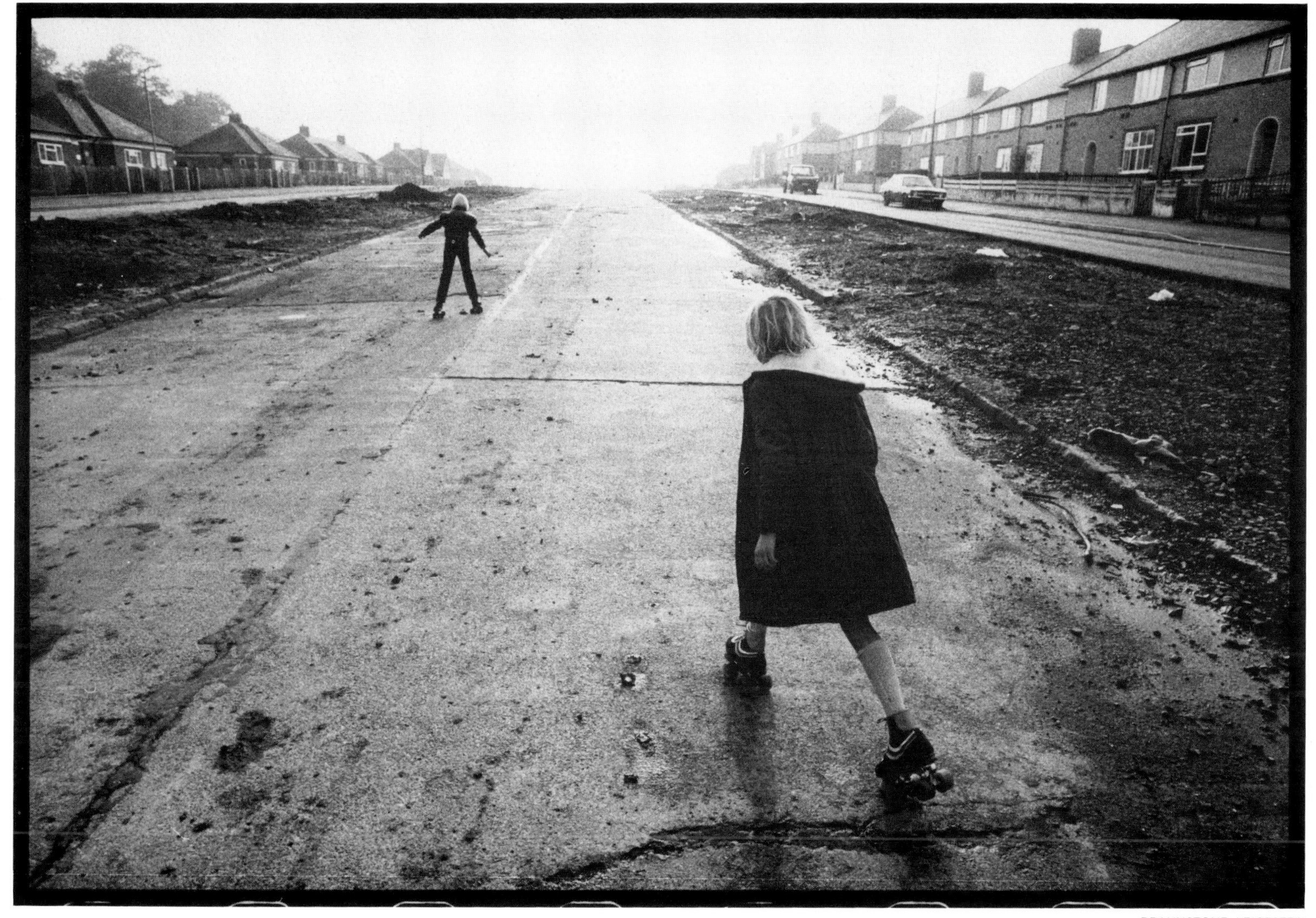

BRAUNSTONE, LEICESTER

MARK POWER

192

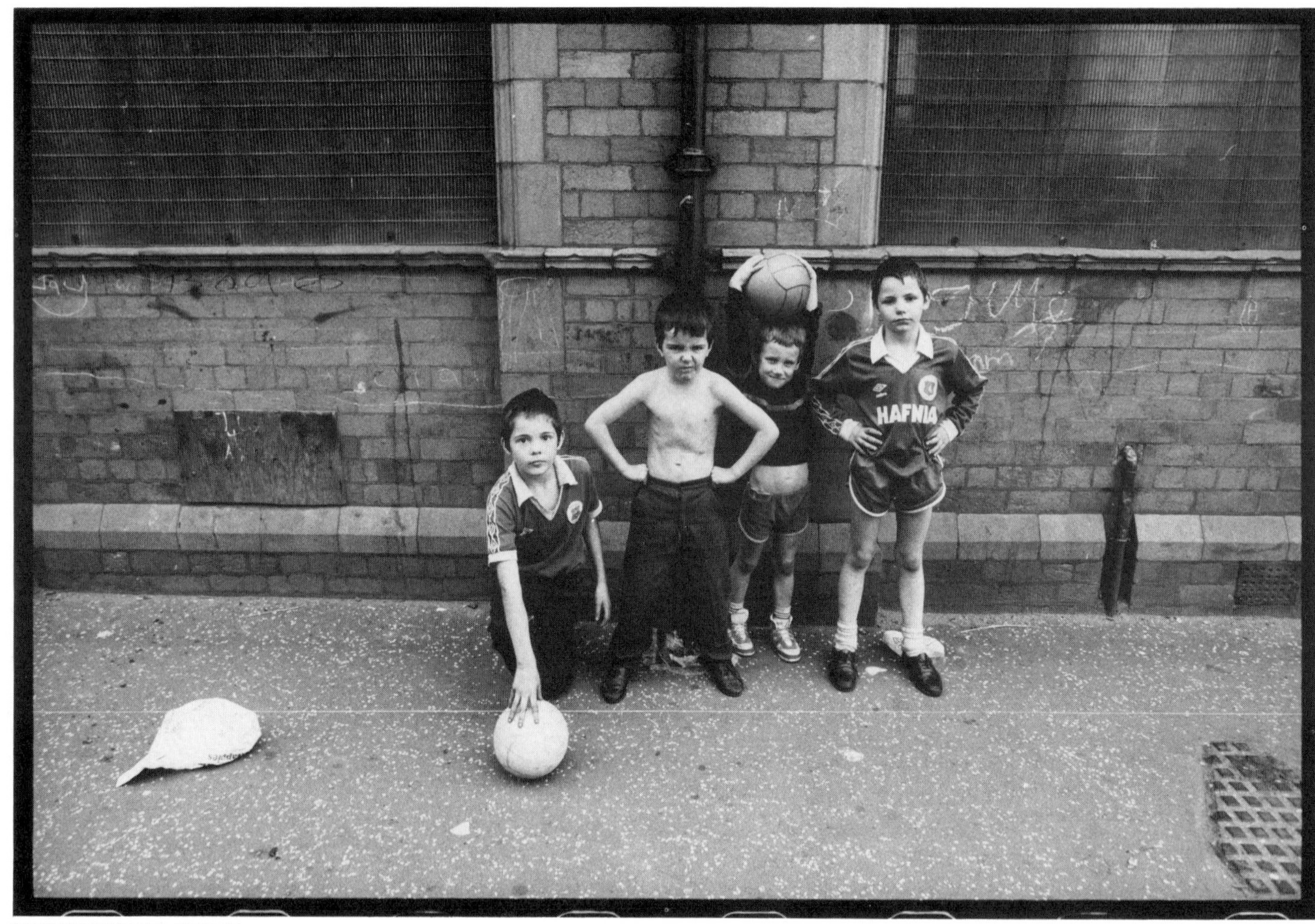

CORONATION STREET, SALFORD

MARK POWER

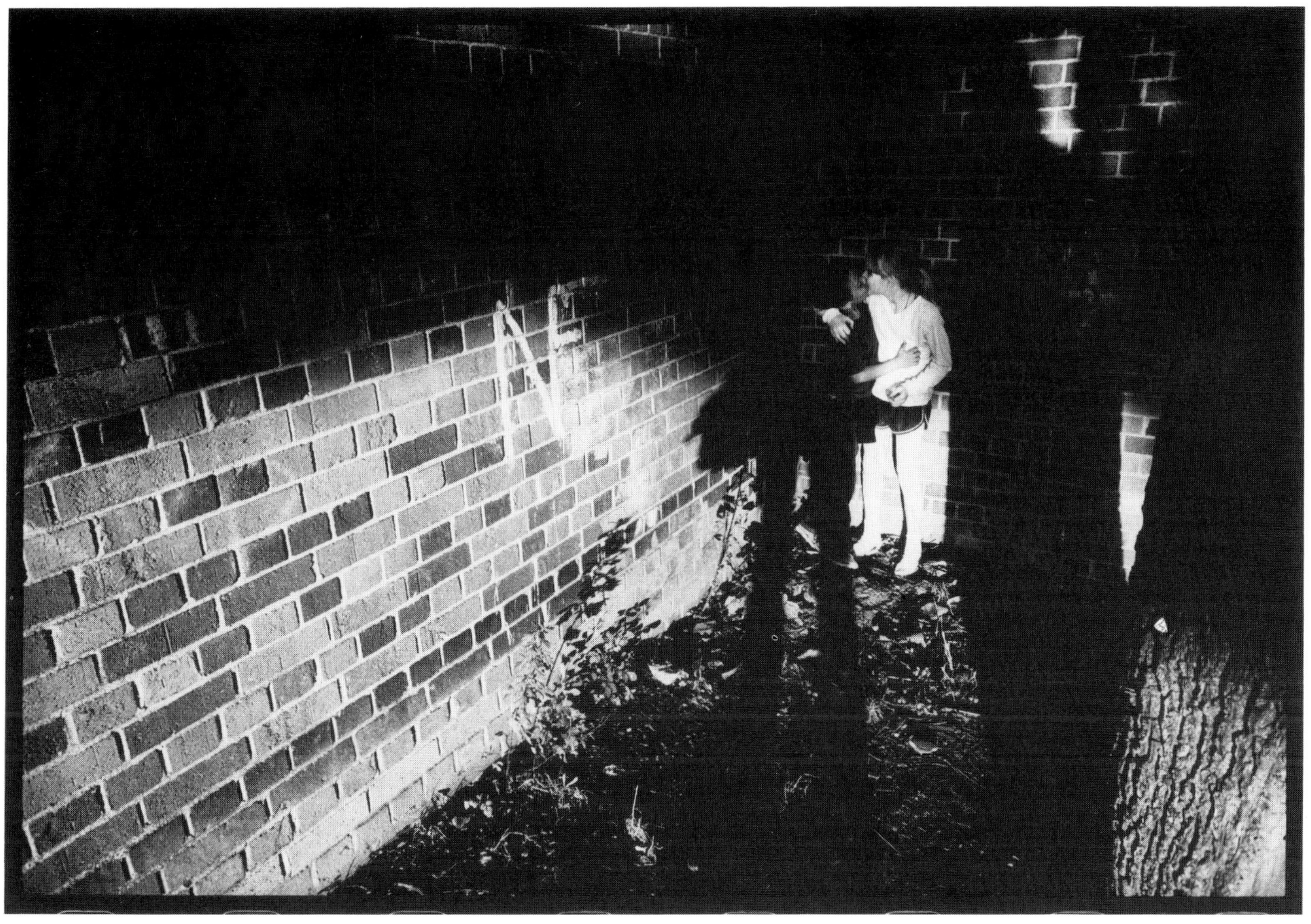

SALFORD

MARK POWER

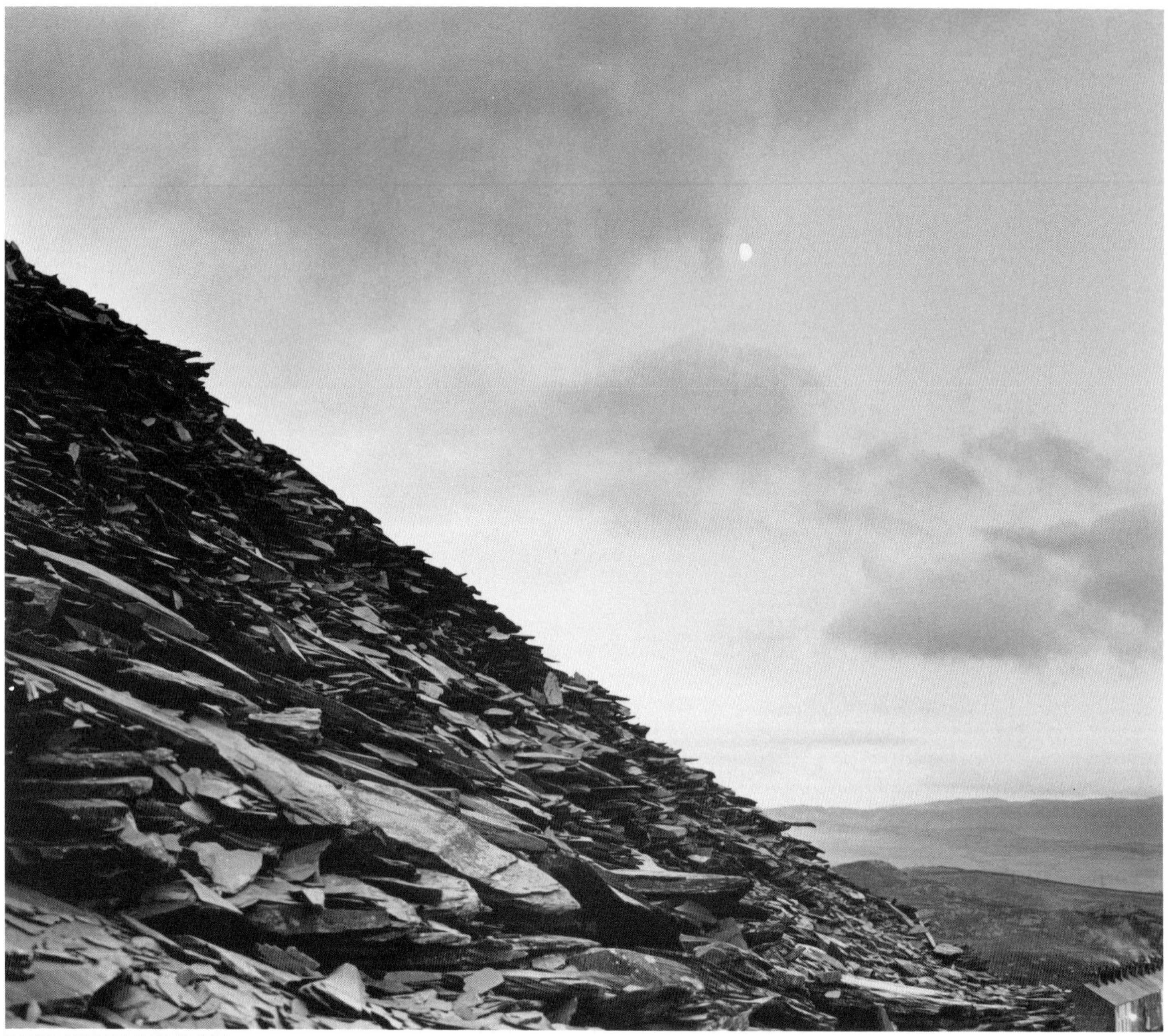
BLAENAU FESTINIOG SLATE QUARRY

ANDREW SOLE GRADUATED 1985 FROM WEST SURREY COLLEGE OF ART AND DESIGN.
TWO PROJECTS IN PROGRESS ARE BRADFORD MILLS AND NORTH WALES SLATE MINES.

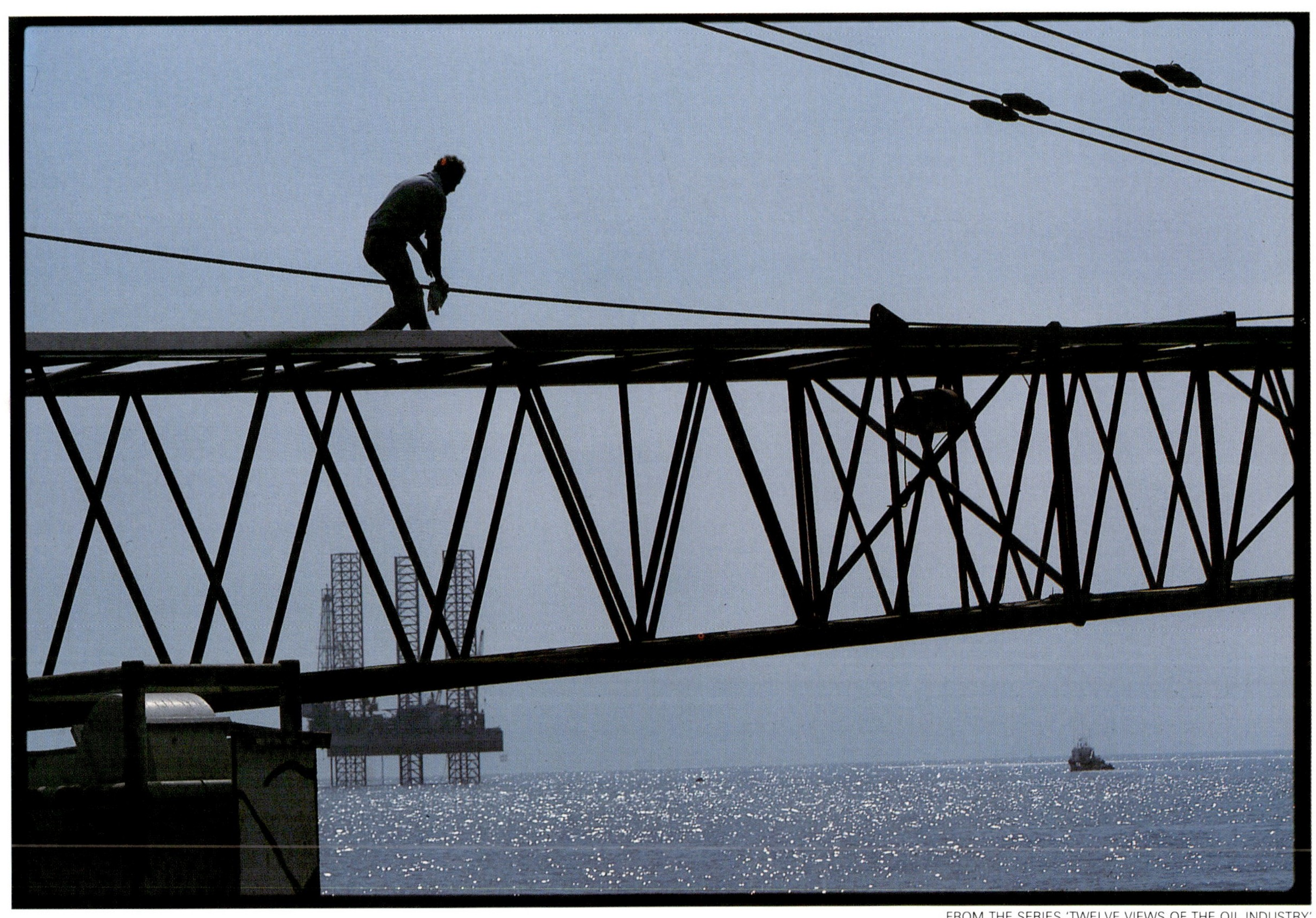

FROM THE SERIES 'TWELVE VIEWS OF THE OIL INDUSTRY'

JOHN CHAMPNEY SAYS HE IS AN 'ATTRACTIVE FAIR HAIRED FATHER OF THREE' AND A PROFESSIONAL PHOTOGRAPHER FROM THE WIRRAL.

196

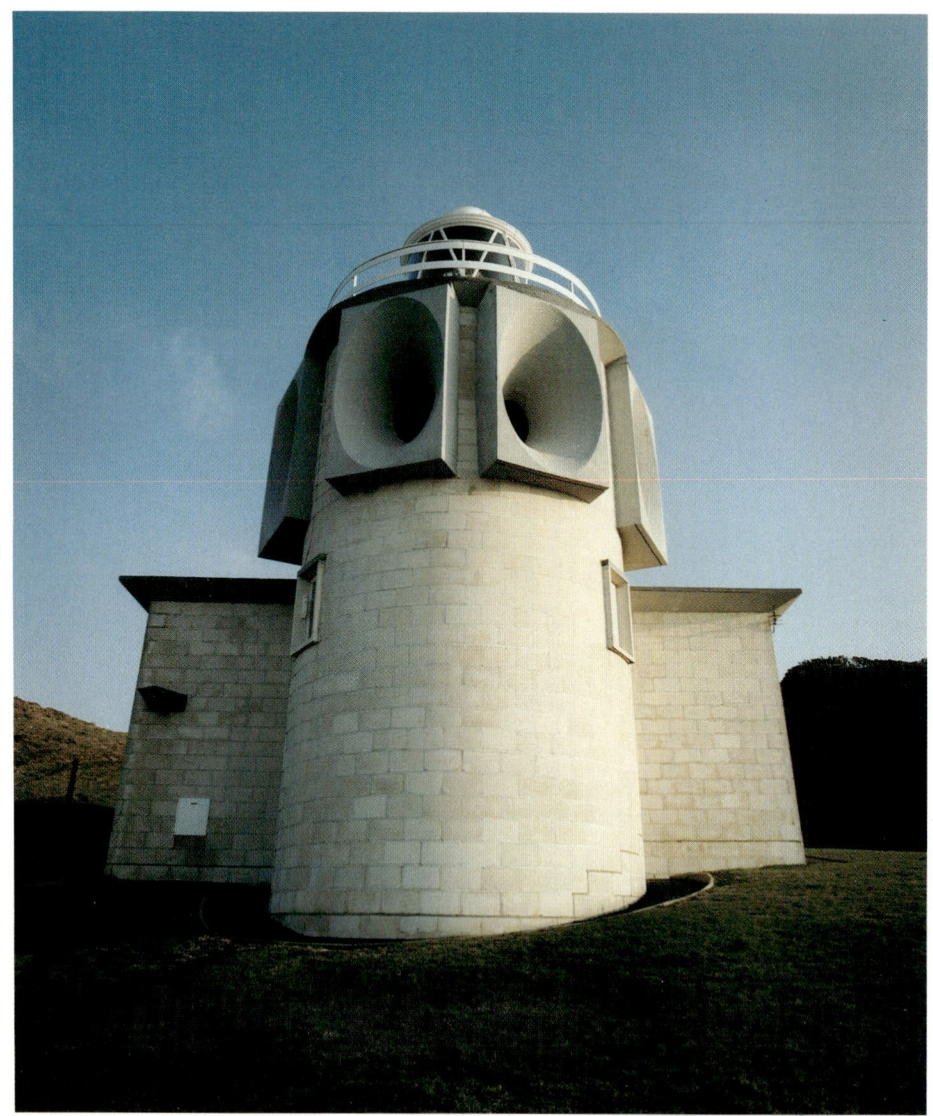

BULL POINT LIGHTHOUSE, NORTH DEVON

HUW DAVIES IS THE PHOTOGRAPHER IN RESIDENCE/FELLOW AT DERBYSHIRE COLLEGE OF HIGHER EDUCATION. HE IS AT PRESENT AT WORK ON A MAJOR EXHIBITION ON BRITISH INDUSTRY. THE PICTURES ARE FROM A RECENTLY COMPLETED SURVEY OF THE AUTOMATION OF BRITISH LIGHTHOUSES.

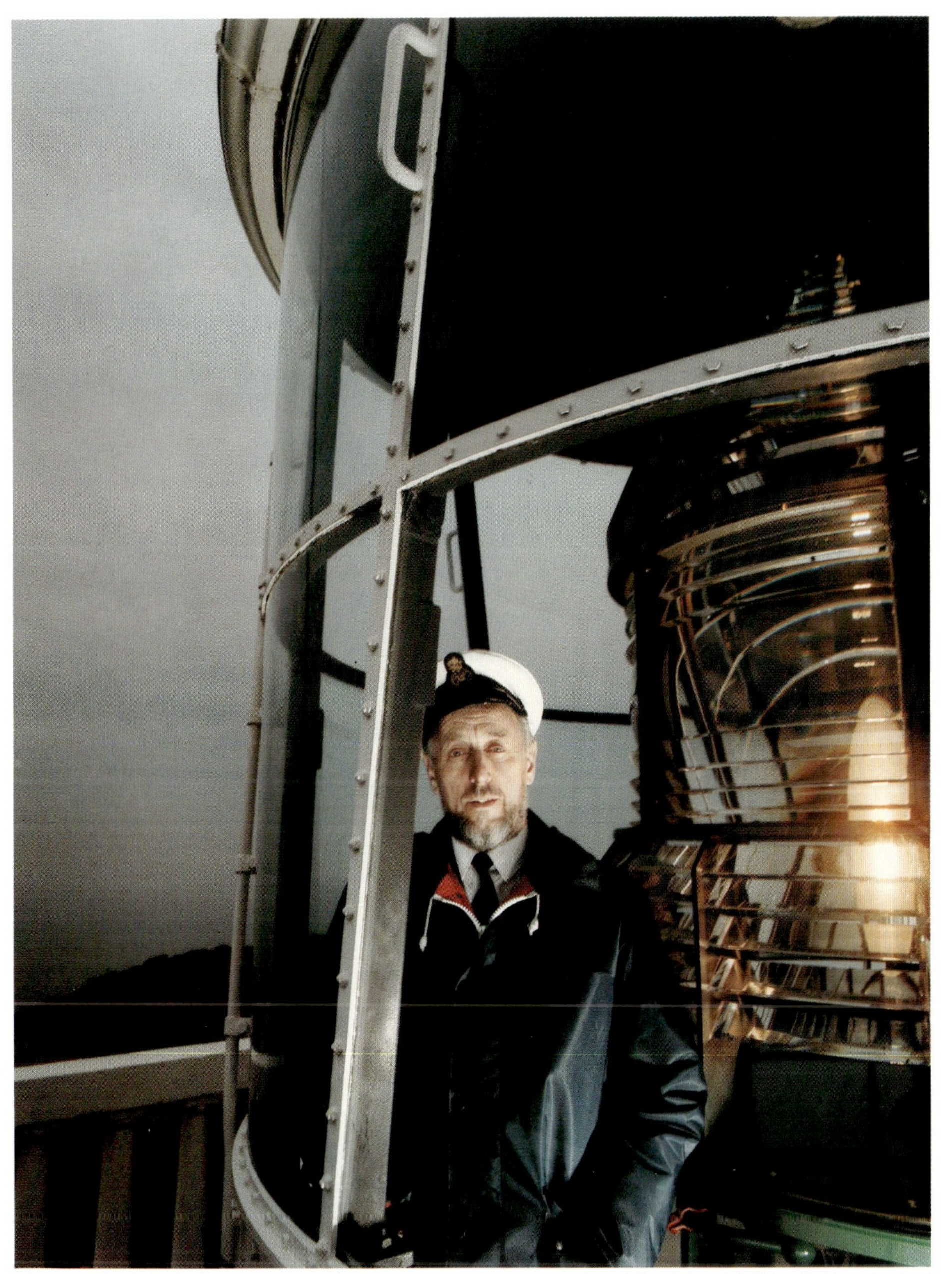

GRAHAM FEARNE, PRINCIPAL KEEPER, CROMER

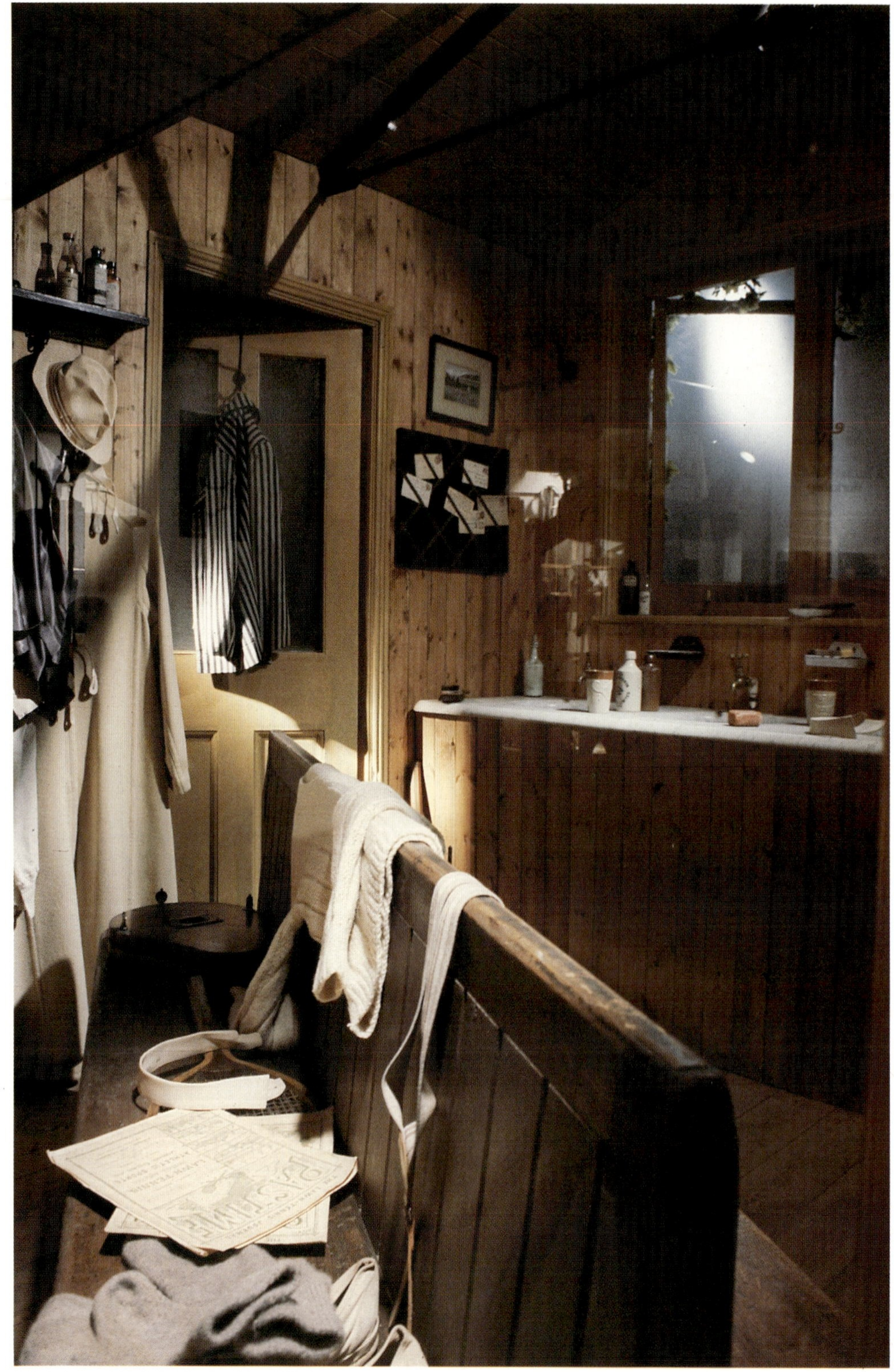

GENTLEMEN'S DRESSING ROOM, WIMBLEDON

MICKY WHITE IS A FREELANCE PROFESSIONAL PHOTOGRAPHER WORKING FOR THE WIMBLEDON LAWN TENNIS MUSEUM. HER PICTURES OF THE VENICE FESTIVAL HAVE BEEN PUBLISHED IN THE WEEKLY *BJP*.

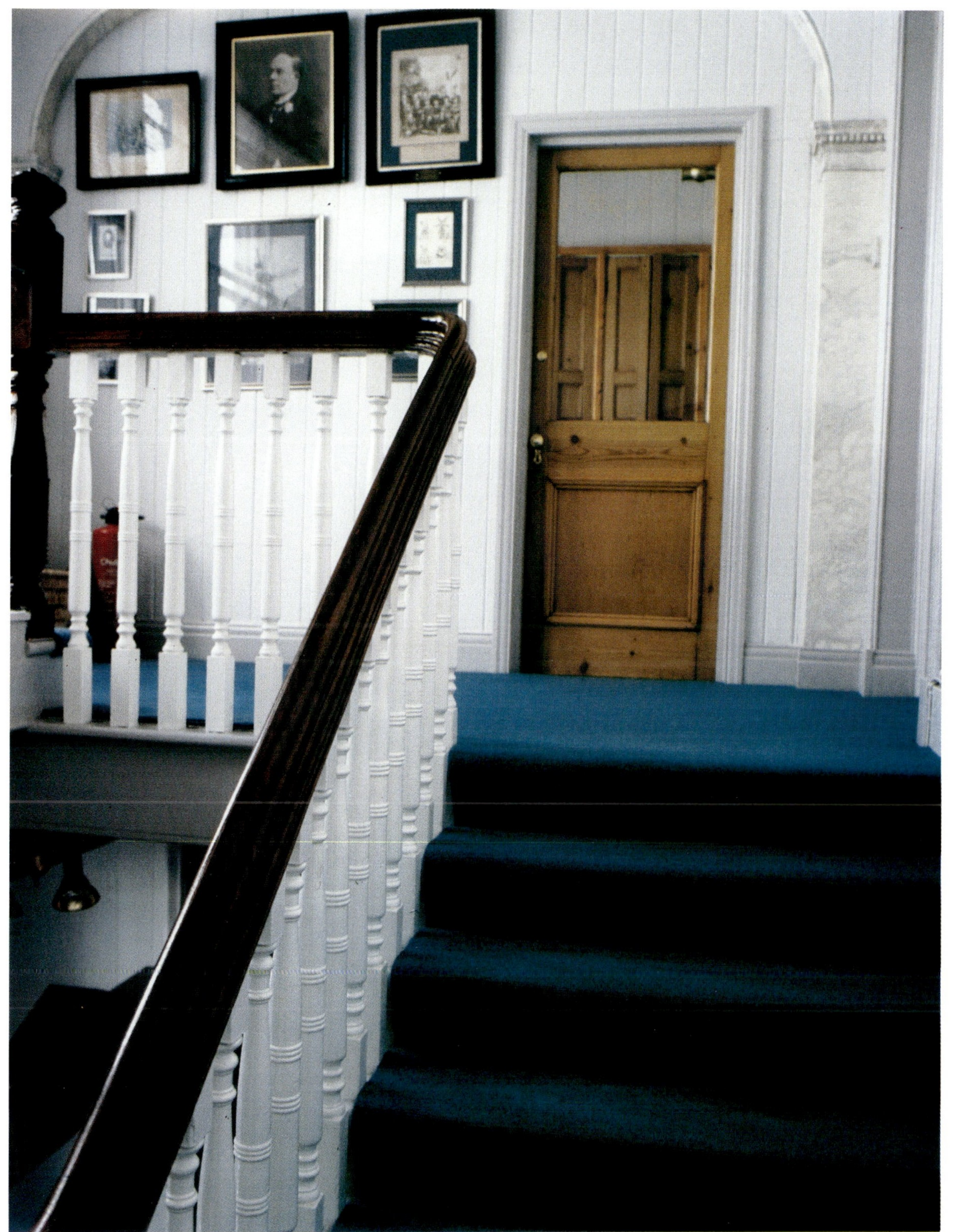

INTERIOR

ANDREW HORSFIELD FROM GATESHEAD IS 19-YEARS-OLD AND WANTS TO SPECIALISE IN FOOD/ STILL LIFE PHOTOGRAPHY. IS LOOKING FOR AN ASSISTANT'S POSITION.

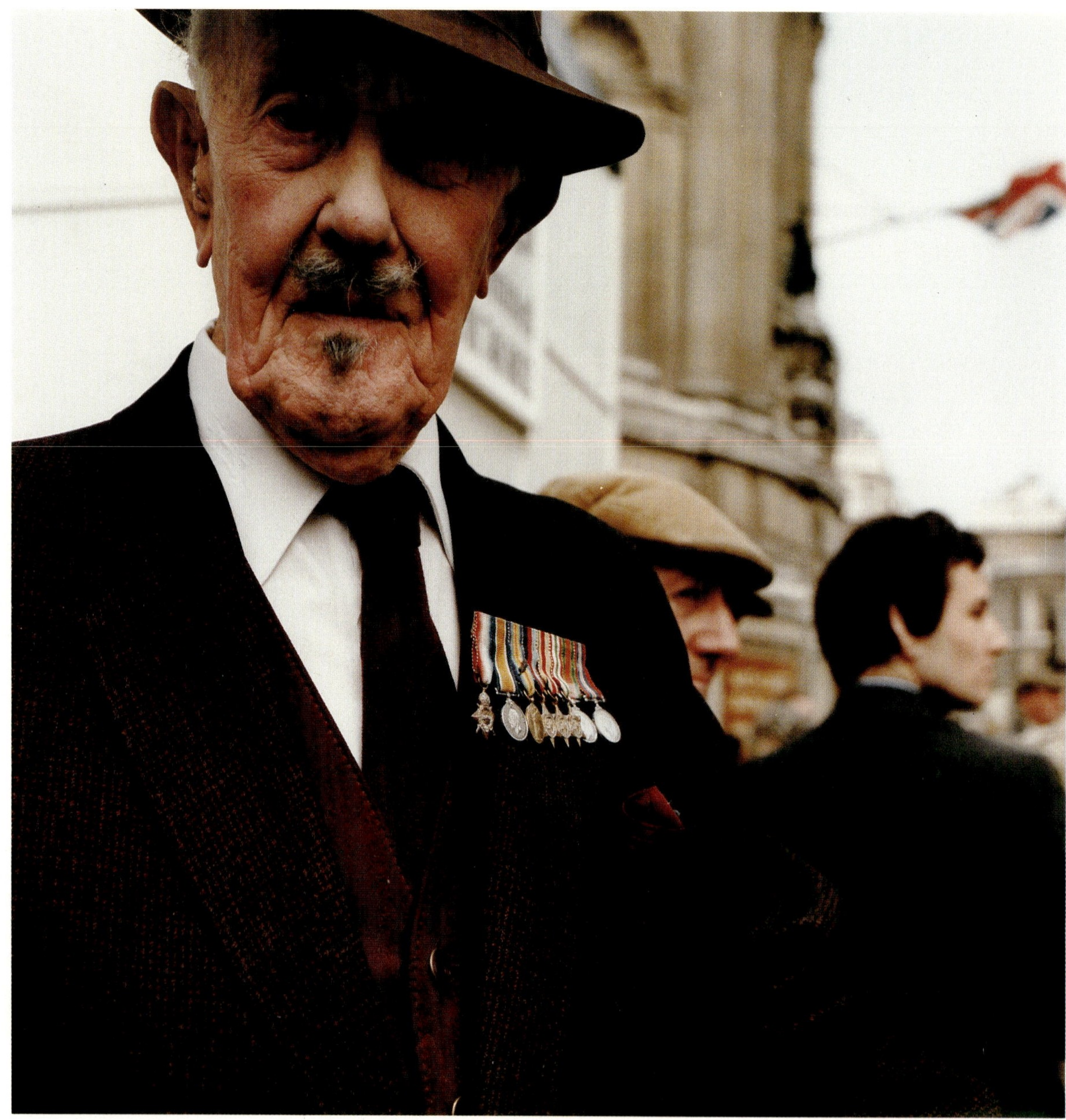

VE DAY CELEBRATION, LONDON

RICHARD BURBRIDGE LIVES IN SUFFOLK BUT IS CURRENTLY STUDYING AT WEST SURREY COLLEGE OF ART AND DESIGN.

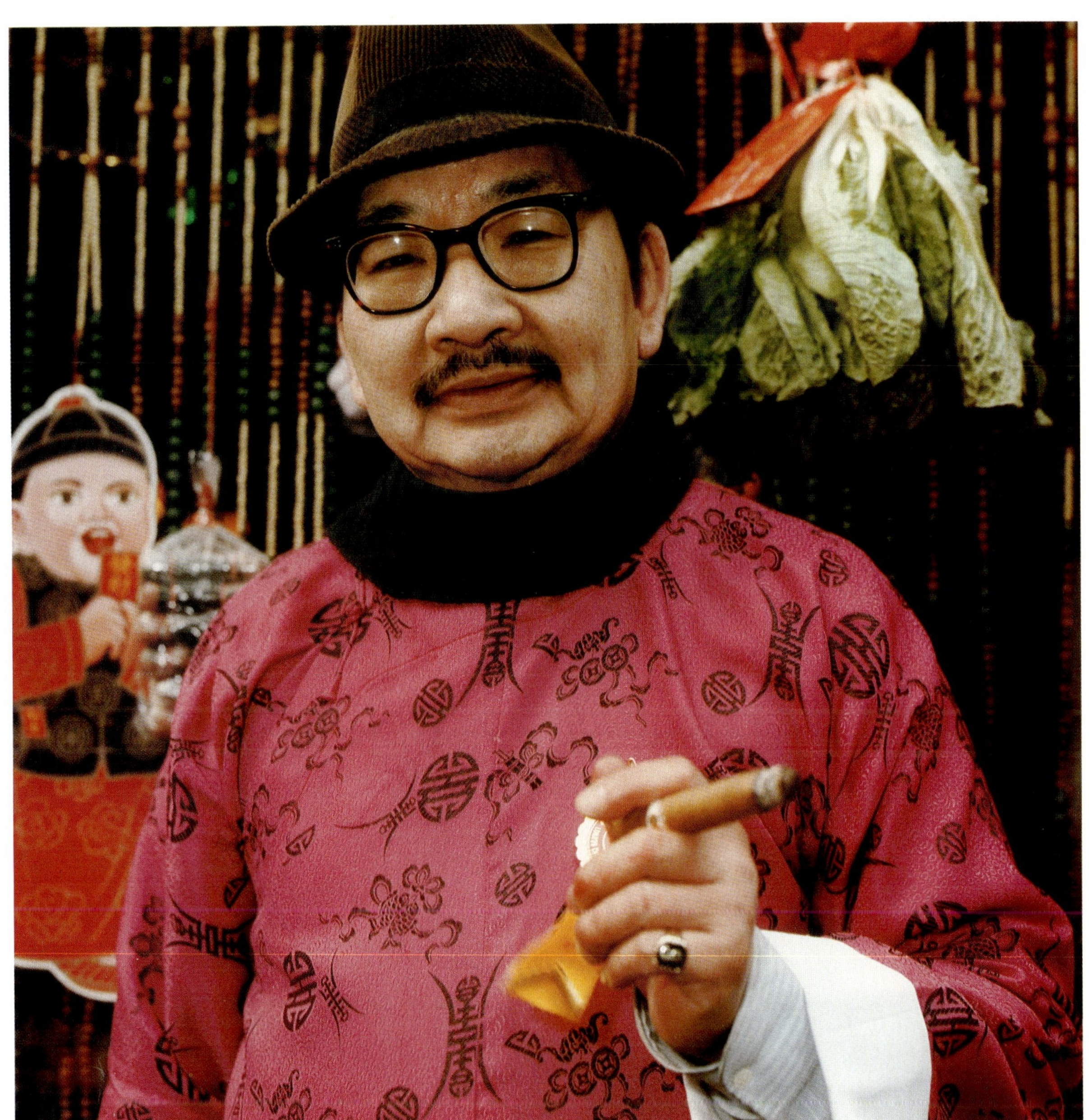

CHINESE NEW YEAR, SOHO

RICHARD BURBRIDGE

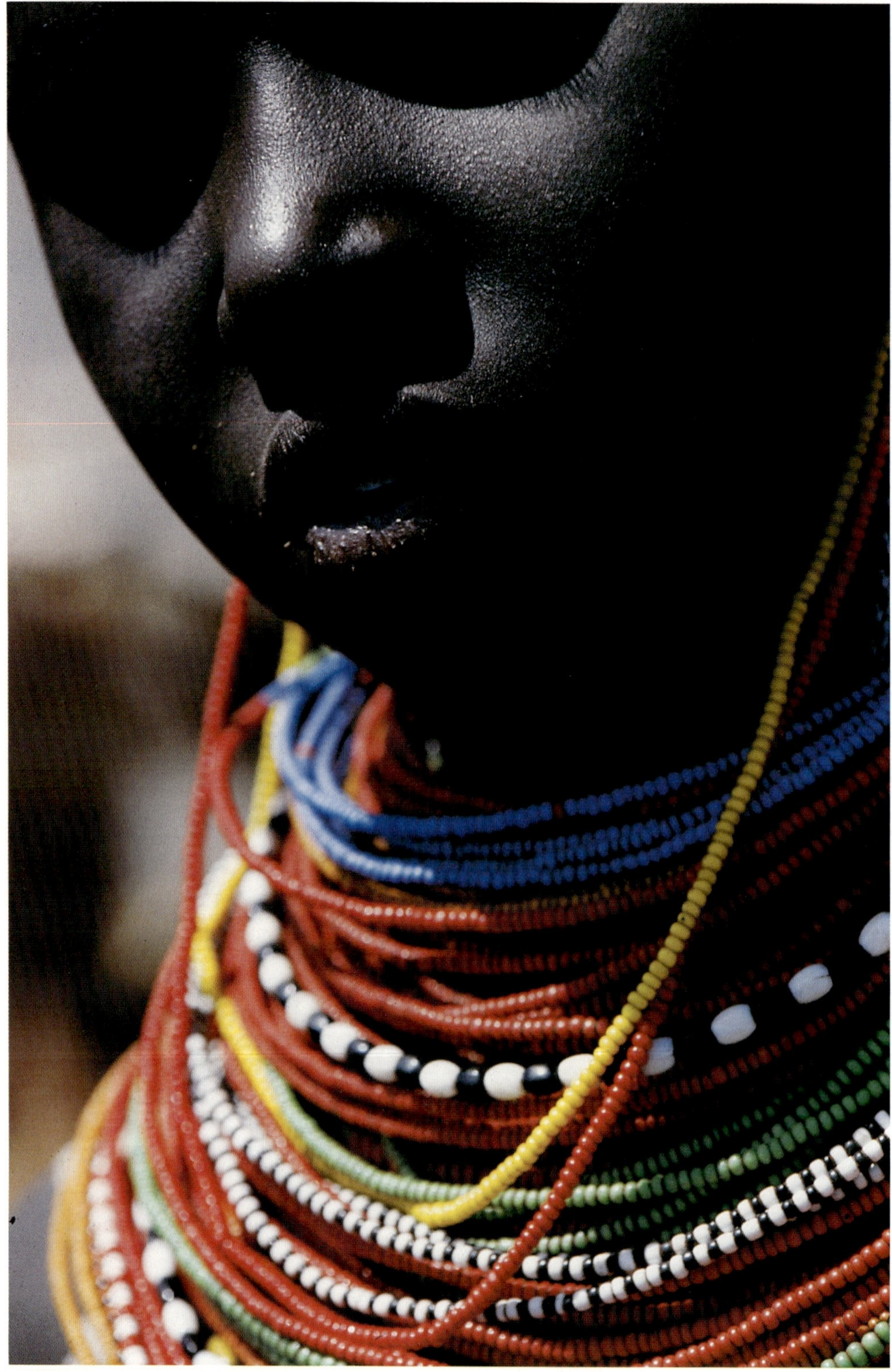

EL MOLO WOMAN, LAKE TURKANA, KENYA

TOM ANG IS A PHOTOGRAPHER AND PHOTOGRAPHIC AGENT SPECIALISING IN TRAVEL PHOTOS.
THIS PICTURE WAS TAKEN WHILE A PHOTOGRAPHIC TUTOR ON A TOUR OF KENYA.

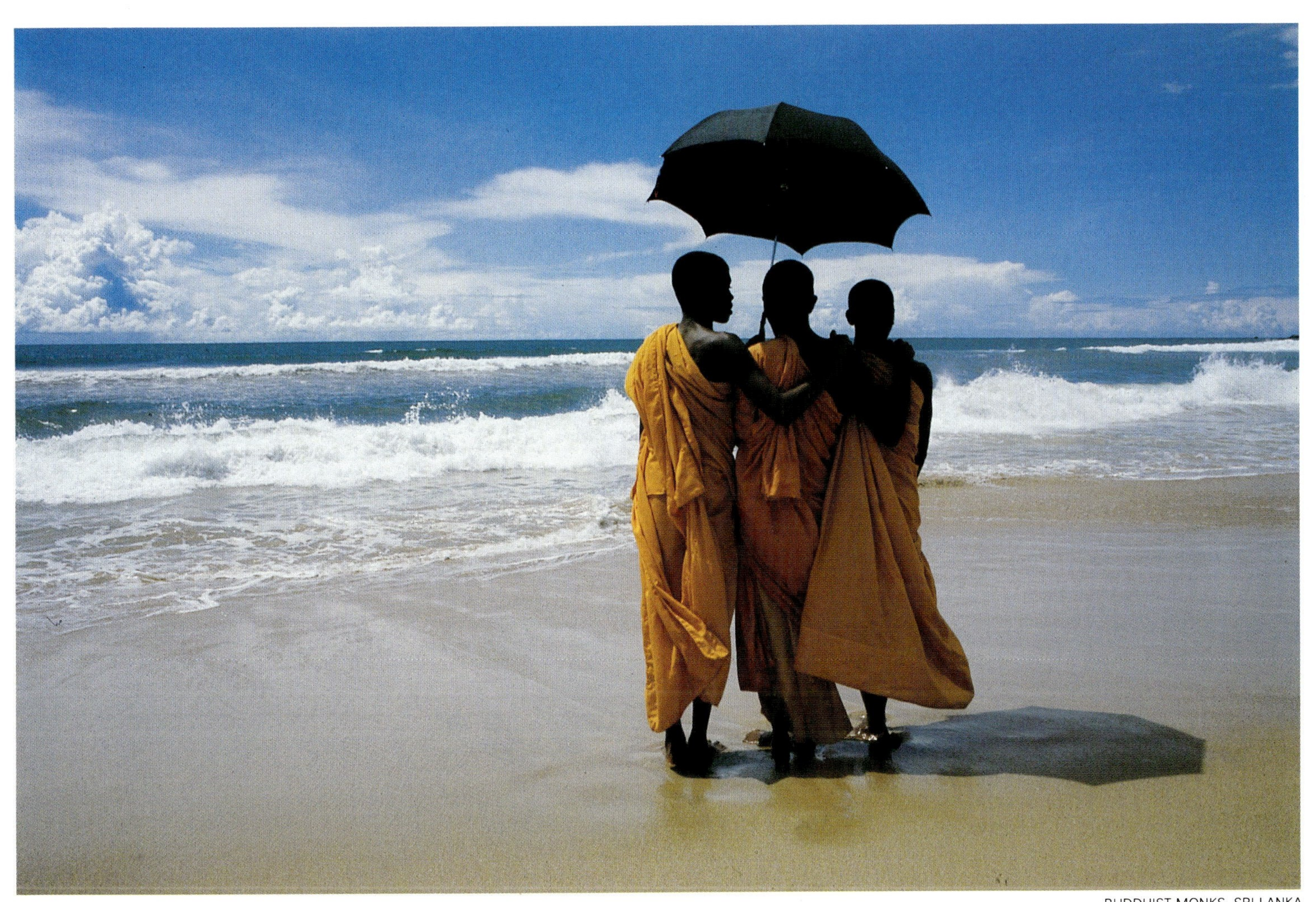

BUDDHIST MONKS, SRI LANKA

NADIA MACKENZIE GRADUATED FROM EXETER COLLEGE OF ART IN 1981. SHE IS NOW WORKING FREELANCE IN LONDON FOR MAGAZINES, DESIGN GROUPS AND PUBLISHERS.

204

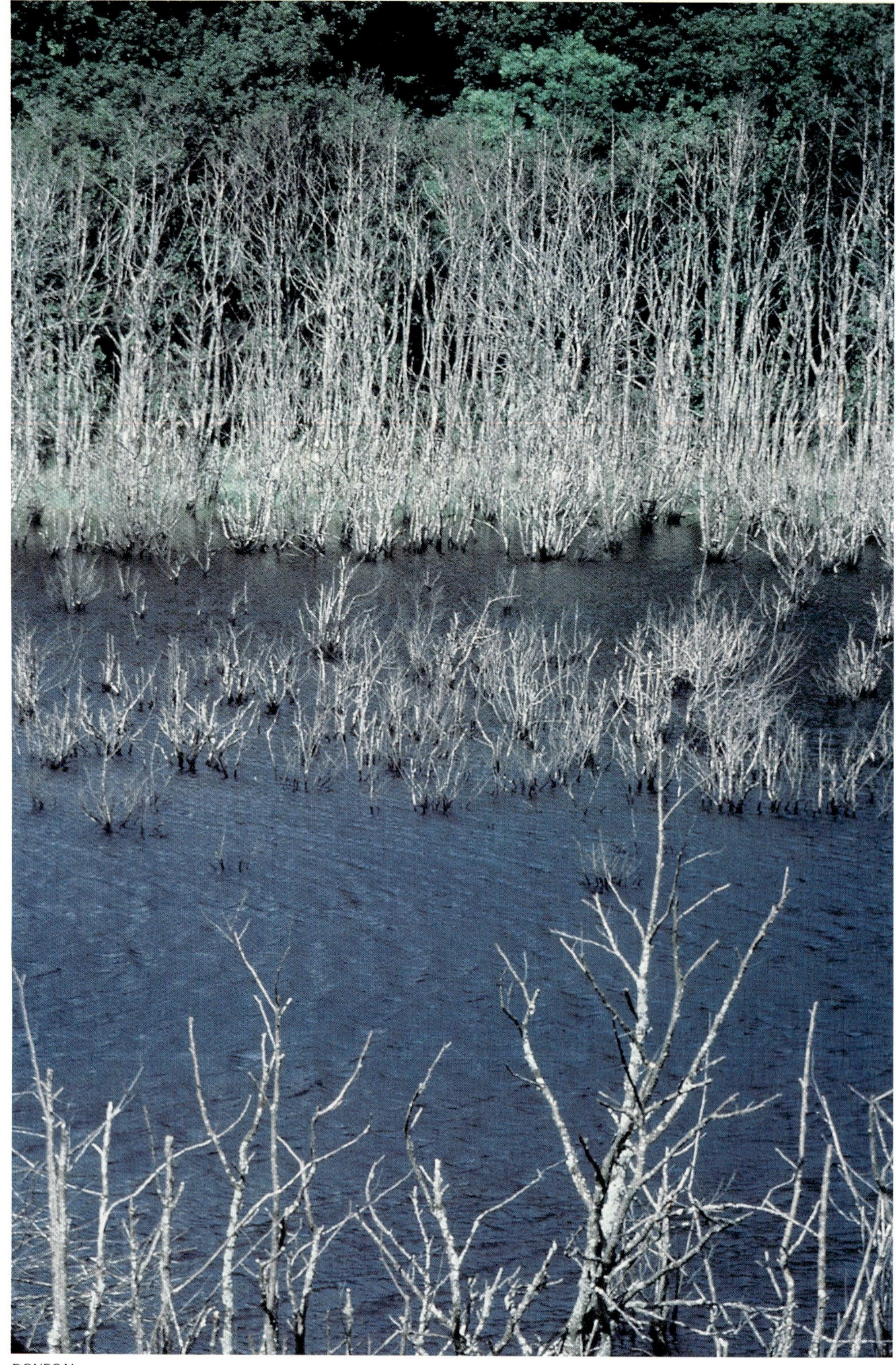

DONEGAL

PAUL DENNISON WAS BORN IN LONDONDERRY, STUDIED AT TRENT AND NOW SPECIALISES IN TRAVEL AND LANDSCAPE PHOTOGRAPHY.

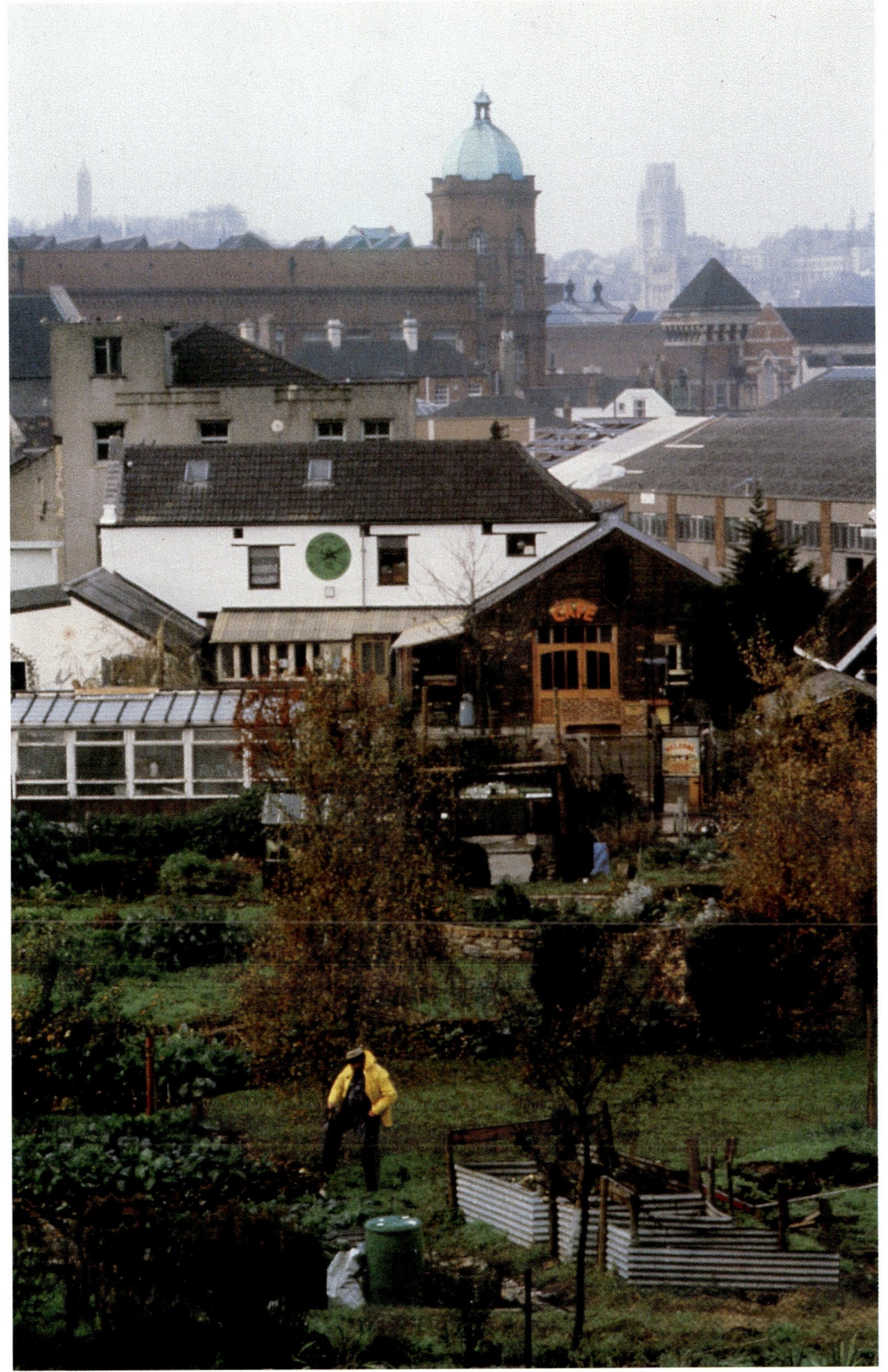

DES AT WINDMILL HILL CITY FARM, BRISTOL

SARAH BROCKLESBY IS A STATE REGISTERED CHIROPODIST WHO TOOK UP PHOTOGRAPHY AND IS NOW STUDYING AT NEWPORT.

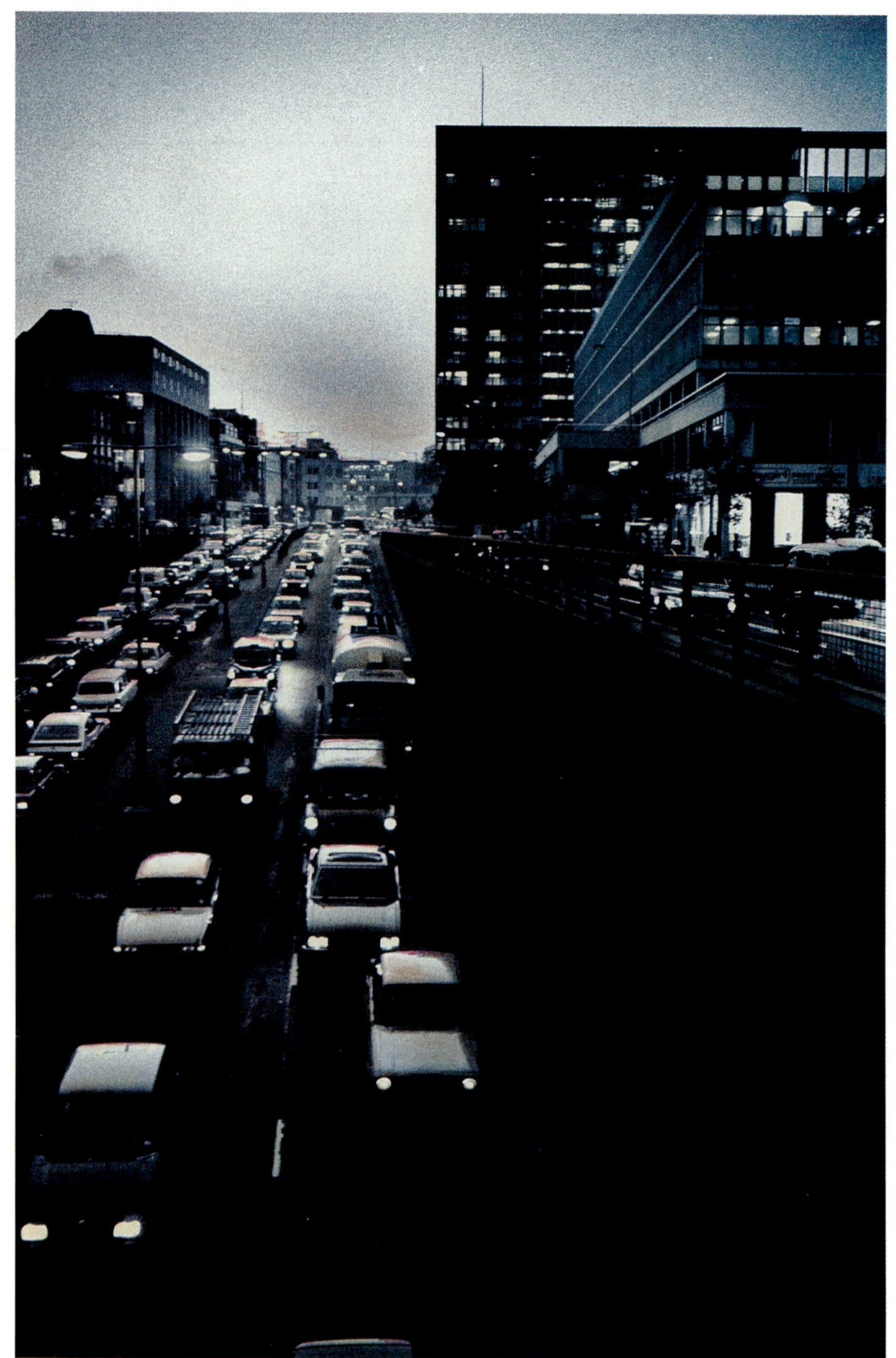

ANDREW CROWLEY STARTED WORK AS A STUDIO ASSISTANT IN PLYMOUTH AND NOW WORKS AS A PRINTER. HE HAS BEEN RUNNER UP FOR THE ILFORD YOUNG PRINTER OF THE YEAR AWARD.

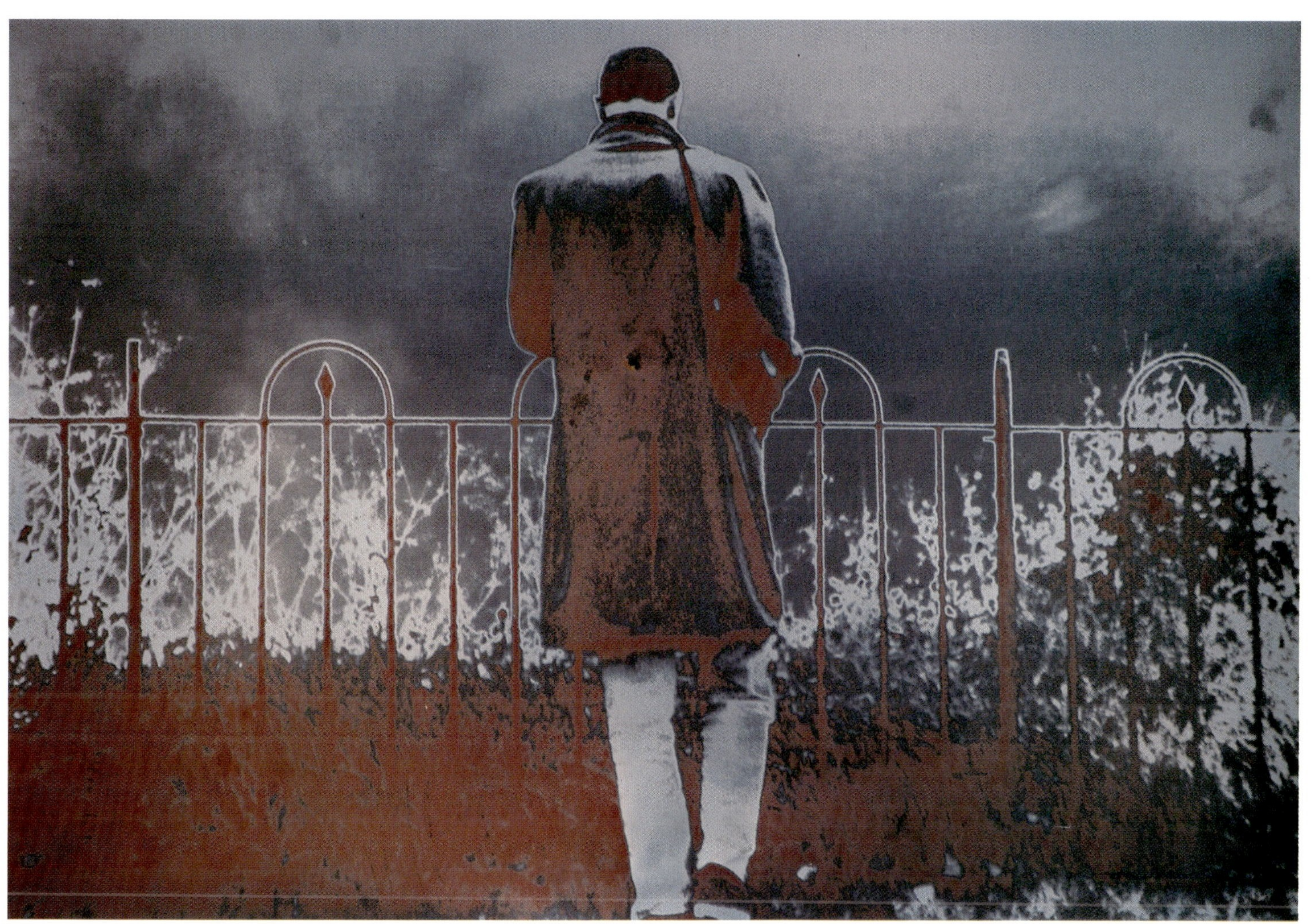

AT THE END OF THE DAY

SUE EVANS IS A SELF-TAUGHT PHOTOGRAPHER BORN AND LIVING IN SOUTH WALES. AT PRESENT UNEMPLOYED SHE HAS SPENT THE LAST TWO YEARS ON HER CHEMICAL MANIPULATIONS.

208

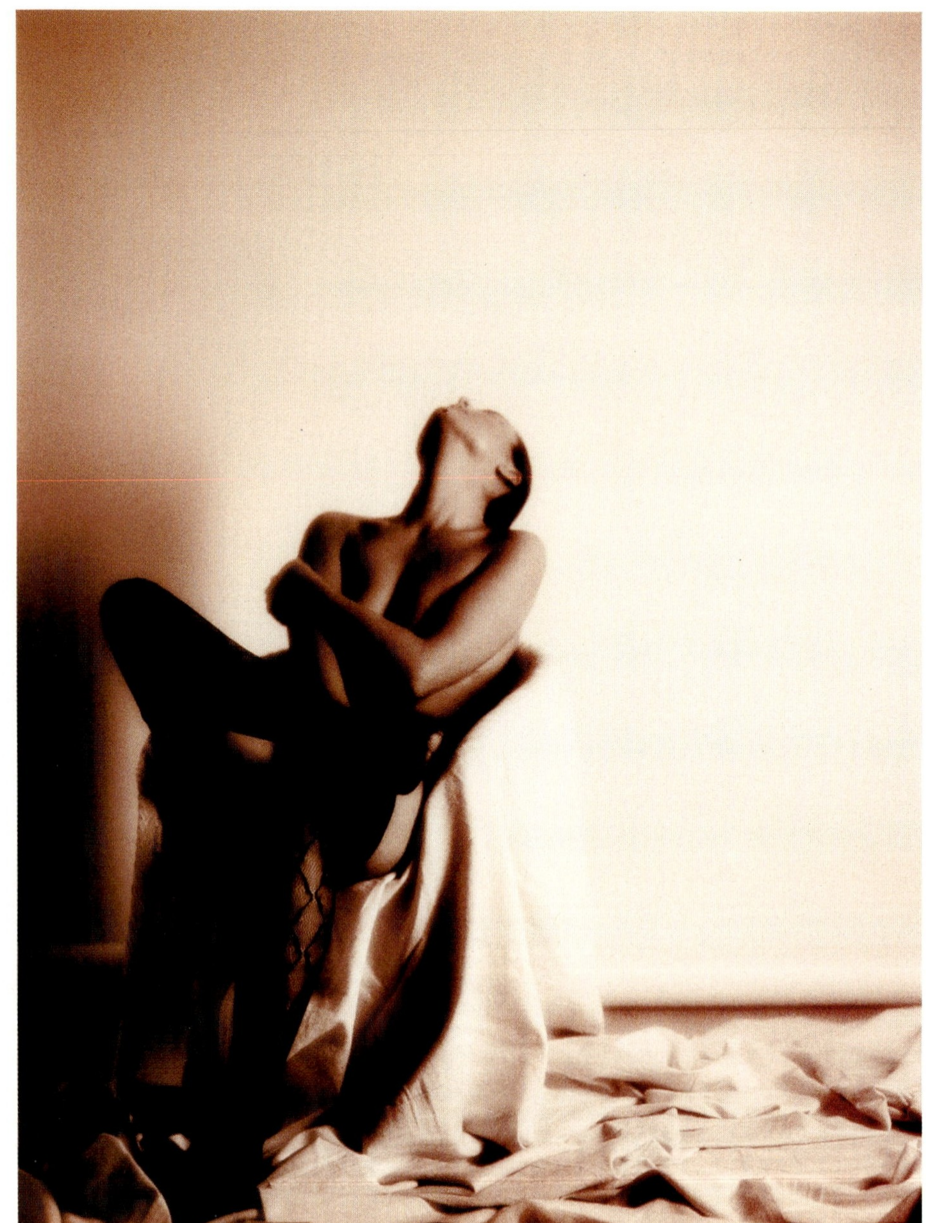

THE PUNISHMENT OF LUSCURY

TWENTY-TWO-YEAR-OLD **HAMISH SCOTT-BROWN** HAS JUST LEFT BOURNEMOUTH AND POOLE COLLEGE OF ART AND DESIGN AND IS STARTING FASHION PHOTOGRAPHY IN GLASGOW.

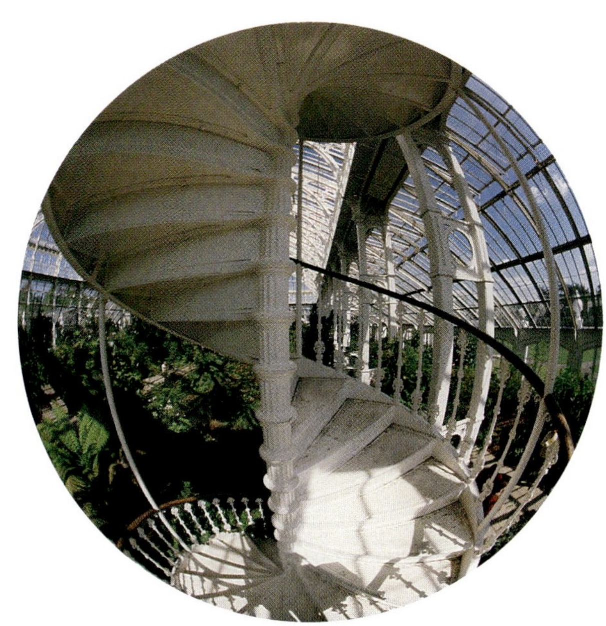

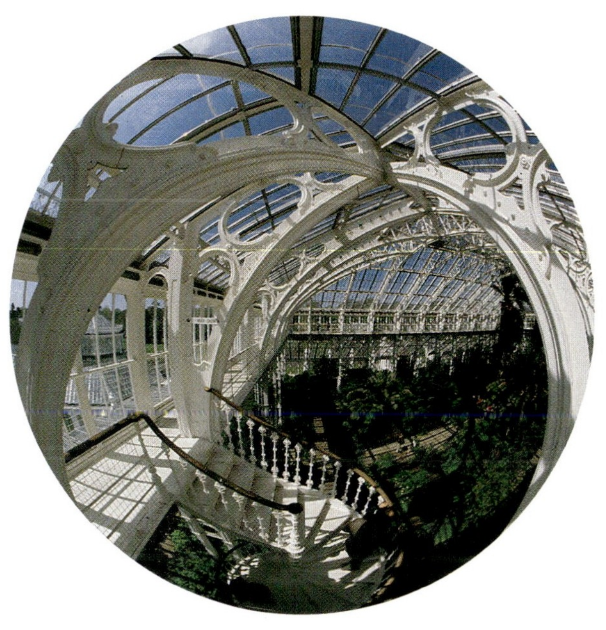

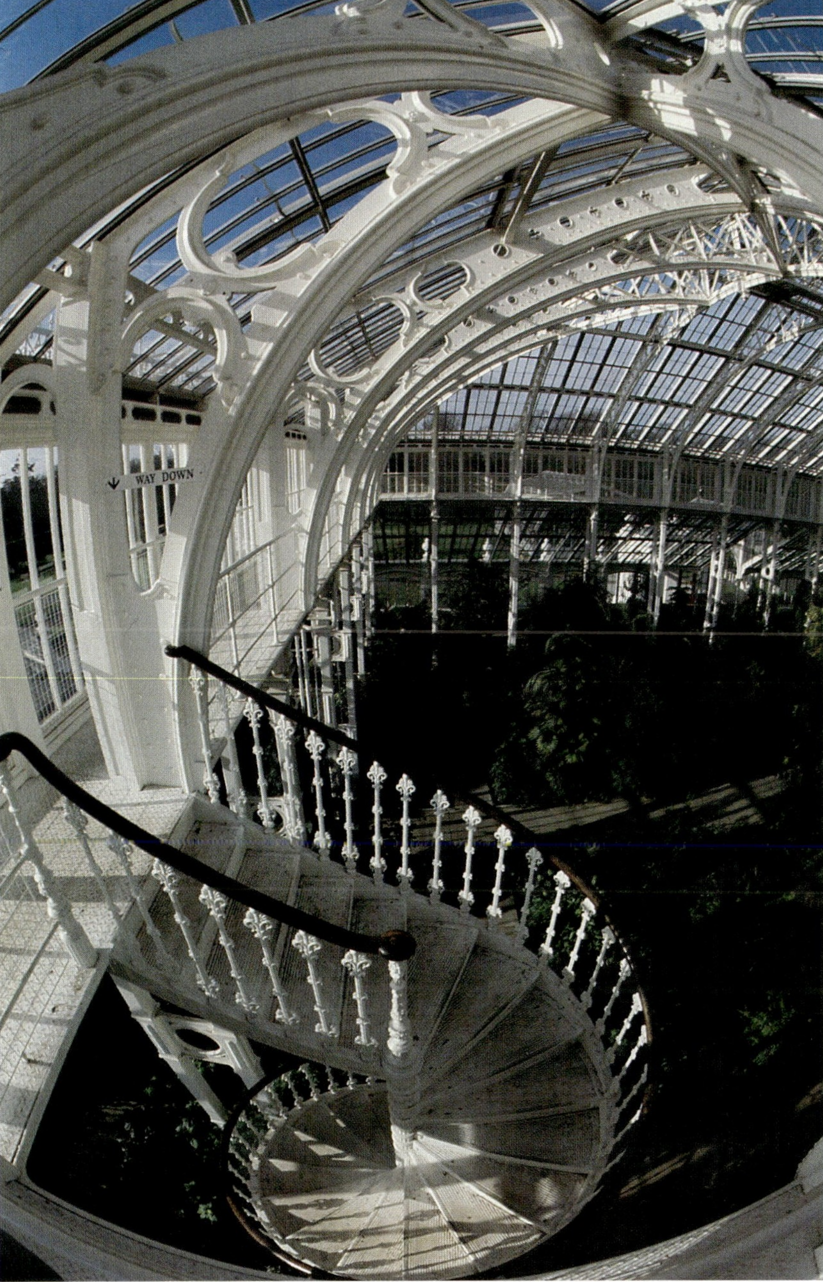

THE TEMPERATE HOUSE, KEW

JULIAN HEATH STUDIED CITY AND GUILDS UNTIL 1975 WHILE WORKING IN STUDIO LIGHTING. HE HAS WORKED IN AMATEUR AND PROFESSIONAL RETAIL AS WELL AS EXHIBITING HIS PHOTOGRAPHS.

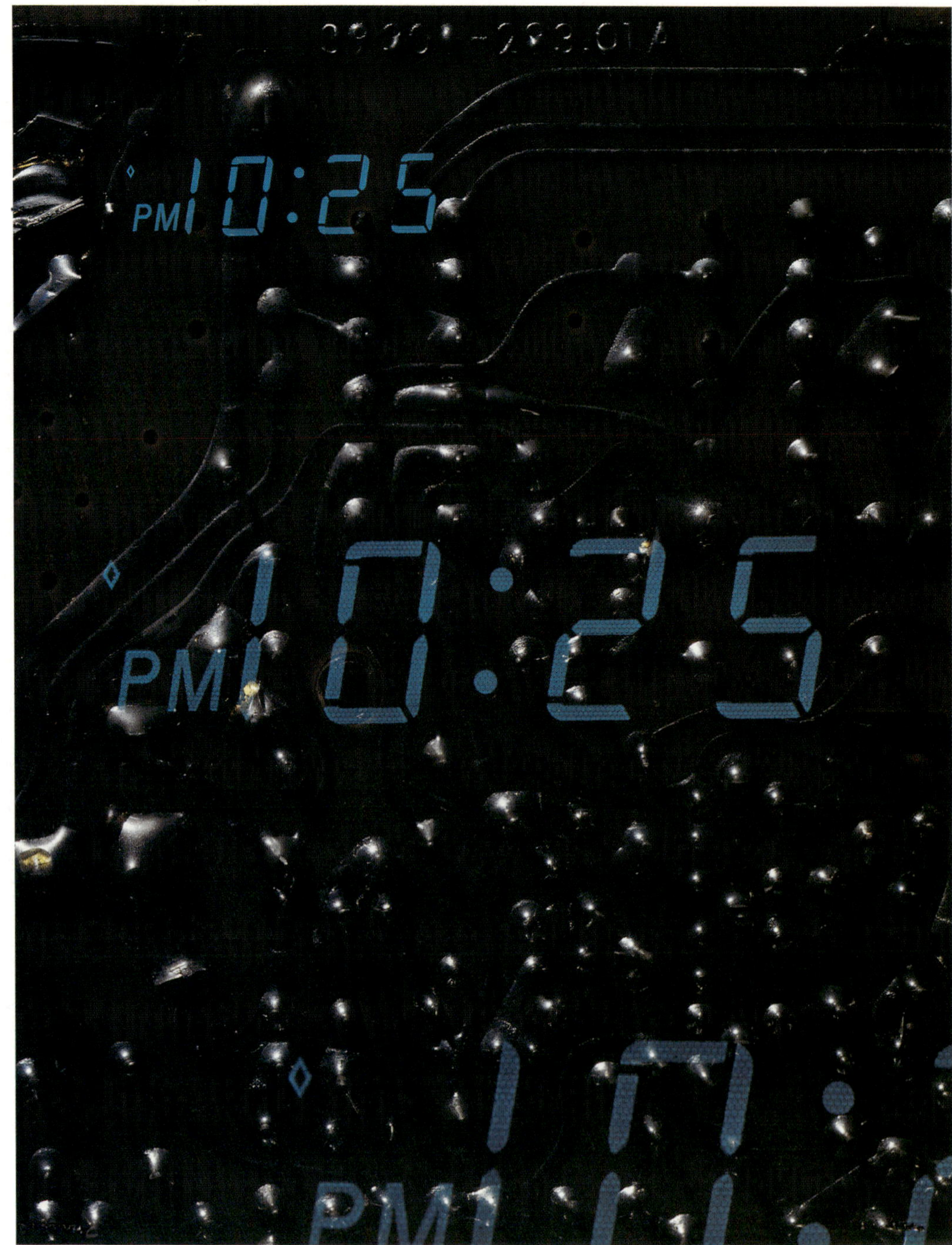

UNTITLED

GREG VIVASH IS 24 AND LIVES NEAR WOLVERHAMPTON. HE SPECIALISES IN ADVERTISING AND EDITORIAL WORK RUNNING HIS OWN MIDLAND COLOUR LIBRARY.

CONTENTS

PICTURE SECTION

WHERE TO FIND PHOTOGRAPHY

Essential information for all who want to know more about photography

Photographic exhibition galleries
Key:

∅ Gallery and/or museum of holography.
● Photographic gallery.
△ Gallery that holds exhibitions of a photographic nature at regular intervals.
□ Gallery that sells original, contemporary prints.
□ Gallery that sells quality reproductions.

United Kingdom

● *AFAEP Gallery,* 9-10 Domingo Street, London EC1Y 0TA. Telephone: 01-608 1441.

△ *Arnolfini Gallery,* Narrow Quay, Bristol BS1 4QA. Telephone: Bristol (0272) 299191.

△ *Barbican Art Gallery,* Barbican Centre, Silk Street, London EC2Y 8DS. Telephone: 01-638 4141 ext 306/346.

● *Cambridge Darkroom Gallery,* Dales Brewery, Gwydir Street, Cambridge. Telephone: Cambridge (0223) 315032.

● *Camera Club,* 8 Great Newport Street, London WC2. Telephone: 01-240 1137.

● *Camerawork,* 121 Roman Road, London E2 0QN. Telephone: 01-980 6256.

△ *Camden Arts Centre,* Arkwright Road, London NW3. Telephone: 01-435 2643.

● *F-stop Photographic Gallery,* 2 Longacre, London Road, Bath.

●■□ *The ffotogallery,* Association of Photographers in Wales, 31 Charles Street, Cardiff CF1 4EB. Telephone: Cardiff (0222) 41667.

● *Fingerprints,* 331 Muswell Hill Broadway, London N10. Telephone: 01-883 6282.

●□ *Fox Talbot Museum,* Lacock, Wiltshire SN15 2LG. Telephone: Lacock (024 973) 459. (Open March to October inclusive).

●■ *Half Moon Gallery,* 119 Roman Road, London E2. Telephone: 01-980 8798.

● *Hamiltons Gallery,* 13 Carlos Place, London W1. Telephone: 01-499 9493.

△ *John Hansard Gallery,* The University, Southampton SO9 5NH. Telephone: Southampton (0703) 559122.

△*Hayward Gallery,* South Bank, London SE1. Telephone: 01-629 9495.

●■□ *Impressions Gallery of Photography,* 17 Colliergate, York YO1 2BN. Telephone: York (0904) 54724.

■□△ *Ikon Gallery,* 58/72 John Bright Street, Birmingham B1 1BN. Telephone: 021-643 0708.

● *Ilford Photo UK Sales Company,* 14-22 Tottenham Street, London W1. Telephone: 01-636 7890.

△ *Institute of Contemporary Arts,* The Mall, London SW1. Telephone: 01-930 3647.

∅ *Light Fantastic Gallery of Holography,* 48 South Row, Covent Garden, London WC2E 8HN. Telephone: 01-836 6423/4.

■ *Marlborough Fine Art (London) Limited,* 6 Albemarle Street, London W1X 3HF. Telephone: 01-405 7841.

■□△ *Midland Group Art Centre,* 24-32 Carlton Street, Nottingham NG1 1NN. Telephone: Nottingham (0602) 582636/7.

● *Mostly Photographic Gallery and Workshop,* 10-11 Market Place off Alexandra Street, Southend-on-Sea, Essex. Telephone: (0702) 352784.

△ *Museum of Modern Art,* 30 Pembroke Street, Oxford. Telephone: Oxford (0865) 722733.

● *National Museum of Photography, Film and Television,* Princes View, Bradford, West Yorkshire BD5 0TR. Telephone: Bradford (0274) 727488.

△□ *National Portrait Gallery,* 2 St Martin's Place, London WC2. Telephone: 01-930 1552.

△ *National Theatre,* South Bank, London SE1 9PX. Telephone: 01-928 2033.

■ *Neal Street Gallery,* 56 Neal Street, Covent Garden, London WC2. Telephone: 01-379 7232.

● *Nikon Gallery,* Nikon House, 380 Richmond Road, Kingston-upon-Thames. Telephone: 01-541 4440.

■□● *Open Eye Gallery,* 90/92 Whitechapel, Liverpool 1. Telephone: 051-709 9460.

△ *Peacock Gallery,* Pinebank House Arts Centre, Tullygally Road, Craigavon BT65 5BY, Northern Ireland. Telephone 0762 41082/41033.

● *Pelling and Cross Showrooms,* 93-103 Drummond Street, London NW1 2HJ. Telephone: 01-380 1144.

● *Photogallery,* The Foresters Arms, 2 Shepherd Street, St Leonards-on-Sea, East Sussex TN38 0ET. Telephone: Hastings (0424) 440140.

● *The Photographers' Corridor,* University College, Main Building, 1st Floor, Cardiff. Telephone: Cardiff (0222) 44211.

● *Photographer's Gallery,* 15 The Pallant, Havant, Hants. Telephone: Havant (0705) 453334.

●■□ *The Photographers' Gallery,* 5 and 8 Great Newport Street, London WC2. Telephone: 01-240 5511.

● *Photographer's Workshop,* 103-104 St Mary's Road, Cowley, Oxford. Telephone: Oxford (0865) 246027.

● *The Photographic Gallery,* Brewery Arts Centre, 122a Highgate, Kendal, Cumbria LA9 4HE. Telephone: Kendal (0539) 235133.

● *Photographic Gallery,* Wigan College of Technology, Library Street Building, Wigan. Telephone: Wigan (0942) 494911.

△■□ *Plymouth Arts Centre,* 38 Looe Street, Plymouth PL4 0BE. Telephone: Plymouth (0752) 660060.

●■□ *The RPS National Centre of Photography,* The Octagon, Milsom Street, Bath BA1 1DN. Telephone: Bath (0225) 62841.

■● *Regent Street Gallery,* Polytechnic of Central London, 309 Regent Street, London W1R 8AL. Telephone: 01-580 202 ext 205.

■ *Howard Ricketts Limited,* 12 Moore Street, London SW1. Telephone: 01-581 4291.

□△ *Science Museum,* Exhibition Road, South Kensington, London SW7 2DD. Telephone: 01-589 3456.

△ *Serpentine Gallery,* Kensington Gardens, London W2 3XA. Telephone: 01-402 6075.

● *Side Gallery,* 9 Side, Newcastle-upon-Tyne NE1 3JE. Telephone: Newcastle-upon-Tyne (0632) 22208.

● *Spectro Photography,* Bells Court, Pilgrim Street, Newcastle-upon-Tyne NE1 6RH. Telephone: Newcastle-upon-Tyne (0632) 322410.

■□● *Stills,* The Scottish Photography Group Gallery, 105 High Street, Edinburgh EH1 1TB. Telephone: 031-557 1140.

●■□ *Sutcliffe Gallery,* 1 Flowergate, Whitby, North Yorkshire. Telephone: Whitby (0947) 602239.

△ *The Triangle,* Aston University Arts Centre, Gosta Green, Birmingham B7 4ET. Telephone: 021-359 3979.

● *The Untitled Gallery,* 173-175 Howard Road, Walkley, Sheffield. Telephone: Sheffield (0742) 340369.

△□ *Victoria and Albert Museum,* South Kensington, London SW7 2RL. Telephone: 01-589 6371.

● *Victoria House Gallery of Photography,* Tayport, Fife DD6 9AR. Telephone: Tayport (08265) 5341.

△ *Watershed Gallery,* 1 Canons Road, Bristol. Telephone: Bristol (0727) 276444.

△ *Whitechapel Art Gallery,* Whitechapel High Street, London E1 7QX. Telephone: 01-377 0107.

∅ *White Light,* 9a Kensington Gardens, Brighton, Sussex.

See *Arts Review Yearbook,* published by Arts Review, 16 St James's Gardens, London W11. Telephone: 01-7530/8533; for Art Exhibition Index, London Gallery Directory, London Public Galleries, Specialist Galleries in London, Regional Gallery Guide, etc.

See Arts Council of Great Britain. Photography in the Arts: Organisations and Projects in Great Britain.

A regular listing of British photographic exhibitions is published fortnightly under the rubric 'On Show' in alternate issues of the *British Journal of Photography.*

See also *Photography North*, a guide to photographers, exhibitions and resources in the Northern Arts region. Available from Northern Arts, 10 Osborne Terrace, Jesmond, Newcastle upon Tyne NE2 1NZ.

Western Europe

● *Aspects/Photo Section,* rue du Président 72, B-1050 Bruxelles, Belgium.
■● *L'Atelier,* 20 Galerie Vivienne, F-75002, Paris, France.
● *Camera Obscura,* Kakbrinken 5, 11127 Stockholm, Sweden.
● *Canon Photo Gallery,* Leidsestraat 79, 1017 NX Amsterdam, The Netherlands.
● *Centre Culturel Americain,* 3 rue de Dragon, 75006 Paris, France.
●□*Contretype,* Rue d'Espagne 103, B1060 Bruxelles, Belgium. Telephone: 02-5384220.
● *Creatis,* 44 rue Quincampoix, 54004 Paris, France.
● *European House of Photography,* Rubens-center, Groenplaats, Antwerpen, Belgium.
∅ *Fielmann Lichtgalerie,* Holstenstrasse 19, D-2300 Kiel, Federal German Republic.
∅ *Fielmann Lichtgalerie,* Moenckeberstrasse 29, D-2000 Hamburg, Federal German Republic.
● *Focus Bilderladen,* Dahlmannstrasse 5, 1000 Berlin 12, Federal German Republic.
● *Fotoforum*, Menzelstrasse 15, 3500 Kassel, Federal German Republic.
● *Foto et Film Centrum,* Mein 50, 2000 Antwerpen, Belgium.
● *Fotogalleria La Rinascente — Il Diaframma/ Canon*, Rinascente Duomo, Milano.
● *Fotogalerie an der Mehlwaage,* 7800 Freiburg, Federal German Republic.
● *Fotogalerie der Staatliche Landesbildstelle Hamburg,* Kielerstrasse 171, 54 Hamburg, Federal German Republic.
● *Fotogalerie Droscher,* Ellchaussee 140, D-2000 Hamburg 50, Federal German Republic.
● *Foto Gallerie 5.6,* St Michielsplasse 14, 9000 Gent, Belgium.
● *Fotogalerie 68,* Cultureel Centrum Kasteel, Postbus 36, Hoensbroek, Netherlands.
● *Fotogalerie Scene,* Bruchstrasse 18, 4500 Osnabruck, Federal German Republic. Tel: 05405-3409.
● *Fotografia,* Mitropoleous 55, PO Box 710, Thessalonica, Greece.
● *Fotowerkstatt,* Luneburger Strasse, 28 Bremen, Federal German Republic.
●□*Galerie Daguerre*, 28 Rue Gassendi — 57 Rue Daguerre, F-75014 Paris, France. Telephone: 1-3221172.
●■ *Galerie Fiolet BV,* Herengracht 86, Amsterdam, Holland. Telephone: 020-23.06.05.
∅ *Galerie fur Holographie,* Basle, Switzerland.
● *Galerie Nagel,* Fasenenstrasse 42, 1000 Berlin 15, Federal German Republic.
● *Galerie Perspektief*, Stationssingel 19b, 3033 HA Rotterdam, The Netherlands.
● *Galérie Perspectives,* 53 avenue de Saxe, 75007 Paris, France.
● *Galerie Photo-Bilder-Laden,* Friedrich-Ebert-Strasse 105, D-23500 Kassel, Federal German Republic.
● *Galérie Photo du Forum,* avenue du 8 Mai 1945, F-95200 Saracelles, France.
● *Galleria Spectrum/Canon,* Balmes 86, Barcelona 8, Spain.
● *Galérie Stieglitz,* Avenue Louise 90, B-1050 Bruxelles, Belgium.
● *Galerie Ton Peek,* Oude Gracht 259, NL-3511 PA Utrecht, The Netherlands. Telephone: 030-312001.
■ *Galerie Wilde*, Auf dem Berlich 6, D-5000 Köln, Federal German Republic. Telephone: 0221 238557.
●■□ *The Gallery of Photography*, 37-39 Wellington Quay, Dublin 2, Eire.
● *Hasselblad Gallery,* Ostra Hamngatan 3, Gothenburg, Sweden. Telephone: 031 171960.
∅ *Hol 3,* Kurfurstendamm 103, 41 Berlin 1000, Federal German Republic.
∅ *Hologram Europe,* (Showroom), Merckthoef 3, 5611 GE Eindhoven, Netherlands. Telephone: (40) 81 46 77.
∅ *Hologram Europe,* 137 Avenue Voltaire, 1030 Brussels, Belgium. Telephone: (2) 24 27 28 4.
∅ *Hologram Gallery,* Prinsgengracht 675, Amsterdam, Netherlands.
∅ *Hologram Gallery,* Lasergrupen Holovision AB, Hagagatan 3, 11348 Stockholm, Sweden. Telephone: 0094-8/32 68 81.
∅ *Hologram Gallery,* Drottninggaten 100, 11160 Stockholm, Sweden. Telephone: (08) 10 5465.
∅ *Holographic Gallery,* Amalienpassage 89, 8000 Munich 40, Federal German Republic.
● *Il Diaframma/Canon,* Via Brera 10, 20121 Milano, Italy. Telephone (02) 806077.
● *Image Center for Fotografie,* Mejlgade 16, DK-8000 Aahrus C, Denmark.
● *Kodak Consumer Center,* 38 Avenue George V, 75008 Paris, France.
● *Leica Galerie,* Ernst Leitz Wetzlar GmbH, 6330 Wetzlar, Federal German Republic.
● *L'Espace Canon,* 117 rue Saint Martin, 75004 Paris, France.
●■ *Marlborough Galerie AG,* Glarnischstrasse 10, CH-8002 Zürich, Switzerland.
∅ *Le Musée Français de l'Holographie,* Forum des Halles, 15-21 Grand Balcon, 75001 Paris, France. Telephone: (1) 296 9605/9683.
∅ *Museum für Holographie Neue Visuelle Medien,* Pletschmuhlenweg 7, D-5024 Pulheim, Köln, Federal German Republic. Telephone: (221) 51 51053/4.
● *Nicéphore,* 8 rue de la Gare, 68540 Böllwiller, France.
● *Nikon Foto Galerie,* Tiefenbroicher Weg 25, D-4000 Düsseldorf, Federal German Republic. Telephone: 0211 41570.
● *Nikon Foto-Galerie,* Schoffelgasse 3, 8001 Zürich, Switzerland.
● *Nikon Galerie,* Getreidemarkt 13, A-1060 Wien, Austria. Telephone: 0222-573197/576727.
● *Octant 20,* 5 rue du Marché Honoré, F-75001 Paris, France.
● *Olympus Galerie,* Grobe Bleichen 31, D-2000 Hamburg 36, Federal German Republic. Telephone: 041-23773247.
● *Paulo Pia Galerij voor Fotografie,* Kammenstraat 57, B-2000 Antwerp, Belgium.
● *La Photo Galérie,* 2 rue Christine, 75006 Paris, France.
● *Photofactory,* Château Neuf, Slemdalsvn 7, N-Oslo 3, Norway.
● *Photogalerie Lange-Irschl,* Türkenstrasse 54, 8000 Munich 40, Federal German Republic.
● *Photogalerie Lichtblick,* Dortfelder Hellweg 15, 46 Dortmund 1, Federal German Republic.
● *Photogalérie Portfolio,* 21 Escaliers du Marché, 1003 Lausanne, Switzerland.
● *Photo-Galerie im Kunsthaus Zürich,* Kunsthaus, Heimplatz 1, 8001 Zürich, Switzerland.
● *Photographic Centre of Athens,* 52 Sina Straese, Athens, Greece. Telephone: 01-3610495/3608825.
● *Polaroid Galerie,* Sprendlinger Landstrasse 109, D-6050 Offenbach, Federal German Republic. Telephone: 0611 8404503.
● *PPS Photogalerie,* Hochhaus 1, Feldstrasse, 2000 Hamburg 4, Federal German Republic.
● *RES Fotogentur and Galerie,* Eichenstrasse 25, 2000 Hamburg 19, Federal German Republic.
● *Rudi Renner Fotogalerie,* Mannhardstrasse 4, 8000 Munich 22, Federal German Republic.
● *Sammlung Fotografis Laenderbank,* Rotenturmstrasse 13, A-1010 Vienna, Austria.
● *Spectrum Photogalerie,* Kurt-Schwitters-Platz, 3000 Hannover 1, Federal German Republic.
●■ *Studio 666,* 6 rue Mâitre Albert, F-75005 Paris, France.
●■ *Texbraun*, 12 rue Mazarine, F-75006 Paris, France.
● *Werkstatt für Fotographie,* Friedrichstrasse 210, 1000 Berlin 36, Federal German Republic.
●■ *Zür Stockeregg,* Stockerstrasse 33, 8022 Zürich, Switzerland.

See also:
European Photography Guide, published in 1984 by *European Photography*, Stargarder Weg 18, D-3400 Göttingen, Federal German Republic. (New edition expected 1987).

North America

● *Alonzo Photo Gallery,* 30 West 57th Street, New York, NY 10019, USA.
■ *Atlanta Gallery of Photography,* 3205 Paces Ferry Place, Atlanta, GA 30305, USA. Telephone: (area code 404) 233-1462.
●■ *Baldwin Street Gallery of Photography,* 23 Baldwin Street, Toronto 130, Ontario, Canada. Telephone: (area code 416) 364-2630.
■ *Jacques Baruch Gallery*, 900 North Michigan Avenue, Chicago, Illinois 60611, USA.
● *Boris Gallery of Photography,* 35 Lansdowne Street, Boston, MA 02215, USA. Telephone: (area code 617) 262-5725.

● *Canon House,* Canon Inc, 776 Market Street, San Francisco, CA 94102, USA. Telephone: (area code 415) 433-5640.

●■ *Carl Siembab Gallery of Photography,* 162 Newbury Street, Boston, MA 02116, USA. Telephone: (area code 617) 262-0146.

● *Castelli Photographs,* 4 East 77 Street, New York, NY 10021, USA.

● *Catskill Center for Photography,* 59A Tinker Street, Woodstock, NY 12498, USA. Telephone: (area code 914) 679 9957.

● *Colorado Photographic Arts Center,* 1301 Bannock Street, Denver, CO 80204, USA. Telephone: (area code 303) 623-4059.

●■ *Corcoran Gallery of Art,* 27 and NY Avenue NW, Washington DC 20006, USA. Telephone: (area code 202) 638-3211.

■ *Kathleen Ewing Gallery,* 3243 P Street NW, Washington, DC 20007, USA.

● *Exposure Photographic Gallery,* 214 East 10 Street, New York, NY 10003, USA. Telephone: (area code 212) 982 6330.

●■ *Focus Gallery,* 2146 Union Street, San Francisco, CA 94123, USA. Telephone: (area code 415) 921 1565.

● *Fotografia Gallery,* 6226 Wilshire Boulevard, Los Angeles, CA 90048, USA.

● *4th Street Photography,* New York, NY 10003, USA.

● *Fraenkel Gallery,* 55 Grant Avenue, San Francisco, CA 94108, USA. Telephone: (area code 415) 981 2661.

●□ *Friends of Photography,* Sunset Centre, San Carlos at 9th, Carmel, CA 93921, USA. Telephone: (area code 408) 624 6330.

∅ *Fringe Research,* 1179a King Street, Toronto, Ontario, Canada. Telephone: (area code 416) 535 3323.

∅ *Gallery 1134,* Fine Arts Research and Holographic Center, 1134 West Washington Street, Chicago, Illinois 60607, USA. Telephone: (area code 312) 226 1007.

●■ *Gallery of Photographic Arts — East,* 2100 Richmond Road, OH 44122, USA.

● *Gallery of Photography,* 453 St Francis-Xavier, Montreal, Quebec, Canada.

● *Gallery 104,* 104 Congress Street, Austin, Texas 78701, USA. Telephone: (area code 512) 474-6044.

∅ *Holos Gallery,* 1792 Haight Street, San Francisco, CA 94117, USA. Telephone: (area code 415) 668 4656.

●□ *International Center of Photography,* 1130 Fifth Avenue, New York, NY 10028, USA. Telephone: (area code 212) 860 1777.

●■ *International Museum of Photography,* George Eastman House, 900 East Avenue, Rochester, NY 14607, USA. Telephone: (area code 716) 271-3361.

● *Jeb Gallery,* 347 South Main Street, Providence, RI 02911, USA. Telephone: (area code 401) 272 3312.

●■ *Kimmel/Cohn Photography Arts,* 1 West 64 Street, New York, NY 10023, USA. Telephone: (area code 212) 799 6675.

● *Klein Gallery,* 356 West Huron, Chicago, Illinois 60610, USA. Telephone: (area code 312) 787 0400.

● *Kodak Photographic Gallery,* 1133 Avenue of the Americas, New York, NY 10019, USA.

●■ *Janet Lehr Inc,* 45 East Street 85 Street, New York, NY 10028, USA. Telephone: (area code 212) 288 6234.

■∅*Library of Congress,* First Street, SW, Washington DC, USA. Telephone: (area code 202) 287-6934.

● *Light Impressions Gallery,* 8 South Washington Street, Rochester, NY 14614, USA.

●■ *Light Gallery,* 724 Fifth Avenue, New York, NY 10019, USA. Telephone: (area code 212) 582 6552.

● *Los Angeles Photography Center,* 412 South Parkview Street, Los Angeles, CA, USA.

● *Maryland Photographic Gallery,* UMBC, University of Maryland Baltimore County, 5401 Wilkins Avenue, Baltimore, MD 21228, USA. Telephone: (area code 301) 455-2353.

● *Midtown Y Gallery,* 344 East 14 Street, New York, NY 10003, USA. Telephone: (area code 212) 674-0325.

● *Milwaukee Center for Photography,* 207 East Buffalo Street, Milwaukee, WI, USA. Telephone: (area code 414) 272-5016.

● *Mind's Eye Photographic Gallery and Bookstore,* 52 Water Street, Vancouver 4, BC, Canada. Telephone 68-4927.

∅ *Museum of Holography,* 11 Mercer Street, New York, NY 10013, USA. Telephone: (area code 212) 925-0526/0581.

●■ *Museum of Modern Art.* 11 West 53 Street, New York, NY 10019, USA. Telephone: (area code 212) 956 6100.

● *Nikon House,* 620 Fifth Avenue, New York, NY 10012, USA. Telephone: (area code 212) 586-3907.

● *Northlight Photographic Gallery and Workshop,* Riverview and Rt 303, PO Box 61, Peninsula, OH 44264, USA. Telephone: (area code 602) 965-6517.

● *Panopticon Gallery of Photography,* 187 Bay State Road, Boston, MA 02215, USA.

● *PDQ Photo Gallery,* 573 N Main Street, Providence, RI 02903, USA. Telephone: (area code 401) 272 7811.

■ *Marcuse Pfeifer Gallery,* 825 Madison Avenue, New York, NY 10021, USA. Telephone: (area code 212) 737-2055.

● *Photocollect,* 740 West End Avenue, New York, NY 10025, USA. Telephone: (area code 212) 222-7381.

● *Photo Gallery,* School of Photographic Arts and Sciences, Rochester Insititute of Technology, One Lomb Memorial Drive, Rochester, NY 14623, USA.

● *The Photographers' Gallery,* 1554 Periwinkle Way, Sanibel Island, FL 33957, USA. Telephone: (area code 813) 472-5777.

●□*Photography Gallery,* 132 South 17 Street, Philadelphia, PA 19103, USA. Telephone: (area code 215) 536-8101.

● *Photographers Gallery,* 236 Avenue South, Saskatoon, Saskatchewan, Canada. Telephone: (area code 306) 244-8018.

● *A Photographer's Place,* 71 Greeme Street, New York, NY 11012, USA. Telephone: (area code 212) 431-9358.

● *Photographers West Gallery,* Dolores at Ocean Avenue, Carmel, CA 93921, USA. Telephone: (area code 408) 625-1587.

●■ *Photopia,* 1728 Spruce Street, Philadelphia, PA 19103, USA.

● *Polaroid Gallery,* 549 Technology Square, Cambridge, MA, USA. Telephone: (area code 617) 577-2000.

●■ *Prakapas Gallery,* 19 East 71 Street, New York, NY 10012, USA. Telephone: (area code 212) 586-3907.

● *Quivira Photograph Gallery,* 111 Cornell Drive SE, Albuquerque, NM 87106, USA. Telephone: (area code 505) 266-1788.

□ *Robert Samuel Gallery,* 795 Broadway, New York, NY 10003, USA. Telephone: (area code 212) 477-3839.

● *San Francisco Camerawork,* 70 Twelfth Street, San Francisco, CA 94103, USA.

● *The Silver Image Gallery,* 92 South Washington Street, Seattle, WA 98104, USA.

● *Soho Photo Gallery,* 30 West 13 Street, New York, NY 10011, USA.

● *Stieglitz Center,* Philadelphia Museum of Art, Parkway at 26 Street, Philadelphia, PA 19101, USA.

● *Vision Gallery of Photography,* 216 Newbury Street, Boston, MA 02116, USA. Telephone: (area code 617) 266-9481.

●△ *Visual Studies Workshop,* 31 Prince Street, Rochester, NY 14607, USA.

● *Weston Gallery,* PO Box 655, Carmel, CA 93921, USA. Telephone: (area code 408) 624-4453.

● *Edward Weston Galleries,* 149 Mercer Street, New York, NY 10012, USA. Telephone: (area code 212) 226-4141.

■ *Wild Visions Gallery,* PO Box 11011, Palo Alto, CA 94306, USA.

●■ *Witkin Gallery,* 41 East 57 Street, New York, NY 10022, USA. Telephone: (area code 212) 355-1461.

■ *Daniel Wolf Inc,* 30 West 57 Street, New York, NY 10021, USA. Telephone: (area code 212) 586-8432.

Other Countries

● *Photography Gallery, Art Gallery of NSW,* Art Gallery Road, Sydney, NSW 2000, Australia. Telephone: (02) 2212100.

● *Australian Centre for Photography,* Dobell House, 257 Oxford Street, Paddington, NSW 2021, Australia. Telephone: (02) 3316253.

● *Department of Photography, Australian National Gallery,* Parkes, ACT 2600, Australia. Telephone: (062) 7124111.

● *Brummels Gallery of Photography,* 95 Toorak Road, South Yarra, Australia.

● *Canon Salon,* Canon Sales Co Inc, 9-9 Ginza 5-chome, Chou-ku, Tokyo 104, Japan.

● *Church Street Photographic Center,* 384 Church Street, Richmond, Melbourne, Australia.

● *The Developed Image,* 391 King William Street, Adelaide, South Australia 5000, Australia. Telephone: (08) 212 1047.
● *Exposure Photo Gallery,* 219 Railway Parade, Marylands, Western Australia 6051, Australia. Telephone: (09) 271 5983.
● *Foto Galeria/Fotoptica,* Rua Bela Cintra No 1465, Sao Paolo, Brasil.
● *Gallery 18,* 18 Mowbray Street, Albert Park, Victoria 3206, Australia. Telephone: (03) 690 6770.
● *Imagery Gallery,* Corner Grey and Melbourne Streets, South Brisbane, Queensland 4101, Australia. Telephone: (07) 448207.
● *Kodak Gallery,* 252 Collins Street, Melbourne, Victoria 3000, Australia. Telephone: (03) 654 4633.
● *Peter Mylonas Gallery,* 11 Logan Road, Woolloongabba, Qld 4102, Australia. Telephone: (07) 391 6922.
● *Photography Gallery, National Gallery of Victoria,* 180 St Kilda Road, Melbourne, Victoria 3004, Australia. Telephone: (03) 62 7411.
● *Nikon Salon,* 5-63-chome, Ginza, Chou-ku, Tokyo, Japan.
● *Pentax Gallery,* 3-21-20 Mishiazabu, Minato-ku, Tokyo 106, Japan.
● *Photoforum Gallery,* 26 Harris Street, Wellington 1, New Zealand.
● *The Photographers' Gallery,* 344 Punt Road, South Yarra, Victoria 3141, Australia. Telephone: (03) 26 6434.
● *Polaroid Gallery,* 3 Eden Park Estate, 31 Waterloo Road, North Ryde, NSW 2113, Australia. Telephone: (02) 887 2333.
● *Snaps Gallery,* 30 Airedale Street, Auckland 1, New Zealand.
● *Visibility,* 642 Station Street, North Carlton, Victoria 3054, Australia. Telephone: (03) 387 7432.

Museum collections of old photographs and photographic items

United Kingdom

Ashmolean Museum, Beaumont Street, Oxford. Telephone: Oxford (0865) 512651.
Barnes Museum of Cinematography, 44 Fore Street, St Ives, Cornwall TR26 1HE.
Birmingham Central Libraries, Local Studies Department, Birmingham B3 3HQ. Telephone: 021-643 2948 (includes Sir Benjamin Stone Collection).
East Anglian Photographic Collection, University of East Anglia, University Village, Wilberforce Road, Norwich NR4 7TJ. Telephone: Norwich (0603) 56161.
Fenton Photography Museum, Strand Road, Port Erin, Isle of Man. Telephone: Port Erin (0624) 834310.
Fox Talbot Museum, Lacock, Wiltshire, SN15 2LG. Telephone: Lacock (024 973) 459. (Open March to October inclusive.)
Grandad's Photography Museum, 91 East Hill, Colchester, Essex. Telephone: Colchester (0206) 64474.
Greater Manchester Museum of Science and Industry, Liverpool Road Station, Liverpool Road, Manchester M3 4JP. Telephone: 061-832 2244.
Imperial War Museum, Department of Photographs, Lambeth Road, London SE1 6HZ. Telephone: 01-735 8922.
Kingston-upon-Thames and Area Central Library, Local Illustrations Collection, Fairfield Road, Kingston-upon-Thames. Telephone: 01-546 2121 (includes Eadweard Muybridge photographs).
Lancashire and Cheshire Photographic Union Collection, c/o Gerald Logan, 20 Warwick Avenue, Newton-le-Willows, Merseyside WA12 8PS.
Maidstone Museum, St Faith Street, Maidstone, Kent. Telephone: Maidstone (0622) 54497/56405.
Museum of the History of Science, Broad Street, Oxford. Telephone: Oxford (0865) 43997.
National Film Archive, 81 Dean Street, London W1V 6AA. Telephone: 01-437 4355.
National Library of Scotland, George IV Bridge, Edinburgh EH1 1EW. Telephone: 031-226 4531.
National Maritime Museum Historic Photograph Collection, National Maritime Museum, Greenwich, London SE10 9NF. Telephone: 01-858 4422.
National Monuments Record (England), Fortress House, 23 Saville Row, London W1X 1AB. Telephone: 01-734 6010.
National Museum of Photography, Film and Television, Prince's View, Bradford, West Yorkshire BD5 0TR. Telephone: Bradford (0274) 727488.
(Includes the Kodak Museum Collection.)
National Portrait Gallery, 2 St Martin's Place, London WC2H 0HE. Telephone: 01-930 1552. The NPG Archive and Library is at 15 Carlton House Terrace, London SW1Y 5AH.
Newbury Museum, Wharf Street, Newbury, Berkshire. Telephone: Newbury (0635) 42400.
The RPS National Centre of Photography, The Octagon, Milsom Street, Bath BA1 1DN. Telephone: Bath (0225) 62841.
Royal Archives, Windsor Castle, Windsor, Berkshire.
Royal Scottish Museum, Chambers Street, Edinburgh. Telephone: 031-225 7354.
Science Museum, South Kensington, London SW7 2DD. Telephone: 01-589 3456.
Victoria and Albert Museum, South Kensington, London SW7 2RL. Telephone: 01-589 6371.
Woolstaplers Hall Museum, High Street, Chipping Campden, Gloucestershire. Telephone: Evesham (0386) 840289.
For further reference see:
Directory of British Photographic Collections, compiled by John Wall and published by Heinemann for the National Photographic Record, London, 1977.
The Merseyside Directory of Photographic Sources, published by Open Eye Limited, 90-92 Whitechapel, Liverpool L1 6EN. 1983.

Western Europe

Bibliothèque Nationale, 58 rue Richelieu, F-75084 Paris, France. Telephone: 01-2666262.
Calcografia Nazionale, via della Stamperia 6, 00187 Roma, Italy.
Centro Studie Archivio della Comunicazione, piazza della Pace 5, 4310 0 Parma, Italy.
Deutsches Museum, Museumsinsel, Munich 26, Federal German Republic.
European House of Photography, Rubenscenter, Groenplaats, Antwerpen, Belgium.
Fotografiska Museet, Box 16382, S-10327 Stockholm, Sweden. Telephone: 08-244200.
Foto-Historama, Agfa-Gevaert AG, 5090 Leverkusen, Federal German Republic.
Fotomuseum Burghausen, Rentmeisterstock, 8263 Burghausen, Federal German Republic.
Gabinetto Nazionale delle Stampe, via della Lungara 230, 00100 Roma, Italy.
Galerie de Photographie de la Bibliothèque Nationale, 4 Rue Louvois, F-75002, Paris.
Gruber Collection/Museum Ludwig, An der Rechtschule, 5000 Cologne 1, Federal German Republic.
Het Sterckshof, Provincial Museum voor Kunstambachten, Hoofvunderlei 160, 2100 Deurne, Belgium.
International Polaroid Collection, Antwerpen, Belgium. For further information and access to the collection contact Polaroid Corporation, 575 Technology Square, Cambridge, Mass 02139 USA. Telephone: (area code 617) 577-2038 or the Publicity Manager of any Polaroid subsidiary company.
Kunsthaus Zürich, Stiftung für die Photografie, Heimplatz 1, CH-8001 Zürich, Switzerland. Telephone: 01-321722.
Leitz-Archiv, Ernst Leitz Wetzlar GmbH, Postfach 2020, D-6330 Wetzlar, Federal German Republic. Telephone: 06441-29-1.
Münchner Stadtmuseum, Photo Museum, 8000 Munich 2, St-Jakobs-Platz 1, Federal German Republic.
Museum Folkwang, Bismarckstrasse 64, 43 Essen, Federal German Republic.
Museum for Holography and New Visual Media, Pletschmühlenweg 7, D-5024 Mulheim/Köln, Federal German Republic.
Musée Français de l'Holographie, 4 rue Baubourg, 75004 Paris, France. Telephone: 0227-15-12.
Musée Français de la Photographie, 78 rue de Paris, 91570 Bièvres, France. Telephone: 6-9411060.
Musée Nationale D'Art Moderne, Centre Georges Pompidou, F-75191 Paris, France. Telephone: 1-2771233.
Museo di Storia della Fotografia Fratelli Alinari, Palazzo Rucellai, via della Vigna Nuova 16, 40123 Firenze, Italy.
Museum für Kunst und Gewerbe, Steintorplatz, 2000 Hamburg 1, Federal German Republic.
Museum voor Fotografie en Cinematographie, Ravensteinstraat 23, Brussels, Belgium.
Musée Nicéphore Nièpce, 28 Quai des Messageries, 71100 Chalon-sur-Saône, France. Telephone: 085 484198.
Neue Sammlung, Prinzregentenstrasse 3, 8000 Munich 40, Federal German Republic.
Photomuseum des Landes Oberösterreich,

Marmorschlössel im Kaiserpark, Postfach 117, A-4820 Bad Ischl, Austria. Telephone: 06132-4422.
Photographic Museum of Finland, Vatt uniemenkuja 4, SF-00210 Helsinki 21, Finland. Telephone: 672382.
Photography Museum, Vilnius Street 118-11, 235400 Siauliai, Lithuanian SSR, USSR.
Photographie Ouverte (Galérie du Musée de la Photographie), 19 rue Huart-Chapel, B-6000 Charleroi, Belgium. Telephone: 071-329783.
Pinacoteca di Brera, via Brera 28, 20121 Milano, Italy.
Preus Fotomuseum, Postboks 124, 3191 Horten, Norway.
Provinciaal Museum voor Fotografie, Karel Oomsstraat 11, B-2000 Antwerpen, Belgium. Telephone: 03-2162816.
Société Française de Photographie, 9 rue Montalembert, 75007 Paris, France.
Rheinisches Landesmuseum, Colmanstrasse 16, 53 Bonn, Federal German Republic.
Stockholms Stadsmuseum, Peter Myndes Backe 6, S-11646 Stockholm, Sweden. Telephone: 08-440709.

For further reference see:
Repertoire des Collections Photographiques en France, published by Editions de la Documentation Française, 29-31 quai Voltaire, 75340 Paris, France.

North America

California Museum of Photography, Watkins House, University of California, Riverside, CA 92521, USA.
George Eastman House, 900 East Avenue, Rochester, NY 14607, USA. Telephone: (area code 716) 271-3361.)
International Center of Photography, 1130 Fifth Avenue, New York, NY 10028, USA. Telephone: (area code 212) 860-1777. (Permanent home for the 'International Fund for Concerned Photography').
Library of Congress, 10 First Street SE, Washington, DC 20540, USA.
Museum of Holography, 11 Mercer Street, New York, NY10013, USA. Telephone: (area code 212) 925-0526.
Museum of Modern Art, 11 West 53 Street, New York, NY 10019, USA. Telephone: (area code 212) 956-6100.
Professional Photographers of America Inc, 1090 Executive Way, Des Plaines, Illinois 60018, USA. Telephone: (area code 312) 299-8161.
Smithsonian Institution, Hall of Photography, 1000 Jefferson Drive SW, Washington, DC 20560, USA.
University of Texas, Humanities Research Centre, Box 7219, Austin, TE 78712, USA (includes the Gernsheim Collection).

For further reference see:
Art Libraries and Visual Resource Collection in North America Directory, compiled for the Art Libraries Society of North America (ARLIS/NA) by Hoffberg and Hess, Neal-Schuman Publishers Inc, New York 1978.
Index to American Photographic Collections, edited by James McQuaid. The index lists over 450 photographic collections in museums, libraries, newspaper archives, etc. The book is arranged for access to 19 000 individual photographers as well as by collection.

Other countries

Art Gallery of New South Wales, Art Gallery Road, Domain, Sydney, New South Wales 2000, Australia. Telephone: (02) 221 2100.
Auckland Institute and Museum, The Domain, Auckland 1, New Zealand.
Australian Museum, 6-8 College Street, Sydney, New South Wales 2000, Australia. Telephone: (02) 339 8111.
Bensusan Museum of Photography and Library, City of Johannesburg Public Library, Market Square, Johannesburg 2001, South Africa. Telephone: 836-3787.
National Gallery of Victoria, 180 St Kilda Road, Melbourne, Victoria 3004, Australia. Telephone: (03) 62 7411.
Pentax Museum, 3-21-20 Mishiazabu, Minato-ku, Tokyo 106, Japan.
Queen Victoria Museum and Art Gallery, Wellington Street, Launceston, Tasmania 7250. Telephone: (003) 31 6777.
Tasmanian Museum and Art Gallery, 5 Argyle Street, Hobart, Tasmania 7000. Telephone: (002) 23 2696.
Western Australian Museum, Francis Street, Perth, Western Australia 6000, Australia. Telephone: (09) 328 4411.

Annuals

United Kingdom

British Journal of Photography Annual, 28 Great James Street, London WC1N 3HL.
Photography Year Book, Fountain Press, 65 Victoria Street, Windsor, Berks SL4 1EZ.

Greece

Photography, Film and Television Annual, Editions Moressopoulos, 21 Vassileos Georgiou Avenue, PO Box 710, Thessolonica.

Japan

Asahi Pentax Annual, 3-21-20 Mishiazabu, Minato-ku, Tokyo 106.

Switzerland

Photographis, 107 Dufourstrasse, 8008 Zürich.

USA

Popular Photography Annual, CBS Magazines, One Park Avenue, New York, NY 10016, USA.

USSR

Photo, Planeta Publications, Petrovka 8, Moscow.

Magazines

Publications of professional associations which themselves have a separate entry in the Directory are not included. The indicator (E) is given when a publication from a non-English speaking country is known to have at least part of the text in English, or appears in an English/American edition.

United Kingdom

Amateur Photographer, Prospect House, 9-15 Ewell Road, Cheam, Surrey SM3 8BZ. Weekly.
Audio Visual, PO Box 109, Maclaren House, 19 Scarbrook Road, Croydon, Surrey CR9 1QH. Monthly.
British Journal of Photography, 28 Great James Street, London WC1N 3HL. Weekly.
Camera Weekly, 38 Hampton Road, Teddington, Middlesex TN11 0JE. Weekly.
Creative Camera, Battersea Arts Centre, The Old Town Hall, Lavender Hill, SW11 5TF. Monthly.
Creative Photography (incorporating Camera), National Publications Ltd, Bushfield House, Orton Centre, Peterborough PE2 0UW. Monthly.
Creative Review, 60 Kingley Street, London W1R 5LH. Monthly.
History of Photography, 4 St John Street, London WC1N 2ET. Quarterly.
Hot Shoe International, 2nd/3rd Floor, 40 St John Street, London EC1N 4AY. Ten issues a year.
The Journal of Photographic Science, 44 Gade Avenue, Watford WD1 7LG. An official publication of the *Royal Photographic Society.* Bi-monthly.
Making Better Movies, 28 Great James Street, London WC1N 3HL. Monthly.
Panorama, Bowman Publishing, 14 Leagrave Road, Luton, Beds. Monthly.
The Photographer, Penblade Publishers Ltd, 1 Gayford Road, Shepherd's Bush, London W12 9BY. The official magazine of the *British Institute of Professional Photography.* Monthly.
Photographers, Impressions Gallery of Photography, 17 Colliergate, York YO1 2BN.
Photographic Collector, The Bishopsgate Press, 37 Union Street, London SE1 1SE. Three times a year.
The Photographic Journal, Royal Photographic Society, The Octagon, Milson Street, Bath BA1 1DN, Monthly.
Practical Photography, Bretton Court, Bretton Centre, Peterborough PE3 8DZ. Monthly.
Professional Photographer, PO Box 109, Maclaren House, 19 Scarbrook Road, Croydon, Surrey CR9 1QH. Monthly.
Reprographics Quarterly, NRCd, Hatfield Polytechnic, Annexe, Bayford, Lower Hatfield Road, Hertford SG13 8LD. Quarterly.
SLR Photography, 38/42 Hampton Road, Teddington, Middlesex TW11 0JE. Monthly.
Ten-8, Aston University Arts Centre, Gosta Green, Birmingham B7 4ET. Quarterly.

35mm Photography, 1 Golden Square, London W1. Monthly.
VFI, King Publications Limited, Film House, 142 Wardour Street, London WC1V 4BR. Monthly.
Which Camera?, Haymarket Publishing Ltd, 38-42 Hampton Road, Teddington, Middlesex TW11 0JE. Monthly.
Widescreen, 48 Dorset Street, London W1H 3FH. Bi-monthly.

Argentina

American Fotografias, Editorial Foco SLR, Monroe 5117, Buenos Aires.

Australia

Audio Vision, Iris Publishing Company, PO Box 143, Mona Vale, NSW 2103.
Australian Camera Craft, PO Box 143, Mona Vale, NSW 2103.
Australian Photography, GPO Box 606, Sydney, NSW 2001 or 432 Elizabeth Street, Sydney, NSW 2000. Monthly.
Industrial and Commercial Photography, GPO Box 606, Sydney, NSW 2001 or 432 Elizabeth Street, NSW, Bi-monthly.
Photo Retailer, GPO Box 606, Sydney, NSW 2001 or 432 Elizabeth Street, Surrey Hills, NSW 2010. Monthly.
Photofile, Australian Centre for Photography, 257 Oxford Street, Paddington, NSW 2021.
Photo Forum, Iris Publishing Company, PO Box 143, Mona Vale, NSW 2103. Monthly.
Photoworld, 1 Bungan Lane, Mona Vale, NSW 2103.
Professional Photography, Iris Publishing Company, PO Box 143, Mona Vale, NSW 2103, Bi-monthly.

Austria

Camera Austria, Forum Stadtpark 1, A-8010 Graz.
Filmkunst, Rauhensteingasse 5, 1010 Vienna.
Der Osterreichische Filmamateur, Neubaugasse 36, 1070 Vienna.
Der Photograph, Salesianergasse 1, 1030 Vienna. Monthly.

Belgium

Cine Dossiers, 30 rue de L'Etuve, 1000, Brussels.
Cinema Belge, 12 rue Paul-Emile Janson, 1050 Brussels.
Clichés, 36 rue du Houblon, B-1000 Bruxelles. Monthly.
Focale, 24 avenue J.S. Bach, 1080 Brussels. Monthly.
Labo Courrier, 204 avenue Brugmann, 1190 Brussels.
Photographie Ouverte, 19 rue Huart-Chapel, B-6000 Charleroi. Monthly.
Snap-Shot, Pacifaciestraat 70, Antwerp 2000.

Brazil

Fotoptica, Avenue Rebougas, 2291, CEPO 5401, Sao Paulo.

Canada

Ovo/Photo, PO Box 1431, Station A, Montreal, Quebec H3C 2Z9. Quarterly. (E).
Photovideo, 177 Bay Street, Toronto M4W 1A7. (formerly *Canadian Photography*).

China

Chinese Photography, 61 Hongxin Hutong Dongdan, Beijing.
Popular Photography, 61 Hongxin Hutong Dongdan, Beijing.

Czechoslovakia

Amatersky Film, Mrstikova 23, 10000 Prague 10.
Fotografie, Diouha trida 12, 11589 Prague 1, Monthly.

Finland

Kaitafilmi, Lonrotinkatu 15, 00120 Helsinki 12.
Kamera Lehti, Kalevankatu 21, A5 00100 Helsinki 10.
Valojuva, Korkeavuorenkatu 2bF 72, 00140 Helsinki 14.

France

Les Cahiers de la Photographie, Lascledes, Brax, F-47310 Laplume. Quarterly.
Camera International, 32 Rue Saint-Marc, 75002 Paris. Quarterly. (E).
Cinema Pratique, 16 quai de la Marne, 75019 Paris.
Contact, 135 rue de Rennes, Paris.
Creatis, 19 rue du Depart, 75014 Paris.
Le Nouveau Photocinema, 189 rue Saint-Jacques, 75005 Paris.
Photo'Argus, 116 Boulevard Malesherbes, 75017 Paris.
Photo Reporter, 30 bis rue Spontini, 75016 Paris. Monthly.
Photo, 63 Champs-Elysees, 75008 Paris.
Le Photographe, 189 rue Saint-Jacques, 75005 Paris.
Photographies, 61 rue de Richelieu, 75002 Paris. Monthly. (E).
Photo Magazine, 189 rue Saint-Jacques, 75005 Paris.
Photo-Revue, 118 bis rue d'Assas, 75006 Paris.
Sonovision, 15 rue d'Aboukir, 75002 Paris.
Le Technicien du Film, 79 Champs-Elysees, 75008 Paris.
Zoom, 2 Rue du Faubourg Poissoniere, 75010 Paris. Five times a year. (E).

German Democratic Republic

Fotografie, Karl-Heine Strasse 16, 7031 Leipzig. Monthly.

German Federal Republic

Amateurfotographie, Fremersbergstrasse 1, 7570 Baden-Baden.
Color-Foto, Leuschmerstrasse 1, 7000 Stuttgart. Monthly.
European Photography, Stargader Weg 18, D-3400 Gottingen. Quarterly.
Fernseh und Kinotechnik, Malvenstrasse 12, 1000 Berlin 45.
Film + Foto, Fachnerstrasse 43, 8000 Muchen 21.
Film 8/16, Oranienstrasse 8, 6272 Niederhausen.
Film-echo und Filmwoche (incorporating *Filmblatter*), Gutenbergstrasse 13, 6201 Nordenstadt.
Filter Foto-Scene Actuell, Postfach 701210, 6000 Frankfurt.
Foto Contact, PO Box 1229 (or Freilingrathring 18-20), 4030 Ratingen.
Foto Creativ, Leuschmerstrasse 1, 7000 Stuttgart.
Foto-Focus, Topferstrasses 29, 6393 Wehrheim/Ts.
Foto-Hobbylabor, Leuschmerstrasse 1, 7000 Stuttgart.
Foto Magazin, Ortlerstrasse 8, 8000 Munchen 70. Monthly.
Foto Popular, G-v-Seidl-Strasse 50, 8022 Grunwald.
Foto-Praxis, Postfach 104849, 2000 Hamburg 1.
Foto-Scene, Hedderichstrasse 43a, D-6000 Frankfurt/Main 70. Monthly.
Fotografie, Rote Strasse 12, D-34 Gottingen. Quarterly.
Foto und Film Hobby, Postfach 1215, 7000 Stuttgart 1.
Fotowirtschaft, Ortlerstrasse 8, 8000 Munchen 70.
Inpho, Postfach 200340, 4000 Düsseldorf.
International Contact, Tienfenbroicherstrasse 69, 4040 Ratingen.
Kamera und Schule, Junger Verlag, Schumannstrasse 161, 6050 Offenbach.
Leica-Fotografie, Stuttgarterstrasse 18-42, 6000 Frankfurt/Main. (E).
MFM Moderne Fototechnik, Teinacher Strasse 34, 7140 Ludwigsberg.
Photo, Sternwartstrasse 4, 8000 Munchen 80.
Photoblatter, Stuttgarterstrasse 18-24, 6000 Frankfurt/Main.
Photo Presse, Postfach 1348, 3510 Hannover-Munchen 1.
Photo-Revue, Schellingstrasse 39, 8000 Munchen 86.
Photo Technik International; English language edition is *Photo Technique International,* Rupert Mayer Strasse 45, 8000 Munchen 25.
Profifoto, Postfach 200340, 4000 Düsseldorf.
Schmalfilm, Markgratenstrasse 11, 1000 Berlin 61.
Video Aktiv, Leuschenstrasse 1, 7000 Stuttgart.
Zeiss Information, D-7082 Oberkochen.
Zoom, Brudermuhlstrasse 6, D-8000 Munchen. Irregular.

Greece

Fotografia, Editions Moressopoulos, 21 Vassileos Georgiou Avenue, PO Box 710, Thessalonica. Bi-monthly.

Hungary

Foto, Lenin Korut 9-11, 1073 Budapest. Monthly.

Israel

Hatzilum, PO Box 1015, Ramat Gan 52109.

218

Italy

European Photofinishers' Tribune, via N. Battiglia 37, 20127 Milan (E).
Fotocultura, viale Ippocrate 97, 00161 Rome.
Fotografare, via Lipari 8, 00141 Rome. Monthly.
Fotografia Italiana, Via delgi Imbriani 15, 20158 Milan.
Fotografia, Belborgo editore, via G Byron, Ferrara.
Foto-Notiziario, via Melloni 17, 20120 Milan.
Fotopratica, via F., Belloni 7, 20129 Milan.
Photo (Italian edition), corso Venezia 18, zoizi Milano.
Photo Made in Italy, via Melloni 17, 1-20129 Milan.
Progresso Fotografico, viale Piceno 14, 20129 Milan.
Reflex, via di Villa Severini 54, 00191 Roma.
Rivista Tecnica di Cinematografia, viale Campania 23, Milan.
Tutti Fotografi, viale Piceno 14, 20129 Milan.
Zoom, (Italian edition), viale Piceno 14, 20129 Milan.

Japan

Asahi Camera, Asahi Shimbun, Tokyo 100. Monthly.
Camerart, Hinode Building 11, 2-Chome, Kyobashi, Chuohku, Tokyo. Monthly. (E).
Camera Mainichi, Mainichi Daily News, 1-1 Hitotsubashi, Chiyoda-ku, Tokyo. Monthly.
Japan Camera Trade News, 18-2 Shibuya 3-chrome, Shibujaka, Tokyo 150. Monthly. (E).
Nippon Camera, 1-5-15 Ningyo-cho, Nihonbashi, Chuohku, Tokyo. Monthly.
Photo International, Meiko Building, 11-11, Shinjuku-1-chome, Shinjuku-ku. Tokyo.

The Netherlands

Focus, Postbus 26, 1087, 1200 BW Hilversum. Monthly.
Foto, Naardersstraat 35, 1211 AJ Hilversum. Monthly.
Foto en Doka, Kroonstraat 150, 6500AA Nijmegen. Monthly.
Foto-Visia, Postbus 16, Nigmegen.
NBJ-Bulletin, Keizersgracht 238, Amsterdam C.
Perspktief, Stationssingel 19b, 3033 HA Rotterdam.
Professionele Fotografie, Kroonstraat 150, 6500AA Nijmegen. Bi-monthly.
Zien, Dresselhuystraat 11a, NL-3039 ZH Rotterdam. Irregular.

Poland

Foto, Krolewska 27, 00950 Warsaw.
Fotografia, Skrytka Pocztowa 169, 00950 Warsaw. Monthly.
Foto Kronika, Skrytka Pocztowa 169, 00950 Warsaw.

Portugal

Foto, Rua Conde de Rio Major 10, 10c/v EF-Alges, Lisbon.
Nova Imagm, Av. Almirante Gago Coutinho 43-1, P-1700 Lisbon.

Spain

Arte Fotografico, Don Ramon De la Cruz 53, Madrid 1.
Cinema, 2002, Ardemans 64, Madrid 28.
Enfoques, Capital, Cordoba 6070.
Flash Foto, Rocafort 39-421, Barcelona 15.
Foto Professional, Fernandez de los Rios 2, 28015 Madrid.
Nueva Lente, Fernandez Ardemans 64, Apartado 8. 425, Madrid.
Photo-Vision, Lopez de Hoyos, 62 Madrid-2.

Sweden

Aktuell Fotografi, Box 1186, S-25111 Helsingborg. Monthly.
Foto, Box 3263, 10365 Stockholm.
Fotonyheterna, Kungstensgaten 20, 11357 Stockholm. Monthly.
Hasselblad, Victor Hasselblad AB, Box 220, 41023 Goteborg 1.
Svensk Fotografisk Tijdskrift, Nytorgsgaten 17, 11622 Stockholm.

Switzerland

Foto Film Ton, Postfach 6766, 8953 Dietikon.
L'Objectif, 12 rue des Mouettes, Geneve.
Photo-Cine Expert/Photo Kino Berater, Route de Bellebouche 13, CH-1246 Corsier.
Photographie, Schlagbaumstrasse 6, CH-8201 Schaffhausen. Monthly.
Schweizerische Photorundschau, 1800 Vevey.

USA

Afterimage, Visual Studies Workshop, 31 Prince Street, Rochester, NY 14607.
American Cinematographer, 1782 North Orange Drive, Hollywood, CA 90028.
American Photographer, 1015 Broadway, New York, NY 10036.
Aperture, Elm Street, Mullerton, NY 12546. Quarterly.
Audio-Visual Communication, 750 Third Avenue, New York, NY 10017.
The Camera Craftsman, 2000 Western Union Avenue, Englewood, CO 8010.
Darkroom Techniques, PO Box 48312, 7800 Merrimac Avenue, Niles, Illinois 60648.
Exposure, Society for Photographic Education, Box 1651, FDR Post Office, New York, NY 10012.
Film-makers' Newsletter, PO Box 115, Ward Hill, MA 01830.
Functional Photography, PTN Publishing Corporation, 101 Crossways Park West, Woodbury, NY 11791.
Hot Shoe International, 303 Fifth Avenue South, New York, NY 10016.
International Photographer, 7715 Sunset Boulevard, Hollywood, CA 90046.
Journal of Biological Photography, Eye and Ear Hospital, 230 Lothrop Street, Pittsburgh, PS 15213. (*formerly Journal of the Biological Photographic Association*).
Journal of Imaging Science, SPSE, 7003 Kilworth Lane, Spingfield, VA 22151. (*formerly Photographic Science and Engineering*).
Journal of Imaging Technology, SPSE, 7003 Kilworth Lane, Springfield, VA 22151. (*formerly Journal of Applied Photographic Engineering*).
Modern Photography, 825 Seventh Avenue, New York 10019, NY 10022. Monthly.
Movie Making, 8490 Sunset Boulevard, Los Angeles, CA 90069.
News Photographer, 170 West End Avenue, New York, NY 10023.
Optical Engineering, PO Box 10, 405 Fieldson Road, Bellingham, WA 98225.
Petersen's Photographic Magazine, 8490 Sunset Boulevard, Los Angeles, CA 90028. Monthly.
Philadelphia Photo Review, Pox 70, Arcola, PS 19420.
Photogrammetric Engineering and Remote Sensing, 105 N Virginia Avenue, Falls Church, VA 22046.
Photography, 210 Fifth Avenue, New York, NY 10010. Ten issues/year.
The Photograph Collector, 127E 59 Street, New York, NY 10022.
Photographer's Forum, 25 W Anpama Street, Santa Barbara, CA 931010. Quarterly.
Photographic Trade News, PTN Publishing Corporation, 101 Crossways Park West, Woodbury, NY 11791.
Photo Lab Management, PO Box 1700, 1312 Lincoln Boulevard, Santa Monica, CA 90406.
Photomarketing, 603 Lansing Avenue, Jackson, MI 49202.
Photomethods, 50 South Ninth, Minneapolis, MN 55402.
Photoshow Magazine, 3818 Brunswick Avenue, Los Angeles, CA 90039.
Popular Photography, 1 Park Avenue, New York, NY 10016. Monthly.
The Print Collector's Newsletter, 205 East 78th Street, New York, NY 10021.
The Professional Photographer, Executive Way, Des Plaines, Illinois 60018.
The Rangefinder, 1312 Lincoln Boulevard, PO Box 1703, Santa Monica, CA 90406.
SMPTE Journal, 901 Meadow Lakes, Eltra Road, Highstown, NJ 08520.
Studio Photography, PTN Publishing Corporation, 101 Crossways Park West, Woodbury NY 11791.
Technical Photography, PTN Publishing Corporation, 101 Crossways Park West, Woodbury, NY 11791. Monthly.
35mm Photography, 1 Park Avenue, New York, NY 10016. Occasional.
Untitled, Friends of Photography, Box 239, Carmel, CA 93921.
Videography, 750 Third Avenue, New York, NY 10017. Monthly.

USSR

Sovietskoie Foto, M Lubyanka 14, 101878 Moscow (Centre).

Venezuela

Foton Viaja, Avenue Maturin 15 altos, Los Cedros, Caracas.

Yugoslavia

Fotografiia film, Ilirska 9, 11000 Belgrade.
Foto Kino Revija, Bulevar Revolucije 44, 1100 Belgrade.

Directories and Guides

Arts Council of GB, Photography in the Arts: Organisations and Projects in Great Britain, 105 Piccadilly, London W1V 0AU.
Art Directors' Index to Photographers. Published by Roto Vision, Geneva. UK Agent: Art Directors' Index, 3A Wychcombe Studios, Englands Lane, London NW3 4XY.
ASMP Book, The American Society of Magazine Photographers, 205 Lexington Avenue, New York, NY 10016, USA. Lists photographers, stock photographs, representatives, models, stylists, locations/sets, prop sources, processors, retouchers, equipment suppliers, advertising agencies, magazines and photo-galleries.

Audio Visual Directory, PO Box 109, Maclaren House, Scarbrook Road, Croydon CR9 1QH. There are five main sections: audio visual equipment, dealers by region, programme production and production services, programme distributors and post-production services. Published annually.

Audio Visual Equipment Directory, National Audio-Visual Association Inc, 3150 Spring Street, Fairfax, Virginia 22030, USA.

Australian Photography Photo Directory, Photo Publishing Co, 432 Elizabeth Street, Sydney, NSW 2000, Australia.

BFI Film and Television Yearbook published by the British Film Institute and available from BFI Publishing, 127 Charing Cross Road, London WC2H 0EA.

British Qualifications, compiled by Barbra Priestley, and published by Kegan Page, 116 Pentonville Road, London N1 9JN. Contains comprehensive listings of educational, professional and academic qualifications in the United Kingdom.
Canadian Industrial Photography, Directory of Goods and Services, French-English, Maclean-Hunter Company Limited, 481 University Avenue, Toronto 2, Ontario, Canada.
Creative Black Book, published by Friendly Publications International Inc, 150 Regent Street, London W1R 5FA. Listings of art directors, major advertising agencies and photographers in the United Kingdom, Western Europe and Scandinavia.
The Creative Handbook, published by Thomas Skinner Directories, Windsor Court, East Grinstead House, East Grinstead, West Sussex RH19 1XE. This is published annually as a comprehensive directory of suppliers to the advertising and graphics industry. The handbook uses the following listings: creative and design consultants, designers, writers, illustrators, photographers, photo libraries, models, stylists, props, locations, photo-processors, art and photo suppliers, audiovisual and video services, art studios, retouchers, typographers, print services, TV and radio production, post production services, music recording services and viewing theatres, exhibition and promotional contractors, employment agencies and advertising agencies. *The Creative Handbook* covers the United Kingdom and *The Creative Handbook — Europe,* from the same publishers, the rest of Europe.

Dictionary of Information Technology, written by Dennis Longley and Michael Shain, and published by Macmillan Reference Books, 4 Little Essex Street, London WC2R 3LF. This encyclopeadic dictionary of over 6000 entries describes all the concepts, systems, technologies, data and organisation in this otherwise complex and confusing area. Here are explained: audio-visual technology (video cassette recorders, electronic news gathering, display techniques); communication technology (telecommunications, broadcasting, data networks and teleconferencing); information systems (eg videotex, teletext), office systems, electronics and printing technology. For each entry it is made clear in which area it is used, distiguishing between meanings acquired in different contexts.
Directory of Commercial Microfilm Services in the United Kingdom published by the National Reprographic Centre for Documentation. Gives alphabetical and geographical listings of bureaux and details of special services.

Directory of Photocopying and Microcopying services, 2nd edn, FID publication 273, International Federation for Documentation, Den Haag, Netherlands.

Directory of Professional Photography and Buyers' Guide, Professional Photographers of America Inc, 1090 Executive Way, Des Plaines, Illinois 60018, USA.
European Photography Guide, published every other year, most recently in 1984, by *European Photography,* Andreas Muller-Pohle, Stargarder Weg 18, D-3400 Gottingen, Federal German Republic. There are two main sections: Galleries and Museums, and Publishers and Magazines. The former includes not only address, opening hours, year of founding and contact name but also details about space available, exhibition area and the average number of photography exhibitions per year. Each entry concludes with a short description of the exhibition programme, any possible specialisation and focal points.

Focus, Annual Buyers Guide, Photomethods, 50 South Ninth, Minneapolis SS40Z, USA. Contains listings and descriptions of products in still photography, cine, video and instrumentation; plus services.

Framing and Art Buyer's Guide, published by Framing and Art Buyer's Guide Limited, 83-87 Bridge Road, East Molesey, Surrey KT8 9HH.

FAB Guide is a source book listing suppliers of art, framing and crafts equipment, materials, services, prints, posters and paintings.

Hollis Press and Public Relations Annual, published annually by Hollis Directories Limited, Contact House, Sunbury-on-Thames, Middlesex TW16 5HG. It provides over ten thousand information sources and media contacts divided into the following sections: news contacts, information sources (public and official), and services for the communications industry.

International Index to Film Periodicals, published annually since 1972 by FIAF, 90-94 Shaftesbury Avenue, London W1V 7DH is a guide to the literature on film that appears during the year in over 100 film magazines. The Index is divided into three main categories: General Subjects, Film and Biography.

London Art and Artists Guide is a comprehensive pocket art guide to London published by Art Guide Publications, 28 Colville Road, London W11 2BS. The guide covers 500 galleries divided into five sections: museums, galleries dealing with pre-1900 art, contemporary art galleries, national centres and institutes and alternative art spaces. Useful art addresses, studios, workshops, evening classes, art supply shops, artists groups, art magazines and art bookshops are also included. The London information covers transport, restaurants area by area, pubs, tea places, parks, markets, music places and sport. Also publishes the *Paris Art Guide*, the *Australian Arts Guide* and *New York Art Guide.*
Madison Avenue Europe, published by Peter Glenn Publications Limited, New York. UK representative: Sweatman and Fordham. Telephone: 01-370 6269. For specialist listings of advertising agencies, publications, PR films, TV and film producers, illustrators, photographic studios and attendant services, model agencies etc. Also includes comprehensive travel information and maps. Cities covered: London, Paris, Amsterdam, Brussels, Copenhagen, Stockholm, Oslo, Milan, Rome, Zürich, Vienna, Madrid, Barcelona and five areas in West Germany. For America see *Madison Avenue Handbook* and *Madison Avenue West.*

Motion Picture and TV Services Directory, Motion Picture Enterprises Publications Inc, Tarrytown, NY 10591, USA. (Semi-annual).
Optical Industry and Systems Directory, Optical Publishing Company, Pittsfield, Masschusetts 11202, USA.

Photography: Sources and Resources by Stephen Lewis, James McQuaid and David Tait. A source book for creative photography published by Turnip Press, Light Impressions Corporation, PO Box 3012, Rochester, NY 14650, USA.
Photographic Trade News, Master Buying Guide and Directory Issue, PTN Publishing Co Inc, 101 Crossways Park West, Woodbury, NY 11797, USA. Issued as part of the annual subscription to *Photographic Trade News.*

The Photography A-V Program Directory by Coleman, Grantz and Sheer. A comprehensive guide to over 3300 audiovisual programmes on photography. Lists films, videotapes, computer programs, sound/slide, microform and related materials. Published by the Photography Media Institute Inc, PO Box 78, Staten Island, New York, 10304, USA.

Photokina, Firmen und Waren (Directory of Firms and Goods), Photokina, Messe-und-Ausstellung GmbH, 5 Koln-Deutz, PO Box 140, Koln, Federal German Republic. Published for use with exhibition and serves as a worldwide index to firms and goods in the photographic industry.

Photographic Directory and Buying Guide, CBS Magazines, 1 Park Avenue, New York, NY 10016, USA.

Photo Trader Directory, Henry Greenwood and Company Limited, 28 Great James Street, London WC1N 3HL. Listings of importers, services etc, etc.

Professional and Industrial Photographic Equipment Catalogue, Photo Publishing Co, 432 Elizabeth Street, Sydney, NSW Australia.

Video Yearbook, published annually by Blandford Press. Comprehensive market guide on video equipment and services.

Willing's Press Guide, published annually by Thomas Skinner Directories, Windsor Court, East Grinstead House, East Grinstead, West Sussex RH19 1XE.

World Design Sources Directory. Published by Pergamon Press for the International Council of Societies of Industrial Design and the International Council of Graphic Design Associations. An inventory of some 250 public and private organisations throughout the world concerned with industrial and graphic design, and to a lesser extent interior design.

The Writer's and Artist's Year Book, published annually by Adam and Charles Black, 35 Bedford Row, London WC1R 4JH. For information of journals, publishers, literary agents, news and press agencies, art galleries, markets for artists, and photographers etc.

Major Text Books

In the following list the emphasis has been on books currently available together with a small selection of older books which are known to be out of print. Out of print books are marked with an asterisk. The *British Journal of Photography Almanac* produced book lists for many years until 1963, and reference should be made to these for earlier definitive text books.

Historical, contemporary and critical

H. J. P. Arnold, *William Henry Fox Talbot.* Hutchinson Benham, 1977.
B. Coe, *A Guide to Early Photographic Process,* Hurtwood Press in association with The Victoria and Albert Museum, 1983.
Van Deren Coke (Ed). *One Hundred Years of Photographic History,* University of New Mexico Pres, 1975.
Van Deren Coke, *The Painter and The Photograph,* rev edn, University of New Mexico Press, 1972.
J. M. Elder, *History of Photography,* Dover Publications, New York, 1980. (Translation of 1932 edition by Edward Epsteam.)
*H. and A. Gernsheim, *The History of Photography,* rev edn, Thames and Hudson, 1969.
H. Gernsheim, *Incunabula of British Photographic Literature,* Scolar Press, 1984.
H. and A. Gernsheim, *L. J. M. Daguerre,* rev edn, Dover Publication, New York, 1968.
H. Gernsheim, *The Origins of Photography,* Thames and Hudson, 1982.
S. Greenough, *Alfred Stieglitz, Photographs and Writings,* Callaway Editions, New York, 1984.
M. F. Harker, *The Linked Ring,* Heinemann, 1979.
I. Jeffrey, *Photography: a concise history,* Thames and Hudson, 1981.
N. Lyons (ed), *Photographers on Photography,* Prentice Hall, New Jersey, 1966.
B. Newhall, *The History of Photography from 1839 to the present,* rev edn, Secker and Warburg, 1982.
B. Newhall, *Photography: Essays and Images,* Secker and Warburg, 1980.
A. Scharf, *Art and Photography,* rev edn, Pelican Books, Harmondsworth, 1974.
P. Tausk, *Photography in the Twentieth Century,* Focal Press, 1980.
D. B. Thomas, *Cameras,* HMSO, 1966.
D. B. Thomas, *The First Negatives,* HMSO, 1964.
E. J. Wall, *The History of Three Color Photography,* 1925, (facsimile reprint, Focal Press, 1970).
L. D. Witkin and B. London, *The Photograph Collector's Guide,* Secker and Warburg, 1979.

Photography — practice and applications

C. R. Arnold, P. J. Rolls and J. C. J. Stewart, *Applied Photography,* Focal Press, 1971.
W. F. Berg, *Exposure: Theory and Practice,* 4th edn, Focal Press, 1971.
E. J. Birr, *Stabilization of Photographic Silver Halide Emulsions,* Focal Press, 1974.
A. Cooke, *Photographic Optics,* 15th edn, Focal Press, 1974.
J. H. Coote, *Colour Prints,* 5th edn, Focal Press, 1972.
O. R. Croy, *Camera Copying and Reproduction,* Focal Press, 1964.
O. R. Croy, *Retouching, 4th edn, Focal Press, 1964.*
M. S. Dinaburg, *Photosensitive Diazo Compounds,* Focal Press, 1964.
*R. M. Evans, *An Introduction to Color.*
*R. M. Evans, *Eye, Film and Camera in Color Photography.*
*R. M. Evans, W. T. Hanson, W. L. Brewer, *Principles of Colour Photography.*
(Focal Press), *The Pictorial Cyclopaedia of Photography,* 2nd edn, Focal Press, 1979.
(Focal Press), *The Focal Encyclopaedia of Photography,* rev edn, Focal Press, 1965.
G. Franke, *Physical Optics in Photography,* Focal Press, 1966.
V. M. Fridkin, *The Physics of the Electrophotographic Process,* Focal Press, 1973.
*J. S. Friedman, *History of Three-Color Photography,* American Photographic Publishing Co, 1948. (Reprint Focal Press, 1970).
H. Frieser, *Photographic Image Recording,* Focal Press, 1975.
J. Hedgecoe, *The Book of Photography,* Ebury Press, 1976.
*K. Henney and B. Dudley, *Handbook of Photography,* Whittlesey House, 1939.
C. I. Jacobson and L. A. Mannheim, *Enlarging,* 22nd edn, Focal Press, 1975.
K. I. Jacobson and R. E. Jacobson, *Developing,* 18th edn, Focal Press, 1976.
K. I. Jacobson and R. E. Jacobson, *Imaging Systems,* Focal Press, 1976.
R. E. Jacobson, S. F. Ray, G. G. Attridge and N. R. Axford (Eds), *The Manual of Photography,* 7th edn, Focal Press, 1978.
M. Langford, *Advanced Photography,* 4th edn, Focal Press, 1980.
M. Langford, *Basic Photography,* 4th edn, Focal Press, 1977.
M. Langford, *The Book of Special Effects Photography,* Ebury Press.
M. Langford, *The Complete Encyclopaedia of Photography,* Ebury Press, 1982.
M. Langford, *Professional Photography,* Focal Press, 1974.
L. Lobel and M. Dubois, *Basic Sensitometry,* 2nd edn, Focal Press, 1967.
*C. W. Miller, *Principles of Photographic Reproduction,* McMillan.
L. F. A. Mason, *Photographic Processing Chemistry,* 2nd edn, Focal Press, 1975.
W. Nurnberg, *Lighting for Photography,* 16th edn, Focal Press, 1968.
W. Nurnberg, *Lighting for Portraiture,* 7th edn, Focal Press, 1969.
A. Rott and E. Weyde, *Photographic Silver Halide Diffusion Processes,* Focal Press, 1972.
G. Saxby, *Holograms: How to Make and Display Them,* Focal Press, 1980.
R. M. Schaffert, *Electrophotography,* 2nd edn, Focal Press, 1975.
J. Sheppard, *Photography for Designers,* 2nd edn, Focal Press, 1976.
D. A. Spencer, *Colour Photography in Practice,* 6th edn, Focal Press, 1975. Revised by L. A. Mannheim and Viscount Hanworth.
D. A. Spencer, *The Focal Dictionary of Photographic Technologies,* Focal Press, 1973.
J. Tait, *Beyond Photography,* Focal Press, 1977.
A. Tyrrell, *Basics of Reprography,* Focal Press, 1972.
G. Veith, *Sensitometric Testing Methods,* Focal Press, 1974.
H. J. Walls and G. G. Attridge, *Basic Photographic Science,* 2nd edn, Focal Press, 1977.

Finding and ordering Books

The Dewey Decimal Classification is the system used by most libraries in classifying articles in periodicals, monographs and documents of all kinds. The numerical classifications for photography based on the *Decimal Classification and Relative Index* are given below. In most libraries shelves will be numbered following this sequence and many bookshops follow (albeit usually much less formally) a similar pattern.

770 Photography and photographs
.1 Philosophy and theory
.11 Inherent features. Composition, colour, form, style, perspective, decorative values, light vision, space, movements, symmetry.
.2 Miscellany
.23 Photography as a profession, occupation, hobby.
.28 Techniques and procedures; including techniques of pinhole photography, of photography without a camera.
.282 Use of cameras. Loading, focusing, exposure, plate and film removal.
.283 Darkroom and laboratory practice, including preparation of negatives (developing, desensitising, reducing, intensifying, rinsing, fixing, washing, drying exposed plates, films, paper).
.284 Preparation of positives. Exposure, developing, rinsing, fixing, washing, drying, retouching, toning, colouring, mounting.
.285 Preservation of negatives and transparencies.
.286 Preservation of positives
.287 Recovery of waste materials
.9 Historical and geographical treatment
.92 Photographers regardless of area, region, place, type of photography.

771 Apparatus, equipment, materials
.1 Studios, laboratories, darkrooms
.2 Furniture and fittings
.3 Cameras and accessories
.31 Specific makes of cameras
.35 Optical parts of cameras
.352 Lenses
.36 Cameras shutters
.37 Focusing and exposure apparatus
.38 Accessories
.4 Developing and printing apparatus
.5 Chemical materials
.52 Support materials
.53 Photosensitive surfaces
.54 Developing and printing supplies Developing reducing, toning, intensifying, fixing solutions.

772 Metallic salt process
.1 Direct positive and printing out processes
.12 Daguerreotype process
.14 Wet collodion, ferrotype, tintype processes
.16 Kallitype processes
.3 Platinotype process
.4 Silver processes

773 Pigment process of printing
.1 Carbon and carbro processes
.2 Powder (dusting-on) processes
.3 Imbibition processes
.5 Gum-bichromate processes
.6 Photoceramic and photoenamel processes
.7 Diazotype processes
.8 Oil processes

774 Holography

775 (Unassigned)
776 (Unassigned)
776 (Unassigned)
777 (Unassigned)

778 Specific fields and special kinds of photography, and related activities.
.2 Photographic projection
.3 Special kinds of photography
.31 Photomicrography
.32 Photography in terms of focus
.322 Telephotography
.324 Close-up photography
.34 Infrared photography
.35 Aerial and space photography
.36 Panoramic photography
.37 High-speed photography
.4 Stereoscopic photography and projection
.5 Motion-picture and television photography and related activities.
.52 Generalities of motion-picture and television photography.
.53 Motion-picture photography and editing
.55 Motion-picture projection
.56 Special kinds of motion-picture photography
.58 Preservation and storage of motion-picture films.
.59 Television photography
.6 Colour photography and photography of Colours.
.62 Photography of colours in monochrome
.63 Direct process reproduction in colour photography.
.65 Additive process in colour photography
.66 Processing techniques, procedures, apparatus, equipment, materials in colour photography.
.7 Photography under specific conditions
.71 Outdoors
.72 Indoors and by artificial light
.73 Underwater
.75 Under extreme climate conditions
.8 Special effects and trick photography
.9 Photography of specific subjects

779 Photographs

Books currently in print are listed in two main references *British Books in Print* (*'BBIP'*) (Whittaker) and the *British National Bibliography* (*'BNB'*) issued by the British Library. These are available in most libraries. Most booksellers use *BBIP.*

The 'ISBN' Standard Book Numbering has been adopted by some thirty countries to fulfil the needs of publishers, booksellers, librarians, wholesalers and others concerned with books who use, or intend to use, electronic data processing.

The International Standard Book Number (ISBN) is administered:
in the United Kingdom by
Standard Book Numbering Agency Limited,
12 Dyott Street, London WC1A 1DF.
Telephone: 01-836 8911.
in the United States by
Standard Book Numbering Agency,
1189 Avenue of the Americans, New York, NY10036.
Telephone: (area code 212) 764-3384.

The number comprises four groups of numbers in the form

0 907191 00 2

The first number indicates the country/language of publication (0 in this case signifies British or other English speaking country origin); the second number group is the publisher number — unique to that imprint; the third group is the serial number within that publisher's productions; and the final single digit (which may be 0-9 or X) is a parity or check digit which allows the whole number to be tested for error. Note that different editions and bindings of the same work may have different serial numbers. The additional prefix 1 came into use for some English-language registrations in 1983.■

This information is a selective listing from a more comprehensive Directory of Photography last published in the *British Journal of Photography,* 7 December 1984-19 April 1985 under the following headings:

1 Art Associations and Councils
2 British Standards
3 Broadcasting
4 Careers and Employment
5 Dealers and Museum Collections of Old Photographs and Photographica
6 Education and Training
7 Galleries and Fine Art Dealers
8 Libraries
9 Photographic Suppliers
10 Picture Libraries and Agencies
11 Professional Associations and Learned Societies
12 Professional Processing Laboratories
13 Publications
14 Publishers and Distributors of Photographic Books
15 Reference Works
16 Scholarships, Awards and Grants
17 Trade Fairs
18 Travel
19 Workshops and Summer Schools

SOURCES FOR COURSES

APART from those establishments which offer regular courses in photography, (listed in *Where to Study Photography, Film and Television,* published by Henry Greenwood and Co Ltd) a number of colleges, art centres, art galleries, scientific bodies and commerical enterprises provide tuition for both amateur and professional photographers as short or even single-day courses. A list of the best known is given here.

Academy of Professional Photography (British Institute of Professional Photography), Amwell End, Ware, Hertfordshire SG12 9HN. Tel 0920 4011. Workshops on all aspects of professional photography. Residential and non-residential.

Bicton Studio Photographic Services, Zoneight, Exmouth, Devon EX8 4EZ. Tel 0395 273311. Workshops and courses on most aspects of photography for amateurs. High standards, beginners to advanced. Details from Brian Allen.

Blackfriars Arts Centre, Spain Lane, Boston, Lincs PE21 6HP. Tel 0205 63108. Occasional workshops on unusual subjects such as pinhole photography.

Brewery Arts Centre, Highgate, Kendal, Cumbria LA9 4HE. Tel 0539 35133. Occasional workshops on colour printing, etc.

British Institute of Professional Photography: see *Academy of Professional Photography.*

Bronica School — Intensive week-end courses for Bronica owners, sited in various centres. Information from Bronica (UK) Ltd, Priors Way, Maidenhead, Berks SL6 2HR. Tel 0628 74411.

Brunel University, Photo Short-Course Unit, Arts Centre, Kingston Lane, Uxbridge, Middlesex UB8 3PH. Tel 0895 37188. Short summer schools.

BFP School of Photography, Focus House, 497 Green Lanes, London N13 4BP. Tel 01-882 3315/6. Intended especially for those hoping to enter the world of freelance photography.

Cambridge Darkroom, Dales Brewery, Gwydir Street, Cambridge. Tel 0223 350725. Courses and workshops throughout the year.

Camden Arts Centre, Arkwright Road, London NW3. Tel 01-435 2643. Summer schools.

Camera Club, The, 8 Great Newport Street, London WC2. Tel 01-240 1137. Occasional one-day courses for beginners and others.

If you have ever wondered where you can improve your skills on a short course, here is your answer

Camerawork, 121 Roman Road, Bethnal Green, London E2 0QN. Tel 01-980 6256. Courses throughout the year.

Colorlabs International, The Maltings, Newmarket, Suffolk CB8 86AG. Tel 0638 664444. One-day wedding photography seminars and master classes. Venues vary.

Counter Image, 19 Whitworth Street West, Manchester M1 5WG. Tel 061- 228 3551. Extensive programmes of courses, workshops and seminars.

Earnley Concourse, Earnley, Chichester, Sussex PO20 7JL. Tel 0243 670392 or 670326. 1 to 5-day courses throughout the year on more popular aspects of photography, including colour processing. Beginners to advanced.

East Ham Computer Graphics Workshop, East Ham College of Technology, High Street South, London E6. Short (6-hour) courses specially designed for artists and designers requiring computer graphics.

European Society for the History of Photography, Karel Oomsstraat 11, B-2000 Antwerp. Organises an occasional international symposium on topics germane to photography.

F.Stop Photography Workshop, 2 Longacre, London Road, Bath. Tel 0225 316922. Lectures, talks and occasional seminars and workshops.

Fenty, Erskine, MPhil CEd Dip BIPP, 168-170 Castle Hill, Reading, Berks RG1 7RP. Tel 0734 509631. Community photographic Workshops, under the title of *Pieces of a Dream.*

Ffotogallery, 41 Charles Street, Cardiff CF1 4EB. Tel 0222 41667. Workshops on landscape and colour photography, etc.

Field Studies Council, Preston Montford, Montford Bridge, Shrewsbury SY4 1HW. Tel 0743 850674. Residential courses, mostly connected with natural history, landscape, etc, 2 to 6 days, at various FSC Centres. From beginners to advanced workers.

Harrow College of Higher Education, Dept of Photography, Film and TV, Watford Road, Northwick Park, Harrow HA1 3TP. Tel 01-864 5422.

Ibiza Photoworkshop, C'Ancielo, Santa Gertrudis, Ibiza. Occasional 'open' workshops. Details from Peter Espé, 21 Petersham Road, Richmond, Surrey. Tel 01-948 1641.

Impressions Gallery of Photography, 17 Colliergate, York Y01 2BN. Tel 0904 54724. Short workshops and courses on various aspects of photography, with the emphasis on B&W processing and printing for beginners and intermediate workers.

International Television Association (ITVA). Courses on various aspects of television and video. Details available from Michael A. Brown, National Administrator, 33 Albury Avenue, Isleworth, Middlesex TW7 5HY. Tel 01-847 1847.

International Centre of Photography, 1130 Fifth Avenue, New York, NY 10128. Tel 212 860 1776. A broad range of workshops, courses and seminars throughout the year, including 10-day study tours in England and 3-week cultural landscape tours in France. Inquiries to the Education department.

Jessop School of Photography, Jessop of Leicester Ltd, Jessop House, 98 Scudamore Road, Leicester LE3 0TF. Tel 0533 20461. Regular Saturday workshops on glamour, flash, colour, freelancing, print quality, etc.

Jolliffe Community Arts Studio, Wyvern Theatre, Theatre Square, Swindon, Wilts SN1 1QT. Tel 0793 26161 ext 3149. Workshops on unusual photographic interests — viz basic exposure with reference to the Zone system; pinhole cameras, etc.

Kodak Lectures, Hertfordshire College of Art and Design, Hatfield Road, St Albans, Herts. A series of lectures on British fine and applied arts. Information and bookings from the Division of Art and Psychology at the College. Tel 0727 64414. Bookings are primarily for the whole series of about twelve lectures.

Kodak Seminars — Occasional series of lectures by well-known photographers as part of Kodak's promotional support for the professional photographer. Details available from Dede Livermore, Kodak Marketing Education Centre, PO Box 100, Gadebridge Lane, Hemel Hempstead, Herts. Tel 0442 61122.

Lansdowne House: see *Picture House*.
Leica School of Photography. Usually limited to ten places, this course is not limited to Leica owners, although Leica and other Leitz equipment is used. Details are available from Lorraine Miller, E. Leitz (Instruments) Ltd, 48 Park Street, Luton LU1 3HP. Tel 0582 413811.

Maine Photographic Workshops, Rockport, Maine, USA, 04856. Tel 207 236-8581. One of America's leading summer schools. Workshops and courses on most branches of photography.

Mazof Workshops, PO Box 256, London N19 4SL. Tel 01-263 3837. Workshops devoted to the techniques of high-speed photography using the Mazof range of products.

Moore, Raymond, Half Morton House, Chapelknowe, Canonbie, Dumfriesshire, Scotland DG14 0YF. Tel 05414 294. A limited number of 4-day workshops each year, each limited to four places.

National Centre of Photography; see *Royal Photography Society*.

National Museum of Photography, Film and Television, Princes View, Bradford BD5 0TR. Tel 0274 727488. Occasional courses on unusual areas of photography.

Newcastle Media Workshops, Bells Court, Pilgrim Street, Newcastle upon Tyne NE1 6RH. Tel 0632 322410.

Newcastle upon Tyne Polytechnic, Ellison Building, Ellison Place, Newcastle upon Tyne NE1 8ST. Tel 0632 326002. New degree in Media Production is now offered.

North Star Studios, 65 Ditchling Road, Brighton, East Sussex BN1 4SD. Tel 0273 601041. Occasional lectures and workshops.

Open Eye Gallery, 90-92 Whitechapel, Liverpool 1. Tel 051-709 9460. Workshops for everyone from beginners to advanced workers. Colour, portraiture, creative photography, Cibachrome, etc. Occasional week-end residential workshops.

Open Frame Community Photography Group, Adult Education Centre, Green Street, Gillingham, Kent ME7 1XA. Tel 0634 576830. Information and training in critical photographic practice.

Oxford Photography, c/o The Photographers Workshop, 103/4 St Mary's Road, Oxford, or 21 London Place, St Clements, Oxford. Tel 0865 245321 for both addresses.

Photogrammetric Society — Occasional symposiums. Details from the Hon Secretary (A.S. Walker), Department of Land Surveying, NE London Polytechnic, Longbridge Road, Dagenham, Essex.

Photographers' Place, Bradbourne, Ashbourne, Derbyshire. Tel 033 525 392. Residential courses mainly on landscape photography. Well-known photographers in attendance. Details from Paul Hill.

Photographers Workshop, Oxford: See *Oxford Photography*.

Photographers Workshop, Southampton Street, Carlton Place, Southampton. Tel 0703 225526. Courses, tuition etc.

Photography at Lansdowne House: see *Picture House*.

Photography at the Metropole, The Arts Centre, New Metropole, The Leas, Folkestone, Kent. Tel 0303 55070. Workshops with well-known photographers.

Photography Workshop, Maritenda, Algarve. Week-long courses for novices and experts. For details telephone 01-858 9352.

Photo Workshops, Ashdale House, 200 Lincoln Road, Peterborough PE1 2NQ. Tel 0733 62030. Seminars and studio sessions sponsored by Courtenay Products and held in different locations throughout the country.

Picture House (formerly Photography at Lansdowne House), 113 Princess Road East, Leicester LE1 7LA. Tel 0533 551310. Regular programmes of lectures and workshops directed by leading British photographers. Courses and in-service support for Leicestershire teachers and students. For further information contact Roger Bradley.

Plymouth Arts Centre, 38 Looe Street, Plymouth PL4 0EB. Tel 0752 660060. General courses on photography, with special classes for young photographers.

Polytechnic of the South Bank, Wandsworth Road, London SW8 2JZ. Tel 01-928 8989. One-day workshops and seminars.

Premises, Norwich Arts Centre, Reeves Yard, St Benedict's Street, Norwich NR2 4PG. Tel 0603 660352. Courses and workshops. For details contact Sue Monypenny.

Richmond Holographic Studios, 4 & 5 Foxton Mews, 48 Friars Style Road, Richmond, Surrey TW10 4QN. Tel 01-940 5525. 1-day seminars and 5-day courses on holography.

Rochester Institute of Technology, Technical & Education Centre of the Graphic Arts, One Lomb Memorial Drive, PO Box 9887, Rochester, NY 14623. A wide programme of seminars and workshops in all fields of photography. Information available from Brenda Reimherr.

Royal Photographic Society, Milsom Street, Bath. Tel 0225 62841. Workshops and courses in Bath and other localities.

Royal Television Society, Tavistock House East, Tavistock Square, London WC1H 9HR. Tel 01-387 1970/1332. Various courses in television production, video, etc.

Resources Centre, Leicester: see *Picture House*.

Soundwell Technical College, St Stephens Road, Bristol BS16 4RL. Tel 0272 675101-4. Short 10-week courses, 2 hours per week, for those wishing to take the City & Guilds exam.

Stills, The Scottish Photography Group Gallery, 105 High Street, Edinburgh EH1 1SG. Tel 031 557 1140. Insensive residential workshops occasionally.

Studio Workshop, 153 Farringdon Road, London EC1R 3AD. Tel 01-278 7633. Workshops centred on large format photography with the Sinar camera system.

Third Eye Centre, 35 Sauchiehall Street, Glasgow. Tel 041-332 7521/4.

Untitled Photographic Gallery and Workshop, 171-175 Howard Road, Sheffield S6 3RU. Tel 0742 340369. Educational courses and workshops. Details available from Stephen Barnett or Matthew Conduit.

Watershed Media and Communications Centre, 1 Canons Road, Bristol BS1 5TX. Tel 0272 276444. Numerous courses in photography and video. Details from Sara Davies.

Wenyon & Gamble, Holography Workshop, The Millard Building, Cormont Road, London SE5 9RG. Tel 01-733 3716 or 01-691 4206. One and 5-day workshops on holography.

West Dean College, West Dean, Chichester, Sussex. Courses on most aspects of photography.

West Surrey College of Art & Design, Falkner Road, The Hart, Farnham, Surrey GU9 7DS. Tel 0252 722441. Occasional colour photography workshops.

Worcestershire Photo Schools, Summerdyne, Cleobury Road, Bewdley, Worcestershire DY12 2QQ. Tel 0299 403260. 1-day, 2-day and 1-week courses for beginners and others in B&W and colour, transparencies and prints.■

A regular listing of dates and venues for the individual courses, workshops and seminars of these establishments is published in Diary, Pinboard or News in the weekly ***British Journal of Photography*.**